THE HOUSE OF COMMONS
IN THE TWENTIETH CENTURY

THE
HOUSE OF COMMONS
IN THE TWENTIETH
CENTURY

ESSAYS BY MEMBERS OF THE
STUDY OF PARLIAMENT GROUP

EDITED BY

S. A. WALKLAND

CLARENDON PRESS · OXFORD

1979

Oxford University Press, Walton Street, Oxford OX2 6DP

OXFORD   LONDON   GLASGOW
NEW YORK   TORONTO   MELBOURNE   WELLINGTON
KUALA LUMPUR   SINGAPORE   JAKARTA   HONG KONG   TOKYO
DELHI   BOMBAY   CALCUTTA   MADRAS   KARACHI
IBADAN   NAIROBI   DAR ES SALAAM   CAPE TOWN

British Library Cataloguing in Publication Data

Study of Parliament Group
    The House of Commons in the twentieth century.
    1. Great Britain.   Parliament.   House of Commons—
    History—20th century
    I. Title   II. Walkland, Stuart Alan
    328.41′07′209   JN673   78–40746

ISBN 0–19–827193–X

*Printed in Great Britain
by
Western Printing Services Ltd,
Bristol*

PREFACE

The task set me by the Editor is simple and pleasant: it is to thank those whose assistance and work have made this book possible. So, very properly, he has removed the temptation for me to spend space on commenting on the feast of historical essays which he has gathered together.

Stuart Walkland put the proposal to the Study of Parliament Group in 1972. The Group is composed of clerks of both Houses of Parliament and of academics interested in the working of Parliament. It has sponsored studies of various aspects of Parliament and has submitted evidence to Select Committees on Procedure. The Group was attracted to the proposal because nothing was available for the present century at all comparable with the famous three-volumed work of Professor Josef Redlich for the nineteenth century. But before the venture could get under way a publisher had to be found and some money made available to cover at least out-of-pocket expenses.

The first thanks of the Group must go, therefore, to the Delegates of the Oxford University Press and to the Social Science Research Council. To the Press we owe not only the greatly encouraging act of faith in deciding to publish the book before any part had been written, and probably at some cost to themselves: they were also tolerant and understanding when the Editor had to explain on several occasions why all the essays were not yet ready for publication, and were helpful in every way. The Social Science Research Council made a grant which met most of the essential expenses and eased the labours of the Editor.

The contributors need no formal thanks. They are members of the Group and all are keenly interested in the well being of Parliament. The Editor, Stuart Walkland, is also a member of the Group but I am sure that it would be the wish of all that we should pass the warmest possible vote of thanks to him. Editors of books based on the contributions of numerous authors have a peculiarly difficult task. The speed with which the volume can be sent to the printers is decided by the speed of the slowest contributors. He is constantly having to bully and persuade the laggards, whilst soothing the feelings of those who submitted their contributions a year, or even two years before. Also he has to ensure that the essays on the different aspects fit together and present a complete and readable account. Stuart Walkland's mixture of diplomatic and scholarly virtues has finally provided this important book.

OXFORD
21 NOVEMBER 1977   NORMAN CHESTER

CONTRIBUTORS

ANTHONY BARRETT is Head of Division, European Parliament Secretariat, formerly a Deputy Principal Clerk in the House of Commons.

R. L. BORTHWICK is Senior Lecturer in Politics in the University of Leicester.

SIR NORMAN CHESTER was the Warden of Nuffield College, Oxford, until 1978.

NEVIL JOHNSON is a Fellow of Nuffield College, Oxford, and Nuffield Reader in the Comparative Study of Institutions in the University of Oxford.

PHILIP LAUNDY is Director of the Research Branch, Library of Parliament, Canada.

DR. GEOFFREY MARSHALL is Fellow and Tutor in Politics, Queen's College, Oxford.

DR. DAVID MENHENNET is the Librarian of the House of Commons.

DR. PHILIP NORTON is Lecturer in Politics in the University of Hull.

DR. PETER G. RICHARDS is Professor of British Government in the University of Southampton.

DR. MICHAEL RUSH is Lecturer in Politics in the University of Exeter.

MICHAEL RYLE is a Principal Clerk in the House of Commons.

DR. COLIN SEYMOUR-URE is Reader in Politics in the University of Kent at Canterbury.

S. A. WALKLAND is Reader in Politics in the University of Sheffield.

CONTENTS

Preface: Sir Norman Chester   v

Contributors   vii

Introduction: S. A. Walkland   1

   I   The organization of Parliamentary parties:
Philip Norton   7

   II   The Members of Parliament:
Michael Rush   69

   III   The Speaker and his Office in the Twentieth
Century: Philip Laundy   124

   IV   The House of Commons and its Privileges:
Geoffrey Marshall   204

   V   Government legislation in the House of Commons:
S. A. Walkland   247

   VI   Private Members' legislation: Peter G. Richards   292

   VII   Supply and other Financial Procedures:
Michael Ryle   329

   VIII   Select Committees and administration:
Nevil Johnson   426

   IX   Questions and Debates: Robert Borthwick   476

   X   Parliament and Mass Communications in the
Twentieth Century: Colin Seymour-Ure   527

Notes on Sources   594

Appendix I
The Department of the Clerk of the House:
Anthony Barrett   596

Appendix II
The House of Commons' Library:
David Menhennet   611

Index   641

INTRODUCTION

S. A. WALKLAND

This volume of essays by members of the Study of Parliament Group was inspired by the massive account of nineteenth-century procedural reform in the House of Commons written at the turn of the century by the Austrian scholar Josef Redlich. The three volumes of his work tell in detail and with remarkable clarity the story of the wholesale transformation of the procedures of Parliament which took place between the Great Reform Act and the end of the nineteenth century. Rules and conventions which had hardly changed since Stuart times responded to what was, when judged by the standards of the eighteenth century, rapid social and political change. It is a fascinating story of how practices and procedures which had their origins in the seventeenth-century constitutional struggles between monarch and Parliament, and which were largely and ingeniously obstructive in character, were changed in the course of seventy years to produce a modern Parliamentary constitution in which a House of Commons confident of its political power gave primacy to the needs of representative governments. We make no apology for confining most of these essays to the same theme of procedural reform and development. Procedure, as the late Sir Kenneth Pickthorn said, is the only constitution that the poor Briton has, and in the sense that it articulates precisely a set of fundamental political relationships this is obviously true. In the absence of a written constitution, and of a bill of rights applied by the courts, it is only through the detailed operation of a Parliamentary constitution that the consensus which lies at its roots can be developed and applied in the day-to-day circumstances of government. A further consideration which prompted the production of these essays is the general lack, until recently, of Parliamentary scholarship this century. Large tracts of twentieth-century procedural development were uncharted, and we hope that the new material which is included here will be useful not only to students of the British Parliament, but to constitutional historians and to anyone whose interest lies in the practice of representative government.

Yet it early became apparent that these essays could not chart the sort of fundamental procedural developments for the twentieth-century House of Commons as those which transformed Victorian Parliaments. In many ways they can be no more than a postscript, albeit a lengthy one, to those changes, describing developments which are only embellishments of the late nineteenth-century structure. The reasons for this are complex—arguably social and political change in the first three-quarters of the twentieth century has approached in magnitude that of the nineteenth, yet its effect on the central institution of British representative government has been nowhere near so marked. This can perhaps mainly be attributed to the fundamental character of the changes produced in the last half of the nineteenth century, and their peculiar aptness for the political structure for which they were devised. This structure has changed little in its basic assumptions concerning the role of Parliament for much of the present century, and has proved equally attractive to modern governments which have felt little impulse to change a set of understandings and conventions which serve their purposes so well. From this stems to a large extent the major characteristic of the twentieth-century House of Commons—its incredible and seemingly innate conservatism in procedural and organizational matters. It is difficult to get completely at the roots of this characteristic. It has something to do with the Commons being essentially a closed corporation, adept, as its history demonstrates, at socializing new classes of membership and defining its role in terms of internally developed rules and conventions. Whatever the causes, the facts of conservatism are easily charted. Long tracts of the history of the Commons this century have seen no development at all—there are, for example, no major and only very minor procedural advances to be noted throughout the whole of the inter-war period, when the House of Commons appeared to consolidate around a minimum conception of its organization barely adequate even for the comparatively limited business of the period. The executive's control over procedural innovation in the Commons, exercised by successive governments this century in remarkable detail, is obviously relevant to any explanation of the slow development of procedure, but the reluctance of government to see major Parliamcntary advances has been continually matched by a similar resistance to innovation on the part of most back-bench M.P.s, and could hardly have succeeded without it.

This alliance in conservatism of both governments and private Members has combined this century to retard even the most moderate and necessary reforms. As subsequent chapters show, an adequate standing committee system for legislation took nearly sixty years to evolve. An Estimates Committee recommended in 1902 was not established until 1912, and only attained a viable role for itself in 1946, after its development had been accelerated by the exigencies of wartime government. A scrutiny committee for delegated legislation, recommended by the Donoughmore-Scott committee in 1932, emerged finally in 1944, similarly requiring abnormal circumstances and a Parliamentary campaign for its creation. The scrutiny of public policy and administration by specialized select committee, widely canvassed in the 1920s and early 1930s, was only accepted in limited experimental form a generation later, and has yet to establish itself as a major function of the Commons. These examples can be multiplied. It is also part of this argument that the flurry of procedural and other developments in the last decade has not essentially altered this picture. Most recent changes have been of a relatively minor character, especially in the sphere of legislative procedure. The growth of secretarial, research, and accommodation facilities for Members, for example, has been the minimum necessary to conform to the expectations of a new generation of M.P.s, and to give some credibility to their role as representatives and critics.

To a large extent this immobility has for its underlying cause the almost purely political nature of the procedure of the Commons. There is in Britain no one definitive theory of Parliamentary government, no detailed conception of the proper role and powers of a representative assembly. Parliament in its long history has responded to so many different political circumstances that no single strategy of Parliamentary government can be regarded as correct. Without anything but the vaguest constitutional guide-lines, which are open to a wide variety of interpretation, political empiricism, and opportunism have dominated the development of the House. Comprehensive and rational schemes of reform have not been well-received, whether emanating from Members, the Clerk's Department, or outside organizations. There has been a widespread feeling that, after having emerged from the turmoil of the nineteenth century, the form of Parliamentary government has been settled, to be developed when absolutely necessary only with considerable caution and circumspection. It has been in the interest of government this century to adopt the narrow view, to sustain a type of Parliamentary proceedings in which its political control has not been threatened, and to discourage developments which might undermine its monopoly of policy. Many of the official Procedure Committees of the House this century have supported this attitude with their findings, often after massive government prompting.

Nothing in the constitutional and political theories of the leadership, at least, of the governing parties has found this situation at all distasteful. Apart from proposals in the 1920s for the municipalization of Parliament, which were for a brief period the official stance on Parliamentary reform of an inexperienced Labour party, the strong conventional Parliamentarianism of Labour in this period has led to a remarkable conservatism in Labour's approach to procedure. The most conservative analysis of Parliamentary government this century is still that of Herbert Morrison, surpassing in this regard even that of Sir Ivor Jennings. Similarly, prompted by such theorists as L. S. Amery, the Conservatives have subscribed to an executive-centred theory of Parliamentary government which is natural to a party hierarchically organized with strong establishment links, sections of which still tend to regard the constitution as a Whig–Liberal invention. Those with the power to implement reform have had no desire radically to change a system which has seemed designed to facilitate their own exercise of power. The result has been a constitution which neither main party has felt called upon to question to any fundamental extent, and which in consequence has been inflexible to a degree in the working of, its central representative institution.

This is not to argue that the House of Commons has remained completely immobile for the last seventy years. As some of the essays show, it could hardly escape being affected by changes in society, in social and political behaviour, and to respond to fresh expectations of its role in a variety of ways. The disappearance after 1900 of informality in its business; increased professionalism both in the House itself and the Parliamentary party infra-structure, which received considerable impetus in the recon-struction periods after both World Wars; the disappearance of the purely social importance of membership of the House; the tendency, especially since 1945, for Members to stay longer in the House and to seek repeated election; all have in some degree changed its character. But essentially it remains an assembly which Balfour would immediately recognize. What, however, has drastically changed and affected the content if not the superficial style of Parliamentary government is the political context within which the Commons operates. The political structure of the country and of the Commons has changed greatly this century, and a Parliamentary system devised for one set of political circumstances has been adopted almost unchanged by a party system which now bears little except superficial resemblance to its late nineteenth-century counterpart. The end result is probably not what the original reformers contemplated.

It would be inappropriate in an introduction to what is primarily a collection of historical essays to enter into the con-troversy surrounding Parliamentary government in Britain in the last decade or so or attempt here to make any profound judgement on the attempts at reform of the House of Commons which have been such a prominent feature of this period. Some of the contributors to this volume have made their views on this question well known elsewhere. A few points are worth making however, since they relate to and complement the theme of this Introduction. The first is that the House as an institution cannot transcend the political forces which inform it and determine its operation and if these have tended in the recent past to diminish its role in national politics the fault does not lie in Parliament.

The second point relates similarly to the political nature of procedure itself. 'Parliamentary procedure is the only depart-ment of State where the old conventions and forms have been ruthlessly set aside from motives of political serviceableness, and where the political division of strength has received adequate legal expression', wrote Josef Redlich in 1908. Full recognition of this truth could have saved a number of twentieth-century

Procedure Committees and a host of individual Parliamentary reformers a good deal of wasted time and effort. The widespread and fundamental Parliamentary changes of the nineteenth century followed and reflected closely important changes in the structure and behaviour of the political parties, and if there is a lesson to be learnt from this it is that successful reform can only take place, and in the past has only occurred, after the political groundwork has been laid. It may be that it is now once more necessary to redefine the relationships between national politics and Parliament, as has happened so many times in Parliament's history, and to revert to the nineteenth-century meaning of Parliamentary, as opposed to purely procedural reform, which meant franchise and electoral reform to change the distribution of political power in the nation. Not the mechanical efficiency of Commons' procedure but its deficiency as a representative institution is perhaps now the problem. It is worth while to ask whether another watershed in Parliament's development has now arrived, when Parliamentary politics and the assumptions on which they have been based have reached the end of their creativeness, and when a new departure analagous to the political changes which brought the present system into being is called for. To say this is not to decry the achievements of the British Parliamentary system this century. Its record has not been ignoble; it has preserved not just the forms but the substance of representative government, in conditions of rapid political change, considerable social stress, and during two great wars, and has survived ideological pressures which were relatively unknown to the nineteenth century. Whatever its present measure of success, the system was developed by statesmen to meet real needs, and any future evolution must build on the strengths as well as avoiding the weaknesses of the existing structure. It is in this spirit that these essays are offered.

I

THE ORGANIZATION OF PARLIAMENTARY PARTIES

Philip Norton

The Development of Organized Parliamentary Parties

Political parties as a feature of political life in Britain are not new, and clearly pre-date, in one form or another, the Reform Act of 1832; Lord Holland's observation, albeit unfulfilled, in February 1830 that 'Party seems to be no more' was merely a recognition of the fact that it had previously existed. With the development of mass suffrage, the nineteenth century was to witness a profound change in the organization and role of political parties. The widening of the franchise in 1832 helped loosen the grip of the aristocracy on political power, transferring it instead to the House of Commons, and producing what has been described as 'the Golden Age' of Parliament in the period between the two Reform Acts. But whereas the increase in the size of the electorate encouraged politicians to develop novel channels of communication with the new electors, the break with the past was far from total—the redistribution of seats had been essentially a conservative one, rotten boroughs were by no means fully abolished, and the franchise was still highly restrictive—and not until the further widening of the franchise in 1867 was the greatest change precipitated: the enlarging of the electorate by 88 per cent (in the boroughs the increase was 140 per cent) produced an electorate too large to be bribed and to be contacted other than through some form of effective mass organization. The result was that 'organised corruption was gradually replaced by party organisation',[1] and both main cadre parties (to use Duverger's terminology) were developed to form mass membership and highly complex organizations. But the formal party organization that was created in response to the mass

[1] R. H. S. Crossman, 'Introduction' to Walter Bagehot, *The English Constitution* (Fontana edition, 1963), p. 39.

electorate was essentially extra-parliamentary (political clubs, registration societies, election funds, constituency associations, the National Liberal Federation, and the Conservative National Union): it was not matched by a corresponding development *within* Parliament. Parties certainly had a profound impact upon Parliament: voters not only had to be contacted, they had to be promised something if their votes were to be forthcoming, and party promises could only be fulfilled if party nominees were returned in sufficient number to, and displayed voting cohesion in, the House of Commons; the consequence of this development was to be party government, with the parliamentary parties acting as a conduit for the transfer of power from Parliament to the executive. But the formal organization of parliamentary parties changed remarkably little: the voting cohesion that the parties developed was facilitated by the operation of the whips, but the whips—both in human and paper form—had been operating in the eighteenth century; they may have increased their effectiveness during the course of the nineteenth century (party loyalty eventually succeeding patronage as their main, but not exclusive, weapon), but they were not new, and they remained the only form of regular party organization within Parliament throughout the century. There were occasional meetings of parliamentary parties—the number increasing during the period between the Reform Acts—but, again, these were not new, and were never held on any regular basis; more structured front benches also developed during the century (collective responsibility on the Government side, meetings of the 'ex-Cabinet' on the Opposition), but again the changes involved no new formal structure, with meetings of some form of 'shadow Cabinet' (though not quite the same as its modern counterpart) having been recorded prior to 1832. With the advent of the twentieth century the formal organization of parliamentary parties hardly differed from that of a century before, and as late as 1908 Lowell was writing that '[T]he whips may be said to constitute the only regular party organisation in the House of Commons, unless we include under that description the two front benches.'[1] Seventy years later, Lowell's description would be unrecognizable.

[1] A. Lawrence Lowell, *The Government of England*, Vol. I (Macmillan, 1908), pp. 455–6.

Whereas the nineteenth century was to witness the development of complex party organization outside Parliament, a similar development within Parliament was to be a feature of the twentieth. The parliamentary party organization of the nineteenth century had been adapted to ensure that Members, as far as possible, loyally supported the line set down by party leaders: party meetings at the beginning of the century had been held by party leaders for the purpose of 'laying down the law',[1] and were still being so used at the beginning of the twentieth; neither of the two main parties had any established machinery for Members to elect the party leader or to help decide the party's course of action. The result was that, even within two elite parties in which deference to party leaders was a feature, 'surprise is sometimes expressed by private members that the chiefs take them so little into their confidence'.[2] The development of parliamentary party organization in the twentieth century was largely to ensure that this situation no longer prevailed, though it was not to be a uniform development, and notably differed between the parties. Indeed, the development of a complex party organization in the Parliamentary Labour Party (a new parliamentary party in 1906 and one of the two main parties by the mid-1920s) and the Conservative Parliamentary Party (one of the two main parties throughout the period covered by our study) may be seen as related to the nature of each party: the emphasis upon intra-party democracy within the Labour Party, an empirical response to events (the policies pursued by the Liberal Government of 1906, periods of Opposition, and internal party crises) within the Conservative Party, though both aided or hindered by the size and composition of their parliamentary ranks. The developments within both parties, though occurring at different times and involving differences in operation and specific structure (as well as effect), nevertheless have had sufficient similarities to allow us to identify four essential elements of parliamentary parties in the twentieth century, namely: (a) party whips, (b) an organized parliamentary party with regular meetings (and, in some cases, written rules), (c) specialized party committees, and (d) the right to

---

[1] A. Aspinall, 'English Party Organisation in the Early Nineteenth Century', *English Historical Review*, Vol. XLI (1926), p. 393.

[2] Lowell, op. cit., p. 456.

elect the party leader(s). All four are essential features of the two largest parliamentary parties in the 1970s, with party whips and regular party meetings—in some instances with elected officers—also constituting features of the smaller ones. In this chapter, we shall consider the development and contemporary position of each of these elements within the parliamentary parties and then consider the effect that they have had upon Parliament and the distribution of power within British political parties having parliamentary representation. We begin therefore with a consideration of each of the essential elements of parliamentary parties, as just identified, in turn.

Party Whips

Party whips, or 'whippers-in' as they were originally known (the name derived from fox-hunting parlance), and the circulation of written whips enjoining the attendance of supporters, can, as we have already noted, be traced back to the eighteenth century; the term 'whipping' itself was known in the first half of the century, and by the last years of the North Ministry not only was whipping being conducted in support of the Ministry but George Byng had come to constitute the 'first regular opposition whip'.[1] During the early nineteenth century the number of Government whips rose from two prior to 1832 to comprise, during the post-Reform Act period, a Chief Whip, who was usually (though not always) secretary to the Treasury, and four or five junior whips who were lords of the Treasury, with three-line whips also being employed;[2] by the end of the century, both Conservative and Liberal whips' offices were well organized, and whipping so refined that even four and five-line whips were being employed.[3] The functions that the whips exercised during this latter period may be identified as three in number within

[1] P. D. G. Thomas, *The House of Commons in the Eighteenth Century* (Clarendon Press, Oxford, 1971), p. 118. See also pp. 113–14.

[2] A. Aspinall, *Three Early Nineteenth Century Diaries* (Williams and Norgate, 1952), p. lii, and Aspinall, 'English Party Organisation in the Early Nineteenth Century", op. cit., pp. 396 and 398.

[3] Josef Redlich, *The Procedure of the House of Commons*, Vol. II (Archibald Constable, 1908), p. 109; Viscount Chilston, *Chief Whip* (Routledge & Kegan Paul, 1961), p. 245.

Parliament and one main one outside Parliament, the parliamentary functions being those of management, communication, and persuasion, and the extra-parliamentary function being that, essentially, of electoral management.

The management function of the whips, their most long-standing function, derived from the Government's need to 'maintain a House' and to obtain a majority in divisions, as well as the desire of the Opposition to keep the Government's majority as low as possible. If the Government was to maintain a quorum and maximize its support in divisions, its supporters had to be advised and encouraged to attend certain sittings and their whereabouts during sitting hours monitored. This task was performed by the whips with increasing efficiency; by the end of the century, the whips could be expected to know the number of supporters remaining in the precincts and the likely Government majority in the event of a division. The main instrument of the whips in performing this function was, of course, the written whip, regularly sent to supporters to request their attendance and indicating the importance attached to the items of business involved. Receipt of the whip, as Lowell noted, also became 'the test of party membership': it signified that the Member was regarded as belonging to the parliamentary party issuing it. With increased Government activity, parliamentary obstruction by Irish Members and greater inter-party conflict toward the end of the century, the managerial function of the whips became increasingly important, both in the marshalling of forces in the lobbies and organizing the business of the House; by the turn of the century the 'usual channels' were well established, with the Government and Opposition Chief Whips in daily contact with one another.[1]

The communicative function of the whips also became increasingly important, very much interrelated to their managerial function: if they were to ensure a full turnout of supporters in a division, it was obviously advantageous to know in advance what Members' views were on the issue in question, and also that the Members were conversant with their leaders' views. The whips thus came to constitute a channel of communication between front and back benches. It was their business, as Lowell

[1] Viscount Gladstone, 'The Chief Whip in the British Parliament', *The American Political Science Review*, Vol. XXI (1927), p. 525.

noted, 'to know the disposition of every member of the party on every measure of importance to the ministry, reporting it constantly to their chief'.[1] From this function may also be seen flowing the Chief Whip's role of adviser to the Prime Minister; he knew the temper of the party and the character of its Members, and could encourage or warn the Prime Minister as to particular appointments. With the growth of Government activity and legislation, the written whips too became important instruments of communication as well as management: the greater the business transacted, and the more complex the legislation debated, the greater the need for guidance. 'Increasing technicality meant Members could no longer advert to their own judgment or experience; the resulting vacuum was filled by party.'[2] The underlining employed in the written whip served both to convey the party line on a particular issue and to indicate the political importance attached to it.

Flowing from both their managerial and communicative functions was the whips' function of persuasion or, as it has more commonly been portrayed, of discipline. To obtain a full turnout of supporters, the whips had to keep their Members advised of when to attend and also to know their views of the issues involved; it was their task to detect any sign of deviation. Indeed, by the turn of the century the practice of Members informing the whips of their intention to vote against the party line at any stage was already operating. Once potential dissenters had been identified, it was the task of the whips to persuade them to fall back into line. The weapons of 'persuasion' at the disposal of the Government whips included the threat of a dissolution (the potency of which was doubtless enhanced by the fact that most Members had to pay their own election expenses), indirectly informing the Members' constituency associations (though, as Lowell noted, direct contact could be counterproductive),[3] the use of patronage, invitations to certain functions, making 'pairing' arrangements difficult, and relying upon

[1] Lowell, op. cit., p. 452.

[2] Hugh Berrington, 'Partisanship and Dissidence in the Nineteenth-Century House of Commons', *Parliamentary Affairs*, Vol. 21 (1967–8), p.370.

[3] Lowell, op. cit., p. 453. Berrington's research also indicates that Liberal radicals who dissented stood to be applauded by their local caucuses, not disciplined. Berrington, op. cit., p. 363.

Members' goodwill in cases where the whips had assisted with election expenses. Merely to recount these weapons in the whips' armoury may nevertheless serve to exaggerate their disciplinary function. The whips often placed emphasis upon the employment of 'tact and persuasion'—the employment of which under the Conservative Chief Whip Akers-Douglas appears to have been valuable in maintaining goodwill in the parliamentary party—and only needed to utilize the foregoing powers on a limited number of occasions; in most divisions, they were merely serving to achieve cohesion among those who wished to be cohesive.

In addition to these parliamentary functions, the function of managing the extra-parliamentary party, with a view to achieving electoral success, also fell to the Chief Whip of each party. They were responsible for ensuring that local organizations were in good working order ready for an election, they had control of party funds which they could use to pay candidates' election expenses in the case of candidates with no great personal wealth (though the 'secret service' fund of £10,000 a year often reputedly used by the Government Chief Whip for this purpose was ended in 1886), and appear to have exercised some influence over the choice of candidates; Campbell-Bannerman's Chief Whip, for example, listed one of his responsibilities as 'suggesting and introducing candidates to constituencies that were in need of them'.[1] By the turn of the century both Chief Whips had supporting organizations, the Conservative Central Office on one side, the Central Liberal Association on the other, but the task of organizing the extra-parliamentary parties—despite some periods of notable effectiveness (as with the Conservatives under Akers-Douglas and Middleton)[2]—was becoming increasingly burdensome for Chief Whips with mounting parliamentary duties. It was these mounting parliamentary duties that were to be responsible for the main changes in the operation and organization of the party whips in the twentieth century.

The main change that we can identify is that the role of the party whips has become increasingly and essentially parlia-

---

[1] Gladstone, op. cit., p. 527. See also the letter from a disappointed candidature-seeker reprinted in Chilston, op. cit., p. 145.

[2] See Chilston, op. cit., *passim*, and Robert McKenzie, *British Political Parties*, 2nd revised edn. (Heinemann, 1964), p. 266.

mentary. Their parliamentary functions of management, communication, and persuasion have not changed as such, but they have become more extensive and time-consuming; their extra-parliamentary function of electoral management has been shed, or, in the case of the newly-formed Labour Party, never assumed.

The parliamentary duties of the whips, as we have already noted, were becoming more burdensome toward the end of the nineteenth century; Government activity and inter-party conflict were on the increase, and, by 1899, the whips were being applied in almost ninety per cent of all divisions. The beginning of the twentieth century further witnessed the final domination of the parliamentary timetable by the Government, and heralded a century when an average of over one hundred Acts were to be passed each year. By 1910, the problems of supervizing the parties in the country as well as in the House were apparent; on the Conservative side, the task of fulfilling both functions was described as being already overbearing (as well as unbearable given the failure to find an adequate successor to Middleton as principal agent), and, on the Liberal side, by the Chief Whip himself as being 'too much for any man'.[1] The Conservative leadership responded eventually to this problem by establishing a committee under the former Chief Whip Akers-Douglas to investigate the party organization; in 1911, in line with the committee's recommendation, the Chief Whip's responsibility for the party outside Parliament was removed. On the Liberal side, a reform of the party's organization was undertaken in 1910, with a Chief Organizer for the party in the country being appointed, but it was not until 1914 that the decision was taken to relieve the Chief Whip of his responsibility for the extra-parliamentary party; however, the First World War and the opposition of the then Chief Whip intervened, and the decision was not implemented.[2] Following the re-uniting of the party after the 1924 election, further organizational reform was undertaken, and responsibility for the Liberal Central Office vested in the post of Chairman of the Party Organisation; the Chief Whip

[1] Neal Blewett, *The Peers, the Parties and the People* (Macmillan, 1972), p. 275; Roy Douglas, *The History of the Liberal Party 1895–1970* (Sidgwick & Jackson, 1971), p. 62.

[2] Cameron Hazlehurst, *Politicians at War* (Jonathan Cape, 1971), pp. 129–30.

remained *ex officio* chairman of the Liberal Central Organisation, but this body now had little responsibility for the extra-parliamentary party (other than candidates), and the duties associated with it were entrusted to someone other than the Chief Whip for a period during the 1930s.[1] With this reform of the party organization, the duties of the Chief Whip became primarily, though not exclusively, parliamentary.

For the burgeoning Labour Party, there was no similar problem to deal with. The Conservative and Liberal parties had (as Tories and Whigs) parliamentary representation prior to the need to develop extensive electoral organizations; on the Labour side, the extra-parliamentary organization existed prior to the creation of the Parliamentary Labour Party, the 'distinct group in Parliament, with its own whips' sought by the Party Constitution. It was thus possible to vest responsibility for the party in the country in the hands of the officers of the party as distinct from the Chief Whip of the parliamentary party. In consequence, the main functions performed by the Labour Chief Whip, as Chief Whip, have always been parliamentary.

The other main change this century affecting party whips has been that their parliamentary functions have become more extensive and time-consuming. The changes in the latter half of the nineteenth-century, coupled with the inter-party dissent generated by the Liberal Government's policies in the 1906–15 period, helped ensure that the whips were well occupied, especially with their managerial function. However, the events of 1921–2, when Sir Austen Chamberlain ignored the warnings of his Chief Whip of Conservative Members' dissatisfaction with the Coalition, suggested to some Conservatives that an additional channel of communication from back to front bench might be advisable. The result, as we shall detail below, was the development in the following Parliament of the 1922 Committee, followed in subsequent Parliaments by the creation of a number of active party committees. It was not long after its formation that the practice developed of a whip attending meetings of the '1922' to announce details of the next week's parliamentary business, with the additional duty of reporting back to

[1] James K. Pollock Jr., 'British Party Organisation', *Political Science Quarterly*, Vol. XLV (1930), p. 173; Sir Percy Harris, *Forty Years in and Out of Parliament* (Andrew Melrose, n.d.), p. 182.

the party leader views expressed at meetings being added in 1924; the practice also developed of a whip being invited to attend each meeting of the specialized party committees. With the expansion of back-bench organization on the Conservative benches, the duties of the Conservative whips thus became more time-consuming. Owing to the size of the Labour and Liberal parliamentary parties during this period—the latter in rapid decline, the former never achieving more than 200 Members except in the 1929–31 Parliament—there was no equivalent development of specialized committees, at least on the same scale; the main expansion in whips' duties was thus on the Conservative side, though the late 1930s did witness a further change affecting both main parliamentary parties: the 'institutionalization' of the Government Whips' Office. Previously, the Government Chief Whip had been assisted at 12 Downing Street by political appointees; Charles Harris, for instance, was private secretary to Conservative Chief Whips from 1919 onwards, both in Government and in Opposition. In 1938, however, agreement was reached between the parties that Harris's experience would be useful to whichever party was in power, and he became a civil servant, henceforth serving as private secretary to the Government Chief Whip of the day (until his retirement in 1961)[1]; the change also apparently marked the beginning of the Government Whips' Office maintaining systematic records, Conservative Governments in the past having taken their papers with them.[2]

The main expansion in the whips' work-load on both sides of the House, though, would appear to have taken place in the period since 1945. In the 1945 Parliament, as we shall examine more fully below, both main parties established specialized party committees on a systematic basis; each committee was attended by a whip. Whipping was also further extended beyond the floor of the House. In pre-1945 Parliaments, little whipping was

[1] He was succeeded by (Sir) Freddie Warren. By 1977, the Government whips' office at Downing Street comprised the private secretary (Warren), two assistants, two secretaries, and two 'paper keepers'. Sir Freddie Warren to author.

[2] F. M. G. Willson, "Some career patterns in British Politics: Whips in the House of Commons 1906–66", *Parliamentary Affairs*, Vol. 24 (1970–1), p. 34.

done in standing committees, and what there was was generally done by the P.P.S. of the Minister in charge of the Bill; in post-war Parliaments, the duties of the whips were extended to cover standing committees, and both Government and Opposition whips are now appointed as a matter of course to such committees; indeed, on major Government Bills, two Government whips may be assigned. These changes were additional to the whips being occupied with their whipping duties on the floor of the House, in the 1945 Parliament in consequence of the managerial tasks associated with the Government's heavy and controversial legislative programme, and in the two succeeding Parliaments in consequence of the small overall Government majorities. Surprisingly, the Government Whips' Office (regardless of the party in power) accommodated these changes without any increase in personnel. From 1900 to 1964 the Government Whips' Office comprised the Chief Whip and between six and nine other whips; not until 1964, when a Labour Government was returned with an initial overall majority of four, was the Whips' Office expanded to a total complement of 15 whips (including the Chief Whip), six assistant whips being appointed in addition to those holding the three Household positions and five holding the junior lordships of the Treasury. Since 1964, when the whips have had to contend with the problems arising from small or non-existent Government majorities (or, in the case of the 1966 Parliament, possibly too large a majority), contentious legislative programmes and growing intra-party dissent on both sides of the House, the Government Whips' Office has never comprised less than a total of thirteen whips. In the 1976-7 session the Government Whips' Office comprised the Chief Whip (parliamentary secretary to the Treasury), his deputy (treasurer of the Household), the two other whips holding Household positions (comptroller and vice-chamberlain), the five whips holding the positions of lords commissioner of the Treasury[1] and seven assistant whips (sixteen in all), the Opposition Whips' Office comprising the Opposition Chief Whip, his deputy, and nine whips. All other parliamentary parties—the Liberal, Scottish National, Plaid Cymru, and Ulster Unionist

---

[1] The formal duties associated with the Household and treasury posts are minimal, although the vice-chamberlain writes a daily report of proceedings in the House for the monarch.

(until May 1977 the United Ulster Unionist Coalition)—each had one whip.

The other main change that we may note in respect of party whips has been their attitudes, and their changing attitudes, toward their persuasive or disciplinary function. At the beginning of the century, the Conservative whips' approach to a potential dissenter would be to try to dissuade him from carrying through his dissent, and then, if he did vote against the party, either do nothing, indicate regret at his action, issue a reprimand, or—in the event of persistent dissent (or absenteeism)—contact his constituency association;[1] some of the weapons in the whips' persuasive armoury we have already noted. In practice, reprimands by Conservative or Liberal whips were rare in the pre-1914 period (though one Conservative Member—Rowland Hunt in 1907—briefly had the whip withdrawn from him), and thereafter the Liberal attitude to cross-voting appears to have become even more relaxed.[2] Perhaps surprisingly, especially given the large Government majorities they experienced, the attitude of Conservative whips tended toward a more disciplinary approach in the inter-war years. The three Conservative Chief Whips from 1921 onwards—Leslie Wilson, Bolton Eyres-Monsell, and David Margesson—were all described by various sources as being disciplinarians, the latter two in particular having reputations for treating dissenters as 'defaulters on parade'; Eyres-Monsell, apparently in anger, briefly withdrew the whip from one Member in 1928,[3] while Margesson was subsequently to be described as 'dictatorial, even ruthless, in his methods'.[4] Only after Margesson was replaced by James Stuart was this disciplinary—and generally unproductive—approach relaxed, and subsequent Chief Whips, with the possible exception of the much-criticized Patrick Buchan-Hepburn, have adopted a more congenial persuasive approach: potential dissenters have been reasoned with, and, if unpersuaded, put in touch with the Minister concerned for further discussion. With-

---

[1] See Sir Ivor Jennings, *Parliament*, 2nd edn. (Cambridge University Press, 1957), pp. 88–9.

[2] Ibid., pp. 89–90.

[3] J. A. Cross, 'Withdrawal of the Conservative Party Whip', *Parliamentary Affairs*, Vol. 21 (1967–8), p. 169.

[4] Obituary in *The Times*, 28 Dec. 1965.

drawal of the whip has fallen into disuse (it was last employed in 1942 and apparently last contemplated in the 1959 Parliament), and rebukes rarely employed; when the Chief Whip admonished a number of P.P.S.s for voting against the Government in 1961, there was a generally unfavourable reaction within the parliamentary party to his action. The main power of the whips is now essentially that of persuasion (as opposed to unproductive threats of disciplinary action and often somewhat pointless post-dissent rebukes), and it is this power which has been increasingly employed by successive Chief Whips in recent Parliaments.[1]

The position has been somewhat different within the Parliamentary Labour Party (hereafter referred to as the PLP). Given the belief in intra-party democracy and the need to maintain a united front in Parliament, the Party Constitution originally required Members to pledge themselves to accept the Constitution and to abide by decisions of the Labour Group in Parliament (somewhat modified in 1911 following the Osborne judgement, while the parliamentary party itself introduced provision for abstention on grounds of conscience), and this was reinforced by the introduction of standing orders by the parliamentary party in 1929; these stated that membership of the PLP involved accepting decisions of the parliamentary party, though recognizing that Members had the right to abstain on grounds of conscience. Such formal provisions, though, were not as valuable to the Labour whips in performing their functions as might be expected: the nature of the party, especially its factional nature, lent itself to intra-party dissent regardless of any written rules. As a gesture, the standing orders were suspended by the parliamentary party in 1946, reimposed in 1952 following dissent on the issue of defence policy, rescinded after the 1959 election and replaced by a code of conduct, re-introduced in 1961 after further dissent and replaced in 1966 by another code of conduct, itself replaced by another code in 1968. Despite such formal provisions, intra-party dissent was and has remained a feature of the parliamentary party, with the whips having no effective disciplinary powers to deal with it; power to discipline Members, usually through withdrawing the whip, is vested in

---

[1] See Philip Norton, 'Intra-Party Dissent in the House of Commons: The Conservative Party in Government 1970–74' (Unpublished Ph.D. thesis, University of Sheffield, 1977), Ch. 6.

the parliamentary party. The experience of the Labour whips during the history of their existence has, in consequence, not altogether been a happy one: in the inter-war years they were faced with having to quickly find their feet in fulfilling their managerial functions (they were described as incompetent by Vivian Phillips during the period of the first Labour Government[1] while the Chief Whip during the 1930s, Charles Edwards, was described as being 'politically a dud' by his own deputy, his work being performed by the PLP Secretary)[2] and having to cope with a 'party within a party', the Independent Labour Party (ILP), prior to its disaffiliation in 1932; in the 1945 and subsequently Parliaments they were faced with continuing dissent, notably from the 'Keep Left' group, to which the parliamentary party responded in the 1950s and early 1960s by withdrawing the whip from the leading dissidents, a move having no apparent deterrent effect. In the 1966 Parliament the Chief Whip himself, John Silkin, urged a more relaxed attitude toward discipline (facing opposition within the PLP liaison committee for so doing),[3] though he himself at one stage attempted to 'suspend' 25 dissenters from party meetings, an action which he had no authority to take. The 1968 code did embody the power of suspension, but, as with withdrawing the whip, the power was to rest with the party meeting; the Chief Whip could recommend such action to the liaison committee, but the committee was free to ignore or modify it. Silkin, at the time that the code was in process of being approved, did use this power to recommend the suspension of 24 of the 25 dissenters, and this was agreed to by the liaison committee and at a party meeting; otherwise, the 'sole disciplinary action the Chief Whip can take off his own bat and without prior consultation with the Liaison Committee is a reprimand'.[4] The Labour whips thus find themselves in the position whereby their main power, like their Conservative counterparts, is that of persuasion, yet a power which, unlike

[1] Quoted in Douglas, op. cit., pp. 177–8. See also McKenzie, op. cit., p. 430.

[2] B. Donoughue and G. W. Jones, *Herbert Morrison: Portrait of a Politician* (Weidenfeld & Nicolson, 1973), p. 240.

[3] See R. H. S. Crossman, *The Diaries of a Cabinet Minister*, Vol. II (Hamish Hamilton/Jonathan Cape, 1976), pp. 95–6.

[4] Douglas Houghton, M.P., 'Labour's disciplines in Party and in Government', *The Times*, 6 Nov. 1968.

their counterparts, they have to employ in a parliamentary party which has a formal code of discipline and, by its nature, is prone to internal dissent. The environment in which they operate is thus somewhat less conducive to the effective employment of their persuasive function than it is for their Conservative opposite numbers.

Organized Parliamentary Parties

Although the twentieth century has thus witnessed important changes in the operation of the party whips—their functions becoming more time-consuming and distinctly parliamentary— the most obvious development affecting parliamentary parties has been their organization into formal bodies, with regular meetings, elected officers, written rules in some instances, and in time, as we shall detail in our next section, a system of subject committees.

Meetings of party supporters in the Commons were not unknown, as we have already noted, prior to the twentieth century. Meetings of Members who supported the ministry were held at the beginning of sessions in the eighteenth century and were continued on an *ad hoc* basis throughout the nineteenth, their number increasing in the period between the two Reform Acts. Their purpose, though, was essentially that of one-way communication: party leaders to followers. The leaders, who summoned the meetings, attended to inform their supporters of decisions already taken, not to seek their advice or invite discussion, and this approach was maintained into the early twentieth century. Although by the turn of the century one section of the Liberal Parliamentary Party (the Welsh LPP) apparently held regular discussion meetings, neither of the two main parliamentary parties as such held meetings which were frequent or for purposes of discussion; what meetings there were, as Lowell observed, were 'held to exhort, not to consult'.[1]

For the newly-formed PLP in 1906, however, such *ad hoc* and hierarchically-based meetings were not to be. The belief in intra-party democracy, which we have already touched upon, and the fact that the parliamentary party was being formed for the first time, contributed to the creation of a more regular,

[1] Lowell, op. cit., p. 456.

organized, and nominally internally more communicative parliamentary party than was the case with the two largest and hierarchically-structured parties. During the 1900 Parliament the Labour Representation Committee had adopted as one of its objects the return of Members who undertook 'to form or join a distinct group in Parliament, with its own whips and its own policy on Labour questions'—even being prepared itself to undertake responsibility for whipping—and following the return of 29 Labour Members in the 1906 election, with the LRC changing its name to that of the Labour Party, a 'distinct group', the PLP, was formed.[1] At its first meeting on 12 February 1906 it proceeded to elect officers, both the holding of an election and actually having officers of the parliamentary party making a distinct change from the practice of the two main parties; Keir Hardie was elected as chairman—an initially tied vote precipitating a regular turnover of chairmen—David Shackleton as vice-chairman and Arthur Henderson as Chief Whip. Of equal importance, it was also decided to hold weekly party meetings (with the officers meeting daily) to 'discuss the business before the House; allocate speakers for the debates; and to receive reports from the various party committees set up to deal with parliamentary activity in its different phases.'[2] This formal, organized structure was also reinforced by the Party's Constitution which required Labour Members to abide by the decisions of the parliamentary party in carrying the aims of the Constitution, thus formally encouraging (if not actually achieving) cohesion among the ranks of the parliamentary party; the party, as Attlee was later to state, 'insists . . . on majority rule'.[3] Although the PLP was to face a number of problems concerning its operation and structure during the first sixteen years of its existence—cohesion was not always easy to maintain (the PLP maintaining an early form of what was later the 'conscience clause' in standing orders, and with internal conflicts being not

[1] McKenzie, op. cit., pp. 388–92. Labour Members in the 1900 Parliament had already started to meet as a group following the election of Crooks and Henderson.

[2] Herbert Tracey (ed.), *The Book of the Labour Party*, Vol. I (Caxton, n.d.), p. 141. The party also secured a room for itself at the Commons and hired a parliamentary clerk (with funds provided by the party's National Executive Committee), while Hardie, the chairman, appointed two P.P.S.s.

[3] C. R. Attlee, *The Labour Party in Perspective* (Gollancz, 1937), p. 109.

uncommon), it suffered from poor attendance by a number of Members who were union officials, had a somewhat difficult time in attempting to establish its relationship with the extra-parliamentary party, and its attempts to establish committees met with only limited success—it continued to maintain itself as a formally organized, though not altogether autonomous,[1] parliamentary party. Its growth to form the official Opposition in 1922 and a minority Government in 1924, while strengthening its authority in relation to the extra-parliamentary party, also presented it with new problems. The conventions of the Constitution, with which it now came fully into contact, were the product of evolutionary adaption, and were based on principles other than those of intra-party democracy. The incompatibility thus arising between the organization of the PLP and certain Constitutional conventions was generally to be resolved, under Ramsay MacDonald's guidance, in favour of the Constitution. In 1922 MacDonald began to be styled not only as chairman but also as 'leader' of the parliamentary party, and in 1924, upon accepting office as Prime Minister, proceeded to employ his prerogative to choose his own Cabinet; while in office, the practice of annually electing the leader, members of the PLP executive,[2] and whips was also abandoned. Cabinet Ministers also refrained from giving the parliamentary party, or organs of it, advance information of their specific intentions, an approach that was to be carried into the 1945 Parliament. Nevertheless, some concessions were made to the principle of intra-party democracy within the PLP, concessions which, in one form or another, have generally been followed since. Party meetings were continued (which Ministers were eligible to attend), and—in order to facilitate better two-way communication between front and back benches, especially given the inclusion of most

[1] There were attempts to have the party conference issue instructions to the PLP, and the PLP was required by the party Constitution to confer with the party's NEC at the opening of each session; its early lack of autonomy is reflected in the fact that the decisions to enter the Asquith Coalition and leave the Lloyd George Coalition were taken against the wishes of a majority of the PLP. McKenzie, op. cit., pp. 400–5.

[2] The PLP executive, first elected in 1923, replaced the PLP policy committee which had comprised the officers of the PLP. In 1951, the executive's name was changed to the Parliamentary Committee to avoid confusion with the party's NEC.

members of the PLP executive in the Government—it was decided 'that, instead of an Executive composed mainly of the officers of the Party, there should be an Executive composed of twelve Members not in the Government, plus three Ministers, to act as a liaison committee between the Party and the Government' (*Labour Party Conference Report 1924*, p. 98). The committee was duly established, electing both a chairman and a vice-chairman. In practice, however, neither PLP or executive committee meetings appear to have achieved their purpose. Ministers, with one or two exceptions, were regarded as aloof and uncommunicative, and rarely attended party meetings; differences of opinion between Ministers and back-benchers were such that the executive committee found it difficult to mediate mutually acceptable compromises, the committee, as Morrison noted, having a hard life.[1] Despite the problems encountered during this first brief period of Government, the idea of having some form of liaison committee was nevertheless carried over to later periods of Labour Government. In 1929, 'it was decided to elect a Consultative Committee to act as a medium of communication between the Ministers and the Members' (*LPCR 1929*, p. 83)— with an identical structure to that of 1924, and equally ineffective[2]—and in 1945, the first full Parliament of Labour Government,[3] a liaison committee with a similar communicative role but very different structure was also established. It comprised a chairman and vice-chairman elected by the PLP (a second vice-chairman being briefly added in the 1950 Parliament), the Leader of the Commons, the Chief Whip, and a Labour peer,[4] and, unlike its predecessors, appears to have had some success in fulfilling a two-way communicative role.[5] Upon being returned to Government in 1964 and 1974 liaison committees were again

[1] Lord Morrison, *Herbert Morrison: An Autobiography* (Odhams, 1960), pp. 104–5.

[2] McKenzie, op. cit., p. 445.

[3] When jointly in Government as part of the wartime Coalition 1940–5, an administrative committee of private Members was formed; the position of Leader of the Opposition went into abeyance, and an acting chairman of the PLP was appointed.

[4] Elected by Labour peers. Labour peers had been first invited to attend party meetings, with one of their number being added to the PLP executive, in 1924, *LPCR 1925*, p. 90.

[5] McKenzie, op. cit., p. 447.

established, that of 1964–70 resembling in composition that of 1945—comprising a chairman, two vice-chairmen (a third being added in 1967), the Leader of the House, the Chief Whip, a Labour peer, and the Secretary of the PLP (not an M.P.), the Party General Secretary also being invited to attend—while that of 1974 was considerably enlarged to comprise a chairman elected by the whole PLP, six back-benchers elected by back-bench Members (the one with the highest vote becoming vice-chairman), the Leader of the Commons, the Chief Whip, four Government Ministers appointed by the Prime Minister (three from the Commons, one from the Lords), and the PLP Secretary, the Party General Secretary, and the Chief Whip in the Lords also having the right (which they exercise) to attend meetings. As with its predecessors, the functions of the committee elected in 1974 were to maintain an effective channel of two-way communication between front and back benches, to decide when party meetings were to be called, to ensure the effective functioning of party subject and area groups, to ease any difficulties between Members and the whips and to ensure proper liaison between the PLP and the party's NEC, though for the first time these functions were committed formally to paper on the initiative of Ian Mikardo. In so far as one of the intentions of enlarging the back-bench representation on the committee in 1974 was to encourage improved liaison through making it more representative of all back-benchers, then this aim would appear to have been dissipated through the dominance of the party's centre–right on the committee; by 1977 no back-bench Member of the Tribune Group was serving on it.

The extent to which the parliamentary party was prone to internal dissent also led to the adoption of formal disciplinary rules which, though occasionally suspended, have since remained in one form or another. The PLP first obtained the power to punish Members who refused to abide by the party Constitution through withdrawal of the whip in the period between 1910 and 1914, but it was not until 1929 that it adopted standing orders on discipline[1] in response to the dissenting behaviour of the Independent Labour Party. The standing orders prohibited Members from voting against decisions reached by the PLP,

[1] The PLP had adopted some standing orders in 1925, but these concerned the organization of the party whips.

though permitting those who had 'conscientious scruples on any matter of Party policy' to abstain from voting; although the standing orders have occasionally been suspended or modified—with some variation to the latitude allowed by the conscience clause[1]—the essential elements (prohibition of voting against party decisions, some latitude to abstain on grounds of conscience) have remained. The purpose for which they were introduced—to increase party cohesion—has nevertheless gone generally unfulfilled. As the research of R. K. Alderman has clearly demonstrated, standing orders have achieved little; when things have gone well for the party they have not been needed, and when things have gone badly, with serious internal dissent, they could not be effectively applied;[2] 'strict party discipline works smoothly', as Michael Foot noted, 'when it is superfluous'.[3] The adoption or amending of standing orders, as Alderman recorded, often increased friction rather than cohesion, but because of the nature of the party the PLP is unlikely to do away with them.[4]

Various other changes, some temporary some permanent, have also taken place in the organization of the PLP. In 1945 it established a series of subject groups (see following section); in Opposition in 1955 Attlee began allocating specific responsibilities to members of the Parliamentary Committee as well as to non-members; a Chief Whip's liaison committee was created after the 1959 election and continued to meet thrice weekly—to consider 'the day to day development of affairs and advise(s) on matters to be raised in the House' (*LPCR 1960*, p. 87)—until 1964;[5] from 1964 to 1970 the PLP met more regularly than had previously been the case in Government (meeting two or three times a month and eventually weekly as a rule, as compared to fortnightly in the Parliaments of 1924 and 1945 and monthly in

---

[1] See R. K. Alderman, 'The Conscience Clause of the Labour Party', *Parliamentary Affairs*, Vol. 19 (1965–6), pp. 224–32.

[2] R. K. Alderman, 'Discipline in the Parliamentary Labour Party from the formation of the Labour Representation Committee in 1900 to 1964' (Unpublished Ph.D. thesis, University of London, 1971), sections A and D.

[3] M. Foot, *Aneurin Bevan*, Vol. 1, p. 456, quoted in ibid., p. 286n.

[4] Ibid., pp. 306–7.

[5] The committee comprised the Chief Whip, the deputy Chief Whip, the leader's P.P.S., and officials of the parliamentary party and the party's headquarters.

that of 1929); and in 1970 the posts of leader and chairman of the PLP, normally combined when in Opposition, were separated, Harold Wilson continuing as leader and Douglas Houghton as chairman. Thus, in the 1970s, the PLP constitutes a highly organized parliamentary party, meeting weekly, with its own elected leaders and officers, liaison committee (in Government), subject groups, and written disciplinary code, the most highly organized of the parliamentary parties.

Despite the early development of the PLP as an organized parliamentary party with regular meetings and officers, it does not appear to have been used as a precedent for a similar development in the Conservative Parliamentary Party; that appears to have been motivated by internal party factors. Indeed, there appears little reason why the Conservative Party should have been interested in the internal organization of the PLP prior to 1922 when the latter was only a minor parliamentary party, and by the time it emerged as the Opposition after the 1922 election the event that was to help lead to the creation of the 1922 Committee had already taken place—the Carlton Club meeting of Conservative M.P.s in October 1922 that led to the downfall of the Lloyd George Coalition. Previously, meetings of the Conservative Parliamentary Party had been held only on an irregular *ad hoc* basis, and despite various attempts to establish some regular discussion forums within the parliamentary party (see below) the only regular party organization in 1922 remained the whips; as one Member of the 1918 Parliament recalled, there was no direct means of communication with the front bench: one had to accept 'unquestionably' the domination of the leadership.[1] However, the events of 1921–2, when Sir Austen Chamberlain ignored information from the whips and representations from junior Ministers about back-bench dissatisfaction with the Coalition, were to provide the incentive for a change in this state of affairs. In the new Parliament returned in 1922, a number of newly-returned Conservatives met on the initiative of Gervais Rentoul and decided to form the Conservative Private Members (1922) Committee 'for the purpose of mutual co-operation and assistance in dealing with political and parliamentary questions, and in order to enable new Members to take

[1] Lord Barnby to author.

a more active interest and part in Parliamentary life'.[1] At a meeting on 23 April 1923 the Committee elected officers— Rentoul being elected chairman—and an executive committee, and proceeded to meet weekly on Mondays throughout the session. It received some co-operation from the then Chief Whip, Leslie Wilson, and it was soon the practice for a whip to attend meetings to announce parliamentary business for the next week; the Committee also began to extend its membership, with twenty or thirty senior Members who had expressed a desire to join 'actively co-operating in its work' by the autumn of 1923. The ranks of the Committee were seriously depleted due to the results of the 1923 election, though it was not until 1925 that it was decided to invite all Conservative private Members to attend.[2] In the 1924 Parliament the Committee had tried to form a more direct link with the front bench, with the idea of meetings being chaired by the party leader; Baldwin had turned the idea down —apparently viewing the Committee as one of the short-lived bodies the party had experienced before, though also, according to one source, because he wished to avoid any similarity with the organization of the PLP[3]—but nevertheless agreed that a whip should attend all future meetings for the additional purpose of reporting back to the leader views expressed thereat. In the same Parliament, the practice was also initiated of reports being received from the various specialized committees that were then in the process of development. The result was that by the end of 1925 the parliamentary party had developed an organized structure which has remained essentially unchanged since: meetings, as a rule, were held on a weekly basis during a session (though there was a period when the '1922' apparently met fortnightly, while during the General Strike it met daily), preceded by meetings of the Committee's executive to draw up the agenda; the business of a meeting would normally comprise the chairman opening the proceedings, a whip announcing the business for the forthcoming week and answering questions

---

[1] Philip Goodhart M.P., *The 1922* (Macmillan, 1973), p. 15; see also Gervais Rentoul, *Sometimes I Think* (Hodder & Stoughton, 1940), pp. 231–9.

[2] Goodhart, op. cit., p. 30.

[3] T. F. Lindsay and M. Harrington, *The Conservative Party 1918–1970* (Macmillan, 1974), p. 64.

about it, reports (if any) from the specialized party committees, discussion on any special matters raised by the executive or Members themselves and/or an address by an invited guest, be it a Minister or outside speaker. Over fifty years later the format of meetings remains the same, and little else has changed. Ministers were apparently not as often invited to meetings in the 1930s as they were subsequently to be and the day of the weekly meeting has changed (meetings being held on a Thursday in post-1945 Parliaments, Mondays and Wednesdays having been favoured in some of the preceding Parliaments), but until 1965 there was little substantive change; the power and influence of the Committee depended largely, as it still does, upon the personality of its chairman as well as the party leader (to whom the former has right of access), and it often acted, as it still does, as arbiter in the event of disputes between party committees and Conservative Ministers; when in power, Ministers were not (and are not) permitted to attend meetings of the 1922 except by invitation (though since 1952 whips have been able to attend as observers), and votes are never taken, the chairman summing up the mood of the meeting. Apart from the appendage of additional specialized committees in the post-war period the only substantive change has been in the method of producing a party leader. Prior to 1965 the party leader 'emerged', in the process of which the 1922 Committee or (more likely) leading members of it may or may not be consulted; in 1965 a new system of election was introduced with the leader being elected by ballot of all Conservative Members. Although the fact that *all* Conservative Members (and not just Conservative private Members) could participate in the ballot meant that the right of election had not been solely acquired by the 1922, though the 1922 officers were responsible for the organization of the ballot, it was in the 1922 that the power now clearly lay. Thus, in the 1970s, the Conservative Parliamentary Party also constitutes a highly organized body, meeting weekly, with its own elected officers, its own elected leader, and specialized subject committees, albeit still less formally organized than its counterpart, the PLP.

While the effectiveness of the 1922 Committee, as we have noted, often depends largely upon its chairman—though, regardless of the chairman, there have been occasions when it has not been notably effective (as in the 1970 Parliament[1]), and less used as a forum for specialized or dissenting opinions than the party committees—it nevertheless appears a somewhat more effective forum for influencing the party leadership than does the PLP on the other side of the House. In part, this may be attributable to the nature of the parties; the Conservatives are able to proceed on the basis of what Punnett has described as 'two-way deference' between leaders and the led,[2] a deference which is essentially alien to the PLP, particularly given its factional nature. The factional nature of the Labour Party also lends itself to left–right divisions across the party as a whole, and thus left-wing Labour Members may bypass the forums of the parliamentary party, dominated by the party's centre–right, to appeal to extra-parliamentary forums such as the party conference. This difference between the parliamentary parties is also encouraged by a number of structural differences: in Government, Conservative back-benchers can take their case to their fellow back-benchers in the 1922, Ministers being ineligible to attend, and without the fear of their arguments being directly voted down; Labour Members, on the other hand, have to contend with the presence of Ministers at PLP meetings—who may argue against them and attempt to make the issue one of confidence—and the possibility of their arguments being voted down, the likelihood of the leadership winning any vote being considerably enhanced by the presence of the Ministers.[3] It is thus not surprising that as a general rule the 1922 Committee is a more (if not always) effective forum for Conservative dissent than the PLP on the other side of the House.

The Conservative and Labour parliamentary parties, though the two largest parties in the House, are nevertheless not the only organized parliamentary parties. Following its rapid decline to third-party status in the 1920s the Liberal Parliamentary Party met regularly, and has since continued to do so, usually on

---

[1] See Norton, thesis, op. cit., pp. 314–15.

[2] R. M. Punnett, *Front-Bench Opposition* (Heinemann, 1973), p. 307.

[3] See James J. Lynskey, 'Backbench Tactics and Parliamentary Party Structure', *Parliamentary Affairs*, Vol. 27 (1973), pp. 35–7. Also note the comments in A. King (ed.), *British Members of Parliament: A Self-Portrait* (Macmillan, 1974), pp. 52–3. Votes at PLP meetings are, however, fairly infrequent.

a weekly basis;[1] it acquired the right to elect the party leader in the 1930s, but lost it in 1976 (see below). All other parliamentary parties in post-war history have also met regularly. The National Liberals met weekly in the 1945 Parliament to discuss policy and, despite the effective merging of their party with the Conservative Party in 1947, continued (as the Liberal Unionist group) to hold weekly meetings into the 1950s; it was not until 1966 that the group (then only four strong) relinquished a room assigned to them in the Commons and became an integral part of the Conservative Parliamentary Party. The Scottish National Party emerged as a parliamentary party in 1974 with seven Members being returned in the February election and eleven in the October election; it now meets weekly on Wednesdays during a session, and, in addition to formally electing its office-bearers, also has its own standing orders. The United Ulster Unionist Coalition came into being as a parliamentary party in 1974 following the rift between the Conservatives and their Ulster Unionist allies. The Coalition met regularly and annually elected a leader and two deputy leaders. It came to an end on 4 May 1977 following the abortive loyalist strike in Northern Ireland, the six official Unionist Members then forming the Ulster Unionist Parliamentary Party; this now meets regularly and elects its own leader. Even the three Plaid Cymru Members returned in October 1974 have found it necessary to meet weekly (usually on Wednesdays) and to keep formal minutes of meetings. Each of the foregoing parliamentary parties also have their own whip, though in the case of the Plaid Cymru Members this does not extend to issuing a written whip. Organized parliamentary parties—even in those instances where the parliamentary party comprises only three Members—are thus a feature of parliamentary life, and in the case of the main parties have been now for over fifty years.

[1] During the leadership of Clement Davies and Jo Grimond there were also weekly meetings of M.P.s, leaders of the party organization and a small number of peers. Under Jeremy Thorpe's leadership a fortnightly Leader's Meeting was held (comprising the leader, party officers, the Chief Whip, and Leader in the Lords), while David Steel as leader consults the head of the party organization and party chairman weekly.

Party Committees

As we have noted, the development of regular meetings of full parliamentary parties was not to be the only one that was to be added to the already-existing structure of the whips to form the regular organization of parliamentary parties: it was to be complemented by the development of specialized party committees. The nature of the specialization of such committees has varied, though, and we may usefully begin by distinguishing three types of committee: *subject* committees, established on a long-term basis to study a particular subject or subjects (e.g. foreign affairs); *attitude* committees, established (usually on a short-term basis) to promote a particular policy or policies; and, lastly, *sectional* or *regional* committees, established on a long-term basis to bring together Members with a common background or constituency interest (e.g. trade union Members and Scottish Members respectively). Whereas, at the turn of the century, few such committees or similar groupings existed, there was to be a remarkable growth of all three types of committees during the decades of the twentieth century, with subject and sectional committees usually being formed as part of the parties' regular structure and with attitude committees being formed intermittently and lacking (in practice) official blessing.

During the first four decades of the century the development of party committees (or less formal groupings) was most marked in the Conservative Party, perhaps surprisingly given the nature of the party, but explicable in terms of its size: a parliamentary party needs a substantial number of Members before it can form effective sub-groupings, and the Conservative Parliamentary Party was the only one to have more than one hundred Members throughout this period. The PLP was too small a parliamentary party to form any effective committees during the first two decades of the century (though it apparently tried), while the Liberal Parliamentary Party started its rapid decline before it had time to experience more than a few unofficial attitude groups and one regional group. Our initial focus of attention, therefore, must be upon developments within the Conservative ranks.

Although it is possible to identify the occasional 'ginger

group' of Conservative Members (of which the 'Fourth Party' and the 'Hughligans' would be obvious examples) as well as at least one sectional grouping (the Liberal Unionists) within the Conservative ranks prior to 1906 (as well as the groupings caused by the split over protection versus free trade), the initial development of recognizable committees was during the period of Liberal and then Coalition Government from 1906 to 1922. They were mainly attitude committees, and were called into being by opposition to the approach (or perceived equivocation) of the party leadership to the reforms introduced by the Liberal Government and, in wartime, by the absence of an effective Opposition. Thus, in the period 1911 to 1914, the parliamentary party experienced the 'Confederacy' (though not confined to M.P.s) to promote the cause of imperialism and keep the party leadership on its toes, the 'Halsbury Club' (comprising peers and M.P.s) opposed to the Parliament Bill, and the Unionist Social Reform Committee which, by 1914, had attracted the support of about seventy Conservative Members and had been sufficiently active to appoint sub-committees; during the period of wartime, the parliamentary party further experienced the Unionist Business Committee, agitating for a more efficient prosecution of the war (and which came to include nearly all Conservative back-benchers not on active service), the Unionist War Committee (established after the parties had entered into Coalition), also designed to press for a more vigorous prosecution of the war and distrustful of Asquith's leadership (meeting weekly, it too represented, as *The Times* noted, 'practically all the unofficial Unionist members in regular attendance at the House'[1]), a small dinner group of seven or eight prominent Conservatives outside the Government with similar views to those of the War Committee, and in July 1916 an 'Imperial Unionist Association' (comprising peers and M.P.s) opposed to an Irish settlement; in the post-war Parliament of 1919–22, the party also experienced the Reconstruction Committee (apparently the successor to the War Committee), the 'Die-Hard' group, essentially opposed to the Coalition and Irish Home Rule, and the 'Young Unionist Group' formed by Lord Winterton and Edward Wood to promote social reform.[2] Such committees and groupings

[1] *The Times*, 12 Apr. 1916.
[2] A 'National Security Union' to oppose Bolshevism and an 'Industrial

varied in their effectiveness, ranging from apparently having no or little effect (the Confederacy?) to clearly having some effect (the War Committee), with others (such as the Social Reform Committee) falling somewhere in between. Although the support enjoyed by the War and Reconstruction Committees has led some observers to view them as the predecessors of the 1922 Committee, their aims clearly place them in the category of attitude committees with essentially short-term aims.

In the pre-war period, these committees would appear to have been supplemented by two sectional groupings (the Irish Unionists and, until 1912, the Liberal Unionists) and, more importantly, by one subject committee, the Unionist Agriculture Committee. This Committee, covering a subject of particular importance to the Conservative Party (and presumably established because of this, rather than in response to a specific event), met fortnightly during parliamentary sessions and was re-established after the war.[1] It was to be the first of many such committees. A number of subject committees were established with official blessing while the party was in Opposition in 1923—though more akin to the policy committees established in the 1964–70 period (extending beyond a parliamentary membership) than purely parliamentary party committees[2]—and were reorganized as parliamentary committees after the 1924 election, apparently on the initiative of the Chief Whip, Eyres-Monsell.[3] The Committee elected their own chairmen (usually members of the Shadow Cabinet while in Opposition) and secretaries, and during the 1924–9 Parliament the committees—on foreign affairs, agriculture, imperial affairs, finance, trade and industry, and the armed forces—operated in a manner which was to

Group' to hold the Coalition to protectionist policies were also formed, though, certainly in the former case, not confined to M.P.s and peers. See, generally, John M. McEwen, 'Unionist and Conservative Members of Parliament 1914–1939' (Unpublished Ph.D. thesis, University of London, 1959), Chs. IV and VI for details of most of the groups in the 1914–22 period.

[1] Jennings, op. cit., p. 374.

[2] See J. A. Ramsden, 'The Organisation of the Conservative and Unionist Party, 1910 to 1930' (Unpublished D.Phil. thesis, University of Oxford, 1974), pp. 255–7, and Lord Butler (ed.), *The Conservatives* (Allen & Unwin, 1977), p. 291.

[3] Harold Macmillan, *Winds of Change* (Macmillan, 1966), p. 159.

become the norm for party committees. The Agricultural Committee (as it was then known) was particularly active: it met weekly on Tuesdays under the chairmanship of Sir George Courthorpe (at some stage it also met fortnightly) and various issues were discussed extending beyond matters solely affecting the Ministry of Agriculture, deputations to Ministers were appointed, sub-committees were established, and Ministers invited to attend the Committee and answer questions—over 150 Members turned up to consider the Minister of Health's Poor Law reform proposals in March 1927.[1] (The Committee was unusual, though, in that it issued official statements of its proceedings.) The subject committees continued to flourish when the party was in Opposition and again when it returned to power in the 1930s, so much so that the whips had to step in to regulate the timing of meetings, committees having tended to choose the most popular (hence overlapping) times for their meetings.[2] The importance of each committee during this period depended very much upon the importance of the subject covered and the strength of its chairman: agriculture was always an important subject to the party and the Committee also benefited from some strong chairmen; its meetings were always well attended. The other two important committees during the 1930s, due to the subjects involved, were the India Committee—which, on occasions, attracted over 200 Members of its meetings,[3] and was rivalled during 1933–5 by an unofficial attitude group, the India Defence Committee[4]—and the Foreign Affairs Committee, which held crowded and often stormy meetings, and was supplemented by a variety of unofficial attitude groupings. The Education Committee, covering a subject which could be unimportant in the party, was also an effective committee under its chairman, Lord Eustace Percy, during this period, whereas for example the Health and Housing Committee under Sir Francis Fremantle was not. Although the parliamentary party also witnessed a number of unofficial attitude groups—

[1] *The Times*, 10 Mar. 1927.
[2] Lord Tranmire to author.
[3] *The Times*, 12 June 1934, 27 Nov. 1934.
[4] It constituted the parliamentary branch of the India Defence League. At one stage it achieved a membership of 84 Conservative Members. Sir Patrick Donner to author. (Donner served as secretary to the committee.)

such as those already alluded to, and also in 1943 the Tory Reform Committee (supported by over 40 Members and a modern version of the Social Reform Committee of 1911–14)— and also at least one regional group,[1] it was the official subject committees which were coming to dominate the main party activity of Conservative Members in the Commons. This domination was to be most marked in the post-war period of 1945 to the present day.

Following the 1945 election, the subject committees (which had continued to operate during wartime) were reorganized and expanded—a total of 16 committees being created, with at least three establishing a number of sub-committees—with the officers being brought together with front benchers in a Business Committee (re-established in Opposition from 1964–70 and since 1974), and each committee being serviced by a member of, initially, the party's parliamentary secretariat and then the research department. During the 1945–50 Parliament committees continued to elect their officers, but in the subsequent Parliament of 1950–1 Churchill instituted the process of appointing chairmen, usually the front bencher covering the committee's subject, and this was continued in Opposition in 1964 and 1974. When the party returned to power in 1951 the committees were continued, though initially reduced in number: there were thirteen subject committees and one regional one in the 1952–3 session, though the defence committee continued with three sub-committees. This number gradually grew again until in 1970, after some variation in number, there were seventeen subject committees (with agriculture having three sub-committees and the Industry Committee one) and five regional committees (including the Ulster Unionists). By 1977 the number had risen to twenty-three subject committees (agriculture still having three sub-committees and the Industry Committee one) and seven regional committees (excluding the Ulster Unionists, no longer part of the parliamentary party). As can be seen from Table I.1, most subject committees (as has been the post-war practice) normally meet on a weekly basis (parliamentary business permitting) and also at a regular time within the period 4.00 to 7.00 p.m., Monday to Thursday; the European

[1] The Northern Group of Conservative Members, apparently established in the 1920s. Macmillan, op. cit., pp. 321–2.

TABLE I.1

Conservative Committees 1977

SUBJECT COMMITTEE	regularity of meetings*	average attendance** (rough estimate)	Comments
Agriculture, Fisheries, and Food Sub-committees:	weekly	20–5	Oldest of the subject committees
Horticulture	as and when required (*c.* 6 times as session)	8	Small, but has some influence
Fisheries	as and when required	10–15	Some influence on policy, though All-Party Fisheries Committee often regarded as more suitable discussion forum
Forestry	as and when required (*c.* 6 times a session)	12	Small, but not without some influence
Arts and Heritage	weekly	5	Influence limited due to nature of the subject
Aviation	weekly	varies	Used as forum for opposing Maplin Development Bill in 1973
Constitutional	weekly (sometimes fortnightly)	5–50	Established in 1976 to cover devolution
Defence	weekly	15–20	
Education	weekly	12	
Employment	weekly	varies	
Energy	weekly	10–30	
Environment	weekly	20	
European Affairs	weekly	20–5	Established in the 1975–6 session
Finance	weekly	20–100	Important committee: taken over briefly by neo-liberal Members in 1972–3 session
Foreign and Commonwealth	weekly	25	Important, long-established committee
Health and Social Security	weekly	10	Has a guest speaker each week
Home Affairs	weekly	12–20	
Industry sub-committee:	fortnightly	15	
Shipping and Shipbuilding	as and when required	6	Influence limited due to nature of the subject
Legal	weekly	varies	

SUBJECT COMMITTEE	regularity of meetings*	average attendance** (rough estimate)	Comments
Media	weekly	6–12	Successor to the Broadcasting and Communications committee in 1976
Northern Ireland	weekly	10–20	Established in 1972
Prices and Consumer Affairs	weekly	12	
Smaller Businesses	c. every 2–3 weeks	10–40	
Trade	weekly	12	
Transport	fortnightly	10	
Urban Affairs	weekly	6–12	Established in 1976. Does not invite guest speakers (under review) preferring to get out 'visiting the grass roots'
REGIONAL COMMITTEE			
Greater London	monthly	8	Normally invites guest speakers
North-West	c. fortnightly	12–13	Sometimes meet in the N. W. Meetings usually held to discuss specific topics
Scotland	weekly	10–16	
Wales	weekly		Much Welsh policy of the party is claimed to originate in the committee
Wessex	about 4 times a year	3–17	Only meets when it is felt a particular subject needs discussing
West Country	weekly	8	Frequently invites guest speakers
Yorkshire	monthly	10	Follows practice of meeting, if possible, in Yorkshire

* Parliamentary business permitting. Committees may also arrange additional meetings if felt necessary. A number of committees—e.g. energy, health and social security, and industry—also have weekly officers' meetings.

** There is no fixed membership.

Affairs Committee, for example, meets at 6.00 p.m. on a Tuesday, the Employment Committee at 5.00 p.m. on a Thursday. Only three committees, the various sub-committees and a majority of the regional committees meet on an intermittent or non-weekly basis. Meetings normally last up to about an hour and are open to any Conservative Member who wishes to attend. Attendances at most meetings would appear to fall roughly in the 5 to 25 category, though large attendances are usually recorded in the event of an important guest speaker—for example, a Conservative Chancellor at a post-Budget meeting of the finance committee—or an important topical issue arising, when attendances can reach three-figure numbers. Guest speakers are a regular feature of most (though not all) committees, and the extensive use made of them was well illustrated by Julian Critchley in describing such committees in February 1971:

> During the week there were 22 meetings which included Mr Arthur Seldon of the Institute of Economic Affairs talking to the Health and Social Security Committee, Baron Edmund de Rothschild to the Finance Committee, and Sir David Barron, the Industry Committee. Besides these guests, Sir Alec attended the Foreign and Commonwealth Affairs Committee, Lord Carrington, the Defence Committee and Peter Walker, the Local Government and Development Committee. By Thursday evening at six o'clock when the weekly meeting of the 1922 Committee . . . took place, the Conservative backbencher would have a surfeit of information.[1]

Some of the regional committees, though, tend to place less emphasis on guest speakers, preferring instead to keep in touch with particular bodies or authorities in their regions, and at least two of the committees follow the practice of holding meetings, where possible, in their provincial area. Certainly, the activity of these committees, which is not insubstantial, has tended to be overlooked. In addition, the subject and regional committees have also been supplemented from time to time by unofficial attitude groups, primarily, for our purposes, short-term parliamentary groups such as the '1970 Group' (opposed to EEC entry) and the Conservative Group for Europe (supporting EEC entry) in the 1970–4 Parliament;[2] other more permanent groupings, such as the Monday Club, Tory Reform Group, and Selsdon Group, fall less within our ambit of interest since they are not primarily confined to the parliamentary party and rarely meet on a purely parliamentary basis.

How influential or functional have such committees been within the parliamentary party? The existence of 'tendencies' as opposed to 'factions' within the party,[3] the emphasis upon

[1] Julian Critchley, M.P., 'Keeping MPs out of mischief', *The Times*, 20 Feb. 1971.

[2] See Norton, thesis, op. cit., pp. 59–61.

[3] For the distinction between these, see Richard Rose, 'Parties, Factions and Tendencies in Britain', *Political Studies*, Vol. 12 (1964), pp. 3–46.

holding office rather than upon party dogma, and the generally more deferential attitude toward leaders exhibited by party members, may be seen as providing the basis for a reasonably harmonious relationship between the committees and the party's front bench, while the structure of the committees has helped make them effective for conveying Members' views to the leadership. The open nature of the meetings has meant that attendance, and not just opinions expressed by regular attenders, can provide a guide to party feelings, the summing up by the chairman (as in the 1922, no votes are taken) means that decisions are not as conclusive as they would be by majority vote[1]— hence Members fearing they are in a minority are not discouraged from expressing their views—and the chairing of the committees by front bench spokesmen when in Opposition has meant that the committees are in a position potentially to influence party policy, a point favourably commented upon by several committee officers in correspondence with the author in 1977; the weekly meetings of the Business Committee in Opposition (on Wednesdays at 6.15 p.m.) also provides the officers of the committees with an opportunity to discuss wider issues, as well as whipping arrangements, with the party leader. In Government, Ministers also appear responsive to the committees, generally preferring the support rather than the dissent of interested Government back-benchers. As one former Minister commented, he always attended meetings of the relevant committee when he was invited to do so when he was in office: it helped, in his own words, to 'keep him on his toes'. Or, as one backbencher noted in a slightly different form: 'No Minister can successfully defend a mistaken policy before such an audience. Most Ministers would rather make a defence in Question Time, for then at least half the House, those sitting behind him, do not want to see him unduly embarrassed. The party Committee thus can act as the most powerful and merciless sanction upon incompetence or maladministration. What greater justification need it have?'[2] Only when a front bencher (or, worse still, the party leader—which appeared to be the case in the 1970–4 Parliament) appears uninterested or unresponsive is tension

---

[1] See Lynskey, op. cit., pp. 34–5.

[2] Richard Body M.P., 'Unofficial Committees in the House of Commons', *Parliamentary Affairs*, Vol. 11 (1957–8), p. 301.

generated between a committee (or committees) and the party leadership, and this within the Conservative Parliamentary Party appears to be the exception rather than the rule.

In the PLP, the position has been somewhat different. For the first two decades of the century, as we have already noted, the parliamentary party was really too small to establish effective regular subject committees; the parliamentary report for 1907 to the Labour annual conference does record the names of convenors for five subject committees as well as five special committees to consider specific Bills (*LPCR 1908*, p. 43), and the report for the following year refers to much 'unseen work . . . accomplished by the respective Committees appointed by the Party' (*LPCR 1909*, p. 29), but no more is subsequently heard of them. A number of sectional groups were formed within the parliamentary party—Dalton records the existence, when he first entered the House in 1924, of a trade union group, a separate miners' group, and the ILP group, as well as a promotional group (the temperance group, 'to which I did not belong'), among 'others'[1]—and during the 1920s when the party was the official Opposition a number of emergency committees were established to consider specific issues (the Government's plans for dealing with unemployment in 1923 and sweated goods in 1925[2]); in the late 1930s a number of advisory committees were also apparently established, but Members sitting in that Parliament have no recollection of them being effective.[3] This failure to develop a system of subject groups similar to that on the Conservative side of the House may be attributable to a number of causes: the existence of a number of committees set up by the party (as opposed to, though sometimes jointly with, the parliamentary party) and other bodies such as the New Fabian Research Bureau and the Fabian Colonial Bureau, the drastic reduction in Labour's parliamentary ranks in 1931, and the background of Labour Members: many were trade-union sponsored or small businessmen, which, given low parliamentary salaries, meant that the latter had to devote much time to

[1] Hugh Dalton, *Call Back Yesterday* (Muller, 1953), pp. 194–5.
[2] *The Times*, 3 Aug. 1923, 27 Aug. 1925.
[3] Lord Shinwell, George Strauss M.P. and John Parker M.P. to author. See also Morrison's comments, Lord Morrison of Lambeth, *Government and Parliament*, 3rd edn. (Oxford University Press, 1964), p. 137.

their outside interests while the former, although attending the trade union group within the parliamentary party, had no specialized knowledge of the sort that would help sustain certain subject groups.[1] Although a reconstruction committee set up in 1943–4 provided the precedent for later groups, it is thus not surprising that a comprehensive system of subject groups was not established until the 1945 Parliament when the parliamentary party had, for the first time, a majority of seats in the House (comparable to the Conservative position in the 1930s) and an influx of intellectuals with specialized interests.

With the return of the Labour Government in 1945, and conditions conducive to the establishment of subject committees, eleven such committees, known as subject groups, were established in October of that year, with a further nine subsequently being added to the list; they covered the main fields of government activity, and a number also established sub-committees 'for detailed examination of particular problems' (*LCPR 1947*, p. 64). These groups, though not meeting on such a systematic basis as Conservative committees, generally met at some time between 4.30 and 7.00 p.m. during sittings, some—such as foreign affairs, finance, and defence—tending to meet more regularly than others, and invited guest speakers, discussed policy items, and circulated papers.[2] Some of these groups did produce interesting and well-attended meetings with good rapport with the relevant Minister—such as the finance group with Hugh Dalton—and play a constructive role in the formulation of Government legislation (as with the 1947 Agriculture Bill), but their general effect was not as great as some Members would have liked. 'Those Members of Parliament who expected that the Groups would give them a chance to take part actively in policy-making have had their hopes rudely dashed. From the start the Ministers made it clear that they did not look on the Groups in this light.'[3] Ministers felt it constitutionally improper to discuss proposed legislation before introducing it in the chamber, and feared (with some justification) that groups might be

[1] The author is grateful to John Parker M.P., who sat in the 1935 Parliament, for drawing his attention to this point.

[2] Donoughue and Jones, op. cit., pp. 368–9.

[3] James Macgregor Burns, 'The Parliamentary Labor Party in Great Britain', *American Political Science Review*, Vol. 44 (1950), p. 859.

unrepresentative of the parliamentary party as a whole; the 'factional' nature of the party also lent itself to tension between groups and Ministers (left-wing group versus a right-wing Minister, as with foreign affairs and Ernest Bevin), as did the attitude adopted by a number of individual Ministers. An attempt to deal with the problems caused by back-bench dissatisfaction and the unrepresentative nature of the groups was made in 1947 by widening the scope of the area groups to include discussion of policy, and not just regional issues, but the attempt was not a success;[1] Members from a particular region who were uninterested in particular policy areas were likely to remain so, while interested Members would presumably already be members of the relevant subject group. The problems initially experienced by the subject groups thus persisted and were exacerbated or, in some cases, encouraged by a number of structural factors: the groups had fixed memberships—only those who joined at the beginning of a session were permitted to vote (though any Member could attend)—and votes were frequently taken; by comparison with Conservative practice, these factors tended to encourage groups that were not necessarily representative of the parliamentary party as a whole and made Members wary of bringing a matter before them if they might be outvoted.[2] In Opposition, front bench spokesmen could be, but were not always, elected as officers of the groups, and thus contact could be less direct than in Conservative committees. The number of groups—18 to 19 subject groups and 10 area groups for most of the 1950s rising to 26 subject and 11 area groups by 1969—and their irregular meeting arrangements (meetings often overlapped or coincided with others), coupled with the view of many back-benchers that such meetings achieved little (policy being made and influenced elsewhere) and were merely utilized by party leaders to keep Members occupied, also helped produce low attendances. The negative attitude of many Labour Members to the groups has thus persisted: Burns noted it in 1950, Lynskey in the 1960s, the Granada TV discussions in the 1970s,[3] while it found expression in some

---

[1] Ibid., p. 860, McKenzie, op. cit., p. 450, *The Times*, 7 and 19 June 1947.
[2] See Lynskey, op. cit., p. 35.
[3] See King, op. cit., pp. 54–5.

Members' correspondence with the author in 1977. Some attempt was made to deal with the problem in the late 1960s, when Harold Wilson held regular meetings with group chairmen, and after the 1970 election when the number of groups was reduced to 16 (a similar attempt at reducing the number having been tried after the 1955 election); by 1976, however, the number of groups had risen to no less than 35. Worried by the apparent continuing malfunctioning of the groups, the PLP liaison committee recommended to the parliamentary party in May 1976 the establishment of a special committee 'to suggest methods by which consultation between the Government and Labour back-benchers could be improved'; the committee, consisting of eight back-benchers, met five times and delivered its report to the liaison committee on July 28 (*LCPR 1976*, p. 65). In its report, it drew attention to the absence of 'effective machinery' for consultation between Government and back-benchers. In future it recommended that the Government should be more forthcoming with information—it wanted Ministers to supply group chairmen with memoranda three times a year outlining the main matters on which their Departments would be concentrating (as well as supplying chairmen with major public documents) and also to consult back-benchers before policy decisions were reached—while it recommended the reorganisation of subject groups to cope effectively with these developments. Thirty-five groups were clearly too many. 'Meetings frequently overlap, rooms are often cancelled at short notice or re-arranged, and the numbers attending are often small, sometimes embarrassingly so. We do not think this is a satisfactory way to organise the back bench side of the consultative process and we believe that it would be sensible to try for a more coherent organisation.' It therefore recommended that the number of subject groups be reduced to 16, organized on a departmental basis, with regular time-slots for meetings and with Members limited to a maximum membership of six groups.[1] These recommendations were discussed at a special meeting of the parliamentary party in November 1976, and, except for reducing the number of groups to 19

---

[1] 'Report of the Special PLP Committee on relations between Government and Back Benchers' (mimeo, 1976, 7 pp.+appendix). It also wanted group chairmen to be consulted on the composition of relevant standing and select committees.

instead of 16, were accepted by the PLP and the Government.[1] The resulting nineteen groups were established for the rest of the 1976–7 session (taking effect in March 1977), and are listed in Table I.2 (the regional groups, though listed, not being affected by the committee's report). How effective these new groups and procedures will be remains to be seen, though given the variables and past experience we have already outlined there is some room for doubt. Writing in mid-1977 one back-bencher was to observe:

Because of the extreme ineffectiveness of consultation within the PLP . . . there is a large degree of scepticism about the latest arrangements. Consultation here—or anywhere else—can only work if there is confidence that everyone wants to make that consultation effective. The poor attendance at our Group—and others—is one indication that such confidence does not exist.[2]

His point concerning attendance is borne out by the figures for average attendances at the reorganized committees in Table I.2, which do not indicate much of an improvement (if any) over attendances (as recorded in the special committee's report) at the unreformed groups in the period October 1975 to June 1976; meetings of groups, as a comparison of Tables I.1 and I.2 clearly demonstrates, also remain less regular than on the Conservative side of the House.[3] Against this, though, must be put the fact that a number of chairmen believe that the groups have exerted some influence upon Government, both before and after reorganization, with at least one chairman believing that his group is having a growing influence upon policy. Regional groups also appear to be active, with most now claiming good liaison with their regional party organization.[4] In general, however,

[1] *The Times*, 16 Sept. and 10 Nov. 1976; Frank Barlow, PLP Secretary, to author.

[2] Labour M.P. (a subject group chairman) to author.

[3] Indeed, it would appear that not all groups are keeping to their allocated time-slots for meetings. Thus, one chairman wrote to the author: 'In practice the . . . Group substantially ignores the time-table and meets when members of the Group suggest to me that it would be desirable, or when I feel it desirable myself.'

[4] The intention that the regional groups should liaise with the regional party organizers was introduced in 1970 'as an attempt to improve Party organisation and strengthen its electoral machinery'. Peter G. Richards, *The Backbenchers* (Faber, 1972), p. 53.

TABLE I.2
PLP Groups 1977 (following reorganization)

SUBJECT GROUP	regularity of meetings*	member-ship	average attendance (rough estimate)	Comments
Agriculture and Food	fortnightly	45	10	Includes former fisheries and forestry groups
Defence and Services	irregularly	69	6–20	
Disablement	7–8 times a year	23	8–10	Escaped being merged with Health group 1977
Employment	fortnightly	51	10–12	
Education and Science	fortnightly	64	20	Includes former arts and amenities group
Energy	once every 3 weeks	67	varies	
Environment	monthly	55	under 10	
Europe	monthly	57	8–10	Not proving successful; pro- and anti-EEC M.P.s prefer other forums for discussion
Finance and Economic	monthly	79	20	Includes former prices and consumer protection group
Health	roughly 3–4 times a month	43	5–25	Rarely invites guest speakers, but has number of working lunches each year (at teaching hospitals etc.)
Foreign and Commonwealth Affairs	weekly	94	15	Has subsidiary groups on Human Rights and Southern Africa
Home Affairs	fortnightly	55	10	Includes former broadcasting and legal and judicial groups
Housing and Construction	once every 3–4 weeks	58	6–10	
Industry	fortnightly	85	9–20	
Northern Ireland	once every 3 weeks	25	varies	Organizes visits, and has close contact with Secretary for Northern Ireland
Parliamentary Affairs		32		
Social Security	monthly	30	12	Avoided being merged with Health group 1977
Trade		73		Has small working group on shipping
Transport	monthly	68	varies	Apparently once managed to have a Transport Minister removed

AREA GROUP	regularity of meetings*	member-ship**	average attendance (rough estimate)	Comments
Eastern	about every 2–3 months	13	varies: up to 10	Active—with deputations, discussions etc.—despite small size
East Midlands	4 times a year	22	8–10	Has started discussing substantive political issues, e.g. in 1976–7 issue of import controls
Greater London	monthly	49	15	
Northern	fortnightly	29	15	Meets as required in the North. Issues covered include shipbuilding, engineering industry, unemployment, etc. Attempts to obtain more jobs and investment in the region
North West		51		
Scotland	fortnightly (executive committee meets weekly)	41	18–20 (executive comm.: 6)	Subjects discussed in 1970s include devolution, unemployment, economic situation, newspaper closures, licensing hours, etc.
Wales	As and when necessary	23	varies	(Has 23 Members, but large proportion of these are Ministers)
West Midlands	monthly	34	10	Topics discussed by group (1976–7) include British Leyland, National Enterprise Board, and machine tool industry
Yorkshire	fortnightly	36	12–15	

* Parliamentary business permitting.
** Membership of area groups comprises all Labour Members from the area concerned. (Labour peers may also join, but their number is excluded from area group membership figures, though included in subject group totals. The number of peers joining a subject or area group rarely exceeds 3 or 4.)

Labour groups still meet less regularly, are not quite so well attended (especially when considered in conjunction with frequency of meetings) and appear to be comparatively less influential than their counterparts on the Conservative side of the House.

One of the variables that has helped produce this position—

the factional nature of the Labour Party—has, however, helped ensure that unofficial Labour attitude groups, such as the 'Keep Left' group and the Bevanites of the late 1940s and early 1950s, their successor, the Tribune Group, and its rival, the Manifesto Group,[1] have been more active and apparent than their Conservative equivalents (in so far as the Monday Club and Tory Reform Group may be regarded as rough equivalents); they are also distinctly more parliamentary groups, meeting regularly as groups of M.P.s (this compares with only intermittent meetings by Monday Club M.P.s on the other side of the House) and discussing tactics and forthcoming parliamentary business,[2] and, on the left, displaying a degree of cohesive dissent in the division lobbies. Whereas the Monday Club now claims less than 15 M.P.s as members (though the Tory Reform Group almost certainly, and possibly the Selsdon Group, can claim more), both the Manifesto and Tribune Groups have over 70 Members each; this means that approximately one in every two Labour Members is a member of either group. The importance of subject and attitude groups within both main parliamentary parties thus notably differs.

As we noted at the beginning of this section, a parliamentary party needs to have a substantial number of Members before it can form effective sub-groupings, and thus the Conservative and Labour parliamentary parties are the only ones to maintain groups *within* their parliamentary ranks. In the first two decades of the century, the Liberal Parliamentary Party did experience one regional group, the Welsh Parliamentary Party, and at least three attitude groups—a Foreign Affairs Committee 1911–14 (an attitude group in that it appears to have existed to promote the views of radical Liberals interested in foreign affairs; it was

---

[1] The 'Keep Left' and Tribune Groups may, to some extent, be seen as less organized versions of the pre-war ILP group. Such groups are not the only ones to be formed in the post-war period; in 1957, for example, 20 or more back-benchers formed a 'ginger-group' to encourage a more vigorous Opposition, *The Times*, 23 Dec. 1957. Then, of course, there were additional groupings not confined to a parliamentary membership, such as the Campaign for Democratic Socialism.

[2] See, e.g., Fenner Brockway, *Outside the Right* (Allen & Unwin, 1963), pp. 79–82, for a succinct summary of the activities of the 'Keep Left' group, and King, *op. cit.*, p. 45, and J. Ashton, M.P. in *Labour Weekly*, 3 Jan. 1975, for details of Tribune Group activity.

about 80-strong in number), a War Committee during wartime which, like its Conservative counterpart, sought a more vigorous prosecution of the war, and in 1918 a 'Radical Committee', formed according to *The Times* to represent the 'advanced section' of the party—as well as the Union for Democratic Control, though this was not confined to the Liberal Party nor to Members of Parliament. Although another small 'Radical Committee' was to be formed after the 1924 election, maintained by about half-a-dozen Members, the drastic reduction in the size of its parliamentary ranks in the inter-war period removed the party's opportunity to develop a system of subject committees, and its total parliamentary strength since 1945 has, like that of other minor parties, generally been less than the average attendance at meetings of a subject group of one of the main parties. Thus committees on which Members of minor parties serve are usually party, and not exclusively parliamentary party, committees.

Forums for electing Party Leaders

Although the weekly parliamentary party activity of Members is based upon the whips, parliamentary party meetings, and (in the two main parties) party committees, the development of parliamentary party organization in this century has not been confined to these: the parliamentary parties have also emerged as forums for electing party leaders. It is, though, a development that has not been uniform between the parties, and one from which one party has already departed.

In the nineteenth-century, although the election of a party leader in one House by party supporters was not unknown—and it was the practice of the Irish Nationalists to elect a chairman[1] —there was no established machinery within either main parliamentary party for the election of a new party leader upon the retirement of the existing leader. It was generally the practice for the monarch's choice of Prime Minister to be formally 'elected' as leader at a subsequent party gathering, and for the

---

[1] Indeed, the Home Rule Members could also claim to have briefly formed an organized parliamentary party in 1874, but the organization planned—a parliamentary committee, and regular party meetings—was not effective. See David Thornley, *Isaac Butt and Home Rule* (MacGibbon & Kee, 1964), pp. 212–17.

former Prime Minister to continue as leader if the party went into Opposition; if in Opposition there was no former Premier to occupy the leadership, then separate leaders were elected in the Commons and Lords. This was the practice adopted by the Liberal Parliamentary Party during its period as one of the major parties prior to the First World War, and by the Conservative Parliamentary Party until as late as 1965. The Constitutional principle of the Prime Minister being the personal choice of the monarch took precedence over any principles of intra-party democracy.

Such a practice was not to be pursued, though, by the newly-formed PLP in 1906. For reasons we have already touched upon, it proceeded at its first meeting to elect not only a chairman but also a vice-chairman and whip, all of whom were subject to annual re-election. Although this introduced the principle not only of election but also of annual re-election—alien to the then main parties—it was the officers of the parliamentary party that were being elected, not the party leader; for the chairman to be considered as 'leader' would, as Snowden noted, be considered 'undemocratic'.[1] Nevertheless, a transition from chairman to leader was to take place sixteen years later when, as we have already outlined, the emergence of the parliamentary party as the official Opposition led to Ramsay MacDonald being designated as 'chairman and leader' of the parliamentary party. As Leader of the Opposition and, shortly afterwards, Prime Minister, it was not difficult for the mantle of PLP leadership to be extended by MacDonald to encompass leadership of the party as a whole; from thence onwards, whenever the PLP elected its leader, it was effectively electing the leader of the whole party. Although this election of a chairman and leader effectively dictated the monarch's choice of Prime Minister after a Labour victory at the polls, the PLP's power of election was severely attenuated during periods of Labour Government; MacDonald, as we have previously described, exercised the Premier's traditional prerogative of choosing his own Cabinet, and the annual PLP election of leader, deputy leader, executive committee, and whips was suspended (though a separate chairman and vice-chairman were elected), a practice which continued in all suc-

---

[1] Quoted in McKenzie, op. cit., p. 301.

ceeding periods of Labour Government. There were some attempts to make the party leader more responsive to party wishes following MacDonald's decision to form a National Government in 1931; in the short term, the TUC and the extra-parliamentary party 'took control of the parliamentary party and disavowed the leadership of MacDonald',[1] and during the 1930s party leaders, Lansbury and then Attlee, were elected who were generally regarded as 'stop-gap' leaders who conceived their roles as party spokesmen rather than leaders, but, in the long term (with Attlee emerging as more than a 'stop-gap' spokesman), very little changed. In 1945, Attlee accepted the King's commission to form a Government without prior consultation within the party, and proceeded to choose his own Cabinet. Subsequent Labour Prime Ministers, Harold Wilson and James Callaghan, have similarly exercised the traditional prerogatives of the office. The basic structure established in the inter-war years—the sessional election of the leader in Opposition, the traditional prerogatives of the Prime Minister being exercised when in office with no sessional election of the leader—has thus been continued. What modifications have since taken place in the electoral rights and procedure of the PLP have generally affected the other elected bodies and persons in the PLP hierarchy, and the method of their election, rather than the position and election of the leader; such modifications as have taken place—some of which we have already touched upon in preceding sections—are detailed below.

Given that modifications have not been fundamental, and that we have already detailed many of them, the electoral practice of the PLP in post-war Parliaments may be conveniently summarized as follows.

When in Opposition the PLP *sessionally* elects:
a leader (generally a formality if the existing leader wishes to continue in office, the exceptions to this being Wilson's challenge to Gaitskell in 1960 and Greenwood's challenge of the following year, both unsuccessful);
a deputy leader (again, generally a formality if the incumbent wishes to continue in office, though George Brown was challenged for the position on two successive occasions following his election to it in 1960);
a chairman (elected since 1970; previously in Opposition the posts of

---

[1] Henry Pelling, *A Short History of the Labour Party*, 3rd edn. (Macmillan, 1968), p. 71.

leader and chairman had—with the exception of the period from 1931 to 1932[1]—been combined);
a Chief Whip (generally a formality, though William Whiteley retired unwillingly from the post in 1955 when other candidates were put forward;[2] it had initially been the practice to elect junior whips, but this was discontinued in favour of appointment by the Chief Whip);
a Parliamentary Committee (known as the Parliamentary Executive until 1951; since its formation in 1923 it has always comprised—except in the 1931 Parliament when the PLP's ranks were seriously depleted[3]— twelve elected Members from the Commons, plus the officers. Its size was increased by the addition in 1924 of the Labour whip in the Lords and later the leader in the Lords and one elected peer).

The foregoing officers and the twelve elected members of the Parliamentary Committee from the Commons are elected by secret ballot under the provisions of standing orders adopted by the PLP in 1953 and amended in 1970, and applicable only when the party is in Opposition. For the election of the officers (i.e. leader, deputy leader, Chief Whip, and chairman), assuming there are two or more candidates for one office, eliminating ballots are held until one candidate has an absolute majority; if there are only two candidates for one office, then the successful candidate will obviously be produced by the first ballot. To be elected an officer or member of the Committee a candidate has to be formally nominated. If more than twelve candidates are nominated for the Committee (as they always are), then a ballot is held in which the twelve candidates receiving the highest number of votes are elected. In the event of a tie for twelfth place a second ballot is held between the candidates involved, and if a vacancy occurs during a session the candidate who came thirteenth in the previous ballot is co-opted to fill it.[4] Ballot

---

[1] Henderson, who lost his seat in the 1931 election, was requested by the PLP to continue as leader, while Lansbury was elected as chairman; Henderson resigned the leadership the following year and was succeeded by Lansbury.

[2] Donoughue and Jones, op. cit., p. 536.

[3] With only 52 Labour Members, it was decided to elect to the Parliamentary Executive only seven Members from the Commons, instead of twelve.

[4] When three members resigned in 1972—Mr. Jenkins as deputy leader, and George Thomson and Harold Lever as elected members of the Committee—Mr. Edward Short was elected deputy leader after a ballot; the vacancies created by Thomson's and Lever's departure were filled by those who came thirteenth and fourteenth in the previous ballot for the Com-

papers are issued to all Labour Members, and they may vote for less than (though no more than) twelve candidates; the provision that all ballots 'must record votes for as many Members as there are seats to be filled', which was adopted in 1953, was abandoned in 1970.[1]

When in Government, the PLP *sessionally* elects:
a chairman (elected by a ballot of all Labour Members):
six back-bench Members to serve on the liaison committee (elected only by back-bench Members of the PLP; previously, as detailed above, the PLP had also elected vice-chairmen, but under this new procedure introduced in 1974 the candidate with the highest vote automatically becomes vice-chairman).

It also elects *upon the retirement of the incumbent from office*:
a leader (that is, the Prime Minister; the first occasion that such an election took place was in 1976 upon the retirement of Harold Wilson);
a deputy leader (who is not necessarily a member of the Government; both George Brown in 1968 and Edward Short in 1976 continued to serve in the post after having returned to the back-benches).

The election procedure employed when in Government is essentially similar to that in Opposition (except for the innovation of the candidate for back-bench membership of the liaison committee with the highest vote becoming its vice-chairman), the six candidates with the highest votes being elected to the liaison committee, and with an absolute majority being required for the election of both the deputy leader and—under the procedure adopted by the PLP in 1976—the leader. The procedures by which Mr. Callaghan won the leadership in Government in 1976 were, as H. M. Drucker has noted, identical to those by which he lost it in Opposition in 1963.[2]

Given the limited powers of election when in Government and some of the other changes that have taken place in the PLP's history—the virtual security of tenure enjoyed by leaders both in and out of Government, the power of the Chief Whip rather than the PLP to choose the junior whips, and the assumption of the power by Attlee to allocate specific responsibilities to members of the Parliamentary Committee and other Members in

---

mittee; Mr. Short's place on the Committee was filled after a ballot due to two candidates having tied for fifteenth place in the previous ballot.

[1] Punnett, op. cit., pp. 113–18 and appendix C.

[2] H. M. Drucker, 'Leadership selection in the Labour Party', *Parliamentary Affairs*, Vol. XXIX (1976), pp. 387–8.

1955 (hence the power to appoint additional front benchers), both the latter changes marking a step away from election by the PLP, junior whips having initially been elected and a 'second eleven' of front benchers having been elected to reinforce the Parliamentary Executive from 1937 to 1940[1]—it has been possible for critics to charge that the PLP has deviated from its original emphasis upon intra-party democracy and that it now resembles in many respects its opposite number, the Conservative Parliamentary Party. Although it is correct to assert that there are now more similarities between the two main parliamentary parties than has previously been the case, the foregoing powers of election nevertheless constitute a significant power on the part of the PLP which is not matched in either the Conservative or Liberal parliamentary parties.

Whereas the basic principle in the filling of offices in the PLP has generally been that of election, from which there have been a number of major deviations, especially in Government, the basis of filling offices in the other two main parliamentary parties has been that of appointment; the only exception among front-bench spokesmen has been the election of the party leader, and in both parties this development was a relatively late one.

Only after its rapid decline following the First World War did the Liberal Parliamentary Party introduce election as a standard practice, and even then it was only to elect a chairman, a post that existed for some time concurrently with that of leader; it was not until 1935 that the practice of electing a leader upon the retirement of the incumbent appears to have been established, and that only after a certain amount of confusion.[2] This power of election remained with the parliamentary party for the next forty-one years, though was not extended to the party spokesmen; these were, and continue to be, appointed by the leader.

For the Conservative Party, the transition from the 'emergence' of a leader to the election of a leader was even longer delayed. From 1900 to 1964 it adhered to its tradition of accepting the personal choice of the monarch when in Government and of the ex-Prime Minister continuing as leader when in Oppo-

---

[1] Punnett, op. cit., pp. 58–9.

[2] See Jorgen Rasmussen, *The Liberal Party* (Constable, 1965), Ch. III, especially p. 40. In 1935 the parliamentary party also elected the Chief Whip, a practice that was not continued.

sition, and on the only occasion in Opposition in this period when it was actually called upon to elect a leader in the Commons—in 1911 following Balfour's resignation—it avoided a ballot through the emergence of an acceptable compromise candidate. Once the leader had 'emerged', he was then formally 'elected' by a party gathering; prior to 1922 this comprised Conservative M.P.s and peers, to which prospective candidates were added for the election of Bonar Law in 1922[1] and all subsequent elections (with the exception of that of Baldwin) until 1965, members of the party's National Union Executive Committee being invited to attend in 1937. For over the first half of the century this process served the party reasonably well. When a leader retired there was usually a generally accepted heir apparent ready to take over, and even when there was not—as in 1911—an acceptable compromise emerged; the only exception was in 1923 when Stanley Baldwin and Lord Curzon were both candidates for the premiership, the party being content to follow its traditional practice of allowing the choice to rest with the monarch. It was a process which had certain advantages: it avoided divisive and public elections (the formal 'election' being unanimous), and in the event of two or more candidates allowed for a weighing of opinion within the party, with the strength of negative attitudes toward the candidates being taken into account. Nominally, the process also permitted for 'soundings' to be taken within the party (and not just the parliamentary party), with all sections being consulted. However, the chief occasions on which these two latter advantages came into play—1957 and 1963—were also the two occasions that led to pressure for change. In 1957 the fact that R. A. Butler was unacceptable to a section of the parliamentary party may have contributed to Harold Macmillan receiving the call to the Palace, but the fact that allowing the Queen to make the final choice involved her in a political decision caused some concern. In 1963 the method of consultation and the disputed results of it caused a serious internal rift within the party, and the party was clearly not unanimous in its choice of leader. The controversy that it engendered encouraged the new leader, Sir Alec Douglas-Home, to institute a very radical departure from traditional practice. He approved

---

[1] Bonar Law underwent the unusual process of first being acclaimed leader by this process *prior* to being called to Buckingham Palace.

a new procedure for the election of the party leader upon the retirement of the incumbent leader, with formal rules to govern the election. Candidates had to be nominated by two Members, and the electorate was to comprise all Members in receipt of the Conservative whip. If, on a first ballot, a candidate received an absolute majority of votes plus fifteen per cent more votes than any other candidate he was deemed elected; failing that, a second ballot was to be held, with new nominations (which could include candidates not in the first ballot), but with an overall majority alone required for election; if no candidate received an absolute majority, a third ballot was to be held limited to the three candidates with the highest number of votes in the second ballot, and with the single transferable vote system of election being employed. In keeping with tradition, though, the successful candidate was to be presented to a party meeting comprising M.P.s, peers, candidates, and members of the National Union Executive Committee. The new rules, officially adopted in February 1965, made no provision for periodic re-election, and were only to be utilized upon the retirement of the incumbent leader. It was not long before they were being employed. In July 1965 Sir Alec resigned the leadership, and the parliamentary party proceeded to elect a new leader; it was the first time since 1846 that the parliamentary party had actually elected a leader, and the first time in its history that it had elected the leader of the whole party. On the first ballot Edward Heath obtained a overall majority, but not one sufficient to satisfy the fifteen per cent requirement; however, his two opponents stood down and he was formally elected on the second ballot. Ironically, almost ten years after his election the use of an election—which had worked so well for him in 1965—was to be turned to Heath's disadvantage. After two successive general election defeats in 1974 pressure began to build within the parliamentary party for Heath to resign or at least offer himself for re-election, a procedure for which there was no provision under the 1965 rules. Heath initially resisted this pressure, but then succumbed and agreed to submit himself to re-election. He appointed a committee under Lord Home to review the rules governing the election of the leader, and on 17 December 1974 this body reported its proposals: the main structure established in 1965 was essentially to remain—though the provision for an extra fifteen per cent of the votes cast on the first ballot was replaced by a requirement of fifteen per cent of all the electors eligible to vote—but with the additional requirement that a leadership ballot should be held between three and six months after a new Parliament had assembled, with annual ballots thereafter within 28 days of the start of each session. The electorate was to remain all Conservative Members, though with more formalized arrangements for consulting peers and, through the National Union, constituency associations. The committee's recommendations were agreed to by the 1922 Committee and Mr. Heath in January 1975, with the first ballot scheduled for 4 February. In it, Mrs. Margaret Thatcher received 130 votes, Mr. Heath 119 votes and Hugh Fraser 16 votes. Mr. Heath withdrew from the contest—the first man to be elected as leader of the Conservative Party, he was also the first to be voted out of the leadership—and in a second ballot in which four newcomers challenged her, Mrs. Thatcher received an overall majority with seven votes to spare. Not only had the party broken with tradition to introduce the principle of re-election, it had also become the first party to elect a woman as leader. Despite this radical departure from past practice, the principle of election is nevertheless only applied to the party leader. The parliamentary party elects no other front bencher; the deputy leader (if there is one) is appointed by the party leader, as are all other front benchers, both in Government and Opposition, the party leader's power of appointment even extending beyond Parliament to encompass the heads of the extra-parliamentary Central Office. Whereas Labour Members can help determine the composition of the Shadow Cabinet through election to the Parliamentary Committee when in Opposition and indirectly influence the composition of any future Labour Cabinet through such election, no Conservative Member can help determine, directly or (to any large extent) indirectly,[1] the composition of the Conservative front bench through election, other than the leader; the only election that they regularly indulge in is for officers and executive members of

[1] A possible indirect influence may be exerted through the election of the leader with unsuccessful candidates receiving a fair degree of support in the ballot being regarded as establishing some claim to a position in the front-bench hierarchy; this does not necessarily mean, in practice, that the claim will be met.

the 1922 Committee, and these positions are not regarded as stepping stones to front-bench promotion.

The introduction of a system of electing the party leader by the parliamentary party in the Conservative Party in 1965— thirty years after the Liberals had done so, and forty-three years after the PLP had effectively done so—marked the beginning of an era in which the parliamentary parties of all three main parties constituted the forums for the election of their respective leaders. It was an era which proved to be short-lived. In 1976 the Liberal Party approved a new system of electing its leader— which had been seriously contemplated in the 1930s[1]—by the extra-parliamentary party. Each constituency was to have a set number of votes (determined by a given formula), with every party member having the right to participate. Given the small size of the parliamentary party there was something to be said for the new system on both practical and political grounds; it transferred the power of election to the party in the country without altogether removing the importance of the Liberal M.P.s who alone could be nominated for election. Once adopted, the new system was almost immediately employed after the resignation of the incumbent leader, Jeremy Thorpe. After a campaign in which the two candidates for the leadership toured the country addressing party meetings Mr. David Steel was elected leader, the first main party leader to be elected by the party's rank-and-file. In the two larger parties there are also signs that the extra-parliamentary activists would prefer a greater voice in the choice of leader. When the new election procedure was adopted by the Conservatives in 1965, the officials of the party's National Union apparently expressed disquiet at their exclusion from the process. When the election procedure was amended in 1975, some provision was made for soundings taken by the National Union among constituency parties to be taken into account, the outcome of the National Union's soundings being reported to the 1922 Executive; the parliamentary party nevertheless remained free to ignore the National Union's findings if it wished to do so, and, in the 1975 election of Mrs. Thatcher, did so on the first ballot.[2] Ironically, as Drucker has

---

[1] See Rasmussen, op. cit., pp. 36–8.
[2] See George Gardiner M.P., *Margaret Thatcher: From Childhood to*

noted, the result of these changes is that the Labour Party now has the least 'open' system of election;[1] the electorate for the purpose of electing the leader remains solely members of the PLP, with no formal provision for consulting the party outside Parliament. Given the nature of the Labour Party it is thus not surprising that there have been calls for change, with some members of the party pressing for the leader to be chosen by the annual party conference or the party's National Executive Committee. Despite the changes within the Liberal and Conservative parliamentary parties, it is nevertheless important to reiterate that the leaders of the two largest parties are still chosen by their respective parliamentary parties; soundings may take place outside Westminster, but the final decision rests with the members of the parliamentary parties. Over and above this, the PLP still remains the forum for electing the Parliamentary Committee in Opposition, with some calls currently being made for the parliamentary party also to have some power to elect Government Ministers when in office. Despite recent events, the right to elect the party leader(s) still rests in the Conservative and Labour parties with their respective parliamentary parties.

The Effect of Organized Parliamentary Parties

Having described the development of organized parliamentary parties during the first three-quarters of the twentieth century, the question then arises: what effect has this development had upon both Parliament and the political parties themselves? It is a question which may conveniently be answered by again looking at the essential elements of parliamentary party organization in turn.

Party whips, the only one of the four essential elements of party organization at Westminster in the twentieth century that is not new, have generally been viewed as fulfilling a positive service on behalf of their leaders—that is, marshalling party supporters in the lobbies—but a negative one for back-bench Members. 'There are', as one Member noted, 'some who believe that the ills of Parliament can be blamed on those silent and

Leadership (William Kimber, 1975), p. 192, and Sir Nigel Fisher, *The Tory Leaders* (Weidenfeld & Nicolson, 1977), pp. 170–1.

[1] Drucker, op. cit., p. 388.

somewhat annonymous M.P.s, who, by dragooning their colleagues into the lobbies, have conspired in the dominance of
Parliament by the executive.'[1] References to the 'tyranny of the
whips' appear popular. In practice, the activity of the whips, as
we have already tried to indicate, is of positive value to both
leaders and their back-bench supporters. Their main functions
are those of communication and management. They exist not
only to convey the views of the party leaders to their colleagues
within the parliamentary party but also to convey the views of
the parliamentary party to the party leaders. If there is widespread disquiet about the line being taken by the front bench,
then the leaders are soon informed and can act upon it. In 1969,
for example, one of the contributory factors to the Labour
Government's decision to abandon its proposed Industrial
Relations Bill was the Chief Whip's announcement in the Cabinet that there was not sufficient support for the measure within
the PLP to guarantee that either a guillotine motion or one to
commit the Bill to standing committee could be carried.[2] On the
Conservative side, if the Chief Whip came to the conclusion that,
on the basis of the whips' soundings within the parliamentary
party, something could not be done, then, as a general rule, as
one former whip noted, that was that: it could not be done.[3]
This communicative role is further enhanced by the fact that it
constitutes a private means of communication, allowing Members to express opinions to the whips that they might be unwilling to express on the floor of the House or other public platform.
The whips' managerial–communicative function of issuing a
weekly written whip is also of positive advantage to Members.
To actively function within Parliament, Members require sheer
information as to what is happening or going to happen and, in
practice, given both the amount and complexity of parliamentary business, some guidance as to what to do. As a one-time
Liberal whip succinctly expressed it: 'A party in the House of

[1] Julian Critchley M.P., 'Westminster's "political cowboys"', *The Times*,
6 February 1971.
[2] John Mackintosh M.P., 'Parliament Now and a Hundred Years Ago',
in D. Leonard and V. Herman (eds.) *The Backbencher and Parliament* (Macmillan, 1972), p. 257.
[3] Ian M. Fraser to author. The exception to this rule was to be during
Mr. Heath's premiership; see Norton, thesis, op. cit., Ch. 6.

Commons can only function as a separate entity if it has guidance. Often in a long and controversial bill there are numerous amendments and divisions: members cannot be in the debating chamber all day, and it is the duty of the whips to advise members of their party, and keep them informed of all that is going on, and to shepherd them into the right lobby.'[1] What life would be like for Members without the whips is demonstrated by the experience of Vernon Bartlett, an Independent Member in the 1945 Parliament, who—lacking information and advice—generally abstained from voting; the lone SNP Member, Mrs. Ewing, similarly encountered difficulties from 1967 to 1970. The 'shepherding' and persuasive functions of the whips have nevertheless helped encourage a negative view of the whips, apparently regarded as being responsible for voting cohesion in the lobbies as a consequence of applying pressure or threatening disciplinary action. In practice (see above), the whips have little disciplinary power—the employment of what little they possess having, in the words of one long-serving Member, 'got pleasurably less' in the twentieth century—and can only ensure consistent cohesion in a party which wishes to be cohesive. Just as a consensus of opinion is a prerequisite for effective party discipline, rather than vice versa, so a parliamentary party with like-minded Members wishing to vote in the same lobby is a prerequisite for the effective functioning of the whips.[2] As we have already contended, the whips generally serve to encourage cohesion among those wishing to be cohesive. On those occasions when some Members may decide to dissent, then the chief power that the whips may bring to bear is that of persuasion; the whips concede that if that fails there is little else they can do,[3] a fact borne out by recent experience.[4] There is, as C. 'Monty' Woodhouse has written, no such thing as the 'tyranny of the whips';[5] they serve to the advantage of both front and back-

---

[1] Sir Percy Harris, op. cit., p. 125.

[2] Cf. Ergun Ozbudun, *Party Cohesion in Western Democracies: A Causal Analysis* (Sage Publications, 1970), p. 336.

[3] See above, and A. King and A. Sloman, *Westminster and Beyond* (Macmillan, 1973), pp. 108–11.

[4] See Philip Norton, *Dissension in the House of Commons 1945–74* (Macmillan, 1975), *passim* and conclusions, especially p. 611.

[5] C. M. Woodhouse, 'Mutiny on the Benches', *Times Literary Supplement*, 12 Mar. 1976.

benchers, and if they did not exist Members of the parliamentary parties would have had to invent them.

The effect of both parliamentary parties and their subject committees may be considered together. Their most obvious effect upon Parliament has been to transfer Members' activity from the floor of the House to private meetings 'upstairs' (i.e. to committee rooms). As early as 1931, when Conservative committees were well established, Sir Austen Chamberlain observed: 'When I have said, "But why are there so few fellows on our benches", I have been told, "Our Committee on India is meeting", or something of that kind.' 'You see these unofficial committees are always crowded', declared Winston Churchill, 'the House empty and unofficial committees full'.[1] With the further expansion of party committees this has been even more marked in post-war Parliaments.[2] The effect of this development should not, however, be misunderstood. It has *not* constituted a further transferance of power from the floor of the House. The main transfer of power from the Commons took place in the nineteenth century when, as we outlined in our introductory remarks, the parties acted as a conduit for its transferance to the executive. The residual power left to Members was their power to occasionally embarrass or threaten the Government's majority in the lobbies, a power which could only be used sparingly; it was not necessarily allied to the need for Members to be present on the floor of the House during most of the parliamentary day. By attending party meetings, Members were not reducing the power of the House; power was no longer exercised through the floor of the House but through party, and by establishing party forums within Parliament Members were, to some degree, regaining a slight measure of influence which they had lost in the nineteenth century. Meetings of parliamentary parties and their subject committees provided Members with forums in which they could privately express their views to their colleagues, and, if necessary, attempt to influence them. Through such forums a number of party Members could express disquiet with their leaders' views in a way that they would be reluctant to do

[1] Quoted in Jennings, op. cit., p. 380.
[2] A fact noted to the author by both George Strauss M.P. on the Labour side, and by his predecessor as Father of the House, Lord Tranmire (Sir Robin Turton), on the Conservative side.

publicly, and by such expression influence their leaders. 'Remember,' wrote Richard Crossman, 'the British Cabinet's concern today is not for its majority over the Opposition, because that is almost automatic, but for its majority inside its own Party. The key to power is *inside* the Party.'[1] The Government has to carry its own parliamentary party with it; if it does not, it faces the possible embarrassment of a public division within its ranks and, in serious cases, the possibility of being defeated in the division lobbies. Governments have generally been prepared to avoid such consequences by responding to disquiet within their parliamentary ranks; when Mr. Heath failed to do so in the 1970–4 Parliament (ignoring both dissent expressed within parliamentary party forums and through the party whips) he suffered a number of embarrassing defeats.[2] Although it may be asserted that such forums are useful for absorbing dissent within a parliamentary party by individual Members, if the 'mood of the meeting' is not favourable party leaders cannot safely ignore it; 'if a committee really blows off steam', commented one Conservative Member in 1972, 'it's in Cabinet the next day'.[3] While, as we have previously observed, such forums are not always effective, Conservative Parliamentary Party forums tending to be more functional than their Labour counterparts (though, as we detailed, some attempt is being made to reduce the malfunctioning of Labour subject groups), they do provide for the exertion of influence by Members which might not otherwise occur. Although a number of Members, particularly on the Labour side, complain about their lack of influence, party forums provide a means whereby *some* influence, albeit limited, may be exercised.

The creation of organized parliamentary parties may also be seen as strengthening the position of party M.P.s in relation to the extra-parliamentary party. Without organized parliamentary parties Members could only operate as individuals (or, in conjunction with other Members, unofficial *ad hoc* bodies)

[1] Richard Crossman, *The Myths of Cabinet Government* (Harvard University Press, 1972), p. 32. See also Anthony King, 'Modes of Executive–Legislative Relations: Great Britain, France and West Germany", *Legislative Studies Quarterly*, Vol. 1 (1976), p. 16.

[2] See Norton, thesis, op. cit., for details.

[3] King, op. cit., p. 49.

attempting to exert influence within party—as opposed to parliamentary party—forums. By forming organized parliamentary parties they are in a position to express themselves as a collective body within their respective parties. This is particularly important in the case of the PLP, which does not exercise the same autonomy within the Labour movement as its counterpart in the Conservative Party. The position of the parliamentary parties is further enhanced by the fact that, if constituting the largest or second largest parliamentary party, they form the Government (or usually so) and potential Government respectively, and this also helps justify their right to elect their party leader, who, as Prime Minister or Leader of the Opposition, relies upon their continued confidence.

The power to elect the party leader held by each of the two largest parliamentary parties is important not only in itself, but also because of the implications flowing from the fact that it is the parliamentary parties, and not the parties as a whole, that exercise it. Members of a parliamentary party operate in a different environment, and may hold somewhat different attitudes, from their party's rank-and-file or members of the party's extra-parliamentary organs. The person they prefer to be the party leader may therefore not be the same person that other members of the party outside Westminster would wish to lead them. Indeed, the choice of a majority of a parliamentary party may not even coincide with the preference of the party 'establishment' within Westminster; had a system of election not been employed by the Conservatives in 1965, it appears possible that under the old system the party 'establishment' would have produced Reginald Maudling as leader instead of Mr. Heath. The importance of this point is clearly demonstrated by the fact that if the power of electing the leader was returned to the party 'establishment' in the Conservative Party or was given to the extra-parliamentary party, or was transferred to the party annual conference or NEC on the Labour side, the current leaders of the Conservative and Labour parties would not be Mrs. Thatcher and Mr. Callaghan respectively, but probably (indeed, almost certainly) Mr. Heath and, possibly, Mr. Michael Foot (or Mr. Tony Wedgwood Benn). In the Conservative leadership election in 1975 Mr. Heath had the support of both the party 'establishment' (the Shadow Cabinet, Central Office

officials, leaders of the extra-parliamentary party, and party
'notables' such as Lord Home) and the extra-parliamentary
party (the National Union soundings indicating that seventy per
cent of constituency associations supported him), and would have
remained leader had the choice rested with either. Unfortunately for Mr. Heath, it did not. 'It was backbenchers, not the
Leader or his Shadow Cabinet, who forced a ballot, and it was
the backbenchers' candidate who emerged triumphant from it.'[1]
The implications for British politics of Mrs. Thatcher replacing
Mr. Heath, as opposed to Mr. Heath continuing as party leader,
are clearly not without significance. Likewise, had the power of
electing the leader in the Labour Party rested with the party
annual conference or more especially the NEC, the 1976 election results for leader would likely have been different, favouring
Mr. Foot or Mr. Benn. Of the Labour Members consulted by
Drucker—all of whom were opposed to removing the power of
election from the PLP—most 'were agreed that Annual Conference selection would simply put the decision in the hands of
the union leaders. This they did not favour. Most thought the
NEC would have chosen either Foot or Benn.'[2] Should the move
to transfer the electoral power to either body be successful (or,
indeed, were there to be any change in the PLP's election procedure—a first-past-the-post system would also have given the
leadership to Mr. Foot in 1976[3]) then, as with the change in the
Conservatives' election procedure in 1975, the implications for
British politics could be profound.

Summary

In summary, the twentieth century has thus witnessed the development of highly-organized parliamentary parties, the essential
elements of each parliamentary party in 1977 comprising whips,
regular meetings of the full parliamentary party (with, in some
cases, written rules and/or elected officers), and, in the case of
. the two largest parties, specialized party committees and the

[1] Gardiner, op. cit., p. 204. See also Fisher, op. cit., Ch. 8.

[2] Drucker, op. cit., p. 388.

[3] On the first ballot Mr. Foot received a plurality of the votes. In practice,
though, had a first-past-the-post system actually operated, some Members
may have taken this into account and voted differently.

right to elect the party leader. This development, which has had a distinct impact upon parliamentary life and British politics, has not been uniform either over time or between the parties. The Liberal Parliamentary Party went into rapid decline at the same time that the development of an organized structure was being undertaken by the other main parties, depriving it of the opportunity to undergo a change in organization on the same scale. In 1976 it also lost its right to elect the party leader, a change which may, largely or in part, be attributable to its small size. The PLP did not develop a regular system of subject committees until the 1945 Parliament, when it had (for the first time) nearly 400 Members, although regular meetings of the parliamentary party had been held since 1906. A system of subject committees was developed in the Conservative Parliamentary Party at the same time in the 1920s that the 1922 Committee was evolving.

The motivation for these changes, as well as their effectiveness, has also differed between the parties. The Conservative Party, a party of hierarchy and wedded to traditional conventions of the Constitution, was content to exist for some time with the whips as the only organized element of the parliamentary party, and subsequent changes may generally be viewed as an empirical response to events, facilitated by the size of its ranks. If the organization of the parliamentary party appeared to be malfunctional, with embarrassing consequences for the party (as with the events of 1921–2 when back-benchers repudiated the views of their leaders, of 1963 when the party was seriously embarrassed by the disputed method of selecting a leader, and of 1974–5 when Members' dissatisfaction with Mr. Heath's leadership began to surface publicly), changes were introduced to correct the malfunctioning. The organization of the PLP, on the other hand, had a guiding principle, that of intra-party democracy, but one which was modified (sometimes drastically) in response to other principles—notably those upon which the conventions of the Constitution were based—as well as to practical circumstances; a parliamentary party, for example, needed a substantial number of Members to sustain a system of party committees. Once established, the effectiveness of the various elements of organization has also differed between the parties. As a party of deference and one based on 'tendencies' as opposed to 'factions'—coupled with a number of structural factors which we have attempted to identify—the Conservative parliamentary organization of whips, 1922 Committee, and party committees has tended to function more effectively than its counterpart of whips, PLP, and subject groups on the Labour side, though both parliamentary parties have encountered problems concerning the election of their respective leaders, the Conservatives in 1963 because of the manner in which the leader 'emerged' (and in 1974–5 due to the absence of any provision for re-election), and in the PLP because of the lack of any provision for the extra-parliamentary party to be formally involved in the process.

The development of complex party organizations in the House of Commons has thus not been uniform between the parties. It has also not been static. Parliamentary party organization has developed and changed over the first three-quarters of the century, and continues to do so. It is essentially dynamic. The 1970s alone have witnessed the transfer of the power to elect the Liberal party leader from the parliamentary party to the party's rank-and-file, the introduction of the provision for a Conservative leader to be subject to re-election, the re-organization of the PLP subject groups, the first election of a Labour leader while in power, and the development of three new parliamentary parties, the Scottish National, Plaid Cymru, and Ulster Unionist Coalition, the latter, created in 1974, undergoing some further change in 1977. Pressure also exists for more change. In the PLP, there is pressure for further reform to increase communication between the front bench and the back-benches and for the election of front benchers to take place in Government as well as in Opposition; there is also a movement in the extra-parliamentary party for the power of electing the leader to be transferred to the annual conference or the party's NEC. The potential for change also exists within the other parties, not only the Conservative and Liberal parliamentary parties, but also, as their ranks decline or swell, the new parliamentary parties of the 1970s. Even with only three Members returned in October 1974, the Plaid Cymru parliamentary party eventually found it necessary to introduce some element of formal organization. If the SNP parliamentary party grows in size, it may witness the actual election of its spokesmen. Given the somewhat more fluid state of party support in the 1970s, there may also be even more parliamentary parties in the future, indeed, a probability should there be electoral reform. Just as the organization of the parliamentary parties in the 1970s bears little resemblance to that of 1900, so party organization at Westminster in the year 2000 (assuming it exists) may be completely dissimilar from that which we currently know.

II

THE MEMBERS OF PARLIAMENT[1]

Michael Rush

'. . . *the House of Commons is not the House of Commons of my time*'. *Mr. Ormsby in* Sybil[2]

Had Mr. Ormsby been looking back over the last seventy or so years, there is little doubt that he would in many respects be quite right. The chamber of the House of Commons, for instance, has undergone some changes in appearance, especially as a result of the rebuilding following its destruction by bombing in 1941. The dark oak woodwork and dark green benches of the old chamber have been replaced by pale grey oak and pale green benches in the new. It is true, of course, that as a matter of deliberate policy the new chamber is exactly the same size and seats no more Members than the old, although the galleries are much more spacious. The new chamber is air-conditioned and is fully-equipped with microphones and a discreet loud-speaker system so that misreadings by *Hansard* reporters, Press Gallery, and public alike are far less likely.

Even so, in appearance the Commons chamber has not changed drastically. A much more striking change to the eye is the presence of women M.P.s, although their number has yet to exceed 5 per cent of the membership in any single Parliament— the largest number being the twenty-nine elected in 1964. This is not to say that the impact of women M.P.s has not exceeded their numbers, but their sartorial impact has probably been greater. Indeed, it is perhaps sartorially that the greatest visual

[1] The author gratefully acknowledges the financial assistance received from the Small Grants Fund of the Nuffield Foundation and the help given by various individuals in gathering and processing the data on which this chapter is largely based. Particular thanks are due to Anthony Hill, who gathered most of the original data and without whose patience and hard work this chapter could not have been written.

[2] Benjamin Disraeli, *Sybil, or the Two Nations* (World's Classics edition, 1926), p. 264, originally published in 1845.

change has taken place. Recalling the Parliament elected in 1900, Lord Winterton wrote: 'The vast majority of . . .[Members] were in morning or frock coats with high stiff collars and wore top-hats on their heads; but there were some deviations from the normal; two or three of the Irish Nationalists were in lounge suits and without hats, and Mr. Keir Hardie was in his well-known tweeds.'[1] It is perhaps worth noting that the mode of dress prevailing at the beginning of the century marked a significant change compared with forty years earlier, as Sir John Mowbray, who entered the House in 1853, noted towards the end of the nineteenth century: '. . . the benches on both sides are thronged with men who wear hats and coats which would have shocked Speaker Denison in 1860 and brought down on their wearers his severe condemnation'.[2]

There are, of course, other senses in which Mr. Ormsby's remark may be interpreted. There is, for example, a sense in which every House of Commons may be described as unique: 'Every Parliament has its own special characteristics, which depend to some extent upon the circumstances under which it came into existence, the authority of the Speaker and the personal influence of the Leader [of the House of Commons].'[3] The political and electoral conditions which create a particular House of Commons, the nature of party representation, the particular individuals who are elected, and the events both inside and outside Parliament which shape and are part of its life, all contribute to this sense of uniqueness. Some may live in the memories of their participants for trivial reasons: a friend of Sir John Mowbray, for instance, described the Parliament of 1860–5 as 'a damnable dining Parliament' because of the frequency with which the House was counted out for lack of a quorum.[4] More seriously, writing of the Parliament elected in 1906, Alexander Mackintosh, a former lobby correspondent, asserted: 'I have never at any other time seen such a House of high expectation

---

[1] Earl Winterton, *Orders of the Day* (Cassell, 1953), p. 10. Lord Winterton was Conservative M.P. for the Horsham Division of Sussex from 1904 to 1951.

[2] Sir John Mowbray, *Seventy Years at Westminster*, ed. Edith Mowbray (Blackwood, 1900), pp. 108–9. Sir John Mowbray was Conservative M.P. for Durham City from 1853 to 1868 and for Oxford University from 1868 to 1895.

[3] Ibid., p. 108.   [4] Ibid., p. 173.

as was elected in January 1906. It contained a great many earnest, eager, sanguine reformers elated by victory.'[1] The House of Commons of 1918–22 will always be remembered as the one which Stanley Baldwin allegedly described as being '. . . filled with hard-faced men who looked as though they had done well out of the war'.[2] Arthur Baker, a former Chief of the Parliamentary Staff of *The Times*, labelled the Commons of 1924–9 'the dull Parliament'.[3] No doubt the Parliament of 1945–50 was a much more exciting affair, beginning as it did with the singing of the 'Red Flag' and Sir Hartley Shawcross's cry, 'We are the masters now.'

Mr. Ormsby's cry is, perhaps, above all one of nostalgia, regret, even criticism, but comparing one House of Commons with another, or examining Parliament over a period of time, is no easy task, for what is experience to one observer, is history to another. No doubt changes take place that are within the compass of an individual's experience, although they often remain matters of opinion. The standard of debate and oratory is one such area:

In more than thirty years great changes have taken place in parliamentary debate . . . Not least of these is the change in the art of speaking and in the quality of debate. In the early twenties there were many real orators in both Houses . . . Today . . . the real orators have diminished to such an extent as to be almost non-existent.[4]

On the other hand the same author asserts, 'The standard of beckbench speaking has not varied greatly since 1919.'[5] The area in which comparisons are at one and the same time easiest and most difficult is that of parliamentary behaviour: scenes of turbulence and disorder are not difficult to document, even though *Hansard* invariably records them as '[interruption]', but it is more difficult to assess the relative degree of such turbulence or disorder in one Parliament compared with another:

When Mr Speaker Clifton Brown . . . retired at the end of the 1950 Parliament, some commentators in the Press suggested that he had had a more

[1] Alexander Mackintosh, *From Gladstone to Lloyd George: Parliament in Peace and War* (Hodder and Stoughton, 1921), p. 225.

[2] Quoted in Roy Douglas, *The History of the Liberal Party 1895–1970* (Sidgwick & Jackson, 1971), p. 132.

[3] Arthur Baker, *The House is Sitting* (Blandford, 1958), p. 207.

[4] Ibid., p. 217.   [5] Ibid., p. 225.

difficult task than any of his predecessors, as for six years he had presided over a turbulent House of Commons with a Labour Government in power. Such inversions of the truth explain why history is so frequently falsified. The 1945 and 1950 Parliaments were like a Sunday School in comparison with the 1906 and two 1910 Parliaments.[1]

There is no doubt that disorder does break out periodically and that some Parliaments may be marked by more frequent disorder than others, but it is by no means unusual for contemporary commentators to describe such outbreaks as 'the worst in living memory' or, even 'unprecedented'. Lord Winterton is quite correct when he states that disorder and violence were far more common in Parliament in the early years of the century, often resulting in the suspension of the sitting. Such occurrences usually take place during periods when the political divisions in the House of Commons are especially sharp. Thus Home Rule Bills were at the centre of disorder and violence in 1893 and 1912–13, as was the Parliament Bill in 1911. The Parliament of 1929–31 was also notable for a number of stormy scenes, including the seizure of the Mace by John Beckett (Labour M.P. for Peckham) in 1930 and the forcible removal in 1931 of John McGovern (ILP M.P. for Glasgow–Shettleston) following his suspension by the Speaker. One indication of the relative decline of disorder is that it is now rare for a sitting of the House to be suspended because of such behaviour among Members. The suspension of the sitting on the 27 May 1976, which was preceded by the brandishing of the Mace by Michael Heseltine (Conservative M.P. for Henley), and the attack in 1972 on the then Home Secretary, Reginald Maudling, by Bernadette Devlin (Independent Unity M.P. for Mid-Ulster, 1969–74) are now exceptions to the general rule that partisan bitterness is confined to verbal and procedural fisticuffs.

Procedurally, in fact, the House of Commons has not altered drastically since 1900. There have been some changes, such as the abolition of the Committees of Supply and Ways and Means, the dates of the Parliamentary session, and minor changes in the hours of sittings, but bills are dealt with in much the same way— the use of standing committees for the committee stage of most bills dating from 1907 and the rules of debate are substantially

---

[1] Winterton, op. cit., p. 42.

the same, and the form of parliamentary business has altered little. Considerably more change, however, has taken place in the parliamentary work-load; a change brought about largely by the enormous increase in governmental responsibilities. It has been pointed out, for example, that of the 718 Parliamentary Questions answered in June 1971, 80–90 per cent could not have been answered in 1900 because they were not the concern of the government.[1] The legislative burden in particular has increased substantially, although this is reflected little in the *number* of Acts of Parliament passed but is illustrated dramatically in the sheer volume of legislation. Public Acts in 1900 amounted to less than two-hundred pages compared with nearly two-thousand pages in 1974. The contrast is even greater in the case of statutory instruments, which have doubled in number since 1900 and which consisted of nearly nine-thousand pages in 1974. The increase in governmental responsibilities is also reflected in the enormous increase in the number of Parliamentary Questions asked each year, in the reduced time allocated to Private Members' Business and the extent to which the government now controls the time and business of the House. The increased work-load has been accommodated by the stricter allocation of time, by the use of more standing committees, and, most of all, by lengthening the parliamentary session from an average of 129 sitting days before 1914, to 163 since 1945, with relatively little change in the length of the parliamentary day.

There are other changes related to the work of the House of Commons to which we will return at the end of this chapter, but there is little doubt that much the greatest change that has taken place this century is in the composition of the House, most notably in the representation of parties. The Irish Nationalists, who regularly constituted an eighth of the M.P.s returned to Westminster earlier in the century, have, of course, disappeared but what might have surprised Mr. Ormsby much more is the decline of the Liberal Party and its replacement as one of the two great parties of the state by the Labour Party.

The decline of the Liberal Party in terms of parliamentary representation was as rapid as it was dramatic: at the height of

---

[1] *Report of the Commission on the Constitution* (*The Kilbrandon Report*), *1969–73* (Cmnd. 5460, 1973), Vol. 1, para. 231.

its power in 1906 it had no less than 399 M.P.s;[1] by 1922 Lloyd George's National Liberals numbered 53 and the Asquithian Liberals, 62, a total of 115; and, although the reunited Liberal Party won 158 seats in 1923, it had already been overtaken by Labour. From a mere two Members in 1900 the Labour Party, helped by its electoral pact with the Liberals between 1906 and 1910 and by the Liberal split in 1916, increased its representation to 57 in 1918, 142 in 1922, and 191 in 1923, when the first Labour Government was formed.

Whilst these changes in the party system should not be minimized, they should not be allowed to obscure the important similarities that remain, especially the extent to which the Commons has been dominated throughout this century by parties in general and two major parties in particular.

Bearing in mind that the Irish Nationalists consistently held some 12 per cent of the seats in the Commons between 1900 and 1910 and that Sinn Fein won 10 per cent in 1918, the extent of party dominance is clearly shown in the right-hand column of Table II.1. Thus any nostalgia for a period since 1900 when a significant proportion of Independent M.P.s were elected to the House of Commons is historically misplaced, however desirable the presence of Independents might be regarded. The largest number of Independents elected this century was in 1945, when 17 M.P.s were returned as Independents and a further 9 with labels such as Independent Conservative, Independent Liberal, and National Independent.[2] Furthermore, it is also clear from these figures that parties other than the Conservative, Liberal, and Labour Parties have had little electoral success with, of course, the important exception of the various nationalist parties. There is some difficulty in defining a party, particularly in distinguishing between a party and an electoral label, which in some cases may be used by a number of candidates who do not necessarily constitute a party. Even so, including such groups of individuals, but excluding for the moment the nationalist parties, the largest single group or number of party representa-

---

[1] The electoral statistics used in this chapter are taken from F. W. S. Craig (ed.), *British Electoral Facts, 1885–1975* (Macmillan, 1976).

[2] i.e. Independent Conservative 2, Independent Liberal 2, National Independent 2, Independent Labour (not to be confused with the Independent Labour Party) 2, and Independent Progressive 1.

TABLE II.1

Proportion of seats in the House of Commons held by the
Conservative, Liberal, and Labour Parties, 1900–1974
(%)

Election	Conservative and Liberal	Conservative and Labour	Conservative, Liberal, and Labour
1900	87·3		87·8
1906	82·8		87·2
1910 (Jan.)	81·5		87·5
1910 (Dec.)	81·0		87·3
1918	77·1		85·7
1922		79·0	97·7
1923		73·0	98·7
1924		91·5	98·0
1929		88·9	98·5
1931		84·9	94·8
1935		88·0	96·7
1945		92·2	95·6
1950		98·1	99·5
1951		98·6	99·5
1955		98·7	99·7
1959		98·9	99·8
1964		98·6	100·0
1966		97·9	99·8
1970		98·1	99·0
1974 (Feb.)		94·2	96·4
1974 (Oct.)		93·8	95·9

Notes:
1. Conservative includes Liberal Unionists 1900–10, Coalition Conservatives 1918, National Liberals 1935 and 1945, and National Liberals and Conservatives 1950–66.
2. Liberal includes Coalition Liberals 1918 and National Liberals 1922 and 1931.
3. Labour does not include Coalition Labour in 1918, nor National Labour in 1931 and 1935, nor 6 unendorsed M.P.s in 1931.

tives elected since 1900 were the 7 Constitutionalists in 1924. Of the clearly defined minor parties the ILP has been the most successful, with 3 Members in 1935 and 4 in 1945, all others being fortunate if they could secure the election of one or two M.P.s. Thus whilst it is true to say that the number of parties represented in the House of Commons since 1900 has never been less than four and has been as high as eleven,[1] the overwhelming majority of seats have been held by the Conservative, Liberal, and Labour Parties.

The nationalist parties constitute an important exception to this rule, however, at least between 1900 and 1918 and, to a lesser extent, since February 1974. As we have already noted, the Irish Nationalists regularly returned 12 per cent of M.P.s between 1900 and 1910 and Sinn Fein 10 per cent in 1918. With 80 or more M.P.s the Nationalists were a distinctive and disciplined group on whose support the Liberal Government had to rely after the election of January 1910, but their number did not fluctuate markedly and they did not constitute a direct challenge to the hegemony of either of the major parties.

The more recent nationalist activity has been more fragmented and has resulted in the election of fewer M.P.s. If the various Loyalist groups which came together to form the United Ulster Unionist Council and their major Ulster opponent, the Social Democratic and Labour Party, are counted as nationalist parties, the proportion of nationalist M.P.s returned in February and October 1974 was 3·3 per cent and 4·1 per cent respectively. Within Northern Ireland the UUUC has achieved an electoral dominance which is comparable with that achieved by the Irish Nationalists earlier in the century: in the two elections of 1974 the UUUC won 11 and 10 of the 12 seats respectively, which amounts to 92 and 83 per cent of the total, compared with the 80 per cent regularly won by the Irish Nationalists in the whole of Ireland. Thus far the Plaid Cymru and the Scottish National Party (SNP) have been less successful, with the former winning 8·3 per cent of the 36 Welsh constituencies and the latter, 15·5 per cent of the 71 Scottish constituencies in October 1974.

The impact of the nationalist parties on the party system has differed in the two periods in which they have been electorally significant. As far as their principal aim is concerned the Plaid Cymru and the SNP are similar to the Irish Nationalists in that they are seeking independence for their respective parts of the

---

[1] This was in 1918 and takes account of the various intra-party groups supporting or opposing the Coalition. The exact number of parties varies according to whether groups such as Liberal Unionists, National Liberals (in 1922 and between 1931 and 1945), National Labour, and National Liberal and Conservatives are treated as separate parties.

United Kingdom, compared with Irish demand for Home Rule, but the situation is more complex in Northern Ireland. The various Loyalist groups are primarily concerned with maintaining the United Kingdom connection but are not necessarily united in the form that they wish this to take, both among themselves and over time. Thus there have been demands for the restoration of Stormont, the creation of a new system of devolution, and for full integration with the United Kingdom. Conversely, the SDLP favours some form of power-sharing devolution and, in the long term, some form of Irish unification.

The main impact of the Irish Nationalists was parliamentary rather than electoral. The parliamentary tactics adopted by Parnell and his followers in the 1880s led to major procedural changes designed to curb obstruction, although from time to time the Irish Nationalists continued to resort to obstruction and disruption. Their *electoral* success did not deprive either of the major parties of the ability to secure a parliamentary majority. Although the Liberal Party lacked an overall majority after January 1910 and the government normally depended on the support of the Nationalists, its minority position was not related to the Nationalist dominance in Ireland and would have existed had all Irish seats been eliminated.

The impact of the more recent nationalist resurgence has been both electoral and parliamentary. The electoral demise of the old Ulster Unionist Party has, in effect, deprived the Conservative Party of a useful, though not necessarily vital, block of seats.[1] From 1922, the first election after partition, the Ulster Unionists never won less than 8 of the 12 Northern Ireland constituencies and as recently as 1959 and 1964 won all 12. The nationalist challenge in Wales and Scotland has affected both major parties, however, although in both cases the longer term impact is likely to be greater on Labour than on the Conservatives. The Plaid Cymru is a less serious threat, although in a period of significant volatility the situation in Wales could change dramatically at a single general election. It is also likely

[1] The same is true of the university seats, which were abolished by the Representation of the People Act, 1948, and which returned only Conservative M.P.s between 1900 and 1910 and Conservative, Liberal, National Liberal, and various Independent M.P.s, but never a Labour candidate, between 1918 and 1945.

that in circumstances of an electoral swing to the Conservatives, Plaid Cymru candidates could deprive Labour of essential votes and facilitate Conservative gains, given the nature of the electoral system.

Of much greater importance is the SNP, which not only poses a serious threat to Labour's hegemony in Scotland but to its ability to secure a majority of seats in the House of Commons. In terms of seats won, the SNP did more damage to the Conservatives in the two elections of 1974, capturing 7 Conservative seats compared with 3 Labour.[1] Whilst far from encouraging for the Conservatives, this tended to confirm their weakening electoral position in Scotland since 1959, of which Labour had hitherto been the main beneficiary. What was ominous for Labour was that in addition to winning 11 seats in October 1974, the SNP had come second in a further 42 constituencies, of which no less than 35 were Labour-held. Neither major party can afford to lose more seats to the SNP but at only three of the elections since 1945 has Labour won a majority of the seats in England and is therefore far more dependent than the Conservatives on winning seats in Scotland to secure an overall majority in the Commons.

The impact of the nationalists in general and the SNP in particular has therefore not only been to make minority government more likely, but threatens to lessen the ability of one of the two major parties to form a majority government more than the other. Thus the two-party system, which seemed firmly established at the beginning of the century, underwent a transformation after the First World War and then seemed even more firmly established after the Second World War, may again be in the process of changing. The situations prevailing after 1910 and after 1974 might seem at first glance similar—a significant number of nationalist M.P.s in the Commons, a third party winning an increased share of the vote, minority government, even a 'Lib–Lab' pact—but the similarities are superficial and misleading. Leaving aside the fact that Labour had a small majority for a period after the election of October 1974, the Irish Nationalists in 1910 were a fairly long-standing and solid

[1] The SNP had previously won the Labour-held constituency, the Western Isles, in 1970, but had lost two other former Labour seats, Hamilton (which it had won in 1967 and lost in 1970) and Glasgow–Govan (which it had won in 1973 and lost in February 1974).

phalanx, not a recent phenomenon; the parliamentary strength of the Labour Party in 1910 owed far more to its electoral pact with the Liberals than the proportion of votes it secured in the country and consequently it had far more seats than the Liberals after 1974; the Liberal Government of 1910 was a majority government in all but name, enjoying as it did the support of both the Irish Nationalists and Labour; and the 'Lib–Lab' pact was an electoral agreement which enabled the Labour Party to reduce the disadvantages that third parties invariably suffer under the simple plurality electoral system, whereas the 1977 pact was a parliamentary agreement and held no such electoral advantage for the Liberals.

The changes that have occurred in the party system since 1900 demonstrate that it is far from immutable but they also demonstrate the tendency to maintain a two-party system. It is not the purpose of this chapter, however, to discuss the extent to which various factors are responsible for a particular type of party system, but there is no doubt that the electoral system is an important factor.[1] In particular, the simple plurality normally militates against third parties, except where they are able to secure some 25–30 per cent of the national vote, or where they have a sufficient concentration of support in particular constituencies or areas of the country. The rise of the Labour Party and the decline of the Liberals illustrates the importance of the electoral 'threshold' of 25–30 per cent. In 1918 Labour secured 20·8 per cent of the vote and won 57 seats, in 1922, 29·7 per cent of the vote and won 142 seats, in 1923, 30·7 per cent and 191 seats; conversely, in 1923 the Liberals secured 29·7 per cent of the votes and 158 seats, in 1924, 17·8 per cent and 40 seats and in 1929, 23·6 per cent and 59 seats. More recently in the two elections of 1974, the Liberals secured 19·3 and 18·3 per cent of the votes and only 14 and 13 M.P.s respectively. The very fact, however, that the Liberals win any seats at all means that they have a sufficient concentration of votes to win a limited number of constituencies but the significance of a concentration of votes as a means of third party success is more vividly demonstrated by the nationalist parties, who naturally concentrate their efforts in their own areas, which, whilst no guarantee, inevitably enhances

[1] See Douglas Rae, *The Political Consequences of Electoral Law* (Yale University Press, 1967).

the possibility of success. Thus in October 1974 the Plaid Cymru won 3 seats with less than 1 per cent of the national vote but 10·8 per cent of the Welsh vote and the SNP won 11 seats with 2·9 per cent of the national vote but 30·4 per cent of the Scottish vote.

In no meaningful sense, of course, is the simple plurality a proportional system, so that the relationship between seats and votes is invariably distorted, especially in elections in which there is widespread third party intervention and support. The principal beneficiary of the electoral bias against third parties is normally the party which wins the largest proportion of the national vote, whose number of seats in the Commons is consequently disproportionately increased at the expense of *all* other parties. In some elections, however, the number of seats won by *both* major parties is disproportionately increased. This may occur either when there is considerable third party support, as in 1929, or, more commonly, when the percentage gap in the national vote between the two major parties is small, as in 1950, 1964, 1970, and the two elections of 1974. Furthermore, it is possible for the 'wrong' party to win, in that the party with the most votes wins fewer seats than its principal opponent, as happened in 1929, 1951, and February 1974. More rarely, it is also possible for *both* major parties to win fewer seats than their proportion of the national vote entitles them, as occurred in the two elections of 1910, when the national vote was narrowly divided between the Conservative and Liberal Parties and the Irish Nationalists had an overwhelming concentration of support in Ireland, including a large number of unopposed candidates.

Obviously, the effect of the electoral system depends very much on the number of parties fighting an election and the support they can secure. As far as the composition of the House of Commons is concerned, however, this means that the number of M.P.s returned by a party can fluctuate considerably from one election to another, as is shown in Table II.2. These party fluctuations are reflected in the percentage turnover for each election, that is the proportion of M.P.s elected at one election who were not returned at the previous election. Thus in elections in which there was a considerable swing to one party, such as those of 1906, 1931, or 1945, the turnover is high. Conversely, in elections in which there is a small swing or which take place only

TABLE II.2

Distribution of M.P.s in the House of Commons 1974, by party

Election	Conserva-tive	Liberal	Labour	Other	Total	Turnover %
1900	402	183	2	83	670	36
1906	156	399	29	86	670	56
1910 (Jan.)	272	274	40	84	670	43
1910 (Dec.)	272	271	42	85	670	15
1918	382	163	57	105	707	65
1922	344	115	142	14	615	53
1923	258	158	191	8	615	33
1924	412	40	151	12	615	36
1929	260	59	287	9	615	43
1931	522	36	52	5	615	48
1935	429	21	154	11	615	35
1945	210	12	393	25	640	74
1950	298	9	315	3	625	33
1951	321	6	295	3	625	12
1955	345	6	277	2	630	19
1959	365	6	258	1	630	25
1964	304	9	317	—	630	31
1966	253	12	364	1	630	16
1970	330	6	288	6	630	30
1974 (Feb.)	297	14	301	23	635	24
1974 (Oct.)	277	13	319	26	635	7

a short time after the previous election, such as December 1910, 1951, or October 1974, the turnover is low. The turnover is also affected, of course, by the number of Members whose constituencies become vacant during a Parliament or who choose to retire at the end of a Parliament. This is particularly noticeable in the elections of 1918 and 1945 which occurred at the end of Parliaments whose life had been extended beyond the normal limit. These two elections were also marked by substantial electoral swings, but in both cases the number of casual vacancies during the life of the two Parliaments and the number of retirements were much higher than usual. The average turnover has also varied at different periods since 1900. Excluding the special cases of 1918 and 1945, between 1900 and December 1910 the turnover averaged 37 per cent, ranging from 15 per cent to 56 per cent; between 1922 and 1935 it averaged 42 per cent, ranging from 33 per cent to 53 per cent; and from 1950 to October 1974 it averaged 22 per cent, ranging from 7 to 33 per cent.[1] To a considerable extent these figures reflect the prevailing electoral conditions and state of the party system during each period. In the early part of the century the two-party system was still firmly established but in terms of party representation the fortunes of the two major parties varied considerably. After the First World War the turnover figures are on average rather higher, reflecting the realignment of the parties. The period after the Second World War has been one of relative electoral stability, resulting on average in much lower turnover figures.

The turnover figures in general and those of 1918 and 1945 in particular would not alone justify using these three periods as a basis for the analysis of the socio-economic composition of the House of Commons since 1900, nor would the argument that the two world wars constitute major historical watersheds. To these factors must be added the electoral circumstances and nature of the party system, which differed significantly in each period and which therefore had a considerable impact on the composition of the Commons. Given the nature of the party system it is important to examine not only any contrast that may exist between M.P.s representing different parties, but also such changes that may have occurred *within* the parties since 1900.

The chapter goes on to examine other aspects of the composition of the House by looking first at the career patterns of M.P.s—at their electoral antecedents in terms of electoral experience, local connections, and local government experience, at what age they were elected, how long they were Members, whether they held ministerial office, and in what circumstances and at what age their careers as M.P.s came to an end; and then at their socio-economic backgrounds in terms of education, occupation, and class. The figures are based on an analysis of the backgrounds of all M.P.s elected in the 21 general elections between 1900 and October 1974. Initially an analysis was made of the M.P.s elected for each party at each election in order to examine both intra- and inter-party changes that may have taken place. For the reasons already stated and from the trends

---

[1] If 1918 and 1945 are included the figures are as follows: 1918–35—average 45 per cent, range 33–65 per cent; 1945–74—average 27 per cent, range 7–74 per cent.

revealed by this examination it was decided that the three periods 1900–10, 1918–35, and 1945–74 were the most appropriate basis for further analysis. Furthermore, because there are important differences in the background of M.P.s representing different parties, election-by-election analysis tends to exaggerate some changes and mask others, given the extent to which party representation can fluctuate from election to election. Of course many changes that have taken place have been part of a gradual process and the election-by-election analysis facilitated their examination. Thus, where appropriate, reference is made to particular elections within the three periods.

Career Patterns 1900–1974

In general the most notable features of the career patterns of M.P.s between 1900 and 1974 is how little they have changed in many respects, in contrast to the greater changes that have taken place in their socio-economic backgrounds. Moreover, relatively speaking the differences between the parties are not very great and this section therefore looks at the House of Commons as a whole, rather than concentrating on the parties.

In the conditions of relative electoral stability that have prevailed since 1945, the concept of the 'safe' constituency has had a wide and justified currency, although in the euphoria of the 1945 landslide a senior Labour official did claim that all Conservative seats were now 'marginal'![1] Subsequent elections were to prove him wrong and, not withstanding some of the massive swings recorded at by-elections in the 1960s and the 1970s, the concept of relative 'safeness' and 'marginality' remains useful and valid. It is a far from new concept, however, as a glance at electoral statistics earlier in the century would show, although post-war electoral research has given it a more precise meaning. For the purposes of this chapter it is sufficient to acknowledge that throughout the century and, of course, earlier, a considerable proportion of constituencies were firmly in the hands of the same party election after election, regardless of the *national* electoral fortunes of that party. Conversely, other constituencies tended to change hands fairly frequently or were at least vulner-

[1] G. R. Shepherd, 'Choosing parliamentary candidates', *Labour Organiser*, Nov. 1945, p. 4.

able to small electoral swings. Although the precise operation of the 'safe–marginal' continuum has varied at different periods since 1900, especially during the realignment of parties after the First World War, in practice it has meant that a substantial majority of M.P.s were elected and re-elected at successive general elections, whilst others served only for a single Parliament or had their careers interrupted by electoral defeat.

Furthermore, as we have already seen, the overwhelming majority of M.P.s represent parties and therefore selection by a local party organization is the first crucial step to a parliamentary career. Historically, the selection and nomination of parliamentary candidates has long been a largely local matter and the development of local party organization in the nineteenth-century did nothing to change it. If anything, the growth of local parties tended to make it more likely that the choice would be made locally, though not necessarily that a local worthy would be chosen. Local magnates and landowners, and, especially in the nineteenth century, local professional and businessmen continued to play a prominent role but increasingly that role was played through the local party and gradually the power to nominate was reduced to the power to veto, finally disappearing altogether. In the period since 1945 the selection of parliamentary candidates has been characterized by a high degree of uniformity in the selection procedures, but before the Second World War and even more so earlier in the century, selection was a more haphazard process. Of much greater importance than this, however, was the part played by money.

Fighting elections costs money and, although the Corrupt and Illegal Practices Act, 1883, did much to eliminate corruption and thus reduce electoral expenses, these were normally borne by the candidates rather than their parties. M.P.s were also expected to give generous financial support to their local parties. Furthermore, before 1911 M.P.s received no remuneration for carrying out their parliamentary duties and at no time after that could a Member's salary be described as generous, especially as until recently M.P.s received only very limited expenses and allowances.[1] It was not until the post-war period that all three

[1] See 'Salaries, Allowances and Pensions' in Michael Rush and Malcolm Shaw (eds.), *The House of Commons: Services and Facilities* (Allen and Unwin, 1974), pp. 161–97.

parties had placed limits on the proportion of electoral expenses that a candidate was required to meet and on the contribution that he made to local party funds. The Labour Party imposed limits as early as 1933, but finance has always been a problem and to some extent candidates sponsored by a trade union or the Co-operative Party retain an advantage over their non-sponsored rivals in selection.[1] The Conservatives imposed similar limits with the Maxwell-Fyfe reforms of 1948.[2] Even so, the low level of parliamentary salaries and allowances often meant financial hardship unless the Member had some additional income or support. In addition, it was not until 1964 that a pension scheme for M.P.s was established, although a hardship fund had existed since 1939. In short, until recently, to become and remain a Member of Parliament, even to contemplate retirement, without financial hardship, meant being wealthy or at least having some means of supplementing a meagre parliamentary salary.

The problem of finance is reflected in the number of un-opposed returns at general elections before 1945: between 1900 and 1935 the average proportion of uncontested seats was 13·2 per cent, ranging from the exceptionally low 1·1 per cent in 1929 to no less than 36·3 per cent in 1900. Between 1900 and December 1910, however, the proportion was 22·2 per cent, compared with 8·0 per cent for the period 1918–35. The Liberal–Labour Pact at the beginning of the century was designed to husband the financial and organizational resources of the two parties, as well as to maximize the anti-Conservative challenge. The Labour Party in particular limited the number of seats it contested earlier in the century. Excluding Ireland, Labour never contested more than 14 per cent of the seats before the First World War, but after the war the proportion rose from 60 per cent in 1918 to 94 per cent in 1929, dropping slightly to 92 per cent in 1935. The introduction of the £150 deposit in 1918 increased, at least potentially, electoral costs and the Labour Party established an insurance fund to cover the risk of lost deposits, whilst between the wars the permission of the National Executive Committee was required before a Constituency Labour Party could contest a by-election. Since 1945, however,

[1] See Michael Rush, *The Selection of Parliamentary Candidates* (Nelson, 1969), pp. 228–39.
[2] Ibid., pp. 28–33.

the largest number of unopposed returns has been four and since 1955 all constituencies have been contested.

TABLE II.3

Electoral experience of M.P.s before first being elected to the House of Commons 1900–1974

(%)

Number of Contests	Period First Elected		
	1900–17	1918–44	1945–74
None	63·3 (542)	63·2 (978)	51·6 (716)
1 Contest	22·7 (194)	21·4 (331)	28·2 (391)
2 Contests	9·2 (79)	9·5 (148)	14·8 (205)
3 Contests			
4 Contests	3·3 (28)	3·5 (54)	4·0 (56)
or more	1·5 (13)	2·4 (37)	1·4 (19)
Total	100·0 (856)	100·0 (1,548)	100·0 (1,387)

In these circumstances it is not perhaps surprising that the proportion of M.P.s elected without having fought at least one parliamentary election is significantly lower in the period 1945–1974 compared with the two earlier periods. The figures in Table II.3 would certainly support the view that before 1945 the financial burden on the individual of fighting elections was a deterrent to embarking on potentially unsuccessful contests, but they also support the views that the competition for parliamentary seats and the demand for candidates with electoral experience have increased.

It is reasonable to argue that the financial factor loomed very large earlier in the century and that this in itself would have reduced the number of would-be M.P.s, but the proportion of M.P.s with no electoral experience has continued to decline since 1945: as recently as 1959 more than half of Conservative M.P.s and two-thirds of Labour M.P.s had had no electoral experience but by October 1974 these proportions had fallen to a third and little more than two-fifths respectively. The removal of the greater part of the financial burden on candidates and M.P.s would not account for this continued trend. There is some evidence that local party selectors may have been seeking candidates with electoral experience, especially in marginal seats, but on the whole electoral experience is more important in the eyes of the aspirant than the selectors,[1] Other factors, such as the frequency of elections, the number of vacancies that occur, and the electoral swing may increase or decrease the likelihood of candidates with no previous electoral experience being elected, but the consistent trend since 1945 would suggest that the competition for parliamentary seats has increased. No doubt this has been facilitated by greater social mobility and the widening of educational opportunities, whilst more uniform and systematic selection procedures have provided a framework for competition. It is, however, difficult to escape the conclusion that the number of would-be M.P.s has increased and that this is the major factor in increased competition.

TABLE II.4

Incidence[a] of local connections between M.P.s and their constituencies 1900–1974

(%)

Type of local connection[b]	Elected at general elections between		
	1900–10	1918–35	1945–74
None	30·6 (449)	37·1 (799)	39·0 (768)
Regional	19·7 (290)	17·1 (369)	16·9 (333)
Area	23·4 (344)	17·6 (380)	16·5 (325)
Direct	26·3 (386)	28·1 (606)	27·6 (545)
Total	100·0 (1,469)	99·9 (2,154)	100·0 (1,971)

[a] Where an M.P. has represented more than one constituency, this has been included in the figures.
[b] For definitions of types of local connections see Chapter appendix, p. 121.

The selection of a parliamentary candidate, however, is seldom attributable to a single factor, particularly something like electoral experience, which is more often seen like most factors as part of an aspirant's general experience and qualifications. None

[1] Rush, op. cit., pp. 71, 91, 94–5, and 220–1.

the less, there is one factor on which both aspirants and selectors sometimes lay great stress—that of local connections.

Although a statute of 1413 required M.P.s to be resident in the county or borough they represented, the provision was largely ignored and the statute was repealed in 1774. The extent to which M.P.s have had local connections with their constituencies has therefore varied. Most M.P.s represent only one constituency during their parliamentary careers, although a significant minority have sat for two constituencies. M.P.s like Sir Winston Churchill, who sat for four different constituencies during his long career, or Sir Frank Soskice (now Lord Stow Hill), who sat for three, are exceptions. However, both cases do illustrate that a Member may represent widely differing constituencies in different parts of the country: Churchill sat for Oldham, Manchester North-West, Dundee, and Epping (later Wanstead and Woodford), whilst Soskice sat for Sheffield (Neepsend), Bebington in Cheshire, and Newport. Conversely, some constituencies are not only represented by M.P.s with close or direct local connections but by a succession of two or more members of the same family. The classic case this century is Southend, which has been represented by a member of the Guinness family since 1912, but there have been others and what may be termed 'family seats' were more common in the earlier part of the century. In the much wider context of regional connections, Scottish, Irish, and Welsh constituencies were and are normally represented by natives of those parts of the United Kingdom, whereas M.P.s of Scots, Irish, or Welsh origin are less of a rarity in English constituencies.

In general, while the proportion of Members with direct local connections with their constituencies has remained constant since 1900, there has been a decline in the proportion with wider connections with the area or region in which their constituencies lie and a corresponding increase in the proportion who have no local connections at all. What accounts for this shift in the pattern of local connections is not clear. It is likely that easier communications has facilitated aspirants seeking candidates further afield, but it is perhaps more likely that it is a further reflection of increased competition: to limit the area of choice is to limit the chances of embarking on a parliamentary career.

In many cases local connections take the form of local government experience in or near the constituency or in the same region. Between 1900 and 1917 and, 1918 and 1944, 37·2 per cent and 37·0 per cent respectively of M.P.s had had local government experience prior to election to the Commons. Since 1945, however, the proportion has risen to 44·0 per cent, a change accounted for by the increase in the number of Labour M.P.s, of whom nearly three-fifths since 1900 have had local government experience, compared with less than a third of Conservative M.P.s, two-fifths of Liberals before 1945 and only a fifth since.

The selection of candidates is undoubtedly a matter of supply and demand, a fact that can be illustrated by most factors which influence the course of selection. In practice, however, it is difficult to distinguish between the two and the age at which M.P.s begin their parliamentary careers is no exception to this rule.

TABLE II.5

Age at which M.P.s were first elected to the House of Commons 1900–1974

(%)

| Age | Period first elected | | |
	1900–17	1918–44	1945–74
Under 30	8·2 (70)	7·8 (120)	4·9 (68)
30–39	26·8 (229)	23·2 (360)	38·7 (537)
40–49	32·8 (281)	31·4 (486)	36·9 (512)
50–59	22·5 (193)	25·8 (400)	15·6 (216)
60–69	8·6 (74)	7·9 (122)	2·9 (41)
70 or over	0·4 (3)	0·5 (8)	0·1 (1)
Not known	0·7 (6)	3·4 (52)	0·9 (12)
Total	100·0 (856)	100·0 (1,548)	100·0 (1,387)

The median age of M.P.s at each general election between 1900 and 1974 has remained more or less constant, ranging between 47 and 52 years, but this masks changes in the age pattern of the House of Commons since 1900. In particular the proportion of Members aged between 40 and 59 has increased, whereas earlier in the century there were generally more M.P.s under 30 and more aged 70 or over. A similar change in pattern may be seen in the age at which Members were first elected: since 1945 three-quarters of the M.P.s were aged between 30 and 49 when first elected to Parliament, compared with three-fifths or less earlier in the century. Conversely, the proportions first elected under 30 and aged 50 or over have declined.

There is no doubt that age is sometimes an important consideration to local party selectors and in some cases upper and lower age limits are applied, often as a means of reducing the number of names under consideration.[1] But age is also a question of supply, in that much may depend on when an aspirant's political ambitions first develop, to what extent his career or occupation facilitates embarking on those ambitions, and, of course, the accidents of the selection process. Some would-be M.P.s are fortunate to be selected for a safe seat held by their party at their first attempt, others are less fortunate. Robert Smillie, for example, fought seven unsuccessful contests between 1894 and 1923 before being elected Labour M.P. for Morpeth. More recently, Neville Sandelson contested eight constituencies between 1950 and 1971 before being elected Labour M.P. for Hayes and Harlington. Since the 1960s a majority of both Conservative and Labour M.P.s—three-fifths and half respectively —were under 40 when first elected to the Commons and the first-time election of M.P.s of 60 or over is now rare. The lowering of the financial barriers and increased social mobility and educational opportunities no doubt facilitated these changes by making younger candidates more readily available, especially in the Labour Party where the change was more dramatic as the traditional trade union candidates were faced with the growing and successful challenge of professional and 'white collar' candidates.

Some parliamentary careers are inevitably short-lived, given the nature of the party system and the electoral system, just as others are correspondingly long. In the safe seats, where selection is normally tantamount to election, a Member is likely to be re-elected until retirement or death, or, more rarely, the Boundary Commission or a quarrel with his local party intervenes. Conversely, to sit for a marginal seat renders the Member vulnerable to swings of the electoral pendulum and, although

[1] Rush, op. cit., pp. 72–3, and 208–9.

some M.P.s survive several Parliaments in marginal seats, many others find their careers abruptly terminated at the polls after a single Parliament.

TABLE II.6

Parliamentary service of M.P.s elected to the House of Commons 1900–1974
(%)

Length of parliamentary service	Period M.P. left Parliament		
	1900–17	1918–44	1945–74
Less than 5 years	15·5 (158)	31·5 (501)	9·9 (111)
5–9 years	23·0 (234)	20·6 (327)	26·1 (291)
10–14 years	25·6 (261)	21·9 (348)	17·0 (190)
15–19 years	14·4 (147)	11·8 (187)	17·9 (200)
20–24 years	9·7 (99)	8·2 (131)	12·9 (144)
25 years or more	11·7 (119)	6·0 (95)	16·1 (180)
Total	99·9 (1,018)	100·0 (1,589)	99·9 (1,116)

The median length of service for M.P.s leaving Parliament between 1900 and 1917 was 11 years, for the period 1918–44 9 years, and for the period 1945–74 14 years. The variation in length of service is considerable, however, ranging from less than a year in each period to 47, 55, and 62 years respectively. Furthermore, as Table 6 shows, parliamentary service reflects the prevailing electoral climate. Thus nearly a third of the M.P.s leaving the Commons between 1918 and 1944 had served less than 5 years and only 14 per cent 20 years or more, whereas the earlier and later periods reflect more stable electoral conditions. It is also probable that the tendency for M.P.s to be initially elected at an earlier age in the post-war period has increased the likelihood of longer periods of service. On the other hand, the growth of electoral volatility in the 1960s and 1970s and the possibility of a significant change in the party system may alter this situation as more M.P.s become electorally vulnerable.

Election to the House of Commons may be the fulfilment of an ambition but for many Members it is the first crucial step to a higher ambition—holding ministerial office. Whether *all* M.P.s have ministerial ambitions is not known, but most must be aware that statistically the odds are fairly heavily against them, however much they hope to prove exceptions to the rule. As governmental activities and responsibilities have grown, however, the chances of holding ministerial office have increased: in 1900 4·9 per cent of M.P.s held ministerial office; by 1975 this proportion had risen to 13·5 per cent. This excludes the unpaid position of Parliamentary Private Secretary and if P.P.S.s are included, the proportions increase to 6·3 per cent and 18·6 per cent respectively.

TABLE II.7

Highest office achieved as an M.P. 1900–1974

(%)

Office	Period M.P. left Parliament		
	1900–17	1918–44	1945–74
None	82·5 (840)	74·8 (1189)	54·7 (611)
P.P.S.	3·5 (36)	7·6 (121)	12·5 (140)
Junior Whip	1·6 (16)	2·9 (46)	4·3 (48)
Parliamentary Secretary	3·7 (38)	4·8 (77)	11·1 (124)
Minister of State	—	0·1 (2)	2·7 (30)
Chief Whip/Deputy Chief Whip	0·7 (7)	0·3 (4)	0·8 (9)
Law Officer	2·3 (23)	1·5 (24)	1·3 (14)
Speaker/Deputy Speaker	0·7 (7)	0·5 (8)	1·4 (16)
Non-Cabinet Minister	0·9 (9)	1·8 (29)	3·2 (36)
Cabinet Minister	4·1 (42)	5·6 (89)	7·9 (88)
Total	100·0 (1,018)	99·9 (1,589)	99·9 (1,116)

(Junior Whip through Cabinet Minister bracketed: 1900–17 = 14·0; 1918–44 = 17·5; 1945–74 = 32·7)

Whether and how soon a Member achieves office is subject to many factors, not least of which is whether his *party* achieves office: no Labour M.P. held office until the wartime coalition of 1915; from 1922 the chances of any Liberal Member securing office diminished rapidly, except in the special circumstances of the National Government formed in 1931 and the wartime coalition of 1940–5, and no Liberal M.P. had held office since 1945, other than as Deputy Speaker. Moreover, even where a party has a reasonable expectation of holding office after the next election, the reality may be a prolonged period in opposition, as was the case with Labour from 1951 to 1964, and even the latter election was won with a very small majority. Similarly, any M.P. whose parliamentary career is interrupted by electoral defeat may find that his chances of holding office have been adversely affected and, whilst it is not true that the longer a Member remains in Parliament the greater his chance of office, it is generally the case that a Member serves a parliamentary apprenticeship before securing his first appointment. Changes of government and periodic reshuffles inevitably enhance the possibility of a ministerial career and this is reflected in the figures in Table II.7 in that a higher proportion of M.P.s actually achieve office relative to the proportion of posts available. The Table also illustrates that, even excluding P.P.S.s, the proportion achieving office has risen from a seventh before 1918 to a third since 1945, although it should be noted that this expansion was apparent during the First World War and the depression years of the 1930s. Not surprisingly, the chances of holding senior office, including membership of the Cabinet, have also increased, but the odds against achieving high office remain formidable and most M.P.s who achieve office at all have to be content with lesser posts.

The majority of M.P.s, however, do not achieve ministerial office or serve the House of Commons as presiding officers. Some become bitter when their ambitions and expectations are not fulfilled, others adjust to the reality and chance of political life. It is an assumption, however, that all M.P.s aspire to office and certainly some secure considerable satisfaction as back-bench M.P.s.

The end of a Member's career in the House of Commons may come about in one of several ways. For most, their membership of the House ends with retirement or electoral defeat: this accounted for approximately two-thirds of the M.P.s who left Parliament between 1900 and October 1974. A further 15–16 per cent died in office, the rest leaving Parliament for a variety of

reasons—resignation, elevation to peerage, succession to a peerage, and, in the case of a small minority, removal or disqualification from membership. The proportions retiring and defeated
have differed in the three periods however. As might be expected

TABLE II.8

*Causes of termination of membership of the
House of Commons 1900–1974*
(%)

Cause	Period M.P. left Parliament		
	1900–17	1918–44	1945–74
Retired	34·9 (355)	32·7 (520)	43·0 (480)
Defeated	31·3 (319)	36·7 (583)	27·0 (301)
Died	15·9 (162)	16·2 (258)	14·9 (167)
Other[a]	17·9 (182)	14·3 (228)	15·1 (168)
Total	100·0 (1,018)	99·9 (1,589)	100·0 (1,116)

[a] i.e. resignation, elevation to the peerage, succession to a peerage, removal
or disqualification from membership of the House of Commons.

in a period of relative electoral instability and party realignment, defeat was the largest single cause of leaving the Commons
between 1918 and 1944. However, since 1945 an increasing
proportion of M.P.s have ended their parliamentary careers
with retirement and this is reflected in the age at which M.P.s
have left the Commons. Well over four-fifths of the M.P.s
retiring since 1945 have done so at the age of 50 or more and
two-thirds retired at the age of 60 or more. The corresponding
figures before 1945 are three-quarters and a half respectively.
Even allowing for causes other than retirement the age at
which M.P.s end their parliamentary careers has tended to
increase since 1945.

No doubt a major contributory factor to this trend is the considerable electoral stability that has prevailed since 1945, but it
is also a reflection of changing attitudes towards a parliamentary
career. In the post-war period being a Member of Parliament
has come to be regarded as an increasingly full-time commit-

ment and a career in its own right. As we have already seen, there is evidence of greater competition for parliamentary candidatures, M.P.s are generally elected at an earlier age, serve longer in the House of Commons, and are more likely to achieve

TABLE II.9

Age of M.P.s on leaving Parliament 1900–1974
(%)

Age	Period M.P. left Parliament		
	1900–17	1918–44	1945–74
Under 30	0·5 (5)	0·4 (6)	0·3 (3)
30–39	7·2 (73)	7·0 (111)	4·8 (54)
40–49	18·9 (193)	18·2 (289)	16·3 (182)
50–59	28·0 (285)	28·9 (459)	25·3 (282)
60–69	29·7 (302)	29·3 (466)	33·7 (376)
70 or over	14·9 (152)	13·3 (211)	18·0 (201)
Not known	0·8 (8)	2·9 (47)	1·6 (18)
Total	100·0 (1,018)	100·0 (1,589)	100·0 (1,116)

office, than was the case before 1945. Earlier in the century the financial burdens on candidates and M.P.s undoubtedly militated against election at an early age of all but the relatively wealthy, regardless of the age at which their political ambitions developed. Many of the younger M.P.s before the First World War were Conservatives with private incomes and not infrequently members of aristocratic families. Even wealthy Liberals often had to establish themselves firmly in their business or professional careers before seeking to fulfil parliamentary ambitions, whilst the majority of Labour M.P.s had served a long apprenticeship in the trade union movement prior to their election and could not have embarked on a parliamentary career without financial help from their unions. It was also more common earlier in the century for men who had had a successful professional or business career to spend their latter days at Westminster, almost as a form of honourable retirement rather than a change of career. For an increasing number of post-war M.P.s however, a parliamentary career was and is no longer an adjunct to nor an interruption of their careers outside the House. Whether their highest ambitions are fulfilled is another matter, but it is doubtful whether many present-day Members would fit the description of one commentator shortly after the First World War:

> ... the number of men in the House of Commons without social or political ambition is remarkably large ... During the day they are engaged in the direction of great industrial and commercial undertakings and in the evening they go down to Westminster for that rest and recuperation which comes within a change of scene and occupation.[1]

Socio-Economic Patterns

In contrast to the career patterns of M.P.s since 1900 their socio-economic backgrounds reflect to a much greater extent the parties they represent, which is only to be expected given the nature of the ideological divisions between the parties and their sources of support. Thus although significant changes have taken place in the socio-economic composition of the House of Commons this century, the most important contrast is between the various parties. Furthermore, important changes have also taken place within parties and these changes are better understood within a party context rather than by looking at the House as a whole.

Before dealing with each party, however, it may be useful to provide a wider historical context to the changes that have taken place in the last seventy or so years by briefly looking at the extent to which the Commons has changed in terms of the representation of economic interests in the seventy years before 1900.

The marked decline of the landed interest and the considerable growth of industrial, commercial, and financial interests, together with a much smaller growth of professional interests and the small but important beginnings of workers' representation are clearly shown in Table II.10. Furthermore, the Commons of 1900 shows a much greater diversity than that of 1832, both in the distribution and number of interests represented. What should be noted in general is that a very considerable

---

[1] Michael MacDonagh, *The Pageant of Parliament* (T. Fisher Unwin, 1921), p. 92.

TABLE II.10

Representation of economic interests in the House of
Commons in 1832, 1868, and 1900
(%)

Economic Interest	1832	1868	1900
Landed interests	52·4 (489)	34·0 (416)	15·5 (205)
Industrial, commercial, and financial interests	27·3 (255)	43·1 (528)	52·2 (689)
Professional interests	20·3 (190)	22·9 (280)	29·4 (388)
Workers' representatives	—	—	0·9 (12)
Miscellaneous interests	—	—	1·9 (25)
Total	100·0 (934)	100·0 (1,224)	99·9 (1,319)

Source: J. A. Thomas, *The House of Commons, 1832–1901: A Study of its Economic and Functional Character* (Cardiff, University of Wales Press, 1939), Section 1, Tables 1–5, and Section 2, Tables 1–6.

The totals exceed the membership of the House of Commons since many M.P.s represented more than one interest.

change in the socio-economic composition of the House of Commons occurred between 1832 and 1900 and it remains to be seen whether a change of similar dimensions has taken place in the ensuing seventy years.

The Conservative Party

Of the three major parties the Conservative Party has undergone least change in its socio-economic composition since 1900 and there is no doubt that the party underwent a much greater transformation between 1832 and 1900. This can be illustrated by an examination of economic representation.

It is important to bear in mind that the shifts in party allegiances in the aftermath of the repeal of the Corn Laws and the emergence of the Conservative and Liberal Parties by the end of the 1860s and the later split over Home Rule in 1886 had significant effects on the composition of the two major parties before 1900. For the Conservatives the loss of many of Peel's former supporters—the Liberal–Conservatives—meant a reduction of the party's representation in industry, commerce, and finance, whilst for the Liberals the defection of the Liberal Unionists meant the loss of its aristocratic element and a further reduction in the landed interests. None the less, the Conservative

TABLE II.11

Representation of economic interests among Tory/Conservative M.P.s in 1832, 1868, and 1900
(%)

Economic Interest	1832	1868	1900
Landed interests	58·3 (123)	47·3 (185)	21·2 (150)
Industrial, commercial, and financial interests	22·3 (47)	30·9 (121)	50·4 (356)
Professional interests	19·4 (41)	21·7 (85)	28·4 (201)
Total	100·0 (211)	99·9 (391)	100·0 (707)

Source: J. A. Thomas, op. cit., Section 1, Table 2 and Section 2, Table 2.

Party and its Tory predecessor demonstrated a remarkable ability to change with the times and by 1900 the Conservative Party could no longer be described primarily as the party of the landed interests, although it is worth noting that as late as 1911 a Conservative M.P. commenting on the selection of Bonar Law as party leader could remark: 'I am concerned at dear Bonar's apparent ignorance of country life now that he is leader of the *country gentleman's party*'.[1]

Since 1900 the Conservative Party has continued to change with the times but as far as its socio-economic composition is concerned, these changes have been less dramatic. Furthermore, none of the changes that have taken place could be regarded as surprising, although that is not to say that they were necessarily inevitable. For example, the proportion of Conservative M.P.s

[1] Quoted Winterton, op. cit., p. 59, author's italics. The term 'country gentleman' was commonly used to describe the occupation of a significant minority of M.P.s, mostly Conservatives, in the late nineteenth and early twentieth centuries.

TABLE II.12

Educational background[a] of Conservative M.P.s 1900–1974
(%)

	Elected at general elections between		
	1900–10	1918–35	1945–74
A *Full-time Education*			
Elementary	—	1·6 (17)	0·6 (5)
Secondary	21·6 (117)	22·1 (230)	23·0 (187)
Elementary/ Secondary plus	1·7 (9)	4·2 (44)	4·1 (33)
Privately	8·9 (48)	6·0 (62)	0·4 (3)
University	64·1 (347)	58·5 (608)	70·1 (571)
Self-educated	—	0·1 (1)	—
Not known	3·7 (20)	7·4 (77)	1·8 (15)
Total	100·0 (541)	99·9 (1,039)	100·0 (814)
B *Public school education*			
'Clarendon' schools[b]	50·8 (275) ⎱ 70·2	35·8 (372) ⎱ 63·8	36·5 (297) ⎱ 76·5
Other public schools	19·4 (105) ⎰	28·0 (291) ⎰	40·0 (326) ⎰
Private schools	11·1 (60)	9·0 (94)	1·3 (11)
Non-public schools	10·7 (58)	16·9 (176)	18·8 (152)
Not known	7·9 (43)	10·2 (106)	3·4 (28)
Total	99·9 (541)	99·9 (1,039)	100·0 (814)
C *University education*			
Oxford	31·1 (168) ⎱ 48·8	22·7 (236) ⎱ 39·3	27·9 (227) ⎱ 50·5
Cambridge	17·7 (96) ⎰	16·6 (172) ⎰	22·6 (184) ⎰
Other British	8·5 (46)	10·6 (110)	11·1 (90)
Service colleges	5·7 (31)	7·1 (74)	7·9 (64)
Overseas	1·1 (6)	1·5 (16)	0·7 (6)
Non-graduates	32·2 (174)	34·1 (354)	28·0 (228)
Not known	3·7 (20)	7·4 (77)	1·8 (15)
Total	100·0 (541)	100·0 (1,039)	100·0 (814)

[a] For definitions see Chapter appendix, pp. 121–2
[b] i.e. Eton, Harrow, Winchester, Charterhouse, Shrewsbury, Rugby, Westminster, St. Paul's, and Merchant Taylors' as defined by the Royal Commission on Public Schools 1864, of which Lord Clarendon was Chairman.

with aristocratic connections has declined from 28·8 per cent between 1900 and 1910 to 13·8 per cent since 1945 and similar patterns of adaptation are found in education, occupation, and class.

Educationally the Conservative Party has changed remarkably little since 1900. Indeed, if the periods before the First World War and after the Second are compared, the most significant change is a fall in the proportion of Conservative Members who had attended 'Clarendon' schools and a marked increase in those who had attended other public schools. Apart from this, the decline in those with a wholly private education (as distinct from those who attended public schools), an increase in those with some further education short of university, and a somewhat larger increase in the proportion of university graduates is only to be expected given educational developments since 1900.

The period 1918–35 seems to be a partial aberration in an otherwise consistent pattern. Two important factors may account for this: first, in 1918 a substantial minority of newly-elected Conservative M.P.s—Baldwin's 'hard-faced men'—came from business backgrounds, had not attended public schools, especially 'Clarendon' schools, and had not been to university; second, increasingly in this period the Conservative Party was recruiting former Liberals and those who would earlier have probably been Liberals, in both cases these included fewer public school products, especially from 'Clarendon' schools, and fewer graduates. None the less, to a very considerable extent the Conservative Party was in 1900, and remains today, an educationally exclusive body and, although there is evidence that it has become more representative of the middle class, it is hardly a middle-class microcosm. Nor does the picture change if the occupational background of Conservative M.P.s is examined, although there has been a notable shift in the distribution of broad occupational categories.

The Conservative Party is now commonly identified as the party of business, just as the Labour Party is regarded as the party of labour, but would be a misleading description before 1918 and not entirely accurate between 1918 and 1945. Before the First World War, the proportion of Conservative M.P.s with business occupations varied from 31 per cent in 1900 to 23 per cent in December 1910. Moreover, any role as the party of business was one which was shared with the Liberal Party until at least 1929, and between 1900 and 1910 in particular there was always a higher proportion of businessmen among the Liberals. There was a substantial influx of businessmen in 1918, as we have already noted, when the proportion rose to 40 per cent but

TABLE II.13

Occupations of Conservative M.P.s 1900–1974

(%)

| Occupationª | Elected at general elections between | | |
	1900–10	1918–35	1945–74
Professions	48·6 (263)	47·9 (498)	34·3 (279)
Business	30·5 (165)	38·1 (396)	53·1 (432)
Workers	—	1·1 (11)	0·5 (4)
Miscellaneous	4·6 (25)	6·1 (64)	9·0 (73)
Private means	15·3 (83)	4·6 (48)	2·9 (24)
Not known	0·9 (5)	2·1 (22)	0·2 (2)
Total	99·9 (541)	99·9 (1,039)	100·0 (814)

ª For definitions of each category see Chapter appendix, p. 122

this subsequently dropped to a third, rising again in 1935 and more especially in the post-war period until by October 1974 nearly three-fifths of Conservative Members had business backgrounds. If anything, the Conservative Party was the party of the professions, since those with professional occupations constituted the largest single group between 1900 and 1935 and a majority between January 1910 and 1931. In practice, of course, the party is relatively diverse and since 1900 there has been some increase in that diversity and a broadening of the party's middle-class base. This is shown in the increase in the proportion with business occupations, in the decline in those with private means, especially those totally reliant on such means as recorded in Table II.13, and, more specifically, by analysing the backgrounds of Conservative M.P.s by means of the Hall-Jones scale of occupational prestige.

That the Conservative Party was and is a middle-class party

as far as the socio-economic background of its M.P.s is concerned there can be no doubt, however much many of those M.P.s may owe their election to the votes of working-class Tories. Furthermore, the figures shown in Table II.14 would not be substantially different if alternative ways of assessing class were

TABLE II.14

Conservative M.P.s 1900–1974 according to the Hall-Jones scale of occupational prestige

(%)

Class[a]		Elected at general elections between		
		1900–10	1918–35	1945–74
Class 1		66·5 (360) ⎱	56·5 (587) ⎱	49·0 (399) ⎱
Class 2		30·1 (163) ⎟	37·1 (386) ⎟	43·3 (352) ⎟
Class 3	middle	2·4 (13) ⎬ 99·0	2·7 (28) ⎬ 97·4	6·8 (55) ⎬ 99·5
Class 4	class	— ⎟	0·8 (8) ⎟	0·2 (2) ⎟
Class 5a		— ⎠	0·3 (3) ⎠	0·2 (2) ⎠
Class 5b		— ⎱	0·4 (4) ⎱	0·2 (2) ⎱
Class 6	working	— ⎟	— ⎟	— ⎟
Class 7	class	— ⎬	0·1 (1) ⎬ 0·5	— ⎬ 0·2
Class 8		— ⎠	— ⎠	— ⎠
Not known		0·9 (5)	2·1 (22)	0·2 (2)
Total		99·9 (541)	100·0 (1,039)	99·9 (814)

[a] For definitions see Chapter appendix, pp. 122–3.

used. There has, however, been some shift in emphasis and Conservative Members are now less concentrated in the upper echelons of the middle class than they were in the early years of the century. Yet the shift is hardly one of marked proportions and tends to confirm the earlier picture of the socio-economic background of Conservative M.P.s since 1900. In short, the Conservative Party has continued to change with the times, but only to a limited extent and, most importantly, in that its composition now clearly reflects its image as the party of business and, especially in the eyes of its opponents, the party of the middle class.

The Liberal Party

It is to a considerable extent at the expense of the Liberal Party that the Conservatives have become identified with the middle class, for the chequered history of the Liberals since 1900 has not only been one of being electorally squeezed between Conservative and Labour, but socio-economically squeezed as well. Like the Conservatives the Liberals had undergone a considerable transformation during the nineteenth century.

TABLE II.15

Representation of economic interests among Whig/Liberal M.P.s in 1832, 1868, and 1900
(%)

Economic Interest	1832	1868	1900
Landed interests	52·8 (321)	26·7 (197)	9·0 (30)
Industrial, commercial, and financial interests	27·6 (168)	49·6 (366)	57·2 (190)
Professional interests	19·6 (119)	23·7 (175)	31·9 (106)
Workers' representatives	—	—	1·8 (6)
Total	100·0 (608)	100·0 (738)	99·9 (332)

Source: A. J. Thomas, op. cit., Section 1, Table 1 and Section 2, Table 1.

It is clear from Table II.15 that even before the defection of the Liberal Unionists in 1886 the landed interests had declined substantially among the Liberal ranks and that by 1900 the Liberal Party's parliamenty representation was drawn almost entirely from business and professional interests. Furthermore, unlike the Conservatives, the Liberals had secured some working-class representation through the 'Lib–Lab' M.P.s. In the socio-economic terms, however, the gap between the Conservatives and Liberals was far from being a gulf: in 1900 both parties were overwhelmingly middle class, a situation which was as little changed in the Liberal Party during the ensuing seventy years as it was among the Conservatives. In the case of the Conservatives there was a considerable degree of continuity of personnel from one election to another, even where substantial breaks occurred between elections, as in 1910–18 and 1935–45, and this was also true of the Liberals until 1923. But the split between Asquith and Lloyd George and the increasing electoral squeeze on the Liberals caused substantial discontinuity of personnel after 1923. Thus only 17·0 per cent of the Liberal M.P.s elected in 1923 but defeated in 1924 were subsequently re-elected, whereas 48·8 per cent of the Labour M.P.s elected in 1929 but defeated in 1931 were later re-elected. Similarly, of the 208 Liberals elected at the five elections between 1923 and 1935 nearly two-thirds served in only one Parliament and only 15 per cent in three or more. In 1945 the Liberals retained only seven of the 22 seats they held in 1935 and only four individuals were re-elected. Since 1945 the situation has improved in that a third of the Liberal M.P.s elected between 1945 and 1974 have served in three or more Parliaments; but against this it must be remembered that the largest number elected at any one election was only 14 and that at four out of ten elections, the number has dropped to six. Moreover, in that time only one Liberal candidate—Emlyn Hooson in Montgomery—has 'inherited' a Liberal-held seat and it is a moot point whether any Liberal constituency in the post-war period could be described as a 'safe' seat except in relation to the re-election of the sitting Member. It is against this background of considerable discontinuity of personnel from 1923 onwards that the socio-economic composition of the Liberal Party needs to be seen.

Like its great rival, the Conservative Party, the Liberal Party is almost entirely middle class in its socio-economic composition but they are far from being indistinguishable. As rivals before the First World War both parties had majorities of M.P.s who were graduates, both drew extensively from the public schools and from Oxford and Cambridge, but the Liberal Party was educationally less exclusive: fewer Liberal M.P.s had attended public schools in general and 'Clarendon' schools in particular and, whilst similar proportions were Cambridge graduates, twice as many Conservatives had been to Oxford and twice as many Liberals were graduates of other British universities. After 1918 this pattern was maintained but it was rather more erratic, probably because of the discontinuity of personnel discussed earlier and the fact that both parties were to a considerable ex-

TABLE II.16

Educational background of Liberal M.P.s 1900–1974
(%)

	Elected at general elections between		
	1900–10	1918–35	1945–74
A *Full-time education*			
Elementary	2·7 (14)	4·2 (15)	—
Secondary	20·1 (105)	25·3 (90)	22·8 (8)
Elementary/			
Secondary plus	3·6 (19)	4·2 (15)	2·9 (1)
Privately	13·6 (71)	10·1 (36)	2·9 (1)
University	57·6 (300)	51·1 (182)	71·4 (25)
Self-educated	0·2 (1)	0·6 (2)	—
Not known	2·1 (11)	4·5 (16)	—
Total	99·9 (521)	100·0 (356)	100·0 (35)

	Elected at general elections between		
B *Public school education*			
'Clarendon' schools	20·5 (107) } 47·4	14·6 (52) } 38·8	14·3 (5) } 51·4
Other public schools	26·9 (140)	24·2 (86)	37·1 (13)
Private schools	21·9 (114)	14·6 (52)	2·9 (1)
Non-public schools	24·0 (125)	39·3 (140)	40·0 (14)
Not known	6·7 (35)	7·3 (26)	5·7 (2)
Total	100·0 (521)	100·0 (356)	100·0 (35)

	Elected at general elections between		
C *University education*			
Oxford	16·3 (85) } 33·6	12·6 (45) } 23·8	25·7 (9) } 48·5
Cambridge	17·3 (90)	11·2 (40)	22·8 (8)
Other British	18·6 (97)	22·5 (80)	20·0 (7)
Service Colleges	2·3 (12)	2·0 (7)	—
Overseas	3·1 (16)	2·8 (10)	2·9 (1)
Non-graduates	40·3 (210)	44·4 (158)	28·6 (10)
Not known	2·1 (11)	4·5 (16)	—
Total	100·0 (521)	100·0 (356)	100·0 (35)

tent recruiting in the same socio-economic fields. Certainly, after 1945 the educational resemblance between the two parties is much closer than that which existed earlier in the century, the principal difference being that substantially more Conservatives have attended 'Clarendon' schools.

TABLE II.17

Occupations of Liberal M.P.s 1900–1974

(%)

| Occupation | Elected at general elections between | | |
	1900–10	1918–35	1945–74
Professions	42·6 (222)	43·0 (153)	40·0 (14)
Business	37·6 (196)	37·3 (133)	51·4 (18)
Workers	1·5 (8)	3·4 (12)	—
Miscellaneous	8·8 (46)	10·4 (37)	5·7 (2)
Private means	6·5 (34)	3·1 (11)	2·9 (1)
Not known	2·9 (15)	2·8 (10)	—
Total	99·9 (521)	100·0 (356)	100·0 (35)

As in the case of education, the Liberal Party is similar to but distinguishable from the Conservatives in occupational background. In the early years of the century the Liberals had a higher proportion of Members with business backgrounds but lower proportions from the professions and those dependent on private means. In the period since 1945, however, the two parties have drawn closer together.

This same pattern is reflected in class terms and Liberal M.P.s since 1900 have been hardly less middle class than the Conservatives. Once again, however, the Liberals were clearly distinguished from the Conservatives earlier in the century in that they were found in greater numbers slightly lower down the social scale, but after 1945 they have become more like their rivals. There can be little doubt that the Liberal Party has found its sources of political recruitment substantially encroached upon by its rivals for power in the state. It had already lost the support of the Liberal Unionists, relatively few of whom returned to the Liberal fold, and its efforts to recruit working-class candidates were not conspiciously successful, even less so after the electoral pact with the emerging Labour Party. After the First World War the Liberal Party found itself increasingly the victim rather than the beneficiary of the electoral system, with the result that the chances of a successful career as a Liberal M.P. declined sharply

TABLE II.18

Liberal M.P.s 1900–1974 according to the Hall-Jones scale of occupational prestige
(%)

Class		Elected at general elections between		
		1900–10	1918–35	1945–74
Class 1	middle class	51·8 (270)	50·3 (179)	45·7 (16)
Class 2		40·3 (210)	37·3 (133)	51·4 (18)
Class 3		3·6 (19) }95·9	6·2 (22) }94·1	2·9 (1) }100·0
Class 4		—	—	—
Class 5a		0·2 (1)	0·3 (1)	—
Class 5b	working class	0·2 (1)	1·4 (5)	—
Class 6		0·8 (4) }1·2	1·4 (5) }3·1	—
Class 7		0·2 (1)	0·3 (1)	—
Class 8		—	—	—
Not known		2·9 (15)	2·8 (10)	—
Total		100·0 (521)	100·0 (356)	100·0 (35)

as the party's prospects of again holding office receded and its ability to retain seats in Parliament diminished. The party therefore faced a growing challenge in the field of recruitment: a number of established Liberal politicians joined the Conservative and Labour ranks in the decade or so after 1918 and both these parties actively recruited candidates who, before 1918, would have been found on the Liberal benches in Parliament. The failure of the Liberal Party to maintain a distinctive political challenge was reflected in its failure to maintain a distinctive socio-economic composition among its Members of Parliament.

The Liberal Unionists

That the Liberal Party might split in the latter part of the nineteenth century was always a possibility, given the presence of both Whigs and Radicals in the same party, but when it came the split was not over issues which traditionally divided Whigs from Radicals, nor did it take the form of a simple Whig–Radical parting of the ways. It is true that the split over Home Rule resulted in most of the Whigs leaving the party but a substantial number of Radicals also joined the Liberal Unionist ranks, including, of course, Joseph Chamberlain, George Goschen, and the veteran John Bright. The Whigs outnumbered the Radicals by about two to one in the election of 1886 but this meant a considerable minority of Radicals given that there were 78 Liberal Unionist M.P.s. The Liberal Unionists retained a separate identity and party organization, but as time passed they co-operated more and more closely with the Conservatives, both electorally and in forming governments, until in 1912 the two parties formally merged as the Conservative and Unionist Party.

By 1900 only 13 of the Liberal Unionist Members elected in 1886 were still in Parliament: in fact, more than three-fifths of the Liberal Unionists elected in 1900 had entered Parliament in 1895 or later. During that time the Liberal Unionists had socio-economically increasingly come to resemble their Conservative allies. Understandably, the Whig presence meant that a considerable number of Liberal Unionists had aristocratic connections—29·5 per cent compared to 28·8 per cent of the Conservatives and 13·4 per cent of the Liberals, but the resemblance goes further.

In every aspect of educational background the Liberal Unionists were closer to the Conservatives: 62·8 per cent were university graduates (Conservatives 64·1 per cent, Liberals 57·5 per cent); 65·4 per cent had attended public schools (Conservatives 70·3 per cent, Liberals 47·3 per cent); 42·3 per cent had attended 'Clarendon' schools (Conservatives 50·9 per cent, Liberals 20·5 per cent); and 43·6 per cent had been to Oxford or Cambridge (Conservatives 48·8 per cent, Liberals 33·5 per cent).

As far as occupation was concerned, however, the Liberal

Unionists showed a closer affinity to the Liberals: 43·6 per cent were members of the professions (Conservatives 30·5 per cent, Liberals 37·6 per cent); and this was of course reflected in the Hall-Jones analysis. Before 1918, however, the proportion of Liberal M.P.s drawn from the professions remained static, at approximately two-fifths, whereas among the Liberal Unionists it had risen to nearly three-fifths in the two elections of 1910, bringing them much closer to their Conservative allies, who experienced a similar increase in these two elections. Thus by the time the Conservative and Liberal Unionists merged in 1912 the principal socio-economic difference between them was the higher proportion of businessmen found among the Liberal Unionists.

In socio-economic terms the Liberal Unionists made little difference to the composition of the Conservative Party, except for introducing somewhat earlier than would otherwise have been the case a greater element of business representation. In the wider context of the House of Commons the Liberal Unionists simply reinforced the overwhelmingly middle-class nature of the Conservative and Liberal Parties.

The 'Lib–Labs'

If the Liberal Unionists tended to be more like their Conservative allies than their erstwhile colleagues, then the 'Lib–Labs' were even more like the growing number of Labour M.P.s than their Liberal allies. The 'Lib–Labs' were one of several manifestations of the Liberal claim to represent the working classes following the extensions of the franchise in 1867 and 1884. There is no doubt that the Liberal Party received widespread working-class support in the latter part of the nineteenth century, both electorally and through the personal support and activity of many early trade union leaders. The party's efforts to secure the election of working-class M.P.s however, were very much less successful: the local Liberal Associations were extremely reluctant to select working-class candidates, even in constituencies in which the Liberal cause stood little chance of success, not least because working-class candidates were seldom able to provide the necessary financial resources other than through a trade union whose funds were inevitably limited. Furthermore, the

'Lib–Labs' faced a growing challenge from the burgeoning working-class and socialist organizations outside the Liberal Party. That challenge culminated in the formation of the Labour Representation Committee (LRC) in 1900 and the Liberal–Labour electoral pact of 1903, which further undermined the position of the 'Lib–Labs', in spite of the fact that there were more 'Lib–Lab' M.P.s than ever before in 1906. The success of 1906 was short-lived, however, and from 24 M.P.s in that election their numbers declined to 10 and 8 respectively in the two elections of 1910, largely as a result of defections to the Labour Party, and those who remained in Parliament after the First World War became fully-fledged Liberal or Labour Members.

The Labour challenge to the 'Lib–Labs' also took a socio-economic form. Increasingly the trade unions became more sympathetic towards and associated with the Labour Party, and the 'Lib–Lab' M.P.s came under great pressure to desert the Liberals and join Labour. The early Labour M.P.s were working class almost to a man and the Labour Party seemed in many respects a more natural home for the 'Lib–Labs'. In fact, two factors tended to inhibit a swift and total transfer of allegiance: the long-standing and sympathetic association of many 'Lib–Labs' with the Liberal Party and an abhorrence of the socialist views held by some of their would-be colleagues in the Labour Party.

Socio-economically, however, there was no significant difference between the 'Lib–Labs' and the early Labour M.P.s: no less than 83·3 per cent of the 'Lib–Lab' M.P.s elected between 1900 and December 1910 had had only an elementary education (Labour 87·1 per cent); 87·5 per cent were workers (Labour 91·3 per cent); and 83·4 per cent were working class on the Hall-Jones scale (Labour 89·1 per cent). Thus, far from forming a socio-economic link between the middle and working classes or between the Liberal and Labour Parties, the 'Lib–Labs' were a weak link between the Liberals and their working-class supporters, a link that could not withstand the challenge from the Labour Party, so ironically sustained by the Liberal–Labour electoral pact.

The Labour Party

In contrast to its two major rivals, the Labour Party has undergone a considerable socio-economic transformation since the
first two Labour M.P.s were elected in 1900. Although the
Labour Representation Committee was formed to co-ordinate
the electoral efforts of a number of working-class and socialist
organizations, the prime mover was the TUC and the great
majority of Labour candidates and M.P.s were financially supported or sponsored by trade unions. In 1906, 70·0 per cent of
Labour candidates and 72·4 per cent of Labour M.P.s were
trade union-sponsored. The Independent Labour Party (ILP),
which was affiliated to the LRC, supported a further 20·0 per
cent of the candidates and 24·1 per cent of the M.P.s. It was
therefore largely through sponsorship that the Labour Party, as
it was known from 1906, sought to overcome the financial problems of fighting elections and maintaining M.P.s. The Labour
Party also secured financial assistance from wealthy sympath-
izers, sometimes to itself, sometimes to its constituent organizations, and sometimes to particular individuals, but the trade
union connection was strong and was reinforced by the passing
of the Trade Union Act, 1913, which reversed the Osborne
judgement of 1909 and legalized the use of trade union funds for
political purposes.

As the proportion of seats contested by Labour rose, the proportion of *candidates* sponsored by trades unions declined, but
this was largely a reflection of the fact that the unions were
primarily interested in helping the Labour Party and themselves
by securing parliamentary representation, rather than merely
providing electoral finance. Thus the overwhelming majority of
union-sponsored candidates stood in constituencies in which the
chances of a Labour victory were high, and until 1924, and again
in 1931 and 1935, a majority of Labour M.P.s were union-
sponsored. Since 1945, however, union-sponsored M.P.s have
constituted between a third and two-fifths of the Parliamentary
Labour Party (PLP).

The majority of early Labour M.P.s were not only union-
sponsored but were also trade union officials, men whose ability
to represent working people and whose working-class credentials

were hardly open to question. As the Labour Party grew, however, its field of political recruitment widened, both in terms of supply and demand. The Labour Party began to attract middle-class candidates and, as the number of Constituency Labour Parties grew after the party reorganization in 1918, there was an increasing demand for such candidates. The impact of both supply and demand became apparent in the general election of 1922, in which there was a marked increase in the proportion of middle-class Labour M.P.s. The analysis of the socio-economic background of Labour M.P.s therefore uses the election of 1922, rather than that of 1918, as a dividing line between the first and second of the three periods used in this chapter.

The educational background of Labour M.P.s generally contrasts strongly with that of the Conservatives and Liberals: many Labour M.P.s had had only an elementary education, only a few had attended public schools, and there were fewer graduates, especially from Oxford and Cambridge. It is to be expected that the proportion of Labour Members with only an elementary education would decline as secondary education became the rule, but the figures in Table II.19 suggest changes which cannot be accounted for simply by the widening of educational opportunity. Moreover, the figures for the period 1945–74 conceal a trend which has continued throughout that period. The proportion of graduates among Labour M.P.s rose from a third in 1945 to well over half by October 1974, whilst the proportion of Oxbridge graduates rose from a seventh to a quarter. In addition, since 1922, the proportion of Labour M.P.s who had attended public schools has been well above the national average. Educationally, therefore, Labour Members have become much more middle class and this has continued in the post-war period.

The change in the occupational background of Labour M.P.s since 1900 follows a similar pattern to that found in education: before 1922 all but a handful of Labour M.P.s were workers, mostly manual workers; between 1922 and 1935 the proportion had declined to not much more than half; and since 1945 it has declined further, to less than two-fifths. By October 1974, in fact, the proportion of workers had declined to less than a third, the proportion drawn from the professions had risen to two-fifths, and those in business and miscellaneous occupations had re-

TABLE II.19

Educational background of Labour M.P.s 1900–1974
(%)

	Elected at general elections between		
	1900–18	1922–35	1945–74
A *Full-time education*			
Elementary	88·4 (76)	55·7 (221)	23·8 (204)
Secondary	4·6 (4)	10·8 (43)	19·4 (167)
Elementary/			
Secondary plus	2·3 (2)	6·3 (25)	13·5 (116)
Privately	2·3 (2)	1·0 (4)	—
University	1·2 (1)	22·2 (88)	42·0 (361)
Self-educated	1·2 (1)	0·7 (3)	0·2 (2)
Not known	—	3·3 (13)	1·0 (9)
Total	100·0 (86)	100·0 (397)	99·9 (859)

	1900–18	1922–35	1945–74
B *Public school education*			
'Clarendon schools	—	4·5 (18)	5·0 (43)
Other public schools	1·2 (1) } 1·2	10·1 (40) } 14·6	15·5 (133) } 20·5
Private schools	2·3 (2)	1·8 (7)	0·1 (1)
Non-public schools	96·5 (83)	78·6 (312)	77·6 (667)
Not known	—	5·0 (20)	1·7 (15)
Total	100·0 (86)	100·0 (397)	99·9 (859)

	1900–18	1922–35	1945–74
C *University education*			
Oxford	—	3·3 (13) } 8·1	11·9 (102) } 18·0
Cambridge	—	4·8 (19)	6·1 (52)
Other British	1·2 (1)	12·8 (51)	23·0 (198)
Service colleges	—	0·7 (3)	0·2 (2)
Overseas	—	0·5 (2)	0·8 (7)
Non-graduates	98·8 (85)	74·6 (296)	56·9 (489)
Not known	—	3·3 (13)	1·0 (9)
Total	100·0 (86)	100·0 (397)	99·9 (859)

mained steady. In short, the PLP had become a much more diverse body occupationally since the beginning of the century and this is reflected in an important shift in the class breakdown of Labour M.P.s.

TABLE II.20

Occupations of Labour M.P.s 1900–1974

(%)

Occupation	Elected at general elections between		
	1900–18	1922–35	1945–74
Professions	2·3 (2)	18·6 (74)	32·5 (279)
Business	4·6 (4)	8·3 (33)	10·8 (93)
Workers	89·5 (77)	56·2 (223)	37·1 (319)
Miscellaneous	3·5 (3)	14·6 (58)	18·9 (162)
Private means	—	1·0 (4)	0·3 (3)
Not known	—	1·2 (5)	0·3 (3)
Total	99·9 (86)	99·9 (397)	99·9 (859)

The Labour Party's historical claim to represent the working-class interests is clearly shown in Table II.21 in spite of the marked decline in the proportion of working-class Labour M.P.s since 1900. It is noticeable, however, that working-class Labour M.P.s were and are drawn overwhelmingly from the skilled and semi-skilled sections of the working class. Historically, this reflects the earlier unionization of skilled workers and the role played by the craft unions in the origins and development of the Labour Party, but it also reflects the higher levels of political participation found among skilled workers. Between 1900 and 1918 the PLP was overwhelmingly working class—an ironical fact, since the conference which established the LRC in 1900, specifically rejected a motion which would have restricted 'Labour candidatures to members of the working class',[1]—but between 1922 and 1935 the proportion fell to less than half and

[1] Henry Pelling, *The Origins of the Labour Party* (Oxford University Press, 1954), pp. 208–9 and David Marquand, *Ramsay MacDonald* (Jonathan Cape, 1977), pp. 67–8.

since 1945 three-quarters of Labour M.P.s have been middle class. Again the proportion of middle-class M.P.s has tended to increase since 1945 and by October 1974 more than four-fifths were middle class.

TABLE II.21

Labour M.P.s 1900–1974 according to the Hall-Jones scale of occupational prestige

(%)

| Class | | Elected at general elections between | | |
		1900–18	1922–35	1945–74
Class 1	⎱	—	⎱ 15·4 (61)	⎱ 23·9 (205)	⎱
Class 2	middle	4·6 (4)	14·1 (56)	23·9 (205)	
Class 3	class	7·0 (6)	11·6 ⎱ 14·8 (59) ⎰ 51·4	19·3 (166) ⎰ 76·3	
Class 4	⎰	—	2·3 (9)	4·2 (36)	
Class 5a		—	⎰ 4·8 (19)	5·0 (43) ⎰	
Class 5b	⎱	46·5 (40) ⎱	24·4 (97) ⎱	13·1 (113) ⎱	
Class 6	working	36·0 (31)	20·1 (80)	9·8 (84)	
Class 7	class	5·8 (5) ⎰ 88·3	2·8 (11) ⎰ 47·3	0·5 (4) ⎰ 23·4	
Class 8	⎰	—	—	—	
Not known		—	1·2 (5)	0·3 (3)	
Total		99·9 (86)	99·9 (397)	100·0 (859)	

None the less, the Labour Party remains clearly distinguishable in socio-economic terms from its rivals: the proportion of Labour graduates has increased considerably, but is still substantially smaller than that found among Conservative and Liberal M.P.s and far fewer Labour M.P.s are Oxbridge products; the proportion of Labour M.P.s who have attended public schools, as we have already noted, has been well above the national average since 1922, but hardly comparable to the proportions of public school Conservatives and Liberals; the proportion of workers has declined, but they still constitute nearly a third of the PLP compared with four Conservatives since 1945 and no Liberals, whilst teachers and lecturers are now the most numerous professional group in the Labour ranks rather than the lawyers among the Conservatives and Liberals; and, in spite of the marked increase in the proportion of middle-class Labour

M.P.s, the Labour Party draws much more heavily than either the Conservatives or Liberals on the lower echelons of the middle class. Furthermore, unlike most Conservative and Liberal M.P.s, many middle-class Labour M.P.s can and do claim working-class antecedents.

The changes in the socio-economic composition of the Labour Party have been marked by dramatic shifts at particular times, followed by a period in which the new trend has been strengthened and consolidated, rather than being a gradual process of change. This was especially the case in 1922 and 1945, when there were significant changes from the previous election. Thus the proportion of graduates rose from a mere 1·6 per cent in 1918 to 17·6 per cent in 1922 and from 18·5 per cent in 1935 to 34·3 per cent in 1945. Similarly, the proportion of workers declined from 89·0 per cent in 1918 to 68·3 per cent in 1922 and from 61·1 per cent in 1935 to 43·4 per cent in 1945.

There is little doubt that after 1918 the Labour Party began to recruit parliamentary candidates in the same field as its rivals, especially the Liberals, but much more importantly it opened up other fields of political recruitment which had been virtually untapped by the Conservative and Liberal Parties. Before 1918, the Labour Party recruited largely from the working class and continued to do so after the First World War, but it also began to recruit candidates from the middle class, including its lower echelons, from which few Conservative and Liberal M.P.s were drawn. This trend of middle-class recruitment was consolidated between the wars and, although it received a temporary setback in the electoral debacle of 1931, this was followed by a further massive boost in the triumph of 1945. The process has continued unabated since 1945, little affected by Labour's defeats in the 1950s and considerably strengthened by the victories of the 1960s and 1970s. In becoming predominantly middle class, however, the PLP has established and retains a broad middle-class image rather than the more exclusive image of the Conservatives and Liberals.

The growth of middle-class recruitment is also reflected in the pattern of union-sponsorship. The proportion of union-sponsored M.P.s has tended to remain constant since 1945, but an increasing number of 'white-collar' unions have sponsored M.P.s in recent elections and many industrial trade unions, such as the

TGWU and NUGMW, now sponsor M.P.s who have no occupational connection with the industries represented by the union and whose background is by most criteria clearly middle class.

How far this socio-economic transformation of the PLP and, in certain respects, of the House of Commons is significant, must be the subject of further research, but suffice to say that it may have profoundly affected the Labour Party's claim to represent the working class and such claims that the House of Commons may have that it is a socio-economically representative body.

The Nationalists

Although the nationalist M.P.s at the beginning of the century and in the 1970s were and are politically distinctive groups at Westminster, they did not and do not differ markedly from most other M.P.s in socio-economic terms. With the exception of the Scotland Division of Liverpool, which was populated largely by Irish immigrants and had a Nationalist M.P. from 1885 to 1929, all nationalist M.P.s represented constituencies in Ireland, Scotland, or Wales, often having close or fairly close local connections with their constituencies. This apart, however, the nationalists have largely reinforced the tendency of the House of Commons to be primarily middle class in its composition, although, like many Labour M.P.s after 1918, they have tended to be drawn from a broader spectrum of the middle class than the Conservatives or Liberals. Thus, whatever their political significance the nationalists, even when present in large numbers, as were the Irish Nationalists, have only had a marginal impact on the socio-economic composition of the House of Commons.

Conclusion

There can be no doubt that the House of Commons has undergone important socio-economic changes since 1900 and that there have been significant changes in M.P.s' career patterns. The Commons is still sometimes described as 'the best club in London'—a term dating from the mid-nineteenth century and, in socio-economic terms, it retains a good deal of the exclusiveness of the club, especially on the Conservative side of the House.

However, as a description of the atmosphere of the House of Commons, the term 'club' was much more appropriate in 1900 than it is now. Not only did many of its facilities resemble those of a club, as was intended by Sir Charles Barry when he designed the Palace of Westminster, but most of its members belonged to a definable social and political élite in whose life the club played a real and significant part. London clubs were at their zenith at the turn of the century and the overwhelming majority of M.P.s were members of one or more clubs. Moreover, the two major parties had clubs with which they were more or less exclusively identified—the Carlton, the Junior Carlton, the Constitutional, and White's for the Conservatives and the Reform, the National Liberal, and Brooks' for the Liberals. Indeed, the defection of the Liberal Unionists in 1886 caused a crisis in Brooks's as rival groups sought to blackball candidates for membership and, although most Liberal Unionists resigned from the Reform and the National Liberal, a significant minority continued to belong to Brooks's.

Between 1900 and 1910 well over four-fifths of all M.P.s belonged to one or more London clubs, including 95 per cent of Conservatives and over 90 per cent of Liberals. In the period 1945–74 the proportion had fallen to little more than two-fifths and, although three-quarters of the Conservatives and three-fifths of the Liberals were club members, this was in direct contrast to only 10 per cent of Labour M.P.s. By 1974 the proportion had fallen to two-thirds of the Conservatives, 6 of the 13 Liberals and 8 per cent of Labour Members. The decline in club membership, even though still high among the Conservatives and to a lesser extent the Liberals, marks a change in style and in the role of the Member of Parliament.

The workload of Parliament and of the individual M.P. has increased considerably since 1900, both in terms of the growth in parliamentary business and the development of the 'welfare officer' role. The legislative burden has grown enormously and the continued existence of disciplined parties committed to the implementation of specific programmes has considerably increased the demands on Members' time, even if it has not necessarily encouraged their active participation. Moreover, the House of Commons has sought to strengthen its ability to scrutinize the actions and policies of the government, notably through the creation of more select committees, which have made further demands upon at least a minority of M.P.s.

Quite apart from this, the burden on individual Members has been further increased as constituents and others have sought the assistance of M.P.s in securing the redress of some grievance or help with various personal problems. In earlier times the help of M.P.s was frequently sought by 'place-hunters' and the like. In 1846, for example, John Bright complained to a friend, '. . . every post brings me twenty or thirty letters—and such letters. I am teased to death by place-hunters of every degree . . .',[1] and as recently as 1918 a Member received the following letter from a constituent:

You're a fraud, and you know it. I don't care a rap for the billet or the money either, but you could hev got it for me if you wasn't so mean . . . That's orl I got for howlin' meself Hoarse for you on pole day, an' months befoar. I believe you think you'll get in agen. I don't. Yure no man. An' I doant think yure much of a demercrat either. I lowas meself riting to so low a feller, even tho' I med him a member of parlerment.[2]

Some elements of the 'welfare officer' role certainly existed before the First World War however: in their book on Parliamentary Questions, Chester and Bowring note that at the beginning of the century it was not uncommon for M.P.s to raise personal constituency cases with Ministers.[3] How far back before 1900 this practice can be traced remains unknown, but it is hardly surprising that as the welfare state developed, so should the 'welfare officer' role. Certainly, the First World War brought with it many attendant welfare problems, especially in areas such as war pensions, with which constituents sought help from their M.P.s and the economic difficulties of the inter-war period did nothing to lessen this development. The 'welfare officer' role was none the less resented by some Members: 'One of the chief torments of a Member's life is the answering of letters, most of which should not have been written . . . No inconsiderable number of the British public appear to think that the chief duty of a Member of Parliament is to attend to their personal claims, and that he should always place these before the needs of the

---

[1] Quoted in MacDonagh, op. cit., p. 68.

[2] Quoted ibid., pp. 69–70.

[3] D. N. Chester and N. Bowring, *Questions in Parliament* (Oxford University Press, 1962), pp. 104–5.

nation.'[1] In the post-war period however, the 'welfare officer' role has become widely accepted by M.P.s, although not without some misgivings.[2]

With the greater workload on M.P.s there have been increases in their parliamentary salaries and expenses and in the services and facilities available to them, although their provision has tended to be piecemeal and belated.[3] The provision of increased remuneration and facilities has been accompanied by an increase in the proportion of full-time or nearly full-time M.P.s who, in many cases, especially on the Labour side of the House, are totally dependent on their parliamentary salaries.

The position of Member of Parliament has undoubtedly become open to more individuals, partly because of the rise of the Labour Party and partly because a private income is no longer a prerequisite of a parliamentary career, and this is reflected in the career patterns of M.P.s and in the socio-economic changes the House of Commons has experienced. But these changes tend to pale beside the greater changes in the party system and to what extent the socio-economic composition of the Commons influences its operations remains an open question, a question which can only be answered in the context of the purpose of Parliament and the role of the Member of Parliament, which is beyond the scope of this chapter. And yet, to little purpose or much, it is no longer true, as John Morley once said, that the life of the M.P. consists of 'business without work and idleness without rest.'[4]

[1] Lord Snell, *Men, Movements and Myself* (J. M. Dent, 1936), p. 213. Lord Snell was Labour M.P. for Woolwich East from 1922 to 1931.

[2] Anthony Barker and Michael Rush, *The Member of Parliament and His Information* (Allen and Unwin, 1970), pp. 189–204. See also Anthony Barker and Michael Rush, 'Political Socialisation in the British House of Commons: A "Generational" View', paper presented to European Consortium for Political Research Workshop, Mannheim, April 1973.

[3] See Rush and Shaw, op. cit., *passim.*

[4] Quoted MacDonagh, op. cit., p. 85.

APPENDIX

Definitions used in this chapter were as follows:

1. Local Connections

(a) Direct connections: including born in the immediate locality, a member of a local government body within the constituency or within which the constituency lies, known to live or work in the locality, a member of the local party.

(b) Area connections: including born in the area or membership of a local government body in an area adjacent to or within the same county as the constituency—generally similar but less specific connections than in (a) above.

(c) Regional connections: known to have connections with a wider area in which the constituency lies, e.g. midlands, north-west, etc.

2. Education

(a) Full-time education:

  (i) Elementary: full-time education terminated at elementary school, including those who had further education at night school, adult education courses, etc.

  (ii) Secondary: full-time education terminated at secondary level, including those who had further education at night school, adult education courses, etc.

  (iii) Elementary/Secondary plus: elementary or secondary education followed by some form of full-time technical or vocational training, including teacher training.

  (iv) Privately: educated by private tutor or similar arrangement.

  (v) University: all graduates, including attendance at the Inns of Court and various military colleges.

  (iv) Self-educated: claimed to have received no formal full-time education.

(b) Public school education:

Public schools were defined as members of the Head-masters' Conference and the Association of Governing Bodies of Public Schools, together with the list of over-seas public schools and the list of principal girls' schools published annually in *Whitaker's Almanac*. Private schools were defined as those schools outside the state system which do not have public school status. The 'Clarendon' schools are Eton, Harrow, Winchester, Charterhouse, Shrewsbury, Rugby, Westminster, St. Paul's and Merchant Taylors', as defined by the Royal Commission on Public Schools, 1864, of which Lord Clarendon was chairman.

3. Occupation

Occupation was defined as the principal or main occupation prior to election to Parliament.

(a) Professions: lawyers, doctors, dentists, school, university, and adult education teachers, officers of the regular forces, and all recognized professions.

(b) Business: all employers, directors of public and private companies, business executives, stockbrokers, farmers, and self-employed businessmen.

(c) Workers: self explanatory, but including non-manual workers not included in any other category and all full-time trades union officials.

(d) Miscellaneous: including housewives, professional poli-ticians, welfare workers, local government officers, insurance agents, journalists, party publicists, professional party organizers, miscellaneous administrators.

(e) Private means: those with a private or unearned income who have no gainful occupation.

4. The Hall-Jones Scale of Occupational Prestige

(a) Class 1: professionally qualified and high administrative occupations.

(b) Class 2: managerial and executive (with some responsi-bility for directing and initiating policy) occupations.

(c) Class 3: inspectional, supervisory, and other non-manual (higher grade) occupations.
(d) Class 4: inspectional, supervisory, and other non-manual (lower grade) occupations.
(e) Class 5a: routine grades of non-manual work.
(f) Class 5b: skilled manual occupations.
(g) Class 6: semi-skilled manual occupations.
(h) Class 7: routine manual occupations.

For a full list of occupations in each class see Abraham N. Oppenheim, *Questionnaire Design and Attitude Measurement* (Heinemann, 1966), pp. 276–84.

III

THE SPEAKER AND HIS OFFICE IN THE TWENTIETH CENTURY

Philip Laundy

The Nature and Continuity of the Speaker's Office

At the turn of the century the traditions and conventions associated with the Speakership were already well established in the form in which we know them today. The nature of the office has changed in no fundamental respect in the years which have since elapsed and the first task of this essay is to summarize those essential features which give the Speakership of the House of Commons its unique character.

The Speaker is a Member of the House of Commons, elected for a constituency in the same way as his colleagues, and chosen by them at the beginning of a Parliament in accordance with the practice of centuries. He is the representative of the House in its dealings with the Crown, the House of Lords, and all its external relationships. He is historically the guardian of the privileges of the Commons and its impartial presiding officer. The Speaker derives his authority from the House which can transact no business until he has been elected, apart from the conduct of the election itself. If a Speaker dies in office the House must elect a successor before doing anything else.

Although freely chosen by the House of Commons, the Speaker's authority depends also on the formal approval of the Sovereign. The historical link with the monarchy is preserved in the ceremony following his election at the beginning of a new Parliament, whereby he seeks the royal approbation of the Commons' choice of himself at the bar of the House of Lords and lays claim on their behalf to 'all their ancient and undoubted rights and privileges'.

It is often suggested by those who oppose any change in the

manner of the Speaker's election to Parliament that the strength of his position lies in the fact that he is an ordinary Member who reached the House of Commons by the same route as the rest of his colleagues. While this argument has a certain validity, no realistic assessment of the office could possibly lead to the conclusion that any ordinary Member is likely to be chosen as Speaker. No ordinary Member has his authority, prestige, and influence, neither would the House vest such powers in an ordinary Member. The choice of the Speaker is a serious business. While he is normally chosen on a non-partisan basis, through agreement between both sides of the House, the proposition that he is the free choice of all the Members has been open to question, as we shall see.

What is, however, indisputable, is the total impartiality of the Speaker once he has been elected. Once in the Chair he becomes in the truest sense a House of Commons man. He sheds all his party affiliations and dedicates himself exclusively to the impartial discharge of his functions. It is inconceivable today that any Speaker would ever be consciously partisan. He might err in a ruling or in his judgement; he might yield to the pressure of an aggressive Member arguing a point of order; but his every action and decision would be motivated by a zealous regard for impartiality and fair play.

A discussion of the Speaker's impartiality normally lays stress on his duty to protect the rights of minorities. This is a duty of which no Speaker ever loses sight, but impartiality also implies a regard for the rights of the majority as well as minorities, and in a modern Parliament no Speaker can ignore the claims of a hard-pressed government striving to achieve its legislative programme. Another phenomenon of modern Parliaments is that minorities have tended to become incorporated within the major broad-based political parties, a fact of parliamentary life which has not been altered by the election of multi-party Parliaments on two occasions in 1974. The Speaker's concern for minorities must thus today extend beyond the traditional concept of what constitutes a minority. A clearly identifiable minority group can always be sure that it will receive a favourable proportion of parliamentary time in relation to its numerical strength. The principal sufferer in the intense competition to catch the Speaker's eye must inevitably be the faithful government or opposition back-bencher who seldom deviates from the party line.

The Speaker's choice of Members to speak in debate, a choice which under modern practice is not open to dispute, is a most important exercise of his impartiality. The very absoluteness of the Speaker's power to call on Members to speak makes it an onerous duty, for the competition to catch the Speaker's eye is so keen that many are inevitably disappointed. The Speaker must weigh many factors, but the final decision as to selection is always his. He must take into account all shades of opinion in the House. He must know the Members who are knowledgeable on the subject under debate. He must take geographical considerations into account and know those Members who have a special interest in the debate because of their constituencies. He must have regard for the rights both of veteran Members and of newcomers. 'He must know who are good debaters, how to provide opportunities for challenge and what Parliament loves to call "the cut and thrust of debate". And all this without any question of party favouritism entering his mind or affecting his choice.'[1]

Another factor which has influenced the Speaker's choice, and which has a bearing on the principle of impartiality, is the custom of according precedence in debate to privy councillors. This custom was much resented by back-benchers, and in 1959 the Select Committee on Procedure recommended its abolition.[2] No formal action was ever taken, however, and although Members continued to complain the Chair for many years continued to feel obliged to honour it.[3] The practice was eventually varied by Speaker Lloyd, who never called two privy councillors from the back-benches of the same party one after the other, but would interpose a non-privy councillor. There is reason to believe that this change has lessened the resentment against privy councillors felt in previous Parliaments.[4]

The need to be impartial obliges the Speaker radically to change his life style. He not only resigns from his party, which of

[1] Horace King, 'The impartiality of the Speaker', *The Parliamentarian*, April 1966, p. 129.

[2] See *Report from the Select Committee on Procedure*, H.C. 92–I, 1959, pp. xvi–xvii.

[3] See for example exchanges between Speaker King and certain Members on 13 Apr. 1970, *Commons Hansard*, 5th series, Vol. 799, col. 1026.

[4] Information supplied by Mr. Speaker Lloyd, 23 May 1974.

itself is a major turning point in a political career, but he also normally resigns from any clubs which may have political associations. He isolates himself from the camaraderie and social life of the House of Commons, and even personal friendships which he may have developed over the years with other members must be submerged in the wider circle that includes every Member. The Speaker is the friend of every Member and he makes a point of always being accessible to them. Dr. Horace King, that most unconventional of Speakers, has written: 'It may be that the social isolation of Mr. Speaker, which has grown up only during the last 100 years, has been carried too far.'[1] However, his own attempts to lessen this isolation while in office were not notably successful. For example, his proposal that he might occasionally take his meals in the Members' Dining Room at the table reserved for the Clerks was dropped following representations from a delegation of senior Members of the House.[2]

With the exception of the Sovereign herself, there is probably no holder of high public office whose prestige exceeds that of the Speaker. An author writing in 1900 saw in the Speaker's office many of the attributes of royalty[3] and although the Speaker is not always immune from press criticism, as will be seen later, what was written then is equally valid today. The Speaker's prestige is deliberately exalted in such a way as to sustain the authority of even a weak incumbent, because all parties recognize the importance of guaranteeing the independence of the office, it being the cornerstone of the parliamentary system. There are few Members who fail to recognize that they share a common responsibility in protecting the integrity of the Speaker's office. An affront to the Speaker is an affront to the House itself, and reflections on his character and actions are punishable as breaches of privilege or contempts.[4] The House itself may criticize the conduct of the Speaker or dissent from one of his rulings only by way of a formal substantive motion introduced for that specific purpose.[5]

[1] *The Parliamentarian*, op. cit., Apr. 1966, p. 128.
[2] Interview with Lord Maybray-King, 13 Sept. 1973.
[3] See Edward Lummis, *The Speaker's Chair* (Unwin, 1900), pp. 6–7.
[4] Erskine May's *Parliamentary Practice* (Butterworth, 18th edition, 1971), pp. 148 and 225. All subsequent references are to the 18th edition.
[5] Ibid., pp. 225 and 361.

Among the outward symbols of his prestige and authority are the robes he wears, the Chair in which he presides, and the ceremony attending him. The perquisites of the office include a house within the Palace of Westminster and a salary equal to that of a cabinet minister.[1] In recognition of his political independence his salary is charged directly to the Consolidated Fund under permanent legislation instead of being annually voted by Parliament.[2]

At the turn of the century the Speaker ranked after all the peers as the first commoner. Today he ranks sixth in the official order of precedence after the Royal Family and ahead of all other peers except those who hold offices which take precedence to his own.[3]

On retirement he is normally elevated to the House of Lords, and if he remains active he takes his seat among the cross-benchers. Speaker Whitley was the only retired Speaker to refuse a peerage during this century. Until recently it was customary to honour a retired Speaker with a viscountcy. In 1971 Dr. Horace King became the first to accept a life peerage which carries the rank of baron. In the light of the contemporary trend which favours avoiding the creation of new hereditary peerages it can be expected that this practice is likely to continue in the future. The Speaker's pension is awarded by special Act of Parliament since no permanent legislation exists for the purpose. From 1832 to the retirement of Speaker Morrison in 1959 it was customary to grant the Speaker a pension of £4,000 a year, an arbitrary figure which came to be regarded as a fixed precedent. Speaker King, in another break with tradition, was the first to be awarded a pension of £5,000 on his retirement.[4]

The Speaker's office is primarily judicial in nature and lawyers have frequently, although not invariably, been selected to fill it.

---

[1] In 1974 £13,000 a year.

[2] See House of Commons (Speaker) Act, 1832, s. 1.

[3] An order-in-council of 30 May 1919 established a revised order of precedence headed by the Royal Family, the Archbishop of Canterbury, the Lord Chancellor, the Archbishop of York, the Prime Minister, the Lord High Treasurer (now a defunct office), the Lord President of the Council, and the Speaker of the House of Commons. See *London Gazette*, 3 June 1919, p. 7059.

[4] See Mr. Speaker King's Retirement Act, 1971.

Of the 22 Speakers who by 1974 had held office since Arthur Onslow all but seven have been lawyers.[1]

As the impartial presiding officer who is called upon to decide points of order, the interpreter of practice and procedure, and the guardian of the privileges of the House, the role of the Speaker is very akin to that of a judge. His decisions stand as precedents in the parliamentary case-law. Such rulings, whether given publicly from the Chair or privately in response to Members seeking his advice, 'in course of time may be formulated as principles, or rules of practice. It is largely by this method that the modern practice of the House of Commons has been developed.'[2]

The judicial nature of the Speaker's office is also evident in his power to rule on the admissibility of bills, motions, and amendments; to invoke the sanctions provided in the standing orders for dealing with disorderly conduct; and in his duty to pronounce the judgement of the House against those who violate its rights and immunities.

He acts in a judicial capacity when he decides, following a complaint of privilege, whether or not the matter should take precedence over the regular business of the day. It is in this capacity that he protects the privileges of the House of Commons from infringement by the House of Lords: for example, by ordering that a bill received from the upper House be laid aside on the ground that it infringes the Commons' financial privilege, or by drawing attention to a Lords' amendment on the ground that it does likewise. His statutory duties under the Parliament Acts 1911 and 1949 (see p. 196) are a further reflection of his judicial functions on behalf of the House of Commons in its relationship with the other House. Another example of the judicial nature of the Speaker's office is to be seen in his role as interpreter of the *sub judice* convention (see pp. 180–4). As with all other matters of procedure, practice, and precedent, the House entrusts its application to the judgement of the Speaker, the impartial guardian of parliamentary law. Just as the judges in the other courts of law are removed from the influence of the

---

[1] In this century Speakers Gully, Lowther, Morrison, Lloyd and Hylton-Foster were lawyers. Speakers Whitley, Fitzroy, Clifton-Brown, and King were non-lawyers.

[2] Erskine May, p. 225.

other arms of government, so has the Speaker been raised above party politics as the supreme arbiter of the law of Parliament.[1]

Many of the procedural powers of the Speaker under the modern standing orders were in existence at the turn of the century, but some have been acquired during the present century. By 1900 it was well-established practice that the Speaker did not participate in debate and never voted in the House except in the event of a tie. In exercising his casting vote, the occasion for which arises very rarely, he does so in accordance with conventions which underscore his impartiality and do not reflect any personal view he might have on the issue in question.[2]

Certain powers designed to control the abuse of procedure were already vested in the Speaker at the outset of the period under review, including the power to accept or refuse a motion for the closure of debate; to accept or refuse a dilatory motion for the adjournment of the House or the adjournment of debate; to decide whether or not an emergency adjournment motion conforms to the requirements of the relevant standing order; to refuse a division if unnecessarily claimed; to curb irrelevance and tedious repetition in debate; and to invoke disciplinary powers in dealing with disorderly conduct.

But while the Speaker's powers may seem formidable he exercises none which the House has not conferred upon him. Although clothed in the raiment of prestige and authority, he is the servant of the House, elected to interpret its wishes as well as its rules and practice. The House is the master of its own procedure and can change it by resolution.[3] The Speaker's rulings are not impositions of his own will but judgements rendered within the

---

[1] See Josef Redlich, *The Procedure of the House of Commons* (Constable, 1908), ii. 148–50. It is only fair to add that one leading parliamentary expert consulted by the author believes this to be an exaggerated assessment of the Speaker's role.

[2] See Philip Laundy, *The Office of Speaker* (Cassell, 1964), chapter II. See also the explanation of Mr. Speaker Lloyd on 12 July 1974 (*Commons Hansard*, 5th series, Vol. 876, col. 1741). The casting vote was twice exercised on the previous day by the Speaker and Deputy Speaker respectively in circumstances where, as it was subsequently revealed, the divisions had been incorrectly recorded and there had been no tied vote.

[3] Except where a particular procedure is necessary to conform to the requirements of a statute such as the Statutory Instruments Act, 1946.

framework of parliamentary law, tempered on occasion by his sense of the mood of the House and the circumstances of the moment. The flexibility of parliamentary procedure is its great and subtle strength. The rules are not intended to be enforced with undiscriminating rigidity in every conceivable circumstance. The House, as Lord Maybray-King has written, 'would not welcome a Speaker who rigidly enforced on every single occasion every jot and tittle of the laws which he administers'.[1]

Members of Parliament are immune from action in law in respect of anything they might say in the course of debate in the House, and the Speaker is the traditional guardian of their right to freedom of speech which is today the most important aspect of parliamentary privilege. However, he also recognizes a duty to protect those who might as a result be attacked with impunity. It is well-established practice that the conduct of the Royal Family and certain other holders of high office, including judges and members of both Houses of Parliament, can only be called into question by means of a substantive motion introduced for that specific purpose.[2] In cases where the practice is less definite the Speaker has taken it upon himself to ensure fair play. On 25 March 1971, in the course of an adjournment debate during which a Member attacked the conduct of a high-ranking British diplomat and his wife, Mr. Speaker Lloyd stated that it is 'a practice of the House not to attack people who are not able to defend themselves' and ruled that 'there has to be a substantive motion if it is to be in order'.[3]

While the ruling might be disputable on the basis of precedent, it seems consistent with the concept of the Speaker's office that in protecting the rights of Members he should also where possible and in the interests of fair play extend a measure of his protection to those they represent.

The principle of continuity in the office of the Speaker was also well established by the dawn of the twentieth-century, a principle which, given the impartial and judicial nature of the office, is clearly both logical and desirable. It has been maintained unbroken since 1841 when Charles Shaw-Lefevre, a

---

[1] See *The Parliamentarian*, op. cit., Apr. 1966, p. 130.
[2] Erskine May, pp. 361–2 and pp. 417–18.
[3] *Commons Hansard*, 5th series, Vol. 814, cols. 893–4.

Liberal who was first elected Speaker in 1839, was unanimously re-elected by a Tory-controlled House of Commons.[1]

However, the conventions associated with the continuity principle are somewhat more vulnerable than is generally believed. They have frequently been subjected to strain, and the fact that they have survived intact over nearly a century and a half is due to circumstances which provoke some interesting speculation. Two factors in particular have been crucial in securing the continuity of the office. Firstly, during the period of what may be termed the modern Speakership, no Speaker seeking re-election in his constituency has ever been defeated at the polls; secondly, during the same period, no incoming majority following a change of government has ever given in to the temptation to replace a sitting Speaker. The Speaker's security of tenure may thus be due in part to an understanding of his role on the part of the electorate in his constituency, at least on those occasions when he has been opposed.[2] It clearly owes something to political restraint on the part of the successful party following a change of government, and also perhaps to front-bench solidarity in the face of back-bench discontent.

But chance has also undoubtedly played its part. In point of fact there is no constitutional or legislative obstacle to prevent a Speaker from being replaced.[3] The electors are free to defeat a Speaker at the polls if he is opposed, as he frequently is, and a new Parliament is free to elect a different Speaker if it so wishes. In the event of one or other of these possibilities occurring, the continuity of the office would receive a severe setback and its future would need to be reassessed.

Consultation in the selection of the Speaker is an important element in the promotion of the continuity of the office and during the twentieth century complaints of lack of consultation concerning the choice of Speaker have frequently been expressed. Sometimes the dispute has been between government and opposition, on other occasions it has crossed party lines. At

[1] See Laundy, op. cit., chapter 4.

[2] The fact that the result in the Speaker's constituency has sometimes run contrary to the national trend may be adduced as support for this idea.

[3] The last time a sitting Speaker was rejected was on 19 February 1835 when Charles Manners-Sutton was unseated after having served as Speaker in the seven previous Parliaments. See Laundy, op. cit., chapters 4 and 30.

the root of such disputes lies the principle that the Speaker is, or should be, the choice of the House as a whole, not of the Prime Minister, not of the government, not of the front benches. This principle is reflected in the tradition whereby the Speaker's nomination is always proposed and seconded by back-bench Members, by a government and opposition Member respectively, in cases where both sides of the House are able to agree on the candidate.

A former Member of the House of Commons, Lord Pannell, has written: 'There have always been disputes involving Speakers of the House of Commons. All my reading of history tells me that they have never been chosen on a rational or procedural basis, but rather have been men who have served the needs of the Prime Minister of the day, and only secondly the political parties. There has been up to now a sort of natural selection—a pragmatic choice.'[1]

It is interesting to examine the record in the light of this judgement.

At the turn of the century the Speaker of the House of Commons was William Court Gully, a Liberal who had first been elected to the Chair on 10 April 1895. On this occasion he was opposed by the Conservative Opposition who proposed a rival candidate of their own thereby giving rise to a highly acrimonious debate.[2]

The complaint of the opposition was that Gully was an unknown and inactive Member whom a moribund government was imposing on the House just before a general election which the Conservatives confidently expected to win. He was elected by the narrow majority of eleven votes and the Conservatives vowed to replace him when their opportunity arose. At the general election four months later they ran a candidate against Gully in his constituency, but the Speaker held his seat and even increased his majority in an election which otherwise went very badly for the Liberals. This was the first real threat to the continuity of the Speakership in many years, but having won the general election the Conservatives relented and Gully was re-elected Speaker unopposed.[3]

[1] Article in *The Times*, 4 Mar. 1972, p. 12.
[2] *Commons Hansard*, 4th series, Vol. 32, cols. 1369–96.
[3] *Ibid.*, Vol. 36, cols. 3–10.

He was re-elected again on 3 December 1900 and as the century progressed the security of tenure of the Speakership became seemingly assured. For 35 years no Speaker was again opposed in his constituency, and not until 1951 was the election of the Speaker again contested in the House.

Gully's successor, James William Lowther, was elected Speaker on 8 June 1905, the first Conservative to be called to the Chair in 70 years. Like Gully himself, he was proposed by a moribund government which was shortly to be swept out of power, but the Liberals raised no objections to his nomination and he was elected unanimously.

The first discordant note to be heard during the early years of the century concerning the selection of the Speaker was raised on 27 April 1921 when John Henry Whitley was first elected to the Chair. On that occasion two Members, Mr. Ronald McNeill and Sir William Joynson-Hicks, rose to complain that insufficient consultation had taken place regarding the choice of the Speaker and that the rights of private Members had thereby been violated. Mr. McNeill referred to a press headline which read: 'The Prime Minister has offered the Speakership to Mr. Whitley'; and he added that the statement 'not very unfairly represents what actually occurred'. He also warned that by selecting twice in succession a candidate who had previously served as Chairman of Ways and Means, the House risked establishing a precedent conferring on the holder of this office the automatic right of succession to the Speakership. The Leader of the House, Austen Chamberlain, intervened in the debate to repudiate both suggestions.[1]

Previous service as Chairman of Ways and Means was one of the factors adduced in support of Lowther when he was first elected Speaker.[2] He was the first of five Speakers to be elevated from the lower Chair during this century, three of whom immediately succeeded him.[3] Previous service as Chairman of Ways

[1] Ibid., 5th series, Vol. 141, cols. 307–18.
[2] See speech of his proposer Sir Michael Hicks Beach, ibid., 4th series, Vol. 147, cols. 1067–8.
[3] Speakers Whitley and Clifton Brown had both served as Chairman of Ways and Means. Speaker Fitzroy was promoted directly from the Deputy Chairmanship since the Chairman himself had declined to accept the nomination. Horace King and more recently George Thomas were promoted from the office of Chairman of Ways and Means.

and Means has never conferred any prescriptive right to the Speakership, but in this century it is certainly a factor which has been taken into account. It is notable, for example, that when the practice was broken in 1951 with the election of Mr. Speaker Morrison, the rival claims of Major Milner were pressed on the ground, *inter alia*, that he had been Chairman of Ways and Means. The Select Committee on Procedure which reported on the method of electing the Speaker in January 1972 made reference to this question and concluded: 'Your Committee are of opinion that there should be no automatic presumption that occupancy of the posts of Chairman or Deputy Chairman of Ways and Means constitutes a qualification for the office of Speaker.'[1]

In the first ten general elections of this century the Speaker was unopposed in his constituency, although it appears that opposition in Speaker Whitley's constituency in 1924 had been seriously contemplated.[2] The convention was broken in 1935 by the decision of the Labour Party to run a candidate against Mr. Speaker Fitzroy in his constituency of Daventry. This decision was deplored in the press and resented by the other parties who jointly nominated Fitzroy as their non-party candidate in the constituency. Stanley Baldwin, Ramsay MacDonald, David Lloyd George, Sir John Simon, and Sir Herbert Samuel all signed a letter denouncing the Labour Party's violation of an established convention. George Lansbury defended the Labour Party's decision on the ground that there was an active Conservative association in the constituency, and he also made the interesting point that the Labour Party was opposed to the principle of the Speaker representing a constituency like any other Member.[3]

The tumult subsided when Fitzroy was re-elected, but in 1938 the Labour Party again announced its intention of contesting the Speaker's seat. This led the House of Commons to appoint a Select Committee in December of that year 'to consider what steps, if any, should be taken to ensure that, having due regard to the constitutional rights of the electors, the Speaker, during

---

[1] *First Report from the Select Committee on Procedure*, Session 1971–2, H.C. 111, page xv, para. 26.

[2] See *Report from the Select Committee on Parliamentary Elections (Mr. Speaker's Seat)*, 1939, H.C. 98, p. 15.

[3] See *The Times*, 27 June and 3 Aug. 1935.

his continuance in office, shall not be required to take part in a contested parliamentary election'.

The Committee, whose membership included Winston Churchill, David Lloyd George, and George Lansbury, called no witnesses but studied the political and constitutional background of the Speakership, its modern evolution, and the practices relating to the Speakership in other democratic countries both Commonwealth and foreign. It considered a number of possibilities, including the creation of a fictitious constituency, the removal of the Speaker to a two-membered constituency, his transference immediately after his election to a seat rendered safe for him, and the prohibition of a contest in his constituency by statute. All were rejected as being contrary to the spirit of the British constitution and it was recommended that no change be made.[1]

This report, followed shortly afterwards by the outbreak of the Second World War which imposed other priorities on Parliament, seemed to dispose of the matter once and for all. However, it is interesting to note that the idea of a special seat for the Speaker was revived on 24 April 1963 when a group of private Members sought leave to introduce a bill under the Ten-Minutes Rule 'for the creation of a constituency to be known as St. Stephen's and represented by Mr. Speaker'. The motion was defeated quite narrowly by 76 votes to 68.[2]

A special relationship exists between the Speaker and his constituency. He never conducts a political campaign, and even when opposed he does not actively fight for his seat. He stands as the Speaker seeking re-election and contents himself with issuing a non-political circular. He does not normally address any public meetings, although Mr. Speaker Fitzroy held one in his constituency in 1935 and warned that the defeat of the Speaker at the polls would be 'the greatest blow to democratic government ever perpetrated'.[3] The Speaker's election statement invariably stresses his impartial role in the parliamentary system

[1] The conclusions of the Committee are set out in the *Report from the Select Committee on Parliamentary Elections (Mr. Speaker's Seat)*, 1939, H.C. 98, paras. 60-1, p. 24.

[2] See *Commons Hansard*, 5th series, Vol. 676, cols. 229-34, also cols. 425-6 where the result of the division, which had been incorrectly recorded, was corrected.

[3] *The Times*, 27 June 1935.

and the fact that he has the same duty as any other Member to look after his constituency.[1]

It has been suggested in the past that the Speaker, because of his political aloofness and the fact that he can neither participate in debate, nor raise matters on the adjournment, nor ask questions in the House, is therefore unable adequately to represent a constituency. This argument is frequently used by those who advocate the creation of a special seat for the Speaker. All the evidence uncovered by this author tends to suggest that there are no grounds for this assumption, a view which was well summarized by the Select Committee appointed to consider the question of the Speaker's seat in 1939.[2]

Speaker Clifton Brown's election communication of 1945 described the idea that the Speaker's constituency is in any way handicapped as 'a mistaken view' and echoed the views of the Select Committee. Speaker Hylton-Foster stated in his election address in 1964 that he had dealt with over two thousand constituency problems by letter and interview in the previous Parliament. In 1970 Speaker King referred to the fortnightly 'surgery' which he held in his constituency and claimed that he dealt with an average of two thousand letters from constituents every year. Speaker Lloyd's election address prior to the first general election of 1974 bluntly described the suggestion that the Speaker's constituency was disenfranchised as 'nonsense'. It pointed out that he had written over 7,000 letters on constituency matters over the previous three years and that he had attended dozens of public functions and seen many constituents personally at his home.

The fact is that the Speaker is probably in a better position than any other Member to seek redress of a constituency grievance since he has readier access to ministers and government departments. His position and prestige give him an added degree of influence. This was the view taken by Mr. Speaker Lloyd who was not in favour of any change in the process whereby the Speaker

[1] See, for example, the election communications of Speaker Clifton Brown, Hexham, 1945; Speaker Morrison, Cirencester and Tewkesbury, 1955; Speaker Hylton-Foster, Cities of London and Westminster, 1964; Speaker King, Southampton Itchen, 1966 and 1970; and those of Speaker Lloyd, Wirral, prior to both general elections of 1974.

[2] *Report from the Select Committee on Parliamentary Elections (Mr. Speaker's Seat)*, 1939, H.C. 98, paras. 37, 38, 39, p. 17.

is elected to Parliament. He believed that the Speaker can represent a constituency more effectively than a minister, and having been both he was in a position to know. He is not bound by collective responsibility and is therefore not inhibited in raising constituency matters, even though he is obliged to raise them privately. He would not hesitate to write a strong letter to a minister if he felt the complaint justified it.[1]

It was nevertheless interesting to learn from Lord Tranmire, a former Father of the House of Commons, that he was disposed to favour the creation of some kind of a special seat for the Speaker. He was not too precise as to how this should be done, but he tentatively suggested either that the constituency of the Cities of London and Westminster, which had been represented by Speaker Hylton-Foster, could be designated as a special seat, or that a special constituency might be created which would enable disfranchised citizens living in the Commonwealth or overseas to vote and that this seat should be reserved for the Speaker. He felt that, despite the report of the Select Committee of 1939, the question of a special seat for the Speaker merited further study.[2]

The next occasion on which a Member was to complain of lack of consultation in the choice of Speaker was on 9 March 1943 when Douglas Clifton Brown was first elected to the Chair.[3] The Member concerned, Captain Cunningham-Reid, alleged that the Speaker had in fact been chosen the previous week. 'It appeared in the press that the Conservative Party had decided that Colonel Clifton Brown should be the Speaker of this House.'[4] He also complained that the Speaker was too much influenced by the party whips in calling on Members to speak and suggested that the opportunity of participating in debate should be decided by ballot.[5] Captain Cunningham-Reid proved to be a lone voice, and even the communist Member, William

[1] Interview with Mr. Speaker Lloyd, 13 Sept. 1973.
[2] Interview with Sir Robin Turton (afterwards Lord Tranmire), 10 Sept. 1973.
[3] It is said that the coalition government of the day favoured Gwilym Lloyd George for the Speakership in 1943 but that the Conservative Party strongly supported Clifton Brown. See, for example, Earl Winterton, *Orders of the Day* (Cassell, 1953), p. 294.
[4] *Commons Hansard*, 5th series, Vol. 387, col. 617.
[5] Ibid., cols. 618–21.

Gallacher, had no criticism to make of the method of electing the Speaker. Mr. Anthony Eden, in the course of his speech congratulating the Speaker-elect, denied that he owed his nomination to any party. He also made the point—although it had not been raised by Cunningham-Reid—that the Chairman of Ways and Means enjoyed no right of succession to the Speakership.[1]

At the first general election following the war, which took place on 5 July 1945, the Labour Party, which was making a determined bid for power, again contested the Speaker's seat. Although the decision was regarded as controversial[2] it did not provoke the same heated reaction as in 1935, no doubt because of the many other weightier matters competing for public attention. In spite of the Labour landslide which followed the election, Speaker Clifton Brown retained his seat at Hexham, although it appears that he automatically assumed that he had reached the end of the road as Speaker because of the election result. Lord Pannell tells the story of how Clifton Brown came to London with a pile of empty suitcases expecting to pack up. 'He freely admitted that after all these years in opposition and with such a triumph, Labour could justly claim a Speaker from their own ranks. Mr. Attlee thought differently and when the view was conveyed to the Speaker, Colonel Clifton Brown wept at what he described as an act of "amazing political generosity".'[3] Although no Speaker had ever been drawn from the ranks of the Labour Party at that time, it appears that the greatly enlarged contingent of Labour back-benchers raised no protests.

Clifton Brown was again elected Speaker in the short Parliament of 1950–1 and retired at the dissolution. He was the first Speaker of the century to retire at the end of a Parliament instead of during the course of a session. He made no personal statement from the Chair, but instead a letter from him was read to the House by his successor at the beginning of the ensuing

---

[1] Ibid., col. 626.

[2] See, for example, R. B. McCallum and Alison Readman, *The British General Election of 1945* (Oxford University Press, 1947), pp. 76–7.

[3] See text of Lord Pannell's broadcast, 'Mr. Speaker', from a series entitled 'Under Big Ben', on the English service of the B.B.C., 30 May 1958; also his article in *The Times*, 4 Mar. 1972, p. 12. Speaker Clifton Brown's daughter, the Baroness Hylton-Foster, confirmed the accuracy of Lord Pannell's account in an interview with the author, 11 Sept. 1973.

Parliament.[1] At least one commentator is on record as criticizing him for staying on until the end of the Parliament,[2] and the Select Committee on Procedure of 1971–2 in its report on the election of the Speaker drew attention to the difficulties which can arise when this happens.[3]

The Conservatives won the general election of 1951 by a narrow majority and the first business of the House was the election of a successor to Clifton Brown. It seems this was an occasion when the consultative process broke down very badly largely due to the fault of the Labour Party leadership. Lord Pannell has given an account of what took place, commenting:

> I was told at the time when Winston Churchill was forming his Government that he had omitted, or forgotten, the claims of W. S. ('Shakes') Morrison. When somebody asked 'What about Shakes?', the old man after a short pause said: 'Offer him the Speakership—he looks the part.'
> The names of Morrison and Hopkin Morris, a Liberal, were put to the Opposition but the latter was really a non-starter. Clem Attlee with Herbert Morrison and Willie Whiteley did not very strongly contest Winston's proposal and brought the recommendation to the Parliamentary Labour Party as a fait accompli on October 31, 1951.[4]

According to Lord Pannell, the Chairman of Ways and Means in the previous Parliament, Major James Milner, had refused the offer of Minister of Pensions in 1945 on the understanding that he had a confident hope of succeeding Clifton Brown as Speaker. At the meeting of the Parliamentary Labour Party of 31 October 1951 a back-bench revolt took place. Mr. Attlee announced that Mr. W. S. Morrison would be Speaker and that the point was not arguable. Lord Pannell reminded him 'that he was no longer Prime Minister but Chairman of our Party and the worst way to start in Opposition was to sell out on a colleague'.[5]

The minutes of the Parliamentary Labour Party for that day record that a considerable discussion took place and that two votes were taken. It was finally agreed by 115 to 107 that the party would acquiesce in the nomination of Sir Charles MacAndrew but that if the Conservatives insisted on proposing

---

[1] See *Commons Hansard*, 5th series, Vol. 493, cols. 171–2.

[2] See Charles Pannell's article in *The Times*, 4 Mar. 1972, p. 12.

[3] *First Report from the Select Committee on Procedure*, 1971–2, H.C. 111, p. xiii, para. 22.

[4] Article in *The Times*, 4 Mar. 1972, p. 12.

[5] Ibid.

W. S. Morrison the Labour Party would nominate Major Milner. The result was the first contested election for the Speakership since 1895.

Mr. Morrison was the first Speaker since Gully who had not previously served as Chairman of Ways and Means and the first of the century to have held numerous ministerial offices. He had served in various governments as Financial Secretary to the Treasury, Minister of Agriculture, Chancellor of the Duchy of Lancaster, Minister of Food, and Postmaster General, and in 1943 he had become the first Minister of Town and Country Planning. In addition he had had the distinction of being included in the cast of 'Guilty Men' of the pre-war era in the celebrated book of that title published in 1940.[1] He had not been very active in the House during the years when the Conservatives were in Opposition but his previous ministerial career was nevertheless regarded by some as an objection to his appointment as Speaker.

According to his widow, Lady Dunrossil, Mr. Morrison never had any ambition to be Speaker. He had been approached in 1943 when Speaker Fitzroy died but had declined, and Lady Dunrossil believes that the approach was probably made by Members who were anxious that the elevation of the Chairman of Ways and Means to the Speakership should not become a precedent. He accepted the offer in 1951 because he believed it was his duty to do so and that Mr. Attlee was committed to supporting him. He had no idea that he was going to be opposed until he arrived at the House on 31 October 1951 just before the election was to take place.[2]

Winston Churchill, newly returned to office as Prime Minister, intervened in the debate to give his own account of the sequence of events, an account which Clement Attlee did not dispute in any material detail. He said it was his understanding that the Labour Party had agreed on 29 October to accept Morrison as Speaker, that he had accordingly approached Morrison who had accepted,[3] and that he, Churchill, thereafter considered

---

[1] 'Cato', *Guilty Men* (Gollancz, 1940).

[2] Interview with Lady Dunrossil, 22 Oct. 1973.

[3] Sir Robin Turton (subsequently Lord Tranmire) in an interview with the author on 10 Sept. 1973 expressed the view that Morrison had been 'dragooned' by Churchill into the Speakership.

himself bound. When the Chief Labour Party Whip raised the claims of Major Milner and Sir Charles MacAndrew on the following day it was too late to go back.[1] In the division which followed the debate Morrison was elected by 318 votes against 251 for Milner, each candidate voting for the other.[2]

Morrison was unanimously re-elected Speaker in 1955 and presided over two Parliaments. Like his predecessor he retired at the end of a Parliament,[3] and this decision was to lead to further consultative difficulties when it came to choosing his successor. The result was that the Speakership again eluded the Labour Party.

It appears that the Conservatives would have conceded the Speakership to the Labour Party provided they chose the candidate, and their choice was Sir Frank Soskice. Sir Frank preferred to decline the offer, whereupon the Conservatives proposed a candidate of their own, Sir Harry Hylton-Foster. This caused great resentment in the ranks of the Labour Party who saw the Conservative action as meaning, in the words of Hugh Gaitskell, 'that there was only one Member of our party who in the opinion of hon. Members opposite was fitted to occupy the Chair'.[4] The opposition proposed no candidate of their own although both Hugh Gaitskell and Charles Pannell registered strong protests during the debate on the election of the new Speaker on 20 October 1959. A Member whose name had been mentioned in informal discussions as a suitable candidate was Bill Williams—'a "natural" with all the qualities' according to Charles Pannell[5]—but Gaitskell explained that no rival candidate was being put forward 'because we do not think it appropriate to make this a party issue in which there is a party battle

[1] See the speeches of Churchill and Attlee, *Commons Hansard*, 5th series, Vol. 493, cols. 12–16.

[2] Ibid., cols. 16–22. In the contest which took place in 1895 between William Court Gully and Sir Matthew White Ridley the candidates both abstained from voting.

[3] Unlike Clifton Brown he took the opportunity of making a farewell statement to the House on 18 September 1959, the day before the prorogation of the final session of the Parliament. Ibid., Vol. 610, cols. 787–9.

[4] Ibid., Vol. 612, col. 8. The Prime Minister, Harold Macmillan, is said to have remarked privately that he favoured Soskice because, like himself, he was a Balliol man. See Charles Pannell's article in *The Times*, 4 Mar. 1972.

[5] See his article in *The Times*, 4 Mar. 1972.

on our very first day'.[1] He added, however, that the opposition would have divided the House on the motion to elect Sir Harry Hylton-Foster had this been in order.[2]

Both Hugh Gaitskell and Charles Pannell referred in the course of the debate to the difficulties which arise when a Speaker retires at the end of a Parliament and the Prime Minister conceded that this seemed to him 'a very fair and a very strong point. There is, of course, a difficulty in timing when a Speaker resigns at the end of a Parliament rather than during a Parliament, because during a Parliament all the consultations and contacts which Members can have are much easier to arrange.'[3] In the light of the difficulties which occurred in 1951 and 1959, and the observations of the 1971-2 Select Committee on Procedure,[4] there is every reason to believe that Speakers retiring in the future will do so during a session so that, in the words of Charles Pannell, 'a known Parliament elects a known personality'.[5]

Sir Harry Hylton-Foster moved straight to the Speakership from the Treasury Bench, which was another ground for criticism in the view of the opposition. He had been Solicitor-General in the previous government but had never held any higher offices of state. Hugh Gaitskell nevertheless saw this as a difficulty, and drew a distinction between a Speaker who had earlier held ministerial office, like Morrison, and one who had been a minister immediately preceding his appointment to the Chair.[6] In making this point he was echoing a view which had been expressed by Gladstone in 1871.[7] The Select Committee on Procedure considering the matter over twelve years later also concurred. They did not find 'that the doubts of witnesses as to

[1] *Commons Hansard*, 5th series, Vol. 612, col. 9.

[2] Ibid. Until the procedure was changed on 8 August 1972 on the recommendation of the Select Committee on Procedure, it was not held to be consistent with modern practice to divide the House on the election of the Speaker when there was only one candidate. See Erskine May, op. cit., p. 260, also *First Report from the Select Committee on Procedure*, 1971-2, H.C. 111, paras. 15 and 16, pp. x–xi.

[3] *Commons Hansard*, 5th series, Vol. 612, col. 9.

[4] H.C. 111, 1971–2, para. 22, p. xiii.

[5] *Commons Hansard*, 5th series, Vol. 612, col. 13.

[6] Ibid., col. 7.

[7] See *Letters of Queen Victoria*, second series (John Murray, 1926–8), Vol. 2, p. 164.

the fitness for the Chair of former Ministers have been realised. They agree, however, with the views expressed by Mr. Gladstone and Mr. Gaitskell that the Speaker should not be elected direct from the Treasury Bench.'[1] Speaker Selwyn Lloyd, who had himself held many high offices of state, was also in agreement with this view. He went further and believed that a Speaker who has previously held ministerial office can offer an advantage to the House. He understands the problems of ministers and knows what goes on in cabinet. This gives him more authority with the government front bench, and he can use his knowledge to the benefit of the back-benches. A former minister, far from being partisan, is likely to make a more efficient Speaker.[2]

Sir Harry Hylton-Foster was by all accounts a reluctant Speaker. As an eminent lawyer his ambitions lay in the direction of the highest offices to which his profession could lead him and he had hoped to become Lord Chancellor. It was at the insistence of Harold Macmillan that he had agreed to accept the Speakership and with it the renunciation of any prospect he might have had of reaching the woolsack.[3] Although he was a man of charm and sensitivity, Sir Harry failed to give universal satisfaction during his occupancy of the Chair. According to Charles Pannell, 'no one tried harder',[4] but several Members expressed the view that he was not a good Speaker. Among them was the Conservative, Robin Maxwell-Hyslop, who felt that neither Hylton-Foster nor his successors dealt firmly enough with the more aggressive Members. He gave notice to his party, and to Sir Harry himself, prior to the latter's sudden and premature death in 1965, that had Sir Harry been re-nominated as Speaker a third time, he, Maxwell-Hyslop, would not have been prepared to support him.[5]

At the general election of 1964 Sir Harry was opposed in his

[1] See *Report from the Select Committee on Procedure*, 1971–2, H.C. 111, para. 27, pp. xv–xvi.

[2] Interview with Mr. Speaker Lloyd, 13 Sept. 1973.

[3] Interview with Lady Hylton-Foster, 11 Sept. 1973.

[4] See article in *The Times*, 4 Mar. 1972. Sir Harry was by all accounts deeply troubled by the responsibilities of the Speakership. It is said that he frequently wrote letters of apology to Members he had been unable to call in debate.

[5] Interview with Mr. Robin Maxwell-Hyslop, 1 Sept. 1973.

constituency, the Cities of London and Westminster, by officially sponsored candidates of the Labour and Liberal Parties. Although a Speaker seeking re-election has been opposed in his constituency at every general election since 1935, the 1964 election was the first since 1945 at which any of the major parties nominated official candidates against him. The experience was repeated in 1974 when Speaker Lloyd also faced Labour and Liberal opponents at both general elections held in that year. In 1950 Speaker Clifton Brown was opposed by an independent. In 1955 Speaker Morrison was opposed by a member of the Labour Party standing without official backing. Speaker King was opposed by an independent in 1966, and in 1970 he faced two opponents, one representing the National Democratic Party and the other an independent. It appears that the Conservatives also gave some thought to running a candidate against him in 1970 but thought better of it.

Sir Harry Hylton-Foster was re-elected in his constituency in 1964 at a general election which was won by the Labour Party by the narrow majority of five seats, shortly afterwards reduced to four by the loss of a by-election. On 27 October 1964 he was unanimously re-elected Speaker. Whether he would have been re-elected had the Labour Party won a more substantial majority is open to speculation. There is reason to believe there would have been back-bench pressure to replace him. Charles Pannell, in a letter written to the author prior to the general election, said that he did not know whether the Speaker was likely to be replaced in the event of a Labour victory. 'I think that the tendency of our Front Bench will be to observe the tradition but if we come back on the 1945 scale with a large majority, then it might be difficult for any incoming Prime Minister to repress the ebullience of his supporters flushed with victory. It might also be rather tough to ask them to give their first vote to keep in a Conservative Speaker.'[1]

Harold Wilson is on record as saying that Sir Harry Hylton-Foster had been assured in the summer prior to the election that a Labour government would wish him to continue in office.[2] Lady Hylton-Foster's recollection is not completely in accord with

[1] Letter to the author, 30 Apr. 1964.
[2] Harold Wilson, *A Personal Record: The Labour Government, 1964–1970* (Little, Brown and Co., American edition, 1971), p. 27.

Harold Wilson's. She is positive that her husband was not approached by the Labour Party prior to the election. According to her he was approached after the election by Mr. Herbert Bowden who expressed the hope that he 'would keep the seat warm'.[1] Sir Harry's second tenure of office was destined to be short-lived. He died suddenly on 2 September 1965, the second Speaker of the century to die while in office.

The death of the Speaker could not have occurred at a more difficult time for the government. The obvious successor, supported by all parties, was Dr. Horace King, the Chairman of Ways and Means.[2] He was to become the first Labour Speaker, ironically at a time when the government with its wafer-thin majority could ill afford to see it depleted even further. Harold Wilson has recorded that 'the Conservatives immediately called for the election of Dr. King, less, we felt, through admiration of his qualities than through voting arithmetic. Their subsequent treatment of him justified this judgment.'[3] Lord Maybray-King himself, however, does not recall any particularly unpleasant episodes during his Speakership.[4] Horace King was elected Speaker on 26 October 1965. A Conservative became Chairman of Ways and Means and a Liberal became Deputy Chairman, thus enabling the government to cling to a precarious majority of three.

When a Speaker dies, the House of Commons is completely out of action until a new Speaker is elected. Sir Harry Hylton-Foster died when the House was not sitting thus further complicating a difficult situation. The Standing Orders make provision for the Chairman of Ways and Means, and if necessary the Deputy Chairman, to take over the Speaker's functions in the event of the latter's unavoidable absence,[5] but no such provision is made in the event of the Speaker's demise. It was in anticipation of such a situation that on 25 February 1953 a Member moved for leave to introduce a bill under the Ten-Minutes Rule 'to provide that in the event of the Speaker's death

[1] Interview with Lady Hylton-Foster, 11 Sept. 1973.

[2] Dr. King did not apparently have the undivided support of his own party and George Thomas is said to have been a competitor for the office.

[3] Harold Wilson, op. cit., p. 135.

[4] Interview with Lord Maybray-King, 13 Sept. 1973.

[5] See Standing Orders 105(2) and (3), 1974 edition. All subsequent references are to the 1974 edition.

the Chairman of Ways and Means shall temporarily exercise the authority of the Speaker'. Leave was granted by 172 votes to 149 but the bill was not proceeded with.[1] In 1972 the Select Committee on Procedure also took cognizance of this problem and recommended:

In the event of the death of the Speaker or his acceptance of office, when the circumstances of his absence have not previously been announced by the Clerk at the Table, to enable the House to continue to sit, the Chairman of Ways and Means should automatically perform the duties and exercise the authority of Mr. Speaker until the commencement of proceedings for election of a new Speaker.[2]

In the debate which took place on the Committee's report on 8 August 1972, the Leader of the House, Mr. Robert Carr, explained that while the government was not opposed to the recommendation, its implementation would require legislation and it was therefore not included in the motion which was put to the House.[3]

Horace King was re-elected Speaker in 1966 and 1970. He retired early in 1971 and the election of his successor proved to be highly controversial, highlighting in a most unusual way the grievance of a number of back-benchers from all sides of the House concerning lack of consultation.

On the basis of the evidence available it appears that the front benches of the two major parties had failed to learn the lesson of previous experience and dealt with the question of the succession to the Speakership as a matter of concern only to the leadership. The Conservatives approached the Labour Party leaders with the names of two candidates, Mr. Selwyn Lloyd and Mr. John Boyd-Carpenter, both former ministers. The Labour Party had no candidate of its own to propose.[4] Mr. Sydney Irving, Chairman of Ways and Means in the previous Parliament, might have been the party's nominee but he had been defeated in the general election of 1970.[5]

---

[1] *Commons Hansard*, 5th series, Vol. 511, cols. 2095–100 and Vol. 514, col. 1717.
[2] *First Report from the Select Committee on Procedure*, 1971–2, H.C. 111, para. 23, p. xiv, and para. 28 p. xvi.
[3] *Commons Hansard*, 5th series, Vol. 842, col. 1666.
[4] Interview with Lord Houghton, 20 Aug. 1973.
[5] Interview with Lord Pannell, 12 Sept. 1973.

There was free speculation in the press concerning the proposed candidates and when the Labour Party leaders expressed their preference for Selwyn Lloyd, Mr. William Whitelaw informed the lobby correspondents that the two front benches had reached agreement on the new Speaker.[1]

The fact that Selwyn Lloyd had held some of the highest offices of state, including those of Chancellor of the Exchequer, Foreign Secretary, and Minister of Defence, did not apparently count against him in the eyes of the Labour Party, a rather curious departure from its attitude on previous occasions. The fact is all the more surprising when one considers the controversial nature of Mr. Lloyd's ministerial career. As Foreign Secretary he had been closely involved in the Suez adventure in 1956 and his policies as Chancellor of the Exchequer cost him his place in the cabinet in Harold Macmillan's dramatic 'purge' of 1962.

He was brought back into the government by Sir Alec Douglas-Home in 1963 as Lord Privy Seal and Leader of the House of Commons and at this point it appears he began to carve out a new parliamentary career for himself. As Leader of the House he was very popular with the Opposition on account of his co-operative spirit and his concern for the improvement of the conditions of Members. He subsequently served with distinction as Chairman of the House of Commons (Services) Committee and as a trustee of the Superannuation Fund of the House. From 1962 onwards he had gradually become more and more detached from political controversies in the House and had devoted himself since that time to the interests of the House and its Members, their remuneration, accommodation, and facilities, acquiring in the process a reputation as a good House of Commons man.[2]

---

[1] See Alan Watkins, 'The fix for the speakership', *New Statesman*, 18 Dec. 1970, p. 823.

[2] This conclusion is derived from interviews with Lord Houghton, 20 Aug. 1973, Lord Pannell, 12 Sept. 1973, and Mr. Speaker Lloyd himself, 13 Sept. 1973. See also the comments of Mr. G. R. Strauss on the occasion of the re-election of Speaker Lloyd to the Chair on 6 Mar. 1974, *Commons Hansard*, 5th series, Vol. 870, col. 14. However, one parliamentary expert who maintains that the prestige of the Speakership has become eroded in recent years believes that Selwyn Lloyd was preferred to John Boyd-Carpenter by the Labour Party leadership because the latter would have

The election of the Speaker on 12 January 1971 was the second contested election of the century and the first to provoke a serious back-bench reaction. After Mr. Selwyn Lloyd had been proposed and seconded by Dame Irene Ward and Mr. Charles Pannell, several other Members rose to speak. Mr. John Pardoe of the Liberal Party was the first 'to express a backbencher's dissatisfaction with the way in which this election procedure has been handled'. He said that his inquiries had led him to conclude that there had been no consultation in any meaningful sense of the word and that no meeting of the Parliamentary Labour Party or of the 1922 Committee had been held to discuss the matter in advance. 'Whatever information was gleaned about the matter by Members of Parliament was gleaned from the pages of the press.' He also expressed a reservation concerning the appointment of a senior ex-minister on the ground 'that he cannot fail to be a figure of controversy'.[1]

Mr. Pardoe was followed by Mr. Robin Maxwell-Hyslop who began his speech by insisting 'that a division can take place on the first nomination without any other proposition being made',[2] and cited precedents to support this proposition. He went on to assert the right of the House to choose its own Speaker and rejected the principle that the front benches should influence the choice prior to the election itself. To the surprise of many he ended his speech by nominating as a rival candidate Sir Geoffrey de Freitas, a prominent Labour back-bencher.[3] Sir Geoffrey was probably more surprised than anybody as he had not been consulted as to his candidature, and before the division took place he rose to declare his embarrassment and to inform the House that he intended to support Mr. Selwyn Lloyd.[4] The purpose of nominating Sir Geoffrey, as Maxwell-Hyslop explained, was to ensure that a division would take place. Another principal participant in the debate was Mr. William Hamilton of the Labour Party, who seconded the nomination of Sir Geoffrey de Freitas. He delivered a fighting speech criticizing his own party leaders for their failure to consult back-benchers

___

been too strong a Speaker and being a younger man would probably have remained longer in office.

[1] *Commons Hansard*, 5th series, Vol. 809, cols. 8–13.
[2] Ibid., col. 14.   [3] Ibid., cols. 14–17.
[4] Ibid., col. 22.

and strongly attacking the principle of electing a former minister as Speaker.[1]

In the ensuing division Selwyn Lloyd was elected by 294 votes to 55, thus revealing a sizeable body of back-bench discontent. Sir Geoffrey de Freitas voted for Mr. Selwyn Lloyd and Mr. Lloyd himself abstained, no doubt in deference to the fact that Sir Geoffrey had declared himself an unwilling candidate.[2]

This was the strongest demonstration of back-bench protest ever to manifest itself in connection with the choice of the Speaker and it was taken seriously. It led to an investigation of the procedure for electing the Speaker by the Select Committee on Procedure and a report recommending changes was tabled on 26 January 1972. The key recommendations were that a Member of the House should preside over the proceedings instead of the Clerk of the House; that he should be equipped with certain powers under the Standing Orders; that a division on the motion to elect a Speaker should be permissible when only one candidate is nominated; and that the new procedure should be embodied in Standing Orders.[3] These recommendations were substantially adopted by the House on 8 August 1972,[4] and the new procedure came into operation for the first time on 6 March 1974 when Speaker Lloyd was unanimously re-elected to the Chair.[5]

The Committee rejected a proposal that the Speaker be elected by secret ballot but concluded 'that the criticisms levelled against the procedure in present use for election of a Speaker are largely justified'.[6]

It recognized that its proposal that the Clerk should no longer preside 'would result in the abandonment by the House of a procedure of some antiquity', but concluded 'that the House is placed in an unduly vulnerable position while the Clerk is presiding over its proceedings' by virtue of the fact that he has no powers under the Standing Orders.[7] The Committee therefore

---

[1] Ibid., cols. 17–21.   [2] Ibid., cols. 22–4.

[3] For full text of the recommendations see *First Report from the Select Committee on Procedure*, 1971–2, H.C. 111, para. 28, p. xvi.

[4] See Standing Order, 103A, 1974 edition.

[5] *Commons Hansard*, 5th series, Vol. 870, cols. 1–16.

[6] *First Report from the Select Committee on Procedure*, 1971–2, H.C. 111, para. 21, p. xiii.

[7] Ibid. See also Sir Barnett Cocks's evidence to the Committee, pp. 32–6.

recommended 'that the retiring Speaker should, if possible, occupy the Chair until his successor is elected' and 'that on all other occasions, including the re-election of a Speaker at the beginning of a new Parliament, the Member with the longest unbroken period of service who is present in the House on the back-benches should occupy the Chair at the election of a Speaker'.[1]

The Committee found that complaints of lack of consultation between party leaders and back-benchers were justified and expressed the hope that the parties would take steps to improve consultation. 'Without this, none of the changes in procedure which Your Committee later recommend will remove the risk of dissatisfaction about the conduct of future elections.'[2]

The Committee thus placed the responsibility for lack of consultation fairly and squarely where it belonged—on the party leaders. In the view of Lord Tranmire, who was Chairman of the Select Committee, there is no reason why consultation should fail and if it does fail it is the fault of the Whips. They are the recognized channel of communication between the back-benchers and the leadership and should take all steps to ensure that the consultative process is thorough and efficient.[3]

Lord Houghton explained some of the difficulties involved in consultation. If it is too widespread it leads to extensive discussion and speculation. Names are bandied about and they are bound to be leaked to the press. A candidate for the Speakership is always an eminent Member of great experience, and he may be reluctant to allow his name to be proposed if he knows it will be a matter for public debate. The House may thus lose the candidate it really wants. Unsuccessful candidates may feel that their prestige has suffered and may retire from active public life. Both Major Milner and Mr. John Boyd-Carpenter accepted peerages shortly after their hopes for the speakership were dashed.[4]

Mr. Robin Maxwell-Hyslop expressed the unorthodox view that the question of consultation should not even arise. He believes that every Member should vote independently at the

[1] Ibid., para. 22, p. xiii.
[2] Ibid., para. 13, p. x.
[3] Interview with Lord Tranmire, 10 Sept. 1973.
[4] Interview with Lord Houghton, 20 Aug. 1973.

election of a new Speaker and that every Member has the obligation to serve as Speaker if called upon to do so. No prior discussion between the Whips' offices should take place and there
should be no anticipation as to who is likely to be nominated. He
also criticized the recommendation of the Select Committee that
the Standing Orders should provide 'that the motions for the
election to the Chair of all candidates subsequent to the first
should be moved in the form of an amendment to the original
motion'.[1] It appears that he envisages a system whereby several
candidates are likely to be proposed without advance notification and that the choice should be made on all of them simul-
taneously by secret ballot, as in a parliamentary election.[2]

Mr. Maxwell-Hyslop's views on this matter do not seem to the
author to be commensurate with the realities of twentieth-
century politics and it is doubtful that many other Members of
Parliament would share them. He is a traditionalist deeply
immersed in historic precedent who sees the Speaker in his
original reluctant role called upon by his colleagues to perform a
duty he has no right to refuse.

The continuity of the Speakership has thus successfully with-
stood all assaults during this century in spite of the vulnerability
of the conventions on which it is based. It has survived attempts
to unseat the Speaker in his constituency; disputes over the
choice of candidate between government and opposition; back-
bench revolts due to lack of consultation; lack of agreement as
to the background required of a candidate and the method of
selecting him. The absence of criteria and the practices which
have developed in consequence tend to validate the judgement
of Lord Pannell that prime ministerial influence has played an
important part in the initial choice of Speaker. It has not necessarily played a decisive part however. Lowther, Whitley,
Fitzroy, Clifton Brown, and King were all chosen, at least in
part, because they had been successful Chairmen of Ways and
Means. In the case of Clifton Brown it is said that Churchill himself would have preferred Gwilym Lloyd George. There is reason
to believe that in 1959 Harold Macmillan would have preferred
a Labour Speaker. And in 1970 Edward Heath left it to the

[1] *First Report from the Select Committee on Procedure*, 1971–2, H.C. 111 para.
28(6), p. xvi.
[2] Interview with Mr. Robin Maxwell-Hyslop, 1 Sept. 1973.

Labour shadow cabinet to choose between John Boyd-Carpenter and Selwyn Lloyd.

It remains to be seen to what extent the new method of electing the Speaker in the House coupled with the hoped-for improvement of the consultative process will bolster the conventions on which the continuity principle has depended in the past. It can be expected, however, that Speakers seeking re-election in their constituencies will continue to be opposed, sometimes by officially-sponsored party candidates, although the experience since 1935 suggests that the party from which the Speaker was originally drawn is unlikely to sponsor a candidate against him. The possibility of a Speaker one day losing his seat must therefore remain. Should this happen there might well be demands for a further inquiry into the method whereby the Speaker is returned to Parliament at a general election.

The Speaker and Procedure

The principal duties of the modern Speaker are to apply and interpret the rules and practice of the House and to maintain order in debate. Specific powers are conferred on him by the Standing Orders and usage of the House for regulating the proceedings. These powers are of great importance and are fundamental to the conduct of parliamentary business. In total they amount to a formidable array and could only be entrusted to one whose impartiality is beyond all question. Although the Speaker cannot impose rules of his own, the influence of the Chair in the shaping of procedure has been profound. The interpretations of the Standing Orders and traditional practice by successive Speakers through decisions given both privately and in the House, their wide discretionary powers in the application of the rules and practice, and the influence of their evidence before Select Committees on Procedure have been major factors in the development and modernization of procedure in the twentieth century. Just as the application of the law is influenced by judicial decision, so the application of parliamentary procedure depends in large measure on the interpretation and discretion of the Speaker. And just as the common law can be modified by legislation, so can the settled practice of the House be altered by amending the Standing Orders.

The powers of the Speaker were already formidable when the century began and they have been extended as it has progressed. The Speaker's control of debate is all-pervasive in its nature; there is no area of procedure in which it does not play a part. For the purposes of this study it has therefore been decided to select for consideration some of those areas of procedure in which the Speaker's control is of especially crucial significance. Firstly, however, there is one important point to emphasize. Unlike the presiding officers of certain other legislative chambers, the Speaker of the British House of Commons exercises no control over the order of business. The daily and weekly agenda of the House is determined by 'the usual channels', that is to say the Leader of the House and the Chief Whips of the government and opposition. There are certain exceptions to this general principle which are dealt with later in this section, but normally the Speaker is bound by the order of business and his task is to ensure that representative debate takes place. In order to do so, as Lord Maybray-King has pointed out, a Speaker has to remember that there are as many 'parties' in the House as there are individual Members, 'because no two Tories are alike, no two Socialists are alike; and that there can even be strange combinations of Tory and Socialist back-benchers against front-bench Tories and front-bench Socialists. Any Prime Minister in Britain knows that he is going to be criticized not only from across the floor, but also from behind.'[1]

Perhaps a fitting point of departure in considering the Speaker's role in relation to procedure would be the question period, since it takes place from Monday to Thursday at the beginning of the parliamentary day and developed as an exception to the normal rules of debate which require that debate can only take place when there is a properly framed motion before the House. The questioning of ministers was already an established practice at the turn of the century. Notice of questions was required, a question to which an oral answer was desired was 'starred' (i.e. distinguished by an asterisk), and supplementary questions were allowed at the Speaker's discretion. A time limit, fixed at forty minutes, was introduced for the first time on 5 May

[1] *Report of the Conference of Speakers and Presiding Officers of Commonwealth Parliaments*, Canada, Sept. 1969, p. 84.

1902 as part of the Balfour scheme of procedural reform. In 1906 a slight extension of time was allotted to questions by allowing them to be taken immediately following prayers and certain routine proceedings and this remains the rule today.[1] The grouping of questions in such a way that those addressed to a particular minister followed each other in succession was also introduced at this time on an experimental basis. This subsequently developed into the rota system which operates today whereby ministers take their turns on specified days to answer questions addressed to them.[2]

The Speaker's control of the question period is exercised largely by convention, the only power specified by Standing Order being that relating to private notice questions.[3] Apart from the weekly business question asked every Thursday normally by the Leader of the Opposition, a private notice question must be justified by urgency and is allowed at the Speaker's discretion.

One of the cardinal rules relating to questions is that they must seek information only on matters falling within ministerial responsibility. However, the Speaker has no power to insist that a minister answer a question. Neither is it his function to decide to which minister a question should be addressed, although this is a matter on which the Table Office sometimes advises Members informally. The position was clearly stated by Speaker Clifton Brown on 4 February 1948 when responding to a point of order relating to the acceptance of questions concerning the nationalized industries.[4] Later, in order to meet certain objections arising from the refusal of ministers to answer questions on the day-to-day administration of the nationalized industries, the Speaker in a ruling of 7 June 1948 proposed a relaxation of the practice to the extent of allowing questions 'on matters about which information has previously been refused, provided that, in my opinion, the matters are of sufficient public importance to justify this concession . . .'[5] On 12 November 1951 Speaker

---

[1] See Standing Order 8(2), 1974 edition.
[2] See Chap. IX below. An account of the origins and development of 'Questions in Parliament' is also available in the book of that title by D. N. Chester and Nona Bowring (Oxford 1962).
[3] See Standing Order 8(3), 1974 edition.
[4] *Commons Hansard*, 5th series, Vol. 446, col. 1816–17.
[5] Ibid., Vol. 451, cols. 1635–6 for full text of ruling.

Morrison announced his intention of following the ruling of his predecessor[1] and this has remained the practice.[2]

Successive Speakers have also taken the view that the grouping of questions for answer by ministers is not a matter for the Chair. Giving evidence before the Select Committee on House of Commons (Procedure) on 15 March 1906, Mr. Speaker Lowther confirmed that the Clerks took their direction from the government with regard to grouping, and added that he would not be very anxious to undertake the responsibility himself.[3] In evidence before subsequent Select Committees on Procedure, Speaker Clifton Brown and Speaker King expressed similar views.[4]

The key duty of the Speaker during the question period is the control of supplementary questions. Under current practice no Member may have more than two questions for oral answer on the paper for the same day.[5] Of these not more than one may be tabled to any minister on that day. There is also an overall limit of eight questions per Member for oral answer in any period of ten sitting days.[6] Even with these restrictions it is impossible to answer all starred questions orally in the time allowed, the volume having grown immensely over the years, and the right to ask supplementaries inevitably limits still further the number that can be reached. Supplementary questions are the essence of question time and it would lose its impact without them. Nevertheless they have to be regulated. At the beginning of the century supplementary questions were not asked as of right. Speaker Gully tended to frown on them as a matter of principle and on 28 June 1901 he ruled: 'Strictly speaking a supplementary question is only in order when it is asked in order to eluci-

[1] Ibid., 493, col. 648.

[2] The appointment on a sessional basis since 1955 of a Select Committee on Nationalised Industries has also assisted the resolution of the problem by providing a further means of parliamentary scrutiny.

[3] First Report from the Select Committee on House of Commons (Procedure), H.C. 89, 1906, pp. 3 and 5.

[4] Second Report from the Select Committee on Procedure, H.C. 58-I, 1946, pp. 36 and 41; Second Report from the Select Committee on Procedure, H.C. 198, 1969–70, p. 49.

[5] See Commons Hansard, 5th series, Vol. 617, cols. 245–6.

[6] These additional restrictions were imposed following a recommendation of the Select Committee on Parliamentary Questions. See Report from the Committee, 1971–2, H.C. 393, p. x, para. 19; and resolution of the House of 18 Dec. 1972, Commons Hansard, 5th series, Vol. 848, col. 1070.

date some ambiguity or to supply some omission in the original answer.'[1] On 15 May 1902 he ruled that a supplementary question could not be based on a written answer,[2] a ruling which had the effect of encouraging Members to star their questions for oral answer. The attitude of the Chair towards supplementary questions relaxed considerably with the election of Speaker Lowther.[3] However, on 5 July 1915 he confirmed the ruling of his predecessor to the extent of saying, in answer to a question as to whether there was a fixed maximum number of supplementary questions permissible, 'that all supplementary questions are out of order and irregular . . . It is entirely a matter of grace.'[4]

Lowther and his successors have all done their best to follow a policy of flexibility although some have been tougher than others in their method of control. Comparing four Speakers under whom he sat Earl Winterton commented that Speakers Lowther and Fitzroy were far stricter in their control of supplementary questions than Speakers Clifton Brown and Morrison, who took the view 'that the remedy was in the hands of the House'.[5]

Speaker Fitzroy, in a memorandum submitted to the Select Committee on Procedure on Public Business in 1931, stated: 'The present rules governing the putting of questions on the paper, and the asking of supplementary questions are very definite. The only difficulty is in getting Members to comply with them.'[6] In his oral evidence to the Committee on 1 July 1931 he indicated 'that nine times out of ten we get through whatever questions are on the Paper' and that he interpreted the rules with great latitude.[7] However, Speaker Fitzroy recognized no automatic right to ask supplementary questions and tended to keep the House on a somewhat tight rein.

Under his successor the practice arose of assuming that the

[1] *Commons Hansard*, 4th series, Vol. 96, col. 264.

[2] Ibid., Vol. 108, col. 372.

[3] See his evidence to the Select Committee on House of Commons (Procedure), *First Report*, H.C. 89, 1906, pp. 3 and 4.

[4] See *Commons Hansard*, 5th series, Vol. 73, cols. 41–2 for full text of this ruling.

[5] Earl Winterton, *Orders of the Day*, pp. 151–2.

[6] *Special Report from the Select Committee on Procedure on Public Business*, H.C. 161, 1931, p. 407.

[7] Ibid., p. 422.

Member asking the original question has the right to the first supplementary. On one occasion Speaker Clifton Brown rebuked Winston Churchill for 'gate-crashing' when, as Leader of the Opposition, he attempted to interpose a supplementary question ahead of the Member who had asked the main question. On that occasion the Speaker said: 'It is always my custom that when an hon. member asks a question he is entitled to the first supplementary . . .'[1]

Giving evidence before the Select Committee on Procedure on 29 November 1945, Speaker Clifton Brown stated in a memorandum:

> I regard the Question hour as a vital part of our proceedings. I would not extend it, neither would I alter the rules governing Questions. . . . Supplementary Questions are important and often elicit unexpected and important points. As a general rule not more than one supplementary by the original questioner should suffice, but on the other hand some Questions may give rise to several legitimate supplementaries. How many is a matter for the Chair, and the rules governing questions should also apply to supplementaries.[2]

Thus the Speaker will call to order a Member who asks a supplementary which goes beyond the scope of the main question, who uses a supplementary question as a camouflage for a statement or expression of opinion, or who puts in the form of a supplementary question a question which the Table Office had rejected as inadmissible. As recently as 24 April 1958 Speaker Morrison reminded the House that although the asking of supplementary questions had become an accepted practice it was not a matter of right. 'It is a matter of discretion and judgment in each case. . . . There is no such right.'[3]

Giving evidence before the Select Committee on Procedure on 24 July 1958, Speaker Morrison confirmed that it was the practice of the Chair to protect the right of a Member to pursue his own question. He indicated that the Chair would intervene 'in the case of particular Members "muscling in" on ordinary parliamentary questions of other members. It is the man's own

---

[1] *Commons Hansard*, 5th series, Vol. 434, cols. 239–40.
[2] *Second Report from the Select Committee on Procedure*, H.C. 58–I, 1945–6, p. 36.
[3] *Commons Hansard*, 5th series, Vol. 586, col. 1149.

"hare"; he finds it, so let him hunt it. I think the proper rule is certainly the old rule.'[1]

However, the evidence given by Speaker King before the Select Committee on Procedure on 11 February 1970 indicated a shift of view on the part of the Chair in the intervening years. He stated that it would no longer be possible to tell a Member that he had no automatic right to follow his own question with a supplementary, and that the situation had even developed to the point where the opposite side of the House was claiming an automatic right to put an additional supplementary. He agreed that the conception of the supplementary question as an automatic right was an innovation, but pointed out that the supplementary was 'very often far more important than the original question'. He acknowledged that an enormous change had taken place and that former Speakers might have regarded 'the question to the Minister as a matter between the Minister and the Member. It has changed since then. Once the original question is asked, it becomes the possession of the House. It is almost certain that somebody on the other side of the House is keenly interested in the topic. If it is politically loaded both sides want politically loaded supplementaries.' He felt that the change had been of value to the House.[2]

The Committee in its report on 'Question Time' reiterated the view that there was no automatic right to ask supplementary questions, and recommended that 'on occasion, Mr. Speaker should feel free not to call such supplementaries'. It added 'that the value of question time would be enhanced if, when a Minister's answer was unsatisfactory, the Member who asked the question had the opportunity to put a second supplementary question', a practice which had disappeared because of the great increase in the volume of supplementary questions.[3]

A number of Members expressed the view that the Speaker's control of supplementary questions was one of his most crucial and significant powers. Every Speaker has employed his own technique, but it is clear that the task has become increasingly difficult with every passing year because of the ever-mounting

---

[1] *Report from the Select Committee on Procedure*, H.C. 92–I, 1958–9, p. 152.
[2] *Second Report from the Select Committee on Procedure*, H.C. 198, 1969–70, pp. 44–5.
[3] Ibid., p. vii.

volume of questions and the modern tendency of following a main question with a supplementary as a matter of course. Reference was even made, during the hearings which led to the report of the Select Committee on Procedure of 1958–9, to 'the growing practice of Members coming with a long supplementary question already written out, typed out, even before they have heard the answer to the question'.[1]

Speakers appeal as a matter of course to the questioners and the ministers to keep their questions and answers short and this constant pressure from the Chair sometimes has its effect. Speaker Lloyd referred however to an occasion when he deliberately allowed a Member to ask a very long supplementary in order to relax a tense atmosphere which had built up in the House. Although he was criticized for having done so, the tension evaporated as a result and he believed more time would have been wasted had he called the Member to order.[2]

Speaker King, in the words of one Member, 'organized questions by the clock'. Speaker King himself explained that as a result of the recommendations of the Select Committee on Procedure he cut down the number and the length of supplementary questions and aimed at getting through a basic 45 main questions each day. He used an indicator which was placed on the Table of the House and showed a minus sign if the question period was dragging and a red minus sign if it was dragging very badly. If progress was good the indicator showed a plus. In this way he was able to decide whether he should accelerate the progress of questions or could allow some flexibility.[3] On certain principles he was quite inflexible. For example, he acknowledged in the House on one occasion that only Scottish Members were entitled to ask supplementary questions on matters related to Scotland. 'It is difficult, almost impossible, for Englishmen to get into Scottish questions while I am in the Chair.'[4]

One Member interviewed described Speaker Lloyd as 'rather weak on questions' in comparison with Speaker King. However, Speaker Lloyd himself explained that he did not believe in the principle of cramming as many questions as possible into the

---

[1] *Report from the Select Committee on Procedure*, H.C. 92–I, 1958–9, p. 154.
[2] Interview with Mr. Speaker Lloyd, 13 Sept. 1973.
[3] Interview with Lord Maybray-King, 13 Sept. 1973.
[4] *Commons Hansard*, 5th series, Vol. 807, col. 1285.

time allotted and allowing only one supplementary to each question. He preferred to judge the mood of the House and to allow a question to be further explored if the House showed a particular interest in it. He took the view that question time becomes too easy for ministers if supplementaries are curtailed too much and it is not the function of the Speaker to protect ministers during question time. He regarded question time as a back-bencher's occasion and did not invariably call on opposition front-bench spokesmen to ask supplementaries.[1]

It was Speaker King's custom to look through questions each day and hold a daily consultation with a senior adviser prior to the question period. Speaker Lloyd held a similar daily meeting. During the Parliament dissolved in February 1974 he rarely looked through all the questions himself although he would always inquire whether there was anything unusual about them or about the groupings. However, the two Parliaments elected in 1974 posed new problems on account of the representation of minority parties. He began to look through all questions likely to be reached because only by this means could he be sure of being fair when calling on Members who wished to ask supplementaries. He also began the practice of urging ministers not to group more than three or four questions for answer at the same time since grouping gives an unfair advantage to some Members over others with earlier questions on the notice paper.[2]

Speaker King initiated the practice of requesting Members to hold over points of order until the end of the question period to avoid cutting into the limited time available. Speaker Lloyd, who expressed the view that the question period was too short, has continued this practice and declines to hear points of order until questions are at an end.[3]

We shall now deal with those powers vested in the Speaker which are designed to curtail debate, counter obstruction, and take account of emergency situations. Most of them were in existence at the beginning of the century and had their origins in the 1880s when the Irish Nationalist campaign of parliamen-

[1] Interview with Mr. Speaker Lloyd, 13 Sept. 1973.

[2] Information supplied by Mr. Speaker Lloyd in the course of correspondence during 1974.

[3] See, for example, his ruling of 27 Jan. 1971, *Commons Hansard*, 5th series, Vol. 810, col. 524.

tary obstruction was at its height. These powers were originally conferred on the Speaker to enable him to deal with an abnormal situation, but so great has been the subsequent increase in the pressure of parliamentary business that they have now become a part of the basic machinery of procedure.

Prominent among the restrictive devices provided for in the Standing Orders is the closure, first imposed on the initiative of Speaker Brand on 2 February 1881 after the longest sitting the House of Commons has ever known.[1] In 1887 the initiative in the application of closure was transferred from the Speaker to the House itself and the rule has remained essentially the same since that time. Under the closure rule the Chair has an absolute discretion in deciding whether or not a motion for the immediate termination of the debate shall be put to the House or committee, as the case may be. Any Member may claim to move 'That the question be now put' and the question is put forthwith 'unless it shall appear to the Chair that such motion is an abuse of the rules of the House, or an infringement of the rights of the minority'. If the Chair accepts the motion it is put to the vote without amendment or debate and if a division takes place not less than 100 Members must vote in the majority supporting the motion in order for it to be carried.[2] If the closure motion is carried the question which was under debate is put immediately, and with the agreement of the Chair any further question may be put which may be requisite to bring the question before the House to a decision.[3]

The operation of closure is thus governed by important safeguards central to which is the authority of the Speaker in protecting the rights of minorities and individual Members. In an article published in 1932, the late Lord Campion, a former Clerk of the House of Commons, illustrated by statistics 'that the power given to the Speaker to refuse closure is a real check on its exercise' and added: 'But the safeguard against the improper use of the closure, provided by the discretionary power vested in the Chair, is more effective than any figures can indicate. The

---

[1] See Speaker's ruling, *Commons Journals*, Vol. 136, p. 50.

[2] In a standing committee the number necessary to render the majority effective for the closure is the number prescribed as the quorum. See Standing Order 65(3)(b), 1974 edition.

[3] See Standing Orders 30 and 31, 1974 edition.

mere knowledge that the power exists prevents the closure being demanded if there is any likelihood that the Chair would refuse it.'[1] This view was borne out by evidence given to the Select Committee on Procedure on Public Business on 16 February 1931 by Ramsay MacDonald who said in reply to a question: 'The closure is never moved now unless it is thought that the Speaker or Chairman will accept it. If he says "I will not accept a closure just now" you never move it.'[2]

Nevertheless, the Speaker is bound to have regard to the problems of a hard-pressed government striving to achieve its legislative programme. Fortunately the agreements reached on allocation of time through 'the usual channels' and the conventions which have developed in relation to the programming of business have rendered this particular duty of the Speaker somewhat less invidious than it once was, at least in relation to government business. Mr. Speaker Lloyd confirmed that the operation of closure on government bills is fairly routine because, unless other arrangements are made through 'the usual channels', it has become standard practice not to allocate more than a single day's debate to the second reading of a government bill.[3] The Speaker can never enjoy complete protection in the exercise of this discretion however. Acceptance of a closure motion by the Chair in relation to government business is a virtual guarantee that it will be carried provided the Whips do their job and ensure the attendance of a sufficient number of Members. The decision therefore inevitably involves the Speaker in favouring one side against the other, no matter how non-partisan he may be in weighing the considerations involved, and he has not always managed to avoid criticism. At least two Speakers during this century have been subjected to motions of censure for having allowed a closure motion.[4]

Different considerations apply in relation to private members' business, where the acceptance of closure can make all the

[1] G. F. M. Campion, 'Methods of closure in the Commons', *Journal of the Society of Clerks-at-the-Table in Empire Parliaments for 1932*, vol. 1, p. 21.

[2] *Special Report from the Select Committee on Procedure on Public Business*, H.C. 161, 1931, p. 14.

[3] Interview with Mr. Speaker Lloyd, 13 Sept. 1973.

[4] On 28 May 1925 (*Commons Hansard*, 5th series, Vol. 184, col. 1591) and on 7 May, 1952 (ibid., Vol. 500, col. 397).

difference to the prospects of a private Member's bill reaching the statute book. The decision with regard to accepting a closure motion on these occasions poses greater difficulties, since the Chair is obliged to balance the desirability of giving a private Member's bill a chance with the necessity of ensuring adequate debate, most private Members' business being taken on a Friday when the hours of sitting are shorter than on other days.[1]

Disputes between Members and the Chair concerning the closure are relatively infrequent, and it is notable that in 1971 the House extended to the Speaker's deputies the power to accept a closure motion on any class of business following a recommendation from the Select Committee on Procedure.[2] The recommendation resulted from evidence given to the Committee by Lord Maybray-King and Mr. Speaker Lloyd, both of whom agreed that this reform, coupled with the appointment of a second Deputy Chairman of Ways and Means, would go far to relieve the burden on the Speaker. The Speaker is therefore no longer obliged to remain in attendance until the end of a sitting in anticipation of a closure motion.

Among other restrictive powers which originated as measures designed to counter Irish obstruction are those relating to dilatory motions, the unnecessary claiming of divisions, and irrelevance and tedious repetition in debate.

Dilatory motions are defined by Standing Order[3] and in the House they consist mainly of motions to adjourn the House or to adjourn the debate when moved for the purpose of superseding the question before the House.[4] Their legitimate purpose is to provide an opportunity to consider a sudden or unexpected development relative to the question before the House. How-

---

[1] Interview with Speaker Lloyd, 13 Sept. 1973. An example of the dilemma which can confront the Chair when private Members' business is under consideration is to be found on 21 November 1958 (ibid., Vol. 595, cols. 1607–20).

[2] See *Second Report from the Select Committee on Procedure*. 'The process of legislation', H.C. 538, 1970–1, p. xx, para. 38 and p. xxxv, para. 70(17).

[3] See Standing Order 28(2), 1974 edition.

[4] Motions for the adjournment of the House are used for a number of purposes and their use as dilatory motions should be distinguished from their other uses e.g., as substantive motions made by ministers for the purpose of holding special debates, as vehicles for seeking emergency debates, and as a means of providing private Members with opportunities to raise matters during the half-hour at the end of each sitting.

ever, they are open to abuse and in the days when they were not subject to restriction they were frequently used for purposes of obstruction. Today this is no longer possible as they are controlled by the discretion of the Chair and certain other restrictions.[1] If the Speaker or Chairman believes a dilatory motion to be an abuse of the rules of the House 'he may forthwith put the question thereupon from the Chair, or he may decline to propose the question thereupon to the House or the Committee'.[2] Modern procedure and the tight programming of parliamentary business have greatly reduced the importance of dilatory motions as a factor in debate.

The power of the Speaker or Chairman to refuse a division which he feels is unnecessarily claimed was originally introduced to counter obstruction from Members calling divisions 'frivolously or vexatiously', to use the words of the original Standing Order of 1888.[3] Today this power is only rarely invoked. The sitting of 25 April 1961 provides an example of its exercise together with some interesting observations relative to it by Speaker Hylton-Foster.[4]

Also designed to counter obstruction is the rule which permits the Chair to direct a Member to discontinue his speech on grounds of irrelevance or tedious repetition.[5] It would of course be impossible to apply this rule rigidly and it was never intended by the House that it should be. Irrelevance and repetition are frequent ingredients of parliamentary debate and are often employed unintentionally, sometimes even legitimately, as, for example, when a Member wishes to emphasize a point.[6] Speaker King has commented shrewdly on the manner in which the Chair uses its discretion in the exercise of this power:

The scope of debate varies to some extent with the person. If some innocent person wanders out of order I hope that none of my colleagues will call him

---

[1] For details see Erskine May, pp. 369–71.
[2] See Standing Order 28(1), 1974 edition.
[3] See Erskine May, p. 390. The current rule is Standing Order 36, 1974 edition.
[4] *Commons Hansard*, 5th series, Vol. 639, col. 371 and cols. 373–5.
[5] See Standing Order 22, 1974 edition.
[6] See Speaker Lowther's comments on this matter in his memoirs: Viscount Ullswater, *A Speaker's commentaries* (Edward Arnold, 1925), Vol.2, pp. 25–6.

to order too soon. I hope they will remember the advice I received from a very old parliamentarian: If a Member gets out of order, let him say something of what he wants to say before you call him back to order. If someone, however, is deliberately using this means and is going out of order to frustrate the work of Parliament, if he is making a speech which is designed to obstruct, then I would say: Apply the rules of order strictly and tie him down to the last sentence and the last comma.[1]

One of the most important powers of the Chair in controlling debate, and one which is allied to the closure, is the selection of amendments, sometimes referred to as the 'kangaroo closure' because it involves 'jumping' over those amendments on the order paper which are not selected. It was first introduced in limited form in 1909 and its exercise required a special decision of the House. Evidence given before the Select Committee on House of Commons (Procedure) in 1914 tended to the view that the selection of amendments should become a permanent power of the Chair. It was contended that the power was necessary in order to deal with obstruction at the committee and report stages of bills and that the Chair would ensure it was exercised with impartiality.[2] Speaker Lowther in his own evidence agreed that it was desirable to restrict the amendments which should be allowed on report, and agreed, albeit reluctantly, that it should become a permanent power of the Chair. He added that on the occasions when he had exercised the power he had consulted both parties: '. . . I simply took their view and called the amendments which they selected.'[3]

Despite Lowther's reservations, the selection of amendments was established as a permanent power of the Chair by Standing Order in 1919. Of all the procedural reforms of the twentieth century, none perhaps expresses more forcefully the overriding confidence the House reposes in its Speaker and Chairmen. The Standing Order[4] allows the Speaker a complete discretion in selecting amendments for debate in relation to any question before the House. It confers similar powers on the chairmen in

---

[1] *Report of the Conference of Speakers and Presiding Officers of Commonwealth Parliaments* (Canada, Sept. 1969), p. 85.

[2] See, for example, the evidence of Ramsay MacDonald, Herbert Asquith, and Sir Courtney Ilbert before the Committee. *Report from the Select Committee on House of Commons (Procedure)*, H.C. 378, 1915, pp. 134, 154, 168–9.

[3] Ibid., pp. 198–9.

[4] Standing Order 33, 1974 edition.

committee of the whole House, permits the Speaker or Chairman to call on a Member to explain an amendment to enable him to form a judgement on it, and defines instructions to committees on bills and motions to recommit bills as amendments for the purposes of the order. In 1971 the Standing Order was amended on the recommendation of the Select Committee on Procedure to enable the Deputy Speaker to exercise the power in the House during the consideration of the business of supply.[1]

All Members interviewed agreed that the power of the Chair to select amendments was a crucial factor in modern procedure, but only one expressed any reservation with regard to its desirability. He took the view that since the selection of amendments determines the speed at which the government secures its business the Speaker is placed in the position of fulfilling a function which normally belongs to the Leader of the House.[2]

Although the selection of amendments can severely tax the judgement of the Chair, successive Speakers since Lowther have seemed content to shoulder the responsibility. Speaker Fitzroy in a memorandum presented to the Select Committee on Procedure on Public Business in 1931 expressed the opinion that the kangaroo 'works quite well, and to the general satisfaction . . . Under the powers of selection the Speaker or Chairman can easily *discern* which amendments are really desired and can readily judge when debate develops into repetition or obstruction, and can accept the closure when it is reasonably demanded. Every amendment of substance can be debated.' The guillotine, by comparison, was unsatisfactory and led to a sense of grievance.[3] He also favoured the extension of the power to the chairmen of standing committees, although he added the caution: 'I find it very difficult to curtail the discussion on the Report when relatively so small a number of Members have had an opportunity of moving amendments, or speaking on them upstairs. It must be remembered that if the powers of the kangaroo are conferred on Chairmen of Committees that difficulty will be still

---

[1] *Second Report from the Select Committee on Procedure*, H.C. 538, 1970–1, p. xx, para. 38 and p. xxxv, para. 70(17).

[2] Interview with Mr. Robin Maxwell-Hyslop, 1 Sept. 1973.

[3] *Special Report from the Select Committee on Procedure on Public Business*, H.C. 161, 1931, p. 406.

more increased.'[1] The power was extended to the chairmen of standing committees in 1934[2] thus further streamlining this method of curtailing debate.

Giving evidence before the Select Committee on Procedure on 14 March 1946, Speaker Clifton Brown opposed a suggestion by the Clerk of the House that standing committees be reorganized with a view to reducing the time spent on the report stages of bills, saying that his power to select amendments was a sufficient safeguard against abuse of the report stage.[3]

Amendments disposed of in committee are very unlikely to be selected on report, a practice based on precedents going back to 1919. Exceptions are made if they raise a principle of particular importance, however. Lord Maybray-King, giving evidence to the Select Committee on Procedure on 17 March 1971, cited two examples of such amendments which he had allowed: 'One was whether a majority jury decision should be valid. . . . The second major question was decimal currency.'[4] In the course of the same evidence Lord Maybray-King stressed the importance of the report stage in the legislative process and indicated some of the problems involved in the selection of amendments. Much of the time is consumed by government amendments and those which the government has pledged itself to consider, selection of which is obligatory.

Thirdly, there are the new points. I am very frank. What has distressed me when I have selected a new point at Report has been to find as the debate proceeded that it was merely a rehashing, a redressing or a retrimming of an old point. What are you going to do to cut down Report stage? You could say that nothing would be discussed on Report except Government Amendments. If you did this tonight, there would be a revolution. Obviously, you could not do that.

His advice to the Committee was not to blame the procedure 'because with every new Parliament we have a keener Parliament than we had in the previous one'.[5]

In the course of an interview Lord Maybray-King stressed

---

[1] Ibid., p. 407.

[2] Standing Order 65(3)(a), 1974 edition.

[3] *Third Report from the Select Committee on Procedure*, H.C. 189–I, 1946, pp. 92–3.

[4] *Second Report from the Select Committee on Procedure*, 'The process of legislation', H.C. 538, 1970–1, p. 47.

[5] Ibid., pp. 47–8.

that before selecting amendments at the report stage the Speaker must study the whole committee report and analyse the amendments, taking as much advice as possible before making his judgement. It was also important to spot those amendments which appeared to be different but which in practice reproduced an amendment which was rejected in committee.[1]

Speaker Lloyd informed the author that he had instituted a new system whereby the Clerk discussed with the opposition the amendments it wished to propose, with a view to determining its priorities. Thus, assuming some amendments have to be dropped, the opposition indicates those it would prefer to see selected. This practice is also followed in cases where a private Member has a number of amendments down. Speaker Lloyd said the system is working well and has given rise to no problems. He also made the point that many difficulties can be overcome if the Chair takes account of what a Member wishes to say and whether or not it would be possible to say it by speaking to another amendment.[2]

Various practices have developed over the years which have assisted the Speaker in maintaining the flexibility which his discretion allows him, and this has been a key factor in the success with which the power to select amendments has been exercised. For example, although he may decline to give reasons for his selection and non-selection, he frequently does offer an explanation of his decisions. It is now normal for the Speaker to indicate his provisional selection in advance, although he is free to make changes if the progress of debate introduces new factors. It is also now normal practice to allow several amendments to be discussed together even though they have not all been selected.[3] Unlimited freedom to consult also assists the Speaker in deciding the factors which must be taken into account in selecting amendments, such as the degree of support which they command, the importance of the principle they raise, the importance with which they are regarded by various sections of opinion, the extent to which they have been discussed in committee, the extent to which they introduce new points, and their relevance to the general content of the bill.

[1] Interview with Lord Maybray-King, 13 Sept. 1973.
[2] Interview with Speaker Lloyd, 13 Sept. 1973.
[3] See Erskine May, p. 442.

Although there appears to be no record of a motion of censure against the Speaker himself in relation to the selection of amendments, the lower Chair has been the subject of such a motion on at least two occasions.[1]

We come now to an area of procedure in which the decision of the Speaker can have a bearing on the order of business. It is open to any Member to seek to move the adjournment of the House for the purpose of debating a sudden emergency and it is the Speaker's duty to decide whether the request conforms to the conditions necessary to justify the setting aside of regular business. This procedure is another which dates from the period of Irish Nationalist obstruction and was first embodied in a Standing Order on 27 November 1882. Previously there was no restriction on the moving of adjournment motions. They could be used as a peg on which to hang a debate on almost any subject; the Speaker had no power to disallow them and they were ready-made weapons of obstruction. The reforms relating to dilatory motions and the introduction of a procedure for holding emergency debates were the methods used to curtail the abuse of adjournment motions.

The emergency adjournment procedure when first introduced was thus a restriction on the rights of private Members. In the modern context, although an emergency debate is not easily granted, it has become a means of protecting their rights. Given the government's control of the parliamentary timetable and the tight programming of business, the existence of the procedure provides the only guarantee that government business may be set aside if the Speaker believes there is sufficient justification and certain conditions are fulfilled. Since emergency debates are frequently in the nature of emergency motions of censure against the government the right to seek such a debate is one which is jealously guarded.

Nevertheless, until the implementation of an important revision of the Standing Order in 1967, it was interpreted with ever-increasing restrictiveness as the century progressed. Prior to the change in the rule, the motion was made for the purpose of discussing 'a definite matter of urgent public importance' and each word of this phrase came to acquire a special and ever-

---

[1] On 21 June 1951 (see *Commons Hansard*, 5th series, Vol. 489, cols. 721–746); and on 1 Mar. 1972 (ibid., Vol. 832, cols. 268–9 and cols. 432–548).

narrower significance in the light of successive rulings of the Chair. In the earlier years of the operation of the rule the criteria for an emergency debate were fairly flexible. On 13 April 1894 Speaker Peel commented: 'What I think was contemplated was an occurrence of some sudden emergency, either in home or foreign affairs.'[1] The latitude permitted by this interpretation is illustrated by the fact that from 1882–1900, 122 emergency debates were allowed under the Standing Order; from 1901–10, 54 were allowed; and from 1911–20, 71 were allowed. Throughout this period the Speaker allowed more than he refused.[2] Thenceforward the number allowed declined markedly. From 1921–30 there were 21;[3] from 1931–40 there were 7; from 1941–50 there were 4; from 1951–60, there were 8; and from 1961 until the revision of the Standing Order there were 4.[4] There were a number of sessions in which none at all were allowed and indeed a few in which none were even sought, so stringent had the conditions become.

This narrowing interpretation of the rule reflected the very great increase in the exercise of government responsibilities under the prodigious volume of administrative powers which has grown up since 1900, and in 1946 the Select Committee on Procedure called for the relaxation of the criteria:

In particular, Your Committee would refer to the refusal of motions because the matters raised by them involved no more than 'the ordinary administration of the law'. This rule was originally intended to refer to the administration of justice in the courts of law, but since 1920 it has been held to cover the administrative action of Government Departments.[5]

This would have been a difficult recommendation to implement because, as one commentator has observed, there is no test which could be applied which would enable the Speaker to make an objective judgement. 'The only ground for selection would be the suspicion of maladministration in a particular

[1] *Commons Hansard*, 4th series, Vol. 23, col. 367.

[2] These figures are taken from a table published in the *Third Report from the Select Committee on Procedure*, H.C. 189–I, 1946, p. liv.

[3] Ibid., p. liv.

[4] See table published in the *Second Report from the Select Committee on Procedure*, H.C. 282, 1966–7, p. 46.

[5] *Third Report from the Select Committee on Procedure*, H.C. 189–I, 1946, p. xviii.

instance; and to proceed upon that basis would be to express an opinion on the merits of the case.'[1]

The Clerk of the House in a memorandum to the Select Committee on Procedure dated 25 February 1966 cited what he described as a classic instance of the restrictive application of the Standing Order: the refusal of an emergency debate relating to the defence of Singapore shortly before its fall in 1942 on the ground that the matter had been urgent for some time and was to be debated fully during the following week.[2] The conditions of wartime, which is a continuing state of emergency, would naturally encourage a restrictive interpretation of the rule, but while the 1950s and 1960s show a considerable increase in the number of emergency debates sought, they reveal no relaxation in the application of the rule by the Speaker until it was changed in 1967.

The memorandum of the Clerk of the House referred to above gives a detailed description of the criteria applied by the Chair before the revision of the rule in 1967.[3] They have been summarized as follows:

In the first place the matter it is sought to discuss must be definite—that is, it must be specific, unambiguous, and based on fact and not on hearsay. It must be urgent—that is, it must be raised at the earliest opportunity and, in the public interest, require the immediate attention of the House. It must be of public importance, and thus raise a larger issue than a purely individual grievance. It must be a matter for which the Government is clearly responsible and on which official information is available. It must call for action which is beyond the ordinary administration of the law, it must be remedial otherwise than by legislation, and it must not be a matter involving privilege or the conduct of persons holding high office.[4]

The interpretation of such criteria imposed a very onerous duty on the Speaker. Given the nature of emergency adjournment debates, the refusal to allow one often gives rise to discontent and the Speaker has on rare occasions been subjected to a

---

[1] Memorandum by the Second Clerk Assistant printed with the *Second Report from the Select Committee on Procedure*, H.C. 282, 1966–7, p. 43; see also ruling of Speaker Whitley, 21 June, 1926, *Commons Hansard*, 5th series, Vol. 197, cols. 40–2.

[2] *Second Report from the Select Committee on Procedure*, H.C. 282, 1966–7, p. 40.

[3] Ibid., pp. 38–9.

[4] Laundy, *The Office of Speaker*, op. cit., p. 60.

motion of censure as a result of his decision.[1] If the Speaker allows the motion it is submitted to the House in accordance with requirements that have remained unchanged in the revised Standing Order.[2]

Giving evidence before the 1946 committee, Speaker Clifton Brown was not enthusiastic about a suggestion that the Speaker should be the judge of 'definiteness', but that the decision as to 'urgency' and 'public importance' should be left to the House. He acknowledged that 'definiteness' was the most difficult factor to judge but felt that it would never be difficult to find 40 Members to agree that a matter was 'urgent' and of 'public importance'.[3]

The House accepted a recommendation from this Committee that, when an emergency debate was granted, the time lost should be made up by taking regular business after 10 p.m.

In 1959 another Select Committee attempted to grapple with the problems of the emergency adjournment procedure. It acknowledged in its report that of all the duties imposed on the Speaker, those concerned with the interpretation of this Standing Order were 'perhaps the most invidious'. The report went on:

The main difficulty in our view lies in the cumulative effect of a long series of restrictive rulings from the Chair over the last sixty years. . . . We therefore recommend that Mr. Speaker be instructed by the House that in future he should be at liberty to disregard rulings which in his opinion unduly restrict the original intention of Standing Order No. 9 as expressed by Mr. Speaker Peel.[4]

This recommendation and four others which followed were not adopted, largely because the guide-lines offered to the Speaker were insufficiently specific.

A breakthrough was eventually achieved by the Select Committee on Procedure of 1966–7 which recommended a revised Standing Order. In a memorandum to the Committee Speaker King acknowledged that the operation of the rule was a cause of

[1] See for example the debate of 29 July 1957, *Commons Hansard*, 5th series, Vol. 574, cols. 878–909.

[2] Standing Order 9(1), 1974 edition.

[3] *Third Report from the Select Committee on Procedure*, H.C. 189–I, 1946, pp. 88–92.

[4] *Report from the Select Committee on Procedure*, H.C. 92, 1959, pp. xviii–xix.

concern because of the rareness with which a request for an emergency debate met the many tests which had to be applied. He referred to various solutions which had been proposed but, while highlighting the problems involved, offered none of his own.[1] Giving evidence to the Committee Speaker King stressed throughout that the Speaker would require very precise guidelines from the House before he could depart from the rulings of his predecessors.[2]

The Committee accepted the importance of the Speaker receiving clear guidance if the rule were to be relaxed and recognized that the main obstacle to any change in practice lay in the formula 'definite matter of urgent public importance' which had come to acquire a special significance in the light of past rulings. They therefore recommended the abandonment of the phrase and its replacement by another, 'specific and important matter that should have urgent consideration', by which a request for an emergency debate would in future be tested. The words were not chosen for any particular significance they had, but solely in order to relieve the Speaker of the need to be bound by past precedents based on interpretations of the former phrase. It was also recommended that the new Standing Order should expressly prohibit the Speaker from stating reasons for his decisions since 'explanations tend to add to the force of precedent, thus diminishing the scope of the standing order'. For the further guidance of the Speaker certain specific relaxations in the interpretation of the new Standing Order were recommended, allowing 'references to any matter that would be in order if the debate were on a motion to take note of the subject under discussion'. Thus the previous prohibitions on the raising of matters calling for legislation, matters of potential as distinct from current ministerial responsibility, and matters involving the criticism of persons who may normally be criticized only on a substantive motion would no longer apply. Matters involving intervention in foreign affairs and the ordinary administration of the law, if not *sub judice*, were also regarded by the Committee as being suitable subjects of emergency debates. The Committee stressed 'the undesirability of debates under the order becoming too

---

[1] See *Second Report from the Select Committee on Procedure*, H.C. 282, 1966–7, pp. 1–3.

[2] Ibid.; see, for example, his answers to questions 23 and 25 on p. 7.

frequent and disruptive', saying that they had in mind an average of five debates a session.[1]

The revised Standing Order proposed by the Committee provided also that the motion should stand over until the next sitting day unless the Speaker directs that it be taken at 7 p.m. on the same day; that notice should be given and that the Speaker may defer his decision until a named hour; and that the Speaker should have regard to the limits of ministerial responsibility or possible ministerial action and the likelihood of the matter being brought before the House in time by other means.[2]

The Standing Order was adopted by the House on 14 November 1967 in the form proposed by the Committee and has given rise to about four debates in a normal session. Lord Maybray-King said that during his Speakership the new rule had worked very well. Speaker Lloyd, however, expressed certain reservations. While acknowledging that he would not wish to return to the old rule, he felt that the new rule had encouraged Members to seek emergency debates far too frequently. Requests are too often made to debate matters for which time should be found through the usual channels; also too many requests are made concerning matters on which the government cannot take effective action. He felt that certain modifications to the Standing Order were called for to curb the frequency with which Members tried to invoke it. He suggested the Speaker might be allowed to rule privately on requests for emergency debates before they could be raised in the House.[3]

Two other occasions when the Speaker's discretion determines the business to be discussed also relate to adjournment motions. Whenever the House adjourns for one of its holiday recesses at Christmas, Easter, Whitsun, and in the summer, one whole day is devoted to the discussion of topics selected by private Members, a motion for the adjournment of the House being used for the purpose. It is the Speaker's duty to decide which of the topics proposed shall be selected for debate and to make a provisional allocation of time to each one.[4]

The Speaker also selects the subject for debate every

[1] Ibid., pp. vii–viii.
[2] Ibid., pp. viii–ix and Standing Order 9, 1974 edition.
[3] Interview with Mr. Speaker Lloyd, 13 Sept. 1973.
[4] See Erskine May, p. 278.

Thursday on the daily adjournment motion. A ballot is held to determine the Members who shall have the right to raise matters on the adjournment on the other days of the week. The motion is debated for half an hour at the conclusion of each sitting and is another back-benchers' occasion for which the competition is keen. Prior to 1955 the Speaker played no part in selecting the subject for discussion and the adjournment belonged to the Members successful in the ballot regardless of the day of the week. On 18 January 1944 Speaker Clifton Brown instituted a system of informal notice of the subjects to be raised during the forthcoming week.[1] On 30 June 1944, after a Member had changed the subject of which he had given notice, the Speaker ruled that 'the Adjournment really belongs to the individual, and the subject cannot have precedence over the individual'. He added, however, that 'it is most inconvenient for Members if the subject is changed . . . and is not quite playing the game'.[2]

In 1955 a new system was instituted as a result of representations from Members that 'no opportunity occurs for raising a matter of immediate topical interest'. The scheme made provision for the retention of the ballot on three days of the week, while the subjects on Tuesdays and Thursdays 'should be selected by the Speaker, who would give priority first, to matters raising individual or constituency grievances, including subjects of which notice has been given at question time, and, secondly, other matters of topical interest'. The rules provided that a Member would not be permitted to change his subject except with the consent of the Speaker.[3] On 9 February 1960 the scheme was modified and since then the Speaker has chosen the subject for discussion on Thursdays only.[4] The scheme was again modified on 7 February 1967[5] and the arrangements currently in force are set out in the 18th edition of Erskine May.[6] A Member successful in the ballot must give 48 hours notice if he wishes to change his subject. On Thursday, as selection relates

---

[1] *Commons Hansard*, 5th series, Vol. 396, col. 42.

[2] Ibid., Vol. 401, col. 978.

[3] For the Speaker's statement of 23 Mar. 1955 and rules of the scheme see *Commons Hansard*, 5th series, Vol. 538, cols. 2076–8.

[4] Ibid., Vol. 617, cols. 245–6.

[5] Ibid., Vol. 740, cols. 1354–5.

[6] Erskine May, p. 356.

to the subject and not the Member, no alteration of subject is permissible without the Speaker's consent.

The precedence of business is determined by the Speaker also on occasions when a Member seeks to raise a complaint concerning parliamentary privilege. Matters of privilege are by custom entitled to precedence over the orders of the day provided two conditions are satisfied: that the complaint is raised at the earliest opportunity and that the evidence presented by the Member making it suggests *prima facie* that a breach of privilege or contempt may have been committed. Under the usage of the House it is the function of the Speaker to decide whether the complaint meets these conditions. It is important to emphasize that the Speaker's power is limited to deciding whether or not there is sufficient justification for giving the matter precedence over other business. Matters of privilege are decided not by the Speaker but by the House, normally after they have been referred to the Committee of Privileges. If the Speaker rules against giving priority to the complaint it is still open to the Member to raise it by way of notice of motion, but it is unlikely to be discussed unless time is provided for it in the normal order of business. Under current practice the Speaker defers his ruling on such matters until the next sitting day without prejudice to their claim to priority.

In 1967 a Select Committee which had been appointed to review the law of parliamentary privilege and the procedure relating to it criticized the existing procedure on the ground that it encouraged the raising of trivial complaints, that it attracted harmful publicity, and that the Speaker's ruling as to whether or not a *prima facie* case is established is open to misunderstanding on the part of the public in that it is frequently believed to be a decision on the merits of the case. The Committee also drew attention to the fact that this was a relatively recent practice.[1] In a memorandum to the Committee dated 20 February 1967 Mr. L. A. Abraham pinpoints 16 April 1934 as the date when the Chair first ruled on the *prima facie* aspect of a complaint of privilege. On that date Winston Churchill raised a question of privilege and following a lengthy exposition of the

---

[1] See *Report from the Select Committee on Parliamentary Privilege*, H.C. 34, 1966–7, paras. 154–8, pp. xl–xli.

case requested the Speaker 'to rule that a *prima facie* case of breach of privilege has arisen'. Speaker Fitzroy ruled accordingly, whereupon Churchill moved that the matter be referred to the Committee of Privileges.[1] Thenceforward, as Mr. Abraham points out, this precedent became set. This in turn led to the reference of a complaint to the Committee of Privileges on the motion of the Leader of the House almost as a matter of course whenever the Speaker ruled that a *prima facie* case existed. Since Speaker Fitzroy was not a lawyer he might unwittingly have provided an argument in favour of appointing lawyers to the Chair! The Committee suggested that the use of the phrase '*prima facie* case' be avoided even if the House rejected its recommendations for the reform of the present practice,[2] and the Speaker has been guided by this advice.[3]

Two further areas of procedure in which the Speaker has important discretionary powers are those relating to anticipation and the raising of matters twice in the same session. Two broad principles exist for the guidance of the Chair: 'No question or bill shall be offered in either House that is substantially the same as one on which its judgment has already been expressed in the current session';[4] and 'a matter must not be anticipated if it is contained in a more effective form of proceeding than the proceeding by which it is sought to be anticipated, but it may be anticipated if it is contained in an equally or less effective form'.[5]

The application of the former principle hinges on the definition of the word 'substantially' and can raise some complex considerations, particularly where bills are concerned. For example, a bill and a motion may raise a similar question, but each has a form and purpose distinct from the other. Two bills may overlap each other in content but whether or not the similarities are 'substantial' for the purpose of the rule may not be easy to decide. On 12 March 1912 Speaker Lowther ruled that a motion raising 'practically the same question' that was discussed

---

[1] *Commons Hansard*, 5th series, Vol. 288, col. 722.

[2] *Report*, H.C. 34, 1966–7, para. 158, p. xli.

[3] See, for example, Speaker Lloyd's ruling of 30 April 1974, *Commons Hansard*, 5th series, Vol. 872, col. 942.

[4] Erskine May, p. 362.

[5] Ibid., p. 365.

on an amendment to the address at the beginning of the session was not in order.[1]

On 21 May of the same year he ruled against a motion for leave to introduce a bill to extend the franchise to women because a bill incorporating the same principle had been rejected earlier in the session.[2] In a private ruling of 4 June 1931, Speaker Fitzroy ordered the removal of the notice of presentation of a bill from the notice paper because leave to introduce it under the Ten-Minutes Rule (now Standing Order 13) had previously been refused.[3] On 4 May 1951 Speaker Clifton Brown announced that a bill which was on the order paper for second reading could not be proceeded with because its subject matter had been dealt with in a bill which had already passed its second reading.[4] However, the Member in charge of the bill was permitted to make a statement before the bill was withdrawn.[5]

The principle relating to anticipation is more straightforward in the sense that there is seldom any doubt as to whether one form of proceeding is more effective than another. For example, a bill or other order of the day is a more effective proceeding than a motion because the former leads to a more concrete result. Similarly a substantive motion is a more effective proceeding than a motion for the adjournment of the House or an amendment; and on 13 March 1946 Speaker Clifton Brown disallowed a supplementary question because it anticipated a subject which was going to be raised on the adjournment motion.[6] Until 1914 it was possible to prevent a subject being discussed under the rule of anticipation by keeping on the notice paper a motion which was never brought up. This misuse of 'blocking' motions is now prevented by a Standing Order giving the Speaker his discretionary power.[7] Thus, for example, on 11 September 1942 Speaker Fitzroy ruled that it would be in order to debate the situation in India on the adjournment motion despite the fact that a motion relating to India stood upon the order paper,

[1] *Commons Hansard*, 5th series, Vol. 35, cols. 1043–4.
[2] Ibid., Vol. 38, cols. 1754–7.
[3] Erskine May, p. 479n.
[4] *Commons Hansard*, 5th series, Vol. 487, col. 1513.
[5] Ibid., cols. 1553–5.
[6] Ibid., Vol. 420, col. 1081.
[7] Standing Order 11, 1974 edition.

since the latter motion was unlikely to be debated within a reasonable time.[1] On 19 June 1918 Speaker Lowther allowed discussion of a matter which was before the Public Accounts Committee although he indicated he had reservations about doing so.[2]

Among the discretionary duties of the Speaker is the application of the convention relating to matters *sub judice*, an area which has given rise to some difficult problems. It is a general principle of parliamentary practice that a matter awaiting judicial decision should not be referred to in debate nor form the subject of a motion or a question to a minister if there is any possibility that prejudicial effect might result. Prior to 1963 no attempt had ever been made to codify this principle. It was a convention, a voluntary restraint self-imposed by Parliament in the interests of justice and fair play, based on precedents dating back to 1844, its interpretation resting with the Chair. The restriction on reference to matters *sub judice* does not apply to debates on bills because legislation is action designed to alter the circumstances on which a court must reach a decision and the right of Parliament to legislate must not be limited. Speaker Clifton Brown gave a private ruling to this effect in 1949.[3] It does apply, however, to motions for leave to bring in bills under the Ten-Minutes Rule[4] and this was specified in the resolution adopted by the House on 23 July 1963.[5]

On 31 March 1926 Speaker Whitley ruled that he had no power to prevent a question in regard to a case which is *sub judice*. 'All that I can do is to suggest that it is not desirable, while a matter is before the courts, that it should be dealt with by debate in the House.'[6] However, the discretion of the Speaker has always been a more crucial factor than this ruling would indicate. The record shows that, both before and since the adop-

---

[1] *Commons Hansard*, 5th series, Vol. 383, cols. 533–4.

[2] Ibid., Vol. 107, col. 430. An excellent example of the flexibility with which the anticipation rule can be interpreted is illustrated by the rulings of Speaker Clifton Brown on 12 and 13 December 1945 relating to the Bretton Woods Agreement (ibid., Vol. 417, cols. 421–2 and cols. 629–32).

[3] See *First Report from the Select Committee on Procedure*, H.C. 156, 1962–3, para. 12, p. v.

[4] Standing Order 13, 1974 edition.

[5] See *Commons Hansard*, 5th series, Vol. 681, col. 1417.

[6] Ibid., Vol. 193, col. 2052.

tion of the resolution of 23 July 1963, the decision as to whether the convention should apply or not has clearly belonged to the Speaker. The problem of the Chair lies in balancing Parliament's right to discuss any matter affecting the public interest with the need to protect individuals whose own interests stand to be affected by the judgements or findings of courts and other tribunals. The problem is compounded by the fact that the Chair is seldom in full possession of the facts of any case and cannot therefore know the extent to which reference to it is likely to have prejudicial effect. Both Speaker Hylton-Foster, giving evidence to the Select Committee on Procedure on 19 February 1963, and Speaker Lloyd, giving evidence to its successor on 23 May 1972, agreed that the Chair should take responsibility for the interpretation of the convention, but they also expressed the view that there was a need for some guidance from the House.[1]

The operation of the convention in respect of criminal cases has always been fairly straightforward unless a capital sentence was involved. This particular problem was largely removed with the abolition of the death penalty for murder in 1965, but previously it had led to extreme difficulties. For example, on 27 January 1953 a substantive motion concerning the refusal of the Home Secretary to recommend a reprieve for a man shortly to be executed was removed from the order paper by order of the Speaker on the ground that it constituted an interference with the royal prerogative of mercy. The attempt of the Member concerned to seek an emergency debate on the matter instead was disallowed for the same reason.[2] Another case which arose on 7 February 1961 led to a motion of censure against the Speaker.[3] The Speaker's ruling was upheld by 253 votes to 60 but the highly unsatisfactory situation, whereby a capital sentence could not be discussed until after it had been carried out, remained unchanged. On 5 March 1946 Speaker Clifton Brown ruled in relation to a criminal case which did not involve a capital sentence that the *sub judice* convention ceases to operate when

[1] See *First Report from the Select Committee on Procedure*, H.C. 156, 1962–3, questions 300, 314, and 329; and *Fourth Report from the Select Committee on Procedure*, H.C. 298, 1971–2, questions 195, 198, 217, 220, and 221.
[2] *Commons Hansard*, 5th series, Vol. 510, cols. 845–64.
[3] Ibid., Vol. 634, cols. 214–22 and cols. 1773–1838.

the verdict and sentence have been announced but again becomes *sub judice* when an appeal is lodged.[1]

Other difficulties which have arisen have related mainly to civil cases and the proceedings of tribunals of inquiry and similar statutory bodies. The first time the convention was applied to a civil action was on 4 December 1961 and the Speaker's ruling on this occasion led to the consideration of the operation of the convention by the Select Committee on Procedure in 1962–3. A question was asked in the House concerning disciplinary action taken against a pilot for refusing to fly in conditions he considered unsafe, but since a writ for libel had been issued in connection with the case the Speaker ruled that the matter was *sub judice*. Objection was taken by some Members on the ground that the safety of the flying public should override other considerations and that since judgement in a civil action is often long delayed the House could be debarred from raising the matter for a long time.[2]

On 8 May 1961 Speaker Hylton-Foster waived the convention in relation to a petition pending before an Election Court so as to enable the House to discuss a matter concerned solely with its own constitution.[3]

The leading precedent in the application of the convention to a body other than a court of law was a ruling by Speaker Lowther on 21 March 1921. It related to the proceedings of the first tribunal established under the Tribunals of Inquiry (Evidence) Act, 1921, to which the House had remitted an inquiry into the conduct of certain government officials. The Speaker ruled that it would not be fair to those officials to discuss their conduct in debate.[4] The Chair has since been guided by this precedent and on 20 November 1962 Speaker Hylton-Foster gave a considered ruling on the application of the convention to tribunals of inquiry, citing Lowther's ruling as the main authority.[5]

The first and apparently the only occasion on which the convention was applied to the proceedings of one of the numerous other statutory bodies empowered to conduct an inquiry (many of them also empowered to take evidence on oath) is to be found

---

[1] Ibid., Vol. 420, col. 303. [2] Ibid., Vol. 650, cols. 911–15.
[3] Ibid., Vol. 640, cols. 34–5. [4] Ibid., Vol. 139, col. 2268.
[5] Ibid., Vol. 667, col. 1013.

in a ruling of Speaker Fitzroy on 12 March 1935. He refused an emergency debate on the loss with all hands of two steamships because the matter had been referred to the Wreck Commissioners for investigation. A list of such bodies is appended to the first report of the Select Committee on Procedure, 1962–3,[1] and the Committee itself commented: 'Your Committee think that the application of the rule to all these bodies as a matter of course would be too restrictive of the rights of Parliament. In their view, in respect of all these bodies each case must be considered on its merits, and they see no alternative to leaving the decision to the discretion of the Chair.'[2]

On 11 February 1953 Speaker Morrison sought to draw a distinction between a judicial inquiry and an administrative inquiry, and ruled that 'a question on a matter which is the subject of an administrative inquiry is in order, or at least, is not forbidden by the rules of order'.[3] However, he did not attempt to define a judicial inquiry and Speaker Hylton-Foster in his evidence to the 1962–3 Committee acknowledged that he found 'some difficulty in applying that distinction. You cannot say that a 1921 Act tribunal is a judicial tribunal. Mr. Speaker Fitzroy's case (relating to the Wreck Commissioners) . . . was obviously an administrative tribunal.'[4]

Speaker Hylton-Foster in his evidence dealt in detail with the problems confronting the Chair in interpreting the *sub judice* convention. He agreed that the starting point for its application in relation to criminal cases and cases before courts martial was the laying of a charge,[5] but that in civil cases the starting point was more difficult to determine.[6] He referred to the damage which can be done by a supplementary question since the Speaker is obliged to hear it before he can rule it out of order 'and then the poison is done'.[7] With regard to the application of the convention to proceedings before tribunals other than courts of law he said 'that I can find no coherent principle, on the precedents, to settle the confines of it', and pointed out the difficulty

---

[1] See appendix 4 of the report, pp. 59–62.

[2] *First Report from the Select Committee on Procedure*, H.C. 156, 1962–3 para. 17, p. vi.

[3] *Commons Hansard*, 5th series, Vol. 511, col. 414.

[4] *First Report from the Select Committee on Procedure*, questions 324 and 325.

[5] Ibid., questions 279 and 280.

[6] Ibid., questions 281–99. [7] Ibid., question 303.

in deciding what constituted prejudice in relation to such cases.[1]

The Committee accepted that the Chair was in need of some guidance from the House, and following upon its recommendations the House adopted the resolution of 23 July 1963 setting out certain guiding principles. To a great extent it confirmed settled practice, but it also took account of the difficulties posed by delays in civil cases and the proceedings of courts martial, and defined the application of the convention to tribunals appointed under the Act of 1921. However, the proviso that the application of the guide-lines was 'subject always to the discretion of the Chair and the right of the House to legislate on any matter' left the Speaker with the ultimate responsibility.[2]

The matter was again referred to the Select Committee on Procedure in 1972 in consequence of difficulties which arose following the setting up of the National Industrial Relations Court which has since been abolished.[3] Giving evidence to the Committee on 23 May 1972 Speaker Lloyd expressed the view that the report of the 1962–3 Committee was too restrictive in its application to civil cases other than those involving actions for defamation, and that as a general principle 'the presumption should be for discussion rather than against it'.[4] The Committee agreed and recommended a relaxation of the application of the convention in accordance with the views expressed by the Speaker.[5] The government-sponsored resolution adopted by the House on 28 June 1972 did not, however, go so far. It simply modified the previous resolution of 23 July 1963 by permitting reference in certain circumstances to matters awaiting or under adjudication in so far as they relate to ministerial decisions.[6]

As was recognized by various participants in the debate on the resolution the discretion of the Speaker must be the deciding factor in every case and there is no way the House can avoid placing this onerous responsibility upon him.

While this treatment of the Speaker's responsibilities in relation to procedure cannot claim to be exhaustive, it has sought to

[1] Ibid., question 322.

[2] For full text see *Commons Hansard*, 5th series, Vol. 681, col. 1417.

[3] See Speaker's ruling of 20 Apr. 1972, ibid., Vol. 835, col. 761.

[4] *Fourth Report from the Select Committee on Procedure*, H.C. 298, 1971–2, p. 38, questions 184, 185, and 186.

[5] Ibid., para. 33, pp. xv–xvi for full text of recommendations.

[6] *Commons Hansard*, 5th series, Vol. 839, col. 1627, for text of resolution.

highlight certain areas where the discretionary powers and influence of the Chair have made an impact of particular significance. The discretion of the Chair is that element of parliamentary practice which enables adjustments to be made as circumstances change. It is the all-important element of flexibility which facilitates the definition of principles, the handling of unforeseen situations, and the resolution of difficulties where the Standing Orders are deficient or the precedents are lacking. It is important to add that the Speaker is relieved of the burden of personal decision in many of the rulings he hands down thanks to the advice available to him through the professional expertise of the Clerk of the House and his colleagues.

Further problems and other duties

'One of the disadvantages of the Speakership is the sense of absence of freedom, which the daily sittings for long hours imposes: the feeling that there is no escape, that you are cabined, cribbed, confined; that, unless very exceptional circumstances should arise, you must be either in the Chair or immediately available in case of your presence being required.'[1]

So wrote Speaker Lowther (afterwards Viscount Ullswater), one of the earlier Speakers of the century, whose successors probably all shared the same feelings. By all available accounts the strains of the Speaker's office are excessive, the principal deterrents being the denial of private life and the adverse effect on health. In the case of Speaker Lowther, it appears his health was equal to the strain, as he continued to lead an active life following his retirement in 1921 and died at the age of 94 in 1949. Some of his successors were less fortunate. Speaker Fitzroy and Speaker Hylton-Foster both died in office. According to various Members of Parliament interviewed, Speaker Clifton Brown's health was visibly declining when he retired in 1951. Speaker Hylton-Foster's widow confirmed that the health of both her husband and her father, Douglas Clifton Brown, suffered in consequence of their duties as Speaker. During night sittings they were unable to go to bed and could only rest briefly on a sofa during periods when they were relieved by their deputies. She added that her husband's great sensitivity to the feelings of the

[1] Viscount Ullswater, *A Speaker's commentaries*, Vol. 2, p. 30.

House contributed to the pressures which led to his early death.[1]

Speaker Morrison maintained 'it is the entertainment that kills' rather than the work in the Chair. He made it a rule to decline any external commitment he was not obliged to fulfil in his capacity as Speaker, and normally refused invitations unless they came from Buckingham Palace or 10 Downing Street. He was handicapped by growing deafness, and although he was occasionally able to turn his disability to advantage when in need of the Speaker's traditional 'deaf ear', this was the principal factor which decided him to retire. His widow did not believe that the Speakership directly affected his health although it may have done so indirectly. Prior to retiring he was given a clean bill of health by his doctors, but nevertheless died shortly afterwards, one year after having been appointed Governor-General of Australia.[2]

Lord Maybray-King described the strains of the Speakership as 'unimaginable' and said he had made a point of retiring before his strength failed. He said that the abolition of the Committee of Supply, which obliged the Speaker to take the Chair on supply days, and other procedural reforms implemented in the mid-1960s had greatly added to the burden of the Chair with the result that he never went to bed when the House sat.[3] Mr. Speaker Lloyd confirmed that the strains were great but said that the appointment of a third deputy, coupled with the fact that the Speaker's deputies are now empowered to accept the closure in the House, had eased the burden and that he himself was seldom in the Chair after 11 p.m.[4]

While isolating himself from the camaraderie of parliamentary life, the Speaker must always be accessible to his fellow-Members. He must get to know them personally, know their background and interests, be sympathetic to their problems, and aware of the kind of debates in which each likes to participate. As a part of the process of promoting direct contact with individual Members the Speaker regularly acts as host to groups of Members. Speaker King said he had initiated the practice of holding a weekly lunch to which he invited about seven

[1] Interview with Lady Hylton-Foster, 11 Sept. 1973.
[2] Interview with Lady Dunrossil, 22 Oct. 1973.
[3] Interview with Lord Maybray-King, 13 Sept. 1973.
[4] Interview with Speaker Lloyd, 13 Sept. 1973.

Members from all parties. On these occasions he encouraged them 'to talk about anything except politics'.[1] Speaker Lloyd continued the practice of holding weekly lunches but the guests were not discouraged from talking politics if they wished.[2] Speaker Clifton Brown was not in the habit of mixing his guests politically as he found his social occasions more successful when the Members present were all from the same political party.[3] Speaker Morrison, who restricted his social activities as much as possible, did not hold weekly lunches, preferring to host larger occasions, such as an annual dinner for the Scottish Members, at regular but less frequent intervals.[4]

The control of debate and the maintenance of order give rise to numerous difficulties for the Chair. Controlling the length of speeches, dealing with spurious points of order, and keeping order in an angry House are all matters which regularly tax the patience, tact, and discretion of the Speaker. All Speakers appeal to Members to keep their speeches short and will not hesitate to interrupt a long speech with an appeal to the Member to wind it up. Front-benchers are usually the worst offenders and it is less easy to apply any form of sanction to them. The House has never adopted suggestions that speeches should be subject to a time limit although the possibility has been discussed from time to time.[5]

Spurious points of order are difficult to control because the Chair is obliged to hear a Member who claims to have a point of order. A Member who abuses his right to raise a point of order can therefore expect to be dealt with very firmly. Sir Lance Mallalieu, who was one of the Speaker's deputies during the Parliament of 1970–4, made reference to this problem at the Third Conference of Commonwealth Speakers and Presiding Officers held in Zambia in September 1973.

. . . I dealt rather fiercely on one occasion with a man who had already made two bogus points of order, and then the third came, and I stopped him at once, and said that the hon. member knew that this was a bogus

---

[1] Interview with Lord Maybray-King, 13 Sept. 1973.
[2] Interview with Speaker Lloyd, 13 Sept. 1973.
[3] Interview with Lady Hylton-Foster, 11 Sept. 1973.
[4] Interview with Lady Dunrossil, 22 Oct. 1973.
[5] See, for example, *Report from the Select Committee on Procedure*, H.C. 92–I 1959, para. 26, p. xv.

point of order and that he knew, therefore, he was cheating at the expense of his colleagues. . . . It is a fierce thing to say; to hold a man up in front of his colleagues in a derogatory manner like that. But I think that is a case where Speakers should perhaps exercise their authority.[1]

At the same conference the then Lord Chancellor, Lord Hailsham, stated the case in favour of an authoritarian Speaker.[2] This view was shared, although sometimes with reservations, by most of the Members of Parliament interviewed. The last of the authoritarian Speakers was Speaker Fitzroy whose military background tended to make him a stern disciplinarian. He never hesitated to impose a sanction. Neither would he explain his rulings nor allow Members to dispute them with him. Lord Tranmire was one of those who favoured the methods of Fitzroy, saying the House always gains by a strong Speakership. Lowther he described as a patriarchal figure who was able to rely on his personal prestige. Whitley was knowledgeable but 'pernickety'. Fitzroy was no intellectual but, according to Lord Tranmire, possessed the qualities of a good Speaker.[3]

It was Speaker Clifton Brown who adopted a policy of flexibility and introduced the practice of explaining and justifying his rulings. The tendency of Members to argue with the Speaker and the consequent exposure of the Chair to the procedural tactics of insistent Members can be traced to his Speakership. The tradition has since grown with the result that Speakers, in the interests of being fair, have sometimes gone too far in explaining their rulings. Sometimes they will concede a point rather than argue since argument is always time-consuming. However, the Speaker who concedes is unlikely to gain in prestige. If he makes a mistake it is usually better to stick to his decision and admit the error later. Speakers have on various occasions apologized to the House without suffering any loss of authority.

Speaker Morrison, although he continued his predecessor's practice of explaining points of order, re-established, in the opinion of Lord Tranmire, the discipline which had been slackened in the time of Clifton Brown.[4] The first year of his

---

[1] *Verbatim Report of the Proceedings of the Third Conference of Commonwealth Speakers and Presiding Officers*, Monday 24 to Friday 28 Sept. 1973, pp. 43–4.
[2] Ibid., pp. 36–7.
[3] Interview with Lord Tranmire, 10 Sept. 1973.
[4] Ibid.

Speakership was particularly arduous but he determined, since his election had been contested, to establish his authority by dealing firmly with those who violated the rules of order. He took the view that a lenient Speaker does not win friends but only gains a reputation for being weak. His widow also observed that those Members with whom he dealt strongly bore him no rancour and were probably among the colleagues who appreciated him best.[1]

Speaker Hylton-Foster, in the view of several Members interviewed, very much wanted to be popular and sought to achieve this by being lenient. One of his severest critics stated that he easily yielded to pressure and that certain Members, well-known for their persistently aggressive tactics, were usually able to wear him down.[2]

Lord Pannell has written of Speaker King that he 'proved to be better than many anticipated' and that the House took to 'his sense of fun. He was a kind man but he could exercise authority, and indeed command, in that last unruly hour when those who have not sat in for the debate come in after having dined not unwisely but too well.'[3]

However, in fairness to Clifton Brown, Hylton-Foster, and other Speakers who have been criticized, it is important to emphasize that the House of Commons was never intended to be run like a military establishment. It is a place where emotions sometimes run high, where anger is frequently and legitimately expressed, where Members are entitled to give vent to strong feelings. The Speaker must judge the mood of the House and decide when greater than normal latitude and tolerance are called for. Speaker King expressed the view that in modern parliamentary conditions the House could never return to the days of an overly authoritarian Speakership.[4] Speaker Lloyd also conveyed the impression that he would rather be criticized for flexibility than for misjudged severity.[5]

In the maintenance of order the Speaker has certain sanctions available to him which are set out in Standing Orders 22–6

---

[1] Interview with Lady Dunrossil, 22 Oct. 1973.
[2] Interview with Mr. Robin Maxwell-Hyslop, 1 Sept. 1973.
[3] Article in *The Times*, 4 Mar. 1972, p. 12.
[4] Interview with Lord Maybray-King, 13 Sept. 1973.
[5] Interview with Mr. Speaker Lloyd, 13 Sept. 1973.

(1974 edition). Standing Order 22 which deals with irrelevance and tedious repetition in debate has already been referred to. Standing Order 23 authorizes the Speaker or chairman to 'order any Member or Members whose conduct is grossly disorderly to withdraw immediately from the House during the remainder of that day's sitting'. The same order together with Standing Order 24 make provision for the more severe sanction consequent upon the 'naming' of a Member. Should the Speaker or chairman consider the conduct of a Member sufficiently grave to warrant a more severe penalty than withdrawal from the House for the remainder of the sitting he will name the Member and thus set in motion the procedure laid down in Standing Order 24. In naming a Member the Chair draws the attention of the House to his conduct and it is the House that imposes the penalty, on motion being made, namely suspension for five days, in the case of a first offence, or as otherwise specified in the Standing Order. The present procedure dates from the 1880s but the Standing Order preserves the right of the House to proceed according to ancient usages should it see fit. Naming a Member virtually assures that he will be suspended from the service of the House, but a division usually takes place on the motion and its rejection would amount to a severe rebuff to the Speaker's authority.

If grave disorder arises in the House—that is to say, disorder of a general nature—the Speaker is empowered under Standing Order 26 to 'adjourn the House without putting any question, or suspend the sitting for a time to be named by him'. This power was invoked for the first time on 22 May 1905 by Lowther when acting as Deputy Speaker,[1] and occasions have regularly occurred throughout the century when the Speaker has been obliged to have recourse to it. Uncontrollable disorder, fortunately, is relatively rare. All Speakers during the century have shown that a touch of wit and humour can frequently avert a potentially ugly situation.

To name a Member is a drastic form of disciplinary action which any Speaker would try to avoid. It is nevertheless interesting to contrast one Speaker's leniency with another's severity. On 25 June 1912 George Lansbury completely lost control of himself following a reply to a private notice question concerning

---

[1] *Commons Hansard*, 4th series, Vol. 146, col. 1072.

the treatment of an imprisoned suffragette. He left his seat and addressed the Prime Minister in grossly disorderly language, and obeyed the Speaker's order to withdraw from the House only after it had been repeated several times.[1] Speaker Lowther, realizing that Lansbury was in the grip of strong emotion, was no doubt reluctant to name him and stretched his tolerance to the limit to avoid doing so. By contrast Speaker Fitzroy's naming of Fenner Brockway on 17 July 1930 seems somewhat severe. On this occasion the latter was unduly persistent in calling for a debate on India, although his language was in no way intemperate. Fitzroy nevertheless named him without first giving him the opportunity to withdraw from the House for the remainder of the sitting. One Member was so outraged by Brockway's suspension that he seized the mace and was thereupon named himself![2]

Speaker King came to the Chair determined that he would never name a Member but found out that there are occasions when the necessity cannot be avoided. On 23 May 1968 he was obliged to name Dame Irene Ward who persisted in obstructing the tellers while they were reporting the result of a division concerning the allocation of time to the Finance Bill.[3] This was the first time a Member had been named in sixteen years and he said the occasion was very distressing for him. While he sympathized with the principle she was trying to uphold, namely that a restriction on the right to debate the Finance Bill was a violation of the traditional rights of Members, he was bound to deplore the manner in which she chose to make her demonstration.[4]

The House of Commons has witnessed many unruly scenes during its long history. One of the worst of the twentieth-century occurred on 5 March 1901 when Speaker Gully, having named twelve Irish Members, called the police into the chamber to remove them bodily, all other attempts to force their withdrawal having failed.[5] The House took this assault upon its dignity greatly to heart and Gully was strongly criticized in the press

[1] *Commons Hansard*, 5th series, Vol. 40, cols. 217–19.
[2] Ibid., Vol. 241, cols. 1462–9.
[3] Ibid., Vol. 765, cols. 893–5.
[4] Interview with Lord Maybray-King, 13 Sept. 1973.
[5] *Commons Hansard*, 4th series, Vol. 90, cols. 691–6.

and elsewhere for the action he had taken. His own confidence was also shaken by the incident and he never fully recovered his prestige. The rule empowering the Speaker to adjourn or suspend the sitting of the House in circumstances of grave disorder had not been adopted at the time Gully was faced with his dilemma. Perhaps he might on his own initiative have suspended the sitting and thus spared the House an humiliating experience. But it is easy to be wise after the event and Gully was faced with the necessity of taking a decision in the stress of the moment.

On 14 April 1938 a member drew attention to a report published on the front page of the *Daily Worker* on the previous day denouncing the Speaker for having advised opposition leaders that it would be out of order to hold a debate on Spain on a motion for the adjournment. The newspaper commented: 'This disgraceful ruling is based nominally on the allegation that there has been "too much talk about Spain already".' The Speaker ruled that a *prima facie* case of breach of privilege had been established and the following motion was moved and adopted after a short debate: 'That the statements complained of contained in the article in the *Daily Worker* are a gross libel on Mr. Speaker, and that the publication of the article is a gross breach of the privileges of this House.'[1] No further action was taken against the newspaper.

A more recent victim of press criticism was Mr. Speaker Lloyd, largely as a result of two incidents which occurred during his first tenure of office as Speaker. The first was the physical attack made in the chamber by Bernadette Devlin upon the then Home Secretary, Reginald Maudling, on 31 January 1972; the second was the menacing of Jeremy Thorpe, the leader of the Liberal Party, on 17 February 1972 after five of the six Liberal Members had voted with the government on the second reading of the European Communities Bill. On neither occasion did he impose a sanction, although in each case he made a statement to the House on the following day.[2] An article in *The Times* referring to both incidents concluded: 'More than all the police and detectives, the House today needs the protection of a strong Chair, prompt in discipline, and a Chair that in turn is strongly

---

[1] Ibid., 5th series, Vol. 334, cols. 1317–20.
[2] See ibid., Vol. 830, col. 239 and Vol. 831, col. 773.

protected by the will and democratic resolve of the chamber it rules.'[1]

In relation to the Bernadette Devlin episode the *Daily Express* published a cartoon by Cummings lampooning the Speaker and bearing the caption 'Maudling! We ought to bring back the troops from Ireland to keep order in the House of Commons!'[2] This kind of criticism of the Chair comes close to touching parliamentary privilege and the cartoon might well have been judged a contempt of Parliament had the House chosen to take notice of it.

What the press fails to take into account in judging these incidents are the exact circumstances of the moment and the implications of any punitive action the Speaker might take. The best interests of the House and the country must always be uppermost in the Speaker's mind. Few of the Members of Parliament interviewed were critical of Speaker Lloyd in his handling of either matter, although there was some disagreement. For example, one Member was more outraged by the manhandling of Jeremy Thorpe than by Bernadette Devlin's assault on the Home Secretary[3] while another took the view that the former incident did not warrant intervention by the Chair.[4] Some Members felt that the failure to name Bernadette Devlin might have set a bad precedent: yet when a similar incident occurred on 4 April 1938 the authoritarian Speaker Fitzroy also imposed no punitive sanction. However, he insisted that both Members involved in the incident apologize, and on the following day he made a statement deploring what had happened in the strongest possible terms.[5]

When strong emotions are aroused it is usually prudent on the part of the Chair to avoid arousing them further. In the case of the Devlin attack, it is a fair assumption that she was seeking publicity and wanted to be named. When the incident took place there was uproar in the House and the Speaker would not have been heard had he tried to intervene. Miss Devlin was bundled out of the chamber by the Opposition Chief Whip and

[1] David Wood, 'Put this house in Order', *The Times*, 21 Feb. 1972.
[2] *Daily Express*, 2 Feb. 1972.
[3] Interview with Mr. Robin Maxwell-Hyslop, 1 Sept. 1973.
[4] Interview with Lord Tranmire, 10 Sept. 1973.
[5] *Commons Hansard*, 5th series, Vol. 334, cols. 6–7 and cols. 195–6.

it would have seemed ludicrous to have named her when she returned about one hour later. The matter would have been reopened, fresh emphasis would have been given to it, and the situation would probably have been exacerbated rather than regulated. Furthermore, the situation in Northern Ireland was extremely tense and anything which might have been seen as an attempt to martyr Miss Devlin could have touched off further violence. Such considerations must inevitably play a part in influencing the judgement of the Speaker, no matter how much one might argue that he is only concerned with what takes place in the House. Perhaps the best vindication of Speaker Lloyd's handling of the affair lies in the fact that a motion of censure against him attracted only four signatories (one of whom was Enoch Powell) and did not come to a debate.

No matter what precautions he might take to hold himself aloof from controversy, no Speaker can protect himself against every eventuality. The matters on which he is called upon to rule are sometimes highly controversial and before rendering an important decision he customarily takes 24 hours for consultation and reflection. This practice arose during the Speakership of Sir Harry Hylton-Foster and can be traced to a sessional order adopted on 8 February 1960 which related to complaints of privilege.[1] The Speaker interpreted the order as allowing him to postpone for 24 hours his ruling as to whether or not a complaint of privilege should take precedence over other business, and although the order was not subsequently readopted the practice has since been followed and applied to other major rulings.

Even when the Speaker retires he can find himself at the centre of controversy and this has happened five times since 1895. On the first four occasions the representatives of the Labour movement in Parliament moved the reduction of the retiring Speaker's pension from £4,000 to £1,000 on the ground that such a pension was not justified in view of the depressed conditions of the working classes. The Speakers concerned were Peel, Gully, Lowther, and Whitley.[2] In 1951 Speaker Clifton Brown was voted his pension without dissent, the social circumstances

---

[1] Ibid., 5th series, Vol. 617, cols. 35–6.
[2] Ibid., 4th series, Vol. 32, cols. 1504–5, Vol. 147, col. 1226; ibid., 5th series, Vol. 141, cols. 895–904, Vol. 219, cols. 535–54.

of the country having changed markedly since Whitley's retirement in 1928.

Speaker Morrison's pension was opposed for an entirely different reason. Shortly after his retirement as Speaker he was appointed Governor-General of Australia and his acceptance of this office was deplored by certain Members of the Labour Party who held the view that a retiring Speaker should retire completely from public life. Speaker Morrison himself was unmoved by this argument. According to his widow he had no idea when he decided to retire as Speaker that he was going to be offered the governor-generalship of Australia, although some of his critics believed that he had had advance knowledge. The then Australian Prime Minister, Robert Menzies, who was a personal friend of the family, deliberately waited until after the election of Morrison's successor before putting forward the proposition.[1]

The matter was first raised in the House on 12 November 1959 when the financial resolution was introduced, and again on the following 18 November when the second reading of Mr. Speaker Morrison's Retirement Bill was moved. The resolution was adopted without a division but in the second debate the dissenting Members pressed their objections to the point of voting against the bill. A large minority opposed second reading which was carried by 300 to 155. There was a further short debate at the committee stage of the bill although no further divisions took place.[2]

The interest of these debates centres on the issue of whether or not it is proper for an ex-Speaker to pursue another career. Some Members felt very strongly that he should not; that his pension was awarded to him on the understanding that he would be living in retirement; that it was not consistent with the dignity of the Speakership to accept a subsequent appointment; and that the guarantee of his impartiality was the fact that he looks to no government for future preferment. Objection was also taken to the principle of paying any pension at all to the former Speaker while he was enjoying the emoluments and perquisites of the Governor-General of Australia. The bill provided for the

[1] Interview with Lady Dunrossil, 22 Oct. 1973.

[2] *Commons Hansard*, 5th series, Vol. 613, cols. 610–20 and cols. 1170–214, and Vol. 614, cols. 219–45.

abatement of one half of the pension in such circumstances, but this was not sufficient to satisfy its critics.

The then Leader of the Opposition, Hugh Gaitskell, while stating that he would not himself oppose the bill, said that he thought it 'more desirable for a retiring Speaker not to accept an appointment of this or any other kind, but to be given a pension fully adequate on which to retire'. He added that if ex-Speakers were not to be debarred from further office it would be desirable to lay down 'what kind of appointments are to be accepted, what kind of appointments we regard as desirable and what kind we do not'.[1] The only other Speaker of the century to accept an appointment following his retirement was Whitley who was appointed Chairman of the Governors of the B.B.C. in 1930.

Among the Speaker's responsibilities are a number imposed on him by statute.

Under the Parliament Acts, 1911 and 1949, which curtailed the powers of the House of Lords, the Speaker has certain duties relating to the certification of bills. The 1911 Act defines a money bill[2] and provides that such a bill when passed by the House of Commons may be presented for the Royal Assent after one month even though the House of Lords has declined to agree to it. The Speaker is required to certify such a bill as being a money bill within the definition of the Act and before doing so 'to consult, if practicable, two members to be appointed from the Chairmen's Panel at the beginning of each session by the Committee of Selection'. The Act provides that the Speaker's certificate is conclusive for all purposes and may not be questioned in a court of law. The delaying power of the House of Lords in respect of almost all other public bills is restricted by the Acts to two sessions or one year, after which they may receive the Royal Assent without the consent of the upper House. In this event the Speaker is required to certify that the provisions of the Acts have been complied with. It is evident that the Speaker's responsibilities under the Acts could be of crucial importance in certain circumstances, although conflict between the two Houses is in practice very rare these days.

[1] Ibid., Vol. 613, col. 1179.
[2] A money bill as defined in the Parliament Act, 1911, does not necessarily coincide with the meaning of the term as employed in the general parliamentary sense. See Erskine May, pp. 788–91.

Under section 4 of the Ministerial Salaries Consolidation Act, 1965, it could fall to the Speaker, should any doubt arise, to decide which political party represented in the House of Commons should be recognized as the official opposition or who should be recognized as the leader of the party.[1] The only occasion on which a Speaker has been obliged to exercise this invidious responsibility was in 1940. Following the formation of the coalition government under Winston Churchill in which the three major parties participated, the small Independent Labour Party claimed that its leader, James Maxton, was entitled to the post and salary of Leader of the Opposition. Speaker Fitzroy rejected the claim.

Among other statutes which impose special duties on the Speaker are the Mental Health Act, 1959, which provides in section 137 for a statutory procedure for vacating the seat of a Member of unsound mind; the House of Commons (Redistribution of Seats Act), 1949 (amended 1958) under which the Speaker is chairman of the four Boundary Commissions; and various Acts of Parliament which provide for the filling of seats vacated during a parliamentary recess. The Regency Act, 1937, names the Speaker as one of a number of persons who, in the event of the incapacity of the Sovereign, might be called upon to declare that the Sovereign is incapable of performing the functions of the office. The British Museum Act, 1753, named the Speaker as one of the museum's principal trustees, but under the British Museum Act, 1963, he is no longer a trustee *ex officio*.[2]

Under the House of Commons (Speaker) Act, 1832, and the House of Commons Offices Act, 1846, the Speaker continues in office for the purposes of the Acts following a dissolution of Parliament until the House elects its Speaker when the new Parliament assembles. This provides for administrative continuity during the interval between Parliaments. Under the House of Commons Offices Act, 1812, the Speaker is a member of the

---

[1] Halsbury's *Statutes of England*, 3rd edn., vol. 6, 1969, p. 816. This provision was originally contained in the Ministers of the Crown Act, 1937.

[2] Other statutes which impose duties on the Speaker include the Church of England Assembly Powers Act, 1949 (amended by the Synodical Government Measure, 1969); the Consolidation of Enactments (Procedure) Act, 1949; the Statutory Instruments Act, 1946; the Parliamentary Oaths Act, 1866; and the National Debt (Conversion of Stock) Act, 1884.

commission which regulates the salaries and conditions of service of the officers and staff of the House. The Act authorizes three members of whom one shall be the Speaker to exercise the full powers of the commission.[1] On 12 February 1970 the commissioners delegated their responsibilities subject to certain broad principles to the Accounting Officer for the House of Commons Vote (i.e. the Clerk of the House).[2] The conditions of delegation reserved certain rights to the Chancellor of the Exchequer but his obligation to consult with the Speaker preserves the administrative independence of the House.

The Speaker is thus the ultimate administrative authority in the House. The Staff Board, on which all five departments of the House are represented, is guided by a Speaker's directive of 17 July 1962 and remains finally responsible to him. He is also advised by the House of Commons (Services) Committee which deals with such matters as the Library, catering, accommodation, and Members' facilities in general. It was first appointed on 7 December 1965 on the recommendation of the Select Committee on the Palace of Westminster.[3]

Within the administrative structure of the House the Speaker heads a department of his own, its principal officers being his Secretary and his Counsel. The latter is the *de facto* head and relieves the Speaker of the day-to-day administration. The responsibilities of the department include the Hansard operation and the Vote Office which handles the distribution of parliamentary papers to Members.

At the end of 1973 the Speaker ordered a thorough-going review of the structure, organization, and co-ordination of the services provided by the five departments of the House,[4] and the

[1] Since this and the three following paragraphs were written, important administrative changes have been implemented altering, among other things, the composition of the House of Commons Commission. See the House of Commons (Administration) Act 1978.

[2] See Erskine May, p. 234.

[3] See *Report from the committee*, H.C. 285, 1964–5, pp. vii–x. Direct control over that part of the Palace of Westminster occupied by the House of Commons passed into the hands of the Speaker on 26 April 1965. See Prime Minister's statement of 23 Mar. 1965, *Commons Hansard*, 5th series, Vol. 709, cols. 328–33.

[4] The five departments were those of the Clerk of the House, the Speaker, the Serjeant at Arms, and the Library, and the Administration Department.

recruitment, terms of service, promotion, and appointment of all staff including those in the highest posts.[1]

During the twentieth century the practice has arisen of referring questions of electoral reform to a conference of Members of Parliament under the chairmanship of the Speaker prior to enacting legislation. The first such conference was convened in 1916 under the chairmanship of Speaker Lowther. Its recommendations[2] led to the most sweeping electoral reforms since 1832, and the Representation of the People Act, 1918, was largely based on them. The most controversial recommendation, which was not unanimously agreed to by the conference, was that women should be enfranchised subject to certain conditions.

In 1929 Lowther, by then Viscount Ullswater, was called out of retirement to preside over a second conference on electoral reform which was permitted to decide its own terms of reference. Proportional representation and the preferential vote were the principal matters considered by this conference, but it failed to agree on any recommendations.[3]

The third conference on electoral reform was convened in 1944 under the chairmanship of Speaker Clifton Brown, receiving its impetus, like the first, from the circumstances arising from a world war.[4] Among the recommendations accepted were those relating to the redistribution of seats and the establishment of the four permanent Boundary Commissions under the chairmanship of the Speaker, and these were embodied in the House of Commons (Redistribution of Seats) Act, 1949. A recommendation that the business and university franchises be retained was not accepted, and plural voting was abolished by the Representation of the People Act, 1948.[5]

The next Speaker to preside over an electoral reform conference was Speaker King who announced its terms of reference to the House on 12 May 1965.[6] This conference worked through

---

[1] See Mr. Speaker Lloyd's statement in the House and subsequent exchanges, 22 Oct. 1973, *Commons Hansard*, 5th series, Vol. 861, cols. 706–11. A report was presented by Sir Edmund Compton on 5 July 1974 and was referred to a select committee for study.

[2] See Cd. 8463.   [3] See Cmd. 3636.

[4] See debate of 1 Feb. 1944, *Commons Hansard*, 5th series, Vol. 396, cols. 1154–369.

[5] See report of the conference, Cmd. 6534.

[6] *Commons Hansard*, 5th series, Vol. 712, cols. 520–3.

three sessions, producing its final report on 9 February 1968. Its most significant recommendation was that the minimum voting age be reduced to 20. However, this was one of the recommendations which was not accepted and the voting age was in fact reduced to 18 by section 1 of the Representation of the People Act, 1969.[1]

On 2 August 1972 Speaker Lloyd informed the House that another conference on electoral law was to be appointed[2] and on 16 March 1973 he announced its composition.[3] Between July 1973 and February 1974 the conference issued three brief reports,[4] the most significant recommendation being that the minimum age of candidature for parliamentary elections should be lowered from 21 to 18 years, thus bringing the minimum age for election into conformity with the voting age.[5]

In the course of the interviews conducted by the author certain reservations were expressed at the tendency of governments to accept some recommendations of electoral reform conferences but to reject others. The purpose of these conferences was to seek agreed reforms through compromise, and the view was expressed that the Speaker's time and that of the other experienced parliamentarians involved was wasted if their recommendations were not accepted. Speaker Lloyd confirmed that his conference, since it held weekly meetings, made considerable demands upon his time.[6] Speaker King also found the work time-consuming, but said that he enjoyed the experience and made no complaint about the fact that the recommendations of his conference were not accepted *in toto*.[7]

In 1919, pursuant to a resolution of the House of Commons on 4 June of that year,[8] a conference was appointed under the chairmanship of the Speaker on a matter other than electoral reform, namely the devolution of powers to subordinate legis-

---

[1] See Home Secretary's statement of 24 July 1968, ibid., Vol. 769, cols. 576–82.

[2] Ibid., Vol. 842, cols. 560–1.

[3] Ibid., Vol. 852, cols. 1625–7.

[4] Cmnd. 5363, 5469, and 5547.

[5] See Cmnd. 5363.

[6] Interview with Mr. Speaker Lloyd, 13 Sept. 1973.

[7] Interview with Lord Maybray-King, 13 Sept. 1973.

[8] See debate on federal devolution, *Commons Hansard*, 5th series, Vol. 116, cols. 1873–974 and 2063–129.

latures within Great Britain. However, the problems encountered proved to be of great complexity, particularly in relation
to the character and composition of local legislatures, and the
conference failed to agree on satisfactory solutions. Its report[1]
was never debated in Parliament.

Another kind of Speakers' conference, which has recently
become a regular institution, is the Conference of Speakers and
Presiding Officers of Commonwealth Parliaments. Possibly the
first occasion on which Speakers and Presiding Officers came
together on a Commonwealth-wide basis was in October 1950
on the occasion of the opening of the new House of Commons'
chamber. The guests included the Speakers and Presiding
Officers of Commonwealth Parliaments and Legislatures and it
appears that Speaker Clifton Brown took advantage of their
presence to convene an informal conference of senior Speakers.
In June 1965 another ceremonial event brought the Speakers
and Presiding Officers of the Commonwealth together again,
the occasion being the 700th anniversary of the Parliament of
Simon de Montfort. A conference presided over by Speaker
Hylton-Foster recorded 'that Speakers should have the opportunity of meeting periodically in conference to discuss their
common problems'.[2]

The establishment of the Conference of Speakers and Presiding
Officers of Commonwealth Parliaments as a regular institution
was initiated by the Speaker of the Canadian House of Commons, Mr. Lucien Lamoureux, with the active support of
Speaker King and others. The first such conference, not being
incidental to any other event, took place in Ottawa in September
1969 at the invitation of the Canadian Speaker. The second
took place in New Delhi just after Christmas 1970 and the third
in Lusaka, Zambia, in September 1973.[3] The pattern of holding
these conferences approximately every two years seems to have
been established, but Speaker Lloyd expressed the view that
once every five years would be more appropriate. He felt, in
view of the Speaker's many other commitments, that no Speaker

[1] Cmd. 692.

[2] *Report of a Conference of Commonwealth Speakers held at Westminster on 16th
and 17th June*, 1965, pp. 4–5.

[3] See Philip Laundy, 'Conferences of Speakers and Presiding Officers',
in *The Parliamentarian*, Oct. 1971, pp. 264–70.

should be obliged to attend more than one such conference during his tenure of office.[1]

On 15 January 1973 Speaker Lloyd attended a conference in Strasbourg of Presidents and Speakers of the European Parliament and the Parliaments of the member states of the European communities. The discussions centred on matters of common interest in connection with the enlargement of the communities. Each participated within the limits of his own authority, and it was noted in the communiqué and the minutes that the Speaker of the House of Commons explained his own special position.[2] Unlike some of his European counterparts he exercises none of the functions which under the British parliamentary system fall to the Leader of the House. It would appear that the role of the Speaker is unlikely to be changed in any way as a result of Britain's entry into the European Common Market, except that his responsibilities for the provision of information to Members might increase. Should the need for a ruling arise as the result of Britain's position in the community, it would probably be referred to the Procedure Committee, as the Speaker might be unwilling to give a firm decision without consulting the wishes of the House.[3]

Sir Ivor Jennings once wrote: 'The qualities required of a Speaker are not really very high, and so great is the prestige of the office, and so careful are all parties to maintain his independence and authority, that any reasonable man can make a success of the office.'[4] He went on to quote Lord Rosebery who wrote to Queen Victoria, in reference to the election of Speaker Gully, that a Speaker is found 'almost invariably, among the mediocrities of the House'.[5]

---

[1] Interview with Mr. Speaker Lloyd, 13 Sept. 1973.

[2] See *European Parliament Bulletin*, 1972–3, special edition 16 January 1973, and Summary Record of the conference.

[3] Interview with Mr. Speaker Lloyd, 13 Sept. 1973. See also *Third Special Report from the Select Committee on Procedure*, H.C. 448, 1971–2. The Committee concluded that 'the entry of Britain into the Communities presents a profound challenge to many of the established procedures of Parliament which, if not adequately dealt with, could leave Parliament substantially weaker vis-à-vis the executive' (para. 9, p. 5).

[4] Sir Ivor Jennings, *Parliament*, 2nd edn. (Cambridge University Press, 1957), p. 65.

[5] *Letters of Queen Victoria*, 3rd series (John Murray, 1930–2), Vol. 2, p. 495.

It is our hope that this essay will have succeeded in demolishing this fallacy. The Speakership is not a job for light-weights. Its duties are onerous and of fundamental importance to the parliamentary system, as we have seen. It calls for qualities of character which will sustain the authority of the Chair and the prestige of Parliament in any situation which might arise. The task is in many respects a thankless one. Impartiality, that quality so essential in a Speaker, while universally applauded does not necessarily give universal satisfaction when it is exercised. A disgruntled Member can all too easily regard an impartial decision as being unjust to himself. The Speaker must accept this with forbearance. He must know when to be indulgent and when to be severe, when to give a flexible interpretation to the rules and when to impose the letter of the law. He must judge the varying moods of the House and take whatever action seems prudent in the circumstances. He should be at all times patient, fearless, compassionate, and judicious, and these are virtues which can be severely tested by the very human institution over which he presides. The qualities which an ideal Speaker should possess are numerous, and can perhaps best be summed up in an observation quoted by Speaker Lowther: 'The office of Speaker does not demand rare qualities. It demands common qualities in a rare degree.'[1]

The Speakership calls for personal sacrifice and a deep sense of dedication. The Speakers of this century have sacrificed their leisure, social freedom, and family life to a very great extent. Some may have renounced alternative ambitions. Several have sacrificed their health, and one or two perhaps even life itself. In their own way they have been men of stature, certainly not mediocrities. Each has made his contribution to the evolution of the office, and its evolution during the twentieth century has further strengthened the foundation on which the British parliamentary system rests.

[1] Viscount Ullswater, op. cit., Vol. 2, p. 298.

IV

THE HOUSE OF COMMONS
AND ITS PRIVILEGES

Geoffrey Marshall

Parliamentary privilege is something more than a topic for the constitutional historian. The exercise by the House of Commons of its traditional privileges in the twentieth century raises important questions about the role of a legislature in relation to the other organs of government. It also impinges upon the rule of law and the liberties of the subject. Clearly many of the crises and conflicts from which the privileges of Parliament took their present shape are of no present concern. The Crown no longer threatens the independence of the Commons. Nor is the dignity of the House menaced by recalcitrant City Aldermen, Sheriffs, or printers. Are, then, all the punitive powers of the High Court of Parliament still essential to the working of a modern legislature? The query might well occur to any foreign observer or native sceptic, noting, as he must, that British parliamentarians, whilst lacking many of the powers and facilities enjoyed elsewhere, yet claim for themselves privileges not conceded to legislative bodies in other democratic political systems. That may not, in the end, be so strange a paradox.

The General Nature of Privilege

Historically, a part of the justification for the privileges of both Houses of the United Kingdom Parliament has rested upon the analogy with judicial practice. A court of judicature has privileges auxiliary to the due execution of its powers. Just as witnesses and judges must speak freely, be protected from molestation, and be released from other conflicting tasks and obligations, so it might be thought necessary to make similar provision for 'the Court of Parliament, the first and the highest court in this kingdom'.[1] The extensive power to punish contempts has a judicial flavour and origin. Yet in reality Parliament in the twentieth century is not a court and a distinction might be made between the powers inherently necessary in a legislative assembly for the direct protection of its legislative function[2] and the wider power to punish an undefined range of contempts that the *lex et consuetudo parliamenti* confers upon the British legislature in its character as the High Court of Parliament. Such a power is not a necessary incident of a legislative body as such and common law did not recognize it as inhering in colonial legislatures.[3] What might have been a distinction of some interest has, however, been obscured by the statutory conferring on Colonial and Commonwealth Parliaments of the powers exercised by the Westminster Parliament. In Australia, for example, s. 49 of the Constitution gives power to the Commonwealth Parliament to define the privileges of the two Houses and provides that until so defined the privileges shall be those of the British House of Commons at the time of the enactment of the Constitution.

The judicial ancestry of the British Parliament's powers has perhaps done something to confuse the concepts of breach of privilege and punishable contempt. The device of conferring Westminster privilege powers on overseas legislatures assumes that the power to punish contempts is itself one of the privileges of Parliament. Yet the terminology is curiously muddled and neither the Committee of Privileges nor individual members have always retained a clear hold upon the distinction made by experts on the Law and Custom of Parliament. Indeed Sir Kenneth Pickthorn, a member not unskilled in constitutional matters, confessed to the Clerk of the House some years ago that the difference eluded him. 'I have been taught often the difference between contempt and breach', he said, 'but I always forget it as soon as I am taught it.'[4] The inability, it should be

---

[1] Hatsell, *Precedents of Proceedings in the House of Commons* (1796), Vol. 1, p. 1.

[2] For example, the power to prevent direct interference or disruption of proceedings by removing non-members or expelling members. See *Doyle* v. *Falconer* (1866) L.R. P.C. 328 and *Barton* v. *Taylor* (1886) 11 App. Cas. 197.

[3] *Kielley* v. *Carson* 4 Moo.P.C. 63. Cf. *R.* v. *Richards, ex p. Fitzpatrick and Browne* (1599) 92 C.L.R. 157.

[4] *Committee of Privileges*, H.C. 247 (1963–4), p. 18.

added, is widely shared and one that afflicts the majority of members, journalists, and academics.

In principle privilege is the sum total of the rights enjoyed by each House collectively and by members of each House individually, designed to secure the proper discharge of their functions and peculiar to them. Some of these rights are mentioned under specific heads by the Speaker at the commencement of every Parliament. These 'ancient and undoubted' rights and privileges are freedom from arrest (and it used to be said, molestation); freedom of speech and debate; access to Her Majesty's person ('whenever occasion shall require');[1] and favourable construction of their proceedings by Her Majesty. Other powers and functions that might also be called privileges could be added to this list. There is for example the right or claim to control their own proceedings. These merge into other entitlements such as the Commons financial and legislative pre-eminence as against the House of Lords, the power of impeachment, and even the right of the Commons to require information from and in the last resort to dismiss the executive. The power to punish for contempt might itself be listed as a specific right or privilege. It is said, however, that the contempt power is not limited to punishments for breach of the specific heads of privilege, at least as these are listed in the Speaker's Petition. Nevertheless, since a contempt is an act or omission that obstructs or impedes either House, or its members or officers in the discharge of their duty (or has a tendency to do so),[2] and since the legislative function is one of free debate and enactment, almost any action that is properly contemptuous will almost certainly be one that directly or indirectly infringes either the privilege of free speech or the privilege of freedom from molestation.[3] The various forms of disobedience to the House's orders such as refusals to attend as witnesses, non-compliance with rules about petitioning, and unlicensed publication of debates, that the Commons has from time to time stigmatized as contempts in its journals[4] have been clearly connected with the proceedings of

---

[1] A collective rather than an individual privilege.

[2] Erskine May, *Parliamentary Practice* (19th edn., 1976), p. 136.

[3] If such a privilege exists (see below, p. 15).

[4] See the points made in the 1967 *Report of the Select Committee on Parliamentary Privilege*, H.C. 34 (1967–8), p. 189.

the House and could have been said to have been interferences with freedom of debate and proceedings. So could the various forms of adverse reflection on the House and its members that have sometimes been denominated constructive contempts. In practice the significance of the insistence on the distinction between contempt and breach of privilege is that it is held that actions may be treated as contemptuous though there is no precedent for the offence and also claimed that the causes of committal for contempt lie outside the jurisdiction of the ordinary courts. This assertion is related to and indeed may be a part of the claim historically made by the Commons that the House is the sole judge of the existence and extent of its privileges. It is the making of this far reaching claim that has led commentators to speak of the unresolved incompatibility, or dualism, between the powers of the Commons and those of the courts.[1] It is difficult, however, to take this dualism seriously. Paradoxically the Parliamentary claim is often buttressed by the citing of judicial decisions or dicta. But respect by the courts for the Houses' jurisdiction in certain areas no more constitutes the existence of an independent power to determine the existence and extent of privilege and contempt powers than does the respect that may equally be accorded to certain discretions of executive officers or bodies. Where the House commits for contempt without stating the ground of commitment or commits for a contempt of the House of Commons generally, it appears that the courts will not inquire into the true ground or as to its sufficiency, but where facts are stated in the warrant the general upshot of the decisions in cases such as *Burdett* v. *Abbott*[2] and *Stockdale* v. *Hansard*[3] is that the courts would in suitable cases declare the committals to be defective as arbitrary or unrelated to any known privilege of the House. The same conclusion is inherent in the admission that the House cannot extend its privileges or create new ones. The determination of whether any particular claim constitutes an application of an existing privilege or an extension and creation of privilege must be assumed by the courts. This is a matter of immediate practical significance under some Commonwealth

---

[1] See, for example, D. L. Keir and F. H. Lawson, *Cases in Constitutional Law* (4th edn.), p. 125.

[2] 14 East 1.

[3] (1838) 9 Ad. & E. 1.

constitutions. Commonwealth courts, even when faced by legislatures that have been given the privilege powers of the British Parliament, have not hesitated to measure them against constitutional requirements. In India, for example, the fundamental rights laid down in the Constitution have been held to protect citizens against arbitrary contempt committals[1] and under constitutional arrangements where special procedures are to be followed for specific legislative purposes the traditional privilege of unfettered control over internal legislative proceedings[2] may have to yield to judicial enforcement of constitutional requirements.[3] Similar considerations might arise in the United Kingdom if there were at any point to be enactment of a Bill of Rights protected by special majority provisions. Meanwhile, it is clear that in recent years courts in the United Kingdom have been increasingly resistant to the notion of an unconfined power in any body to determine the limits of its own jurisdiction. Neither House of Parliament can lay claim to any assistance from the principle of Parliamentary Sovereignty, since neither the Commons nor the Lords alone is the sovereign legislative body. So although the Commons have by resolution attempted to insist upon their sole jurisdiction in matters of privilege the claim is not one that in the last resort can be defended. It has been said that 'the decisions of the courts are not accepted as binding by the House in matters of privilege'.[4] But the answer to that is that the House is not a body entitled to decide what is or is not legally binding and its resolutions on that issue do not affect the matter. Sir William Anson drew a proper conclusion in writing that 'the Courts will not be deterred from upholding private rights by the fact that questions of parliamentary privilege are involved in their maintenance and—except as regards the internal regulation of its proceedings by the House, Courts of Law will not hesitate to inquire into alleged privilege, as they would into local custom, and determine its extent and application'.[5]

[1] An interesting example is described in Duncan B. Forrester, 'Parliamentary Privilege—an Indian Crisis', *Parliamentary Affairs* (1965), p. 196.

[2] See Enid Campbell, *Parliamentary Privilege in Australia* (1966), Chapter 5 (Control of the Internal Proceedings of Parliament.)

[3] This is an inference that can be drawn from *Bribery Commissioner* v. *Ranasinghe* [1965] A.C. 172; cf. *Clayton* v. *Heffron* (1960) 105 C.L.R. 214.

[4] Erskine May, op. cit., p. 201 and Chap. XI generally.

[5] *Law and Custom of the Constitution* (5th edn.), i. 196.

For the purpose of surveying applications of privilege in the twentieth century it may be convenient (though the categories overlap) to examine the rights of the Commons under four heads: first, the freedom from arrest and legal process; secondly, the freedom of speech, debate, and proceedings in the House; thirdly, the freedom from intimidation or molestation; and, fourthly, the freedom to punish as contempts breaches of privilege under any of the stated heads, plus an indeterminate class of obstructions and indirect interference whether by speech, action, or writing.[1]

Freedom from Arrest and Legal Process

The immunities of members from arrest and from other legal processes have as their fundamental purpose the securing of members' attendance in the House and the assertion of the House's prior claim to their services. Exemption from attendance as a witness and from jury service clearly stand upon this basis. Freedom from arrest now exists only in civil matters, though it is not always easy to know what is a criminal cause and what is civil. Detention by the Executive, as when Captain Ramsay, M.P., was interned under the 1939 Defence Regulations, was held by the Committee of Privileges not to involve any breach of the member's immunity. As to arrests for contempt of court it may be necessary to determine whether the contempt is primarily of a civil character or primarily related to a criminal charge. The difficulty has not presented the House of Commons with any insuperable problem but the potential difficulty is illustrated by a case arising in the Australian Federal Parliament in 1971. A member, having laid an information alleging assault against a police constable, was ordered to pay costs after the information was dismissed and was imprisoned for forty days in default of payment. The House of Representatives Committee of Privileges, sought in vain for British precedents and, having received conflicting legal advice, held that the imprisonment was imposed to enforce performance of the duty of payment and was primarily

---

[1] These 'freedoms' comprise a mixed collection of what jurisprudentially ought to be classified as privileges, powers, and immunities. The freedom of speech is a legal immunity. The freedom to punish contempts is a legally protected power.

civil in nature although imposed by a court that in general had been exercising a criminal jurisdiction. Hence the imprisonment was a breach of the House's privileges.[1]

In 1957 the Judicial Committee of the Privy Council was called upon to resolve an important uncertainty about the limits of another form of immunity, namely, freedom from being impleaded in a civil suit. In general a series of statutes has long since abolished the general privilege. In 1770 the Parliamentary Privilege Act declared that actions could be commenced against members of Parliament and their servants and that these should not be interfered with on grounds of privilege. The question at issue in 1957 was whether an application for a writ alleging libel by a member in the course of a proceeding in Parliament could be treated as a breach of privilege. The Judicial Committee held that the Act of 1770 had not intended to include actions for words spoken in the course of Parliamentary proceedings amongst those actions that should not be stayed by privilege, since this would implicitly have been to abrogate the freedom of speech of members confirmed in the Bill of Rights. The Judicial Committee held that in the light of this the Commons would not be precluded by the 1770 Act from treating the issue of such a writ as a breach of privilege. They left open the possibility, however, that any such action by the House might infringe the common law right of the subject to have recourse to the courts for legal remedies.[2]

About the residual but significant legal immunities of members in civil matters it would be possible to feel a measure of doubt. Arrest in civil causes is an infrequent occurrence but if it is merited why should it not be undergone? Extension of the immunity to forty days before and after the session[3] seems to have been originally intended to cover the period required for the farthest-flung members to reach Parliament and return home.[4] Despite the uncertainties of modern road, rail, and air

[1] *Report relating to the commitment to prison of Mr. T. Uren, M.P.* (Parliamentary Paper No. 40, 1971) (Australia).

[2] In *Re Parliamentary Privilege Act, 1770* [1958], A.C. 331; cf. S. A. de Smith, Parliamentary Privilege and the Bill of Rights', (1958) 21 *Modern Law Rev.* 477.

[3] *Goudy* v. *Duncombe*, 1 Exch. 430.

[4] The notice of summons required in Magna Carta was forty days and the custom of extending immunity to a similar period was intended, it

facilities, this now seems an unduly cautious extension of the immunity.

Freedom of Debate and Proceedings

Freedom from external control or interference with what is said and done within the walls of Parliament is perhaps an important special case of the wider privilege of exercising exclusive control over internal proceedings. The notion that 'Whatever is done within the walls of either assembly must pass without question in any other place'[1] is, to the extent that it is true, a breach in the general rule of law. How far it is true is unclear. Ordinary criminal acts unconnected with the legislative function would not enjoy immunity. Possibly Sir Alan Herbert went too far in supposing, on the analogy of the House's ability to circumvent the licensing laws,[2] that members could indulge without penalty in a wide variety of immoral and illegal activities,[3] but possibly there are other regulatory statutes that might be difficult of application in the Commons and there may be minor criminal violations such as physical assaults during the course of debate that are arguably connected with the proceedings of the House. For words spoken in debate or in committee, however, there is no doubt that members (and in addition officers and witnesses giving evidence before committees) are immune from all civil and criminal penalties. The privilege is confirmed in Article 9 of the Bill of Rights in the declaration that 'the freedom of speech and debates or proceedings ought not to be impeached or questioned in any court or place out of Parliament'. In consequence members are protected from the normal consequences of the law relating to libel,[4] sedition,[5] official secrecy, and

seems, to secure the protection of a member 'eundo, morando, et exinde redeundo' (Anson, *The Law and Custom of the Constitution* (5th edn., 1922), i. 165).

[1] *Per* Lord Denman in *Stockdale* v. *Hansard* (1839) 9Ad. & E. 1 at p. 114.

[2] *R.* v. *Graham-Campbell ex p. Herbert* [1935] 1 K.B. 594.

[3] See 'Crime in the Commons' (*Uncommon Law*, 6th ed. 1948), pp. 420–1.

[4] *Dillon* v. *Balfour* (1887) 20 Ir. L.R. 600. Nor can evidence be given of words spoken in the House in actions alleging libel by members committed outside the House. See *Dingle* v. *Associated Newspapers Ltd.* [1960] 2 Q.B. 405, and *Church of Scientology of California* v. *Johnson-Smith* [1971] 3. W.L.R. 434.

[5] *R.* v. *Eliot, Hollis, and Valentine*, 3 State Trials 294 (1629).

obscenity. Control of possible abuses of the wide facility for un-inhibited speech will, it is hoped, be exercised by the House itself.

In the case of Mr. Duncan Sandys in 1938 the House asserted its privileges to avert the threat of a prosecution for a refusal to reveal the member's sources of information on a national security matter which he had made the subject of a Parliamentary question.[1] Mr. Sandys's case also raised obliquely an issue of some difficulty and importance, namely what transactions besides the delivery of speeches in the House or in committee are to be included in the ambit of 'proceedings in Parliament'. The Select Committee on the Official Secrets Acts in 1939 said (in the light of the Sandys decision) that the term might cover the asking of a question and the giving of written notice of a question or the discussion of the terms of a question with another member. If a minister who has been questioned asks for further information any letter written to him will, so the Speaker ruled in 1958, be privileged. Thus some activities of members that do not take place literally in Parliament may be so related to the procedure of Parliament as to be Parliamentary proceedings for this purpose. Neither the courts nor the House have ever determined where the limits of this principle lie. An extreme interpretation would imply that the protection is enjoyed by anything a member does, in or out of the House, that is related to his Parliamentary function. But this would be arguably overbroad and it would be difficult, particularly at election times, to distinguish between the member in his capacity as member and his capacity as party representative. In 1958 the House determined that an allegedly defamatory letter written to a minister about the operations of a nationalized industry board and passed by the minister to the Board was not a proceeding in Parliament (though the Committee of Privileges had taken the opposite view[2]). The decision caused for a while some perturbation amongst members about the peril in which they might stand by passing on defamatory letters from constituents both to ministers and to non-Parliamentary agencies—such possibly as the police or public corporations.[3] However the fears raised in the London Electricity

---

[1] H.C. 146 (1937–8); H.C. 173 (1937–8).

[2] *Complaint of Certain Actions of the London Electricity Board*, H.C. 305 (1957).

[3] See Donald Thompson, 'Letters to Ministers and Parliamentary Privilege', 1959 *Public Law* 10.

Board case seem to have abated. In passing on constituents' letters, members are protected by qualified privilege,[1] and the belief that they might lose such privilege if their correspondents were motivated by malice (a view expressed in 1958) now appears to be unfounded.[2]

A constitutional iconoclast (if there be any) might even raise the question whether the absolute privilege that is conceded in judicial and quasi-judicial bodies[3] and in some few confidential relationships (such as those between litigants and legal advisors) is really justified in a deliberative assembly. Any such heretical view would no doubt be assailed by each and every member of both Houses on a number of grounds. It would be argued that the Grand Inquisitors of the Nation would be disabled from carrying out their essential functions if it were not possible for them to speak freely and frankly and without fear of legal consequences about matters of public concern. One answer might be that a society that took free speech seriously would concede that right to all citizens (as the United States does). If, on the other hand, our own concept of free discussion is one in which we think the rights of private and public persons to vindicate their reputations have been rightly balanced against the benefits of unhindered licence in speech and communication, is it clear beyond all question that elected persons should have a permit for potentially malicious and damaging utterance that ordinary citizens are denied? Qualified privilege will, after all, protect words not spoken with malice. Undoubtedly there have been scandals and misdemeanours exposed that might not have been exposed had members not believed themselves to be protected by an absolute immunity. The episodes involving Mr. John Profumo that led to the Denning inquiry of 1963 are sometimes offered as an example. But it might be wondered how many such examples there are that a member speaking without malice

---

[1] See *R. v. Rule* [1937] 2 K.B. 375; *Beach v. Freeson* [1972] 1 Q.B. 14.

[2] *Meekins v. Henson* [1964] 1 Q.B. 472. A member's correspondent may not himself be protected if his letter is not on any Parliamentary matter, even if he communicated it within the precincts of the House. *Rivlin v. Bilainkin* [1953] 1 Q.B. 485.

[3] As also to investigatory bodies such as the Parliamentary Commissioner and tribunals of inquiry (Parliamentary Commissioner Act 1967 s. 10(5); Tribunals of Inquiry (Evidence) Act 1921 s. 1).

under the protection of qualified privilege would find it impossible to reveal by speech or question. And in any genuine calculation of public policy ought not such examples to be weighed against the damage done by the possibility of unrestrained accusation presently enjoyed? Neither members nor ministers, particularly when moved by fervour or partisan feeling, invariably choose their words with sober deliberation. Many instances come to mind. When Mr. Michael Foot, Secretary of State for Employment, referred to one of Her Majesty's judges as a 'trigger-happy judicial fool'[1] many outside and some inside the House felt such words to be a misuse of absolute privilege. But there is no guarantee that the House will restrain its members, particularly where condemnation of persons outside the House cuts along party lines. Members would probably suggest that even with qualified privilege there would be a spate of time-consuming (although hopeless) attempts to involve them in litigation. There is no reliable evidence on which such a fear could be grounded. It is often forgotten that other deliberative assemblies such as local councils, in which equally free and often fierce debate about the affairs of public and private bodies is carried on, have never enjoyed absolute privilege for their proceedings and there is no spate of defamation actions. Nor are local representatives noticeably inhibited from speaking freely in council.

Some obvious problems have arisen and may in future arise from the broadcasting and televising of Parliamentary proceedings. The Committee on Defamation in 1975 thought that in the case of live television or sound broadcasts absolute privilege should apply for the words of the broadcast but that qualified privilege would be appropriate for television pictures transmitted, since these might be the subject of editorial selection and that the same consideration should apply to any edited sound broadcast.[2] On the other hand, the Joint Select Committee on

---

[1] *The Times*, 20 May 1975.

[2] Cmnd. 5909 (1975). The Parliamentary Papers Act, 1840 gives absolute protection to reports of Parliamentary proceedings published by or under the authority of Parliament. At common law qualified privilege is enjoyed by any unauthorized report if fair and accurate. The same is true of a summary or a Parliamentary sketch if made without malice. *Wason* v. *Walter* (1868) L.R. 4 Q.B. 73; *Cook* v. *Alexander* [1973] 3 W.L.R. 617; cf.

the Publication of Proceedings in Parliament recommended in 1969 that only qualified privilege should apply to all forms of television or radio broadcasts. The authors of the recommendation obviously thought that neither the BBC nor the IBA had any ground for apprehension in relaying the honest and forthright sentiments promulgated at Westminster.

The House's privilege to treat any publication of its proceedings whatsoever as a breach of privilege or contempt has been long abandoned in practice and in 1971 the House formally resolved that it would entertain no complaint in respect of the mere publication of its debates or proceedings except where they or any committee proceedings are expressly prohibited from publication by the House. The publication of the proceedings of a select committee before it has reported to the House remains however, a matter about which members continue to feel excitement. In 1975 *The Economist* obtained and printed a draft report of the Select Committee on the Wealth Tax, and the Select Committee determined this to be a breach of privilege damaging to the work of Parliament.[1] Arguments for such a conclusion are not easy to supply. When examined they tend to rest upon the analogizing of premature disclosure of committee conclusions to the bringing to bear of improper pressure on the committee's members. Indeed, both privilege in general and the punishment of contempts turn essentially upon the need to keep members free from improper pressures of a kind that obstruct them in the

the Memoranda by the Clerk of the House and the Attorney-General, submitted to the Select Committee on the Broadcasting of Proceedings in the House of Commons, H.C. 146 (1966), (Appendices 37 and 38, and paras. 41-7 of the Report).

[1] In *The Times* (9 Dec. 1975) Mr. Bernard Levin suggested that this was 'self-important nonsense of exactly the kind that M.P.s in general are dangerously given to'. The Committee in this case recommended the banning of the Editor of *The Economist* and another journalist from the House of Commons for six months and suggested that the Committee should be empowered to impose fines in such cases. For further recent instances in which publication of unreported proceedings or draft reports have been held to be a contempt see H.C. 357 (1967–8) and H.C. 180 (1971–2). The first involved an article in the *Observer* about biological warfare, giving an account of proceedings in the Select Committee on Science and Technology and the second disclosure in the *Daily Mail* (in an article entitled 'The Million Pound Queen') of increases in the Civil List proposed in a draft report laid before the Civil List Committee.

execution of their representative function. The retention of privilege and contempt powers can plausibly be defended only in so far as it is possible to define and identify such pressures.

Freedom from and Right to Punish Intimidation and Molestation

The Speaker's Petition traditionally made reference to freedom from 'arrests and molestations' and it seems probable that the principle reference of 'molestation' was originally to interferences with attendance at the House by legal processes rather than by other forms of intervention. Analytically, however, it seems more convenient in dealing with twentieth-century aspects of privilege to group freedom from arrest with other forms of immunity from legal process and to characterize freedom from molestation as the subject matter of a separate head of privilege. In his evidence to the 1967 Select Committee Mr. L. A. Abraham cast doubt on the existence of such a privilege, suggesting that most forms of molestation of members were in any case unlawful and that to speak of a privilege (or immunity) from such acts was 'an absurdity in terms'.[1] It is not the case, though, that all or even most attempts to influence or bring pressure to bear on members by improper means are illegal, and there does seem some utility in grouping together such lawful but threatening or intimidating forms of intervention especially to contrast them with more indirect forms of alleged interference or obstruction by means of words or writings that merely scandalize or are held to bring the House and its members into disrepute. It is true, of course, that both types of action may be treated by the House as contempts, so it makes little difference whether all such interferences are treated as different varieties of contempt or whether they are thought of as breaches of the

---

[1] *Report from the Select Committee on Parliamentary Privilege*, H.C. 34 (1967–8), p. 93. Mr. Abraham pointed out that reference to molestation had been omitted from the Speaker's Petition since 1866 and the Select Committee agreed with him that the expression 'freedom from molestation' ought to be discontinued (para. 112). Sir Gilbert Campion treated the privilege as an existent one, however (see his memoranda in H.C. 181 (1945–6), p. 33, and H.C. 36 (1946–7) p. 62). Perhaps the expression 'freedom to punish molestation' would meet the criticism that it is merely an aspect of the contempt power. Cf. Jordan's case (below pp. 16–18).

privilege of freedom from molestation or direct or indirect intimidation and obstruction.

Such molestation might be very roughly broken down, on a descending scale of seriousness, into seven categories. We might distinguish the following:

(1) Actual physical assaults or violent intimidation
(2) Threats of assault or violence
(3) Physical, though non-violent, obstruction
(4) Threats of future penalties or legal action
(5) Intimidatory denunciations or threats of exposure or adverse publicity
(6) Bribes or financial inducements
(7) Political pressures or threats of electoral or constituency action

Examples can be found in all these categories in privilege issues raised by members during the present century.[1] As to assaults, there seem to have been few reported instances except by members on each other. In 1946 Mr. Piratin and Mr. Lucy exchanged blows within the precincts of the House and were held to be guilty of contempt and censured by the House.[2] In 1972, however, Miss Bernadette Devlin assaulted the Home Secretary in the Chamber without incurring any form of penalty. (In the interval between the two episodes there has perhaps been a perceptible increase in the degree of public tolerance extended to ideological militants whose feelings get the better of them.) Threats of violence by outsiders have been equally rare. In 1960 it was reported in the House that threats had been made against the life of Sir Leslie Plummer; and in 1967 the Committee of Privileges decided to take no action against a body described as the 'Free Wales Army' who were alleged to have threatened the lives of two Welsh members and 'all the traitors who have sold Wales out to England'. The words used were thought by the Committee to constitute a contempt.[3] What constitutes a 'threat' to a member (or for that matter to anybody) is a matter of some

---

[1] It is noticeable that these cases are heavily concentrated in the more recent period, perhaps as a result of the increase since 1945 in the activity of pressure groups and public participation in policy making. Other explanations are conceivable, such as the possibilities that members have become more sensitive or that their activities in recent times are inherently more likely to provoke molestation.

[2] H.C. 36 (1946–7).

[3] H.C. 100 (1967–8).

philosophical difficulty. The difficulty is illustrated by the case of Mr. Charles Pannell in 1960.[1]

In July 1960 Mr. Pannell put down a question in the House in which he condemned the distribution of fascist pamphlets in Leeds. Several days later he received a letter from a Mr. Colin Jordan, organizer in chief of the British National Party, which concluded with the words 'No doubt when you clamour for our prosecution . . . you would do well at the same time to take into account the possibility that in the resurgent Britain of tomorrow, it may well be you and your racial renegades who face trial for your complicity in the coloured invasion and Jewish control of our land.'

When summoned before the Committee of Privileges Mr. Jordan agreed that he intended to influence Mr. Pannell's opinion and conduct, but argued that his letter did not contain any threat against the member. He had, he thought, commented in a legitimate way on a historical possibility, as he might have done had he suggested that the Government might do well to take note that certain courses of action might lead to the possibility of violence. No conduct on the part of himself or his party was concerned, he said, but merely the future contingency of a new constitutional regime with new laws. The Committee concluded that Jordan's conduct did constitute a breach of privilege in that it was intended to influence the member's conduct in Parliament by improper means and to deter him from pursuing his Parliamentary activities;[2] but they did not elaborate on what it was that made Jordan's letter improper or threatening. In other cases the Committee has used such phrases as 'conduct having a tendency to impair an M.P.'s independence in the future performance of his duty'.[3] All persuasion and warning is of course an attempt to influence, but is what makes it an improper incursion on the member's independence of action a matter of its verbal form, or its effect on the recipient's mind, or the intention of the communicant, irrespec-

[1] H.C. 284 (1959–60).

[2] H.C. 284 (1960). It is to be observed that the Committee referred to the conduct as a breach of privilege (presumably of freedom from molestation or intimidation) and not as a contempt. The case is a good illustration of conduct that is held to be intimidation or molestation without being illegal.

[3] H.C. 118 (1946–7) (W. J. Brown's case).

tive of whether his communication takes the form of a statement, prediction, or invective, and irrespective of its actual deterrent consequences? The Clerk of the House in Jordan's case did not think it relevant that the member did not feel deterred nor that there was a lack of any reality in the state of affairs envisaged by the writer (though Jordan's 'resurgent Britain' was regarded by him as 'within the realms of possibility'). Whether the envisaging of a state of affairs entirely outside the realms of possibility or of the writer's control can be said to constitute a threat is a matter on which further precedents are needed. A letter stating an intention to stick pins in an effigy of the Prime Minister might help to advance the argument.

A category of action closely related to the predicting or threatening of future adversities or legal penalties is that which includes attempts to influence members by publicizing their votes or conduct with a view to instigating adverse political or electoral reaction. In 1946 a number of constituents posted notices in Westminster stating their intention to publish the names of members who voted in favour of bread rationing in a forthcoming debate as being 'public enemies and dictators'.[1] The offenders on this occasion were a group calling themselves the 'Face the Facts Association', but their chosen mode of publicizing the facts was held to be improperly intimidatory. So also was the attempt of a newspaper in 1956 to persuade readers to telephone a member and acquaint him with their views.[2] The Committee in that case suggested that whether a communication to a member of Parliament amounted to an improper interference depended on the nature and manner of the communication—a proposition that illustrates, if nothing else, the flexibility of the concept of contempt. In this case there was perhaps an

---

[1] H.C. 181 (1945–6).

[2] H.C. 27 (1956–7). A similar 'gross breach of privilege' took place in 1935 when the League for the Prohibition of Cruel Sports sent a questionnaire to members with a letter reading 'If we do not hear from you we shall feel justified in letting your constituents know that you have no objection to cruel sports.' See 301 *H.C. Deb.* 5s. col. 1545. In 1975 an unsuccessful submission was made by Mr. Marcus Lipton that a *Daily Telegraph* advertisement was an improper attempt to influence M.P.s in the discharge of their duties. The advertisement contained the words 'Send a telegram to your M.P. c/o House of Commons London, S.W.1. Ask him to vote Heath in next weeks ballot, signed "Friends of Ted Heath".'

element of physical obstruction in that the collective attempts of a large number of telephone communicants could be held to have in effect immobilized the member's telephone and obstructed him in the carrying out of his constituency duties.

Obstruction itself is another clear category of contempt with unclear boundaries. In the past some members have taken a wide view of it arguing that it has occurred when the police or traffic regulations have temporarily interfered with their access to Westminster.[1] When, on the other hand, significant impediments were placed in the way of M.P.s in 1975 as the result of a two-week strike by industrial civil servants that interfered with the delivery of Parliamentary papers, *Hansard*, and the House's heating and lighting facilities, it was regarded as a matter for congratulation that the unofficial strikers and pickets had not brought the work of Parliament entirely to a halt. *The Times* report noted that 'as no members were actually molested in carrying out their duties it was generally considered that the pickets were not a breach'.

Two other groups whose obstructive activities have been handled in a manner perhaps best described as diplomatic, are students and party whips. In April 1969 a sub-committee of the Select Committee on Education and Science visited the University of Essex to inquire into the relationship between the University and its students. The sub-committee discovered what it was almost immediately since their first session was disrupted, the table at which they were sitting was overturned, and the members were physically obstructed, jostled, and handled.[2] The matter was referred to the Committee of Privileges and the Clerk to the House, Sir Barnett Cocks, reminded them of resolutions of both Houses that 'The assaulting, insulting or menacing any Member of the House . . . is an high infringement of the privilege of this House, a most outrageous and dangerous violation of the rights of Parliament and an high crime and misdemeanour.'[3] The Committee's conclusion was that nothing

---

[1] e.g. H.C. 244 (1950–1) (Mr. J. Lewis's case). The Committee of Privileges, however, found no breach of privilege to have occurred in this instance.

[2] Clutched, in particular, by the legs (evidence of Mr. Gilbert Longdon). H.C. 308 (1968–9), p. 6.

[3] L.J. (1718–21); C.J. (1732–7) 115.

should be done.[1] It would be a venturesome and idle speculation to ask whether the same conclusion would have been reached if the Essex events had taken place in, say, a police station, a newspaper office, or a meeting of a local chamber of commerce. The Committee report on the Essex case points out that the Commons should invoke its contempt powers only when it is 'absolutely necessary for the due execution of its powers'. What is felt to be necessary and absolute is, no doubt, in great measure a variable matter much affected by custom and convention. Some pressures go almost unnoticed by reason of their familiarity. So much could certainly be said of the threats, menaces, and inducements of the party system. Their impact on the independent judgement of the member of Parliament is of rather more consequence than the minatory letters, postcards, and editorials with which so much privilege history is taken up. But whips and Party leaders, though occasionally challenged at times of political excitement, are not regarded as an impediment to free will. At the time of the Suez crisis when it was suggested by Opposition members that 'unexampled pressures' had been used to force Government supporters into line, the Speaker gave it as his view that the activities of whips and the usual channels had never been regarded as a breach of the privileges of the whole House.[2] A similar view was expressed (by Mr. Speaker Selwyn Lloyd) on 9 April 1975 that arrangements made within political parties would be unlikely to raise questions of contempt or privilege. The occasion was an attempt by Mr. Michael English, M.P., to persuade him that the cabinet guide-lines laid down for the conduct of ministers in the House during the course of the Common Market referendum campaign ought to be referred to the Committee of Privileges. Nor was the Committee of Privileges assembled to consider the propriety of Mr. Harold Wilson's colourful announcement to potentially dissident members of the Parliamentary Labour Party in 1967 that persistent unruly conduct might lead to the withdrawal of 'dog licences'.[3]

---

[1] H.C. 308 (1968–9), p. vi.   [2] 578 *H.C. Deb.* 5s. col. 408 (1956).

[3] The statement was made at a meeting of the Parliamentary Labour Party. Mr. Wilson's words were 'All I say is "Watch it!" Every dog is allowed one bite but a different view is taken of a dog that goes on biting all the time. . . . Things happen to that dog. . . . He may not get his licence renewed when it falls due.' (*The Times*, 3 Mar. 1967.)

A crucial area in which a degree of uncertainty still prevails is that in which attempts are made by constituents or pressure groups to influence the conduct of members. Action by way of financial threats or inducements in their simplest form undoubtedly constitutes contempt. In terms of the Commons' resolution of 1695,[1] 'the offer of money or other advantage to any member of Parliament for the promoting of any matter whatsoever, depending or to be transacted in Parliament, is a high crime and misdemeanour and tends to the subversion of the English constitution'. The relationship of financial payments to particular matters or votes in the House is probably important since many members receive money or money's worth at least partly in return for services—such, for example, as advice in relation to Parliamentary matters generally.

Whether under the present law improper payments to members are capable of amounting to bribery is a matter of some difficulty. In 1976 the Royal Commission on Standards of Conduct in Public Life[2] concluded that neither the Public Bodies Corrupt Practices Act, 1889, nor the Prevention of Corruption Act, 1906, could be applied to members of Parliament, since they were not agents or members of public bodies as defined in these Acts. In 1916, however, the Acts were extended to 'local and public authorities of all descriptions', and it might be argued that Parliament is a public body at least of some description. There is also the possibility that the taking and giving of financial inducements may be common law offences. Perhaps because corruption of members has been dealt with as a contempt, prosecution has not been taken in this country, though in Australia the High Court and state courts, basing themselves on English precedents, have concluded that members are persons holding offices of public trust and confidence and that bribery of them and attempted bribery are common law offences.[3]

It has also been argued that any prosecution for bribery would, if the payments were for a member's services in the House, be in respect of Parliamentary proceedings and therefore ruled out by the protection given to such proceedings by privilege and by the Bill of Rights. This argument seems misconceived,

---

[1] C.J. (1693–7) 331.
[2] Cmnd. 6524 (1976), pp. 96–9.
[3] See, for example, *R. v. Boston* (1923) 33 C.L.R. 386.

since the relevant transaction is not the potential proceeding in Parliament but the taking of the bribe outside Parliament. Some acts of members outside the House may, we have seen, be deemed to be a part of the House's proceedings if inherently related to the discharge of a member's duty as a member in the House. But it is difficult to see that taking a bribe outside, or for that matter inside, the House bears any relation to his duty.

In 1947 the House resolved that it was inconsistent with the duty of a member of Parliament to enter into any contractual agreement with an outside body, of a kind that limited his complete independence and freedom of action or that stipulated that he should act as a representative of such a body in relation to matters transacted in Parliament. It is, however, difficult to reconcile this principle with the accepted fact that many members receive financial assistance from associations of constituents or trade unions and that such bodies are entitled to terminate such agreements if they believe the member to be acting in a way that no longer serves their interests. This was the question at issue in the dispute in 1946 between Mr. W. J. Brown and the Civil Service Clerical Association.[1] Brown's contract with the Association provided that he should deal with all questions arising in the work of the Association which required Parliamentary or political action (though adding that he should be entitled to engage in his political activities with complete freedom). Disagreement developed, however, between Mr. Brown and his sponsors and they resolved that his financial support should be terminated. The Committee of Privileges accepted that they were entitled so to act, though Brown had argued that the Association's action was calculated to influence him improperly in the exercise of his Parliamentary duties. Several points may be noted. As the Committee pointed out, where a member voluntarily places himself in such a relationship he must be taken to have accepted its possible termination as a matter which would not influence him in his Parliamentary duties, and be taken to require no protection against a bona fide

[1] H.C. 118 (1946–7). For the subsequent Commons debate and resolution see 440 H.C. Deb. 5s. cols. 284, et seq. Cf. the case of Mr. W. A. Robinson (H.C. 85 (1943–4)) in which the National Union of Allied and Distributive Workers threatened to end the member's sponsorship if he did not resign his seat. No breach of privilege was found.

attempt by the outside body to bring the relationship to an end. Again, it may be important that the member's agreement in this particular case specifically provided for his freedom of action and also that the termination of the financial support was not directed to any particular vote or action in the House of Commons. Brown's case, therefore, does not provide a ground for saying that in no circumstance will termination or a threat to terminate financial support to a member be improper. The Committee in that case pointed out that a decision to terminate relationships with a member might in practice be a powerful factor in inducing him to change his course of conduct and that an outside body is not entitled to use its agreement or the payment of money as an instrument by which it seeks to control the conduct of a member or to punish him for what he has done as a member.

In recent years a number of Trade Unions or Trade Union leaders appear to have overstepped the boundary line of propriety more clearly than did Mr. Brown's civil service association. In 1967 the Transport and General Workers' Union declared that its sponsored members would risk losing the union's financial subvention if they supported the Labour Government's prices and incomes policy. In the following year Mr. Will Howie resigned from the Draughtsmen's and Allied Technicians' Union after a similar threat, but neither case was raised in the House. The Common Market issue also led to complaints of union pressure. At the conference of the Transport and General Workers' Union in Scarborough in 1971 the executive secretary was reported as saying that 'any Labour M.P. backed financially by the Union should seek support elsewhere at the next general election if they voted for entry'. In 1974 and 1975 complaints were made by members about pressure exerted by the National Union of Journalists and by the National Union of Railwaymen. However, the Union Secretary of the N.U.J. apologized, as did the General Secretary of the railwaymen's union who had said of the union's sponsored members: 'The M.P.s know that when I am talking about the railways there is no area in which they can deviate from what we are expecting of them.' In June 1975 an equally uncompromising set of resolutions was passed by the Yorkshire Area Council of the National Union of Mineworkers stating that sponsorship would be withdrawn from any member who refused to accept union guide-lines. The guide-lines were to the effect that no miners' M.P. should vote or speak against union policy on any issue affecting the coal industry, or campaign or work against union policy on any other major issue.[1] This policy was announced by Mr. Arthur Scargill, and complaint was made in the House both against Mr. Scargill himself and the area council. The Committee of Privileges reported in October 1965 that a serious contempt had been committed but that no further action need be taken since the national executive of the union had repudiated its area council's policy. The area council and Mr. Scargill, however, continued to maintain that the resolutions would remain the policy of the Yorkshire N.U.M. Their defiance was described by *The Times* as 'a challenge to Parliament which Parliament cannot allow to pass'. It was, however, allowed to pass. Nobody suggested that Mr. Scargill should be brought to the Bar of the House and be invited to purge his contempt, in the manner of lesser contemners in times past. *Tempora mutantur.*

The position of members faced by demands for resignation by their constituents, or threats of future action to unseat them in consequence of their Parliamentary activities, has never been squarely considered by the Committee of Privileges. Two well-known cases were those of Mr. Nigel Nicolson in 1956 and Mr. Dick Taverne in 1971, forced into resignation by constituency caucuses because of their votes in the House during the Suez crisis and the E.E.C. membership debate respectively.[2] It is generally assumed that demands for resignation or threats not to readopt a sitting member do not constitute contempt or breach of privilege. Members, understandably, are not inclined to submit such cases for the Privilege Committee's arbitrament, but it seems possible to argue that in a suitable case the threat to take such action against a member (say in relation to a particular forthcoming vote in the House) might in the light of the Committee's existing precedents and dicta constitute improper interference with the freedom of action of a member.

[1] *The Times*, 26 June 1975.
[2] Both members set out their experiences in detail in *People and Parliament* (1958) (Nicolson) and *The Future of the Left* (1974) (Taverne).

Freedom from and Right to Punish Adverse Reflections on the House and its Members

A final class of cases involving speech, writing, or communications may be discerned in which the essence of the offence committed is not so much its intimidatory effect as its impact on the reputation or dignity of the House or its members or officers and the presumed interference with the House's capacity to carry out its function if it is lowered in public esteem. In effect, this is a form of seditious libel, an offence whose existence can only coexist with a public right of free expression if narrowly circumscribed. One limiting principle, which is analogous to that defining constructive contempts against courts or judges is that the offence consists in impugning the fairness, impartiality, or competence of the body concerned, or the imputation of improper motives, rather than in mere denunciation, even where robust and inaccurate.[1] Many of the examples of contempts listed in Erskine May under the heading of 'Reflections upon Members' fall into this category, consisting in such offences as imputing corruption or partiality to members or to the Speaker or chairmen of committees. Another limiting principle is that any punishable adverse reflection upon an individual member should relate to him in his Parliamentary capacity rather than in his personal character or non-Parliamentary activities. These distinctions may be obscured, however, to the extent that two other categories of speech or writing are brought within the ambit of contempt, namely 'gross calumny or foul epithets' and 'misrepresentation of Members' Proceedings'. The original resolutions in the Commons against misrepresentation were in fact linked to the prohibition on publication of members' names.[2] Bearing in mind the House's historical concern for its

---

[1] See, for example in relation to contempt of court *R*. v. *Metropolitan Police Commissioner, ex p. Blackburn* (*No. 2*) [1968] 2 Q.B.150. On imputations against Parliament cf. Viscount Kilmuir, *The Law of Parliamentary Privilege* (1959), p. 16.

[2] See Commons' resolution of 22 Apr. 1699: 'That the publishing of names of the members of this House and reflecting upon them, and misrepresenting their proceedings in Parliament is a breach of the privilege of this House and destructive of the freedom of Parliament' (C.J. (1699–1702) 767).

dignity and the fact that its members are politicians and members of a profession peculiarly apt to feel misrepresented, it is not difficult to see that they may not always have been relied upon to keep a firm hold upon the distinction between contempt and condemnation. A rough count of cases since 1900 that have been considered by the Committee of Privileges reveals perhaps twenty to thirty cases that could be classified under the heading of adverse reflections upon members or officers. Most of them have occurred since 1945 and have involved criticisms or accusations made by newspapers or public speakers, many of them members of Parliament. A glance at some selected examples illustrates that it has not always been easy to distinguish alleged imputations of wrongful or partial conduct from reflections on the competence and political judgement of members or of policies endorsed by them. Perhaps the clearest cases that concern competence or propriety are those that involve accusations of drunkenness or financial corruption. Mr. Stanley Baldwin referred in 1926 to the need for delicacy in discussing the manner in which members conducted themselves. In an assembly of over six hundred men, he said, it was perfectly obvious that there would be cases where men forgot themselves. 'But we do not talk about it. We draw a veil of reserve over it.'[1] On occasion, members reporting on their experience of Parliamentary life have neglected Mr. Baldwin's advice. In that same year Dr. Salter had said that he had seen many members drunk in the House and that 'no party was exempt'.[2] In 1930 Mr. E. Sandham said that Labour members got 'stupidly drunk' and accepted bribes from money-lenders and other private interests.[3] In 1947 Mr. G. Allighan wrote an article in which he alleged that the proceedings at party meetings were sold to newspapers by members under the influence of drink:[4] and in 1965 Mr. A. Duffy remarked that he had seen Conservative M.P.s 'half drunk' during debates.[5] All were found by the Committee of Privileges or by resolution to have committed grave contempts or perpetrated gross libels.[6]

---

[1] 199 *H.C. Deb.* 5s. col. 720. [2] Ibid., cols. 561–6, 709–31.
[3] H.C. 187 (1929–30). [4] H.C. 138 (1946–7).
[5] H.C. 129 (1964–5).
[6] A severer penalty of fine and suspension was inflicted on an earlier

Alleged financial impropriety has not invariably been a matter of straightforward bribery, but turned upon the relationships between members and special interest groups or their representatives. In 1960 the activities of a public relations firm employed by the Government of the Central African Federation in offering free travel and hospitality to M.P.s was raised in the House, but the Speaker ruled that no prima facie breach of privilege was revealed by the alleged facts. In 1965 a reference to the financial interests of some Conservative members was referred by a narrow majority in the House to the Select Committee. The Chancellor of the Exchequer, Mr. J. Callaghan, had said (in a weekend speech) that he did not think of them as the honourable member for X, Y, or Z. 'I look at them and say "Investment Trusts", "Capital Speculators" or "That is the fellow who is the Stock Exchange man who makes a profit on Gilt Edge". I have almost forgotten their constituencies but I shall never forget their interests.' Mr. Callaghan told the Committee that he had no offensive intention in making these remarks and no action was taken.[1] In 1974, however, Mr. J. Ashton was found guilty of a serious contempt against the House as the result of articles and radio comments about the alleged practice of members making certain services available to outside interests for payment. In the radio broadcast Mr. Ashton had said that if a firm needed publicity to apply pressure to a minister or to launch a campaign it was easy to hire an M.P. He knew of half a dozen who were approachable. Their services could be hired and they could be asked to raise matters in the House.[2] Later Mr. Ashton apologized for unintentionally bringing the House into disrepute, though attempting to justify what he had said.

Accusations of partiality against the Speaker, or of misconduct by committee chairmen[3] are easy to locate within the traditional

offender who had said that members were 'accompanied in their counsels by Bacchus' (Hall's case, C.J. (1547–1628) 122–6).

[1] H.C. 269 (1965).

[2] *The Times*, 30 Apr. 1974.

[3] See, for example, the complaint by Mr. Robert Maxwell in 1969 of the *Sunday Times*' description of his chairmanship of the Commons Catering Sub-Committee. ('It displays all the classic movements in Maxwell's repertoire—the Amazing Leap from the Wings with Loud Promises of Modern Efficiency; the Masterly Treatment of Accounts and the Rapid

boundaries of constructive contempt. A more doubtful category of cases is perhaps that in which members claim that their motives or the nature of their activities or arguments in committee or in the House have been distorted or misrepresented. Such accusations may go partly to the motives of members, or contain insinuations of lack of frankness or insufficient concern for the public interest, or they may principally relate to such alleged failings as political partisanship or the pursuit of mistaken or dangerous policies. A number of cases illustrate this difficult category. In 1972 complaint was made by members of a Commons select committee that an article in the *Sunday Times'* colour supplement entitled 'Shell Versus Parliament; a Study in Parliamentary Impotence' had misrepresented the proceedings in committee. It was argued that the article must constitute a breach of privilege because it distorted what happened in Committees of the House.

Similar resentment was felt by members in 1956 when a number of privilege complaints arose from press and radio criticism of the decision to issue supplementary petrol coupons to M.P.s when petrol rationing was introduced in the aftermath of the Suez operations. The principal offender was the *Sunday Express* which, in a critical editorial, remarked that petrol rationing would pass M.P.s by in a time of general hardship. Members, it was said, had not protested about their special treatment and the public should make it plain that they would not tolerate politicians who were more interested in privileges for themselves than in fair shares for all. The Committee of Privileges thought that these views were intended to hold members up to public obloquy and to charge them with contemptible conduct and self-interest. The editor, Mr. John Junor, had, they concluded, been guilty of a serious contempt in reflecting upon all members of the house.[1] Mr. Junor was ordered to attend at the Bar, where he apologized for his conduct in diminishing the respect due to the House and weakening its authority.

It would not be going too far to say that the Junor case did more to bring the House's privilege jurisdiction into disrepute

Disappearance, just before the audience begins to throw things.') H.C. 478 (1968–9); H.C. 185 (1969–70). The Committee found the article derogatory but not a contempt.

[1] H.C. 38 (1956–7).

than any other exercise of it in the twentieth century. Several other cases of press and radio comment were referred to the Committee at the same time, including a cartoon in the *London Evening News*, and an article in a provincial newspaper alleging that M.P.s had been 'too kind to themselves' and were 'muzzling comment' through the action of the Committee of Privileges.[1] It was not thought by the Committee that these comments were contemptuous though they seemed to embody an accusation of partiality and disregard of constitutional principle at least as severe as that levelled by Mr. Junor.

There is a noticeable clustering in the incidence of privilege complaints at particular periods in the post-war history of the House of Commons. They have the appearance of being stimulated by situations in which government majorities are small and political partisanship high. The period from 1950 to 1956 was one such period. Another seems to have occurred between 1964 and 1966. In 1965 Mr. Jo Grimond suggested that there might be a connection between the restraints of the party system and the touchiness of the House about protocol, privilege, and the Standing Orders. A comment in the *Spectator* at about the same time saw an explanation for the frequency of privilege cases in the state of the parties. 'In a House almost equally divided, the strains upon members are great. The hours are long, frustration accumulates, tempers grow shorter and tactical manœuvres to discomfort the other side assume an unreal importance.'[2]

The comment was made after a debate in the House on the case of Mr. William Warbey. In February 1965 Mr. Warbey complained that articles in the *Spectator* and the *Daily Telegraph* were defamatory and calculated to deter him from carrying out his Parliamentary duties. The passage in the *Spectator* stated that on a visit to Hanoi his hotel expenses had been paid by the Vietnam Fatherland Front. The Speaker ruled that the passage complained of did not prima facie raise a matter of privilege, but a motion to refer the issue to the Committee of Privileges was put down by Mr. Sidney Silverman. Mr. Silverman's motion

---

[1] H.C. 74 (1956–7) and H.C. 39 (1956–7) ('Complaint of a drawing and text in the "*Evening News*" newspaper').

[2] The *Spectator*, 26 Mar. 1965. Cf. Colin Seymour-Ure, 'The Misuse of the Question of Privilege in the 1964–5 Session of Parliament', *Parliamentary Affairs*, 1965, p. 380.

averred that the statements made about Mr. Warbey were an attack upon his honour, integrity, good faith, and loyalty in the discharge of his Parliamentary duties and, by implication, upon those of the many honourable members who had from time to time paid visits to foreign countries in pursuit of their obligations as members. On a free vote Mr. Silverman's motion was narrowly defeated, the Government Chief Whip and seven other ministers voting in favour of it, against the advice of the Solicitor-General who in the debate reminded the House that in 1887 *The Times* had referred to a group of Irish members as 'midnight murderers' and got away with it.[1] After the Speaker had ruled against his original complaint Mr. Warbey tried again without success to argue that a postcard he had received was an attempt to intimidate him and inhibit him from expressing his views in the House. The postcard—signed 'Realist'—ran: 'Dear Mr. Warbey, Listening to your comments on TV I formed the opinion that you are only in the Labour Party to further the Communist cause. Be good enough to admit this and change your party!'[2]

In considering reflections on members an obvious difficulty is that of distinguishing between attacks on the member in his Parliamentary and extra-Parliamentary or private role.[3] The

[1] *The Times* had commented that certain members drew 'their living and their notoriety from the steady perpetration of crimes for which civilisation demands the gallows' (311 *Parl. Deb.* (1887) I col. 286). The Speaker ruled no prima facie breach of privilege, there being presumably no direct connection between the matters charged and the members' Parliamentary duties (though it could well be thought that the reputation of Parliament as a whole would be diminished in the public mind if its members were widely thought to be homicidal criminals).

[2] *The Times*, 24 Mar. 1965. On the same occasion the Speaker declined to give any guidance to Brigadier Terence Clarke, M.P., who asked for a ruling on what members should do when they received such postcards. They regularly got postcards (he added) signed 'Lulu'.

[3] What, for example, of a general attack on the personal ability of members or groups of members? An example is the complaint raised by Mr. Emrys Hughes on 12 April 1960 about reflections on 'the women members of the House'. The Speaker's wife in a speech reported in the press had expressed the view that 'Women do not have enough education to become politicians.' She added 'I know that many Labour members of Parliament who had no education have done extremely well, but they have bothered to find out things for themselves and read up what they do not know. Women do not.'

matter may be even more complicated, since it may not always be obvious whether an adverse reference is to the member as an elected representative merely or to his party political character, or to the alleged failings of the Government of which he may be a part. This precise question was posed by the complaint raised in 1964 against Mr. Quintin Hogg. Mr. Hogg, then Secretary of State for Education and Science, in a public meeting said that the Government had not since coming into power pursued a reactionary or illiberal policy. 'Nevertheless,' he went on, 'our elbows have been jarred in almost every part of the world by individual Labour members' partisanship of subversive activities. This is the party which is now seeking power.' Mr. George Wigg submitted that the minister had committed a gross calumny and a contempt against the House in asserting that some of his colleagues had been engaged in subversive activities. Reflections upon members, the particular individuals not being named or otherwise indicated, were, he said, declared in Erskine May to be equivalent to reflections on the House. In the House Mr. Hogg maintained that in his speech he had been referring to the Labour Party as a whole (rather than the Parliamentary Labour Party) and to its penetration by elements that he regarded as subversive. Before the Committee of Privileges he argued that he had not intended to say even that any Labour Party member was engaged in subversion but only that they had engaged in 'partisanship of subversive activities'. The Committee accepted Mr. Hogg's interpretation of his speech and found that no breach of the House's privilege had occurred. There had been no contempt in the sense that ignominy had been cast on it as an institution. They recognized the principle enunciated by Erskine May that reflections on particular individuals might be equivalent to reflections on the House itself. The principle, however, was not, they concluded, free from doubt as to the limits of its scope and application. It might be that it related only to the conduct of a member or members in the transaction of the service or business of the House or within its precincts. It was by no means clear that reflections on members otherwise than in respect of their conduct within the precincts of Parliament or in the transaction of the service or business of the House could properly be regarded as reflections upon the House itself. It was also uncertain whether a person accused of imputations upon members that might amount to contempt of the House could justify his conduct on the basis that the imputations were in fact true.[1]

The report of the Committee in Hogg's case raises two important questions about constructive contempts that consist in adverse reflection upon members of the House. Even if the imputations made against a member are in fact in relation to conduct in the House (as they were in Junor's case)[2] why should they not be permissible if—as the Committee in Hogg's case asserted—privilege should not be used so as to inhibit the free expression of opinion about the affairs of the nation? The conduct of affairs in the House and the conduct of the House itself is an important aspect of public affairs. Unlike other forms of contempt (such as threats or intimidation) there is an obvious question that arises about the category of alleged contempts that consists in statements either of fact or opinion about the House or its members—namely whether they are true or false. Are such statements capable of constituting a contempt of the House irrespective of their truth or falsity and should those accused of contempt be permitted to justify their allegations? This among

[1] H.C. 247 (1963-4). In November 1976 somewhat similar accusations against a number of Labour members were referred to the Privileges Committee but the Committee declined to pursue them. Mr. Iain Sproat, M.P., alleged in a speech outside the House that about thirty Labour M.P.s were in an 'unholy alliance of crypto-Communists'. Another group of Labour members had also issued a statement suggesting that some of their colleagues were 'undercover political agents for alien political creeds'. (*The Times*, 18–19 Nov. 1976.)

[2] Two other cases of accusations against members may be compared with Hogg's case, in both of which it might be considered that the accusations of subversive intent did relate to activities in the House. One was the case of Colm Brogan (H.C. 112 (1947–8)), in which it was alleged that secret sessions in the House were useless since defence information would be given to the Russians by twenty-nine secret supporters of the Communist Party. Another was Fitt's case (H.C. 462 (1966–7)), in which the *Protestant Telegraph* newspaper called Mr. Gerard Fitt, M.P., an 'arch traitor' who had gone to Westminster 'for permission to mount mayhem in Northern Ireland'. No action was recommended in either case. No explicit answer was given to the contempt or breach of privilege question in Brogan's case, but the statements about Fitt were found to constitute a breach. In 1953 a *Sunday Express* article was referred to the Committee on the ground that in describing an all-night session it made reference to women members 'snoring' in a retiring room H.C. 171 (1952–3).

other issues was one of the questions on which the Select Committee on Parliamentary Privilege, set up in 1967, was ordered to report.[1]

The 1967 Select Committee and its Report

In November 1967 a select committee was set up 'to review the law of Parliamentary Privilege as it affects this House and the procedure by which cases of privilege are raised and dealt with in this House and to report whether any changes in the law of privilege or practice of the House are desirable'. Evidence was heard from a large number of individuals and groups representing the press, the broadcasting organizations, the Parliamentary Lobby, the Law Society, and the Bar. The major questions considered by the Committee related to the procedure of the House, the retention by the House of its existing jurisdiction in contempt cases, and the position of persons called to give evidence in their own behalf before the Privileges Committee. The question of justification by those charged with contempt by reason of adverse reflections on the House was one of the issues on which some disagreement was registered by witnesses. The Clerk of the House suggested that the question of allowing a defence of justification had never been definitely decided by the House.[2] The Committee had power to inquire into the facts surrounding and reasonably connected with the matter of a complaint. If a witness wished to submit a defence of justification in an appropriate case it would appear to be for the Committee to decide whether they would hear it. The Attorney-General was in agreement and, though saying that he knew of no case in which an accused person had attempted to tender such evidence,[3] thought that it ought in principle to be permissible. A memorandum by Mr.

[1] The members of the Committee were Messrs. Bellenger, Deedes, Edelman, English, Foot, Hogg, Hooson, Kershaw, Pannell, Ramsden, Silkin, and Strauss.

[2] H.C. 34 (1967–8) p. 5.

[3] Perhaps the cases of Dr. Salter, Mr. Hogg, and Mr. Colin Jordan were such cases, though justification was combined in the two latter cases with explanation. Is it both the truth of facts and the fairness of comment that is in question? Cf. the report of the Committee in Allighan's case, H.C. 138 (1946–7), where it was suggested that publication of discreditable matters for the purpose of putting an end to them might constitute a defence.

L. A. Abraham, however, suggested that all the Parliamentary precedents indicated that in proceedings for contempt of Parliament in the seventeenth- and eighteenth-centuries the truth of a libel would not have been a defence, any more than it would have been a defence at common law in criminal prosecutions for libel; and there was no evidence that the passage of time had made any difference. Investigation of the facts would give ill-disposed persons an opportunity of making defamatory statements in circumstances of absolute privilege and the function of contempt proceedings was to prevent obstruction of the House in the performance of its functions—a matter to which justification was not relevant. Neither of these considerations if intended as a defence of the practice of not permitting justification, at least as to matters of fact, seems very persuasive. What has to be explained is how the making of true statements about members' conduct could be considered to prevent the *proper* functioning of the House. The opportunity offered to irresponsible people to make allegations under the protection of absolute privilege would be subject at least to the restraints of cross examination and is no greater than the opportunity that occurs daily in every case heard in the ordinary courts.

In the matter of raising privilege complaints in the House a memorandum submitted by the Study of Parliament Group suggested the adoption of a practice originally recommended by the Select Committee on Procedure of 1959, namely that precedence over the orders of the day should not be withheld from matters of privilege if raised not less than twenty-four hours after the first opportunity for so doing. If in addition members were to follow the practice of apprising the Speaker privately of their intentions, his opportunity for consideration might deter them from bringing up, for fear of losing their opportunities, matters which on reflection might not be thought worth pursuing. The Study of Parliament Group also made two additional and radical proposals. The first was that contempt should be defined so as to include, first, all forms of direct interference with, or obstruction of, Parliamentary machinery such as molestation of witnesses, assaults, disorder, and misconduct in the House, disobedience to orders of the House; and secondly, physical and financial threats calculated to coerce or penalize members' votes or attitudes by attempts at bribery or other improper forms of financial inducement. But it should exclude (they argued) all other forms of political pressure brought to bear by individuals, interest groups, or constituencies, enforced by electoral sanctions or threats of such sanctions. It should also exclude all adverse reflections, attacks, or allegedly defamatory statements made in speeches, writings, or broadcasts, together with the remaining constructive contempts mentioned in Erskine May, such as distorted reports or misrepresentation of debates. The professions often made by the Committee of Privileges (as in Mr. Hogg's case) about the importance of not inhibiting free speech were not, they suggested, easily reconcilable with the attitudes of individual members in seeking the protection of privilege against critical speeches and writings, especially at times of acute party controversy.

They added:

We believe the reputation of Parliament to be sturdy enough to withstand without special protection anything which is said, written or broadcast about it. Defamatory statements about individual members are subject to the law of libel, but the legislature ought not as an institution to be more in need of protection than any other part of the constitution such as the Crown. In principle the Crown and Parliament are protected by the law of seditious libel. A conviction, however, for that offence in modern times requires proof of language 'calculated . . . to promote public disorder or physical force or violence in a matter of State'.[1] There seems no reason why Parliament should wish to impose in its own defence a severer control on the freedom of speech than the general law of the land.[2]

A second proposal made by the Study of Parliament Group was that the House should transfer its jurisdiction over contempt cases to the courts. The arguments for such a course of action were that consideration by the House of complaints of contempts against itself or its members amounts to a denial of natural justice which is compounded by the lack of any provision for legal representation. To the response that violation of the principle *nemo iudex in sua causa* is inherent in the situation of any court that exercises a contempt power, it was suggested that the punishment of contempts against courts and judges was tied closely to the notion of immunizing adjudicative processes from public pressure or influence and was not exercised even there without facilities for appeal. 'The House of Commons', on the

---

[1] *Rex* v. *Aldred* (1909) 22 Cox 1, p. 3.
[2] H.C. 34 (1967–8), p. 192.

other hand, it was urged, is not, in substance, a judicial body. An assembly of six hundred and thirty members cannot be and is the wrong sort of body to carry out an essentially adjudicative process, namely the resolution of an individual case arising under the law and custom of Parliament. Even adjudication by a legislative committee may be thought objectionable in principle.'[1] It was considerations of these kinds, it was argued, that had led the House to commit the adjudication of disputed election petitions to the courts (by the Parliamentary Elections Act of 1868). It would be necessary to provide a definition of contempt either by setting out a number of general heads of the offence (thus following the method adopted in the Privilege Laws of many Commonwealth legislatures[2]) but omitting any reference to slanders or libels on the House; or, alternatively, to adopt a general statutory definition of the offence based upon that given in Erskine May ('an act obstructing or having a direct tendency to obstruct either House in the execution of its functions') omitting any reference to 'indirect tendency'. Offences committed by members within the House and possibly outside the House could be left within the House's jurisdiction.

The Select Committee reported in December 1967 and its recommendations were as follows:[3]

1. The expression 'Parliamentary Privilege' in its customary sense should be abolished. The House should speak of its 'rights and immunities' rather than 'rights and privileges' and of 'contempt' rather than 'breach of privilege'. The Committee of Privileges should be renamed 'The Select Committee of House of Commons Rights'.

2. In the future exercise of its penal jurisdiction the House should follow the general rule that it should be exercised (a) in any event as sparingly as possible and (b) only when the House is satisfied that to exercise it is essential in order to provide reasonable protection for the House, its Members or its Officers, from such improper obstruction or attempt at or threat of obstruction as is causing, or is likely to cause, substantia interference with the performance of their respective functions.

3. In the ordinary case where a Member has a remedy in the courts he should not be permitted to invoke the penal jurisdiction of the House in lieu of or in addition to that remedy. Nor should he normally be permitted to do so to defeat another's remedy. But the House should retain

[1] Ibid. 194.
[2] See Appendix IV, of the Select Committee Report (on Privilege Jurisdiction in Commonwealth Legislatures), H.C. 34 (1967–8), pp. 176–87.
[3] See summary of recommendations, ibid. xlix–li.

the ultimate power to punish improper obstruction or an attempt or threat of improper obstruction of its functions and those of its Members and Officers, whenever this may be essential in the public interest.

4. In dealing with complaints of contempt the House should be guided by the general principles set out (in 2 above).

5. It should be open to the House, in deciding whether or not a contempt has been committed, to take into account either the truth of, or reasonable belief in the truth of, the allegations made, provided that they had been made only after all reasonable investigations had taken place, had been made in the honest and reasonable belief that it was in the public interest to make them and had been published in a manner reasonably appropriate to that public interest.

6. Legislation should be introduced to extend and clarify the scope of the defences of absolute and qualified privilege which are available in the courts to actions brought against Members and others.

7. The immunity of Members from arrest in civil suits should be abandoned and legislation should be introduced for this purpose.

8. The Speaker should be informed whenever a Member is arrested in the course of civil litigation, in the same way that notification is given when a Member is arrested on a criminal charge.

9. The immunity of Members (and Officers of the House) from jury service should be retained.

10. The immunity of Members and Officers of the House from attendance as witnesses should be retained, to the extent only that Mr. Speaker upon being informed of the service upon a Member or Officer of the House of a subpoena to attend court as a witness should be empowered in the name of the House in appropriate cases to require the attendance of the Member or Officer at the House in priority to the requirements of the subpoena. Legislation for this purpose should be introduced.

11. The immunity of Members and Officers of the House from appointment as Sheriff should be abandoned and Members (and Officers of the House) should be free to accept the office of Sheriff in all cases which would not subject them to disqualification.

12. The use of the expression 'freedom from molestation' should be discontinued insofar as it is used to describe a right of Members separate and distinct from the rights which are protected by the ordinary penal jurisdiction in contempt.

13. The right to impeach should be formally abandoned, and legislation should be introduced for this purpose.

14. All resolutions prohibiting the reporting of proceedings of the House should be formally rescinded and all rules of practice analogous to them should be abandoned.

15. The rules governing public admission to the House and its Committees and to other bodies established by or under authority of the House should be amended to provide that;

    (a) save in the case of the House itself or a Standing Committee, strangers should be excluded unless it is otherwise decided;

    (b) unless the House specifically order otherwise in any particular case, the decision whether to permit strangers to attend should be made by a majority of those voting in the relevant Committee or other body concerned; and

(c) unless the House or the parent Committee or other parent body order otherwise in any particular case, tho decision be made by a majority of those voting in the relevant Sub-Committee or other subordinate body concerned.

16. (i) The reporting of the proceedings of the House or of any Committee or Sub-Committee of the House should not of itself be considered as capable of being a contempt if strangers are admitted to the proceedings; but (ii) the disclosure or publication without the required authority of reports of the proceedings of the House, its Committees or Sub-Committees from which strangers are excluded should be capable of being held to be a contempt.

17. The following conduct should not of itself be regarded as being capable of constituting a contempt of the House and the House should resolve accordingly;

(a) to publish in advance of publication of the relevant Notice Papers;
   (i) how any Member in fact voted in a division
   (ii) the contents of any Parliamentary Question or Notice of Motion which has in fact been tabled;

(b) to publish the expressed intention of a Member to vote in a particular manner (or to abstain from voting) or to table a particular Parliamentary Question or Notice of Motion.

18. The resolution of 21st April 1837 should be rescinded, and in its place the House should resolve in terms of the principles expressed in paragraphs 134 and 135, subject to the general rules for the guidance of the House proposed in paragraph 48.

19. The House should retain its penal jurisdiction.

20. The present procedure for raising complaints of contempt should be replaced.

21. Whenever a complaint of contempt is entertained or is ordered to be investigated by the Select Committee of House of Commons Rights, the rules set out in the Report[1] should apply.

22. Legislation should be introduced to enable the Select Committee of House of Commons Rights to authorise legal aid in appropriate cases in dealing with complaints of contempt.

23. Legislation should be introduced to empower the House to impose fixed periods of imprisonment and fines and to remit, suspend or vary any such penalty.

24. A Member who speaks upon a specific topic in which he has a financial interest, whether direct or indirect, ought to disclose such interest, and the fact that his failure to do so without good cause should be capable of being considered a contempt should be clearly understood by Members.

---

[1] These provided for rights of legal representation and cross-examination of witnesses in proceedings in the Committee of Privileges.

The new procedure proposed for initiating complaints provided that a member should inform the Clerk to the Committee of Privileges of the details of his complaint and that the Committee should inform him whether they had decided to entertain and investigate the complaint. If the Committee declined to entertain the complaint a motion might be placed on the order paper to direct them to do so, which if signed by not less than fifty members would be voted on at the earliest practical opportunity. If not securing the minimum number of signatures, such a motion would enjoy no greater priority than any other private member's motion unless the Government gave time for its consideration. The proposal was well adapted to allowing privilege questions to be raised without wasting the time of the House or giving undue publicity to seekers of it. Many of the other minor recommendations also plainly reflected a desire to clarify and tidy up the margins of the subject. Most of the more fundamental suggestions made to the Committee, however, such as the proposals to codify contempts and breaches of privilege and to transfer jurisdiction to the courts were rejected.

In some ways, therefore, the Committee's conclusions represented an anti-climax. The Committee's wish to dispense with the term 'Parliamentary Privilege' as being inappropriate to modern times was perhaps one of the odder recommendations in the Report. Substitution of the phrases 'rights and immunities', 'contempt of the House', and 'penal jurisdiction' for 'privilege', 'breach of privilege', and 'power to punish for breach of privilege' respectively, was intended to remove the impression that members constitute a 'privileged' class.[1] But perhaps misconceptions about usage, even if commonly held, ought not to govern the matter. In one sense the term 'privilege' may be used to point a contrast with a facility enjoyed as a right. The soldier's leave, said to be a 'privilege rather than a right' is nevertheless not thereby undeserved. A 'privilege' may also carry the idea of a power or facility exercised as an adjunct of some specific role, office, or status. But neither by derivation from *privilegium*, nor in any other way, does its meaning contain any necessary implication of *unmerited* reward or access to facilities. The phrase 'the privileged classes' is of course simply a casual abbreviation for some such phrase as 'the classes enjoying *un-*

[1] *Report*, p. vii.

deserved privileges'. It can hardly be supposed that anyone who is seriously concerned with the processes of government is in such a conceptual fog as to be unconscious of this, and it seems unnecessary to adjust a whole section of existing constitutional vocabulary for the sake of anyone else. One might as well stop talking about 'select' committees on the ground that they sound intolerably exclusive.

Adjectival trouble, moreover, seems possible if the Committee's suggestion were to be adopted. Are privileged words or occasions to become 'immunized' words or occasions? Is there not something to be said for keeping the link with qualified and absolute privilege as used in the law of defamation, especially since the Committee made frequent use of these terms in discussing the extent to which speech and proceedings should be protected from libel suits?[1]

In discussing the penal jurisdiction of the House the Committee recognized the validity of the criticism that members have in the past attempted to invoke the House's power to punish contempts and breaches of privilege in cases which are trivial or where other remedies (e.g. in the courts or by complaint to the Press Council) are open to them.

They were confident, however, that members could be persuaded in the future to use such remedies. Criticism of members and of the House was, they agreed, the life blood of democracy 'however strongly it may be expressed and however unjustifiable it may appear to be' and the sensible politician, they suggested, 'expects and even welcomes criticisms of this nature'. If legislative assemblies were indeed filled with such sensitive and liberal-minded men there might be much to be said for the Committee's optimism. But the Committee almost immediately gave cause to doubt even their own convictions of the value of free speech. For they went on to imagine the possibility that an 'unjustifiable and improper attack' might be made on members by a newspaper ('a powerful organ of the press') and that newspapers might conceivably persist in such attacks. For such cases the residual power of the House to imprison in self-defence should, the Committee felt, be retained with the addition of the power to fine. This jurisdiction should, it was emphasized, be

[1] See ibid., xxvii–xxviii.

invoked only when the House was satisfied that it was essential to provide reasonable protection for itself from actions which constituted improper obstruction and a substantial interference with the performance of the functions of the House or its members and officers. If such a general principle were adopted by resolution of the House for the future exercise of its powers, much of the present uncertainty and confusion which now exist would, the Committee suggested, be removed. The existing and substantially similar definition of contempt set out in Erskine May, however, has not succeeded in restraining members of the House of Commons from giving effect to the belief that vigorous or violent criticism of their conduct is an obstruction of the House in the performance of its functions.

In rejecting any proposed transfer of contempt jurisdiction to the courts, the Committee argued that the functions and duties of the House and its members were in a constant state of flux and alteration and only the House could really know what their limits were. Moreover, they said, the balance between the freedom of the individual and the protection of the House involved considerations of a political character which might vary from time to time, and judges would be embarrassed by the need to take such considerations into account. The House, too, might be embarrassed if its prima facie decision on a complaint referred to the courts was not upheld. Finally, it was argued, there was no need of any appellate procedure since the House had to endorse the Committee of Privileges' decision and would see that justice was done. In other words, the House as a whole could be said to constitute 'an adequate protection of an appellate character'.

It would not be true to say that the Committee were without support for their conclusions on this point. Three important witnesses presented arguments in favour of the *status quo*. The Attorney-General was against any yielding up of the House's jurisdiction, on the ground that it would 'in some measure deprive the House of the right to regulate its own proceedings'. The Clerk of the House was against such a course since it would waste time; and Mr. L. A. Abraham opposed it in part because 'the judges would be free from the restraint which the recognition of the difficulty of being impartial in one's own cause imposes on the House'.

In several memoranda presented to the Committee, comparisons were drawn with the practices of the United States Congress. The final section of Sir Barnett Cocks's memorandum, for example, suggested that the privileges of Congress were based on those of the British Parliament and that there did not appear to have been any wide divergence either in practice or interpretation of their privileges from those of the United Kingdom. It was conceded, however, that Congress does not take action against criticisms or misrepresentations of members' speeches and that 'in modern practice, there is considerable reluctance to pronounce against newspaper or public criticism of members'. That, indeed, might be thought an understatement. Comparisons were also drawn in Mr. L. A. Abraham's evidence which suggested that American practice, both as to the ambit of contempt powers and as to the direct exercise of a penal jurisdiction, could be regarded as in major respects similar in principle to the traditional practice of the British Parliament. In both memoranda, it might be argued, that what was omitted was of memoranda, it might be argued that what was omitted was of more importance than what was mentioned. In the first place, it cannot be asserted with any plausibility that attacks by speech or writing on Congress are today treated as 'offences of the same species' as assaults or obstructions to legislative proceedings which flow from refusals to testify or produce documents. In Mr. Abraham's memorandum, *Canfield* v. *Gresham*,[1] a decision of the Supreme Court of Texas in 1891, is cited as suggesting that they may be so treated. So is the American author of an article[2] written in the 1920s contending that anything that 'stirs the passions and arouses the righteous indignation of legislators or of a deliberative body as a whole was truly an obstruction of its proceedings as any physical interference'. But *Marshall* v. *Gordon*[3] repudiated the notion that a libellous written attack constituted an obstruction to the legislative process, and the concept of constructive contempt by writing, which the American colonial assemblies and Congress at an earlier period certainly embraced as enthusiastically as Westminster, can surely

[1] (1891) 19 South West. Rep. 390.
[2] C. S. Potts, 'Power of Legislative Bodies to Punish for Contempt', 74 *Univ. of Pennsylvania Law Review*, 691.
[3] 243 U.S. 521 (1927).

not be kept alive in the face of the First Amendment and the Supreme Court's elaboration in more recent times of the right to criticize public officials,[1] including legislators.

A somewhat similar criticism might be offered of the suggestion that support can be found in American doctrine for the retention of Parliamentary power directly to commit offenders. Mr. Abraham quoted Hallam's view that no man would wish to take away Parliament's coercive authority and suggested that not very different views were expressed by Chief Justice Warren in *Quinn* v. *U.S.*[2] In that case (which upheld a constitutional objection taken by a witness to questions put by a Congressional Committee) the Chief Justice remarked that 'without the power to investigate—including of course the power to compel testimony, either through its own processes or through judicial trial —Congress would be seriously handicapped in its efforts to exercise its constitutional function wisely and effectively'. But it may be doubted whether in this passage Chief Justice Warren was expressing any view about the relative wisdom of Congress retaining coercive power in its own hands as against any other procedure. He was merely asserting the propriety of the Congressional power to inquire and investigate as an implicit right inherent in its legislative function. He was certainly not expressing any views on the merits of the procedure for punishing refusal of testimony by citation to the federal courts as against direct imposition of punishment by Congress. It is constitutionally open to Congress to take such action but it does not now do so. Chief Justice Warren himself stated the current practice in *Watkins* v. *New York*.[3] 'Since World War II the Congress has practically abandoned its original practice of utilizing contempt proceedings at the bar of the House. . . . The Congress has instead invoked the aid of the federal judicial system in protecting itself against contumacious conduct. It has become customary to refer these matters to the United States Attorneys for prosecution under criminal law.'

---

[1] *New York Times* v. *Sullivan* 376 U.S. 254 (1964); *Garrison* v. *Louisiana* 379 U.S. 64 (1964); *Gertz* v. *Welch* 418 U.S. 323 (1974).

[2] 349 U.S. 155, 160 (1955).

[3] 354 U.S. 178, 207 (1957). The original statute penalizing refusals to testify or produce papers was passed in 1857 and the relevant sections are set out in 2 U.S. Code 192 and 194.

There does not seem therefore to be a strong case in present Congressional practice for retention of a direct penal jurisdiction by the House of Commons, whatever other arguments there may be for it.

More important, perhaps, is the fact that outside the power to compel testimony relevant to its legislative purposes, Congress would be inhibited by the Bill of Rights from any use of its penal powers to restrict written or spoken attacks on the legislature whether by individuals or by 'powerful organs of the press'. Freedom of speech at this point is given a preferred position. It is not delicately balanced against the supposed effects on the performance of legislative functions as judged by legislators themselves.

Action since 1967

The reaction of three successive governments to the Report of the 1967 Select Committee has been lethargic. Between December 1968 and 1969 a number of motions based on some of the less important recommendations in the Committee's Report were placed on the Order Paper, but they met with criticism and were not pursued. On several occasions Mr. Michael Foot pressed for action. On 28 April 1969 he opposed a motion to refer a complaint to the Committee of Privileges, adding that he would 'oppose all such proposals until the question of Privilege has been examined properly and the House has dealt with it (and) we should not submit any further case to the Committee of Privileges until that committee has been reformed'.[1] Mr. Foot repeated his threat after an inconclusive debate in July 1969[2] saying that he would 'resort to direct action' and oppose every request for a matter to be referred unless the Government gave a clear pledge that they would deal with the matter in the next session.[3] The then Leader of the House, Mr. Fred Peart, promised that there would be decisions taken by the Government on the Committee's Report.

[1] 782 *H.C. Deb.* 5s. col. 963.

[2] 786 *H.C. Deb.* 5s. cols. 825–13; cf. Colin Seymour-Ure, 'Proposed Reforms of Parliamentary Privilege: An Assessment in the Light of Recent Cases', *Parliamentary Affairs* (1970), p. 221. This article assesses the way in which privilege complaints, arising after the Committee's Report, might have been dealt with if the Committee's proposals had been adopted.

[3] 788 *H.C. Deb.* 5s. cols. 222–4.

In 1970, however, there was a change of government and in July 1971 the Conservative Leader of the House, Mr. William Whitelaw, tabled a number of motions on privilege. In the course of the debate[1] he told the House that many of the Committee's recommendations were not being proposed for implementation either because the Government disagreed with them or because they would require legislation. The House went on to approve several resolutions of a minor character to do with the publication of debates, select committee proceedings, and division lists. The Resolution of the House of 3 March 1762[2] was declared no longer to be a barrier to the publication of the debates and proceedings of the House (which it had not been for some time) save where the proceedings should have been conducted behind closed doors or expressly prohibited from publication. In addition select committees were given power to authorize witnesses who had given evidence to them to publish it and the Speaker was authorized to give such permission for a select committee no longer in existence (the provision being designed to avoid the possibility that evidence might be held permanently in limbo if never embodied in a committee's report to the House).

Thus, ten years after the Committee began its work, two small pieces of absurdity had been formally dispatched, but nothing done to implement the Committee's main recommendations. The future historian may well see in this something characteristic of English constitutional development.

[1] 821 *H.C. Deb.* 5s. cols. 922–95.

[2] The resolution had declared 'That it is an high Indignity to, and a notorious Breach of, the Privilege of this House . . . for any Printer or Publisher of any printed Newspaper . . . to give therein any Account of the Debates or other Proceedings of this House or any Committee thereof . . . and that this House will proceed with the utmost severity against such offenders.'

V

GOVERNMENT LEGISLATION
IN THE HOUSE OF COMMONS

S. A. Walkland

Writing in 1905, Josef Redlich summed up in a few sentences
the transformation in British Parliamentary government which
had taken place during the nineteenth century.

In the British Cabinet today [he says] is concentrated all political power, all
initiative in legislation and administration, and finally all public authority
for carrying out the laws in kingdom and empire. In the sixteenth century
and down to the middle of the seventeenth this wealth of authority was
united in the hands of the Crown and its privy council; in the eighteenth
century and the first half of the nineteenth Parliament was the dominant
central organ from which proceeded the most powerful stimulus to action
and all decisive acts of policy, legislation and administration; the second half
of the last century saw the gradual transfer from Crown and Parliament into
the hands of the Cabinet of one after another of the elements of authority
and political power. This process took place side by side and in organic
connexion with the passing of political sovereignty into the hands of the
House of Commons, supported as it now was by an electorate comprising
all sections of the population.[1]

In the case of the legislative process, this period essentially saw a
nationalization and centralization of legislative initiative in the
hands of the government, a massive supplementation of Private
Bill procedure by government-introduced Public General Acts,
and a marked diminution in the opportunities for private
Members to legislate. The new pattern appears to have been set
by the mid-nineteenth century. Sir Charles Wood, speaking in
the year 1885, is reported to have said 'When I was first in
Parliament, twenty-seven years ago, the functions of the government were chiefly executive. Changes in our laws were proposed
by independent members, and carried, not as party questions,
by their combined action on both sides.' Redlich comments:

At that time, it was not the business of the executive government to initiate
fresh laws; the speech from the throne did not embody a programme of

[1] Josef Redlich, *The Procedure of the House of Commons*, i. 208.

legislation. In the course of a generation all was changed . . . The main cause of the throwing upon the Government the chief, it may be said now the exclusive, initiative in all legislative problems is the great complexity of modern legislation, which at every turn is confronted by difficulties and considerations as to countless economic and social problems and vested interests. The formation of modern central and local authorities in England has led to the construction of an executive machinery, the intricacy of which corresponds to the involved needs of modern society, but which gives much cause for consideration upon any change in existing law. And as legislation has become more complex, Parliament and the public have become more critical. Bills are now reproduced, summarised and criticised by newspapers, are made the subject of comment by countless bodies, are studied by constituents, and therefore cannot be disregarded by members. It is scarcely possible, except for the Government, to satisfy all these conditions.[1]

Legislative procedure in Parliament was radically simplified between 1830 and 1880 to facilitate the scrutiny and criticism of government programmes of legislation and to assist in the sifting of information and the determination of facts which was an essential feature of the deliberative stage of the legislative process. A traditionally obstructive procedure, dating in its major forms from the seventeenth-century conflicts between Parliament and the Stuart monarchs, was transformed into a procedure which facilitated constructive criticism of the financial and legislative proposals of politically responsible governments, whilst severely restricting the opportunities of private Members to legislate. The Liberal assumption behind the new legislative procedures was that Parliament as a representative body was competent to dispose of all matters coming before it without according any procedural formalities to the organized interests who were affected by particular measures. The procedure which was evolved to control legislative proceedings in the Commons was designed to secure fair discussion, adequate deliberation, and general efficiency in the disposition of legislative matters without giving consultative rights to outside individuals and groups, as had been common under the processes of Private Bill legislation. A. Lawrence Lowell, the American commentator, writing in 1908, echoes Redlich in his description of the great procedural rationalizations of the previous forty years, legislative procedure at the turn of the century being

one of the many striking examples of adaptation in the British political

---

[1] Redlich, op. cit., p. 122.

system. A collection of rules that appear cumbrous and antiquated, and that even now are well-nigh incomprehensible when described in all their involved technicality, have been pruned away until they furnish a procedure almost as simple, direct and appropriate as any one could devise. Many old forms remain, but they have been shorn of their meaning, and often amount to nothing but entries in the journal.[1]

In 1970, Mr. John Mackintosh, M.P., a member of the Procedure Committee of the House of Commons, in a memorandum stating why in his view a further examination of public bill procedure was necessary, contrasted the legislative process in Parliament in the period from the second Reform Act to the outbreak of the 1914–18 war with that of the present day. He wrote:

The kernel of the problem is this. The existing procedure—1st reading, 2nd reading, Committee stage, Report stage, 3rd reading, House of Lords' amendments, etc.—was designed for a period when the legislative proposals were simple, often tentative, and when they were remodelled during the passage of the measure through the House. They were designed for a period when it was considered improper for outside interests to lobby civil servants or government Departments; they lobbied Members and put their case through such Members on the floor of the House.

This is a 'golden age' perspective of Victorian Parliamentary government which loses some of its attraction when it is realized that the same view was prevalent some seventy years ago in relation to an even earlier period of Parliamentary government.[2] It is in any case difficult to agree with this analysis of the late nineteenth-century legislative process. The characteristic of simplicity claimed for the statutes of this period cannot be applied to the major bills of successive nineteenth-century reforming ministries, as Redlich was aware, whilst contemporary accounts of the drafting process and of Cabinet control of the details of legislation show that by the time bills were introduced into Parliament the process of legislative ossification was well advanced. Lowell refers to the practice of legislation by reference and by delegated powers as 'having been carried very far' by the

---

[1] A. Lawrence Lowell, *The Government of England* (New York, 1908), 278.

[2] See Lowell, i. 317, where he remarks 'It was formerly maintained that the House could exercise a great deal of freedom in amending bills, without implying a loss of general confidence in the Cabinet', and cites Todd, *Parliamentary Government in England* (1869), ii. 370–2. Todd himself places the period of greatest legislative freedom for the House of Commons in the twenty years ending in 1850.

turn of the century, and is supported in this by Sir Courtney
Ilbert, the eminent Parliamentary Counsel to the Treasury,
whose book *Legislative Methods and Forms*, published in 1901,
marked an advanced stage in the development of the legislative
process in Britain. Practices of group consultation by the
government, whilst not so intensive as at the present day, were
common, following on the growing national organization of
interest groups in the later nineteenth century. But in particular
Mackintosh's view that legislative measures were extensively
remodelled during their Parliamentary passage is largely refuted
by Lowell, from whom Table III.1 of legislative amendments
carried against the government for each year from 1851 to 1906
is reproduced:

TABLE III.1

*Number of amendments to government bills (not including
the Estimates) carried against the government whips acting
as tellers in each year since 1850**

1851 . . . 9	1865 . . . 4	1879 . . . 1	1893 . . . 1
1852 . . . 2	1866 . . . 2	1880 . . . 0	1894 . . . 0
1853 . . . 6	1867 . . . 8	1881 . . . 0	1895 . . . 0
1854 . . . 7	1868 . . . 7	1882 . . . 1	1896 . . . 1
1855 . . . 5	1869 . . . 2	1883 . . . 3	1897 . . . 0
1856 . . . 7	1870 . . . 2	1884 . . . 3	1898 . . . 0
1857 . . . 4	1871 . . . 4	1885 . . . 4	1899 . . . 0
1858 . . . 2	1872 . . . 8	1886 . . . 2	1900 . . . 0
1859 . . . 1	1873 . . . 4	1887 . . . 1	1901 . . . 1
1860 . . . 4	1874 . . . 0	1888 . . . 1	1902 . . . 0
1861 . . . 6	1875 . . . 0	1889 . . . 0	1903 . . . 0
1862 . . . 6	1876 . . . 0	1890 . . . 0	1904 . . . 2
1863 . . . 4	1877 . . . 0	1891 . . . 1	1905 . . . 1
1864 . . . 2	1878 . . . 0	1892 . . . 0	1906 . . . 0

* See Lowell, op. cit., i. 317, Note 2.

There is a drop in the annual figures of successful amendments
carried over the period of fifty-odd years, and particularly after
the tightening of party organization in the 1870s, but none of
the totals, in relation to the volume of legislation in any one
year, is particularly significant. Only four cases of successful
amendments carried against the government occurred between

1897 and 1906. These figures do not tell the whole story, since many amendments would have been accepted without a defeat, but it is not a picture of an independent Parliament reshaping legislation in the teeth of Ministerial intransigence. Lowell makes the general point which emerges from these figures that without Ministerial consent Parliamentary amendment of legislation was not on the whole possible. The overwhelming majority of bills in the period covered by Lowell's figures were sent to Committee of the Whole House rather than to standing committee, and in the former party votes were the rule. In 1899, for example, 91 per cent of the divisions in Committee of the Whole House were on strict party lines, and figures for other years are comparable.[1] Lowell himself, after his detailed study of the late Victorian legislative process, comes to the surprisingly modern conclusion that 'to say that at present the cabinet legislates with the advice and consent of Parliament would hardly be an exaggeration'.

At the outset of the period covered by this essay, Cabinet legislative organization was casual in the extreme. Cabinet committees were occasionally used in the late Victorian period for the work of preparing bills. On the other hand, it was common practice for Ministers to tackle the drafting of clauses themselves, aided by draftsmen from the Office of Parliamentary Counsel to the Treasury, which was established in 1869. By 1892, according to Mackintosh, Liberal Cabinets had developed a definite system. At the opening meetings of the Cabinet in the autumn 'a list of measures was prepared and all the more intricate ones were handed over to Committees'.[2] This seems to have been as much a device to prevent Ministerial argument in full Cabinet as a functional way of relieving the burden of the Cabinet's work. Lord Morley in 1909 described the process: 'The Cabinet . . . settles the principles of the Bill, then refers it to a committee of that body; the committee thrashes out details in consultation with all the experts concerned and at command; the draft Bill comes to the Cabinet, and it is discussed both on

---

[1] See ibid., i. 323, Note 4.
[2] J. P. Mackintosh, *The British Cabinet* (London, 1962), p. 251.

the merits and in relation to Parliamentary forces and Parliamentary opinion.'[1] It is apparent that by the first decade of this century civil servants and Cabinet committees were used quite freely, although the machinery for operating below the level of the full Cabinet had not been completely developed. Before 1914 the Prime Minister and the full Cabinet still took far greater interest in, and were far more influential in preparing, the main heads of most bills of medium importance than is the case today, a situation which reflects the rather amateur and informal organization of pre-1914 Cabinets and the comparatively lighter load of administrative and legislative supervision which they were responsible for than that which is borne by modern Cabinets. The development after 1918 in Cabinet organization for the detailed preparation and formal approval of bills is in line with the general modern development of the Cabinet which is described by Mackintosh—an evolution from a governing institution to an appellate body, moderating and co-ordinating the claims of active Departments through powerful committees.

Similarly in the late Victorian period the House of Commons was reluctant to delegate legislative scrutiny to smaller bodies, and had to be pressed by government to differentiate its legislative structure. The pace of development of a legislative committee system was exceptionally slow, tentative, and cautious, and demonstrates the innate conservatism of the House of Commons at its most pronounced. Redlich made the theme of the nineteenth-century procedural changes in the House of Commons which he described in such detail the transformation of procedure into a political weapon in the hands of governments, and this is well illustrated by the development of standing committees. On the whole the initiators of change in Parliamentary legislative practice were successive governments, often with the collaboration of the Opposition front bench. Mediators of change were the Procedure Committees of the House which were usually set up at government instigation, and which responded to Ministerial pressures. The Chairmen's Panel also contributed to discussions of procedure, especially as this bore on the powers of standing committee chairmen. Back-bench opinion throughout most of the period covered by this essay was on the whole much more reluctant than front bench to recognize the need for

---

[1] Quoted ibid., pp. 251–2.

an extensive legislative committee system, and the attitude of back-benchers to this type of procedural change is worth noting. The practice of taking the committee stage of bills in Committee of the Whole House instead of in standing committee was long defended on the grounds that every M.P. has a right to consider a bill with special reference to his own constituents, and to move whatever changes he considered necessary in their interests. This basic attitude was continually complemented and reinforced by a strong conviction on the part of many M.P.s that the main forum in which governments should justify their activities and be subjected to political criticism was the plenary House, committees, whether standing or select, being regarded as devices which allow governments to escape legitimate political confrontation. Thus Balfour in 1907 criticized the new Liberal government's policy of sending the major controversial bills of that session to standing committee. The argument was in fact similar to the argument over 'bills of first-class constitutional importance' in the Parliament of 1945–50. Proposals to expedite legislation through the House in addition usually attracted criticism from M.P.s who, in the classic dictum of Lord Salisbury, equated more legislation with more taxation, or other undesirable results. In 1882 W. H. Smith objected to 'bill-spinning machines' and in 1907 Lord Robert Cecil and Sir William Anson exhorted the House to remember that it was not 'merely a legislative machine'. Lt.-Col. Lockwood in the same debate found support for the view that apparently 'the object of the government . . . is to produce as much legislation as possible in a given time out of the Parliamentary machine. . . . The government are applying the wrong remedy. The remedy is to produce less legislation but of a better sort.' This point of view has been expressed whenever the system of standing legislative committees has been extended; in 1919 Sir William Joynson-Hicks commented: 'After all, the House of Commons is not a mere machine for grinding out legislation.' Even in 1934, when changes in the legislative committee structure were initiated by a Conservative-dominated National government, and criticism was hence subdued, Winston Churchill could say: 'Parliament is not a mere apparatus for passing bills. A not less important function is preventing bad bills from passing. . . . It seems to me to be absolutely essential that people should not try to shape our procedure as if perfection would be attained when legislation was most easy.'[1] Repeatedly, reform of the legislative organization of the House has had to overcome the conviction that either the legislative potential of politics has been exhausted, or that the limits of the capacity of the House for legislative work has been reached. Thus Lowell, in 1908, remarked: 'There can be no doubt, however, that the legislative capacity of Parliament is limited, and the limit would appear to be well-nigh reached, unless private Members are to lose their remnant of time, or debate is to be still further restricted. . . .' He continues:

The limited capacity of Parliament to pass statutes is not felt as a pressing evil, because the period of great remedial legislation is over. The transition from the political and industrial conditions of the eighteenth century has been accomplished, and the consequent change in laws and institutions has been, in the main, effected. The demand for radical legislation is, therefore, comparatively small, and for the time at least the process of making law can afford to run slow.[2]

Opinion in the 1931 Select Committee on Procedure on Public Business was similarly practically unanimous that the House attempted too much in the field of legislation, and that the volume should be reduced. Baldwin himself warned the Committee of the danger of trying to pass too much rather than too little, and was echoed by Sir Eyres-Monsell, Winston Churchill, and Lloyd George.

Ironical though in retrospect such opinion becomes, it was against this background of reluctance to contemplate increases in the legislative burden of Parliament that the slow and piece-meal development of the legislative committee system of the Commons took place from 1907 onwards. Although in the period 1882 to 1907 the House had a rudimentary standing committee system, this first experiment was confused, both as to function

---

[1] These quotations can be multiplied. With a Labour government in office in 1945 proposing further streamlining of the standing legislative committee system, the Opposition was less restrained. At that time Churchill said: 'It would be a great mistake to think that all you have to do to improve the procedure of the House of Commons is to make it able to turn out the largest number of bills in the shortest amount of time. This is alright if you are working a sausage factory; it is not quite the same in regard to matters which affect the lives and happiness of vast numbers of people throughout the country.'

[2] Lowell, op. cit., i. 326.

and procedure, and by the latter date the House had no experience of using committees for the main legislative stage of
most bills, or of the problems of integrating committees into the
mainstream of the Commons' legislative organization. The result
was that a full legislative committee system, with adequate
powers to control its own business, took the next forty years to
evolve. This accomplishment owed nothing to any theory of
Parliamentary organization, but much to the exigencies of
politics.

The first standing committees date from 1882, when Gladstone introduced proposals, approved in temporary Standing
Orders, for two committees on bills. The rationale for this development came largely from Erskine May, whose support for an
enlarged committee structure of the House can be traced in
articles and evidence to Procedure Committees from 1848
onwards. As is common in the history of the development of
Commons' procedure, political exigency succeeded where argument had failed, and May's suggestions were taken up by
Gladstone as a possible means of bypassing Irish obstruction in
the plenary House. Prior to 1882 the time taken by the committee stage of bills in Committee of the Whole House had
increased substantially, and standing committees offered some
means of speeding up the legislative process. Two standing committees were set up, one to deal with bills 'relating to law and
courts of justice and legal procedure', and the other with bills
concerning 'trade, shipping and manufactures'. Each of the
specialized committees consisted of between 60 and 80 M.P.s as
a central core, to which up to 15 additional Members were
added in respect of a particular bill. Members were nominated
by the Committee of Selection, which also nominated a Chairmen's Panel of between four and six M.P.s who acted as chairmen of the committees. The temporary Standing Orders were
operative until the end of the 1883 Session. They were renewed
for the following Session, but only the Committee on Law met
and in 1885 the Standing Orders lapsed completely. A Procedure Committee of 1886 foreshadowed later developments by
recommending a division of the House for legislative purposes
into four standing committees, to which all bills would be
referred unless the House otherwise ordered. The proposal was
too advanced to secure acceptance at the time; when in 1888

standing committees were resuscitated after more obstruction in the previous Session, a return was made to the system which had been established six years earlier.

It is important not to over-emphasize the change in the legislative procedure of the Commons that the early standing committees made. Lowell gives statistics of the limited use made of the committees between 1888 and 1907, when the structure was revised. On average only one in seven public bills were referred to them in this period. In the sixteen years from 1888 to 1903, 1,080 public bills were enacted, of which only 109 passed through the hands of the committees. During the eight years from 1896 to 1903, this was the case with 73 bills out of 446. Statistics also show that a bill had a better chance of being enacted if it went to standing committee rather than to Committee of the Whole, but this was largely due to the non-contentious nature of the bills referred, at least until the turn of the century. Lowell remarks about the early standing committees:

> The most important government bills, and especially those of a highly controversial nature, are not referred to committee at all. . . . To select committees a few public bills are referred, and those as a rule are certainly not of a controversial character. The only difficulty arises in the case of the standing committees. When he first proposed these in 1882, Mr. Gladstone said that they were not intended to consider measures of a partisan character; and it has been generally recognised ever since that very contentious bills ought not to be referred to them.[1]

Lowell mentions the debate on a 1904 bill to restrict alien immigration, which went to the Standing Committee on Law. No Member disagreed with the general principle concerning the use of standing committees; the only difference was over the test of contentiousness. In the 1900 Parliament, however, it seems that as a result of increasing pressure on the House a practice of referring more contentious legislation to the committees began, which in 1905 precipitated some criticism from the Chairmen's Panel. Stating that in their origin the committees had been intended to deal only with such classes of legislation as consolidation, improvement of various branches of statute law, etc., the Panel's Report went on to say that during the previous few years it had become the custom to refer to them

[1] Lowell, op. cit., i. 318–19.

'a different class of bill for which their procedure was not intended or adapted'. They referred to instances of political obstruction in committee, and concluded that in the event of such bills still being referred to committee the chairmen should have the same power of closure as that enjoyed by the chairman of the Committee of the Whole House, and suggested the consideration of rules restricting the duration of speeches and limiting their number.[1]

Largely as a result of the Report from the Chairmen's Panel and the confused situation which has given rise to it the government appointed a further Procedure Committee in 1906. In its Second Report the Committee largely followed the proposals of the 1886 Hartington Committee, and suggested that all bills except Finance, Consolidated Fund, and Appropriation bills, and bills for confirming provisional orders should be sent to a standing committee after second reading unless the House otherwise ordered. They differed from the 1886 Committee in recommending that the number of legislative committees of the existing type should be increased to not less than four (instead of dividing the whole House into four committees). This increase in number was to be accompanied by abandoning the system of functional specification for the committees in favour of designating them simply alphabetically, since no systematic referral of bills according to subject matter seems to have been followed with the Committees on Law and Trade. The quorum was to be increased, and the allocation of a bill to a particular committee was to be in the hands of the Speaker, with the provision that government bills were to have precedence on all but one of the committees. At the same time the 1906 Committee tackled the problem of committee procedure, recommending that in order to deal with the difficulties imposed by sending controversial legislation to standing committee the chairman should have power to deal with irrelevance and repetition and to accept motions for the closure. Further, following the Report of the Chairmen's Panel, it was proposed to make the procedural position clear by ordering that proceedings in standing committee were to be analogous to proceedings in a Committee of the Whole House, instead of as in a select committee.

[1] See the 1908 edition of Redlich, Supplementary Chapter by Sir Courtney Ilbert, iii. 211.

The proposals of the 1906 Procedure Committee were built on by the government, who brought them to the House of Commons in 1907. Virtually all the Committee's recommendations were adopted by the government, apart from the increased quorum and the broad stipulation about standing committee procedure.[1] They were approved by the House only after four days of debate and the use of a guillotine resolution, the main amendments offered to them by back-benchers aiming at excluding various classes of bills from those which were to go to standing committee. The government resisted all amendments, and adhered to the broad principle recommended by the Committees of 1886 and 1906 that except for finance and provisional order bills all bills should go to standing committee unless the House otherwise ordered. This was a considerable reversal of existing practice, which was wrung by the government out of a reluctant House with some difficulty.

It is obvious that the substitution of 'contracting out' for 'contracting in' was of major importance, and if it had been carried to the extreme would have meant the removal of the committee stage of nearly all bills from the floor of the House to standing committee. Government spokesmen were forced to explain that this was not their intention, and that, in the words of Campbell-Bannerman, 'the Government have no desire to send the great measures of the session, which almost necessarily are controversial, to Grand Committee'. In the period to 1914 governments retreated somewhat from this principle. In 1908 the Coal Mines (Eight Hours) (No. 2) Bill was sent to standing committee, and in 1911 the first great social measure, Part II of the National Insurance Bill, was also considered in standing committee, a landmark in its development. Yet the general

---

[1] As a result, until 1940, the Standing Orders explicitly provided that procedure in standing committees 'shall be the same as in a select committee unless the House shall otherwise order'. Standing committee practice, however, left these provisions well behind, and in general from their inception the committees assimilated their procedure to that of Committee of the Whole House. This was largely done by the use of the chairman's discretion, but the gap between theory and practice caused constant difficulty. For a full discussion see G. M. Higgins, 'The origin and development of the Standing Committees of the House of Commons, with special reference to their procedure, 1882–1951' (Unpublished B.Litt. thesis, University of Oxford, 1953).

principle strongly influenced the policy of successive governments, and produced a more sparing use of the new system than
otherwise might have been the case. In the period from 1907 to
1914 the number of government bills sent upstairs only roughly
doubled from its low pre-1907 figure.[1] The main beneficiary of
the new committee system was private Members' legislation, the
number of private Members' bills dealt with by standing committee being multiplied three or four times in the period to
1914.

It might appear that the 1907 change whereby standing committees were designated alphabetically represented the introduction of non-specialized committees for legislation, although
exactly the same provisions as before, that the Committee of
Selection in nominating the members of standing committees
'shall have regard to the classes of bills committed to such committees, to the composition of the House, and to the qualifications of the members selected' were retained in the new Standing
Orders. But it would appear that practice overruled the injunc-
tion concerning particular classes of bills, and in the practical
working of the system the change to non-specialization seems to
have occurred before 1907. One of the new standing committees,
however, was specialized both in subject matter and personnel—
the Scottish Standing Committee. First set up in 1894, after
Gladstone's retirement, it was renewed for the 1895 Session, but
with the return of the Conservatives to power it was allowed to
lapse. In 1907 it was revived as one of the four standing committees approved. Pressure for its re-establishment began as soon
as the Liberals returned to power, and Campbell-Bannerman
took the opportunity afforded by the comprehensive reforms of
1907 to re-establish the Committee. Containing all Members
sitting for Scottish constituencies, together with fifteen other
M.P.s, it was empowered to consider all public bills relating to
Scotland, a rather wider competence than its predecessors had

---

[1] See Higgins, op. cit., pp. 70–3. The number of government bills dealt
with in standing committee for each year from 1900 to 1914 was as follows:

1900 . . . 8	1905 . . . 0	1910 . . . 3
1901 . . . 5	1906 . . . 15	1911 . . . 12
1902 . . . 3	1907 . . . 18	1912 . . . 7
1903 . . . 8	1908 . . . 15	1913 . . . 10
1904 . . . 5	1909 . . . 10	1914 . . . 13

possessed. It was to prove a permanent part of the legislative machinery of the Commons.

Between 1906 and 1946 no Procedure Committee dealt exclusively with legislative procedures in the House, and no exhaustive examination of the Parliamentary legislative process was undertaken. In a particularly unheroic period in procedural matters most changes, either in Standing Orders or in practice, were made quietly and pragmatically. In substance the cumulative effects of the inter-war changes was not great—they extended the logic of the legislative structure which was devised in 1907 and produced a committee system with the minimum competence necessary to deal with the legislative burden of the period. Progressive changes were made in both the structure and procedure of standing committees, which nevertheless by 1939 still left a number of problems unsolved.

Changes in structure affected the number of committees, their size, and their patterns of membership. Procedural changes revolved largely around the powers of committee chairmen. So far as structure was concerned, this period saw an increase in their number, a progressive diminution in their size, and a pattern of membership which more closely reflected the political realities of the Parliamentary legislative process. As the system developed, it was more closely absorbed into the mainstream of Parliamentary political life, and subjected in large degree to the same pressures which affected the floor of the House. In particular, the continuous diminution in the size of standing committees throughout the period, which was reflected also in a smaller quorum, is only partly explicable in terms of securing adequate attendance by M.P.s of more numerous committees—it also reflected a change in attitude whereby M.P.s accustomed themselves to relegating detailed scrutiny of bills to smaller and comparatively unrepresentative bodies.

In 1913–14 a Procedure Committee was established specifically to deal with private Members' use of the time of the House. Owing to the outbreak of the First World War, the Committee only issued a chairman's draft report, which suggested, *inter alia*, the extension of the use of standing committees. It recommended that the committees should not necessarily be limited in number to four, and that their size should be reduced possibly to between 40 and 50 M.P.s with 10 Members added for each bill. The quorum should approximate to one quarter of the whole committee. It was also proposed that committees should be able to sit while the House was sitting without a specific order permitting them to do so. These concepts, and others relating to procedure, formed the basis of changes introduced by the government in 1919, to accelerate the post-war reconstruction legislation which had been promised by all parties in the 1918 election. In 1919 the Standing Orders referring to the committee system were thoroughly overhauled. Six standing committees were provided for instead of four. The size of the nuclear membership was reduced from between 60 and 80 members to between 40 and 60; the number of M.P.s added for each bill was more closely specified at from 10 to 15. This provision applied also to the Scottish Grand Committee. Committees were also empowered generally to sit 'during the sitting and notwithstanding any adjournment' of the House, on any day on which the House sat. The size of the Chairmen's Panel was similarly increased from between four and eight to between eight and twelve. This trend was carried even further by an amendment moved by a private Member and adopted by the government which became the curious Standing Order 49A, which provided that the House might adjourn to facilitate the work of standing committees. A short-lived but interesting change provided that 'other business' as well as legislation might be referred to the committees, the other business in question being the consideration of the annual financial Estimates. This experiment ran into difficulties—despite their theoretical select committee procedure standing committees proved inappropriate bodies for detailed expenditure investigation when it was decided that they had no power to call witnesses. Towards the end of 1919 the Chairmen's Panel submitted a private report to both government and House in which they maintained that the taking of the Estimates in standing committee had been a failure, and pointing out that if the practice was not repeated it would be possible to reduce the number of standing committees from six to five. In addition they proposed that the nucleus should be reduced again to between 30 and 50 members, with not less than 10 nor more than 35 members added in respect of any bill. It was hoped that this change, by increasing the proportion of added members and reducing the number of the permanent nucleus, would produce better attendance and improve the quality of committee work.

The Select Committee on Estimates was re-established in 1921, and the practice of sending Estimates to standing committee was discontinued. Apart from this, the government took no action on the Panel's Report. Five years later the Panel submitted another special report to the House, reiterating its earlier recommendations. As a result, in 1926 Standing Orders were amended to reduce the number of standing committees from six to five, and to re-order their membership along the lines previously recommended.

No further changes in Standing Orders relating to standing committee structure were made until 1933 and 1934, after the Select Committee on Procedure on Public Business had sat. The changes on the whole were relatively minor. Standing Order 49A was repealed without ever having been used; it would seem that no government wished to admit that the House was so under-occupied, although a similar Order was resuscitated in 1945. The main changes were those which recognized that for some considerable time standing committees had been non-specialized and overwhelmingly political bodies, subjecting bills to much the same sort of scrutiny as they would have received from the plenary House. As has been mentioned earlier, when the House carried out its reformation of the standing committee system in 1907, it apparently considered that each committee would continue to specialize by subject, as had theoretically been the case since 1883; the relevant Standing Order providing that in nominating members for committees the Committee of Selection would *inter alia* have regard to 'the classes of bills' which were sent to each committee, and to the qualifications for dealing with that kind of bill possessed by the members nominated. These were the criteria which were repealed in 1933; in practice they had been disregarded since 1907, except in the case of the Scottish Committee. Under the changed Order of 1933, the nucleus of a committee was to consist of members chosen with regard to the composition of the House only, with strict regard to the balance of party strength. The added members for each committee were to be chosen for their qualifications, for the specialized knowledge or interest they could bring to committee debate on a particular bill. Only in 1933 did the House retreat from the theoretical possibility of having all its standing committees specializing in bills of a particular subject-matter. The retention of dual selection at this time seems difficult to justify; the ease with which members could be made to join or leave the nucleus meant that specialists could be included in it as readily as in the other part. Although the Committee of Selection after 1933 was instructed to have regard to the composition of the House when nominating the nucleus, in fact it always did so when nominating the added members as well. It was only however in 1960 that the logic of this situation prevailed, and two-part membership was abolished.

The halting and cautious development of the structure of the standing committee system from 1907 to 1939 was mirrored in the development of its procedure. This largely centred around the powers of committee chairmen to control debate, and to determine the consideration of selected amendments. As early as 1905 the Chairmen's Panel recommended that in addition to the power of ending debate already possessed by committee chairmen, the principle of closure should become a part of committee procedure. The Procedure Committee of 1906 similarly recommended that in order to deal with difficulties imposed by controversial legislation the chairmen of standing committees should have power to deal with irrelevance and repetition and to accept motions for the closure. These proposals were accepted in 1907, when Standing Orders were amended. Otherwise progress was slow. In 1911, when Part II of the National Insurance Bill was referred to standing committee, the power to select amendments for debate was granted to its chairman, although it was emphasized at the time that this step was not to be regarded as a precedent. Further proposals, of a minor nature, were made by the 1914 Procedure Committee, but the problem of the inadequacy of the chairman's powers, particularly in regard to the selection of amendments, persisted beyond the 1919 changes and the Report of the 1931 Procedure Committee. It was only resolved in 1934.

The 1930s, then, ended with a Commons' legislative committee structure which had only lately developed as a significant part of the Parliamentary legislative process. Although the 1907 Standing Orders had provided for most bills to be automatically sent to standing committee, the practice in the inter-war years had still been to retain many major measures on the floor of the House for their committee stage, and in terms of quantity the bulk of legislation was also dealt with in Committee of the Whole. During most of the period of the Second World War standing committees were not appointed. The diminished share of legislation carried out by statute as opposed to order during the war and the fact that the House took to meeting in the morning explain the reduced need and opportunity for standing committees to meet. In the 1944–5 Session three committees were set up, including the Scottish Standing Committee, to deal with aspects of a legislative programme. These were appointed according to the rules and understandings of the pre-war period.

The Procedure Committees which dealt with the Parliamentary legislative process from the turn of the century were largely supportive in character, developing a system which was as much a reflection of government interest in the Commons' legislative procedure as with the rights and opportunities of back-benchers. The most clear-cut example of a supportive procedure inquiry came in 1945–6, when an investigation into the organization and working of standing committees followed massive government prompting. In many ways the intensification of Commons' procedures which were brought about in the immediate post-war period were the Parliamentary reflection of a systematic gearing up of the legislative process in general, undertaken by the government to deal with a large programme of economic and social reform. Before 1939 the rather casual and reluctant approach of the Commons to legislative committee work had matched the fairly loose executive organization for the planning and production of a legislative programme. Between the wars rudimentary standing Cabinet arrangements were made to advise on bills. This function fell to a Home Affairs Committee of the Cabinet, which was set up in 1918 to prevent the small War Cabinet from being swamped by domestic business during the last year of the war. It considered all items of domestic legislation, both in their policy implications and their form and drafting. Some policy matters, when important or particularly controversial, still went to the full Cabinet. The Home Affairs

Committee (its name was changed after the formation of the War Cabinet in 1940 to the Home Policy Committee) also planned and kept under review the government's legislative programme for a Parliamentary Session. In 1940 the functions of supervising form and policy were separated, a distinct Legislative Committee of the Cabinet being devised for the task of scrutinizing the detailed form of bills, and to plan a legislative programme.

After the war the Cabinet legislative organization was still further differentiated. In 1945 the new Labour government, with a large and pressing legislative programme to achieve, took the legislative arrangements of the Cabinet in hand and remodelled the machinery of legislative planning.[1] The functions of the Legislation Committee were split, and the important task of planning the content and strategy of the legislative programme for both individual Parliamentary Sessions and the full five years of a Parliament was given to a new and small Future Legislation Committee, with the Leader of the House of Commons as chairman of both the new Committee and the Legislation Committee. This legislative structure seems to have lasted in essence, although later governments do not appear to have retained such a rigid distinction between the Legislation Committee and the Future Legislation Committee. With the establishment of this structure the planning and introduction of legislation fell into a definite routine. The normal practice was for a Department which had obtained the approval of the Future Legislation Committee for a particular bill to work out the heads of the bill itself, as an instruction to Parliamentary Counsel. They would then be circulated to other Departments for observations, and to an appropriate policy committee of the Cabinet. At some stage in the preparatory process a draft of the bill was submitted to the Legislation Committee of the Cabinet, a technical agency with the task of advising on the form, wording, and acceptability of a particular measure. It was chaired by the Leader of the Commons, and included among its members the Lord Chancellor, the Law Officers of the Crown, the Chief Whip, and a limited number of Departmental Ministers. The Ministers whose bills came up for discussion were also

[1] See Lord Morrison of Lambeth, *Government and Parliament*, 3rd edn. (London, 1964), Chapter XI, 'The Legislative Programme'.

present, as were Parliamentary Counsel. The Committee thus contained elements which could examine a bill from two points of view—the legal, and the political and strategical. Before publication in final form, some bills might go to the full Cabinet, or again to the appropriate policy committee for final scrutiny. During the heavy legislative Sessions of the 1945–50 Parliament, the Legislation Committee was hardworked. Morrison shows how many drafts of the important bills introduced during this Parliament were necessary: Coal Industry Nationalization Bill, 13; Transport Bill, 21; Electricity Bill, 15; Iron and Steel Bill, 12; Town and Country Planning Bill, 23.

With such a complex and careful structure of legislative planning, it is not surprising that some acceleration of Parliamentary legislative procedure was similarly sought, in a reshaping of the operations and a distinct upgrading in importance of the legislative committee structure. In line with the generally empirical development of this system which has been traced so far, the main changes were in practice rather than in theory, attempting to effect, in Herbert Morrison's words 'a change of attitude . . .'

It was necessary [Morrison recalled] for the (standing) committees to accept the view that they must do something like a real day's work when required instead of just a few hours. It was necessary to develop the doctrine and practice that the House should split up into committees to carry through Bills, which would otherwise have occupied a full House with a smaller output. Unless Standing Committees took this view any attempt to develop them into useful parts of the legislative process . . . would break down.[1]

The point of departure for the government was a report to the Cabinet by a committee of the wartime coalition government, which had considered Parliamentary procedure towards the end of hostilities. This was presented to the Select Committee on Procedure which was set up in August 1945, almost as soon as the Labour government took office. The personnel of the Committee was carefully chosen, including Gaitskell and Clement Davies, the leader of the Liberals. The Opposition did not oppose the appointment of the Procedure Committee, although they had reservations about the government's intentions. There seems to have been a general feeling amongst Conservatives that, once in power, the Labour government would proceed by means

[1] Morrison, op. cit., p. 223.

of wide enabling Acts, leaving the great mass of legislative detail to be filled in by statutory order. As *The Economist* in August 1945 observed, 'There has been so much loose talk among Socialists in the past about their intention of proceeding by enabling Acts and cutting out discussion that any Tory could be forgiven for thinking, as Mr. Churchill manifestly thinks, that a major assault on the liberties of the people is in prospect.'[1]

The Committee's main term of reference was 'to consider schemes for the acceleration of proceedings on Public Bills', and the urgency was seen to be such that it was empowered to sit during the summer recess. It produced its Report in just over a month, and this was concerned almost wholly with the working of standing committees. It was based to a considerable extent on the government memorandum mentioned above, which, primarily, was designed to secure the committal of more bills to standing committee. In effect it was seeking to have the 'great measures of the Session' so dealt with, the major change it proposed from pre-war practice. This would require no change in the Standing Orders, only a change in convention. The exception was that 'bills of first-class constitutional importance' should be retained on the floor of the House. What exactly was covered by this phrase was not explained, and its definition was subsequently to provide considerable scope for controversy. The main objection to such a major change in practice, as was put repeatedly in evidence to the Procedure Committee, was the probable need for a longer Report stage for major bills dealt with in standing committee instead of on the floor of the House. The reason for this, as the Speaker indicated to the Committee in his evidence, was the need to safeguard the right of all Members, at some stage, to influence the details as well as the principle of legislation. It was suggested that longer Report stages would mean that other changes would save less time on the floor of the House than the government memorandum seemed to suggest. Despite these difficulties, the Procedure Committee in its Report endorsed the main proposal concerning greater use of standing committees, feeling that the change 'would result in an acceleration of Public Business, despite the fact that some increase in time may be required on Second Reading and at the Report Stage'.

[1] *The Economist*, 25 Aug. 1945.

Not surprisingly, since it had instigated them, the government accepted the majority of the Procedure Committee's First Report. In November 1945 the necessary changes in Standing Orders were introduced as Sessional Orders rather than as fully revised Standing Orders. This gave the innovations a slightly lesser degree of permanence, which accorded with the Procedure Committee's recommendation that the proposals should be accepted initially on an experimental basis. Further proposals of the Procedure Committee were designed to enable standing committees to deal with the greater legislative burden that was envisaged for them. The number of standing committees was to be increased, and as a corollary their size was to be reduced. It was proposed that instead of the existing five committees, which included the Scottish Committee, as many standing committees should be appointed as was necessary, with a reduction in size of the nucleus of permanent members rather than in the quota of added personnel. The Committee was made well aware by the Clerk of the House of the difficulties—of accommodation, committee staff, and personnel—which would attend such a change, and also considered other disadvantages, such as that on small committees it is difficult to maintain a government majority, that small committees are comparatively unrepresentative of Commons' opinion, and that the position of small parties is seriously weakened. After much argument the Procedure Committee agreed to a reduction in size of an unspecified number of committees, and that the reduction should affect the committee nucleus. The figures suggested were a nucleus of 20, with up to 30 added members, with a quorum reduced to 15. These figures were accepted by the government and embodied in Standing Orders. Objections made in the debate on the proposals to the comparatively small size of the new standing committees were overridden.

The third proposal in the government memorandum considered by the Procedure Committee was that standing committees should sit longer and more often than pre-1939. The suggestion that the length of committee sittings should be increased from two to two-and-a-half hours met with little opposition, but a linked proposal that standing committees should meet on an additional day each week raised objections, largely because of the burden it would put on Ministers. Oddly enough, to deal with this problem the Procedure Committee revived the discredited notion that the House should adjourn on one or more days in the week to let standing committees sit in the afternoon and evening. Such a provision had been embodied in Standing Orders in 1919, but had been repealed, unused, in 1933. Nevertheless, this proposal was included in the Procedure Committee's Report, together with an extension of the length of standing committee meetings and a proposal that, abnormally, standing committees should be empowered to sit three mornings a week. All these changes were accepted by the government and embodied in the new Sessional Orders. The Opposition made little objection.

Of all the changes in committee organization and practice considered by the 1945 Procedure Committee the scheme for applying the guillotine to standing committee proceedings proved the most contentious. This, however, was no more than a natural corollary of the proposal to send major bills to standing committee, and ultimately its logic was accepted. It was realized that the usual method of maintaining a time-table by voluntary agreement between the parties would not work in the case of ultra-contentious legislation. After canvassing a number of alternative ways of administering Allocation of Time Orders, the Committee came down in favour of a business sub-committee of the standing committee, consisting of the chairman and seven other members chosen by the Speaker. In this way the detailed allocation of time to the stages of a bill would be carried out by M.P.s who were familiar with its details. The provisions which they made would need to be approved only by the parent committee, and would not make demands on the time of the House. This procedure was in essence accepted by the government, and amendments put down by back-benchers were resisted.

The sum total of the changes in committee structure and procedure in the immediate post-war period was fairly modest in proportions, designed mainly as improvements in the existing system and not as an attempt fundamentally to redraw it. In this sense they met the immediate wishes of the government even if not those of some radically-minded back-benchers and clerks of the House. An opportunity to discuss more fundamental proposals was taken by the Procedure Committee using as its basis of discussion a memorandum put in by Sir Gilbert Campion, the

Clerk of the House. Campion's proposals were not restricted to legislative procedures, but were a comprehensive and inter-related scheme covering most aspects of public business. Their essence was a specialized committee structure which would com-prehend legislative, financial, and administrative scrutiny, rationalizing the *ad hoc* committee arrangements of the House in a comprehensive and logical scheme. Its reception was mixed, and the main proposals proved unacceptable, both to the Pro-cedure Committee and the government—not surprisingly, since a taste for comprehensive reform on theoretical lines has never been a noticeable characteristic of the House of Commons. The entire Third Report of the Procedure Committee of 1945–6, although it led to nothing, is best seen as a reaction against the excessive domination by the government of the Procedure Com-mittee's earlier deliberations.

After the 1945–6 reforms, bills were referred to standing com-mittee, any one of which, pre-1939, might have been retained on the floor of the House, with the government quite satisfied to get it through as the major measure of the Session. To take the outstanding post-1945 Session in terms of legislative output, in 1946–7 the Transport, Town and Country Planning, Electricity and Agriculture Bills were all sent to standing committee. As Higgins remarks, of these the first three, and probably the last, depending on the Parliamentary situation, would have been dealt with in Committee of the Whole before 1939, and the government would have been happy to get one or at the most two through by the end of a Session.[1] Other important bills con-sidered in standing committee and passed in the 1946–7 Session included the Companies Bill, the Fire Service Bill, the Civic Restaurants Bill, and the Cotton (Centralised Buying) Bill, all of them too controversial to have been sent upstairs in earlier periods. In addition the Town and Country Planning (Scotland) Bill and the National Health Service (Scotland) Bill were con-sidered in the Scottish Grand Committee. This output would have been quite creditable for a full five-year Parliament before 1939. It is in the size, complexity, and controversiality of the bills considered by post-war standing committees that the main difference with the pre-1939 situation lies, rather than in the actual number of bills sent upstairs. Figures show an increase in

[1] See Higgins, op. cit., p. 98.

the number of bills referred to standing committee by the Labour government, but as a proportion of the bills considered in any one Session the rise in numbers is not phenomenal.[1]

Given the political controversy surrounding Labour's use of standing committees in the 1945–50 Parliament, and Conservative suspicion that they were used to steam-roller major controversial measures through the House, some diminution in their use might have been expected when the Conservatives returned to office in 1951. An analysis of the period from 1945 to 1959, covering four Parliaments, shows that there was no marked change in the use of standing committees, especially in the practice regarding the 'major measures' of a Session. Despite a comment by Jennings to the effect that 'the practice, since 1951, under Conservative governments, has been to refer all major bills to a Committee of the Whole House',[2] the change does not appear to have been as striking as one might have expected. If one takes major bills to be those attracting the longest second reading debates in each Session, then the difference as between, say, 1945–50 and 1955–9 is almost non-existent. Nor is there much difference in the proportion of government bills sent to standing committee in any one Session. Between 1945 and 1950 an average of just over 29 per cent of government bills were dealt with in standing committee in each Session, whereas for the period 1955–9 the figure declines to just over 28 per cent.[3] It would seem that Conservative governments found the reforms of 1945–6 as convenient as did their Labour counterparts.

Nor was there much difference in the use of Allocation of Time Orders to restrict and focus debate in committee. Conservative administrations in the 1950s used the guillotine more

---

[1] The number of government bills dealt with each Session in standing committee from 1930–1 to 1950–1 are as follows. Obviously there were special circumstances operating in 1931–2, 1944–5, and in 1950 and 1950–1.

1930–1 ... 18	1934–5 ... 13	1938–9 ... 16	1947–8 ... 21
1931–2 ... 9	1935–6 ... 11	1944–5 ... 7	1948–9 ... 28
1932–3 ... 14	1936–7 ... 15	1945–6 ... 27	1950 ... 3
1933–4 ... 16	1937–8 ... 12	1946–7 ... 15	1950–1 ... 9

[2] Sir Ivor Jennings, *Parliament*, 2nd edn. (1957), p. 270.

[3] See R. L. Borthwick, 'The Standing Committees of the House of Commons: A Study of Membership, Procedure and Working between 1945 and 1959' (Unpublished Ph.D. thesis, University of Nottingham, 1967), pp. 95–8.

liberally than the 1945–50 Labour government, who only applied it to three bills.[1] Nevertheless the guillotine was one evidence of the increasing institutionalization of standing committees in this period. The constant change in practice regarding controversial legislation and the standing committees was also mirrored in the internal discipline of the committees, which largely centred around the practice of whipping. Whipping occasionally was not unknown in the early standing committees after 1882, but largely to secure attendance and not to obtain members' votes. In fact the freedom from party discipline in the early committees was regarded as a virtue, as fostering a spirit of impartial consideration of legislation, a less formal and more purposive procedure and debate on the merits of the case. On the other hand, freedom from party discipline could only last so long as the bills referred to standing committee were not party-controversial, and if it were not important to the government how a point was decided. After 1902, however, when more controversial legislation was sent to standing committee, there was at first no increase in whipping in committee, the government usually using the Report stage to secure reversal of a committee decision unfavourable to it. Practice in the inter-war period seems to have been confused and haphazard. Whipping in committee was the exception rather than the rule, and it would seem that governments did not make as much use of standing committees as they could have done because they had better control of the floor of the House than of the committees upstairs.[2] Evidence to the Select Committee on Procedure on Public Business of 1930–1 implied that it was extremely rare for a Whip to attend a standing committee (except in the case of the Scottish Grand Committee, where the Scottish Whip, sitting for a Scottish constituency, was automatically a member of the committee). Higgins has investigated the period 1931–9, and concludes that the arrangements made for whipping in committees in these years were haphazard and followed no discernible

---

[1] These were the Transport Bill and Town and Country Planning Bill in Session 1946–7; and the Iron and Steel Bill in Session 1948–9. For a full discussion of the post-war use of the guillotine see John Palmer, 'Allocation of Time: The Guillotine and Voluntary Timetabling, *Parliamentary Affairs*, Summer 1970, Vol. xxiii No. 3.

[2] See Jennings, op. cit., p. 275.

pattern. The general absence of Whips on committees in this period might have been connected with the size of the government majority in the 1930s, but there can be no explanation for the decisions which were taken. As Higgins points out, it was not necessarily the most important bills of the Session which were whipped during their committee stage—in the 1931-2 Session, for example, the Town and Country Planning Bill was not whipped. In Session 1932-3 the unimportant Sea Fish Industry Bill was whipped whilst the Road and Rail Traffic Bill and the Agriculture Marketing Bill were not. After 1935 some important bills tended to attract Whips at the committee stage, but on the whole in this period practice was not uniform.

The main change came after 1945, with the gearing up of the legislative process which involved a more ambitious use of standing committees. It was confidently predicted that well-whipped majorities would steam-roller legislation through the committee stage, but for the first two Sessions whipping arrangements in committee were by no means perfect. It took some time for the Whips' Office to get properly organized, and until 1947, as Higgins remarks, 'Whips seem to have been included in the main body of the committee or among the added members haphazardly.'[1]

Occasionally the Minister's Parliamentary Private Secretary was put on to act as unofficial whip, but in some cases when a Whip was omitted so was the P.P.S. In the 1946-7 Session, two of Labour's key bills, the Agriculture and Electricity Bills, were not whipped in committee, and in each case the task fell to the P.P.S. After 1947, however, as Higgins remarks, 'the spectacle is one of machine-like efficiency, every government bill of the following four sessions having a Whip on the committee considering it'. Similar arrangements were made by the Conservative government after 1951, and the procedure is now standard.

Whether the presence of Whips on standing committees has made much difference to their proceedings is open to question. The effect of whipping on attendance of government supporters is difficult to assess. Adjournments for lack of a quorum are in any case fairly rare on government bills, and were almost equally rare in the pre-war period. The post-1945 Labour government

---

[1] See Higgins, op. cit., pp. 124-5.

was occasionally defeated in committee despite the presence of the Whip. But whilst revolts occasionally took place 'the massed battalions were there when required', and standing committee is now too integral a part of the legislative process for governments not to take all precautions against defeat. There is plenty of evidence that whipping has helped on numerous occasions to maintain the time-table on a bill.

Changes since 1946 in the legislative procedures of the House have been relatively minor, but interesting in their implications, especially since in this period they have rested in part on two major investigations by the Procedure Committee of the legislative process in Parliament. In 1951 the size of standing committees was slightly reduced, to safeguard the position of a government with only a small overall majority. Not much then happened for almost a decade. In 1956 a Select Committee on Procedure was set up, and re-appointed in the following Session. Slight reductions in the number of members required for a quorum and for the closure resulted, largely on the basis of government prompting. Changes in the composition of the Scottish Standing Committee were also made at this time. In 1958 a further Procedure Committee was established, on a private Member's motion, with wide terms of reference. The motive behind the setting up of the Committee was a re-examination of Sir Gilbert Campion's comprehensive scheme of reform of 1946, and his successor as Clerk of the House, Sir Edward Fellowes, produced similarly wide-ranging proposals for the Committee's consideration. As in 1946, these elicited little enthusiasm; in their Report the Procedure Committee accepted the need for a further reduction in the size of standing committees, particularly those dealing with minor bills; more importantly, they proposed a change, long overdue, in the method of appointing legislative committees—the distinction between nucleus and added members should be abolished. The implications of this move are dealt with below. Later developments in procedure were canvassed by the Committee at this time, in particular the taking of the Report stage of bills in standing committee, and the removal of the Finance Bill, or sections of it, from the floor of the House to committee. In the event the Report stage of all bills continued for the time being to be taken on the floor; some experimentation with the Finance Bill was agreed to by the government, but later dropped. In the government's final statement only the point relating to the membership of standing committees was adhered to; the size of committees was enabled to vary between 20 and 50 members, and the numbers for the quorum and closure were brought into line at a third of the membership.

It cannot be said that there was any marked change in the use of standing committees between 1945 and 1959. All the changes which were made concerned points of detail; wide-ranging schemes of reform were not well received, and the pragmatic development of the Commons' legislative system continued. After 1945, as has been noted, the use of standing committees for the committee stage of bills increased greatly, and with the growth of confidence in this procedure the House has been more and more ready to entrust committee proceedings to a small number of M.P.s. The minimum size of a standing committee was reduced in 1968 to sixteen, which (with a quorum of one third) allows some legislation to be examined in detail with only five M.P.s and the committee chairman present. An extra Scottish Standing Committee has been provided for, and more than one chairman can now be appointed to a standing committee for more demanding bills. A major change, brought about in 1968, has been the amendment of Standing Orders to allow the Finance Bill and other bills imposing taxes to be taken in standing committee of the maximum size of fifty. After having been canvassed in the 1950s, the use of standing committees for the Report stage of small bills has also been introduced. It had long been resisted on the grounds that the House as a whole should have an opportunity to review the work of a committee on a bill; in 1967 Report committees were introduced for small bills whose second reading had also been taken in committee. Safeguards exist against the indiscriminate use of this procedure —objections by twenty Members are sufficient to block the reference to committee. Report committees have not been much used, since bills regarded as suitable for this treatment take little time on Report in any case. A further attempt to save time on the floor of the House has been made by providing that no debate, but a vote if demanded, should be permitted on the Third Reading of a bill. A motion supported by only six

Members, however, is sufficient to secure a debate, and this procedure has been much used recently.

Many of these comparatively minor reforms were canvassed in the course of the two procedure inquiries into legislation to be held in the last ten years. These were a comparatively modest inquiry into 'Public Bill Procedure, etc.'[1] in the 1966–7 Session, and a more fundamental and wide-ranging investigation of 'The Process of Legislation'[2] in Session 1970–1, an inquiry designed to match in depth the well-received First Report of the Procedure Committee of 1968–9 on the control of public expenditure and administration. The 1966–7 inquiry saw only a few witnesses, and in general its Report was conservative, limiting itself to minor recommendations designed to save the time of the House. Increased use of Second Reading committees, the taking of some Report stages and some statutory instruments in committee, and the restriction of debate on Third Reading were all recommended, and subsequently largely accepted. In each case the Committee proposed safeguards which would enable a small number of Members to prevent a bill or statutory instrument from being removed from the House or not debated. A recommendation which was to be taken up later by the 1970–1 Procedure Committee was concerned with bringing the House in at an earlier point in the legislative process. Observing that 'Parliament is entitled to have its views taken into consideration, whenever possible, at a sufficiently early stage in the formulation of . . . (legislative) decisions', the Committee went on to say that 'There are several improvements in procedure that could be made to this end, both by debates in the House and by the work of Committees.' It canvassed the extended use of White Papers before the introduction of legislation, and examination of proposed bills by the existing select committees of the House. In addition it proposed the use of *ad hoc* select committees to consider future legislation, although the Leader of the House, Richard Crossman, was careful in his evidence to restrict this possibility to legislation in social or technical fields. The development of this

[1] *Sixth Report from the Select Committee on Procedure*, 1966–7, 'Public Bill Procedure, etc.', H.C. 539.

[2] *Second Report from the Select Committee on Procedure*, 1970–1, 'The Process of Legislation', H.C. 538.

type of pre-legislative scrutiny by the House in this century is dealt with below.

This recommendation marked the limit of the Procedure Committee's more adventurous forays. It turned down abruptly a proposal by the Study of Parliament Group for a much wider degree of delegation in legislative matters, which would have confined the House normally to the consideration of the broad principles of bills only, and in general the Committee cannot be regarded as being radical in its proposals. Nevertheless, this was the first occasion since the early years of this century that the House devoted an entire procedure inquiry to legislative business. Certain statistics were revealed in the course of the inquiry which are worth noting and commenting on. In the mid-1960s the average number of days in the House in each Session occupied by legislation (including private Members' Bills and the Finance Bill) was 73 out of an average number of sitting days of 160. This included Second Reading debates, sittings on some bills of Committee of the Whole, most Report stages, and most Third Readings. A number of hours equivalent in time to a further 80 days of average length were spent in standing committees.[1] In evidence the Leader of the House and the Opposition Chief Whip maintained that this proportion of the time of the House spent on public bills was about right, and the Committee agreed. It is difficult to trace in the Committee's reasoning any criteria which allowed them to make this assertion; the Study of Parliament Group's contention, that the balance of government activity had shifted and now favoured administration as against legislation, and that therefore the House should improve greatly its opportunities for administrative scrutiny whilst reducing its legislative pre-occupations, was completely ignored by the Committee.

The Committee also noted some interesting statistics concerning the handling of legislation by the Commons which testified to the success of the system established in 1907 and expanded in 1946. The volume of statute law enacted by Parliament had risen from 202 pages in 1900 to 1,817 pages in 1965, reflecting well on the assiduity of the Commons in legislative matters. Evidence given to the Committee by the Leader of the House, First Parliamentary Counsel, and the Clerk of Public

[1] *Report*, paras. 4 and 5.

Bills established that it was possible for time to be found in the House for all bills to which the government of the day attached significance; and that with the use of Second Reading Committee procedure there was no backlog which could not easily be cleared. The Committee, however, was concerned with the uneven spread of legislative business over a Session; in particular the queue of bills in the autumn waiting for Second Reading, and the compression of standing committee work into the first months of the calendar year. It made some recommendations, which in the event were not adopted, for overcoming this situation—the holding over of bills which had received Second Reading in one Session to allow them to go straight to committee in the following Session, and the relaxing to some extent of the rules which operate to discourage certain classes of bills from being introduced in the House of Lords.

This was a useful and business-like inquiry which has been overshadowed to some extent by the more comprehensive study of the process of legislation undertaken by the Procedure Committee in Session 1970–1. This was primarily concerned to promote more vigorously some of the more radical proposals of the 1966–7 inquiry, in particular those which would have enlarged the competence of the House of Commons to enter more positively and constructively into the process of public legislation. The list of witnesses it heard and the information it gathered were considerable; it was nevertheless influenced by the views of a few members, in particular Mr. John Mackintosh, and by a memorandum from the Study of Parliament Group. The main emphasis of the Report was on the need for the House to be able to debate and to scrutinize fields for possible legislation, or actual proposals for legislation, prior to the introduction of bills. The Committee noted that in 1967–8, of 48 public bills, 11 were based on a White Paper, 6 on a published report, and 15 on a public statement. But of these important sources of legislation, the House only debated one White Paper, one report, and four statements. The corresponding figures for 1968–9 were 44 public bills (excluding financial, consolidation, and private Members' bills) of which 8 were based on a White Paper, 8 on a published report, and 11 on a public statement. Only 3 White Papers, 3 reports, and 5 statements were debated. The Committee noted with regret that neither the Labour nor Conservative government had given the House an opportunity of expressing its opinion on the earlier Procedure Committee's proposal for pre-legislative scrutiny by select committees, to consider specific matters which might subsequently form the basis of legislation. These would exclude 'certain matters of basic party controversy' not considered suitable for this type of investigation. Taking account of the generally non-controversial character of the matters suggested for consideration by pre-legislative committees, the Procedure Committee believed that there would be advantage if pre-legislation committees were appointed jointly with the House of Lords.

Although the Committee cited some of the evidence on the work of pre-legislation committees this century put in by the Second Clerk Assistant and the Clerk of Public Bills, the weight of this evidence did not support the Procedure Committee's proposals. It is worth while devoting some time to examining the use since 1900 of select committees of the House in the process of legislation, as opposed to the more usual standing or 'grand' committees. Select committees were the normal way of doing House of Commons' business for much of the nineteenth century; numerous authorities have shown the extent of the use of these devices by Victorian Parliaments before reliance came to be placed on Royal Commissions and Departmental advisory agencies. The use of select committees by the Commons to ascertain facts before the introduction of legislation declined steeply towards the end of last century. It was the victim of the rise of party organization and political control of the Commons by the government after the 1867 Reform Act, and the creation of the modern Civil Service, which removed from Parliament most of its responsibility for the preparation of legislation. Select committees associated with legislation did not disappear entirely in this century, however, but the procedure became exceptional.

Select committees have been used in two ways in relation to public bills. A committee can be appointed to inquire into a public matter with a view to making recommendations on the scope of future legislation. This was standard nineteenth-century practice, and this type of select committee has recently been termed 'pre-legislative'. Alternatively, a public bill can be committed to a select committee after the Second Reading stage. Procedure in a pre-legislation select committee follows that of any other select committee. The committee's report can either refer generally to the outlines of the proposed legislation, or, as was done on one occasion this century, a draft bill can be annexed as an appendix to the report.[1] Procedure in a select committee to which a bill is referred after Second Reading follows a standard pattern (except in the case of 'hybrid' bills). Such a committee has the usual powers to send for persons, papers, and records, and to take evidence on the bill. The rules which govern the admissability of amendments are the same as for a Committee of the Whole House or a standing committee, but the chairman does not have the power of selecting amendments or of accepting closure.[2]

In their Memorandum to the Procedure Committee in 1970–1 the Second Clerk Assistant and the Clerk of Public Bills analysed the occasions between 1900 and 1970 when select committees had been used, either with a view to making recommendations on legislation, or to take a stage of a bill after Second Reading. In the case of pre-legislation select committees, a distinction was made between those committees which resulted in identifiable legislation, and those where no resultant legislation could be identified. In general, greater value seems to have been obtained from pre-legislation committees than from select committees to which bills were referred. Nearly half of the pre-legislation committees gave rise to successful legislation (21 bills in all), whilst of the 35 bills committed to select committees after Second Reading between 1900 and 1970 only 10 became Acts of Parliament.[3] Of these two were rather special as constituting regular reviews of discipline in the armed forces, and other successful bills had had some prior consideration of their content in pre-legislation committees.

From the survey conducted for the Procedure Committee the limitation of the pre-legislation committees which have operated this century appear fairly clearly although the Committee seems to have ignored them—they have on the whole dealt with narrow

---

[1] See Appendix 1 to *Report of the Select Committee on the Army Act and the Air Force Act*, H.C. 223, 1953–4.

[2] See *Second Report from the Select Committee on Procedure*, 1970–1, H.C. 538, Appendix 1, Memorandum by the Second Clerk Assistant and the Clerk of Public Bills.

[3] Ibid., para. 91.

and complex issues, and were concerned with the rights and interests of only a relatively small minority of the electorate. The other consideration is the lengthy and time-consuming nature of the practice—four months seems to have been the shortest time for which a pre-legislative committee deliberated in the period 1900–70, and a period of two years between the appointment of a committee and the enactment of legislation seems to have been common.[1] There would be obvious difficulties in widening the scope of the practice, as has been urged, to deal with more substantial proposals for legislation. In the case of select committees to which bills have been referred after Second Reading, much the same considerations apply. Committal of a bill to a select committee involves an extra stage in legislative proceedings; after the bill has been reported from a select committee it stands committed to a Committee of the Whole House. Any alteration in this, such as regarding the select committee stage as a substitute for standing committee or Committee of the Whole would mean that the bill would have been examined by a smaller number of Members than is at present the case with most bills. The extra time which a select committee stage would entail, especially if it took evidence from outside interests, would make the proper distribution of business in the House almost impossible. So far as practice this century goes, bills were committed to select committees after Second Reading in cases where additional information was required in socially or technically complicated situations.[2] In at least ten cases the subject-matter of the bill had already been considered by a Royal Commission or a pre-legislation select committee. In general, the select committee device in this century has not been particularly successful. In the period 1900–39 few bills committed to select committees passed their remaining stages, and in the post-1945 period only

[1] See ibid., Annex G, 'Pre-Legislation Select Committees, 1900–1970', Part 1, 'Select Committees which resulted in identifiable legislation'.

[2] It has been suggested that occasionally tactical considerations might have been a reason for referring a bill to a select committee. Particularly in the period 1900–14 in five cases the reason given was congestion of business in the standing committees, and in some instances this sort of referral was regarded as a holding operation. The practice was not regarded with any great enthusiasm. Joseph Chamberlain was quoted as saying in 1906 that 'to send a bill to a select committee was a specious device on the part of those who did not wish to legislate', Lowell, op. cit., p. 52.

those bills which had received some prior consideration were successful.[1] The 1956–7 Obscene Publications Bill spent four months in a select committee without reaching the stage of detailed consideration. It was only after a pre-legislation committee in the following Session that a bill based on the committee's findings was successful, and that bill went to a standing committee and not a select committee.

The Procedure Committee in the 1970–1 inquiry also canvassed the possibility of some 'post-legislative' scrutiny by the Commons of the way in which particular bills were implemented, and this proposal to some extent rested on the reasoning which the Study of Parliament Group had expressed in the course of the 1966–7 procedure inquiry. The actual recommendation reads:

Post-legislation committees should be appointed where necessary to enquire into difficulties in the application or interpretation of statutes and consequent delegated legislation within a short period of their enactment; where appropriate such committees should be appointed as joint committees of both Houses of Parliament.[2]

No action has so far been taken on this proposal; whether, given the difficulties of manning even the present range of committees in the House, time and Members could be found for this sort of scrutiny, which would in any case have to be highly selective, is doubtful. Apart from this, the Committee made numerous proposals, twenty-six in all, bearing on the normal Parliamentary procedures on both primary and delegated legislation. Most of these were technical, dealing with Allocation of Time Orders, the need for explanatory memoranda for bills, increased use of the legislative potential of the House of Lords by a waiver of 'the ancient and undoubted privileges' of the House of Commons, and increased use of select committees for the committee stage of 'suitable' bills. One gets the impression of a Procedure Committee attempting two things—primarily to increase the scope of the participation of the Commons in the whole process of public legislation, and secondly, by a series of minor and common-sense reforms, to squeeze the last measure of efficiency from the existing system. Apart from these sorts of reforms it is difficult

[1] See H.C. 538, Annex F, 'Public Bills committed to Select Committees, 1900–1970'.
[2] Ibid., Para. 70, Recommendation (2).

to see how the system's potential could now be extended. One of the Committee's suggestions, that Standing Order 40 should be amended to enable bills to be committed in part to a standing committee and in part to a select committee, points the way to more flexibility. This proposal is dealt with more fully later.

Some broad characteristics of the Commons' legislative structure as it has developed this century can now be briefly noted. Conforming to a deeply felt, if seldom articulated, sentiment of the bulk of M.P.s, the entire thrust of the reforms in standing committees since 1907 has been against specialization. The sentiment was expressed curtly enough by the Speaker, Douglas Clifton Brown, when he gave evidence in 1946 to the Select Committee on Procedure which was examining the memorandum by Sir Gilbert Campion on Parliamentary reform, which would have produced a rigorously specialized committee system for legislative and financial purposes. The Speaker's memorandum stated quite bluntly 'Specialist Committees do not appeal to me'. A sentiment which he elaborated in evidence as follows:

I shudder at the idea of, say, all our financial experts being put onto a finance committee. It does not seem to be the right principle of Parliament. We want to consult experts and then bring our common sense as ordinary people to bear, and that is why I am frightened of a specialist committee. You get a collection of cranks, probably, on most subjects . . .[1]

As has been stated, the formal requirement concerning the identification of committees with distinct classes of bills was repealed in 1933; some element of specialist membership remained with the increasingly ineffective stipulation for two-part membership of committees until 1960, when standing committees ceased to have any permanent membership. It follows that 'specialization', when referred to in the context of standing committee membership, is a fairly casual concept, revolving mainly around the occupational experience and constituency links of M.P.s, and is indicated to some extent by the frequency with which Members seek appointment to standing committees on particular types of bill. In a few well-defined areas of legislation, such as agriculture, a small but definite degree of specialization

[1] *Third Report of the Select Committee on Procedure*, 1945–6, Evidence: Qs. 128–9 *et seq.*

can be discerned, with about one in six members appointed to standing committees dealing with agriculture bills showing a distinct interest, in the sense of seeking continual committee appointments, over a prolonged period of time. In most well-defined legislative fields there are small groups of M.P.s who can be regarded as specialists. The group usually includes Members with experience in office of the relevant Department, i.e. the Minister, the Parliamentary Secretary, and Parliamentary Private Secretary. The occupational experience of back-benchers plays a major part, which is often joined with membership of the appropriate Parliamentary party committee or subject group. A further line of approach to specialist bias is provided by constituency interest. On the other hand, it is often difficult to make the connexion between previous occupational interest, constituency interest, and committee appointments. What constitutes the link in the case of, for example, pensions and national insurance bills, or housing bills, is often difficult to discover. Relevant experience in a shadow capacity, professional experience, experience of office in a party committee, are recurring factors. In general, however, there is little evidence of continuity of committee membership within those areas of legislation which originate a sufficiently large number of bills for analysis.[1]

Recent reforms in standing committee structure have in any case deprived the system of any institutionalized bias which might have existed in favour of continuity and specialization. Since 1960, when the concept of two-part membership disappeared, standing committees have ceased to have any permanent membership. Separate committees are nominated for each bill, and the turnover of members between bills has the effect of minimizing the continuity of membership of the committees. For example, an analysis of two standing committees taken at random—Committees A and F in Session 1966–7—shows that Committee A met on eight bills, and Committee F on nine. The membership of Committee A fluctuated from 21 to 51 for different bills, and over the Session involved 218 M.P.s. Only

---

[1] For a fuller discussion of specialization in legislative matters in the House of Commons see Borthwick, op. cit., pp. 135–52, and Richard Kimber and J. J. Richardson, 'Specialisation and Parliamentary Standing Committees', *Political Studies*, Vol. 16, No. 1, February 1968.

26 M.P.s were on more than one bill in Committee A. In regard to Committee F, the membership varied from 21 to 31 in the course of the Session. A total of 209 Members served on Committee F; of these 44 were appointed to the Committee for more than one bill. Standing Committee A had seven different chairmen for its eight bills, one chairman being appointed for two bills. Committee F had seven different chairmen for nine bills, two chairmen each taking two bills. Committee A had two Clerks of the House in attendance, except for two bills when only one Clerk was appointed. Four Clerks in all dealt with the Committee during the Session. Committee F had twelve Clerks usually two Clerks to a bill.

It is difficult to see what significance the identification of standing committees by letter has, except for Scottish bills where there is some considerable continuity of membership. In general there is little continuity on the committees from bill to bill, either in Members, chairmen, or Clerks. The effect is to produce in any one Session a multiplicity of anything up to 70 separate standing committees, each with a life which can vary from a single day's sitting to a few months' association. On rare occasions a committee may consider only one major bill in the course of a Session. But long sittings on a bill are the exception rather than the rule. The Commons' talent for the *ad hoc* cannot be better illustrated than in the present standing committee arrangements. It is evident that built-in discontinuities militate against committees achieving any corporate sense which can be developed, as has occurred in other legislatures, over a continuous period of common association.

So far no attempt has been made to offer even a general analysis of the effects of Parliamentary scrutiny and examination of the four thousand-plus government bills which have been considered by the House of Commons this century. Until very recently there has been very little empirical analysis of the way the House handles legislative matters, largely, it can be suspected, because the slow and undogmatic process of accommodation between the executive and Parliament which has fashioned legislative procedures since 1900 has seldom thrust them into constitutional or political prominence. One major difficulty is that there are no real uniformities, despite a repertory of legislative procedures which at first sight appears limited and inflexible. In fact the system provides for a considerable degree of flexibility. As Professor Griffith has pointed out, Second Reading debates in the Commons can vary 'from the formal, the cursory and the brief, to extended examination of the principles and sometimes of the details of government bills'.[1] An analysis which Professor Griffith made of the time spent on the floor of the House on Second Reading for government bills during the three Sessions 1967–8, 1968–9 and 1970–1 showed that out of 146 bills 37 took less than an hour, 13 between one and two hours, 16 between two and three hours, and 20 between three and four hours. The rest took longer, the Industrial Relations Bill in 1970–1 occupying the House for more than twelve hours. Thus more than one third of the bills in these three Sessions were debated on Second Reading for less than two hours. Nearly another third were debated for between five and seven hours, which, as Griffith remarks, is the normal period for 'policy' bills, the debate beginning around 4 p.m. and ending at 10 p.m. The same disparity of treatment can be found at the committee stage. Normally there is considerable variation—committee proceedings can vary from a single morning sitting to deliberations over some months. As has been said, long sittings on a bill are the exception rather than the rule. For example, the average number of sittings per bill of Standing Committee A in the 1966–7 Session was 8, and this figure was swollen by the 25 sittings devoted to the complex Agriculture Bill and the 19 sittings on the important Criminal Justice Bill. In the same Session the average for Standing Committee F was only four sittings per bill, and of the nine bills dealt with by this Committee four took only one sitting, and two took two sittings. The total of 48 bills dealt with in standing committee in 1968–9 took 246 sittings—an average of five sittings per bill. Only nine involved more than 10 sittings each. Many of the bills were the subject of voluntary agreements. In general, non-controversial legislation is dealt with very expeditiously by the House. In the 1968–9 Session, for example, of the 50 government bills which were dealt with by the House of Commons 18 took under five hours for all their stages, the average for each bill being 2 hours 28 minutes; less

[1] J. A. G. Griffith, *Parliamentary Scrutiny of Government Bills* (London, 1975).

than ten hours was spent on each of 25 out of the total of 50 bills.[1] It would seem that little scope now exists for saving the time of the House in legislative matters, short of a probably unacceptable degree of legislative delegation to Ministers.

When one turns to the actual process of Parliamentary amendment, one finds that the scope and degree of this is hotly contested. Writing in 1968 on the legislative process in general, this writer concluded, after admittedly a fairly superficial survey of post-1945 Parliaments, that the result of attempts at amendment of government bills by Parliament was not marked, and it was subsequently argued that some other explanation must be sought for the continued interest of Members in the legislative process, their willingness to serve on fairly powerless standing committees and to put down extremely large numbers of amendments, the majority of which having no hope of even being selected, let alone of being accepted.[2] This conclusion was challenged by Professor Frank Stacey in his book *The British Ombudsman*, which contained a detailed account of the Parliamentary amendment of the Parliamentary Commissioner for Administration Bill of 1966. Parliamentary discussion of this bill led to important changes, both in the Commons and the Lords. This bill, however, was in a special category, inasmuch as it introduced a reform which was of special concern to M.P.s, and was not strictly speaking a partisan measure. But Stacey also cites the Transport Bill of 1968, which was a major government bill strongly supported by the Labour Party. In its passage through Parliament it was extensively amended, attracting about 700 changes. Many of these, however, were Ministerial amendments introduced as a result of imperfect drafting or incomplete consultation at earlier stages. Stacey's conclusion, that there is a great deal of variation in the handling of government bills by Parliament, is impeccable but not particularly helpful. As he says, 'Some bills are perfunctorily discussed and little amended, some bills are extensively discussed and little amended, some bills are extensively discussed and extensively amended.' But a clearer perspective emerges by aggregating Parliamentary amendments over a period of legislation. Professor Griffith[3] has

---

[1] See H.C. 538, Appendix 9, para. 10.
[2] S. A. Walkland, *The Legislative Process in Great Britain* (London, 1968).
[3] Griffith, op. cit.

calculated that in the 1967–8, 1968–9, and 1970–1 Sessions, private Members moved 3,510 amendments to government bills in committee, of which only 171 were agreed to. Whereas of 907 amendments moved by Ministers 906 were agreed to. Amendments forced on Ministers by dissenting back-benchers, either on the floor of the House or in standing committee, are an even smaller proportion of the amendments moved. The number of issues on which the government was defeated in standing committee as a result of back-bench dissent were 10 for the whole of the 1959–64 Parliament, 2 in the 1964–6 Parliament, 10 in the 1966–70 Parliament, and 23 in the 1970–4 Parliament. Many of these amendments were subsequently reversed, either whilst still in committee or on Report. This of course is not a complete measure of Parliamentary influence, since most amendments accepted by Ministers do not require the sanction of Ministerial defeat. Mr. Valentine Herman has noted, in a study of the fate of amendments moved in Committee of the Whole during one recent Parliamentary Session, that only those amendments which contain policy differences that basically separate the Government from the Opposition are unlikely to be accepted by the government.

All other Opposition amendments, however, the Government is likely to accept, incorporate or accommodate in one way or another into its legislation. Although the Government draws up the details of its legislation without consultation with the Opposition and exerts tight control over what amendments are accepted, the Opposition is able to make its mark on both the principles and details of this legislation. . . .[1]

Perhaps a somewhat too rosy view—further explanation is needed of the discrepancy between the actual legislative effort exerted by the Commons and the often puny results. There is an 'inwardness' about the operation of standing committees which is only explicable in terms of the private political and cultural character of the Commons. Proceedings are stylized—even ritualized—to a considerable degree. Bills serve as a focus for the process of defence, clarification, explanation, and justification of government policy which it is the role of the Opposition to elicit,

---

[1] Dick Leonard and Valentine Herman (eds.), *The Backbencher and Parliament* (London, 1972), Chap. 4, Part II, 'Backbench and Opposition Amendments to Government Legislation', p. 155.

and which the moving of particular types of amendments serves to facilitate. What is more, this sort of legislative proceeding does not seem to have altered much in essence in the course of a century. The position today, in much more hectic circumstances and with considerably accelerated proceedings, seems much as it was described by Lowell seventy years ago, based on analysis of late Victorian Parliaments.

Reference has already been made to the fairly intense Parliamentary interest in legislative procedure in the last ten years. In addition to two Procedure Committee inquiries, in 1975 the Renton Committee, working from a different angle, reported on the preparation of legislation. The Procedure Committee of the House of Commons which was appointed in 1976 is certain to devote a considerable amount of time to legislative procedure, as is the parallel investigation in the Lords. Interest in the process has been heightened by the comparatively large number of heavily contentious bills which have been a feature of the 1970s, and which have demonstrated the fragile nature of the consensus on which current legislative procedure in Parliament is based. It has been the conventional wisdom of the last few years that successive governments have overloaded the Parliamentary legislative machinery, which has resulted in proposals both by the Renton Committee and the government that recourse should be had to more delegated legislation, by the use of enabling bills conferring much wider powers on Ministers than is now regarded as desirable—'framework legislation', to use the term favoured by the Leader of the House in 1976. It is doubtful, however, whether the legislative situation in Parliament warrants such a drastic innovation, which is objectionable on many grounds. The number of bills enacted in recent sessions has remained more or less constant from year to year; even the heavy Sessions of 1974–5 and 1975–6 were not outstanding in this regard. Careful Cabinet planning would appear to match the exigencies of policy to Parliament's legislative capacity fairly precisely. It does not appear from the statistics that Parliament has suddenly been asked to deal with unprecedented legislative problems. Much legislation, indeed most of it, is uncontentious and administrative in character; what has perhaps given the impression of overload has been the high incidence of major and contentious bills in this period, such as the 1971 Industrial Relations Act, the Immigration Act of the same year, the 1972 European Communities and Housing Finance Acts; other controversial measures introduced by Labour governments from 1974 onwards have demonstrated that a period of government by small majorities heightens feelings of deep and important differences when a minority or near-minority government uses its precarious control over the House of Commons to settle by legislation contentious industrial and political issues.

   The theme of legislative overload has in any case been a fairly constant one throughout the period covered by this essay. It has seldom resulted in drastic innovation in the Parliamentary legislative process, and it is likely that the present discontents of back-benchers in this sphere have deeper causes. One constant theme of the last ten years has been that the purely adversary character of the legislative procedure of the Commons, seen at its most formal in standing committee proceedings, denies back-benchers a constructive and major role in legislative policy making. Proposals for an investigative evidence-taking stage in the process have been a constant factor in most criticisms of present procedure in recent years. Richard Crossman has put the criticism characteristically forcefully:

> . . . the whole procedure of a Standing Committee is insane. What is the sense of starting at the beginning and working line by line through each clause when in many cases there is no-one there who understands what they mean? If we had a Select Committee at which I could be cross-examined on the main policy and the Committee could get down to discussing the controversial issues, that would be far more constructive. . . .[1]

Crossman was referring to the committee stage of the Local Government Bill, measures of which sort perhaps lend themselves more to the select committee approach than others. What seems practically certain at the time of writing is that the current Procedure Committee will recommend something along these lines as an extra stage in the process. Whether the consequent loss of government control over a section of legislative proceedings will be acceptable remains to be seen. There is pressure on the Procedure Committee from a number of directions, and their

---

[1] R. H. S. Crossman, *The Diaries of a Cabinet Minister*, i, 561.

resolution will not be easy. It seems likely, however, that changes will be conservative in scope and effect; the legislative procedure of the Commons has throughout this century conformed fairly closely to the political structure of Parliament. Without some modification of this it is hard to envisage major reforms.

VI

PRIVATE MEMBERS' LEGISLATION

Peter G. Richards[1]

A private Member's Bill is a proposed piece of public legislation
introduced by a back-bencher. There are three procedural
avenues for such legislation. A Member can enter the ballot held
under Standing Order 6 for the right to introduce Bills. A
Member can give notice of his intention to introduce a Bill after
question time on a Tuesday or Wednesday in accordance with
Standing Order 13, when a ten-minute speech may be made in
its favour. The third course is for a Member to introduce a Bill
without either of these preliminaries under Standing Order 37;
this category is sometimes known as unballoted Bills. The greater
part of this chapter will be concerned with Bills initiated through
the ballot for this group embraces almost all private Members'
legislation of importance. No parliamentary time is normally
available for the Ten-Minute Rule Bills and the unballoted
Bills so they fail for lack of time unless they are so uncontroversial
as to pass through without debate 'on the nod'. However,
Standing Orders 13 and 37 are still of value so it is well to open
an examination of private Members' legislation with an account
of the alternative methods of promotion.

The ballot under Standing Order 6 is held on the second
Thursday of each session. Members who so wish enter their
names. By convention, Ministers do not. The Speaker is responsible for arranging the ballot. The number of names drawn
depends upon the amount of time available. The Standing
Order decrees that ten Fridays will be made available for the
balloted Bills. However, each year a sessional order is passed
which supersedes this part of the Standing Order so the amount
of time allowed and the number of names drawn has varied.

---

[1] I am grateful to Mr. Peter Cockton for his assistance with the collection
of historical and statistical material. His help has been invaluable.

Members successful in the ballot introduce their Bills on the fifth Wednesday of the session. At this stage the Bills are only in dummy form. Members need the three-weeks grace in order to decide the subject of their attempted legislation. They also have to decide which Friday to choose for the Bill's introduction. Half the allocated Fridays are devoted to second readings; the other half are devoted to later stages of Bills, report stage, third reading, or the consideration of Lords' amendments. The Bills which have advanced furthest along the path to the statute book have priority. On the later Fridays if no Bills are ready for their report stage etc., then further Bills can be brought forward for second reading—but this is unlikely to happen. Since the first Bill on a second reading Friday may take all the time available, it follows that the second and subsequent Bills due for consideration may make no progress. At the time of writing twelve Fridays are available for balloted Bills so the first six Members to have their names drawn can be certain that their Bills will at least be discussed. In all twenty names are drawn so Members 7–20 have either to try and choose a Friday when there is hope that earlier Bills will not consume all the time or to pick up an idea that is so trivial or uncontroversial that it may get a second reading without discussion.

The difficulty of finding time for a second reading debate is only the beginning of the procedural problems facing a Bill's sponsor. If a measure is even mildly controversial he needs to secure a favourable vote. Opponents may try to 'talk the Bill out' by continuing the debate at 4 p.m. when the main business on Friday must end. The sponsor may claim to move that 'the question be now put' at 4 p.m. and the Speaker will permit a vote if he is of opinion that a reasonable amount of time has been given to the debate. He will always allow a vote on the first Bill of the day. He will probably not allow such a vote on a second or subsequent Bill. Even if a vote is obtained, there is the further difficulty of marshalling supporters. On Fridays the claims of constituencies and the week-end provide powerful counter-attractions to attendance at Westminster. And a sponsor may need not merely a majority over his opponents but also a minimum of 100 supporters, for the motion 'that the question now be put' needs 100 'Ayes' to succeed. In January 1971 the Divorce (Scotland) Bill was delayed (it was ultimately lost through lack of time) when the closure failed with a vote of 71 to 15 in favour.[1]

The next obstacle may be delay caused by a queue of Bills awaiting consideration in standing committee. To avoid the queue it is good tactics for a sponsor to seek an early Friday for a second reading debate. By convention a standing committee reflects the opinion of the House so that the supporters of a Bill should be in a majority on the committee stage. Opponents may cause discussion to be protracted but they cannot usually insert amendments which are hostile to the central purpose of a Bill. Yet a filibuster in committee can kill a Bill by ensuring that there is no time left for its later stages—witness Sir Cyril Black's campaign against the Sunday Entertainment Bill, 1968. Again there may be a queue of Bills awaiting a report stage back in the Chamber. This is another major hurdle and some Bills are lost for lack of time at this juncture. Once the report stage has been passed the outlook is brighter because, at least in more recent years, the House of Lords has not been so hostile to measures promoting social reform.

In essence the situation is that a highly controversial private Member's Bill cannot hope to succeed unless the Government provides additional time. The question of whether extra time should be provided is considered below.[2]

The other categories of private Members' Bills can be described more briefly. Any Member can take advantage of the Ten-Minute Rule by handing in prior notice of his intention to introduce a Bill after question time on a Tuesday or a Wednesday after the fifth week of the session; this delay is required in order to maintain the priority of Bills promoted through the ballot. The notice must be given not less than five and not more than fifteen days in advance.[3] No Member may have more than

---

[1] *H.C. Deb.*, Vol. 810, col. 1547. (All references to Commons Debates are from the 5th series, except where otherwise stated.)   [2] pp. 326–7 below.

[3] These time limits were first introduced in 1970 in order to prevent any repetition of the events of November 1969 when Robin Maxwell-Hyslop stayed at the Commons overnight to be first in the queue when the Public Bill Office opened to receive notices under this Standing Order. He handed in 70 notices on behalf of himself and other Conservative Members in order to pre-empt all the time available during the session. After protests in the Chamber, Opposition leaders agreed that 14 days should be made available for Labour Members. See *H.C. Deb.*, Vol. 792, cols. 639–50 and Vol. 807, cols. 165–9; also *Select Committee on Procedure, First Report*, 1969–70, H.C. 141.

one such notice in effect at any one time. Not more than one Bill can be introduced under this system on any day. On some Tuesdays and Wednesdays the facility is not used, but this 'waste' is now less frequent.[1] The sponsor of such a Bill can make a ten-minute speech to outline the purpose of his measure and urge its acceptance. A single speech of similar length may be made in opposition. The Bill may be unopposed; alternatively there may be a division. Unless the Bill is defeated it will be read a first time, it will be printed and is ready to go forward for a second reading. At this stage it is unlikely to make further progress because the second reading of Bills introduced under the ballot have priority on private Members' Fridays.[2] As a result of some procedural fluke a little time may become available:[3] the Government may provide extra time for discussion: the Bill may be uncontroversial and be passed 'on the nod'. These things happen but rarely. The purpose of the Ten-Minute Rule is not to provide new opportunities to legislate. Rather the purpose is to allow Members to draw attention to a problem and to test opinion in the House. A twenty-minute debate at 3.30 p.m. at the time when attendance in the Chamber is high provides maximum publicity.[4] If the Commons react favourably to a Ten-Minute Rule Bill it may pave the way for a similar Bill introduced under the ballot in a later session. Alternatively it may stimulate Government action. The support given to Leo Abse's Bill to reform the law on homosexuality persuaded the Wilson Government to find time for a private Member's Bill on

[1] *Select Committee on Procedure, First Report*, 1969–70, H.C. 141, p. 3.

[2] This priority does not extend to the later stages of Bills. So on a Friday set aside for the later stages of private Members' Bills, the report stage of a Ten-Minute Rule Bill or an unballoted Bill would have priority over the second reading of a balloted Bill.

[3] One such example is the Bill introduced by Graham Page in 1957 to obviate the need to endorse cheques. *H.C. Deb.*, Vol. 568, cols. 1504–18.

[4] In 1970 the Commons rejected by 52 votes to 167 a proposal that Ten-Minute Rule Bills be taken at 10 p.m. instead of 3.30 p.m. The change in time would have reduced substantially the publicity given to these Bills by the mass media. See *H.C. Deb.*, Vol. 807, cols. 165–94. The proposal came from the *Select Committee on Procedure, First Report*, 1969–70, H.C. 141. In the short session 1965–6 these motions were taken at 10 p.m. Between February and November 1967 they were part of the experimental morning sittings. When regular morning sittings lapsed the Ten-Minute Rule motions returned to the period after question-time.

this subject.[1] Sir Gerald Nabarro's Tobacco and Snuff (Health Hazards) Bill, 1970, is another unusual illustration of the value of this procedure. His Bill, *inter alia*, required health warnings to be printed on cigarette cartons. At the time the Government were trying to obtain a voluntary agreement with British tobacco companies that this should be done. To bring pressure to bear on the tobacco industry the Government allowed Nabarro's Bill a second reading 'on the nod'. The Ministry then achieved a voluntary agreement with the industry.[2]

Members may also introduce a Bill by merely presenting it to the House without any preliminaries under the terms of Standing Order 37. Most Government Bills are also introduced by this method. A Member who has notified his wish to bring in a Bill is called by the Speaker; then the Member takes his 'dummy' Bill to the Clerk of the House who reads the short title of the Bill. This constitutes a first reading. There is no question before the House, no debate, and the Bill is printed. A Bill presented by a back-bencher in this way, like a Ten-Minute Rule Bill, will make no further progress unless one of three things happen. The Bill may be so uncontroversial as to be passed without debate. However, when the second reading is called at 4 p.m. on a Friday it requires only a single Member to shout 'Object' for further progress to be totally blocked. A dearth of other business on a private Members' Friday may provide unexpected time for debate: this is most unusual. The third possibility is that Government time may be made available for debate on the Bill. This may happen if Ministers are broadly in favour of the measure but the Government as a whole does not wish to be officially associated with it. Sydney Silverman's Bill to abolish the death penalty in session 1964–5 is the leading example.[3]

[1] Peter G. Richards, *Parliament and Conscience* (Allen & Unwin, 1970), pp. 76–9.

[2] At this stage Ministers urged that the Bill be withdrawn. Sir Gerald refused to withdraw and the Bill ultimately failed at the report stage through lack of time.

[3] At the 1964 election the Labour Party pledged itself to find time for a private Member's Bill on this subject which traditionally had enjoyed a 'free' non-party vote. This promise was repeated in the Queen's Speech after Labour had won the election. So Silverman's Bill had the unique distinction for a back-bench measure of being mentioned in the Gracious Speech from the Throne.

Individual peers may also promote legislation. Should a private peer's Bill pass all its stages in the House of Lords it then becomes available for consideration by the Commons. Any Member may give notice that he wishes to take up such a Bill. This action is taken as the equivalent of a first reading. The Bill is then printed and is ready for second reading. Next comes the familiar difficulty that no time is available. Few private peers' Bills reach the statute book; those which do are non-controversial and pass the Commons without discussion. Thus the role of a back-bench sponsor of such a Bill is nominal.[1]

The growth of Government control over the timetable of the House of Commons during the nineteenth century has been described elsewhere in this book. By a resolution passed on 25 June 1852 the orders, i.e. the Bills, proposed by private Members were to have precedence on Wednesdays at a short sitting from noon to 6 p.m. This arrangement was incorporated into Standing Orders in 1861 and with minor modifications remained in force until the end of the century. At this period Tuesdays were set aside for private Members' motions. The Wednesdays were not sacrosanct. Whenever there was heavy pressure of ministerial business, the Government could introduce a motion to enable a private Members' day to be taken over for official purposes. In 1887 the Government took every Wednesday before Easter.

Priority for private Members' Bills on Wednesdays depended upon the order in which they were submitted at the commencement of the session. Thus Bills submitted on the first day of a session had priority over all other later Bills. The priority as

---

[1] The Sunday Theatres Act, 1972, is an exception to the rule. This private peer's Bill to permit Sunday opening of theatres was sponsored in the Commons by Hugh Jenkins. Perhaps surprisingly it obtained a second reading 'on the nod' and joined the queue of Bills awaiting attention by standing committee. Subsequently Hugh Jenkins moved a motion that the committee stage be taken in the Whole House. The following interchange then took place (*H.C. Deb.*, Vol. 835, col. 1015): 'Mr. Speaker: Committee what day? Mr. Jenkins: Now, Sir. Mr. Speaker: I am bound to point out that this is unusual and, I think, inconvenient as Hon. Members have had no warning. Nevertheless, I will put the Question.' No Members present objected. The committee stage and third reading were agreed without a word and the Bill became an Act.

between Bills submitted on the first day was decided by ballot. The precise origin of the ballot and the rules applicable to it are obscure. Standing Orders merely record that the arrangements for it shall be made by the Speaker. The draw gave priority to Members rather than to Bills and at least by the 1880s the number of names drawn was less than the number of Bills submitted on the first day: no doubt this was because at some stage the ballot became meaningless since Bills with a very low priority had no chance at all of passing unless they were unopposed. There is no official record of the number of names drawn. This remains true today. The number has varied from time to time at the discretion of the Speaker. In the twentieth century the number drawn has depended upon the amount of time made available for private Members' legislation.

Before 1894 the ballot was held in the Chamber on the first day of the session at 4.30 p.m.[1] However, at the very end of the 1893–4 session the Speaker proposed that the draw be held elsewhere than in the Chamber in order to save the time of the House.[2] Instead, the ballot was to be held in Grand Committee Room E on the second day of the session. The Speaker, in co-operation with the Clerk of the House, also prepared a plan to alter the ballot procedure which was designed to prevent alliances of Members in favour of particular Bills. The scheme was to print with the Vote the Notices for Bills handed in on the first day, so that Members were required to submit not merely their names for the ballot but also the title of a Bill. The Commons had not been consulted about this idea which secured, in effect, that the ballot was between Bills rather than between Members. Such an arrangement would have frustrated the established practice whereby groups of Members were formed to promote particular Bills, the method being that the Member who introduced the Bill was the one in the group who had drawn the most favourable place in the ballot. Clearly this form of co-operation would be impossible if the titles of Bills had to be submitted the day before the ballot. The Speaker's plan caused tremendous confusion at the start of the 1894 session and was widely deplored. In effect, it changed the procedure without having been submitted to the House for approval. It was

---

[1] Erskine May, 13th edn. (1924), p. 232n.
[2] *Parl. Deb.*, 4th series, Vol. 21, cols. 1129–30.

promptly abandoned and never reintroduced. The conduct of the ballot was subsequently determined by a motion moved by the Leader of the House

That no Bills, other than Government Bills, be introduced in anticipation of the ballot; and that all Members who wish to ballot, whether for Bills or Motions on the first four Tuesdays of the session, do hand in their names at the table during the sitting of the House on the first or second day of the session. . . . That the ballot for the precedence of the said Bills or Motions be taken on the third day of the session at a convenient time and place to be appointed by Mr Speaker and that the introduction and first reading of Bills on the fourth day be taken before Questions . . .

This new arrangement gave a Member a little more time to consider the subject of his Bill or time to decide between introducing a Bill or proposing a Motion.

Yet the difficulty facing private Members' legislation was not simply that of the ballot. The fundamental problem was shortage of time on Wednesdays. As a result few Bills were discussed at second reading and fewer still achieved the Royal Assent. A Bill needed a good place in the ballot to gain a second reading debate; to get through the later stages it needed to be largely uncontroversial and so could pass an unopposed business after midnight on a Government day or after 5.30 p.m. on a Wednesday.

However, in 1888 came three changes in procedure which did facilitate the discussion and passage of private Members' legislation. The first derived from Resolution No. 3 of the 1878 Select Committee on Public Business. A new Standing Order, No. 12, provided 'That after Whitsuntide, Public Bills, other than Government Bills, be arranged in the Order Book so as to give priority to the Bills most advanced, and that Lords' Amendments . . . be placed first, to be followed by Third Readings, Consideration on Report, Progress in Committee, Bills appointed for Committee and Second Readings.' Thus this arrangement gave precedence towards the end of the session to those Bills which had already progressed furthest along the road to the statute book. Another change in 1888 made it a little easier to force the House to come to decisions. Before 1888 a closure of a debate could be obtained only if 200 Members voted for it or, alternatively, if at least 100 Members supported the closure and not more than 40 opposed it. The new rule, Standing Order 26, required only that 100 Members need vote in the majority for the closure of the debate to be carried. Granted the normally low attendance at discussions on private Members' legislation, this modification was not unimportant. Another innovation in 1888 was the nomination, in accordance with Standing Order 47, of two Standing Committees to deal with the committee stage of Bills. One Committee was concerned with matters of trade and manufacture, the other with law and legal procedure. A Bill, including a private Member's Bill, could be referred to a Standing Committee by order of the House after it had obtained a second reading. Taken together these moves did a little to assist private Members' legislation as can be seen from Table IV.1.

TABLE IV.1

Fate of Private Members' Bills 1887–1890

Session	Total Bills	Failed to secure Second Reading	Failed after Second Reading	Royal Assent
1887	125	114	7	4
1888	92	84	5	3
1889	95	79	5	11
1890	111	97	7	7

Another development in 1888 was the introduction of what are now known as Ten-Minute Rule Bills. A new Standing Order 16 provided

That on Tuesdays and Fridays, and if set down by the Government on Mondays and Thursdays, motions for leave to bring in Bills and for the nomination of Select Committees, may be set down for consideration at the beginning of Public Business. If such Motions be opposed, Mr. Speaker, after permitting, if he thinks fit, a brief explanatory statement from the Member who moves and from the Member who opposes any such Motion respectively, may, without further debate, put the Question thereon.

So a Member could obtain the right to ventilate the merits of a Bill. If his Bill was opposed there could also be a division which would test opinion in the House. The value of this procedure has been discussed above.[1] It is not very expensive in terms of parlia-

[1] pp. 295–6.

mentary time and it adds elements of variety and unpredictability to the business of the Commons.

Under the important procedural reforms promoted by Arthur
Balfour in 1902 the day for private Members' Bills was changed
from Wednesday to Friday. The Government seemed to believe
that Wednesday was a more valuable day than Friday and so
should be used for official purposes. Attendance on Friday was
more difficult to sustain. The Liberal Opposition argued against
change. Their Leader, Sir Henry Campbell-Bannerman, deplored the fact that the business of the Commons was being
adjusted to meet the fashion in London society for a week-end in
the fresh air of the country; he also suggested that fashion was
fickle and could well change.[1] It was also argued that the ability
to relax on Wednesday enabled Members to recover from the
late sittings on Monday and Tuesday and reinvigorated them
for the Government business to be taken on Thursday and
Friday. The move to Friday was seen as a further downgrading
of the rights of back-benchers and the significance of their power
to initiate legislation. In an attempt to mollify the critics,
Balfour did stress that under the new arrangements it should be
less necessary for Ministers to take over private Members' days
for Government business. Nor would they lose two hours on Ash
Wednesday, when the House met at 2 p.m. rather than noon, to
enable Members to go to church.[2] The House accepted the
Government proposals so after 1902 private Members' Bills had
priority on Fridays before Whitsun and on the third and fourth
Fridays after Whitsun when the later stages of Bills were to be
taken (Standing Order 4).

Further development of the Standing Committee system came
in 1907. Standing Order 46 then ruled that a Bill should be
committed to a Standing Committee unless the House decided
otherwise. The number of these Committees was increased from
two to four. Functional specialization was ended but it was
decreed that Government business should have priority at three
of the Committees, leaving one for private Members.

To revert to the raiding of private Members' time by the
Government. After 1902 the Balfour Government did, in fact,
avoid further incursions. But the temptation remained strong for

[1] *Parl. Deb.*, 4th series, Vol. 102, cols. 549 et seq.
[2] Ibid., col. 1002.

any Government facing heavy pressure on the parliamentary timetable. At this period the parliamentary session normally opened in February and ended in August. The congestion of business was greatest at the beginning and the end of the session. The initial difficulty was that a large amount of routine financial business, the votes on supply, the Army and Navy Estimates, the Civil Estimates, and the Consolidated Fund Bill, had to be completed before the end of the financial year. So the Fridays before Easter were always potentially at risk and the Asquith Government took all or most of them in 1910, 1911, and 1913. During the First World War there were no sittings of the House on Fridays and no private Members' Bills. In 1919 Bonar Law moved a sessional order 'That, until the House otherwise determines, no Public Bills other than Government Bills be introduced, and no ballot be taken for determining the precedence of such Bills.' However, on this occasion the House rebelled and Ministers retreated.[1] After a short delay a ballot was held on 17 March.[2] Two years later the Government again succumbed to the pressure of financial business and acquired all Fridays before 31 March.[3] In 1928–9, 1931–2, and 1934–5, complex or controversial Government legislation deprived private Members of any chance to legislate. The other factor that caused variation in the time available to back-benchers was, of course, the length of the session (see Table IV.2).

Apart from almost permanent uncertainty about the availability of time, two other issues were of central importance. One was the difficulty of obtaining the passage of Bills which had been favourably received at second reading. The other was the question of how priority should be allocated to private Members' Bills.

The first of these matters was considered by a Select Committee in 1914. Its Report suggested only that the problem be reconsidered by another committee in the following session, by which time the outbreak of war effectively eliminated such discussion. However, the Chairman of the 1914 Select Committee, Sir Thomas Whitaker, did make detailed proposals for major procedural changes in the later stages of Bills. The number of Fridays devoted to these later stages should be increased from two to eight. A Bill, if reported without amendment from a

---

[1] *H.C. Deb.*, Vol. 112, col. 109.   [2] Ibid., Vol. 113, col. 1476.
[3] Ibid., Vol. 138, cols. 101, 795.

Standing Committee, should go straight forward to a third reading, omitting the report stage. A Bill which had been amended at the committee stage might be remitted to the same or another Standing Committee for its report stage if the House passed a motion to this effect. Such a Bill might have a truncated

TABLE IV.2

Time available for Private Members' Bills

Session	No. of days	Session	No. of days
1906	8	1924–5	13
1907	13	1926	14
1908	17	1927	13
1909	13	1928	17
1910	6	1928–9	—
1911	5	1929–30	19
1912–13	13	1930–1	15
1913	9	1931–2	1
1919	12	1932–3	16
1920	12	1933–4	14
1921	7	1934–5	—
1922	8	1935–6	11
1923	12	1936–7	15
1924	15	1937–8	16

Source: *Select Committee on Procedure Report*, Appendix I, 1938–9

debate on third reading in which only three 15-minute speeches would be allowed, including one from a Government representative, provided that the House passed a motion approving this procedure by a two-thirds majority. A Bill which had passed the committee stage might be carried over to the next session of a Parliament and be permitted to continue its progress from the point already reached. The first four Fridays could be devoted to private Members' Bills carried over from the previous session and priority given to the Bills according to the support each of them had received. Thus Sir Thomas Whitaker produced a sophisticated scheme which tried to ensure that Bills which had widespread support were not lost through lack of time or obstruction by a small minority.[1]

[1] 1914 (H.C. 378) vii, paras. 30–7.

Thirteen years later in 1927 another Select Committee faced the same problem by trying to classify Bills as contentious and non-contentious.[1] However, it is only possible to classify a Bill in this way after it has been discussed. One proposal was that the test of contentiousness could be the vote on second reading and that priority for private Members' Bills after Whitsun should be arranged to vary inversely with the size of the hostile vote at second reading, Bills unopposed at second reading being taken first. This idea did not find favour with the Committee. It noted that sometimes the amount of opposition to a Bill did not become apparent until after the second reading. Sometimes also a controversial Bill slipped through the second reading stage unopposed due to the inattention of Members. The scheme also would seem to encourage unnecessary speech-making on uncontroversial measures. An alternative was for the decision to be left to an impartial observer; it was suggested that the Speaker, on the recommendation of the Chairmen's Panel, should certify which bills were non-contentious and they would then be starred by the Government and taken through their later stages as exempted business after 11 p.m.[2] This device was not adopted partly because the Speaker did not wish to be burdened with this type of decision. Instead the Committee proposed that the number of Fridays devoted to the later stages of Bills be increased from two to four—a minor but useful reform that was adopted by the House.

It is peculiar that the Standing Orders governing private Members' times should have remained unchanged since 1927 when they have not been effective since 1939. Each year since 1939 they have been superceded by a sessional order. From 1939 to 1948 no time at all was provided for private Members, the result of the wartime emergency and the heavy programme of legislation initiated by the Labour Government in the immediate post-war period. After 1945 the back-benchers did not surrender their rights without protest. In 1945 A. P. Herbert, the Independent Member for Oxford University, threw a bundle of thirteen Bills, fully drafted and ready for presentation, on to the floor of the Chamber to add colour to his objection to the motion that gave absolute priority to Government business.[3] On the

---

[1] 1927 (H.C. 102) vi.   [2] Ibid., Q.157.
[3] A. P. Herbert, *Independent Member* (Methuen, 1950), pp. 374–6.

Labour benches there was also much regret at the continued loss of private Members' time.[1] Finally in 1948–9 the Government relented and allowed ten Fridays for back-benchers' Bills, but no time was allowed for motions. In the brief 1950 session there were five Fridays for motions but none for Bills. Since 1951 private Members have had the use of twenty Fridays each session for Bills and motions except when the session has been cut short to hold a general election.[2] From 1951 to 1967 the Fridays were divided equally between Bills and motions; from 1967 to 1970 the ratio was changed to sixteen for Bills and four for motions; in 1970 the ratio became twelve for Bills and eight for motions.[3] Between 1951 and 1967 the last four Bill Fridays were reserved for later stages; since 1967 half the Bill Fridays have been used for this purpose. Since 1951 the number of names drawn in ballot has been 20 except in 1966–7 when it was 26 and between 1967–8 and 1969–70 when it was 27.

Changes have been made in the procedure to help Members to prepare their Bills. As noted above, at the end of the nineteenth century Members were required to introduce their Bills the day after the ballot; by 1953 the interval had become six days and now it is three weeks. So Members who succeed in the ballot have a reasonable time to decide how to use their opportunity. In 1972 Greville Janner used the time interval to consult with teenage schoolchildren in his constituency about the subject of his Bill: the result was a measure to require the installation of warning devices in the homes of elderly and disabled persons. Even after the three-week interval Members have only to present their Bills in dummy form. The final draft can be submitted nearer the date for the second reading. Another change has been made in the time scale for Bill Fridays. In the 1950s Bills and motions were taken on alternative weeks. Now the arrangement is that the first six Fridays after the Christmas recess are used for second readings and then there is a gap after which six more Fridays give priority to later stages. This system allows Members

---

[1] *H.C. Deb.*, Vol. 413, col. 133 et seq., Vol. 430, col. 93 et seq., and Vol. 443, col. 88 et seq.

[2] The Wednesday time for motions was surrendered to the Government. These changes were based on the recommendations of the *Select Committee on Procedure, Third Report*, 1945–6 (H.C. 189) ix, p. xvii.

[3] Since 1959 four extra half days have also been available for motions.

more time to get their Bills drafted and the gap in the middle provides a breathing-space when the details of Bills which gain a second reading can be examined in Standing Committee.

Drafting of legislation is a highly specialized art only understood fully by the limited group of official draftsmen. So Members need help in preparing their Bills. Sometimes they get aid from friends in the legal profession; sometimes from legal advisers to voluntary organizations; sometimes from the Clerks in the Public Bill Office. But if the subject matter is complex, inadequate drafting is an obvious target for criticism. It can also waste valuable time at the committee stage and the report stage. The Select Committee on Procedure proposed in 1971 that the Members who win the first ten places in the ballot should be entitled to the assistance of official draftsmen or alternatively should get financial help towards the cost of professional assistance.[1] The Government response was to offer a grant of up to £200 to each in the first ten places.[2] Except as an economy measure there is no good reason for restricting this assistance to the first ten. The chance of a balloted Bill becoming law depends at least as much on its subject matter as its priority in the ballot. Thus in session 1970–1 of the seven balloted Bills to succeed, four had been drawn within the first ten places: in the following session four of the eight to succeed were within the first ten.

In recent years the main controversy surrounding procedure on private Members' Bills has been over how far the Government should provide additional facilities for them, not in terms of drafting but in relation to parliamentary time. It has been common practice for the Government to provide a little time towards the end of the session to deal with Lords' amendments. But the assistance provided by the Wilson Labour Government was much more extensive. The Bill to abolish capital punishment was debated in Government time. For other measures, e.g. those relating to homosexuality, abortion, and divorce, additional parliamentary time was created by holding morning sessions or all-night sessions. Sometimes additional Standing Committees were provided. When challenged to explain what principles guided Ministers' decisions on whether to arrange extra time, the leader of the House, Richard Crossman, ex-

[1] *Second Report*, 1970–1 (H.C. 538), para. 54.
[2] *H.C. Deb.*, Vol. 825, col. 651.

plained: 'The considerations include the state of the Government's own programme; the prospects for the bill in private members' own time and the effect on other private members' legislation; the amount of interest in and support for the measure and possibly the progress the bill has made. The Government's attitude to the bill is also relevant.'[1] When the Conservatives took office in 1970 there was a sharp change of policy and it was made clear that no official assistance would be forthcoming save in exceptional circumstances. Between 1964 and 1970 the Labour Government gave some assistance for 23 of the private Members' Bills which became law.[2] Help was provided for back-bench sponsors from all parties and usually took the form of additional facilities at the committee stage. In contrast, between 1970 and 1972 a single Bill was assisted; this was a measure concerning vasectomy, promoted by a Labour Member, Phillip Whitehead, which had been delayed by a technicality when Lords' amendments were being considered. In 1973 came a fresh development when the Labour Opposition used half a Supply Day to provide time for William Hamilton's Anti-Discrimination Bill to obtain a second reading which was ultimately achieved without a division. On a previous Friday the Bill had been the second item on the Order Paper and no decision had been reached as the Speaker refused the closure on the grounds that there had been inadequate time for debate. This precedent of using a Supply Day could be important in relation to any Bill favoured by the Opposition and on which the Government and its supporters were neutral or divided. Indeed, should the Conservative attitude to private Members' legislation continue to be less sympathetic than that of the Labour Party, the total effect could be substantial. Controversial social measures may be assisted by the Labour Party; subsequently, if attempts are made to modify or repeal such measures, the reaction is likely to fail through lack of time.

Table IV.3 attempts to summarize the success of private Members' Bills over the last seventy years. It shows the numbers for each type which were introduced and passed into law in sessions selected at roughly five-year intervals. Two gaps in the series are caused by two world wars. As noticed above, no pro-

[1] Ibid., Vol. 745, col. 1152.
[2] Three private peers' Bills were also assisted.

vision for non-balloted Bills was available in session 1948–9. No session can claim to be typical but when choosing those to be analysed one avoided sessions obviously abnormal in relation to private Members' time.

TABLE IV.3

Success of Private Members' Bills, 1906–1972

Session	All Private Members' Bills[1]		Balloted Bills		Ten-Minute Rule Bills		Unballoted Bills	
	Intro-duced	Passed	Intro-duced	Passed	Intro-duced	Passed	Intro-duced	Passed
1906	189	5	41	—	3	—	145	5
1911	223	14	25	1	12	—	186	13
1921	75	14	21	2	4	—	50	12
1926	81	13	31	8	19	2	31	3
1930–1	94	6	24	3	28	2	42	1
1935–6	41	7	27	5	4	1	10	1
1948–9	23	5	23	5	—	—	—	—
1953–4	28	13	19	11	8	1	1	1
1958–9	42	21	20	8	12	5	10	8
1963–4	79	27	20	13	40	5	19	9
1967–8	74	13	26	8	35	3	13	2
1971–2	72	12	20	9	39	—	13	3

A number of tendencies emerge clearly from the figures. There is a dramatic fall in the number of unballoted Bills after the First World War, a fall which is largely explained by the exclusion of Members from Southern Ireland. The 1930s, 1940s, and early 1950s were lean years, but since then there has been a growth in activity. A higher proportion of balloted Bills have been successful. More minor measures have been slipped through outside the ballot procedure. Since the 1960s the popularity of the Ten-Minute Rule procedure has greatly increased—another indication of greater back-bench vigour. But what these figures cannot show are the nature and sources of unofficial legislation—matters which are analysed in the following section.

Ideas which form the basis of private Members' Bills come from

[1] Excluding private peers' Bills.

four sources: the enthusiasms of individual Members, party policy, interest groups, and official quarters. The last category may be said to include Government departments, the Law Commission, and the reports of official inquiries. More than one, but rarely more than two, of these stimuli may be operative in any particular measure. Naturally a Member must approve of the legislation he sponsors but often he will adopt a cause suggested by another Member or an interest group. A Member who wins a high place in the ballot is now the target for much lobbying. Sir Alan Herbert has given a delightful description of how he secured the introduction of his Matrimonial Clauses Bill by Sir Rupert, then Mr., De la Bère:

Two other Members with Bills in their beaks descended on us and tried to carry him off. But I was able to claim priority and bullied them away. He, too, already had a Bill in his hand, an innocent little thing about municipal elections, which the Whips had given him. My heart sank when I saw that: but I did not know Mr. De la Bère.[1]

Thirty years later Leo Abse wished to liberalize further the divorce law and had to obtain co-operation from colleagues who had won a good place in the ballot—William Wilson for the unsuccessful Bill in session 1967–8 and in the following session Alec Jones who sponsored the measure that became the Divorce Reform Act, 1969.

The second source mentioned above, the party policy element, has receded. Irish Members used this procedure until 1914 as a useful means to parade the grievances of their countrymen. In the inter-war period Labour Members used private Members' Bills as a vehicle for party propaganda. They introduced a Prevention of Unemployment Bill six times between 1919 and 1927, and a Bill to nationalize coal mines four times between 1924 and 1938. A Workmen's Compensation Bill was produced regularly between 1932 and 1939. In the period before the General Strike Conservative Members were active in introducing measures to restrict trade union activity. Clearly, Bills based on party policy will never be passed unless they emanate from Government supporters. And the Government benches are likely to feel that their policies can be translated into law most

[1] *The Ayes Have It* (Methuen, 1937), p. 84. Sir Alan's unsuccessful attempt to find a Member to introduce his Bill on Newfoundland in 1948 is described in his *Independent Member*, pp. 425–8.

effectively by ministerial legislation. To use the ballot procedure for party purposes is frustrating and unproductive. Since 1948 this view has been fairly widely accepted by Members.

A tradition has developed that party whips are not used officially in private Members' time. A move to impose a Government whip against the Matrimonial Property Bill 1968 caused such a storm of protest among Labour Members that the idea was dropped. Ultimately the Bill was withdrawn in return for a promise of Government legislation in the following session.[1] Ministers will always be able to block a measure if they are strongly hostile to it, but their view may triumph only after difficulty and embarrassment. Bromhead has given a detailed description of the problems caused to the Labour Government by the Hairdressers' Registration Bill, 1949, before it was defeated at the third reading.[2] The Women's Emancipation Bill, 1919, which sought to give the vote to women between the ages of 21 and 30, got even further: it passed all stages in the Commons, in spite of Cabinet hostility, before being defeated in the Lords. However, the Upper House can no longer be regarded as a secure longstop always ready to defend the community against social change. More recently its willingness to accept changes in the laws governing abortion, homosexuality, and Sunday observance preceded that of the House of Commons.

Members who wish to make a positive contribution to the legislative process will avoid using Fridays for staging party battles. Table IV.4 demonstrates that a high proportion of balloted Bills now enjoy multi-party support. It should be noted that a Bill promoted by Government supporters does not necessarily have ministerial approval.

There is also an important constitutional restriction on the subject matter of private Members' Bills. Where a Bill imposes a fresh charge on the Consolidated Fund it requires a financial resolution to be passed after its second reading, a resolution that must be proposed by a Minister of the Crown and is sometimes known as the Queen's Recommendation. This rule is an important safeguard of the probity of public life. No back-bencher can introduce legislation designed to produce direct financial bene-

[1] Richards, *Parliament and Conscience*, p. 152.
[2] P. A. Bromhead, *Private Members' Bills in the British Parliament* (Kegan Paul, 1956), pp. 181–7.

fits for his constituency or other sections of the community. Yet the rule is not as restrictive as it may appear at first sight. Whether a Bill does need a financial resolution is a complex question.[1] One is not required where the type of expenditure to be incurred can be regarded as authorized by existing legislation. The position, stated broadly, is that a private Member can

TABLE IV.4

Balloted Bills—Party or Non-Party

Session	No. of Bills	Bills sponsored by Members of more than one party	Bills sponsored by one party[2]				Bills sponsored by a single Member
			Cons.	Lab.	Lib.	Irish Nat.	
1906	41	21	1	1	7	7	4
1911	25	10	8	—	4	(1)[3]	3
1921	21	7	9	2	2		1
1926	31	9	10	10	—		2
1930–1	24	10	5	8	—		1
1935–6	27	6	11	10	—		—
1948–9	23	6	7	8[2]	—		2
1953–4	19	14	2	3	—		—
1958–9	20	9	4	6	—		1
1963–4	20	13	5	2	—		—
1967–8	26	10	5	6	(1)[3]		5
1971–2	20	13	3	4	—		—

promote a Bill that increases the total of public spending providing that its main purpose is not the imposition of a fresh charge on the public revenues. Thus an increase in administrative cost is regarded as incidental. And where a private Member's Bill authorizes new avenues for local authority expenditure which may also impose fresh burdens on the Exchequer through the general grant to local government the practice is for a Minister to move the necessary financial resolution.

This financial safeguard has had an effect on the nature of pressure groups which interest themselves in private Members'

---

[1] Erskine May, 18th edn. (Butterworth, 1971), pp. 733–48.

[2] Including one Bill sponsored by the 2 Communist Members with Labour support—Piratin had won a place in the ballot.

[3] One Bill was sponsored by a single Irish Nationalist, and one Bill was sponsored by a single Liberal. These Bills are counted in the last column.

legislation, for the procedure is useless to those who wish to press for higher pensions, higher family allowances, or more generous grants and subsidies. With these exceptions the activity of interest groups in relation to private Members' Bills has increased steadily. In part this is a reflection of the growing importance of voluntary groups of all kinds. To an increasing extent politicians get their ideas from non-party sources; they provide a sieve through which ideas must pass. Meanwhile the growing strength and sophistication of interest groups improves the quality of assistance they offer to Members who sponsor their proposals. Sir Ivor Jennings has given details of the campaign by the National Association of Local Government Officers to secure superannuation rights for their members which produced an Act in 1922.[1] Later attempts to strengthen this measure failed but ultimately the Government was persuaded to produce a compulsory and comprehensive scheme in 1937. Temperance and animal welfare groups have been very active in pressing their respective causes. And groups are not only concerned to promote legislation; they may wish to block it. The Lord's Day Observance Society has a long history of attempting to defeat legislation which would liberalize laws relating to behaviour on Sunday. Sometimes a Bill becomes a battleground between groups with opposed views. The proceedings on the Abortion Act, 1967, became a struggle between the Abortion Law Reform Association and the Society for the Protection of the Unborn Child.

A Member who wishes to use good fortune in the ballot to place a measure on the statute book is well advised to use the fourth source of inspiration—official quarters. Government departments are conscious of minor defects and anomalies in the law that they wish to correct when the opportunity arises. Such items are often uncontroversial. If a Member adopts one he may well get his Bill through Parliament with little trouble. Also possibly uncontroversial, but probably more technical, are proposals by the Law Commission which was established in 1965 to advise the Lord Chancellor on questions of law reform. Their reports may be the subject of either ministerial or back-bench legislation. An example of their work is the Domicile and Matrimonial Proceedings Bill, 1973, introduced by Ian Mac-

[1] *Parliament*, 2nd edn. (Cambridge University Press, 1957), pp. 193-4.

Arthur. Reports of commissions or departmental committees may also provide the stimulus for back-benchers' Bills. Less frequently the report of a parliamentary select committee may do so; the Theatres Act, 1968, introduced by George Strauss was based on the report of a joint select committee of both Houses.[1]

What, then, emerges from these various channels, pressures, and restraints? What does private Members' legislation seek to do? The character of these Bills is so diverse as to defy precise description, but five main categories are discernible. Table IV.5 is an endeavour to make a subject classification of balloted bills in selected sessions over the past seventy years. Bills have been divided into those concerned with constitutional matters, local government, control of individual behaviour, control of group behaviour, and law reform including legal procedure. In addition, there is a miscellaneous column for items that do not fit in easily elsewhere. It will be noted that the number of constitutional Bills has fallen; this is largely because the controversies about the franchise have faded. It will also be noted that Bills of this kind were (almost) never passed as they tended to lead to party clashes. Bills relating to individual behaviour have grown in number. Some of these impose new restraints: others remove restraints. The next category refers to the control of social or economic groups and covers such matters as labour legislation and standards of commercial and professional behaviour. Law reform is another traditional object for private Members' legislation and such Bills have a fair chance of becoming law.

The richness and variety of argument stimulated by this class of parliamentary business cannot be shown by statistical analysis. It is, indeed, a changing panorama of our social and economic history. Bills discussed in the Edwardian period to control the import of exotic plumage required for ladies' hats have no place in the 1970s. Conversely, the more recent debates on Bills concerned with sexual matters would have been regarded as impossible and intolerable before 1914 and perhaps before 1939. Temperance Bills have disappeared as the puritan spirit has waned. The modern style of concern with welfare is reflected in Bills which seek to authorize a far wider range of social protection and social provision.

[1] 1966–7 (H.C. 503 or H.L. 255).

TABLE IV.5
Subject Matter of Balloted Bills

Session	Constitutional	Local Government	Social Control		Law and Legal Procedure	Miscellaneous	Total Bills
			Individual	Collective			
1906	6	7	4	17	3	4	41
1911	5	1	3	12 (1)	1	3	25 (1)
1921	3	2	8	3	1	4 (2)	21 (2)
1926	1 (1)	5	6 (2)	11 (2)	5 (2)	3 (1)	31 (8)
1930–1	1	5 (1)	8	9 (2)	1	0	24 (3)
1935–6	3	2	10 (3)	4	5 (1)	3 (1)	27 (5)
1948–9	2	1	13 (3)	3	2 (1)	2 (1)	23 (5)
1953–4	2	0	9 (6)	3 (1)	5 (4)	0	19 (11)
1958–9	0	0	7 (1)	9 (4)	4 (3)	0	20 (8)
1963–4	1	2 (1)	8 (6)	6 (4)	1 (1)	2 (1)	20 (13)
1967–8	1	3 (1)	14 (5)	5 (1)	3 (1)	0	26 (8)
1971–2	1	0	9 (5)	3 (1)	4 (2)	3 (1)	20 (9)

Numbers in brackets show the numbers of bills to become law.

It is widely accepted that issues of conscience which involve moral or religious attitudes are peculiarly suitable for private Members' legislation because they arouse differences of opinion which transgress the normal patterns of party allegiance.[1] From the viewpoint of the whips such matters should be either avoided or put on a free vote basis. Temperance and Sunday observance were natural conscience issues. So were the marriage laws, slowly liberalized through back-bench initiative. The Deceased Wife's Sister Act, 1907, and the Deceased Brother's Widow's Marriage Act, 1921, both permitted marriages previously forbidden. Sir Alan Herbert's more extensive Marriage Act, 1937, was the most famous private Member's Bill of the inter-war period. Other important measures coming in this category are the Obscene Publications Act, 1959, the Legitimacy Act, 1959, the Sexual Offences Act, 1967, the Abortion Act, 1967, and the Divorce Reform Act, 1969.

On such issues Government inactivity is understandable. Other back-bench legislation has dealt with matters where ministerial inertia is less excusable, e.g. the Summer Time Act, 1925, the Transport Lighting Act, 1928, the Hire Purchase Act, 1938, and the Inheritance (Family Provisions) Act, 1938. The back-bench attempts to pass a daylight-saving law started in the Edwardian era. Another reform successfully achieved after a long delay was Harold Lever's Defamation Act, 1952, based on the 1945 Report of the Parker Committee, the Parker Committee itself being established as a consequence of an unsuccessful private Member's Bill in 1938. Thus unofficial Bills can be useful even when they do not become law. Sir Gerald Nabarro withdrew his Clean Air Bill in 1955 in return for a promise of Government legislation the following session. Edward Bishop did the same with his Matrimonial Property Bill in 1968. Sometimes all a sponsor can achieve is a promise of an official inquiry. In 1951 Mrs. Eirene White withdrew her Matrimonial Causes Bill after the offer of a Royal Commission upon the divorce laws. More recently in 1970 the appointment of the Younger Committee on the privacy of the individual followed the withdrawal by Brian Walden of his Bill on this subject.

So the range and impact of back-bench legislation is wide. It

---

[1] For full discussion see Richards, *Parliament and Conscience.*

does not and should not impinge on major issues of party controversy. It may not propose new categories of public expenditure. Subject to these limitations there is a wide field open for
back-benchers. Members are increasingly conscious of this
opportunity.

Attitudes among Members towards private Members' legislation have varied over the years. The prevalent nineteenth-
century view was that it was a valuable right which emphasized
the independence of the legislature. Equally, it was admitted
that the procedure was unproductive because so few unofficial
Bills became law. The changes in Standing Orders in 1888 and
the discussions of the 1914 Select Committee were both attempts
to make more effective use of the time available. However, the
difficulty of getting private Members' Bills on to the statute book
was not merely a matter of procedure for another major obstacle
was the type of Bill many Members insisted on promoting.
During this period many Bills related to regional problems or to
the personal enthusiasms of individual Members. Irish Members
produced measures to deal with the grievances of Ireland. Non-
conformist Members produced temperance Bills to promote
their cause in specified areas. Each year James Bryce sponsored
a Bill to facilitate access to mountains. None of these Bills could
command majority support in the Commons. They induced
boredom because the arguments for and against became pain-
fully familiar. In these circumstances private Members' Bills
remained important largely as a symbol of the rights of back-
benchers.

During the 1920s criticism of the procedure became more
basic.[1] Right-wing opinion was potentially hostile to fresh
legislation and, therefore, to supplementary channels for legislation. Left-wing opinion felt that, in an ideal world, legislation
should come from a Labour Government in full command of the
parliamentary timetable. So the 1930 Select Committee on
Procedure heard opposed opinions. Mr. Winston Churchill
thought it should be made difficult 'for all sorts of happy thoughts

---

[1] The following paragraphs are based on Chapter 10 of my *Parliament and
Conscience*.

to be carried on to the statute book'.[1] The Labour Chief Whip thought that time spent on private Members' Bills was 'very largely wasted'.[2] Lloyd George was more favourable because he felt that the procedure offered an opportunity to discuss new ideas and new topics.[3] Writing towards the end of the 1930s, Harold Laski was hostile. He argued that if a matter were important enough to require legislation then responsibility for the legislation should rest with the Government; in any case legislation will not pass unless the Government approves of it. The private Member as a sponsor of legislation was in a hopelessly weak position: A. P. Herbert had been forced to accept damaging amendments to his Divorce Bill and 'the truncated measure which resulted will probably prevent the serious rationalisation of the marriage laws for many years to come'.[4] This is a searing criticism. Yet it ignores two vital points. If a Government wishes to evade a moral issue, the private Member is the only alternative source of initiative within the rules of parliamentary procedure. Secondly, it is at least as valid to claim that a limited reform prepares the way for subsequent and wider reform as it is to claim that limited reform impedes subsequent and more radical change—especially on matters affecting religious belief and social values where behaviour patterns change slowly.

Critics of back-bench legislation can argue that it produces bad laws and/or that the time spent on it could be better used in another way. The latter view used to be popular in left-wing circles. The private Member was thought to be a nineteenth-century irrelevance. Once a Labour Cabinet was elected with a clear majority in the Commons it must then set about the task of achieving socialist reconstruction of the country. No time could be spared for the trivia which back-benchers might wish to see on the statute book. Essentially this was Laski's view and the view of the Attlee Labour Government in the immediate post-war years. But experience bred disenchantment. By 1948 the energy of the Government was seen to flag and the possibility that back-benchers could contribute usefully to the total of legislation became difficult to deny. So time was again made

---

[1] *Procedure on Public Business, Special Report*, Q.1530, 1930–1 (H.C. 161), viii.

[2] Ibid., Q.718.   [3] Ibid., Q.893.

[4] *Parliamentary Government in England* (Allen & Unwin, 1938), p. 166.

available for private Members' Bills after a gap of nine years, Sir Ivor Jennings's comment became increasingly acceptable: 'The fact that much Government legislation is either vote-catching or of a departmental character renders desirable the provision of time for other measures.'[1]

The challenge to back-bench legislation between 1967 and 1970 was quite different in character. The objections were right-wing rather than left-wing. Nothing was heard about trivial time-wasting; instead the complaint was that the Government allowed back-benchers to have glorious and irresponsible free-dom to force through changes in the basic fabric of our social life. Five separate yet complementary arguments in this approach can be distinguished.

1. The Government is succeeding in obtaining the passage of controversial laws without accepting responsibility for them.
2. Measures are passed at a stage when insufficient study and debate has been devoted to the issues involved.
3. Constituents do not know the views of parliamentary candidates on non-party issues: Members, therefore, have no mandate.
4. Important votes on private Members' Bills are taken on Fridays or in all-night sittings when attendance is low.
5. Private Members' Bills are badly drafted and do not—in the case of complex measures—operate as intended.

These propositions will be considered in turn.

1. The Government is succeeding in obtaining the passage of controversial laws without accepting responsibility for them. This was the basic challenge. It was claimed that permissive social legislation was unpopular with many electors, including Government supporters; that were the Cabinet to espouse these causes openly it would have lost support; that because these causes were keenly pressed by many Labour Members the Cabinet let them go ahead while dodging responsibility.[2] No

---

[1] *Parliament*, p. 373.

[2] A development of this thesis was that the Government gave a green light to back-benchers on social issues to provide an outlet for their crusading energies and so divert them from criticism of Government policy. But left-wing opposition to ministerial policy continued unabated and most Members closely concerned with these measures were not noted for extreme political opinions.

back-bench initiative that arouses great passion can succeed unless the Government arranges extra time and this, it was argued, implies not merely neutrality but covert support. The counter-argument is that the supply of extra time merely allows the Commons to reach a decision; a Bill allowed such a facility might be successful or it might be defeated. All the measures allowed extra time have passed because Ministers judged correctly the broad wishes of the House. If a Government aided a Bill that failed it could be accused of pushing it or of wasting Members' time.

The main issue, however, is Laski's theme that all legislation should be Government legislation. Here one must face the fact that British parties, if not class parties, are differentiated by their economic policies rather than by moral attitudes. It is 'bread-and-butter' issues which excite the electors; votes are won and lost over matters of material well-being. Immigration is the only social controversy likely to have a significant impact on voting behaviour.[1] Capital punishment and a few other issues could have a slight effect where a Member had played a prominent role in a campaign for reform. But attitudes on these social questions traverse economic divisions and take second place to them. If our party system resembled more closely a European model, it might be that social issues could fit neatly into the established party complex. A Roman Catholic party with a generally conservative, private enterprise approach to economic issues could be expected to oppose legislation on abortion and divorce, but to support Sunday entertainments, the abolition of capital punishment, and the reform of the law on homosexuality. Britain does not happen to have that kind of Conservative Party. Religious differences are submerged in a two-party system. Any Government, Conservative or Labour, must offend some of its supporters if it dares to approach issues of this nature. The consequent inaction can breed festering social problems. The alternative is to set aside the party dimension and for Parliament to decide as a Parliament and not merely as a body recording Cabinet decisions. Responsibility moves away from Cabinet to Parliament. This is not a new or revolutionary tendency but a movement towards older ways.

[1] David Butler and Donald Stokes, *Political Change in Britain* (Macmillan, 1969), Chap. 15.

2. Measures are passed at a stage when insufficient study and debate has been devoted to the issues involved. This is an obvious line of attack against any proposal for reform. Any subject may be illuminated by further research: levels of knowledge can always be improved. Public participation in any discussion is always incomplete and fuller discussion and understanding will always be desirable. Unless law is to be treated as immutable, at some stage decisions must be taken and votes determine the outcome. But the plain fact is that Parliament does not rush ahead on conscience issues. Capital punishment had a Royal Commission. Departmental committees had considered homosexuality and Sunday observance. A Joint Select Committee had reviewed theatre censorship. The Law Commission had reported on the divorce laws. Documents had been issued by the Established Church on homosexuality, abortion, and divorce. It seems probable that no private Member's Bill on an issue of conscience could succeed without some preliminary inquiry of this kind. One Bill that failed to pass, that on Sunday entertainments, departed most clearly from the recommendations of the preceding inquiry.

3. Constituents do not know the views of parliamentary candidates on non-party issues: Members, therefore, have no mandate. Without question, this statement is correct. But is it relevant? It has been argued above that the electorate is more concerned with economic issues than other matters. To put this in another form, electors are more concerned with party than non-party issues. Votes are cast on party lines because parties differ on matters which are felt to be most important. It is ridiculous to suppose that many voters would change their allegiance because a candidate said he would vote this way or that on a private Member's Bill. In reality, the level of public knowledge of party policies is low. Opinion studies have shown repeatedly the limitations of public understanding and the extent to which people do not agree with the policies of the party they support. No parliamentary candidate can foresee all issues that will be presented to Parliament in the coming four or five years. No parliamentary candidate should be willing to guarantee that his views will not change in the light of changing circumstances. The British tradition of democracy is based on representation not on the unfree actions of mandated delegates.

The public can express opinions on any issue through pressure groups, the mass media, and personal communication with their elected representatives. But the decisions remain with Members. Voters who are displeased with Members have a possibility of redress at the next general election. Even then, almost all will make a choice in accordance with an individual perception of *party* principles or programmes.

4. Important votes on private Members' Bills are taken on Fridays or in all-night sittings when attendance is low. In general, this statement is accurate. However, if a Bill excites public interest, the attendance of Members improves. The number voting in the critical division on the abolition of capital punishment was 529; on homosexual law reform 348; on abortion 254; on divorce law reform 293. But as all these Bills were given additional facilities by the Government, of the divisions noticed above only that on abortion took place on a Friday. The safeguard against legislation by a small minority is the closure rule which requires the presence of 100 supporters to force a decision. In fact, the amount of attention and concern in the Commons over major private Members' Bills is probably greater than that devoted to much Government legislation. The numbers voting on Government Bills are higher because normally the party whips are on both sides of the House: the back-bench sponsor of a Bill can make no such claim on party discipline or loyalty. How much Government legislation, in the absence of the whips, could ensure the presence of 250 Members? A great benefit of legislation without party whips is that it offers Members freedom, not merely in terms of how to vote but whether to vote at all. Those who do stay and vote are those who feel most strongly about a subject and, one hopes, are the most fully informed about it. Is there any advantage to be gained from filling the division lobbies with extra Members who are relatively indifferent and uninformed about the matter to be decided?

The criticism that Members do not bother to vote can be linked with proposition 2 that decisions are taken with inadequate preparation. This raises the further question of how far existing law has been the result of careful deliberation in Parliament. Both theatre censorship and Sunday observance were based on eighteenth-century statutes which were passed largely for reasons that today are totally unacceptable, i.e. political and religious intolerance. The nineteenth-century law on homosexuality was, indeed, a late-night rush, virtually undebated. Abortion law had become uncertain and depended upon judicial decisions rather than parliamentary decisions. Only in the cases of capital punishment and divorce could the existing law be said to be the result of full consideration by a democratic assembly. But law is accepted as legitimate in Britain because it is the law, not because of the conditions under which a law was made. In any case, a private Member's Bill which survives all the obstacles offered by parliamentary procedure has at least as good a claim to validity in democratic terms as the law which it replaces.

5. Private Members' Bills are badly drafted and do not—in the case of complex measures—operate as intended. Amateur drafting could cause legal confusion and waste parliamentary time. In practice, this is not a serious problem because Members do get help—from the Clerks, from voluntary bodies, or from official sources. Also since 1971 those who gain the top ten places in the ballot can have financial assistance to obtain professional advice. Whether a piece of legislation works as intended is a matter which affects government legislation as well as private Members' Bills. It is an issue that is likely to arise over any controversial topic, e.g. industrial relations, race relations, or the breathalyser law.

The arguments against private Members' legislation were not persuasive. Indeed, since 1970 they have faded away. But is it really possible for Parliament to play a more constructive role in law-making? J. S. Mill's dictum must not be forgotten: 'a numerous assembly is as little fitted for the direct business of legislation as for that of administration'.[1] Ninety years later Professor J. A. G. Griffith regarded the task of Parliament in legislation as that of 'examination, criticism and approval'.[2] It is quite clear that Parliament as a whole cannot master the details of a problem or draft complicated proposals for new legislation. Initial spadework must always be done by small groups of people with specialized knowledge and skill. The task for Parliament is to accept or reject the main heads of proposals prepared in this way. The question is whether the preparatory

[1] *Representative Government* (1881), Chap. IV.
[2] See his penetrating article 'The Place of Parliament in the Legislative Process', *Modern Law Review* (1951), Vol. 14, pp. 279–96 and 425–36.

work necessarily has to be done within Government departments or be presented by Ministers to Parliament on the basis that the prestige of the Government is linked to the fate of the draft legislation.

If one accepts the value of private Members' legislation and its importance to the work of Parliament, the question remains whether procedure could be improved. This matter falls into two parts. The first is how the Bills selected for discussion should be chosen. The second is whether the rules governing their discussion could usefully be amended.

To organize priority for Bills through a ballot is to relegate decisions to luck. This is an obvious target for criticism. The fortune of the draw may give top places to Members with idiosyncratic ideas which are unlikely to gain the support of the House. Should this happen, it is arguable that valuable time and opportunities have been wasted. An alternative procedure would be for Bills to be introduced in the form of motions; priority for Bills could then be determined by the number of supporters each motion attracted within a given period. This is a very old idea: one version of it was proposed by Mr. Bryce in the Commons as early as 1888.[1] By this means the most popular Bills would go to the head of the queue and have an excellent chance of becoming law. Judged by a productivity criterion of the number of laws passed, it is certain that this method would give the best results. The dangers are that the legislation passed would be trivial in character or that the majority party would dominate proceedings, perhaps by design or perhaps not. Minority interests would be squeezed out. It is arguable that this would be unfortunate. Unorthodox opinions can only gain support if they are freely ventilated and their advocates given a good chance to persuade others. Popular ideas and non-controversial items already have an advantage over less popular ideas in that they can more easily find a sponsor. One doubts whether this advantage should be made absolute.

Professor Ramsay Muir suggested to the Select Committee on Procedure in 1930 that the allocation of time for private Members' Bills should be determined by a committee which would

[1] *Parl. Deb.*, 3rd series, Vol. 322, cols. 1775–7. The same suggestion was made by the Clerk of the House, Sir Gilbert Campion, to the Select Committee on Procedure, 1945–6.

choose the Bills it felt to be most worthy of discussion.[1] But upon what basis could a committee fix priorities? If it preferred Bills with the widest support, it would, as argued above, discriminate against minority interests and new ideas. If it adopted any other method, the committee could be accused of pushing forward personal preferences or, more probably, holding back personal *bêtes noires*. The ballot is an imperfect technique but the alternatives all suffer shortcomings at least as grave.

Another possibility is that subjects for private Members' Bills should be given preliminary consideration by a Select Committee which would take evidence and hear witnesses. This raises wider issues, considered elsewhere in this volume,[2] about the value of pre-legislation committees. During this century there have been five private Members' Bills based on the reports of Commons' Select Committees: Savings Banks Acts Amendment Bill, 1904, Performing Animals Bill, 1923, Employment of Disabled Ex-servicemen Bill, 1924, Nursing Homes (Registration) Bill, 1927, and Obscene Publications Bill, 1959.[3] The Theatres Act, 1968, which abolished the censorship powers of the Lord Chamberlain was based on the recommendations of a Joint Select Committee of Lords and Commons. More often Select Committee recommendations have formed the basis of Government legislation. Certainly if there is any urgency about the implementation of such recommendations it is unsatisfactory to leave them to the uncertainties of the ballot.

An alternative is for a private Member's Bill to be submitted after second reading to a Select Committee rather than to the normal Standing Committee. The Select Committee procedure provides opportunities to hear evidence and canvass opinion. It is also more expensive in terms of Members' time and produces delay. Since the start of this century 27 private Members' Bills

---

[1] 1930–1 (H.C. 161) viii, p. 256. The following session the Procedure Committee proposed that, as the session proceeds, the Committee of Selection could give priority at the committee stage to Bills which seemed likely to command general assent. No action was taken on this recommendation which is also open to the objections made in the main text. See 1931–2 (H.C. 129) v, p. xvii.

[2] See Chap. VIII.

[3] *Select Committee on Procedure, Second Report*, 1970–1 (H.C. 538), Appendix 1, pp. 276–80.

have been subjected to this procedure: only four became law.[1] This technique has fallen out of favour and has been used only twice since 1931.[2] It is clear that the Select Committee process means almost certain death to a private Member's Bill.

A variety of other proposals have been made to assist the preparation and passage of private Members' Bills. The ballot could be held, not at the start of the session, but at the end of the previous session. The Procedure Committee of 1970–1 felt that this change would give successful Members three months in which to prepare their Bills. Second readings could also be taken earlier in the session.[3] The Committee also suggested that a Member might use a place won in the ballot to adopt a Bill that had passed through the Lords early in the session.[4] A proposal made by the Study of Parliament Group to the same Committee —but not accepted—was that the sponsor of a private Member's Bill should be able to move that his Bill go before a Second Reading Committee, subject to the same conditions as apply to Government legislation. To prevent queue-jumping such a motion would have to be taken at the moment when a Bill is called for second reading under existing procedure. For the same reason this provision should not apply to non-balloted Bills until after the last second reading Friday for balloted Bills.[5] Another simple idea is that a second Standing Committee should be nominated to deal with private Members' legislation. This would reduce the waste of time caused by Bills queuing for attention at the committee stage. It would also remove the incentive to waste time on non-contentious business in order to delay controversial legislation.

John Parker suggested to the 1970–1 Procedure Committee

---

[1] Ibid., pp. 271–6.

[2] One was the special case of the Obscene Publications Bill. After second reading in session 1956–7 it was submitted to a Select Committee which failed to complete its work. Next session a Select Committee was appointed to continue examination of the subject. Its recommendations became the basis of a successful Ten-Minute Rule Bill in 1958–9. The second was the Anti-Discrimination Bill, 1973, designed to secure equality between the sexes: at the time this Bill received a second reading a parallel measure was before a Select Committee in the Upper House.

[3] *Second Report*, 1970–1 (H.C. 538), paras. 52–3.

[4] Ibid., para. 54.

[5] Ibid., Appendix 6, para. 11(ii).

that for private Members' Bills the number of Members required to support a successful closure motion should be reduced from 100 to 50.[1] The absence of party whipping in private Members' time makes it far more difficult to secure the attendance of Members. A lower minimum for the closure would sometimes help to secure a second reading and would be even more useful at the report stage of a measure contested by a small minority. Why should a 100 Members be required to defeat the filibustering tactics of, say, a dozen Members determined to prevent a change which is generally acceptable to opinion in the House? On the other hand, it is arguable that controversial measures should not be passed when the overwhelming majority of Members are absent. Fifty Members constitute only 8 per cent of the House. This is perhaps too small a proportion to be allowed to pass a new law which does arouse argument.

It is sometimes argued that Bills which fail to complete their parliamentary journey during one session should be allowed to continue in the next from the stage already reached—save when a new Parliament has assembled. Sir Thomas Whitaker, Chairman of the 1914 Procedure Committee, made a proposal on these lines.[2] The sessional 'cut off' does seem arbitrary and unnecessary. But Bills carried over would eat into the ration of private Members' time in the following session. A sessional carry-over would substantially increase the influence of Lords' amendments. The tyranny of the timetable does force issues to a conclusion. To allow a carry-over would remove the sense of urgency and could well increase delays to legislation rather than decrease them.[3]

The main need for private Members' Bills is more time: not more time in general, but more time when it is needed to avoid bottle-necks or avoid filibustering by a minority. Essentially these problems apply to the committee stage and the report stage. As noted above, the solution at the committee stage is to organize an additional committee as required by the pressure of business. The problem at the report stage is more difficult and possibly cannot be solved by formal adjustments to the rules of

[1] Ibid., Appendix 2, para. 26.
[2] 1914 (378) vii; pp. vii–xi.
[3] Cf. evidence of John Silkin, Labour Chief Whip, to the 1966–7 Select Committee on Procedure, *Sixth Report*, 1966–7 (H.C. 539) xvi, Q.439.

the House. The Study of Parliament Group suggested to the 1970–1 Procedure Committee that where a private Member's Bill had passed the second reading and had emerged from committee unchanged in its major features, then 'the Government should be encouraged to feel an obligation to allow the House to come to a decision by, if necessary, permitting a late sitting after ten p.m.'.[1] It was argued that the additional burden on the House would not be large because only one or possibly two measures a year would require this facility. On the other hand it is unrealistic to expect Ministers to support a Bill in this way if they (or some of them) heartily dislike it.

Yet public opinion, at least informed opinion, is becoming more sensitive to the opportunities provided for unofficial legislation. Recent years have seen a substantial increase in pressure groups of all kinds and important social changes have been secured through private Members' legislation. Encouragement is given to more people, more groups, to press their ideas for reform upon Members. As a result Members themselves are far more conscious of their personal right to promote Bills; more of them enter the ballot and those who are successful give more care to their choice of subject. The choice of a topic in the public mind will attract substantial publicity. The level of attention secured by the modern-style suffragettes led to the use of Opposition time in 1973 to secure a second reading for the Sex Discrimination Bill after it had failed for lack of time on a second reading Friday. This can be a precedent for finding more time to debate measures which capture public imagination. There is a feeling, both inside and outside Westminster, that legislation need not be a monopoly of Ministers supported by Civil Service advisers and party whips. It is arguable that a healthy Parliament needs a measure of freedom combined with an element of unpredictability. Before the second reading debate on the 1969 Divorce Bill the Speaker asked Members who wished to contribute to let him know privately whether they were for or against the measure as otherwise he could not ensure a balanced debate:[2] his request illustrates sharply the abnormal freedom and reality of the subsequent discussion. When the party dimension is set aside, Members are forced to think for themselves

[1] *Second Report*, 1970–1 (H.C. 538), Appendix 6, para. 11 (iv).
[2] *H.C. Deb.*, Vol. 758, col. 810.

about the questions at issue. Private Members' legislation puts Parliament at the heart of the decision-making process. It is good for society as it enables problems to be faced that might otherwise be ignored. The agenda of the Commons is helped to reflect more fully the fears, the desires, and perhaps the illusions of the electorate.

*

VII

SUPPLY AND OTHER FINANCIAL PROCEDURES

Michael Ryle

Introduction

The basic principles of Parliamentary control of expenditure

Most Gracious Sovereign,
We, Your Majesty's most dutiful and loyal subjects the Commons of the United Kingdom in Parliament assembled, towards making good the supply which we have cheerfully granted to Your Majesty in this Session of Parliament, have resolved to grant unto Your Majesty the sum hereafter mentioned . . .

In these words, which are the first part of the enacting formula for all Consolidated Fund and Appropriation Bills, are embodied the major principles of Parliament's responsibilities for public expenditure as they first evolved in medieval times, became established in the time of the Tudor monarchs, and received their conclusive political endorsement on the battlefields of the Civil War. These same principles have governed the role of the House of Commons[1] in respect of the authorization and control of public expenditure throughout the period with which this work is concerned.

However, the manner in which the principles have been applied has not remained unchanged. And examination of these changes further resolves itself into two levels of analyses. First, what rules of procedure have from time to time been framed to regulate the exercise of the House's responsibilities in respect of public expenditure? And, second, how have these procedures been used in practice (that is, the use Members of Parliament have made of the powers and opportunities the rules confer on

---

[1] This Chapter is, of its nature, primarily concerned with the House of Commons. Unless otherwise indicated the term 'House' so refers.

them)? It will be the main purpose of this Chapter to seek to answer these questions.

But first we must be clear what are the basic principles of financial procedures. They stem from and to some extent define both the relationship which has historically evolved between the Crown and Parliament and that which exists between the two Houses of Parliament. As stated by Sir Thomas Erskine May,

The Sovereign, being the executive power, is charged with the management of all the revenue of the State, and with all payments for the public service. The Crown, therefore, acting with the advice of its responsible ministers, makes known to the Commons the pecuniary necessities of the government; the Commons, in return, grant such aids or supplies as are required to satisfy these demands; and they provide by taxes, and by the appropriation of other sources of the public income, the ways and means to meet the supplies which they have granted. Thus the Crown demands money, the Commons grant it, and the Lords assent to the grant: but the Commons do not vote money unless it be required by the Crown; nor do they impose or augment taxes, unless such taxation be necessary for the public service, as declared by the Crown through its constitutional advisers.[1]

It will be noted that these principles govern both authorization of expenditure and taxation. However, in this Chapter, we are primarily concerned with public expenditure, and therefore explanation of the principles will be limited to their application in this respect.

Before setting out the precise general rules of financial procedure we must clarify certain terms. Not all forms of public expenditure fall within the scope of financial procedure. Some are excluded from it altogether: for example, today, the current account expenditure of the nationalized industries. Others fall in it for some purposes but outside it for others: for example, expenditure by local authorities is not subject to direct Parliamentary control but the House of Lords' legislative powers in respect of provisions affecting charges born on local rates are restricted by procedural rules.[2] Those forms of public expenditure which are subject to Parliamentary financial procedures, or have to be authorized by Parliament in specified ways, are

---

[1] Erskine May's *Treatise on the Law, Privileges, Proceedings and Usage of Parliament*, 19th edn., p. 695 (hereafter cited as 'May'). The quotation here given is from the latest edition, but the words are substantially the same as in the earlier editions edited by May himself.

[2] See May, p. 797 and pp. 356–7 below.

called 'charges upon public funds' (or sometimes 'charges upon the public revenue') or commonly simply 'a charge'.

Charges are exclusively limited to, first, payments out of moneys provided by Parliament, i.e. moneys voted each year, in response to the presentation of estimates, in what is known as business of Supply, which are eventually to be paid out of the Consolidated Fund, and, secondly, moneys authorized by statute to be paid directly out of the Consolidated Fund (or, since 1968, the National Loans Fund, from which loans are made to nationalized industries and other bodies) without further Parliamentary sanction.[1] Thus, payments out of certain other funds, although public in the sense that they are raised by public revenue and regulated by statute, do not constitute a charge and provision for them is thus not subject to the financial procedures of the House. Examples of such other funds have been the revenues of the Church Commissioners, the present National Insurance and the former National Insurance (Industrial Injuries) Funds, funds created within an industry for purposes beneficial to that industry (e.g. as proposed to be set up by the Cotton Industry Bill 1938, the Betting Levy Bill 1960–1, and the Industrial Training Bill 1963–4), and, above all, payments from local rates except in so far as they attract grants from central Government funds.

One other matter requires clarification. To constitute a charge, the proposal involved must either be for a new expenditure, for an increase in the amount to be spent under existing legislation, for an extension of the time during which expenditure may be received, or an extension of the purpose for which expenditure is currently authorized. No special forms of procedure apply to proposals to reduce existing charges.

We can now outline the main rules of financial procedure as they have applied in this century.[2] The first fundamental rule is that 'a charge does not acquire full validity until authorized by legislation; it must originate in the House of Commons and, if it constitutes a service paid for out of moneys provided by Parliament, must be appropriated in the same session as that in which the relevant estimate has been laid before the House'.[3]

---

[1] Until 1948 charges upon the revenues of India were also included.
[2] For detailed explanation of these rules, see May, Chapter XXVII.
[3] Ibid., p. 702.

This enshrines the historically established pre-eminence of the Commons in respect of expenditure: the Crown cannot incur expenditure without the legislative sanction of the Commons and not only has the total to be approved by them, but the detailed appropriation of the total sum to individual service requires Parliamentary sanction each session.

This rule also implies that the role of the Lords is restricted to assenting to or rejecting charges approved by the Commons and they cannot themselves initiate or amend such charges.[1] This was laid down in the resolution of the Commons of 3 July 1678:

That all aids and supplies, and aids to His Majesty in Parliament, are the sole gift of the Commons; and all bills for the granting of any such aids and supplies ought to begin with the Commons; and that it is the undoubted and sole right of the Commons to direct, limit and appoint in such bills the ends, purposes, considerations, conditions, limitations and qualifications of such grants, which ought not to be changed or altered by the House of Lords.[2]

The second fundamental rule is that 'a charge cannot be taken into consideration unless it is demanded by the Crown or recommended from the Crown'.[3] Historically, as explained by Erskine May, this stems from

the long period when the King enjoyed a non-parliamentary revenue which was expected to provide for the ordinary needs of government, and when no legal sanction fettered his discretion in disposing of the supplementary revenues granted by Parliament. During all this period the Commons, as a body traditionally in favour of royal economy, naturally abstained from taking the initiative in offering money to the Crown. The practice of demand proceeding grant had accordingly solidified into an invariable rule before Parliament began to take steps to appropriate its grants to the purposes for which they were demanded.[4]

Thus, without need for a specific standing order, the rule restricting the grant of Supply, or the annual grant of moneys for specific years, to that requested by the Crown became and remains a fundamental feature of the House's financial procedures.

Following the adoption of the practice of appropriation, which began in 1668 and became regular by the end of the seventeenth

---

[1] At least in theory. Modern methods or circumventing this rule in some respects are described below, pp. 357–8.

[2] *Commons Journals* (1667–87), 509.

[3] May, p. 702.　　　　　　　　　　[4] Ibid., p. 706.

century,[1] the House increasingly found itself faced with requests, either by petitions from outside Parliament or directly from the King's Ministers, to authorize expenditure on specific purposes. This was not an ancient practice and to bring the treatment of such requests into line with the established doctrine that the demand of the Crown regularly preceded the grant of Supply, the House passed self-denying resolutions restricting its consideration of proposals involving a charge to that recommended by the Crown. The first such resolution was passed in 1706 and became a standing order in the following form: 'That this House will receive no petition for any sum of money relating to public service but which is recommended from the Crown.'[2] Originally this was applied only to charges proposed to be made directly on the Consolidated Fund, but later, in 1866, it was extended to apply also to provisions seeking to authorize payments to be made out of moneys to be provided by Parliament, i.e. by later Supply proceedings. The rule is now embodied in Standing Order No. 89 as follows:

This House will receive no petition for any sum relating to public service or proceed upon any motion for a grant or charge upon the public revenue, whether payable out of the Consolidated Fund or the National Loans Fund or out of money to be provided by Parliament or for releasing or compounding any sum of money owing to the Crown, unless recommended from the Crown.

And the same rule has, in substance, been in force throughout the period with which this work is concerned.[3]

This rule is of the greatest importance in relation to the proceedings of the House as, in effect, it means that only Ministers (who now, of course, act in the name of the Crown) are able to secure the enactment of provisions involving new charges. It also means that Members are not able, by amendment, to increase charges beyond those authorized by the Crown; most amendments to bills that may be moved by the Opposition and by back-benchers are therefore restricted to amendments to reduce expenditure. The varying operation of this rule, in practice, is one of the themes of this Chapter.

[1] Ibid., p. 206.
[2] *Commons Journals* (1711–14), 417.
[3] Until 1948 charges upon the revenues of India also required the recommendation of the Crown.

These first two rules—relating to the legislative authorization and appropriation of charges and the financial initiative of the Crown—concern the roles of the Crown, the Lords, and the Commons, and involve legislation. They are therefore wider in their impact than the procedures of the Commons alone. There are, however, two other long-standing rules of lesser importance that are internal to the Commons and are designed to ensure that special care is given to financial business. Both rules have been modified considerably in their recent application, but in some form or other have been enforced throughout the period we are considering.

The first is that 'a charge must first be considered in the form of a resolution which, when agreed to by the House, forms a necessary preliminary to the bill or clause by which the charge is authorised'.[1] Formerly, under an ancient standing order dating from 1707, such resolutions had first to be considered in a committee of the House, but since 1966 the requirement that charges must originate in committee has been abandoned.[2] The significance of this rule is that it requires expenditure to be considered at a stage preliminary to legislation and, in particular, enables Ministers (as only they may move for such resolutions) to limit, in advance of its detailed consideration, the expenditure that may be authorized by a bill. The operation of this rule is another of the themes of this Chapter.

The second subsidiary rule is that 'not more than one stage of a bill founded upon a charging resolution can be taken on the same day',[3] although partial exemptions to this rule, both by standing order in respect of Consolidated Fund Bills[4] and by *ad hoc* orders of the House, have been common in recent years.

The basic procedures for Parliamentary control of expenditure

So much for the principles and the rules, as they had evolved historically by 1900 and, indeed, as they apply today. Now we outline the principal procedures through which the House of Commons has concerned itself with public expenditure in this century. Later we describe how they operated at different times.

---

[1] May, p. 702.   [2] See p. 410 below.   [3] May, p. 702.   [4] S.O. No. 93.

First, it must be noted that where the rules refer to the Crown in modern times this must be read as a reference to the Ministers of the Crown. But subject to that the principles still apply. As Erskine May puts it,

The financial relations between the Crown and Parliament took shape during the period while the King still governed through ministers responsible to himself, and the House of Commons only exercised a negative control through its power to withhold supplies. These constitutional relations have been maintained in essential continuity, despite the establishment of Cabinet government dependent upon the support of the House of Commons.[1]

What has changed, as we consider in the next section of this Chapter, is the concept of control.

The House exercises control of public expenditure in four main ways. First, there is the annual process—known as the business of Supply—in which the House considers and approves the Government's annual expenditure requirements which are presented to the House in the form of estimates.

The process is as follows. In the Speech from the Throne at the beginning of each session the Queen,[2] addressing for this purpose only the Members of the House of Commons, states that 'Estimates for the public service will be laid before you.' Thus the Queen's Recommendation is, in effect, signified to the annual estimates. The main estimates are presented and Supply resolutions authorizing expenditure in accordance with those estimates are moved by Ministers and must be agreed before the end of the session. When they have been agreed, Consolidated Fund Bills are ordered in to give legislative authority to the proposed totals of expenditure for the relevant years; the last such bill of each session also provides for the appropriation of all moneys voted in that session to the specific services as provided for in the estimates. In addition to the main estimates, the House is asked to approve Votes on Account (which authorize sufficient expenditure for about the first four months of the financial year —which starts on 1 April—pending the voting of the final estimates), supplementary estimates (to cover additional expenditure to that requested in the original estimates including provision for new services, the need for which had arisen since

[1] May, p. 695.
[2] To avoid confusion we have used the term 'Queen' throughout this Chapter except when the actions of a particular Sovereign are referred to.

the ordinary estimates had been presented), and excess Votes (to give retrospective authority for expenditure incurred in excess of the voted provision in a previous financial year). Thus in each full session the House will approve (though not in this order) excess Votes for year 1, supplementary Votes for year 2, and Votes on Account, main Votes, and supplementary Votes for year 3.[1] The varying extent of Parliamentary control of expenditure by the voting of Supply in these ways is one of the main themes of this Chapter.

The second procedure by which the House controls public expenditure is by legislation in respect of specified services. Continuing authority for expenditure on a service may be granted by Act of Parliament, which will also authorize the source of such expenditure. Thus, for example, legislative authority may be given for payment 'out of money to be provided by Parliament' (i.e. by later Supply resolutions and, ultimately, Consolidated Fund and Appropriation Acts) of grants to farmers for certain agricultural subsidy purposes. Or payments may be authorized directly from the Consolidated Fund for the service of the National Debt or for salaries of certain high officers such as the Speaker and the judges (these are known as 'Consolidated Fund Standing Services'). Or, more recently, periodic payments may be authorized directly from the National Loans Fund for the purpose of making advances on loans to the nationalized industries and certain other bodies.[2]

In accordance with the rule requiring that a charge on public funds must first be considered in the form of a resolution, any bill which seeks to authorize such a charge (i.e. payments out of money to be provided by Parliament or out of the Consolidated or National Loans Funds) requires what is termed a 'money resolution'. The stage at which such a resolution is made has varied,[3] but their nature and purpose has basically remained the same. Money resolutions, which, in accordance with the second of our fundamental rules, must be recommended from the Crown and thus can only be moved by Ministers who act on

---

[1] A 'Vote' is the term used to describe the money provision for each service as set out in the estimates.

[2] The National Loans Fund was created by the National Loans Act 1968; prior to this such advances were made from the Consolidated Fund.

[3] See pp. 355, 386–7, 404, 419–20 below.

behalf of the Crown, set limits to the expenditure which may be authorized by the bill to which they relate. This can be done in various ways. The resolution may restrict the total amount that may be paid e.g. 'advances not exceeding £20 million', or the rate of a grant e.g. 'payments not exceeding £10 per year for each pig kept by a farmer', or the purposes e.g. the payment 'of any sums required to enable the Secretary of State to give financial assistance to a voluntary organization concerned with homelessness or matters related to homelessness', or it may combine any two or three of these restrictions. Alternatively, a money resolution may be completely open and authorize the payment out of money to be provided by Parliament of any expenses of the Secretary of State under the proposed Act. In this latter case the actual financial restrictions on expenditure are left to be fixed annually by the Appropriation Act.

The significance of money resolutions for the working of Parliament is twofold. First, they retain control of expenditure in the hands of Ministers. A private Member's bill, for example, may include provisions imposing a charge (provided that this is not the main object of the bill[1]), but such provisions cannot become effective unless the Government move a money resolution authorizing this charge, nor can any bill be amended by either House to increase public expenditure beyond the level the Government is prepared to countenance as expressed in the money resolution. And second, money resolutions thus regulate the acceptability of amendments: amendments to any bill which are 'outside the money resolution', i.e. would impose a charge greater or wider than that authorized by the resolution, are out of order. Thus, the framing of money resolutions can substantially condition the nature of the debate on the bill at the committee and report stages. A narrow or tight resolution will considerably restrict debate (especially as Members normally seek to increase rather than reduce expenditure), while a totally open resolution will impose no restrictions. As this means, in effect, that Ministers can effectively limit the competence of the House and restrict the scope of debate in respect of bills authorizing expenditure (and, in this century, such bills have become increasingly numerous and important), the drafting of money

[1] See the present S.O. No. 91 and p. 404 below.

resolutions is a matter of considerable significance and has, on occasions; been controversial.[1]

The third method by which the House exercises some measure of control over public expenditure is by restricting the borrowing powers of certain public bodies. This is a more recent development and applies today particularly to the nationalized industries. Under numerous statutes ceilings are set to the amounts which these bodies may borrow and in many cases the source of their borrowing, e.g. only from the Secretary of State and from other bodies with his consent, is also restricted. However, it is normal to provide for the limit to be raised, by resolution of the House, up to a further statutory ceiling; if further borrowing is required when the latter ceiling is reached, a further Act of Parliament is required. The imposition of restrictions on the borrowing powers of nationalized industries and other bodies in this way has enabled the House to exercise some control over capital expenditure (although some borrowing may be employed to finance losses on current account) in the public sector which falls outside the field of Government expenditure of voted money.

We have described three ways in which the House exercises direct control over public expenditure. The fourth method is more indirect. Public expenditure decisions reflect a political response to demands and circumstances. Some of the factors of the equation are largely fixed and cannot be readily varied by politicians (the number of children, for example), but others are variable and are either responsive to alterations in the level of expenditure (size of classes in schools) or themselves largely influence that level (decisions on the school entry and leaving ages). Thus the level of state expenditure on public education, for example, is continually at issue, and the decisions are essentially political. As such they can be regularly raised in Parliament. And the nature of the Parliamentary discussion, which both reflects to some extent public opinion and also conditions electoral opinion, must consequentially influence Ministers' decisions. Thus, the House exercises some control over public expenditure simply by discussing it.

The discussion takes place at different levels. First, it should

[1] See pp. 402–4, 419 below.

be emphasized, specific expenditure proposals, as incorporated, for example, in the annual estimates, are simply the financial reflection of policy decisions already taken and of work that it is planned to do or of payments that will be made in accordance with that policy. Indeed the annual estimates are not even a full reflection of that policy, but simply an indication of the bills that will fall due for settlement in any one year: a major decision on the ordering of new warships, for example, may have little effect on the estimate for several years, while other decisions may make an immediate and continuing impact. Thus, the majority of debates on policy matters (for there are few serious questions of policy—apart, perhaps, from criminal law, civil rights, etc.— that do not involve expenditure) are in part debates about expenditure irrespective of the form or occasion of debate. Thus, the House indirectly controls expenditure whenever it debates Government policies—including those policies incorporated in bills or statutory instruments—or whenever Ministers are questioned about the conduct of their departments.

There are also various procedures by which the House may turn its attention more specifically to expenditure. For many years, as we shall see, Supply debates were always held on motions to approve various provisions in the estimates, and these were occasions when the Government's expenditure policies or spending practices could be reviewed. There are also debates on money resolutions and borrowing-powers bills and orders. In other words, the procedures by which public expenditure is formally sanctioned by the House are also used as occasions for exercising indirect control by seeking to influence future policy and administration. Debate on, for example, the estimates for road construction, will very seldom lead to any change being made in the Vote concerned: the Government will be authorized to spend on roads the sums it asked for in its estimates. But the arguments in the debate—and the continuing arguments within Whitehall, the parties, and, perhaps, within the Cabinet that the Parliamentary debate both reflects and stimulates—may well lead to a change (either up or down) in the road construction programme in the following years.

The amount, range, and complexity of Government expenditure have all increased in this century: the total of Supply grants appropriated by Parliament in session 1900 was £154,858,066;

in session 1976–7 it was £40,891,322,686·47. Even allowing for inflation (nearly twentyfold over this period) the grow this enormous. In 1900 Navy and Army expenditure comprised nearly 70 per cent of the total, and the only Civil Votes exceeding £1 million were those for the Inland Revenue, the Post Office, the Board of Education (and related services in Ireland and Scotland), the Royal Irish Constabulary, and grants in aid and other services for the colonies. In 1977, defence, although itself greatly swollen, only comprised about 17 per cent of the total. In 1900 there was little or no expenditure on overseas aid (apart from colonial administration), assistance to industry, export credit guarantees, employment services, support for nationalized industries, housing services, a national health service, national insurance and supplementary benefits, or rate support grants for local authorities, which are the major expenditure services today. Nor were the expenditure services so complex at the turn of the century. The Victorian and Edwardian M.P.s did not have to consider how to control expenditure on highly technical projects which take many years to develop such as nuclear reactors or supersonic aircraft; they did not have an elaborate system of agricultural and industrial subsidies; they were not troubled by technical problems of resource allocation; and the mesh of the social security safety net was not as fine as that provided by the complex structure of social services we offer the citizen today. Thus, the nature, as well as the volume, of public expenditure, as is well known, has greatly changed in this century.

In the face of this change the House has become increasingly aware of the inadequacy of simple debating procedures for scrutinizing public expenditure. Not only is it impossible to cover the whole of the field by debates on the estimates, and not only is it too difficult in debate to probe, in any depth, the details of any one service, but even debates on major policies affecting expenditure are somewhat hollow if Members are not informed of the facts, figures, and complexities of the problem. Ministers are, of course, fully briefed—or can be—on these matters. In an attempt to arm themselves, and also in an attempt to exercise a more detailed control over expenditure than debate on the estimates permitted, Members have turned increasingly to the use of select committees, i.e. committees with power to call for oral and written evidence (particularly, in this context, from civil servants concerned with departmental expenditure), to deliberate and to produce reports.

The last method by which the House has sought to control public expenditure, therefore, has been through financial committees especially appointed for this purpose. The first of these antedates the period we are considering. The principle that not a penny of public money should be spent by Ministers or Government departments without Parliamentary sanction lies at the heart of our constitution; it is the fount of Parliament's power, authority, or influence. It was therefore natural, that, for many years, a principal weapon of Parliamentary control was the annual audit of the departments' accounts to ensure that the limits on expenditure on the several services, as set by Parliament in the Appropriation Act, had not been exceeded. But here again Members found that they were not able to satisfy themselves simply by reading the accounts which were laid before them. They wished, for example, to ask for explanations of any discrepancies or apparent overspending—and to question these officials who were responsible. A more systematic and sophisticated procedure was required, and so the Public Accounts Committee came to be set up in 1861 and continues to this day.[1]

Ex post facto scrutiny, however, although necessary is not sufficient. The fact that money has been spent correctly as provided for in the estimates does not guarantee that it has been spent wisely or well: the estimates themselves may have been carelessly prepared or, indeed, may reflect policies which merit re-examination. Various attempts have been made to improve the scrutiny of the estimates themselves—and more recently of the underlying policies and expenditure programmes of which the estimates are the annual reflection—by the appointment of select committees, namely the Estimates Committee (first appointed in 1912), the wartime National Expenditure Committees, and the present Expenditure Committee. The evolution of these Committees as means of exercising some detailed, if indirect, control of expenditure is one of the themes of Chapter VIII. It must also be borne in mind, however, as a parallel development to the development of the other methods of con-

---

[1] For an account of the evolution of this and other financial committees, see Basil Chubb, *The Control of Public Expenditure* (1952).

trolling or debating expenditure with which this Chapter is concerned.

The concept of control of expenditure

It is appropriate, at this stage, to clarify what is meant by 'control of expenditure' and to apply this concept to the workings of the House. In its strictest sense control implies a rational and deliberate process in which alternative ends are appraised, one of them is selected, and then all necessary steps are taken to ensure that that end is actually achieved. Applied to expenditure, this means considering alternative policies, deciding the pattern, levels, and phasing of expenditure for each service, publishing these expenditure plans and then securing that the money is spent on the services selected in the volume and at the times so planned. It should be emphasized, incidentally, that control, thus conceived, does not just mean reducing or stopping expenditure. A driver controls a car by use of the steering wheel and accelerator as well as the brake; and so it is with public expenditure. Some critics talk as if 'bringing Government expenditure under better control' is synonymous with cutting services and administrative costs. This is not necessarily so: there can be controlled increases as well as controlled decreases.

Looked at in this way it is clear that the House can never exercise complete control over public expenditure. In the first place, because of the fundamental rule that all proposals for expenditure must be recommended by the Crown (i.e. Ministers) this means that although the House may consider alternative policies the actual choice and publication of the desired end is left to Ministers. Furthermore, the House's control, at this stage, is restricted to the use of the brake. It can reduce or refuse a request for expenditure (be it in an estimate or a bill). It cannot increase it—or, in the case of a charge in a bill, not beyond a level which the Government have permitted in the money resolution. And finally, of course, the House have only the most indirect control over the actual spending of the money; at this stage it can only advise and seek to verify that the money has been spent as authorized.

There is, however, a looser sense of control in which the House plays a real part. Like a policeman controlling the traffic (who has little control over the directions drivers wish to take, but has certain powers to stop vehicles and who can advise the best routes) the House can and does exercise influence over the volume and pattern of Government expenditure. As the Study of Parliament Group said in evidence to a Procedure Committee in 1965, speaking of the role of Parliament generally, 'Parliamentary control means influence, not direct power, advice, not command, criticism, not obstruction, scrutiny, not initiative and publicity, not secrecy.'[1] Thus, in addition to its limited powers of direct control, the House also exercises a considerable amount of indirect control through these processes of scrutiny and criticism—by debate, by work of select committees, and by questions in the House.

The relative importance of direct and indirect controls in different periods is one of the themes of this Chapter. But it is essential to note the interrelationship of the two processes. As we shall see, in this century the independent exercise by the House of direct controls—reductions in the estimates or alterations in the terms of money resolutions for example—appears to have been very sparing.[2] In nearly all cases the estimates have been approved as presented by the Government and likewise the expenditure provisions of bills go through largely unamended. But this does not mean that the historically formal powers of the House—the right to refuse or reduce expenditure (and taxes) requested by the Crown—is meaningless.

In the first place the possibility of the House withholding Supply—even if it be an ultimate deterrent which is never used and is unlikely to be used—must nevertheless exercise some restraint on Government. It symbolizes the ultimate authority of the House and cannot lightly be disregarded. It is on this basis, for example, that the House has founded its claim to have select committees for the detailed examination of Government expenditure—both before and after the money is spent. It is true, however, that, in this century at least, the main political thrust has been towards greater Government expenditure, not less. As

---

[1] *Fourth Report from the Select Committee on Procedure*, 1964–5 (H.C. 303), p. 139.

[2] Even in 1908, Lowell could only record two occasions in the previous twenty years when an estimate had been reduced without the consent of the Government (*Government of England*, Vol. I, p. 346).

Sir William Harcourt said in 1896, 'It is not the House of Commons that restrains the extravagance of the Government—it is exactly the other way round.'[1] Only on defence, and then only from one element of one political party, has there been sustained pressure for reduced expenditure. In practice, therefore, it must be admitted that the House's right to refuse or reduce expenditure has lent little weight to the exercise of indirect influence.

The second relationship, however, is more fundamental and is of crucial importance to an understanding of Parliamentary procedure and practice in the twentieth century. The fact that the formal sanction of the House has to be given to all requests for expenditure submitted by Ministers, and has to be specifically given at a number of distinct stages—Supply resolutions, Consolidated Fund Bills, money resolutions, etc.—means that time has to be given in the House for the consideration of motions embodying such formal sanction. And time is the real weapon of the House in its critical capacity, especially of an organized Opposition. This means that the opportunity is secured of debating the policies, administration, and acts of Government, before the Government is given the sanctions it seeks. As we shall see, a certain number of days have to be set aside each session for considering (in varying degrees of directness) the Government's requests for Supply as set out in the estimates. The Government may get its way in the end, but the House, and especially the Opposition, are first given an opportunity to raise the issues that they believe need to be publicly debated—and to advance, publicly, their alternative policies. This is the modern manifestation of the ancient principle that the raising of grievances must proceed the granting of Supply.[2]

This relationship, the fact that the *power* of the House of

---

[1] *Hansard*, 24 Feb. 1896, col. 960.

[2] Lowell put it well: 'The whole initiative, as regards both revenue and expenditure, lies with the government alone. The House has merely power to reject or reduce the amounts asked for, and it uses that power very little. Financially, its work is rather supervision than direction; and its real usefulness consists in securing publicity and criticism rather than in controlling expenditure. It is the tribunal where at the opening of the financial year the ministers must explain and justify every detail of their fiscal policy, and where at its close they must render an account of their stewardship.' (*Government of England*, Vol. I, p. 288.)

Commons to exercise direct control (by voting or refusing financial sanctions) secures the *opportunity* for the House to exercise indirect control (by publicly debating and criticizing the policies and acts of Government that involve expenditure) lies at the heart of our Parliamentary system. It is in this sense that Parliamentary procedure may be said to be the cement of the constitution holding the fabric together. How this cement has been used and what uses have been made of the building it holds up—the content as well as the framework of control—is another of the themes of this Chapter.

The concept of control has one other dimension—that of the levels and stages at which it is exercised. As the Select Committee on Estimates put it in its 1958 Report on Treasury Control of Expenditure, control of Government expenditure operates at four levels. First there is the total of expenditure; then the optimum balance of expenditure within that total between the major services, so that greater value could not be obtained from the total by reducing the amount spent on one service and increasing spending elsewhere; next the more precise control of the expenditure on individual policies and services; and, lastly, control of expenditure by individual spending departments to ensure that there is the optimum use of money within each service.[1]

These are broad distinctions and the borders between them may often be blurred. But they provide the background to the continuing questions of at what stage Parliamentary control—both direct and indirect—can most effectively be exercised. To what extent can Parliament control the total of expenditure or influence the balance of expenditure between major services? Is Parliamentary control more effective when directed to the totals for specific individual services, as when voting Supply? What contribution can Parliamentary scrutiny, especially by committees, make to the economic expenditure of public money within departments?

There is also a range of questions relating to timing. When Parliament is concerned with individual items and projects and the whole spectrum of detailed administration, the required expenditure can be examined on an annual basis and piecemeal,

[1] *Sixth Report from the Select Committee on Estimates*, 1957–8 (H.C. 254), para. 9.

as provided for in the estimates (although with major and highly technical projects which are developed over a period of years, this is less appropriate). But when it comes to considering totals and the balance between services, it becomes increasingly necessary, as the Plowden Committee of 1961 argued, to look at 'public expenditure as a whole, over a period of years ahead, and in relation to prospective resources'.[1] In other words piecemeal decisions on separate expenditure proposals on an annual basis have to be replaced (or at least supplemented) by greater concern with long-term programmes and the planned growth (or reduction) of expenditure over a period of years. This has been increasingly realized and practiced by the executive. The extent to which Parliament itself has moved away from the traditional concern for 'the saving of candle-ends' (which Gladstone thought 'very much the measure of a good Secretary to the Treasury'[2]) to a concern for public expenditure planning in the broader sense is again a theme of this Chapter.

Parliamentary Procedures for Control of Expenditure in 1900

We examine in this Chapter the state and development of Parliamentary financial procedures and control of expenditure in three periods: 1900–19, 1919–45, and 1945 to the present day. To avoid repeating procedural matters in each period we will first describe the procedures as they were in 1900—and indeed, in many aspects, still are today. We thus both clarify the starting point and describe the salient features of the House's financial procedures throughout our period. And only changes in procedure need be described in later sections of this Chapter.

Students of Parliament in this period are deeply indebted to a great Austrian scholar, Josef Redlich. His three-volume work, *The Procedure of the House of Commons*, first published in English in 1908, is a fascinating and clear picture of the historical development of Parliament and of the way it worked at the time he was writing. He succeeded, as few others have done, in not only describing the precise rules and procedures of his day but also in putting some flesh on the bones and showing how these

[1] *Report of the Committee on Control of Public Expenditure*, 1961 (Cmnd. 1432), para. 12.

[2] Sir Algernon West, *Recollections: 1832 to 1886*, vol. ii, p. 82.

rules and procedures worked in practice. He also relates, in a lucid manner, the legal purity of the rules to the reigning principles and political theories of his age. (Lowell also achieved something of the same thing in his *'Government of England'* (1908) (Chapters IX to XXI), and later Sir Ivor Jennings's *'Parliament'* (1939) again answered the need to describe procedures and practice together in the inter-war period. It is to be regretted that no such work exists on the British Parliament today.)

There is therefore no need for a detailed description of the practices of 1900 for Redlich and Lowell have done this (and for even more details of procedure, reference should be made to the eleventh edition of Erskine May's *Parliamentary Practice* of 1906). The main features must, however, be set out.

Supply procedure—the Balfour reforms

Supply procedures, as they were in 1900, had recently been modified fundamentally by the Balfour reforms.[1] These were first embodied in a resolution passed by the House in 1896, which had been passed again with certain modifications in following sessions.[2] Until that year there had been no limit on the number of days that might be devoted to business of Supply; in the course of a session, each Vote had to be moved in the Committee of Supply and could be debated. The Government chose the order in which they were to be considered, and normally they were put down in numerical order of classes. Balfour argued that this meant that much time was wasted each year in discussing the earlier Votes in Class I—repairs to royal palaces, etc.—while some of the largest Votes were hurried through with little comment at the end of the session.[3] But the increasing volume and complexity of Government expenditure—and the presence of the Irish Members—led to increasingly extended discussions, often late into the night and often concentrated at the end of the session and often prolonging that session into August (continuation after 12 August was particularly unwelcome, as Balfour wittily demonstrated, although Balfour also

[1] A. J. Balfour was then First Lord of the Treasury and Leader of the House of Commons.

[2] It was to become a standing order in 1902 (see pp. 360–1 below).

[3] *Hansard*, 20 Feb. 1896, cols. 729–30.

produced statistics indicating that the total number of days spent on Supply before 1896 was, on average, not greatly different from the number he proposed should be available under his new rule[1]). After considerable debate[2] it was agreed to limit the number of days available for the main elements of Supply business and to provide that all Votes that had not been agreed to by the last of these 'allotted' days would then be voted on without further debate under what came to be known as the Supply guillotine.

We will observe how this packaging of Supply business came to be modified over the years, and also the changing nature of Supply debates. But the fundamental importance of the new procedures must be emphasized from the outset. In the first place, while it no doubt reduced the tedium of long-drawn-out debates on every estimate (or at least the threat of such) it also greatly extended the control of the Government over the House[3] (which had by then become firmly established by the priority given to Government business, at the expense of private Members' motions and bills). There had already been an erosion of private Members' basic opportunities for raising grievances before voting Supply when the rule was passed in 1882 which made it no longer necessary to have a debatable motion for the Speaker to leave the Chair every time the House wished to resolve itself into Committee of Supply to consider the estimates; since that year such motions were only required on first going into committee on the Army, Navy, and Civil Service estimates, i.e. only three times a session. But the 1896 procedure went considerably further and completely removed the open-ended aspect of Supply procedure which had until then meant that the House's power to refuse or modify Supply was a very real weapon of direct control of expenditure in the hands of the House. As a leading financial expert of the day, Chester Bowles, M.P., said in 1902,

Up to recent years, . . . the Opposition and Members interested in particular votes always had a power of bargaining with the Government of the day, and with the Leader of the House as representing that Government. Since

---

[1] *Hansard*, 20 Feb. 1896, cols. 731–2.

[2] Ibid., 20, 24, 25, and 27 Feb. 1896.

[3] Redmond said that nothing had so facilitated the general business of the House and the Government as this rule (ibid., 15 Feb. 1900, col. 118).

the Government must obtain all the Votes before closing the session . . . it was possible, so long as the time devoted to Supply was unlimited, to extort concessions as the price of acquiescence. But since the new sessional order limiting the number of days to be given to the annual estimates, things are wholly different.[1]

On another occasion he argued that the effect of the rule was to deprive private Members of all power.[2]

There was, however, another feature of Balfour's package which was to the advantage of the critics of the Government, although this was not fully appreciated at the time (although Balfour himself saw the possibility). Once the Government was guaranteed that it would obtain its Supply Votes for the session on days of its choosing, in a limited number of days and by a convenient date, it ceased to be so concerned with how these days were used. And this facilitated the gradual transformation of Supply days from being occasions for considering Government requirements (the Votes) to being essentially Opposition business days. It also stimulated the House's search for other ways of looking in detail at the estimates. This is to anticipate our story, and it did not all happen at once, but the important general conclusion is that while the Balfour reforms of 1896 (as later modified) undoubtedly weakened the House's direct control of expenditure, they also led to improved opportunities and procedures for exercising indirect control and influence.[3]

Consideration of the estimates

The main features, then, of Supply procedure in 1900 were as follows. First, immediately after the debate on the Address had been completed at the beginning of each session, the House set up the two ancient committees of the whole House—the Committee of Supply and the Committee of Ways and Means— that were concerned, respectively, with considering the Crown's requests for expenditure as presented in the estimates and so authorizing grants of money for the Army, Navy, and Civil Services, and, parallel to this, considering the Crown's proposals

---

[1] *Minutes of Evidence* given before Select Committee on National Expenditure, 1902, Q.1028.

[2] *Hansard*, 15 Feb. 1900, col. 120.

[3] See also Gordon Reid, *The Politics of Financial Control* (Hutchinson and Co., 1966), pp. 69–75.

for raising revenues and so authorizing taxes and for authorizing payment into and out of the Consolidated Fund. The Chairman of these Committees (called the Chairman of Ways and Means) could then be chosen by the Committees themselves (although in the case of more than one candidate the choice would be made by the House itself, as it is today).[1]

By a resolution of 1821, the Navy and Army estimates had to be presented before 15 January if Parliament had met before Christmas, or (as was much more normal in those days) within ten days after the opening of the Committee of Supply if Parliament did not assemble till after Christmas. It was also expected that the Civil Service estimates would be presented at the same time. The estimates, when presented, stood referred to the Committee of Supply.

The form of the estimates was decided by the Government, subject to the requirements of the Exchequer and Audit Departments Act 1866, although it was already established that major changes would not be made without the prior approval of the Public Accounts Committee. The estimates were made up of separate Votes (each of which had to be approved by the Committee of Supply) stating the total grant thereby demanded, and each Vote was divided into sub-heads and items (which did not require to be approved by the Committee, but which could be separately considered, if so desired, by process of amendments).

In addition to the ordinary annual estimates for each service, other estimates were presented. A Vote on Account was presented each year for the Civil Services, to authorize necessary expenditures on current services (new services were not normally permitted to be authorized by a Vote on Account) in the financial year beginning on 1 April, pending agreement to the ordinary estimates by about the end of July.

Votes on Account were not, however, required by the Army and the Navy as the constitutional principle which insists that each grant of Supply shall be devoted exclusively to the object for which the grant is made was, with the sanction of the Treasury and subject to annual legislative approval, waived in their case; instead the practice was to agree to certain Votes

[1] May, 11th edn., pp. 603-4.

for these armed forces (usually those relating to pay) before the beginning of the financial year and to permit the departments concerned to use the money so voted for any service for which they had presented an estimate pending the grants for the Army and Navy being completed later in the year. In addition, Votes 'A', authorizing the maximum numbers of men who might serve in the armed forces, also had to be passed each year before the end of March (and on the Vote A for the Army being agreed to, the Army Annual Bill, which continued for one more year the Army Discipline Acts 1879 and 1881, was ordered in).

Supplementary estimates were frequently presented and excess Votes were sometimes required. And occasionally application was made for a Vote of Credit to cover extraordinary naval or military charges or other exceptional expenditures.

The procedure for considering the estimates was as follows. Pursuant to the standing order first passed in 1882, whenever the Committee of Supply stood as an order of the day, the Speaker left the Chair without putting any question unless, on first going into Supply on the Army, Navy, or Civil Service estimates respectively, an amendment was moved or any question raised relating to the estimates proposed to be taken.[1] Thus, there were occasions each year for general debates on the two armed services in the course of which there were separate debates on particular aspects as defined in an amendment. There was also a debate on a civil subject as selected by the mover of an amendment. The right to move an amendment was governed by a ballot (similar to the periodic ballot for private Members' motions) but there were several restrictions on the acceptability and debatability of amendments.[2]

The sessional resolution of 1900 (similar to that first passed in 1896) governed the debates in Committee of Supply, and modified ancient practice. By a long-standing custom, the Committee of Supply had always been placed among the orders of the day for Mondays, Wednesdays, and Fridays. The sessional resolution now said that it was automatically to be first business on Fridays unless the House otherwise ordered

---

[1] S.O. No. 17 of 1900.   [2] May, 11th edn., pp. 608–10.

on a Government motion to be decided without amendment or debate. Furthermore, not more than twenty days, to be taken before 5 August, were to be allotted for consideration of the annual estimates for the Army, Navy, and Civil Services, including Votes on Account (but excluding supplementary estimates, excess Votes, and any Vote of Credit). This could be extended to twenty-three days if the House agreed. On the last but one of these allotted days the Chairman was directed at the end of the day to put to the Committee the questions necessary to dispose of all Votes not yet agreed by it, without further amendment or debate. Thus, on all these allotted Supply days (plus those on which supplementary estimates etc. were considered) the Committee would debate resolutions authorizing grants for particular services, and might also consider and, if desires, vote on amendments to reduce (but not to increase) these grants. Consideration of Votes might be completed and reported to the House, or might be adjourned. However, whenever the Committee of Supply had come to any resolutions, it was always necessary for them to be reported to the House itself and to be set down for a consideration by it on a future day. This was normally done without amendment or debate,[1] but under the new procedure it was also provided that on the last allotted day at 10 p.m. the Speaker would put, without further amendment or debate, every question necessary to dispose of all the outstanding reports from the Committee of Supply.

Consolidated Fund Bills

Even when agreed to by the House, however, the resolutions of the Committee of Supply, sanctioning grants as provided for in the estimates, did not convey full authority for expenditure. Two further steps were required. First, a resolution had to be agreed to in the Committee of Ways and Means to authorize the necessary payment out of the Consolidated Fund to permit the required grants to be made (sometimes called a Ways and Means 'spending' resolution, to distinguish it from the fiscal resolutions with which that Committee was normally con-

---

[1] Redlich, *Procedure of the House of Commons* (1908) Vol. III, p. 142.

cerned). And on the 'spending' resolution being agreed to by the House (again on a later day) a Consolidated Fund Bill was ordered in, for the second requirement was that the resolutions be given full legislative sanction.

There were normally two Consolidated Fund Bills each session. The first, passed before the end of March, authorized the Treasury to issue specified sums out of the Consolidated Fund, and apply them towards making good the Supply granted to the Sovereign for the service of two (and sometimes three) financial years. First, the Bill would deal with the excess Vote requirements (if any) for the previous financial year; second, it would authorize the supplementary estimate expenditures for the year just ending; and third, it would authorize the moneys required on account for the Civil Services for the next financial year plus the moneys so far voted for the Army and Navy. The Bill also authorized the Treasury to borrow, up to the limit of the total of the permitted issues, any money needed for the Consolidated Fund.

The second Bill was called the Consolidated Fund (Appropriation) Bill, which, on enactment, became the Appropriation Act. It was normally passed at the end of July or beginning of August and it sanctioned the issue out of the Consolidated Fund of the money necessary to complete the grants for the current financial year (i.e. the total estimate requirements as originally presented in the ordinary estimates, plus any supplementary estimates later presented, but less the amounts already voted on account or voted in advance for the Army and Navy). It again made provision for the necessary Treasury borrowing. In addition, however, the Appropriation Bill dealt with other matters. First, it appropriated all sums granted in the session (both by the first Consolidated Fund Act and by the current Bill) to the several services, in accordance with the Votes agreed to by the Committee and the House. Second, it authorized the additional appropriation of moneys received by departments from fees, sales, etc.—what are known as appropriations in aid. Third, it sanctioned the temporary use (subject to Treasury authority) of the moneys voted for the Navy and Army for purposes other than those for which they were voted (i.e. virement between service Votes). And, lastly, in accordance with further resolutions passed in a committee and agreed to by the House (the so-called 'Monk Resolutions') the Bill retrospectively sanctioned the Treasury approval of the virement between service Votes made in the previous year.

Both Consolidated Fund Bills were, of course, debated. The debates on second reading permitted review by Members—especially by back-benchers—of Government policy and administration. Debate at the committee stage was strictly limited by a succession of Chairman's rulings to the effect that, as the Bill was simply endorsing what the House had already decided in agreeing to the Supply resolutions, it was not open to the Committee to amend it. There could also be a debate on third reading. Historically, the Royal Assent to the Appropriation Act marked the end of Parliament's work of the session and Parliament would normally be prorogued at the same time. But there were occasions, in 1882 and 1893 for example, when the Houses simply adjourned for the summer recess after the passing of the Act and resumed for further business in the autumn.

Money bills and money resolutions

We now turn to the financial procedures applied in 1900 in respect of bills involving expenditure. All bills were, at that time, ordered in after a motion, that leave be given to bring in a bill, had been agreed to by the House.[1] But, in accordance with the basic rule that provisions imposing a change must be first considered in a committee, committees of the whole House were required to consider proposals for expenditure before they were incorporated in legislation. The committees were appointed by a motion for the House to resolve itself into a committee on a future day to consider the matter specified in the motion. This motion could be debated or amended, but the Speaker would not put the question unless a Minister of the Crown or a privy councillor signified that the motion was recommended by the Crown (hence securing the Crown's—i.e. Minister's—initiative in proposing expenditure).

When the main object of a bill was the creation of a public charge (i.e. it was a money bill) this procedure was used before

---

[1] The standing order permitting the simple presentation of a bill without motion was not made until 1902.

the bill was introduced. The committee of the whole House would thus be appointed on one day; on another day it would agree to the founding money resolution; on a third day the House would agree to the report of the committee; and thereupon a bill would be ordered to be brought in. Thereafter the proceedings on a money bill were the same as for other bills except that, in accordance with another of the basic financial rules, bills ordered in on money resolutions from committees were not allowed to pass through more than one stage at the same sitting of the House.

Where, however, the charge created by the bill was subsidiary to its main object (the administrative expenses of a Minister, for example) the royal recommendation and the preliminary committee proceedings were not necessary prior to the bill's introduction and the bill could be ordered in on an ordinary motion for leave to bring in a bill. But in this case the clauses or provisions of the bill which sought to create a change were printed, in the first print of the bill, in italics 'to mark that they do not form part of the bill, and that no question can be proposed thereon, unless vitality has been imparted to these provisions by a committee resolution'.[1] It was then necessary for a committee to be appointed to consider a money resolution covering the proposed charges and for the money resolution to be agreed to by the House before the italicized parts of the bill could be considered by the committee on the bill. Debate on second reading was not restricted, however, and the procedure for agreeing the money resolution was deferred till after the bill had been read a second time. As already explained[2] the terms of the money resolution conditioned the acceptability of amendments in committee and on report.

The role of the Lords

Although we are only concerned in this Chapter with the procedures and practices of the House of Commons, the role of the Lords—and relations between the two Houses—on questions of public expenditure are, as the events of 1909 to 1911 were to prove, material to our story. In 1900 the theoretical

---

[1] May, 11th edn., p. 560.   [2] See p. 337 above.

powers of the Lords were still unrestricted by statute. There were, however, a number of well-established conventions which limited their exercise, and also further practices which averted inconveniences that would result from a too rigid application of these conventions.

The basic position of the Lords in 1900 in financial matters was stated in the then current edition of Erskine May: 'The responsibility discharged by the Lords in the grant of supplies for the services of the Crown, and in the imposition of taxation, is concurrence, not initiation.'[1] This position was founded on the Resolution of 1678—'all aids and supplies . . . are the sole gift of the Commons'—which we have already quoted in full[2] and which set out the financial privileges, as they are called, of the Commons. For over 200 years this position had been generally accepted by the Lords, and although on occasions they had flexed their muscles and taken steps which had infringed the Commons privileges—most notably in 1860 when the Lords rejected the Paper Duties Repeal Bill—they always accepted the supremacy of the Commons in financial matters. As Redlich said, regarded historically the right of the Commons 'to control expenditure was somewhat later in arriving at full maturity than the right of exclusive granting of supplies; but from 1688 to the present day it has continued to grow in strength step by step and has been carried to its farthest conclusions.'[3]

To be more specific, the Commons claimed privilege (and still do today) not only in respect of national taxation and expenditure (although they did not claim privilege in respect of sectional funds, such as Church revenues). But with regard to these changes in respect of which they did claim privilege, the Commons treated as a breach of privilege by the Lords any alteration, whether by increase or reduction, of the amount of a charge on or of its duration, mode of assessment, levy, collection, appropriation, or management; and, in addition, any alteration in respect of the persons who pay, receive, manage, or control it, or in respect of the limits within which it is

[1] May, 10th edn., p. 540.

[2] See p. 332 above.

[3] *The Procedures of the House of Commons*, p. 120. He was writing in 1908: perhaps his reference to the Commons rights being then carried to their farthest conclusions was a little premature.

leviable.[1] Thus, the provisions of a bill may be deemed to create a charge for purposes of invoking the financial privileges of the Commons against the Lords, which would not constitute a charge for the purposes of Commons' financial procedures.[2] Put bluntly, the Lords may not meddle in money matters—or at least not without the connivance of the Commons.

The operation of those rules and the extent to which the Commons were prepared, in practice, to tolerate breaches of their financial privileges can best be shown by looking respectively at the restrictions on the Lords' rights to initiate, amend, and reject bills.

It would be completely contrary to constitutional usage for the Lords to initiate a bill which contained provisions which would infringe the Commons' privileges. When on rare occasions this has occurred, whether by accident or design, the Commons either laid aside the Lords' Bill or postponed it for six months.[3] And, except for certain long-established relaxations in respect of the imposition of fees and pecuniary penalties and in respect of certain types of charges in private bills,[4] the Commons never waive their privilege in relation to public bills sent down by the Lords and only rarely in relation to private bills. Usually, when it has become apparent that a Lords' bill would be regarded as infringing the privileges of the Commons if it were sent to them, the bill has been withdrawn in the Lords before it was passed.[5]

Few bills involve no expenditure whatsoever. It will be apparent, therefore, that if the principle that the Lords may not initiate expenditure provisions of any kind and in any way were applied in every sense, few bills could originate in the Lords. This would be highly inconvenient. Two expedients have therefore been adopted to circumvent this obstacle. The first device is to leave out, at the third reading in the Lords, all those provisions which would infringe the privileges of the

[1] See May, pp. 796–8.   [2] See p. 330 above.
[3] May, p. 798, notes only eight cases before 1900 since this rule was established.
[4] See ibid., p. 799.
[5] Cases in this century include the Outdoor Relief (Friendly Societies) Bill 1904, the Local Government (Adjustments) Bill 1913, the Riot (Damages) Bill 1922, and the Legal Aid Bill 1963.

Commons so that the bill is sent to the Commons with some blanks. The omitted provisions are, nevertheless, included in the first print of the bill in the Commons, but marked by underlines and brackets to show that they are not part of the bill. The missing provisions are then inserted as amendments in the Commons and ultimately the Lords agree to these Commons' amendments. The second expedient works the other way round. Before the bill leaves the Lords a provision is inserted which, in effect, nullifies the other expenditure provisions of the bill and states that nothing in the bill shall impose a charge on public funds. This provision is then left out by the Commons by amendment in committee and, when this amendment is agreed by the Lords, the bill is in an effective form.

Both these devices are of long standing, dating back at least to the first half of the nineteenth century. However, the latter, which is particularly helpful when it is difficult to disentangle the charge provisions from the rest of the bill, used to be rarely employed and the only examples given of its early use are to cases where the charge provisions could be readily left out without destroying the sense of the bill.[1] Today, such 'privilege amendments', as they are called, are regularly inserted in Lords' bills 'to avoid questions of privilege' in the Commons, even if they would, if enacted, make a nonsense of the bill. Thus here, as elsewhere, although the basic principles remain unchanged, the practical application of the rules has varied greatly.

The position is different in respect of Commons' bills. Here, of course, the Commons can include whatever expenditure provisions they wish, subject to the recommendation of the Crown. The powers of the Lords differ, however, according to the nature of the bill. If the bill be a 'bill of aids and supplies', i.e. a bill for granting Supply or the ways and means of raising Supply (in this century this has primarily meant the annual Consolidated Fund Bills and Finance Bills, although in recent years there have been other bills which have been treated as bills of aids and supplies, e.g. when the primary purpose was the levying of a tax[1]), then no amendment by the Lords is tolerated in accordance with the terms of the resolution of 1678.

---

[1] May, 10th edn., pp. 548–9.   [1] See May, pp. 801–2.

The Lords, therefore, must pass such bills without amendment (or reject the bill) and, nowadays, they do not even go into committee on such bills.

The Lords may, however, amend other bills, and such amendments may infringe the Commons' financial privileges. If they do this, the Commons, when they come to consider the Lords' amendments, may either reject the amendment (in which case it is the established practice to state that the reason for the rejection was that the amendment infringed the privileges of the Commons) or they may waive their privileges and accept the amendment. Already, by 1900, the practice of waiving privilege and accepting Lords' amendments which deal with expenditure, especially in a manner incidental to the main purpose of the bill (e.g. administrative expenses), was well established—and so it remains today.

Lastly, we consider the powers of the Lords to reject bills imposing charges. Here the constitution is clear and simple. As the 1893 edition of Erskine May's *Treatise* said, 'The legal right of the Lords, as a co-ordinate branch of the legislature, to withhold their assent from any bill whatever, to which their concurrence is desired, is unquestionable',[1] and this power— including even the power to reject bills of aids and supplies— had long been recognized by the Commons. It is important to note, however (benefiting, as we do, from knowledge of what was to come), that up to 1900, apart from their rejection of the Paper Duties Repeal Bill of 1860, the Lords had never rejected measures exclusively relating to Supply and Ways and Means. (Because of the 1860 case the practice was adopted, before the end of the nineteenth century, of including all tax proposals in a single Finance Bill—but that is another story.)

In general, by 1900, the powers of the Lords in relation to expenditure were already greatly constrained, but were by no means negligible.

1900–1919: Developments and Practice

Changes in Supply procedures

The major development in the procedures of the House for

---

[1] May, 10th edn., p. 550.

handling Supply business in the period before the First World War was, of course, the codification of those procedures in the new standing orders made in 1902. These set out in a somewhat more complete and sophisticated form the Balfour rules as agreed by the House in 1896.[1] The new Supply standing order was, however, but one of a number of changes in the rules and practices of the House which were designed to rearrange business to give greater priority to Government business and to streamline, in various ways, the processes of legislation and other business. Some of these reforms were highly controversial at the time—though now long accepted as sensible ways of disposing of business and avoiding time-wasting and repetition. As Balfour said, until the nineteenth century 'the difficulty was not to check the flow of oratory but to induce it to flow at all'; by the end of that century it was less desirable to have numerous occasions for debating every matter.[2] However, this was not readily accepted in 1902 and debates on the new rules were continued over a period of more than fifteen days spread throughout the session.

Much attention was therefore directed to these new proposals and, in the general debate on the rules,[3] not much attention was paid to the proposed Supply standing order: the House had had experience of the system by then for six years and the original strong objection to any form of restriction of debate on Supply had somewhat evaporated. Sir William Harcourt, for example, speaking for the Opposition, admitted that the new Supply procedure had been operated fairly and well towards all parties.[4] However, when the actual resolution relating to business of Supply came before the House, numerous amendments were moved. In particular, attention was drawn to the growing practice of passing Votes under the guillotine without discussion.[5] In the end it took four sittings before the House would agree to the new Supply rule.

The main differences between the original 1896 rule and the standing order made in 1902 were as follows (although some of these had been incorporated in earlier sessional resolutions):

[1] See pp. 347–52 above.
[2] *Hansard*, 30 Jan. 1902, cols. 1351–2.
[3] Ibid., 6 and 7 Feb. 1902.   [4] Ibid., 7 Feb. 1902, col. 716.
[5] See e.g. Redmond, ibid., 24 Apr. 1902, cols. 1275–7.

(i) the normal Supply day was to be Thursday instead of Friday;

(ii) three additional allotted days could be added, even after 5 August;

(iii) the business of Supply was to end at midnight on allotted days;

(iv) but no non-Supply business was to be taken before midnight;

(v) not more than two allotted days were to be devoted to consideration of the Vote on Account, in committee, and on reports;

(vi) while consideration of supplementary estimates was still excluded from the allotted days, a rule was made that new estimates must be considered at least two days before the Committee of Supply finished its work.

Apart from the fundamental objections of those who were opposed to guillotining consideration of Supply, the most important points that emerged from the debate on the new rule were the questions of the order in which the estimates would be considered by the House and of who should decide which estimates to put down for consideration on each allotted day. The granting of Supply to meet the requirements of the Government was, of course, Government business and it had always been accepted that the Government had the right to decide the order in which the Supply Votes were considered, although it would seek, to some extent, to meet the convenience of the House and the wishes of Members. As Balfour said in 1896, no 'Government would ever try so to manipulate the arrangement of the Votes as to divert the discussion of what they believed to be dangerous topics.'[1]

Before the system of allotted days and the guillotine was introduced in 1896 all Votes were liable to be debated and thus, in theory, the order in which they were taken might not appear important. In practice, however, the Votes were by and large taken each year in the order in which they were presented in the estimates, although it was the custom to separate out the Votes relating to Ireland (which appeared in various classes of the estimates) for consideration together to ensure one or two Irish

[1] Ibid., 24 Feb. 1896, col. 1027.

days each session. This had the effect of ensuring that the Votes in the Class I of the Civil estimates were fully considered each session but usually resulted in later Votes being taken hurriedly in August when Members were exhausted and anxious to rise for the summer recess. This was described by Balfour as restriction of Supply debate by putting Members on the rack and involving 'physical torture': he preferred the guillotine.[1] Indeed, one of his avowed purposes was to ensure a better balance in the consideration of the estimates. The introduction of the new procedures would make it possible, in his view, to revise the order in which Votes were considered.

At an early point Balfour made it clear that he would be willing, in return for the certainty of the Government being granted its Supply in a specified number of days and by a convenient date, to concede to the House, and indeed to the Opposition, the right to choose the Votes to be debated on each allotted day. When opening the debate he had not gone so far. He was anxious to ensure that important Votes were properly debated or not left to fall under the guillotine without discussion. He recognized that leaving the selection of Votes to the Government might be criticized, and he had toyed with the idea of leaving this selection to a committee of the House, but in the end he advised the House to leave the discretion with the Government. He was confident that no Government would try to manipulate the business of the House so as to avoid criticism, and he instanced the way time had always been provided for debating the Irish estimates on days convenient for Irish Members.[2]

By the end of the debate in 1896, however, Balfour was persuaded to go a little further. In the light of later developments his words may be seen to be significant enough to merit quotation in full:

My idea is that if the time-limit be twenty days, or whatever period the House fixes, it should be left to the Whips of the two sides—and mainly, let me say, to the Whips of the Opposition—to determine the order in which the Votes would be taken. I would put that suggestion even more strongly. I would say let it be left entirely to the Opposition Whips, if there were not such questions as the Army and Navy, on which hon. Gentlemen on this side would desire some opportunity for speaking and on which, perhaps,

---

[1] Ibid., 20 Feb. 1896, col. 735.   [2] Ibid., cols. 727, 729.

there is not the same desire for debate on the other side. But, at all events, so far as the Government is concerned, we have no desire to interfere with the convenience of private Members, whether on this side or the other side, as to the mode in which these twenty days should be allocated.[1]

Thus, from the beginning, Balfour was aware of the two sides of his package deal. The Government would be guaranteed its Supply business: the Opposition, or at least Members generally, would be able to choose the subjects for debate.

Balfour explained how the selection of Votes was arranged in 1900. In response to criticism about the time given to Irish Votes he said that he was anxious to see the time allotted fairly between the different Votes, but this could only be done by co-operation between the various parties, and within parties: the selection of Irish Votes, for example, was left entirely to the Irish Members. He went on, 'I am always ready to place Votes in the order in which the main body of the critics of the Government are desirous of seeing them.'[2]

Thus, by the time of the 1902 debate, the theme of who should select the Votes for debate had been thoroughly aired. But it was still not settled to the satisfaction of all Members. Redmond, for the Irish Members, complained of too many Irish Votes coming under the guillotine.[3] Gibson Bowles, a trenchant critic of the Balfour reforms, argued that the Votes selected for debate should be varied year by year so that, over a period, all would be debated;[4] he also suggested that the selection might be left to the Public Accounts Committee (of which he was a member) and he moved an amendment to this effect.[5] Balfour had several times indicated his personal willingness to accept selection by committee, but he did not think this was acceptable to the House, and so it proved.[6]

The most important—and, as it now appears, surprising—reaction to the Balfour proposals was that of the official Opposition. They were far from eager to accept the plate that Balfour proffered. Sir Henry Campbell-Bannerman, the Leader of the Opposition, argued that the House ought not to divest the Government of the day of the responsibility properly

---

[1] *Hansard*, 24 Feb. 1896, col. 1026.
[2] Ibid., 15 Feb. 1900, cols. 123–4.
[3] Ibid., 24 Apr. 1902, cols. 1278–84.
[4] Ibid., cols. 1307–8.
[5] Ibid., 25 Apr. 1902, cols. 1380–2.
[6] Ibid., cols. 1357, 1382–4.

attaching to it of deciding how Votes should be dealt with in Committee of Supply. 'For that reason he had always had an objection to the kindly proposal the Leader of the House had often made, that the selection of the particular Votes to be taken on particular days should be left to a committee, and even a committee of those opposed to him in politics': the Government should determine what should be done.[1] And Sir William Harcourt, formerly Chancellor of the Exchequer in the Liberal Government, said that 'the only principle we can act upon is to leave the whole responsibility of these matters on the Leader of the House . . . he has much better means of ascertaining the views of hon. Members than any committee . . . if you trust the Leader of the House, I think it is far better.'[2]

Thus, it is clear that even the Opposition themselves were slow to recognize that the limitation of Supply days and the guillotine procedure made it possible to convert Supply debates into official Opposition occasions when they could choose the topic for debate and bring matters of their choosing, rather than that of the Government, before the House. Because for hundreds of years the consideration of Supply had been essentially Government business (as indeed it still is formally today), the House was unwilling, at first, to accept the opportunities the new procedure offered. As we will see, the recognition of Supply days as Opposition days developed only slowly.

The only other changes in Supply procedure in the period up to 1919 were relatively minor. In 1906, following a select committee inquiry, a number of major changes were made in the hours of sitting of the House. As a result the rule that provided that Supply business should continue to midnight, but not after, was amended so that such business ended at 11 p.m.[3] And in 1918 the standing order was again amended to include reference to the Air Force estimates. The standing order relating to the procedure for the Speaker leaving the Chair on the House resolving itself into the Committee of Supply was also amended so as to permit a debate on the Air Force on the first occasion each session when the estimates for that service was to be considered (as with the Army, Navy, and Civil Service estimates).[4]

---

[1] *Hansard*, 11 Apr. 1902, col. 84.   [2] Ibid., 25 Apr. 1902, col. 1382.
[3] Ibid., 3 Apr. 1906, cols. 404–6.   [4] Ibid., 13 Feb. 1918, cols. 233–5.

The Parliament Act 1911

There was, of course, one other procedural change—and one of constitutional importance—in this period. The story of the Parliament Act 1911 and of the events leading up to it is too well known and well documented to need repeating in this Chapter. But the fundamental changes in the powers of the House of Lords that were embodied in the Act stemmed from a threat by that House to the financial supremacy of the Commons (though not, as it happens, in respect of expenditure) and they include the formal curtailment of the Lords' powers in respect of certain legislation authorizing expenditure.

Section 1 of the Parliamentary Act 1911 reads as follows:

'Powers of House of Lords as to Money Bills

1.—(1) If a Money Bill, having been passed by the House of Commons, and sent up to the House of Lords at least one month before the end of the session, is not passed by the House of Lords without amendment within one month after it is so sent up to that House, the Bill shall, unless the House of Commons direct to the contrary, be presented to His Majesty and become an Act of Parliament on the Royal Assent being signified, notwithstanding that the House of Lords have not consented to the Bill.

(2) A Money Bill means a Public Bill which in the opinion of the Speaker of the House of Commons contains only provisions dealing with all or any of the following subjects, namely, the imposition, repeal, remission, alteration, or regulation of taxation; the imposition for the payment of debt or other financial purposes of charges on the Consolidated Fund, or on money provided by Parliament, or the variation or repeal of any such charges; supply; the appropriation, receipt, custody, issue or audit of accounts of public money; the raising or guarantee of any loan or the repayment thereof; or subordinate matters incidental to those subjects or any of them. In this subsection the expressions 'taxation,' 'public money,' and 'loan' respectively do not include any taxation, money, or loan raised by local authorities or bodies for local purposes.

(3) There shall be endorsed on every Money Bill when it is sent up to the House of Lords and when it is presented to His Majesty for assent the certificate of the Speaker of the House of Commons signed by him that it is a Money Bill. Before giving his certificate, the Speaker shall consult, if practicable, two members to be appointed from the Chairmen's Panel at the beginning of each Session by the Committee of Selection.

It will be seen that the bar on the House of Lords amending 'money bills' is not absolute and, if such amendments were made, the Commons could consider them. Nor was the power of the House of Lords to reject a 'money bill' abolished—only the consequences of such rejection. It should also be emphasized that the definition of a 'money bill' was narrow and precise. The requirement that such a bill should contain *only* certain financial provisions means that many bills which are commonly thought of as money bills—for example a bill the main object of which is the creation of a charge on public funds—are not so treated for the purposes of the Parliament Acts: while some bills which do not impose a charge may yet be certified as a 'money bill' under the provisions of the Act. Nor does the definition coincide with that of the financial privileges of the Commons so that a bill may contain privileged matters but not be a money bill. And, finally, it is possible for a bill of aids and supplies to contain matters which prevent it being certified under the Parliament Act; indeed it is the case that, more often than not, the Speaker's certificate has been withheld from a Finance Bill. These distinctions are clearly spelt out in the current edition of Erskine May.[1] The editors conclude 'As the framers of the Parliament Act did not realise the inconvenience of using an established term [i.e. "money bill"] in a new and partly different sense, the resulting ambiguity must be frankly recognised.'[2]

In practice, however, the provisions of the Act regarding 'money bills' have created little difficulty and criticism has seldom been voiced of the Speaker's action in giving or withholding his certificate. The respective powers of the two Houses, in respect of expenditure, are now clearly established: the Commons have both the right of initiative and the final say.

Use of Supply debates

So far we have dealt mainly with the formal procedure. It is now time to look at how the House—and in particular the official Opposition and back-bench Members—used these procedures. What matters were debated? To what extent and

---

[1] May, pp. 806–10. [2] Ibid., p. 810.

in what ways did the debates relate to control of expenditure? Sessions of 1903, 1914, and 1918 have been examined in some detail.

It was then the practice for sessions to run from February to August, with sometimes a short spill-over in the autumn. Debate of Supply (and in this term we include debates on the various stages of Consolidated Fund Bills) occupied a large part of the time of the House. In 1903, for example, Supply was debated on 39 days (although not always for the full day). The Committee of Supply sat and debated on 27 days, reports of Supply resolutions were debated in the House on 6 other days, on 3 days there were debates on motions for the Speaker to leave the Chair for the House to resolve itself into Committee of Supply, and Consolidated Fund Bills were debated on 3 days. This constituted a large share of the 115 days on which the House sat that session. And in 1914, Supply was similarly debated on 42 days out of a session of 130 days' duration. The continued devotion of a high proportion of the time of the House to consideration of Supply, after the adoption of the new Supply procedure involving the guillotine, may appear surprising. But it should be remembered that, in this period, there were a number of Supply debates which could not be taken on allotted days (in particular debates on supplementary estimates) and, in the earlier years in particular, reports of the Committee of Supply were frequently debated on days which were not 'allotted days' under the standing order. Furthermore, throughout these years, all parts of the House—Ministers, Opposition, and back-benchers—clearly regarded extended debates on the Government's estimates as one of their main functions. Even during the war no opportunity was neglected for looking critically at the conduct of the Government, both in respect of the war itself and other matters, by debating Supply.[1]

Throughout this period Supply debates tended to be concentrated into the months of February and March (supplementary estimates, Votes A and other selected money Votes for the armed forces, and the Civil Services and Revenue Departments Vote on Account), and in July and August (remaining Votes). In 1903 for example, there were Supply debates on 16 days in

---

[1] See pp. 377–80 below.

March and 10 days in July and August. In 1914 the corresponding figures were 19 days in February and March and 12 days in
July and August. However, the extended end-of-session pile-up,
of which Balfour had complained, was successfully removed by
his new procedure.

The effect of the guillotine is interesting. The number of
estimates to be voted (and, of course, their value) increased
significantly over this period. In 1903 there were (excluding
all supplementary estimates) 18 Navy Votes (including Vote
A), 18 for the Army, and 113 for the Civil Services and Revenue
Departments. Of these, 4 Army, no Navy, and 56 Civil Services
and Revenue Departments Votes were agreed to without
debate in Committee of Supply under the guillotine at the end
of the session (although one or two of these had previously
been debated). In other words nearly two-thirds of the Votes
were either debated at some stage or had been placed for debate
but in fact agreed to without discussion. In 1914 there were still
18 Navy Votes, and 17 Army Votes, but the number of Civil
Services and Revenue Departments Votes had risen to 131.
Of these, 10 Navy, 11 Army, and 123 Civil Services and
Revenue Departments Votes were passed in committee under
the guillotine (although of these Votes, 8 had previously been
debated but not agreed and there is some evidence that the
practice of keeping estimates 'open' for further debate instead
of voting them had begun[1]). Thus, in the period up to the war,
the proportion of debated Votes fell markedly and the proportion guillotined correspondingly increased. Examination of
individual debates confirms this development. There was a
clear tendency, over this period, to select fewer estimates for
debate and to have fuller debates on those important estimates
which were chosen. This is important evidence of the move
(which we will see throughout the period covered by this
Chapter) away from detailed consideration of individual
estimates towards broader consideration of policies.

There was, however, another development which inclined in
the opposite direction. Matching the growth in the number of
Government services which was roughly reflected in the
growing number of Votes (in 1914, for example, there were

---

[1] See pp. 395–6 below.

estimates for Old Age Pensions, National Insurance, and Labour Exchanges which did not exist in 1903) and in the growth of public expenditure, came an increasing prevalence of supplementary estimates (all of which had to be separately considered in committee and on report). In 1903 there were 1 Army and 11 Civil supplementaries; in 1914 there were 1 Navy, 1 Army, and 14 Civil supplementary estimates (excluding the special additional Votes A at the beginning of the war); and in 1918 there were 1 Navy, 1 Army, and 24 Civil supplementaries.

The most important question, however, is what use did the House make of its Supply procedures in terms of the subjects debated. First we note the obligatory debates. Each session there had to be, before the end of March, debates in the House on the motions 'that Mr. Speaker do now leave the Chair' for the House to resolve itself into Committee of Supply or the first occasion when the Navy and Army (and, from 1918, the Air Force) estimates, respectively, were to be considered. These were traditionally occasions for an annual statement by the Ministers concerned, followed by a general debate on their service (there was also opportunity, on an amendment, to consider a specific topic). Alternatively, these general debates could be held in Committee of Supply when considering the Votes A for the Navy and Army (and from 1918 for the R.A.F.). In addition, time had to be provided for debate on the pay Votes of the services and such other Navy and Army Votes as were required to provide enough money for those services pending the final agreement to all the estimates in August.[1]

Furthermore, all supplementary estimates (and excesses) had to be placed for debate as they could not fall under the guillotine. And although it was not, of course, obligatory for the House to debate all of them, it was, at least at the beginning of this period, the practice to examine the majority. It should also be remembered that these 'obligatory' debates in Committee of Supply were liable to be repeated on the report of the committee's resolutions—indeed, this often happened on the service estimates.

For the remaining occasions, however, there was a wide

[1] See pp. 350–1 above.

choice as to what could be debated. Let us see how it was used in the selected sessions.

The Supply business of 1903 began with two days in committee on supplementary estimates. The subjects actually debated included

Marlborough House (overhaul of drains)
Prisons (conveyance and diet of prisoners)
Mercantile marine (repairs to steam launches)
Consular Service (cost of telegrams)
British Protectorates in East Africa (debate on policy)
Valuation and boundary surveys in Ireland
Board of Education
Commissioners for National Education (Ireland) (teaching Irish language and history)
Colonial Office (costs of Premiers' conference)
Colonial Services (maintenance of South African constabulary)
Army pay (Somaliland expedition)

And on report of the resolutions for these estimates, there were further debates on Colonial Services and Army pay.

The four days 9, 10, 11, and 12 March and part of 18 March were devoted to debates on the Army, which (following soon after the Boer War) was a major issue of the day. On the motion for the Speaker leaving the Chair there was a full debate on an amendment relating to the training of officers and men, and a further debate on the role of the Volunteers. On Vote A, in committee, and on the Pay Vote there was a wide debate on general policy and especially on the size of the Army. An attack on the level of Army expenditure was mounted by the Liberal Opposition (aided vigorously by a young Member, elected as a Tory, called Winston Churchill). Both the Prime Minister and the Leader of the Opposition spoke on several occasions. And amendments to reduce the size of the Army by 27,000 men and, correspondingly, its expenditure by £710,000, were negatived on divisions. Another Vote relating to retired pay, pensions, etc., was debated in some detail and agreed to.

On 16, 17, 18, and 23 March, the Navy estimates were likewise considered. Matters raised included Navy training, tactics, equipment, recruiting, buildings at naval bases, pay of dockyard workers, etc. Again, an amendment (moved by back-benchers) to reduce Naval expenditure by substantial amounts was negatived on a division. Other Votes were taken without much debate, and although some Members complained that the estimates were being rushed, the Prime Minister, Balfour, said that these 'technical Votes' had often been passed without discussion.

Next came the Vote on Account for Civil Services and the Revenue Departments (i.e. Inland Revenue, Customs and Excise, and the Post Office). By the decision of the Government, but designed to meet what it believed to be the wishes of the House, the Colonial Office Vote was put down first (i.e. out of the normal sequence). This permitted a broad debate on South Africa (following a recent visit by the Colonial Secretary, Joe Chamberlain). There was also time for a debate on education and for a short debate on agriculture before the question was put, pursuant to the standing order. A few days later, the report stage of the Vote on Account permitted a number of unrelated matters to be raised (including agriculture, South Africa, lawlessness in the Highlands, and Balkan affairs). And finally the second reading of the Consolidated Fund Bill provided an opportunity for a general debate (on an amendment moved by Dilke) on native labour and taxation in South Africa. The committee and third reading stages of this Bill was not debated. Thus the provision of Supply to be voted by the end of March was completed.

Two further days were then spent in committee on further service estimates, and a number of detailed matters were debated, including works services, the latest rifle, payments to contractors, wages of employees at Woolwich, pensions of naval widows, medical services, naval prisons (including the salary of a particular prison chaplain), naval building, the provision of beds for boy ratings (hammocks were said to be bad for their backs), seamen's food, and provision of weapons for the militia (the withdrawal of lances from active service was deplored by some Members, and the development of balloons welcomed by others).

The major consideration of the Civil estimates began with the motion for the Speaker to leave the Chair. This was the occasion for a debate on a balloted amendment relating to working-class housing; Kier Hardie raised the working of the

Truck Acts; and the salaries of senior civil servants and Scottish fisheries were also debated.

From after Easter to the end of July the Committee of Supply sat regularly once or twice a week, mostly for consideration of Civil estimates. The matters debated were

Royal Palaces
Royal Parks
Houses of Parliament Buildings
Diplomatic and Consular Buildings } debated on same day
Public Buildings (Great Britain)
Agriculture
Government printing
Treasury services

Board of Trade (railway rates, hours worked by railwaymen, railway accidents, registration of ships, radio on ships, and many other matters)

Army operations in Somaliland

The Post Office, and } two days' debate
Post Office Packet Service

Dockyards (manning, repairs, and construction programme)

Law and Justice (Supreme Court expenses, Land registry, Prisons, county courts)

Customs and Excise (import of milk)
Inland Revenue
Post Office Packet Service
Post Office Telegraph Service
British Museum } debated on same day
National Gallery
Wallace Collection
Grants in aid of Science
Temporary commissions

Local Government Board (general debate including speed limit for motor cars, public health and adulteration of milk)

Education (Scotland)

Home Office (health and safety in industry, Factory Acts, vivisection, Metropolitan police, etc.)

Naval shipbuilding and construction programme

Boards of Education (working of new Education Act, dismissal of a senior civil servant, children's health)

Irish Education (Ireland)
Agriculture (Ireland) } debated on same day
Crime and Prosecutions (Ireland)

Foreign Office

Colonial Office (South Africa, Canadian tariffs, } debated on same day
Malta, Tristan da Cunha, Fiji)
Embassies, Missions, and Consular Service

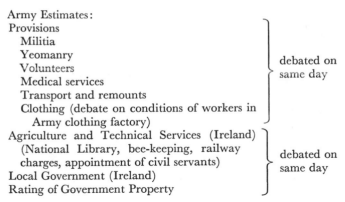

Army Estimates:
Provisions
  Militia
  Yeomanry
  Volunteers   debated on
  Medical services   same day
  Transport and remounts
  Clothing (debate on conditions of workers in
    Army clothing factory)
Agriculture and Technical Services (Ireland)
  (National Library, bee-keeping, railway
  charges, appointment of civil servants)   debated on
Local Government (Ireland)   same day
Rating of Government Property

On 10 August the outstanding Supply resolutions were reported, and there were debates on foreign affairs(Macedonia), Uganda (with the Prime Minister intervening), Cyprus, an explosion in Woolwich, pay of ordnance factory workers, rating of Government property in Ireland, and the problems of the Scottish Highlands. On 11 August, the second reading of the Consolidated Fund (Appropriation) Bill enabled many matters to be raised; in particular much anxiety was shown by front-bench Liberals about the prospects of tariff reform but the Speaker refused to allow debate on future (and hypothetical) legislation. And on 14 August the third reading of the Bill provided an opportunity for debates on religious education (opened by Lloyd George), Macedonia, tariff reform (answered by the Prime Minister), Irish workhouses, and other questions. Thus, Supply for the session was completed and Parliament was prorogued.

In general it will be seen that Supply debates were used in 1903 for three main purposes. First, there were whole day's debates on the general administration of all of the major departments of State (although many matters of detail were also raised in these debates). Second, there were shorter debates on many more detailed aspects of administration and public expenditure (especially on the Navy and Army Votes and those for public buildings etc., and on supplementary estimates). And third, there were a few major debates on specific topical issues of current political importance, e.g. size of the Army, South Africa, the Somaliland expedition, and naval construction.

Another general feature is the repetition of certain themes, either because of political topicality (e.g. size of army and South Africa) or because questions raised on one occasion but not answered may be raised again on another occasion. This repetition of debate was facilitated by the duplication of opportunities created by the report stage of Supply resolutions. And repetition was particularly prevalent in debates on the Navy and Army because many issues (e.g. the size of the Army) could be properly raised at least seven times—on the motion for the Speaker to leave the Chair, on Vote A in committee, on Vote 1 (Pay etc.) in committee, on Vote A on report, on Vote 1 on report, on the second reading of the Consolidated Fund Bill, and, finally, on the third reading of that Bill. Clearly, this multiplication of opportunities was welcomed by some Members (after all the procedures were originally intended to ensure ample opportunities to debate each issue). But, equally, it also made for untidy debate. We will see how, over the years, the opportunities have been reduced and tidiness enhanced.

Let us now see whether the use of Supply occasions had changed by 1914. Again, four days were devoted in committee at the beginning of the session to debates on Civil supplementary estimates:

Agriculture and Technical Services (Ireland) ⎫
Houses of Parliament Buildings ⎪
Registry of Friendly Societies ⎬ debated on same day
Registrar-General ⎪
Board of Lunacy in Scotland ⎭
Colonial Services (wide debate on policy in relation to Somalia)
Miscellaneous Irish Votes ⎫ debated on same day
Scottish Education ⎭

On all of these many details were raised, and amendments to reduce the estimates were moved and negatived on divisions.

The treatment of the Army and Navy supplementary estimates, however, was different. In each case a single question was put for all the supplementary estimates for the service and this permitted a wider debate on the need for the supplementary estimates and new developments. In the case of the Army, for example, there was a fairly wide debate on the provision of aeroplanes. Two-and-a-half days were spent on the service supplementary estimates.

Report of Supply on 4 March enabled the House to debate certain foreign loans. Consideration of the Vote on Account on 5 March in committee provided the occasion for a whole day's debate on the operation of the National Insurance Act. And the report of the Vote on Account on 16 March permitted a debate on housing at Rosyth and several other matters.

The services debates followed the same pattern as in earlier years. The respective Ministers presented their estimates on the motion for the Speaker to leave the Chair (Churchill, introducing 'the largest Estimate for Naval expense ever presented to the House' created another record by speaking for two-and-a-half hours). Amendments were moved by Members who had been lucky in the ballot ('shortages of military forces' and 'selection of Naval Officers' were their chosen topics) and there were major debates, extending in each case over two days, on the Army and the Navy. On Army Vote A there was a debate on reserved forces and on Vote 1 (Pay etc.) a debate on the problems of married soldiers. But the debate in committee on the Navy Vote A and Votes 1, 2, and 3 was taken formally as the allotted time had been taken by an emergency debate on the Curragh Mutiny. On report of the Army Votes there was a debate on the size of the Army and an extremely muddled debate on the Royal Flying Corps and military discipline in the light of the events at Curragh. And again, the Navy Votes were agreed without debate.

The second reading of the Consolidated Fund Bill was the occasion for a major debate on the Curragh Mutiny and the actions of the Secretary of State for War (Seeley, who was forced to resign). And on third reading there was another major debate on the Government of Ireland.

The motion for the Speaker to leave the Chair for the Civil estimates enabled the House to have another debate on the National Insurance Act, and so the House turned to the Civil estimates and other outstanding Votes. The matters debated were

Housing conditions in Ireland
H.M.S.O. and Parliamentary printing
Houses of Parliament Buildings (restoration   } debated on same day
   of roof of Westminster Hall)

Post Office wages—two days' debate

Home Office (general debate, but especially on suffragettes)

Agriculture

Local Government (especially housing)

Foreign Affairs (on 29 June, the day the murder of Archduke Ferdinand of Austria was announced. The event was only mentioned in passing and relations between the great powers of Europe were not debated. The main topic was the Near East)

Prime Minister's salary (Ministers and civil servants dealings in shares) ⎱
Inland Revenue (pay of civil servants) ⎰ debated on same day

Post Office (telephone service)

Board of Trade (Shipping and railways)

Foreign Affairs (wide ranging but European problems hardly mentioned even though this was on 10 July 1914!)

Navy (pay of dockyard workers, etc.)

Colonial Office and Colonial Service ⎱
Education ⎰ debated on same day

Scottish Land Court ⎱
Board of Agriculture for Scotland ⎰ debated on same day
Fisheries (Scotland)

European War

And so the House finished its Supply work as it was caught up by the growing avalanche that swept Britain into the war. On 4 August all outstanding Votes were agreed to in committee without further debate and on 15 August they were similarly agreed on report. On 6 August the first Vote of Credit[1] of £100,000,000 was passed in the Committee of Supply and also supplementary Votes A for the Navy and Army. (It is significant of British attachment to constitutional process that even at the moment of crisis the formal procedures for sanctioning a growth in the size of the armed forces of the Crown were meticulously observed—as indeed they were throughout the war.) On the same day, debate on the second reading of the Consolidated Fund (Appropriation) Bill enabled back-benchers to raise sundry matters of current concern. Then on the following day the Vote of Credit and Votes A were agreed on report, the Bill was amended in committee to appropriate the additional sums and numbers that had been voted (this was one of the rare occasions when it has been possible to amend a Consolidated Fund Bill), and the Bill was read the third time, when again

---

[1] See p. 378 below.

numerous separate matters were raised. Finally, before the session closed, the House was recalled in September and a supplementary Vote A was agreed for the Army, permitting a further 500,000 men to be recruited. Appropriately there were debates on recruitment of soldiers both in committee and on report.

The session of 1914 was the last peace session before the war, but inevitably the use of Supply debates showed a growing interest in defence questions (although, oddly, foreign affairs did not bulk particularly large). Ireland was also a recurring theme. In general, compared with 1903, it is clear that Supply time was beginning to be used more by the official Opposition for debating questions of policy and current political issues (e.g. the National Insurance Act, suffragettes, the Curragh Mutiny) rather than being used by Members at large for scrutiny of the estimates. Whole day's debates were again devoted to reviews of the work of each of the major departments (except the Colonial Office and the Board of Education who shared a day), and no less than three days were spent in debating various aspects of the Post Office. But there were fewer short debates directly concerned with the estimates: only 16 Civil estimates (excluding supplementaries) were selected for debate, compared with 33 in 1903.

A few other aspects of Supply debates in 1914 are worth noting. Again, a number of debates were muddled, covering two or three topics at once. For example, in the middle of a debate (on the report of the Vote on Account) on housing at Rosyth a Member was able to turn the attention of the House to the political situation in South Rhodesia. And there was uncertainty about the scope of debate on Votes A compared with the pay Votes. Another factor which disturbed the systematic examination of Supply was the very frequent interruption of Supply debates at 8.15 p.m. for debate on opposed private business, which sometimes absorbed the remainder of the sitting.

Supply continued to be debated throughout the war. Indeed, one gets the impression that Members were anxious to cling on to as many opportunities as possible for holding the Government to account, not only for the conduct of the war itself, but also for the increasing problems of their constituents, whether they be in uniform or not. However, in the earlier years there was some reduction in the number of allotted days, namely to 17 in 1914–16, to 15 in 1916, and to 16 in 1917–18, but in 1918 the full 20 days were again made available.

Technically, the main change in the Supply system in the war was that only token sums of £1,000 were voted for each of the Navy, Army, and Air Force estimates and also for some Civil estimates, e.g. those for the Ministry of Munitions and the Ministry of Shipping. This meant that the conduct of these departments was still liable to debate and their Votes had to be agreed by the House; but the great bulk of the Government's expenditure on the war was provided for by Votes of Credit which were voted in blocks and which did not have to be accounted for in detail to the House. The Vote of Credit resolution of 7 March 1918, for example, read as follows:

> Vote of Credit, 1918–19.
>
> *Resolved*, That a sum not exceeding £600,000,000 be granted to His Majesty, beyond the ordinary Grants of Parliament, towards defraying the Expenses which may be incurred during the year ending the 31st day of March 1919 for general Navy, Army, and Air Services, in so far as specific provision is not made therefor by Parliament; for the conduct of Naval and Military Operations; for all measures which may be taken for the security of the country; for assisting the Food Supply, and promoting the continuance of Trade, Industry, Business, and Communications, whether by means of insurance or indemnity against risk, the financing of the purchase and resale of Foodstuffs and Materials, or otherwise; for relief of Distress; and generally for all Expenses, beyond those provided for in the ordinary Grants of Parliament, arising out of the existence of a state of War.[1]

The war sessions were not typical, however, so perhaps it is not necessary to examine our selected session of 1918 in the same detail as we did those of 1903 and 1914. It is important to emphasize, however, that Votes of Credit were specifically excluded by the standing order from being taken on allotted Supply days and as four such Votes were taken (in March, June, August, and November) and as each Vote was debatable (and was debated) in committee and on report, and as each Vote had to be given statutory authority by a Consolidated Fund Bill (with two debated stages for each Bill), the House was given, in effect, 12 extra days (allowing for two Consolidated Fund Bills being required in a normal session) for debating

[1] *House of Commons Journal*, 1918, p. 29.

questions of interest to the Opposition parties and back-benchers. It is interesting to note how these days were used.

On each of the four occasions there was at least one day's general debate on the conduct of the war (with the Chancellor of the Exchequer addressing himself in particular to the financing of the war effort). Other matters raised in 1918 on the Votes of Credit and Consolidated Fund Bill debates were

Government—press relations
Relations with Russia and Japan ⎫
Conduct of courts-martial   ⎬ debated on same day
                     ⎭
Control of national expenditure ⎫
Venereal disease   ⎬ debated on same day
Contracts for a certain chemical ⎫
League of Nations   ⎬ debated on same day
Prisoners of War   ⎭
Naval and military pensions ⎫
War losses (grants)   ⎬ debated on same day
War-trading profits   ⎭
Problems of transition to peace (on 12 November)
Agriculture and food supplies in Ireland
Shipbuilding ⎫
Banking   ⎬ debated on same day
Labour relations ⎭
Foreign Affairs

and many other separate questions were raised in the debates on the Bills.

There was also, however, the ordinary Supply business. There were the usual debates on the armed forces estimates, permitting general reviews of each service and also enabling numerous detailed problems, e.g. individual cases, to be raised. Two days were spent in committee on an increased number of Civil supplementaries and more time on report, and many details of the estimates were scrutinized. And there were wide-ranging debates on the Vote on Account. The estimates or matters that were debated on the main Civil estimates were as follows:

Royal Parks ⎫
Houses of Parliament Buildings ⎪
Legal buildings   ⎬ debated on same day
British Museum   ⎪
Consular buildings   ⎪
Employment exchanges ⎭

Local Government Board
Ministry of Pensions
Ministry of Food
Post Office
Agriculture (Scotland) and other Scottish Votes
Aliens (Police and Home Office Votes were taken formally)
Board of Agriculture
Secret Service (part of a day)
Board of Trade (coal rationing) } debated on same day
Foreign Office

It will be seen that the number of separate Civil Votes selected for debate was (as in 1914) only 16, and the number of days devoted to debate on the main Civil estimates was reduced to 10 as compared with 14 in 1914 and 16 in 1903. This was, no doubt, a reflection of the natural major interest in defence matters but was also made possible by the provision of other opportunities on the Votes of Credit etc. However, the result was that in 1918 it was no longer possible to have a separate day's debate on each of the main departments. Yet again, however, Supply time was used for a few topical political debates e.g. Government–press relations and the Ministry of Information (Lord Beaverbrook had been appointed to head this department), defence contracts, and, of course, the conduct of the war. But less time than in the pre-war days was spent on scrunity of individual estimates.

One detail is worth noting. On 11 July the Police and Home Office Votes were taken formally (i.e. without debate) in Committee of Supply, so that a debate could be held on the question of aliens or a motion for the adjournment of the House. This was a forerunner of a method of proceeding that was to become more popular in later years.

We have looked at the matters debated in Supply time. Looking at this period as a whole, the question must now be examined as to who chose those subjects for debate.[1] The answers (for there are different answers for the different types of business) must be tentative: the published records give us clues (who opens debates, for example) but no conclusive proof. Some trends are, however, evident.

[1] For an interesting discussion of this question, covering the whole of our period, see Anthony Barker, 'Party and Supply', *Parliamentary Affairs*, Spring 1964, Vol. xvii, No. 2.

Navy and Army estimates were, throughout the period, put down in accordance with the needs of the Government (certain Votes had to be agreed by the end of March), although they appear to have consulted with the Opposition on convenience of dates. Similarly, all Civil supplementary estimates had to be placed for debate; which estimates were actually debated was, in 1903, very much left to back-bench Members on either side, but by 1914 there are signs that the official Conservative Opposition wished to concentrate on certain topics (a whole day on Somalia for example).

The main occasions for choice, therefore, were the topics for debate on the Vote on Account and Consolidated Fund Bills and the selection of the main Civil estimates. In 1903 the topics were 'placed' by the Government for the Vote on Account in committee to give priority to three matters (South Africa, education, and agriculture) on which there appears to have been some generally expressed desire for debate. And on report of that Vote a number of unrelated topics raised by back-bench Members were debated. On the Consolidated Fund Bills the opening subject appears to have been chosen by (and the debate opened by) the official Opposition, but after that (if time permitted) other Members raised other topics.

By 1914, however, it appears that these occasions had been largely taken over by the official Opposition. All four days in March (two on the Vote and two on the Bill) were used by them for major debates of their own choosing. Only in August (at the outbreak of war) were debates on the Bills used primarily by back-benchers. The 1918 session is not typical or helpful from the point of view of this analysis. A coalition Government was in power and the Opposition was fragmented. It was noticeable, however, that both Asquith and Ramsay MacDonald played a prominent part in the broader Supply debates (just as Mac-Donald and Redmond had in 1914).

As far as the selection of the main Civil estimates was concerned, the evidence suggests that in the period up to 1914 the official Opposition came increasingly to choose the topics for debate. Balfour, as we have already shown,[1] had always been ready to leave the selection of topics to the House (though how

---

[1] See pp. 362-3 above.

'the House' should make this choice was never very clear), a sentiment which he repeated in 1903[1]. However, the official Opposition (as also already shown[2]) were at first reluctant to accept a direct responsibility on this matter. An exchange in 1903 is revealing. Complaint was made that a certain Vote was not to be discussed (some aspects had become *sub-judice*) and of the short notice given of the Votes that were to be taken. Balfour said that 'he always desired to put down the Supply which, as far as he could gather, the House desired to discuss'.[3] He was not able to give a firm pledge, however, that a particular Vote would come on; there might not be time for it.[4] And when another Member complained about 'private arrangement' in the choice of Votes to be placed for debate, the Government Chief Whip explained how it worked: he had had differing representations from 'Rt. Honourable Gentlemen opposite' as to what should be taken; the aim was to take the major departments in turn, but the choice was limited; he had tried to meet the general wishes of Members 'in accordance with Parliamentary etiquette'; and he regretted any inconvenience caused.[5]

It is clear from this evidence (as well as a general reading of the debates and examination of the topics chosen) that although the Opposition were consulted in 1903 the final selection of topics still lay with the Government. The practice of Governments appears to have been to put a large number of the estimates down, ensuring that there was at least a day for each of the main departments and to leave to the House how much time was spent on every estimate. Certainly all the main estimates were debated and a number of less important ones were not debated, although they had been placed. Equally, few votes of importance fell under the guillotine without debate.[6]

The same could not be said of the debates of 1914, although again all the main departments were covered. There appears to have been a much greater effort to select topics for a whole day's debate, rather than covering many estimates at the wish of individual Members.[7] The evidence suggests that the official Opposition (now of course the party formerly led by Balfour)

---

[1] *Hansard*, 18 Mar. 1903, col. 1115.   [2] See pp. 363–4 above.
[3] *Hansard*, 21 May 1903, col. 1363.   [4] Ibid., col. 1365.
[5] Ibid., cols. 1365–6.   [6] See particularly, 2 July 1903.
[7] See p. 377 above.

were playing a much more positive and selective role, there were references to topics being put down for debate at the request of the Opposition,[1] and Opposition spokesmen more often opened the debates. We may not have reached by 1914 the total acceptance of Supply days as 'Opposition days', but this concept was nearing recognition.

Thus, Lowell's statement that 'what departments shall be examined is determined by the critics themselves' which he made in 1908 appears to have been fulfilled. But he went on to say 'if an excessive proportion of the time devoted to supply is consumed in the ventilation of small grievances, that is due to the fact that the criticism is conducted, in the main, by individual Members of the House, and not by an organised Opposition'.[2] We now turn to consideration of how the criticism was conducted and the nature of the debates.

Supply debates—at least in Committee of Supply—throughout this period appear to have been much more informal than the equivalent debates today. Members frequently spoke more than once (as they were entitled to do). Ministers also frequently intervened and might also speak several times on each question, much as in a standing committee today. However, participation was not restricted to back-benchers and departmental Ministers. In both 1903 and 1914 senior Ministers, including even the Prime Minister and the Chancellor of the Exchequer, frequently took part, even on debates on relatively routine matters, and equally the Leader of the Opposition would weigh in. All of this led to lively debate. There was much genuine argument and little delivery of previously prepared speeches that had little reference to the previous course of the debate (this appears to have been less true of the multi-topic debates held on Consolidated Fund Bills and other occasions).

The informal and vigorous nature of Supply debates was reinforced in committee by the conduct of the Chairmen. Although they were usually strict in enforcing the rules of relevance (particularly in debates on supplementary estimates[3]), they were not restrictive in application of other procedural rules. They frequently allowed motions for the

---

[1] E.g. *Hansard*, 10 July 1914, col. 1393.
[3] Lowell, *The Government of England*, Vol. 1, p. 345.
[3] See pp. 384-5 below.

adjournment of debates etc. to be moved, which would then be very briefly and orderly debated and decided. And they willingly allowed amendments to reduce Votes or items of Votes to be moved, often without notice, even though this sometimes narrowed the scope of debate (again a point they enforced) until the amendment was disposed of. Quite frequently, especially in 1903, a number of amendments were moved to reduce individual items within an estimate before the estimate as a whole was voted on.

This made, of course, for spirited debate. However, it also encouraged untidy debate. Members tended to be concerned with detail and the topic of debate would frequently change. Only on big occasions—when there was a clear political issue or general policy at stake—did a general theme emerge. There was also a lot of repetition of debate, spreading sometimes over several days.[1]

The nature of amendments—and their fate—is worth examining. Most amendments, both in committee and on report, were for token reductions (usually £100) in an item of a Vote or in a whole Vote. This was, in effect, a peg on which to hang a debate and a division (even if the Member would really have preferred to increase the estimate). But in 1903 there were a number of cases where Members moved genuine substantial reductions, especially in respect of the numbers of soldiers and sailors and of Army and Navy expenditures. By 1914, however, this practice appears to have died out: all amendments were for token reductions and, indeed, fewer amendments were moved. Many of these amendments were pushed to divisions, but always unsuccessfully. In the three years in question the Government majorities always held and no estimate was actually reduced in committee or on report.[2]

In looking at the nature of Supply debates we must again distinguish between the occasions. Debates on supplementary estimates were strictly controlled by the Chair and only exceptionally (e.g. for a new service) could policy be discussed.

[1] See p. 374 above.

[2] However, on 20 July 1905, the estimate for the Irish Land Commission was reduced by £100 following a Government defeat, and in 1919 provision for alterations to the Lord Chancellor's bathroom had to be reduced following the defeat of the Government in a standing committee (*Hansard*, 31 July 1919, col. 2323).

Debate was thus concentrated on details and matters of administration (like the cost of telegrams to Venezuela in 1903). There was also some genuine discussion of the estimates; Ministers, for example, were required to explain why more money was required. However, even here, there was little attempt to go through the estimates item by item or to attempt any systematic critique of the expenditure proposed by the Government; attention was more frequently focused on the failure to keep the expenditure within the limits originally authorized. Many supplementary estimates were agreed after very short debates—perhaps just a few questions and answers by the Minister. Debate on supplementaries tended to be more cursory in 1914 and 1918 than in 1903.

On all other occasions, Supply debates tended to be more concerned with administration or policy rather than with the estimates themselves.[1] There were few references to detailed items of the main estimates in 1903 and even fewer in the later years. In 1903, however, many different administrative aspects were selected for short debates within each estimate or group of estimates. By 1914 and 1918 there were more broad debates, perhaps on an amendment to reduce the Minister's salary, in the course of which separate administrative details could be debated. And, finally, in the later years, there was more emphasis on general policy than in 1903.[2]

In general, we may sum up on the use of Supply procedure in the period 1900 to 1919 in this way. By the first years of the century the House had already ceased to examine each estimate in detail and seriatim. The new guillotine procedures had both encouraged and made possible a more balanced review of Government administration that concentrated on the major spending departments and their work. Although the Government continued to be responsible for arranging the debates on Supply, the Government's critics, both Opposition and backbench, were beginning to ensure that time was mainly spent on debating estimates of their choosing. And the fact was increasingly appreciated that the numerous occasions on which

---

[1] A fact of which Bryce complained in the debate on the Balfour reforms (*Hansard*, 24 Apr. 1902, cols. 1901–2).

[2] Dilke had forecast that this would be the effect of the new rules (ibid., col. 1284).

Supply could be debated provided excellent occasions for Parliament to examine policies and administration, as well as financial details.

By 1914 all these trends had been carried further. The official Opposition were now using Supply days to focus attention on the policies of the Government which they wished to debate, as well as reviewing more systematically the work of departments. And the war years up to 1918 simply reinforced these features. The necessary availability of Supply debates throughout the war was an essential feature of the preservation —even at the time of gravest crisis—of our Parliamentary democracy. And so Supply time came to be accepted as essentially House of Commons (if not yet 'Opposition') time, and not just the occasion for voting the Government the money it needed. By 1918 the modern concept of Supply was firmly established. We will see later how it was further developed.

Money resolutions

Money resolutions appear to have caused few problems during this period and they were not very numerous—about a dozen per session. If the main purpose of the bill was to authorize or impose a charge on public funds then such a bill had to be founded on a resolution. Theoretically each stage of this procedure was debatable. First, a Minister moved for the appointment of a committee on a future day, but in practice there was no debate at this stage. Second, on the day appointed, the House accordingly resolved itself into committee to consider the resolution; at this stage the terms of the resolution and the need for the bill to be founded on it was normally debated, sometimes at some length. And third, the resolution was reported on a later day, often without further debate,[1] and the bill was ordered in on the resolution being agreed to. The terms of such resolutions were normally broad and covered all the matters proposed to be included in the bill. Frequently, however, the resolutions also specified the maximum amount of the grants or loans to be made under the bill, and this sometimes provoked discussion.

Where the creation of a charge was subordinate to the main

[1] A proposal was made by Balfour that no debate should be permitted at this stage (*Hansard*, 30 Jan. 1902, col. 1356), but it was not then acceptable.

object of a bill the necessary money resolutions did not have to be considered till after the bill's second reading. Such resolutions were usually drawn fairly broadly in this period ('any expenses of the Minister' or some similar words) and were often agreed without debate at any stage.

Development of Financial Committees

The increasing tendency of Members to use Supply debates for discussing questions of policy and administration was already apparent at the beginning of the century. Thus it was clear that debates on the estimates were no longer purely financial and that the House was no longer exercising much scrutiny or any direct control over the details of public expenditure as set out in the estimates. Bryce complained about this in the debate on the new Supply standing order.[1] And another Member, Edmund Robertson, complaining that Balfour's proposals would do nothing to increase the control of the House over expenditure, proposed that the estimates should also be referred to a select committee for detailed examination, and that that committee should report on them before they came before the House.[2] The Government agreed that this proposal should be further considered and a select committee was appointed.

The Report of the Select Committee on National Expenditure of 1903[3] is one of the important milestones in the development of the House's financial procedures. The Committee noted the growing volume of Government expenditure (it had doubled in twenty years) and took note, without itself commenting, that a number of experienced witnesses had concluded that the effect of discussions in the Committee of Supply was to urge increased not decreased expenditure. And it concluded that a select committee system was needed to strengthen the House's financial control. The Committee's conclusions on this matter are worth recording in full (it also indicates the view of Members at that time of the nature of Supply debates):

But we consider that the examination of Estimates by the House of Commons leaves much to be desired from the point of view of financial scrutiny. The colour of the discussions is unavoidably partisan. Few questions are discussed with adequate knowledge or settled on their financial merits.

[1] Ibid., 25 Apr. 1902, cols. 1301–2.   [2] Ibid., 11 Apr. 1902, col. 107.
[3] H.C. 242 (1903).

670 Members of Parliament, influenced by party ties, occupied with other work and interests, frequently absent from the Chamber during the 20 to 23 Supply days, are hardly the instrument to achieve a close and exhaustive examination of the immense and complex estimates now annually presented. They cannot effectively challenge the smallest item without supporting a motion hostile to the Government of the day; and divisions are nearly always decided by a majority of members who have not listened to the discussion. Your Committee agree in thinking that the Estimates are used in practice —perhaps necessarily by the Committee of Supply—mainly to provide a series of convenient and useful opportunities for the debating of Policy and Administration, rather than to the criticism and review of financial method and of the details of expenditure. We are impressed with the advantages, for the purposes of detailed financial scrutiny, which are enjoyed by Select Committees, whose proceedings are usually devoid of party feeling, who may obtain accurate knowledge collected for them by trained officials, which may, if so desired, be checked or extended by the examination of witnesses or the production of documents; and we feel it is in this direction that the financial control of the House of Commons is most capable of being strengthened.

After a full discussion extending over several meetings, the Committee, on a division, agreed to an amendment proposed by Winston Churchill (who was, throughout, a very active member of the Committee) recommending the appointment of an Estimates Committee, which had been proposed to them by Gibson Bowles, an enthusiast for detailed financial scrutiny. This Committee, which would work in close partnership with the Public Accounts Committee, should not have power actually to reduce or amend the estimates (Members were anxious that a small committee should not infringe the prerogatives and responsibilities of Ministers and of the House), but, so far as possible, examine selected estimates and report on them in time for its report to be debated with the estimates concerned in the Committee of Supply.

What resulted from this Report—the appointment of the Estimate Committee in 1912 and of the National Expenditure Committee—is described elsewhere in this book.[1] Nor is there space in this Chapter to examine how these Committees worked. It is important, however, to emphasize that from the beginning of our period the House was aware that debates of the estimates in Committee of Supply and on report did not provide effective procedures for the House to exercise control of

[1] See Chapter VIII.

expenditure. Other measures were needed 'to enhance the value of discussion in Supply and enable the House of Commons more effectively to exercise control over the details of National Expenditure' (as the Committee of 1903 put it). But equally, the further control then proposed was indirect rather than direct. The Select Committee would not be allowed to alter the estimates; and the House, as we have seen, would never do so.

1919–1945: Developments and Practice

Changes in Supply procedures

The Balfour reforms (one man's reform is another man's phobia, but as these changes eventually proved broadly acceptable perhaps the term can be tolerated) survived well the tests of both fierce political fighting before 1914 and the different circumstances of the war years. And so it was that major changes in Supply procedure which had been strongly opposed when they were first introduced came to be accepted as a normal, and most important, feature of the British Parliamentary system. The essential feature of these procedures which made them acceptable was, of course, that they offered advantages to both Government and Opposition parties and, by 1924 at least, all three major parties had had experience of both sides of the bargain and found it fair.

There were, however, two occasions when the arrangements for Supply business were reviewed by the House. In 1918 the Committee on National Expenditure, in its Ninth Report, considered the financial procedures of the House.[1] It conducted a thorough review by means of detailed questionnaires to a large number of experienced and expert witnesses (the answers make fascinating reading for historians and students of procedure) and considered such matters as restricting debate on motions for the Speaker to leave the Chair, on report stages of Supply resolutions, and on Consolidated Fund Bills so as to avoid duplication of debates. The Committee concluded that 'the existing procedure of the House of Commons is inadequate to secure proper Parliamentary control over the national expenditure'.[2] But it concentrated its proposals for procedural reform

[1] H.C. 121 (1918).   [2] Ibid., para. 29.

on strengthening the Estimates Committee system,[1] on enabling the reports of that Committee to be debated in the House together with the relevant Votes, and in urging that divisions on amendments to reduce estimates in Committee of Supply (particularly those recommended by the Estimates Committee) should not be treated as issues of confidence. The National Expenditure Committee did not favour curtailing any of the opportunities for debating Supply or any change in the number of allotted Supply days, and its only recommendation for a change in Supply procedure itself was that there should be Votes on Account for the Navy, Army, and Air Force (it would be many years before this was agreed to[2]).

There was another occasion for considering Supply procedure in 1932. A Select Committee on Procedure had carried out a major survey of current procedural problems, had received wide-ranging proposals for change, and had taken evidence from the majority of the most senior and experienced Members of the House (including the Speaker and the Leaders of the major parties) and from senior officers of the House. Its Report,[3] however, was a disappointing document, which touched on many topics but examined few in depth. In regard to financial procedures, it re-echoed the anxieties of the 1918 National Expenditure Committee and its conclusion that the Committee of Supply was unsuited for detailed scrutiny of expenditure proposals. The Procedure Committee recognized the valuable function it played, however, in securing opportunities for debate of grievances and of many questions of policy (which 'crowded out' questions of finance). Its remedy, once again, was to seek to improve indirect control of expenditure by strengthening the Estimates Committee.[4] The Procedure Committee's only recommendation regarding Supply procedure was that at least three allotted Supply days each session should be set aside for debates on the reports of the Public Accounts and Estimate Committees.[5]

It is not surprising, therefore, that in our second period—up to the end of the Second World War—we see no major changes in Supply procedure of a permanent character but rather a

---

[1] See Chapter VIII.
[2] See pp. 411 below.
[3] H.C. 129 (1931–2)
[4] See Chapter VIII.
[5] H.C. 129 (1931–2), para. 10.

period of consolidation. Indeed, in the whole of those years, the relevant standing orders were amended only three times, and in all cases the amendments were relatively minor.

The first amendment, which was made in 1919, was a new standing order which enabled the House to deal more expeditiously with its financial business in two respects.[1] First, it permitted the House to consider forthwith resolutions authorizing issues of money out of the Consolidated Fund when reported from the Committee of Ways and Means. These were nearly always a formality and went undebated, but hitherto the report stage had to be taken on a later day. (Another standing order was also passed permitting reports of Ways and Means Resolutions to be considered after the moment of interruption (then eleven o'clock) though opposed.) And second, it made similar provision for Consolidated Fund Bills so that the third reading (which was nearly always debated) could be taken on the same day as the committee stage (which was seldom debated). These were the first moves towards the telescoping of financial procedures which was to be a major feature of later procedural reform.[2] They were not substantially opposed at the time.

In November 1933 a number of purely drafting improvements were made and the opportunity was taken to remove an anachronism, namely the requirement embedded in the 1902 order, that Supply should stand as first business in the House on Thursdays. This rule had frequently been set aside by order of the House, and it was generally accepted that the standing order should leave the timing of Supply business in the Government's hands, as with other business (although there might be consultation with the Opposition).

A slightly more important change was made a year later in response to the recommendation of the Procedure Committee of 1932. In November 1934 an amendment was agreed to, without opposition, to permit Supply days to be used for debates on the reports of the Public Accounts and Estimates Committees, although Baldwin, in commending the idea, emphasized that such debates should not be held automatically (as the Committee had proposed); regard should be had to the content of

[1] *Commons Journal*, 20 Feb. 1919, p. 40.   [2] See pp. 409–11 below.

the reports.[1] Attlee for the Opposition (whose territorial rights might be thought to be being infringed by this proposal) said that there might well be occasions when the possibility of having debates on these reports would be generally welcomed, though he did not think it should be allowed to restrict the Opposition; if there was pressure on Supply days, he hoped the Government would use the provision of the standing order that permitted up to three extra allotted days.[2]

We referred to 'no major changes of a permanent character' because, as it happens, there was one major change made right at the beginning of this period which proved ephemeral. The Government did not accept the recommendations of the National Expenditure Committee for the appointment of an Estimates Committee (although, later, an Estimates Committee of a rather different type was appointed[3]). It proposed instead, in 1919, as a sessional experiment, a radical system (which had not found favour with the National Expenditure Committee) under which all the estimates, on being presented, except the Votes A and Votes 1 (i.e. pay) for the Navy, Army, and Air Force, should be automatically referred to a standing committee which should consider them 'in accordance with the customary form of procedure of the Committee of Supply' (i.e. by ordinary debate: the Committee would not deliberate, have powers to hear evidence, or to make reports). The Committee would have power to reduce the Votes by amending the Supply resolutions, and the resolutions it came to were to be considered by the House as if they had been agreed by the Committee of Supply.

It would, however, be open to Ministers to move that specified estimates be considered in Committee of Supply, and, if this was agreed, they would then be debated in that Committee in the normal way, and withdrawn from the Standing Committee. For this purpose, and also for the consideration of the Votes A and 1 of the defence services, the Government proposed to leave twelve allotted Supply days (instead of the twenty in the standing order). And lastly it proposed to abolish the debatable motions, and amendments thereto, for the Speaker to leave the Chair on the House first going into

[1] *Hansard*, 15 Nov. 1934, cols. 2170–1.   [2] Ibid., cols. 2174–5.
[3] See Chapter VIII.

Committee of Supply on each of the main branches of the estimates.

These proposals were regarded with some dismay by the House.[1] Members feared loss of valuable opportunities for raising policy matters in the Chamber; they feared that debates upstairs would go unreported; and, in general, they were anxious lest the House be relinquishing one of its major powers over the executive—that of raising grievances before voting Supply. It became apparent, however, that the Government's main worry was the way Supply took up so much floor time at the beginning of the session (i.e. in January to March) when all Ministers were anxious to launch and progress their legislation. The main matters the Government wished to remove from the floor were therefore the supplementary estimates which had to be voted by March (having accepted that the Votes A and 1 of the services had to remain downstairs). And for the same reason it wished to be relieved of the four debates on moving the Speaker out of the Chair. The Government were less worried about days later in the session and so Bonar Law, the Leader of the House, sensing the House's anxiety, willingly gave in and agreed that the full twenty days should be restored.[2] In the face of this generous concession the House agreed to the experimental proposal; Members might, indeed, be gaining opportunities for getting at Ministers.[3]

On the face of it, the experiment appears to have been fairly satisfactory from all points of view. Although it was agreed after all to take most of the supplementary estimates on the floor of the House, only six days, before the end of March, were spent in Committee of Supply in 1919. This contrasts with 18 days in 1920, to which should be added four days on moving the Speaker out of the Chair. On the other hand, back-benchers also gained. Standing Committee C considered estimates (including, for example, those hardy annuals of Royal Palaces, Royal Parks, Diplomatic and Consular Buildings etc.) on 20 days and debated, in all, 47 separate Votes.[4] The debates in committee were, however, not reported—as had been feared—and no doubt that was one of the reasons why the experiment was not repeated in the following sessions.

---

[1] *Hansard*, 20 Feb. 1919 cols. 1256–92. 2 Ibid., col. 1276.
[3] Ibid., cols. 1291–2.   [4] And see footnote 2 on p. 384.

Indeed the practice of using standing committees to debate estimates in 1919 remained an aberration until, much later, procedures were developed for considering certain Scottish estimates in the Scottish Grand Committee.[1]

Use of Supply debates

Apart from this, however, Supply days were now well established under the new procedures, and it is not necessary to examine their use in this period in the same detail as we did for the previous years. However, a comparison of certain years is again instructive, as, although the procedures were little changed, the use made of them did develop significantly. We have chosen 1924, 1934–5, and 1943–4.

The Supply season of 1924 began, as usual, with consideration of supplementary estimates. The equivalent of about six days were devoted to these, in committee and on report. Altogether there were 17 Civil supplementaries; nearly all of these were debated, but most attention was given to those on which it was possible to debate the policy (e.g. a new Vote for the Post Office underground railway in London). Otherwise the topics debated at length reflected the political concerns of the day, principally unemployment, housing, the building of a railway in East Africa, and a recent outbreak of foot-and-mouth disease. In most of these debates the Chair exercised a fairly tight control and confined the debate to details of the supplementary estimates. Wider debate was of course permitted on the Vote on Account. The topics chosen in 1924 were German reparations, the Road Fund, and, once again, unemployment.

Two days were devoted to debates in committee on each of the armed services and two more on report. These were broad policy debates (although Members also raised details, including constituency cases). There was a major debate on the size of the Army (when a substantial reduction was proposed and negatived); other major topics included the cruiser construction programme and the Singapore naval base.

The debates on the March Consolidated Fund Bill were

---

[1] See p. 408 below.

topics chosen by the Opposition parties. On second reading Conservative spokesmen opened debates on industrial disputes, housing, and foot-and-mouth disease. But on third reading the Liberals had their turn and held debates on reparations and security and on the problems of ex-servicemen.

The debates between April and the end of July on the main estimates ranged widely. Some were specific policy debates, e.g. food production, free rail travel for M.P.s, the League of Nations, the problem of unemployment (debated three times), the Government handling of a strike by London Transport Underground workers, relations with France and the reparations issue (debated twice), and the Sudan. Others were reviews of the work of different departments, e.g. the Home Office and the police, the Board of Trade, the Scottish departments of agriculture and education, various Foreign Office matters agreed through the usual channels, and the Board of Education. And in a few cases there were more detailed discussions of the financial or administrative aspects of the actual estimates, e.g. Inland Revenue and Diplomatic and Consular Buildings, compensation claims for enemy action, and expenditure by the diplomatic and consular service. At the end of July 128 Votes were agreed to under the guillotine.

The Supply business concluded with two-and-a-half days' debate on the Consolidated Fund (Appropriation) Bill. On the first day of the second reading the House turned to consider a number of topics raised by back-benchers but after five of these had been debated the House was counted out. The following day Lloyd George used the resumed debate on second reading to open a major debate on relations with France (there were talks going on at Prime Minister level) in which Ramsay MacDonald was obliged to intervene. And finally on third reading there was a major debate arranged by the Conservative Opposition on the Anglo-Soviet Treaty.

One procedural feature of Supply debates in 1924 is of interest. About half the debates on the main estimates finished without the Vote being agreed to (as it nearly always had been before the war); the debate was either adjourned or 'talked-out'. This enabled estimates to be 'kept open' so they might be considered again if the Opposition parties so chose. Thus, the Ministry of Labour Vote was considered on four occasions and the Foreign Office Vote on three. Another feature was that there were few debates on the report of Supply resolutions; most of the Votes were agreed on report under the guillotine. And another change from earlier practice was a reduction in the number of amendments moved; the usual practice was for the Conservative Opposition to move simply one token reduction of the Minister's salary for the purpose of voting against some aspect of Government policy, but they seldom moved reductions to specific items on sub-heads as had formerly been done.

In 1934–5, consideration of supplementary estimates still loomed large; indeed the number of such estimates—27—was growing, and they were debated in committee on seven days (there was very little debate on report). On the other hand less time was devoted to the armed forces. There was only one day each for the Air Force, Army, and Navy estimates. On each day there were debates on the motion for the Speaker to leave the Chair with balloted amendments (light aero clubs, the Territorial Army, and sloops for convoys being the respective topics) and then the Votes A and elected money Votes were agreed after short debates. There were two days debates on the Vote on Account on topics chosen by the Opposition—unemployment and commodity speculation.

On the main estimates there were again debates on current issues of policy and on the general conduct of departments, but there was less attention to specifically financial aspects of the estimates. The estimates chosen were those for

Public buildings and the Royal Jubilee
Foreign Office (thrice)
Treasury (thrice)
Transport
Education
Dominions Office
Health (Scotland) ⎫
Agriculture (Scotland) ⎬ same day
Police (Scotland) and other Scottish Votes
Home Office
Health
Board of Trade
Special Areos
Colonial Services ⎫
Mines ⎬ same day

Two procedural features are worth noting. First, by 1934–5 it had become the normal practice to keep all the estimates 'open' rather than agreeing the Vote at the end of the debate. Second, a new procedure was creeping in, namely that of taking Supply formally so that a debate could take place on a motion moved by the Opposition, to which the Government could move an amendment. This was done on two occasions that year. It was to become more popular in later years and foreshadowed the use of Supply days today.

When Britain was at war again, the practice of voting massive Votes of Credit for the war effort instead of substantive estimates was revived, though token Votes were still granted so as to give Parliamentary sanction to the services concerned; this also ensured that any aspect of Government could still be raised on a Supply day. There was, however, one technical difference from the procedures employed in the First World War. Instead of continuing to vote substantive Votes A (which had to be periodically increased as the armed forces grew), the Votes A in 1939–45 simply authorized 'such numbers of officers and men as His Majesty may deem necessary'; this avoided the need for supplementary Votes.

The Supply business of 1943–4 opened with a supplementary Vote of Credit for the financial year 1943–4, another Vote of Credit for the same year, and a Vote of Credit (of £1,000 million) for 1944–5. There were three further Votes of Credit of similar sums in the course of the session. These provided additional debating occasions for considering wider issues (for they could not be taken on allotted Supply days). War finance was explained by the Chancellor of the Exchequer on each occasion and opportunity was taken by critics of the coalition Government (Nye Bevan being well to the fore) to debate the conduct of the war. Other topics raised on these days included rehabilitation and aid for European countries, the concept of 'unconditional surrender' and civil aviation.

Twenty-one Civil supplementary estimates were presented on which there were short debates on detail on two days; the main discussion was on the policy of the new Ministry of Reconstruction and on the Foreign Office. On report of the supplementary Votes there was a policy debate on civil aviation.

Somewhat surprisingly only three days were devoted to the

Navy, Army, and Air Force estimates—but perhaps the House had had enough debate on the war on other occasions. On each occasion, in addition to a broad survey of the work of the service concerned by the responsible Minister and a general debate, there was a debate on a balloted motion; this time the topics chosen were civil aviation, army pay and allowances, and education of naval personnel—clearly, by 1944, Members were turning their thoughts away from the battlefields.

Similarly on the Vote on Account the topics debated on two days were essentially peaceful, namely, infant mortality and housing; on the second of these occasions, the report of the Vote on Account was taken formally and there was a debate on a Government motion. Finally, Supply to be granted by March was completed by the Consolidated Fund Bill. The second reading debate was opened by Churchill who made a statement on his Government policy regarding war medals, which led to a debate. The third reading was not debated.

The topics chosen for debate on allotted days on the main estimates were as follows:

Research and Science Colonial administration (twice)
Agriculture in Scotland
Foreign and Dominion affairs
Fuel and power
Detention of Captain Ramsay and operation of Regulation 18B (on motion)
Employment policy (on motion)
Housing and health in Scotland
Location of industry
Ministry of Food
Ministry of Information (broadcasting, propaganda, and censorship)
Disposal of surplus Government property
Ministry of Labour
Ministry of Pensions
Ministry of War Transport
Public Education (Scotland)

On the second reading of the Consolidated Fund (Appropriation) Bill there was a whole day's debate on India.

Most of these debates were wide, rather than concentrating on a specific topic. There was less attention (no doubt because of the existence of a coalition Government) to matters of party political controversy, and there were few proposed amendments or divisions. Indeed, in the absence of any substantial organized Opposition, many of the debates were opened by statements by Ministers.

Procedurely, there were again two occasions when Supply was taken formally so that there might be debates on motions. And in this year all the Votes were kept open, and only actually voted under the guillotine.

There was, however, one important procedural innovation. Under the traditional practice in the Committee of Supply each estimate was considered separately and the question was proposed on the whole Vote (though the scope of debate could be narrowed by amendments). But it was not possible to debate more than one estimate at once as that would involve more than one question being proposed (which the basic procedures of the House do not permit). Some difficulty had therefore been experienced, before the war, in debating topics to which more than one estimate was relevant, for example education as a whole (because there were separate votes for Scotland and England) or Foreign and Dominion affairs. The Chair had sometimes ruled out of order references to services borne on other Votes even though they were closely related by subject to the Vote being considered. However, in 1942, a new procedure was devised by Mr. (later Sir Edward) Fellowes, then Second Clerk Assistant. Under this the House could consider a schedule of token sums of £10 drawn from different Votes relating to a specified service or topic. These became known in the procedural trade as 'Fellowes schedules' and for a number of years served a useful purpose in making it possible to refer to a number of different estimates and yet remain in order. In 1943-4, Fellowes schedules were used on eight of the allotted Supply days.

Looking generally at the use and nature of Supply debates in the years 1919 to 1945, and comparing them with the years before the First World War, several distinct patterns can be discerned. First, until the war at least, there was a growth in the number of Civil supplementary estimates and hence in the number of days that had to be devoted to Supply in addition to the twenty allotted days. However, there was a corresponding falling off in the 1930s of the number of days devoted to the service estimates, so more time was spent on debating the growing number of main Civil estimates.

Because the estimates were not presented until about the beginning of February, Supply continued to be concentrated into the spring and summer months. Even though the House now regularly met in the late autumn and sat till Christmas, no Supply debates could be held in this period. This became a cause of complaint to Opposition parties, but we must wait till our next period to see the solution.

The nature of Supply debates moved steadily further away from the financial examination of the details of estimates towards either specific policy debates or broad reviews of particular departments. By the 1930s the debates on the main estimates were nearly all full day's debates on one estimate at a time, and the short debates on a number of estimates, when details of administration were examined and when amendments were moved to reduce individual items, had vanished. Throughout this period, indeed, amendments were almost entirely limited to token reductions to enable the Opposition to register votes of protest against the Government and its policies.[1] But even this was beginning to prove too restrictive to the House by the later years of this period. Members no longer wished to be confined to debating specific estimates, and new devices (like the Fellowes schedule) to permit wider debate were adopted. Alternatively if the House wished to debate policy in a way that enabled it to vote on and express a clear opinion it could do so by taking Supply formally and then debating a motion; this was done on seven occasions between 1929 and 1939.

The increasing use of Supply days to review specific policy issues and major areas of administration (with unemployment and foreign policy well to the fore in this period) may well be linked with the increasing acceptance that the choice of topic for debate on the main estimates rested with the Opposition (they had less choice over supplementary estimates and the armed services, which had to be debated each year). At the beginning of this period Baldwin could still speak on one

---

[1] From 1919 to 1938–9 inclusive, an amendment to reduce a single vote was moved on about 70 per cent of allotted Supply days (H.C. 122 (1965–6), pp. 42–4).

occasion of certain Foreign Office topics being 'agreed through the usual channels',[1] but in 1919 Bonar Law had accepted that the main value of Supply debates was in enabling topics of the Opposition's choice to be debated, whether the Government wished it or not.[2] And by 1934 Baldwin too said categorically that the Opposition chose the subject of debate on Supply days.[3] Indeed, by the end of this period the practice was well enough established to be enshrined in Erskine May itself: the guillotine system, wrote Lord Campion in his 1946 edition, had succeeded 'in transferring the initiative in the criticism of administrative policy to the Opposition'.[4]

The element that had been squeezed out, of course, were the back-benchers. It was they who had previously raised the wide variety of less major topics and held debates on the details of the estimates.[5] By the 1930s they had lost almost power of initiative on allotted Supply days, and their only chances were on the supplementary estimates (where, if they tried to discuss policy they were frequently ruled out of order) and on the Consolidated Fund Bills—and even then the first debate was normally on a topic selected by the official Opposition.

In the earlier years of the 1920s, however, there had been a little more flexibility. For one thing, with coalition and minority Governments (as in 1924), 'the Opposition' was less clearly defined (especially when there were two Liberal factions), and, as Bonar Law had complained in 1919, this made the system of 'Opposition initiative' difficult to work.[6] Joynson Hicks, on the same occasion, urged that Government back-benchers should also have a say in selecting topics for debate when there was no effective Opposition. And indeed in 1924 (and again in 1943-4, for very different reasons) there appears to have been a fair variety of sources of inspiration and initiative, including (in 1924) Lloyd George, Asquith, and Conservative back-benchers, as well as the official Conservative Opposition. In general, however, by the 1930s the full rights of the official Opposition were unchallenged.

---

[1] *Hansard*, 7 July 1924, col. 1812. [2] Ibid., 20 Feb. 1919, col. 1275.
[3] Ibid., 15 Nov. 1934, col. 2171. [4] May, 14th edn., p. 287.
[5] On this theme, both before and after the Second World War, see Barker, 'Party and Supply', op. cit.
[6] *Hansard*, 20 Feb. 1919, col. 1275.

The changing scope of Supply debates between the wars was reflected in changes in the style of debate. More and more the debates became set pieces, with each Member who took part simply making one speech. By 1934–5 and 1943–4 few of the characteristics of committee proceedings—namely greater informality, Members (and particularly Ministers) speaking more than once, short debates, and examination of detail—survived in the Committee of Supply (except sometimes when considering supplementary estimates).

A more systematic arrangement of debates was, however, becoming apparent, especially when, as in the later 1930s, the selection of topics was almost entirely in the hands of one party. The repetition of debate which had been a feature of pre-war Supply business—with many topics being raised on report as well as in committee—had almost disappeared, except where, as a matter of policy, the Opposition wished to return to a theme of continuing political interest, such as unemployment.

To sum up, it may be said that by the 1930s Supply days were being used as they are today, namely as the occasion for arranged and formal debates on policies and areas of administration chosen by the official Opposition of the day. They were thus essentially concerned with indirect rather than direct control of expenditure.

Money resolutions

Until 1919 the Crown's recommendation for money resolutions had been signified to a motion for the House to resolve itself into a committee on a future day to consider making provisions for expenditure in relation to a specified piece of legislation. This 'setting-up motion', as it was called, was usually in very broad terms and was drafted by the Public Bill Office of the House of Commons. The terms of the money resolution itself, which was moved without previous notice appearing on the order paper and which was based on the setting-up motion, were usually equally general. In 1919 it was decided to introduce an alternative procedure under which notice could be given of the actual money resolution and when this was done the House automatically went into committee without need for a setting-up motion. The Crown's recommendation was then signified to the resolution itself. All of this made the drafting of money resolutions more important, and responsibility for this was transferred to the Treasury. The new procedure was embodied in a standing order in 1922 and after that date the old procedure fell into disuse. Another change in 1922 permitted the report of such a resolution to be considered forthwith.

These apparently innocuous changes were to prove important. We have already explained how the drafting of a money resolution can condition the acceptability of amendments to bills.[1] As the House became increasingly occupied in considering bills for extending public expenditure, especially in relation to such matters as unemployment relief and assistance to industry on which many Members wished to increase public spending, Ministers became anxious about the growth of amendments to bills intended to those ends. Their newly-acquired responsibility for drafting money resolutions gave them a useful weapon in limiting debate, and especially proposals for expenditure, to those matters which suited the Government of the day.

Throughout the 1920s, money resolutions became increasingly tight, sometimes repeating almost exactly the wording of the bill in a way that made any amendment to broaden or increase the financial purposes of a bill almost always out of order. These resolutions often took up two or three columns of the *Commons Journals*. Not surprisingly Members raised objections and in 1934 even the Speaker was moved to express his concern, saying 'not only has the limit been reached but it has been rather exceeded by the amount of detail which is put in a money resolution'.[2] But, despite verbal instructions by the Prime Minister,[3] the problem became worse. There was particular difficulty over very tight money resolutions for the Tithe Bill of 1936 and the Special Areas (Amendments) Bill of 1937, and finally the Government were persuaded to appoint a select committee to examine the problem.

The Select Committee on Procedure relating to Money Resolutions went into the matter most thoroughly and reported on every aspect of the problem in 1937. The Committee appreciated that it would not be desirable to go back for every

---

[1] See pp. 337–8 above; for a fuller discussion of the political significance of money resolutions, see Gordon Reid, *The Politics of Financial Control*, pp. 84–92.

[2] *Hansard*, 3 Dec. 1934. col. 1236.   [3] H.C. 149 (1936–7), para. 5.

resolution to the old system of totally open resolutions. On the other hand it was 'sensible of the danger of allowing an undue encroachment by the Government upon the sphere of the House by reducing the functions of the latter in respect of financial legislation to purely restrictive criticism'. To avoid this, the Committee argued that the terms of a money resolution should be wider than the terms of the bill to which it related.[1] And it recommended that the House should pass a declaratory resolution to this effect which would guide the draftsmen and which should be enforced by the Chair. In the end, although the Government would not agree to such a declaratory resolution as it believed this would conflict with the fundamental principle of the Crown's initiative in regard to expenditure, it accepted the main line of the Committee's argument and instructions were given by the Prime Minister to the Parliamentary draftsmen accordingly.[2] But the effect of this, before war broke out, cannot easily be judged. Certainly a number of tight resolutions continued to be moved.

One important procedural change was made, however, following another recommendation of the 1937 Report. A standing order[3] was made changing the old practice whereby bills whose main object was the creation of a public charge had to be founded on a financial resolution (which was thus debated before the terms of the bill were published). To avoid repetition of debate, such bills, if presented by a Minister, might be introduced in the normal way and the consideration of the money resolution could be deferred till after second reading, as with bills which involved a charge subsidiary to the main purpose. This has proved a successful and generally acceptable simplification of our procedures.

Financial committees

The development of committees is described in Chapter VIII. Here it is only necessary to remind readers that, parallel to the decreasing use of Supply business for direct control of expenditure and the growing attention of the House to policy rather than the estimates, there was a growing desire to seek closer

[1] Ibid., para. 9–10.
[2] For the terms see *Hansard*, 9 Nov. 1937, cols. 1595–6.
[3] Now S.O. No. 91.

vigilance over the estimates by examination by select committees. This concern had been expressed in the Report of the National Expenditure Committee of 1918.[1] Following this the Estimates Committee was revived, but was unable to work either broadly or in depth. And, despite further expressions of anxiety by the Procedure Committee of 1931–2,[2] little improvement was achieved until the war. Then, at last, a relatively effective committee—the National Expenditure Committee—was appointed which, working through subcommittees, were able to carry out a number of effective and useful inquiries into various aspects of Government administration and expenditure.[3]

It should be emphasized, however, that the work of these Committees had nothing to do with the voting of Supply. Despite various arguments and proposals to the contrary, no satisfactory procedure has ever been devised for linking detailed examination of the estimates by select committees with the debating or passing of those estimates by the House. This is partly a matter of time. If a committee are to examine thoroughly the estimates which are presented in February or March, it is almost impossible for it to finish its work in time for its reports to be considered in debates on the estimates before the end of July—and clearly all debates cannot be deferred till then. It is also a question of political management. The Opposition wish to debate matters that interest them politically, not necessarily those estimates or topics on which a select committee has made a report.

In fact the two processes were really quite distinct. The House debated policy: the Select Committee looked at administration and the execution of policy. There was no good reason why the two should be brought together. Indeed, the only move made to that end in the inter-war years was to permit debates on the reports of the Estimates Committee (and the Public Accounts Committee) to be held on allotted days. And, in practice, even this provision remained unused.

[1] H.C. 121 (1918), see pp. 389–90 above.
[2] H.C. 129 (1931–2), pp. xiii–xiv.
[3] See Chapter VIII, p. 466

Since 1945: Developments and Practice

Changes in Supply procedure

The inter-war years had been a period of consolidation after the major changes at the turn of the century. The period since 1945, by contrast, was once again a time of fundamental revision of Supply procedures—although, as we will see, the changes were perhaps more of form than of substance. The restiveness of Members in relation to Supply procedure is demonstrated by the fact that, from 1946 to the time of writing, there were no less than twelve reports of various Procedure Committees that dealt in one way or another with the business of Supply and most of their recommendations were embodied in changes in the standing orders. Some of the alterations were of minor or ephemeral importance, often being overtaken by later ones. Here we describe the principal changes in procedure in this period.

In 1946 the then Clerk of the House, Sir Gilbert Campion (later Lord Campion who is entitled to be acclaimed as one of the architects of post-war Parliamentary procedure, another being, of course, Herbert Morrison) and his senior colleagues prepared and laid before the Procedure Committee a comprehensive set of proposals for reforms of the procedure of the House.[1] He gave much attention to the business of Supply. He started from the premise—proved by the experience of how Supply days had been used in this century—that consideration of Votes in Committee of Supply were simply pegs on which to hang debates on 'administrative policy'. He also stated as a confirmed practice that the Opposition had the right to choose the subject for debate on Supply days and also on consideration of Consolidated Fund Bills. And he accordingly made a number of proposals designed to spread the consideration of Supply more evenly over the session, so that some allotted supply days could be taken earlier than had previously been possible, and to permit the type of debate necessary for consideration of administrative policy. His proposals were broadly agreed to by

[1] Appendix to the *Third Report of the Select Committee on Procedure*, 1945–6, (H.C. 189).

the Select Committee[1] and eventually, with some modification, by the House.[2] The changes made were as follows:

(i) All Supply business (apart from Votes of Credit and Consolidated Fund Bills) could be taken on allotted days. Supplementary estimates and excess Votes were brought under the guillotine and the debates on moving the Speaker out of the Chair on first going into Committee of Supply on the various branches of the estimates would also qualify for consideration on allotted days. The number of allotted days was increased to 26;

(ii) To help ensure that allotted days were spread more evenly over the session and to ensure that supplementary estimates and the Vote on Account were obtained by the end of March, an additional guillotine was required. This would fall in Committee of Supply on a day not earlier than the seventh allotted day, being a day before the 31 March. Similarly, on the eighth day, the reports of resolutions would be put without further debate. Thus the Opposition could ensure that they had at least eight Supply days before the end of March;

(iii) The motion that Mr. Speaker do now leave the Chair could be moved, by a Minister, on any allotted day. It was envisaged that the traditional debates on first going into committee on the Navy, Army, Air, and Civil estimates would continue, and on these occasions there would still be a ballot for an amendment moved by a back-bencher. But there could be other occasions when debates were held on this motion, and on those occasions amendments moved by the Opposition could be moved. This would enable the Opposition to take some of their Supply days early in the session before the estimates had been presented and so go a long way towards spreading Supply more evenly over the session; and

(iv) Debate on motions for the Speaker to leave the Chair should be allowed to include 'such incidental references to legislative action' as might be 'relevant to any matter of administration then under debate' when enforcement of the ancient prohibition against discussing legislation when considering Supply would, in the opinion of the Speaker, unduly restrict the discussion (enforcement of this rule had sometimes

---

[1] Ibid., paras. 17–23.   [2] *Hansard*, 2 Nov. 1947, cols. 1634–5, 1654–94.

created problems in the inter-war years). In this way, the changing nature of Supply debates—from financial examination to debates on policy—was formally recognized.

The next change was in 1948 when the system of referring certain Scottish estimates to the Scottish Standing Committee (later renamed the Scottish Grand Committee to avoid confusion with Scottish Standing Committees on bills) was adopted. The estimates were referred on a Government motion, but this has always reflected the selection made by the Opposition with regard to the estimates they wished to debate. Debate was confined, however, to six days, and the Committee could only report that it had considered the estimates, i.e. it had no power to approve, reject, or amend the estimates (unlike the Standing Committees that considered estimates in 1919). This procedure continues to the present day and has proved generally popular and useful. It enables the Scottish Members to debate the policies and administration of Scottish Ministers in the cosy seclusion of a committee room upstairs and in the intimate company of their fellow Scotsmen, and it spares the rest of the House from having to spend time on purely Scottish business.

Certain changes in the consideration of defence estimates were made in 1957 following the report of a Procedure Committee.[1] These did not involve amendment of the standing orders but simply of practice. First, the practice of moving the Speaker out of the Chair for a general debate on each of the Navy, Army, and Air estimates (and of interrupting the general debate for a limited debate on a specific subject chosen by a Member who had been successful in the ballot) was abandoned.[2] The general debate on the service estimates was then taken on the Votes A and one other day was devoted to debating selected money Votes of all three services. The ballot for a motion on going into committee on the Civil estimates was similarly abandoned in session 1960–1.

In 1959–60 the Monk Resolutions authorizing virement between votes of the Navy, Army, and Air estimates[3] were

---

[1] *First Report from the Select Committee on Procedure*, 1956–7 (H.C. 110).

[2] The disadvantages of the balloted amendment were made apparent when one Member was able to use the debate on the Navy estimates in 1952 for raising the desirability of reforming the spelling of the English language.

[3] See pp. 353–4 above.

brought within the ambit of Supply business on allotted days. This, in effect, meant that they were no longer debated[1] as they could now be taken under the guillotine.

Major changes, however, came in 1966 and 1967. Again the catalyst was a report from a select committee, this time the Report of the Select Committee on Procedure of 1965–6 on Financial Procedure.[2] And this time the architect of reform was the then Clerk Assistant, Mr. (later Sir David) Lidderdale. He started from the finding that

> no real financial scrutiny of the estimates takes place at all on allotted days . . . and it is many years since the House itself attempted such scrutiny. So far as debate is concerned, allotted days are used for the discussion of Government administration and policy, sometimes within the framework of estimates and sometimes not. In form, however, every such debate has somehow to be tied on to the business of Supply.

This was not a new development, and for many years the forms of Supply (debates on estimates) had proved suitable for the kinds of debates Members wished to hold. 'Within the last twenty-five years, however, their suitability appears to have greatly diminished. The discrepancy between what the Committee or House wishes to do, and the forms through which it has to do it, produces a series of anomalies and unrealities in Supply proceedings.'[3] And he then adopted the simple approach of proposing changes of form to match the reality of debate rather than (as some critics have always desired) seeking to change the nature of the House's work to suit the forms (saying, for example, that in Committee of Supply Members should debate the details of the estimates). In general, he argued, the House should 'abandon any pretence' that it exercised control over national finances through the traditional Supply procedures. It should rather develop such control by improved use of select committees, and should let Supply days be seen to be what they had increasingly become, namely days for debating matters—of any nature—of the Opposition's choice.[4]

---

[1] Ellis Smith, a Labour Member from Stoke-on-Trent and a leading devotee of this somewhat esoteric procedure, had for several years assumed the mantle of the financial purists of earlier years, such as Chester Bowles, and insisted that these resolutions were at least discussed briefly; few other Members showed much interest.

[2] H.C. 122 (1965–6). [3] H.C. 122 (1965–6), p. 27. [4] Ibid., p. 32.

The Committee endorsed these views and the House agreed with nearly all Mr. Lidderdale's recommendations. The main changes that were made were as follows:

(i) the old rule that charges must originate in committee was repealed, and thus the Committee of Supply was abolished (and also the Committee of Ways and Means and committees on money resolutions); this also had the effect of ending debates on the motion that Mr. Speaker do now leave the Chair;

(ii) Supply days were to be held in the House, sitting as such, and the business taken on these days could include debates on substantive motions and motions for the adjournment of the House as well as debates on estimates;

(iii) it was to be made clear, by a note on the Order Paper, that the subject for debate on Supply days was chosen by the Opposition;

(iv) a third guillotine was introduced on a day not earlier than the sixth allotted day, being not later than 6 February, for voting the Civil Vote on Account and winter supplementary estimates (which had recently proved necessary); this ensured a more even spread of Supply days over the session;

(v) the three guillotines were to fall at 10 p.m., so giving a full day's debate and the questions on outstanding votes were to be put *en bloc*, but opportunity to vote again stselected Votes was preserved (although this procedure has only been used twice);

(vi) the third reading of Consolidated Fund Bills was made no longer debatable, and the second reading debate was to be reserved, in future, entirely for back-benchers (and in 1968 a system was introduced by the Speaker for determining by a ballot the priority of Members in raising topics);

(vii) in compensation for the loss of days on the third reading of Consolidated Fund Bills (one stage had often been taken formally to permit debate on an Opposition motion or on the adjournment[1]), the number of allotted days was increased from 26 to 29; and

(viii) Consolidated Fund Bills were to be brought in on the House agreeing to the Supply resolutions instead of the anachronistic Ways and Means 'spending' resolutions.

It will be seen that, while in form these changes were substantial

[1] H.C. 122 (1965–6), pp. 82–5.

(and indeed, as one well-known radical Member, Mr. W. W. Hamilton, acknowledged, procedurally revolutionary), the practical realities of Supply debates were little altered. The classic features of the Balfour reforms were preserved in that the Government was still guaranteed its money Votes by a given date and in a determined number of days. The only real change was that, in future, the Opposition could choose the form as well as the topic of Supply debates and at times of the year convenient to them. However, the jettisoning of what another radical, Emrys Hughes, christened the 'mumbo-jumbo' of Parliamentary proceedings was generally welcomed.

Only two other changes in Supply procedure in this period need be noted. In 1969, after consideration by the Procedure Committee,[1] the system of voting money for the armed forces was fundamentally altered. A Defence Vote on Account was introduced which had, of course, to be passed by the end of March and was therefore made subject to the March guillotine. This meant that it was no longer necessary to devote a day in the spring to debates on the armed forces money Votes, although the three Votes A continued. It also meant that the ancient form of Monk Resolutions for authorizing virement between the service Votes could be abolished. In future Parliamentary, and Treasury, control of these estimates would be on the same lines as with the Civil estimates. And finally, in 1973, the Defence Vote on Account was transferred to the autumn and so might be taken at the same time as the Civil Vote on Account. This permits a better spread of defence debates.[2]

One major development in the control of public expenditure since the war which, however, has had little effect on the use of Supply days and none on Supply procedure must also be mentioned. In 1958 the Estimates Committee made a report on Treasury Control of Expenditure.[3] This argued the need for major changes in the Treasury's approach in several ways which were relevant to Parliamentary control: there should be more systematic reviews of continuing commitments as well as of new services; the Treasury should take 'forward looks' to

---

[1] H.C. 411 (1968–9).
[2] See *Third Report of the Committee on Procedure: Debates on Defence*, 1972–3 (H.C. 257).
[3] H.C. 254 (1957–8).

measure the consequences of current policies in terms of estimates for a number of years ahead and should encourage the development of planned programmes of expenditure on major services, especially capital expenditures; and the value of different services should be compared with each other with a view to obtaining the optimum balance of expenditure. After much internal argument within Whitehall, the Treasury agreed to a further internal review under Lord Plowden. And the Plowden Report on the Control of Public Expenditure was presented in 1961.[1] The Plowden findings were very much in line with those of the Estimates Committee, particularly in their emphasis on the need to plan expenditure as a whole over a period of years ahead and in relation to prospective resources (para. 12).

Following Plowden, new winds blew through the Treasury. The earlier emphasis on annual estimates and 'candle-end economies' gave way to the Public Expenditure Survey (PESC) and (later) Programme Analysis and Review (PAR). And in 1963 the first Public Expenditure White Paper, giving estimates of expenditure for the years 1963 to 1968 on the basis of the Government's current policies and programmes, was presented to the House. Thus the House, too, was given an opportunity of looking at expenditure planning over a period of years, instead of simply the annual estimates. No change was made in the arrangements for actually voting Supply; this was still done on an annual basis. The House could debate the White Papers (and they could be analysed by select committees) and hence the opportunities for indirect control of expenditure were to some extent augmented. But no provision was made for obligatory debates on the Government's plans (the suggestion was turned down by the Procedure Committee in 1966[2]) and the extent of debate has varied from session to session.

Use of Supply debates

Although the post-war period has been characterized by basic changes in Supply procedure, the actual use made of Supply debates has, with one important exception, changed little.

---

[1] Cmnd. 1432.   [2] H.C. 122 (1965–6), para. 10.

Only the form, not the content, has altered significantly. This may be shown by analysis of four selected years: 1946–7, 1956–7, 1966–7, and 1976–7.

In 1946–7, which was the last session before the introduction of the March guillotine, 8 days or part days were devoted to considering 40 Civil supplementary estimates; three days were spent before March on each of the defence services Votes A and associated money Votes; and two days (one in committee and one on report) were used for the Vote on Account, when there were debates on foreign affairs and manpower distribution as chosen by the Opposition. The subject of debates on the main estimates were as follows:

House of Commons	Coal situation
Foreign Affairs (twice)	Public education (Scotland)
Housing in Scotland	Fisheries (Scotland)
Board of Trade (twice)	Functions of Ministry of Supply
Ministry of Food	Housing
Post Office	Colonial administration
Productivity of labour	Germany and Austria
Treasury	Education

Twelve of these debates were held on Fellowes schedules, so permitting reference to more than one estimate and a topic-focused debate (such as that on productivity).

In 1956–7 there was one day on a supplementary estimate for the Army and only one day for Civil supplementaries, when colonial services and the Foreign Office were debated. One day each was devoted to Votes A and the money Votes for the armed forces. Both stages of the Civil Vote on Account were taken formally, permitting debates on Opposition motions on National Insurances benefits and on the disclosure of Budget secrets.

The topics for debate on the main estimates were

Power resources	Ministry of Health
Colonial territories in Africa	Ministry of Transport and Civil Aviation
The Royal Air Force	Cyprus
The Navy	Industry in Scotland
The Army	Roads programme
Suez situation	Foreign Service and Ministry of Defence
Water undertakings	Health (Scotland)
Racial policies in Africa	Treasury
Home Office	

Eight of these debates, those on the work of individual departments, took place on single Votes. Fellowes schedules were used on six occasions. On two occasions the 'peg' was a motion for the Speaker to leave the Chair. And on one occasion a Vote was taken formally to enable a debate on Suez to be held on an Opposition motion. It should also be noted that no allotted days were taken before February.

By 1966–7, the pattern had changed again. The session opened early—in April 1966—because of the general election and six allotted days were taken in the summer. A second Supply series of 29 allotted days commenced in the autumn. Six days were taken before Christmas, when there were debates on the adjournment or on motions. And the winter supplementaries were taken under the guillotine (for the first time) on 30 January 1967. Eight more days were taken before the March guillotine fell, including four days for the defence services (three for Votes A when there were general debates, and one for miscellaneous money Votes when details were raised). The remaining allotted days were used for debates on the adjournment on topics of the Opposition's choosing or on motions. The subjects of motions were

Family poverty	National airport policy
Problems of regions	Industry and employment in Scotland
FIII aircraft contract	Government policy towards the aircraft
Prices and incomes (twice)	industry
European communities	Further nationalization
Deficit of British Railways	Economic affairs

On no occasion was a Fellowes schedule used, and no debates on the main Civil estimates were held on single Votes.

The pattern was similar in 1976–7. Various forms of proceeding were used. There was a brief debate on the defence winter supplementaries in December when an amendment moved by some Government back-benchers to reduce defence expenditure by some £273 million was negatived on a division (an unusual procedure in recent years). And debates on the Departments of the Environment and of Transport and on the Ministry of Agriculture took place on Votes with amendment to reduce the Ministers' salaries. Otherwise all Votes (even the Votes A) were taken without debate, either under the guillotine or forthwith, at the beginning of a sitting, pursuant to a special order made that day (this has become customary in recent years). There were debates on motions for the adjournment of the House on the following topics:

Crime prevention (twice)
Unemployment in the North West
Child benefit scheme
Self-employed persons (tax exemption)
Education standards
Employment in the South West
The economy in Wales
Burden of personal taxation
Teacher training colleges in Scotland
(on which the Government were
defeated)
The Army
Mobility of the disabled
The construction industry

The R.A.F.
Belgrade meeting of the
Helsinki Final Act
The Royal Navy
Job opportunities for young
people
Conditions of service in the
armed forces
Housing in England and Wales
Fisheries policy
Recruiting methods and
techniques of S.L.A.D.E.
Problems of large towns and
cities

And there were debates on substantive motions on the following topics:

P.A.C. Reports and related papers
The salary of the Secretary of State
for Defence
The reform of Government (topic
chosen by the Liberals)
Strengthening of Ulster security
forces (topic chosen by the
United Ulster Unionists)

Report of the Select Committee
on Overseas Development
The salary of the Prime Minister
(topic chosen by the Scottish
Nationalists)
Various EEC documents.

Various features of the use of Supply time in this session are worth noting. First, for political reasons, there was an exceptionally large number of debates on the adjournment. Second, on several occasions there were two separate topics on one day. Third, as in other sessions since 1974, two days were devoted to debates initiated by the various minority parties. Fourth, the defence Votes A were taken formally so that the usual defence debates were spread out, instead of being concentrated in the pre-Easter period. Fifth, there was a great range of topics, but few broad debates (and very few, compared with earlier periods, on foreign affairs); most debates were on specific policy issues. Sixth, allotted days were spread very evenly over the year. And finally, there was one extremely rare occurrence on a Supply day—a defeat for the Government. It was quite an eventful session.

Once again we must risk some generalizations about the use of Supply time in these years. The important exception to the general picture of little substantial change since the war is, of course, the virtual disappearance of debates on the supplementary estimates. And this has happened despite an overwhelming growth in the number of supplementary estimates. In recent years supplementary estimates have had to be presented for the majority of Votes simply because of inflationary increases in pay and prices.[1] This has tended to mask genuine supplementaries incorporating new services or expenditure additional in real terms to that originally estimated. Perhaps partly for this reason, but no doubt mainly because supplementary estimates rarely have great political appeal, they are nowadays very seldom chosen by the Opposition for debate on a Supply day.[2] Similarly the individual money Votes for the armed services no longer have to be taken before the end of March. All these Votes, which used to be debated regularly, now fall under the guillotine. And hence we may have witnessed the final demise of the last surviving 'financial' debate on a Supply day.

Throughout this period, whatever the form of proceeding (single vote, Fellowes schedule, motion or adjournment debate), it has become increasingly the case that debates have been on aspects of policy (apart perhaps from two days each session used for debating the reports of the Public Accounts and other Select Committees).[3] Even the rather general survey of the affairs of a selected department, which continued to be popular for several years after the war, has now almost gone. And even the debates which have been held since 1970 on the Government's 'forward look' Public Expenditure White Paper have often been turned into a political debate by the moving of an amendment on some aspect of policy. The over-all level of

[1] In 1977 there were 21 excess Votes for 1975–6 and 149 supplementary estimates for 1976–7.

[2] They enjoyed a brief revival of popularity in the 1960s when the Estimates Committee made a point of reporting on the winter and spring supplementaries before they were debated in the Committee of Supply.

[3] Since 1960–1, it has become regular practice for the Opposition to give up two of their days for such debates, while the Government have given one of its days for the same purpose.

expenditure has frequently been debated, but rarely the balance between services. Nearly all Supply debates, therefore, are now on specific issues of policy on which the Opposition of the day wishes to focus attention. They may involve money (e.g. the F111 contract) or they may not (e.g. racial policies in Africa). But they are all and always issues of the day.[1]

It may be asked, therefore, what the significance of the different forms of proceedings may be. The answer would seem to lie, almost entirely, in the realm of Opposition tactics. A debate on the adjournment, for example, is less specific, and less committed in detail (though a specific title is now placed on the Order Paper), and does not permit an amendment—though there may be a division. An amendment to reduce a Vote (amendments to reduce Ministers' salaries have become more popular in recent years) serve as a good focus for a party division, but again are not susceptible to a Government amendment. But a specific motion, while having the attraction of spelling out clearly the Opposition point of view on policy, usually attracts a Government amendment designed to sub-stitute the Government's point of view. Clearly there are times when this last weapon may be preferred by the Opposition—but not always, as the analysis of 1976–7 shows.

With the final establishment of the straight policy debate, the last vestige of the older style of committee debating has also disappeared (and, indeed, since 1966, the debates have not been held in committee at all). Thus there are today a series of prepared speeches; there are few amendments (other than to motions); and debates tend to be confined to the theme chosen by the Opposition rather than ranging widely over all the affairs of a selected department.

One other change must be mentioned. Until 1966 it was possible to debate both the second and third readings of Con-solidated Fund Bills and, from 1946, the choice of the principal subject to be debated (or of motions to be moved after the stage of the bill had been taken formally, as it often was) had, by convention, been left mainly with the Opposition; only after

[1] For another analysis of Supply debates up until 1963–4, see Anthony Barker, *Political Studies*, Vol. XIII, No. 1, Feb. 1965, pp. 45–64. He gives details showing the falling number of debates related in any way to estimates or expenditure, and the growth of debates held on motions.

their selected topic had been debated could back-benchers raise matters of their choosing (and even that was impossible, of course, if the bill had been taken formally). Thus back-bench opportunities had been severely limited on these bills.[1] Since 1966, the debate on third reading has been abolished, but the debate on second reading is reserved for back-benchers.[2] There are now normally two 'broad' bills a year—the first Consolidated Fund Bill of each session, which enacts, *inter alia*, the two Votes on Account and so covers all services, and the Consolidated Fund (Appropriation) Bill—and one narrow bill. Nearly all debates on broad bills last all night and cover some dozen different topics. Even on narrow bills, major topics may sometimes be raised (if there is a new service for example) and they too often go on late.[3] Despite some protest against long sittings which was echoed by the Procedure Committee of 1971–2,[4] the opportunities provided for private Members by these bills remain popular (the number of those entering the ballot nearly always exceeds those who are eventually called) and the system has remained largely unchanged.

Money resolutions

Two major changes in procedure for money resolutions were made in this period. First, by a standing order passed in 1960, debate on such resolutions was restricted to three-quarters of an hour if entered on at or after the moment of interruption (10 p.m. on Mondays to Thursdays and 4 p.m. on Fridays). And second, as with the other financial committees, the committee stage was abolished in 1966 so that since then motions for such resolutions have always been moved in the House. This meant the loss of the report stage, but in practice this made little difference as it had rarely been debated.[5] One other minor change made in 1966 was to permit the Queen's Recommendation to be signified in advance instead of requiring the presence of a senior Minister to signify it in the House (which

---

[1] For detailed statistics see H.C. 122 (1965–6), pp. 82–6.
[2] See p. 410 above.
[3] For statistics to 1970–1, see H.C. 217 (1971–2), p. 53.
[4] Ibid., paras. 12–20.
[5] H.C. 122 (1965–6), p. 37.

may have been a slight relief for Ministers and certainly relieved the Government Whip on duty of an extra anxiety).

In the earlier years after the war, there continued to be some anxiety about money resolutions being framed so tightly as to unduly restrict the scope of amendments to the bill. The Procedure Committee of 1957 said that 'Governments tend to err on the side of strictness' as was evidenced by the fact that since the war there had been twenty-seven occasions when a second resolution had had to be tabled.[1] But as the years went on, less interest was paid to money resolutions. By 1965 the then Clerk Assistant could report that they frequently were passed 'on the nod' or with only a few words of explanation.[2] And this remains true today. It is difficult to be precise on this matter, but it certainly appears that money resolutions are usually drafted today more broadly than before or immediately after the war. Indeed, the totally open type (authorizing 'any expenses of the Secretary of State') is frequently moved. Thus money resolutions are once again—as they were before 1914— a matter of little concern to the House on most occasions (although sometimes Members discover too late—when their amendments are ruled out of order in committee as being outside the money resolution—that they should have taken their chance to protest when the resolution was agreed to).

One other change has recently been made which, although of theoretical constitutional importance, has had little practical effect to date. It had long been held that a bill whose main object was to impose a charge could not be introduced in the House of Lords, and if such a bill were to be sent to the Commons, it would be laid aside.[3] It was agreed by the Commons in 1972, however, that, if such a bill were passed in the Lords it could be taken up by a Minister in the Commons (although the normal devices would have to be used to avoid infringing the Commons' financial privileges[4]). This meant that, if so desired, the Government could start a money bill in the Lords (i.e. the sort of bill that prior to 1938 had to be founded on a resolution in the Commons), provided that it moved a money resolution to cover the expenditure provisions of the bill after

[1] H.C. 110 (1956–7), para. 13.   [2] H.C. 122, loc. cit.
[3] See pp. 356–7 above.
[4] See pp. 357–8 above. And see present S.O. Nos. 58A and 91(2).

second reading in the Commons. Theoretically this was intended to assist the balancing of the Government's legislative programme between the two Houses. In practice the procedure has so far only been used once.[1]

Financial committees

The work of select committees, including the financial committees on Public Accounts, Estimates, and Expenditure, since the war has been well documented.[2] It is only necessary here to underline one or two salient developments and features.

The first is, in a way, a significant non-event. Despite several recommendations by a variety of experts, in particular Sir Gilbert Campion (as he then was) in 1946, there has been no merger between the Committee (originally the Estimates Committee and now the Expenditure Committee) concerned with looking at plans for future expenditure and hence, inevitably, current policies and practices as well, and the Committee (the Public Accounts Committee) charged with examining how money has been spent which is equally inevitably led into what is now being done to remedy defects it has discovered. Parliament has insisted on keeping the two tasks separate, and certainly the Committees work in very different ways and employ different methods. The 'double bite' approach has been criticized, but clearly it also enriches Parliamentary scrutiny by enabling Members to approach the problem of scrutiny of public expenditure in more than one way.

The first major development that did occur was the reappointment of the Estimates Committee in 1945 but this time, as with the wartime National Expenditure Committee, with the power to work through subcommittees, although for many years these were not specialized by subject matter. Next came

---

[1] Overseas Pensions Bill [Lords] 1973.

[2] See especially Basil Chubb, *Control of Public Expenditure* (1952); David Coombes, *The Member of Parliament and the Administration; the case of the Select Committee on Nationalised Industries (1966);* Nevil Johnson, *Parliament and Administration: the Estimates Committee 1945–65 (1966)*; Ann Robinson, *Parliament and Public Spending* (1978); and evidence given to the Procedure Committee of 1968–9 and published in their *Report on Scrutiny of Public Expenditure and Administration* 1968–9 (H.C. 410). And see Chapter VIII.

the creation of the Select Committee on Nationalised Industries in 1956–7, extending the House's system of scrutiny by committee to public expenditure by the industries which, although not mainly vote-borne, was nevertheless subject to some degree of Ministerial and Parliamentary control (especially capital expenditure financed by borrowing). The Committee has been especially interested in the relations between Ministers and the industries. In 1971 the Expenditure Committee replaced the Estimates Committee. Its terms of reference are somewhat broader and it is permitted to consider policy as well as administration. Like the Estimates Committee it works through subcommittees, but each of these (now six in number) specialize in a particular field of Government. One of these—the General Sub-Committee—has paid considerable attention in recent years to the planning and control of public expenditure and especially to the relation of these matters to the national economy. Other subcommittees—especially that on Defence and External Affairs—have been concerned with examining expenditure planning over a period of years (as recommended by the Plowden Committee) in addition to looking at specific areas of defence expenditure.

Lastly, the Public Accounts Committee has continued its work, though it too has broadened its approach in recent years —carrying out, for example, inquiries in greater depth than was traditional into some aspects of research and development (the Ferranti and Bristol–Siddley inquiries) and into university expenditure. Both the PAC and the Expenditure Committee have shown great interest in the Treasury's new system of cash limits for controlling public expenditure. And it may well be that this will have some effect on the form of the annual estimates, which might, in its turn, affect supply procedure. So it will be seen that, even as we write, the situation is in flux—as indeed it has been since Balfour started his procedural reforms in 1896.

Conclusions

The first three-quarters of this century has been a period of great change in procedural forms and also in the substance of debates in regard to Parliamentary control of expenditure. But the fundamental rules described at the beginning of this Chapter[1] are still central today, although their application has been modified. The constitutional realities embodied in these rules are, of course, the supremacy of the Commons over the Lords; the limitations of the Commons' powers in relation to those of the Government; and the guarantee of numerous opportunities for debate of Government policies and actions before the Government is given legislative authority for its expenditure.

It is on these foundations that the House's historical concern for control of expenditure has been founded. The procedures for expressing this concern have, however, changed markedly in this century. They have moved a long way from the provision of numerous occasions for considering specific Supply Votes to which genuine amendments could be moved (with each stage duplicated in committee and on report) to the securing of somewhat less numerous, but guaranteed, occasions for holding debates on matters of the Opposition's choosing but not necessarily related in any way to the voting of Supply. In other words the changes in financial procedures represent a considerable reduction in occasions for exercising direct controls of expenditure while retaining numerous opportunities for more indirect control.

The substance of financial control, as expressed in the use made of Supply days, has also changed. There has been a move away from discussion of details (the so-called 'candle-ends' approach) towards a broader concern with the administration of the many services which involve expenditure. And there has been a considerable move away from scrutiny of the annual estimates towards discussion of policies, including the development of policies over the years.

Mr. Anthony Barker, in his study made in 1965, concluded that 'As soon as the Opposition could choose their attack and forget the problem of staying within the rules of order in debate on real votes proposing real sums, the House in effect reached the end of financial control through Supply.'[2] This is certainly partly true: some Supply debates today, as Barker showed then, do not relate in any way to expenditure. But it is not the

---

[1] See pp. 331–4. [2] *Political Studies*, op. cit. 60.

whole truth. Debates which deal with policies for expenditure should not be lightly dismissed in this context. Control by criticism of policy is an essential part of the control of expenditure, for, as Gladstone emphasized, expenditure decisions flow from policy decisions. Thus, the use of Supply for policy debates—and the parallel use of financial committees for considerations of policy and administration—as means of exercising indirect control over expenditure remains important. At the very least, the reactions of Members of the House of Commons to the Government's expenditure proposals on every subject and at every level and as planned, developed, and executed over a period of years cannot be ignored by any group of Ministers. If it does nothing else, the House acts as the litmus paper by which the probable acceptability of Government policy by the wider public can be tested. In this process, Supply proceedings are as relevant today as they were when Balfour introduced his structural reforms at the turn of the century. For even then there was little genuine detailed and direct control of expenditure by the House.

Thus, we may sum up the modern evolution of Parliament's role in relation to control of public expenditure in this way. The Government's own approach has, as expressed in the Plowden Report, moved steadily away from concern with annual estimates and the piecemeal appraisal of individual services towards a greater concern for more systematic control of the total of expenditure over a period of years and a more deliberate review of the balance of expenditure between services and across the board. To some extent this is reflected by Parliament. Increasingly the general level of public expenditure is kept under review. And the policies for individual services and the total of expenditures at that level are often debated on Supply days or scrutinized by committees. The House has found it less easy to develop methods of matching the vital political decisions of Ministers regarding the balance of expenditures within an agreed over-all total (where, in other words, to cut or where to increase) with equally important occasions for Parliamentary debate of these same political discussions.[1] But here, too, within

[1] For a fuller discussion of this, see the author's 'Parliamentary Control of Expenditure and Taxation', *Political Quarterly*, Vol. 38, No. 4, 1967, pp. 435–46.

the framework devised by Balfour, Supply procedures could provide the opportunity if Members so desire.

For it should not be thought that changes in the substance of Supply business have been caused by procedural changes. Rather, to quote Barker again, 'the overwhelming impression gained from a study of the Committee of Supply's performance since 1896 is one of practical flexibility—of fitting the procedure to the political needs of the day'.[1] Thus procedure has remained the servant not the master. The use that Members make of procedure is the all-important factor. And the changes that have been made in Supply procedure, at least since 1902, result on the whole from the changed wishes of Members as to how to use Supply days not vice versa.

There has, however, been one change of major constitutional importance (and one not directly related to control of expenditure) that if not created by the Balfour reforms was at least made possible by them. Although, as we have seen,[2] Members were slow to recognize it, the adoption of the Balfour package made it possible for Supply days to be converted from days on which Members as a whole had the chance to debate the various policies, proposals, and actions of the Government on what were still Government motions into days on which the official Opposition have the right to raise in the House any matter of their own choosing and in their own terms. Supply debates at the beginning of the century really belonged to Members at large—back-benchers on either side as well as the Government and Opposition. All elements played a part in raising matters for debate, and, essentially, they were debates on Government business. Supply days by the end of our period had almost completely become official Opposition days— something that did not exist at all in the nineteenth century. This is, perhaps, the most important single change in the working of the House of Commons in this century. And it happened, almost by accident, as a result of procedural changes made for quite different reasons.

Thus, we may conclude by emphasizing that the basic and unchanged rules of financial procedure have provided the foundations of the modern balance of rights and opportunities

---

[1] Barker, *Political Studies*, Vol. XIII, No. 1, p. 51.
[2] See pp. 363–4 above.

between Government and Opposition within the House. And the formal powers preserved for Members by Supply procedures have secured for them that continuing opportunity for criticizing the executive which is the peculiar prerogative of the House of Commons.

VIII

SELECT COMMITTEES AND ADMINISTRATION

Nevil Johnson

From about 1700 onwards the form of committees of the whole House almost completely took the place of that of real committees in respect of bills and financial proposals. From that date real committees have been only applied to investigation and preliminary work, and as organs in the direct legislative process have been smitten with atrophy. Josef Redlich.[1]

There would be but a modest touch of hyperbole in the suggestion that the history of select committees of investigation and scrutiny in the twentieth-century House of Commons amounts to little more than an examination of the consequences of the atrophy to which Redlich referred, though in relation to times near to the present it would have to comprehend such efforts as have been made to raise these committees out of the peripheral role into which they long ago fell. Writing at the beginning of this century Redlich had no doubt that the important procedures of the House were those which affected the handling of business on the floor and he had some wise things to say about why the House had come to attach such significance to its plenary proceedings. But as an experienced continental jurist[2] he was struck by the absence of 'real committees', i.e. bodies with a limited membership, some degree of permanence, and charged with taking decisions on legislation, subject, of course, to the right of the whole to amend their decisions. Instead, for the consideration of bills there were (and still are) pseudo-committees, that is to say the whole House

---

[1] *The Procedure of the House of Commons* (Archibald Constable, 1908, 3 vols.), Vol. II, p. 211, in a note on the history of House of Commons committees.

[2] It is worthy of note that no Englishman has subsequently produced a better book on the procedure of the Commons than the three volumes written by this distinguished Austrian.

debating under a 'committee' procedure, and the beginnings of what we are now familiar with and call standing committees operating more or less as a committee of the whole in miniature. For the rest there were few traces in the House of that organized dispersion of responsibility for actual decisions which comes to mind when we consider the committee systems of those legislatures which have been shaped either by continental European or by American traditions. At best there were but fragments of 'real committees' in the guise of select committees charged with specific investigatory duties preliminary to decisions which the House might or might not care to take. And only one of these select committees revealed permanence, that on Public Accounts which had first been established in 1861.

Before we turn to look at the uses made of select committees of investigation in the period before 1914 it is worth recalling again the reasons why this atrophy of real committees had taken place, for they remain relevant even though the circumstances which produced them lie all of two hundred years in the past. During the Long Parliament something in the nature of executive committees emerged, for only by this means could Parliament hope to discharge the burdens of actual government which it had assumed in the course of the struggle with the Crown. Yet this development really went against the grain of parliamentary conventions which had already struck root, including in particular the claim of the whole House to sovereign authority and the principle of the equality of all Members. Already in Cromwell's time Parliament began to revert to its earlier procedures protective of the claims both of each Member and of the whole House, and this tendency was reaffirmed even more clearly after the Restoration. However, faced with a slow growth in the number of bills to be considered and grants of money and taxes to be approved, the House might well not have been able to sustain its opposition to a regular division of labour within itself but for two political discoveries of outstanding importance. I refer, of course, to party government and to the emergence of a cabinet exercising the functions of the Crown and responsible to Parliament. It is well known that neither of these political practices was firmly and clearly established even by the mid-eighteenth century, let alone in the closing years of the seventeenth. Indeed it is reasonable to hold that they do not assume a recognizably modern form until after 1832. Nevertheless the lineaments of such political practices and of the constitutional theories they came to support were present when the constitutional conflicts of the seventeenth century were resolved in the settlement of 1688–9: party (or faction as it was pejoratively called for many years) as a means of organizing opinion and a ministry founded on organized opinion and subject to the approval of Parliament. It was by these means that 'the subordination of the whole conduct of the affairs of state to the will of the House of Commons'[1] became attainable. And it was as a direct consequence of this constitutional development that within the House a permanent and specialized distribution of functions to committees was held to be unnecessary. Indeed, the non-development of such a system was entailed by the underlying constitutional concepts and forms of political behaviour: the claim to sovereignty explicit in the settlement of 1688 could make sense then and for many years to come only if Parliament and the House of Commons in particular saw itself as a unified institution in which no part could claim an authority in competition with that of the whole. It is still recognizably this doctrine which finds expression in recent years in the arguments put to the House and to its Procedure Committees on the matter of 'real committees' by men as diverse in their party sympathies as Herbert Morrison, R. A. Butler, J. Enoch Powell, and Michael Foot. The institutions of the late seventeenth century were built to last.

Whilst this retrospect of parliamentary history may have served to underline what have been the decisive constitutional obstacles in the way of the emergence of permanent committees with effective powers, there is, however, one facet of the modern objections to such developments which calls for an historical correction. And this too has some bearing on the use made of select committees early in this century. I refer to the distinction drawn between policy and administration. Since 1945 much has been made of the argument that policy is essentially the preserve of the Executive and of the House as a whole, whilst committees of investigation should be limited to administration, or to put it the other way round, should be prevented from expressing judgements on matters of policy. Let us leave on

1 Redlich, op. cit., p. 211.

one side the conceptual puzzles associated with distinguishing between policy and administration. What is of more practical interest is to note that in the nineteenth century this particular distinction would not normally have been made: there was no magic in policy which in some way marked it off as unsuitable for committees of the House of Commons to touch. It was not thought that the prerogatives of the House were encroached on if, subject to the control of the House, policy issues were handled directly or indirectly by select committees. After all, committees being by definition subordinate instruments of the House, whatever they said on 'policy' was for further consideration and decision by the House. There was, therefore, less inclination to stick up those 'Keep off: Policy' signs which became almost a stereotype reaction in the period from 1945 to roughly 1970, a reaction which still finds expression from time to time in the discussion of committees and their uses.[1]

In this connection the big change that has taken place is in the role of the Government. It is understandable that when the House was more powerful than it is now there was little hostility in principle to referring even politically sensitive matters to a select committee for inquiry. It is when the Government has asserted control over the House that the picture changes: to reserve 'policy matters' for the House becomes a way of protecting the Government's position and of safeguarding its business.

The years before 1914

The beginning of the twentieth century is in some respects a convenient and significant starting-point for a study of the changing uses of select committees. This is because the years between 1896 and 1903 are marked by those major procedural innovations, sponsored chiefly by Mr. Balfour, which had the

[1] It is worth remembering that even the Estimates Committee, first set up in 1912, was in its second and third years of life not excluded from considering policy, though it is true that when appointed in 1912 the 'economies consistent with policy' qualification was added to assuage fears expressed chiefly by the Opposition. A note to this effect is contained in a memorandum presented by Captain C. Diver to the Select Committee on Procedure, 1945–6. *Third Report*, H.C. 189–1, 1946, *Minutes of Evidence*, p. 229.

effect of confirming formally the claims already advanced by Governments in the 1880s to control a large part of the time available on the floor of the House for the purpose of securing the passage of their public bills and financial measures. As a consequence of thus recognizing that precedence was to be accorded to the needs of the Government over those of the private Member, the problem which was continuously to worry Parliament in the twentieth century was already delineated in outline at least. Essentially this problem resolves itself into the question: if it is the Government which dominates and controls the course of business in the House, subject to some recognition of the claims of the Opposition or alternative Government to an allocation of time for the purposes of public criticism, what then is the role of Parliament as an institution distinct from the Government, and in particular what is the role of the five hundred or so Members[1] who belong formally neither to the Government nor to its shadow? Much of the argument about committees from 1931 onwards has been directed to proposing answers to this question. But since the position of the Government and its relationship with the Commons as a whole rested on sound constitutional theory—as we have already indicated—it is not surprising that no new and satisfactory answer to the question has been found. And since few have been prepared to challenge the fundamental elements in the definition of constitutional relationships out of which the modern House of Commons emerged, it is also not surprising that in the search for answers to this question most of the participants have been content to travel hopefully rather than indulge a desire to cut corners too quickly in an attempt to reach their preferred destination.

However, in the years before 1914 there is little evidence to show that many Members of Parliament were yet acutely sensitive to their growing weakness *vis-à-vis* Government and the party Whips on both sides. The establishment of committees of inquiry, scrutiny, and investigation was regarded generally as simply a normal procedure for the discharge of certain parts of the business of the House. Such committees were not seen in the context of an argument about 'reforming' the House and

---

[1] Earlier this century when Governments were smaller, the number of back-benchers was considerably more than 500.

restoring to back-benchers the influence they had already lost to the advantage of the Government and the official Opposition. Nor is this entirely surprising, for select committees were used in a way which still gave considerable opportunities for service to the House and conferred both influence and prestige on many of those who were involved in them. This was possible because, despite the omens of the Balfour procedural reforms, the realities of political life in the House changed only slowly and, at any rate until the shock of the First World War occurred, the style and habits of an earlier age lingered on. And this means that select committees continued to be used in a manner not markedly different from that familiar throughout the second half of the nineteenth century. What, therefore, were they used for? And to what extent can we describe their tasks as scrutiny of administration?

To understand the role of select committees other than those concerned with procedure and matters of a domestic nature inside the House of Commons itself, it is useful to take a look at what two notable authorities on the British Parliament and system of government said about them. I refer again to Redlich, whose great work on Procedure was published in an English translation in 1908, and A. L. Lowell, whose study *The Government of England*, first came out in the same year.

Redlich distinguished select committees from standing and sessional committees, the latter including the Committee on Public Accounts. He described the functions of select committees as the preparation of legislative material and the investigation of questions of fact or law upon which the House wished to be informed. 'The task of a select committee is accordingly investigation and nothing more: it stands in the sharpest contrast to the work of a committee of the whole House.'[1] However Redlich qualified this summary of the role of select committees by pointing out that they did indirectly contribute to legislation by arranging material upon which bills might later be founded.

Lowell followed Redlich in identifying select committees as the largest class of 'real committees', by which he meant committees different from a committee of the whole House. He too noted that they might prepare the ground for a bill, conduct

[1] Op. cit., Vol. II, p. 187.

an inquiry, or consider a bill already before the House, though in the latter event the work of a select committee could save no step in procedure owing to the need to subject such a bill to the usual committee and report stages on the floor. Both Redlich and Lowell agree in pointing out that the powers of select committees—to send for persons and papers—stem logically from their investigatory function, and that the judicial procedure of taking evidence is likewise a natural consequence of the tasks chiefly assigned to them. Lowell observes too that committees are often concerned with 'some grievance, some alleged defect in the law or in administration', a point of emphasis which was intended to refer to the historical experiences of such committees rather than to be prophetic in respect of the future.

Generalizing on the basis of these judgements of the part played by select committees before 1914 it is possible to distinguish the tasks assigned to them as follows:

(a) The investigation of alleged abuses. These might be faults of administration, matters of public concern for which the Government might to some degree be held responsible, or allegations of misconduct on the part of known individuals holding public office.

(b) Inquiries into areas of public policy on which action was being demanded. The findings might influence considerably such measures as the Government would then propose.

(c) Consideration of actual bills, these usually being measures straddling the normal lines of party division and calling for a testing of public opinion by the examination of witnesses.

(d) The continuing scrutiny of financial rectitude, provided at that time in a more or less judicial manner by the Public Accounts Committee, the only select committee on public business which had permanence.

These then were the main categories of select committee work and to some extent they have remained so, though as we shall see some of them have declined in importance and, more generally, the categories have tended over the years to become blurred and more recently to be subsumed under a single general category of administrative scrutiny. But before illustrating how these tasks were performed in the pre-1914 Parliaments, it is necessary to stress that select committee procedures were applied also to private bills and that it was not uncommon for the House of Commons to join with the Lords in the consideration of private measures (as indeed it did also for the investigation of questions of public concern). It has to be remembered too that private legislation was more significant in quantity in the early years of the century and that through its select committee scrutiny of such measures the House was performing tasks which in several other countries might have fallen either to a central judicial body like the Conseil d'État in France or to courts of administrative jurisdiction. Apart, however, from noting the essential procedural similarity between committees on private bills and those established for essentially investigatory tasks, we shall pay no further attention to this aspect of select committee uses.

Let us now illustrate how these categories of select committee work were represented in a few of the sessions before 1914. The 1905 session was marked by five reports from select committees in addition to four reports and over 800 pages of evidence from the Public Accounts Committee. There was a select committee on Foreign Ships (Statutory Requirements) which reported in favour of applying certain domestic requirements to foreign ships using British ports.[1] Its fifteen members included Reginald McKenna and Bonar Law. The select committee on the Post Office (Telephone Agreement) had twelve members. It took extensive evidence and deliberated at length, being fairly sharply divided over its recommendations.[2] Essentially the report validated agreements already made by the Postmaster-General with the National Telephone Company which were to result in 1911 in the creation of what was virtually a national telephone monopoly. Then there was a committee going back to 1904 on the Registration of Nurses which published a large quantity of evidence and reported in favour of a scheme for the state registration of nurses.[3] The select committee on Workmen's Trains had been going even longer, since 1903. Basically this was an inquiry into the working and administration of the Cheap Trains Act of 1883, an extraordinary tribute to both the rigidity of class divisions in Victorian Britain, and to the ingenuity of the well-to-do in devising measures of economic relief for the lower orders of society.

[1] H.C. 266, 1905–6.   [2] H.C. 271, 1905–6.   [3] H.C. 263, 1905–6.

Though the committee laboured long and hard, it was not able to produce many practical proposals.[1]

Here then are four examples of committees working chiefly in preparation of possible legislative action, though in one case (the Post Office agreement) executive action had effectively committed the House already. There was also a committee of the same kind on Protection of Life from Fire, but it met too late to take evidence in the 1905 session. In the category of committees to consider actual bills was that on the Trade Marks bill. This committee met frequently between March and July 1905 and gave the bill a thorough scrutiny.[2] As well as reporting in the usual way the committee provided draft amendments to the bill. No other bill appears to have been sent to a select committee in this session, though two House of Lords select committees on bills did present reports which were published by the House of Commons. Nor was there any committee set up to investigate allegations of serious abuses in public affairs, though there was clearly a public concern and grievance element in both the inquiry into the registration of nurses and that into the Cheap Trains Act.

As far as the Public Accounts Committee is concerned it is worth noting that its four reports were exclusively concerned with the army and navy, a circumstance to be explained by the continuing aftermath of the South African war. The emphasis was indeed on rectitude and candle-ends, a typical example being the committee's concern that the writing-off of 337,704 lbs. of jam in Durban should be explained. It was: the committee learnt that 1,350,816 tins of jam thought as a result of a clerical error to contain 16 ozs. each had in reality contained only about 12 ozs. per tin. So nothing had really been wasted and the committee had no cause for anxiety.

The 1912–13 session provides rather more diversity and indeed illustrates very clearly how extensively select committees were still used under all the categories indicated above. A committee was set up to inquire into common land, though it did not report until the following session.[3] The same goes for a committee on Motor Traffic, prompted by the increase in road accidents in the metropolis, which issued a long report and

[1] H.C. 501, 1905–6.   [2] H.C. 231, 1905–6.   [3] H.C. 85, 1913.

over 450 pages of evidence in the 1913 session.[1] A committee on Patent Medicines was established and conducted so exhaustive an inquiry that its report did not finally appear until 4 August 1914.[2] By that fateful date the fact that G. T. Fulford, the proprietor of Dr. Williams' Pink Pills for Pale People, had left a fortune amounting to £1·11 million, one of the items uncovered by the committee, had no doubt lost some of its urgency as a ground for reforming the legal framework for the control of what was clearly a serious exploitation of human ignorance and gullibility. Yet undoubtedly this kind of social inquiry did contribute to the advancing tide of public regulation of private economic activity which the First World War was to push forward so decisively. Another major select committee was that on Wages and Conditions of Employment of Post Office Servants which reported late in 1913. This was a monumental work, with a report of 289 pages, over 600 pages of written memoranda, and over 1,700 pages of oral evidence.[3] Few contemporary select committees could claim to rival this one in the extraordinary thoroughness with which the inquiry was conducted and the remarkable degree of technical detail assimilated in the conclusions.

Apart from these four examples of committees set up to prepare the ground for legislation, there were eight select committees on bills, chiefly of a private or local nature, though not exclusively so. A few of these were joint committees with the Lords. In addition there were reports from the Public Accounts Committee and the first slender report from the newly established Estimates Committee. But this session was also marked by three committees set up to inquire into specific allegations of abuse and misbehaviour. One was the famous committee on the Marconi Wireless & Telegraph Company Agreement which conducted an immense inquiry into the allegations of share speculation brought against Lloyd George, Rufus Isaacs, and Herbert Samuel. The report of 1913[4] finally absolved those concerned of improper behaviour, though it was opposed by the Conservative minority on the committee, a fact which underlines the limitations of a purely party committee for

[1] H.C. 278, 1913.   [2] H.C. 414, 1914.   [3] H.C. 268, 1913.
[4] H.C. 152 and 185, 1913. These were final reports, following four preceding volumes of evidence published in the 1912–13 session.

such a judicial task. There was too an inquiry into the vacation of a parliamentary seat by a Member holding a contract (this one being chaired by the Prime Minister, Asquith) and the committee on the Putumayo Atrocities. This latter was also not able to report before the following year. The inquiry concerned the alleged involvement of British companies in the gross mal-treatment of Indian-rubber plantation workers in Peru and Colombia. Though the committee could express moral censure and adjure the British diplomatic services to advise companies strongly against such entanglements, there was clearly very little that a British Government could do in such matters.[1]

A survey of other years before 1914 would reveal a similar picture. Select committees were used fairly extensively for the first two tasks mentioned above. Despite the bitterness of party divisions at this time, there was evidently still an overarching sentiment of solidarity in the House which made it appear feasible and desirable to use select committees for certain tasks which nowadays would certainly be assigned to official com-mittees or royal commissions. No doubt a factor of some importance was the greater attention being given to social problems after about 1905. This is reflected in the relatively large number of select committee inquiries into social problems which might be amenable to public control and regulation. It is worth noting that this happened despite party differences and was not held to be ruled out by a Government claim to responsi-bility for policy. In addition it hardly needs to be pointed out that there was here no bar on policy considerations: on the contrary the committees were expected to review the problem referred to them and the current state of the law, and then to make proposals.

Alongside these forms of investigatory activity there was a modest amount of what was to become regular administrative scrutiny *par excellence* (the fourth category above). The Public Accounts Committee had an established position as a watch-dog for financial probity. Its reports and hearings were extensive, concentrating almost entirely on correct appropriation, observ-ance of the proper financial procedures, and the avoidance of waste.[2] The Estimates Committee, established in 1912 but

[1] H.C. 148, 1913.
[2] The best account of the evolution of the Public Accounts Committee is

foreshadowed in the National Expenditure Committee of 1903, was intended to occupy what some people (Churchill amongst them) regarded as the middle ground between *post mortem* control of spending and straight policy argument about how much for what purposes. On this middle ground, it was hoped, that somehow or other 'the merit of expenditures' could be analysed and in this way some kind of control be established which might make up for the withdrawal of the Committee of Supply from anything definable as 'financial control'. The initial experience with the Estimates Committee was disappointing and in 1914 it was forced into oblivion by the suspension of normal estimating methods. But the dilemmas it faced were not to be resolved for a long time, if indeed they ever have been.

Apart from the investigatory work of the kind described, select committees were also used with some regularity for the scrutiny and amendment of bills. As already indicated it was bills on relatively technical subjects (e.g. forgery, trade marks) or with a strong moral content (e.g. Sunday shop opening) which went to such committees. Moreover, select committees on bills were often run jointly with the Lords, a circumstance which reflected the substantial flow of measures down from the Lords to the Commons. Major measures introduced by the Government did not, of course, go to select committees. Quite apart from the fact that it was expected that these would be contested between the parties on the floor of the House, there was also the difficulty that the intercalation of a select committee stage would have served to prolong a legislative process which was still far longer than we have become accustomed to in recent years.

Perhaps the most striking fact brought out by a consideration of committees at the beginning of this century has, however, nothing to do with what they did, but concerns how they did it. The procedure of oral evidence-taking and of the consideration of written memoranda had already been long established and was adhered to punctiliously. In the heavy quarto volumes of these years we can pursue the magisterial dialogue which

in *The Control of Public Expenditure*, by Basil Chubb (Oxford University Press, 1952). It deals *inter alia* with the setting-up of the Estimates Committee.

went on at a measured pace between Members of the House and those summoned to assist them in their investigations. It is not without significance for later arguments about select committees that apparently matters of great legal or technical complexity were often mastered by Members who were rarely 'experts' and worked with no more than the support of clerks of the House. But, of course, there were differences in the circumstances of Members as compared with fifty years later. A higher proportion consisted of men in established professional positions—lawyers, accountants, stockbrokers, bankers, etc.— and there is some evidence that they were particularly active in select committee work. Such people were often skilled in the technique of interrogation and accepted as a matter of course that what they did would be done thoroughly. There was little disposition to seek popularization or even simplification of the questions put to them for inquiry. Moreover, there were fewer party and constituency burdens falling on Members, so that those who went in for select committee work could devote relatively more time to it than is thought to be practicable now.

On the other hand, there is little doubt that the method of inquiry by select committee was (and remains) time-consuming and somewhat haphazard. The practice of questioning witnesses ensures that the same ground is gone over many times and that much effort is expended on presenting points which could often be grasped quickly if put down on paper or expounded in informal discussion. This can all be observed in the record of the proceedings of the years before 1914. It is in respect of this procedure and its effects that the persistent conservatism of the House of Commons is most fully revealed. One change there has been, however, and that concerns the range of witnesses summoned. Before 1914 the majority came from the public services, and only in the case of issues affecting private interests was there an effort either to summon those directly involved or those held to represent various segments of public opinion. There was on the whole an economy in the calls made on witnesses: the committees evidently preferred to explore problems in depth with officials having actual responsibility rather than to invite opinions at large. This stands in some contrast with the tendency since 1965 to widen the net and to call upon a heterogeneous range of witnesses who may or may not have much direct responsibility for the matters under review.

The Waning of Select Committee Inquiry: 1914–1939

The First World War had profound effects on both the functions of government and on the social structure of British politics. In many respects the years between 1900 and 1914 were an Indian summer. Parliamentary life still retained many of the characteristics it had had in the Victorian age, despite the fact that the ground rules for a different relationship between Parliament and the Executive had already been laid down. Thus there were still few doubts about the virtues of the parliamentary system and little serious anxiety about the value of the roles which a Member of the House could assume. The major functions of the House were discharged on the floor and there was still no strong tide of opinion which held that within this framework the majority of individual Members lost all prospect of exerting an effective influence. The relatively frequent use of select committees for the investigation of matters of public concern showed that Governments and party leaders acted on the assumption that the House contained people who could and would make a useful and constructive contribution to the ongoing evolution of public policy when acting within a procedural framework which moderated the stresses of competing party loyalties.

In the years after 1914 there was no sudden and decisive shift away from these parliamentary habits. But long-term influences were at work which steadily undermined what might be called the complementing of the floor of the House by select committee activity. The powers of government increased sharply after 1914, many of them being exercisable by regulation. Though wartime powers were largely removed after 1918, the tendency for Governments to seek more power for social and economic regulation could not be reversed, nor could the rising tide of delegated legislation by statutory instrument. Thus the House of Commons found itself gradually confronted by a structure of powers over which its own supervisory influence was in decline and for the determination of which its direct approval became less and less necessary. Moreover, the familiar party landscape was profoundly changed by the collapse of the Liberal party, the emergence of the Labour party, and the disappearance of the Irish. And even the Conservative party experienced substantial changes in the composition and character of its parliamentary representation as a result of the party's entanglement with Lloyd George between 1916 and 1922. Thus the stability and social homogeneity of the parliamentary élites were weakened and there emerged a narrower and more uncertain basis for drawing back-benchers into the kind of investigatory and advisory work traditionally performed by select committees. Finally, it must not be forgotten that the 1920s witnessed the consolidation of the modern Civil Service under the complete control of the Treasury, and that politicians found themselves confronted with economic problems which were increasingly unresponsive to the measures they applied.

In a context marked by such changes we find that select committee activity slowly declined and half-way through the inter-war period parliamentary methods of government were themselves subject to some challenge. Some use continued to be made of *ad hoc* committees to inquire into matters of public policy, but such references became less frequent and virtually faded out in the 1930s. There was in 1923, for example, a select committee on Betting Duty which examined betting law and got as far as concluding that the imposition of a tax on betting was feasible.[1] The occasional use of select committees for inquiry into allegations of misconduct persisted, an example being the 1923 committee on Navy and Army Canteens which examined the alleged misapplication of profits made by the Navy and Army Canteen Board after acquisition of the Expeditionary Forces Canteen.[2] Another and rather different case was the committee set up in the 1937–8 session to inquire into the Official Secrets Act and the manner in which it had been applied to a Member, Mr. Duncan Sandys.[3] This case, however, was hardly distinguishable from an issue of parliamentary privilege. A somewhat unusual example of select com-

---

[1] H.C. 139, 1923. The report stood in a line of inquiry and discussion which resulted eventually in Churchill's ill-fated betting tax of 1926. (See *The Limits of Administration*, by C. Hood (John Wiley & Sons, 1976), Chap. 10 for full details.)

[2] H.C. 117, 1923.   [3] H.C. 173, 1937–8.

mittee work, and more in the old style, was the 1932–4 joint committee with the Lords on Indian Constitutional Reform, the proceedings of which extended to four volumes and were destined to have a considerable influence on the legislation of 1935 for the future government of India.[1] This was a committee containing major party figures such as Attlee, Austen Chamberlain, and Hoare. To some extent the reference of such a problem to a joint select committee reflected the Government's realization that the handling of the future of India could not be restricted to the Government itself and the fact that the Conservative party was seriously divided on the issues at stake.

The reference of bills to select committees was also in decline. A Matrimonial Causes Bill was so referred in 1923, a typical example of the kind of 'moral' question which it was thought appropriate to take out of the usual party framework and on which 'public opinion' might with advantage be consulted by an evidence-taking body.[2] Joint committees continued to be used too for the same purposes, and again the legislation usually came into a category which set it outside the bounds of party commitment—the Collecting Charities (Regulation) Bill and the Food and Drugs Bill in the 1937–8 session for example.

The only continuing addition to select committee work was the re-establishment of the Estimates Committee in 1921. The fledgling committee had gone into abeyance in 1914 after getting off to an uncertain start. By 1917 there was sufficient disquiet in the Commons about the lax control of current spending to ensure that the Government agreed to the appointment of a National Expenditure Committee with broad powers to review expenditure, to ascertain where economies might be made consistent with existing policies, and to examine the form of accounts. The committee had twenty-six members, was intended to work through sub-committees, and had the unusual power to appoint additional persons to serve on any sub-committee, though it does not appear to have used it. The National Expenditure Committee operated far more like a free-ranging inquisitorial body than any previous select committee. Its procedures were less formal, it penetrated into departments, it heard many witnesses but did not consistently publish

[1] H.C. 112–I, 1932–3, and H.C. 413, 1933–4. [2] H.C. 118, 1923.

verbatim evidence, and it took little account of the distinctions between policy and administration, which were already affirmed more sharply in the field of general financial and administrative scrutiny than in respect of the other categories of select committee work. For a while the National Expenditure Committee was tolerated by the Government, but by late 1919 had fallen into disfavour and at the end of 1920 was not renewed. But it was impossible to leave a void and so the Estimates Committee was re-created in July 1921, though only in the face of the patent hostility of the then Chancellor of the Exchequer, Mr. Austen Chamberlain.

The 1917–20 Expenditure Committee is perhaps most significant for two reasons. One was the manner in which it used sub-committees, demonstrating that such a division of labour could extend substantially the range of investigations undertaken. The other was the shift which took place within the expenditure remit to inquiries which concentrated on administrative methods and organization, and thus came to make a contribution to a more informed analysis of how government agencies were actually operating and of the problems encountered in the pursuit of policies which were in many cases ill-defined or merely implicit in particular programmes of action. Unfortunately neither of these lessons to be derived from the experience of the National Expenditure Committee were to have much influence on the reconstituted Estimates Committee. Though this was set up as a relatively large committee of twenty-four members, later expanded to twenty-eight, it did not make regular use of its power to set up sub-committees, and what is more, it reverted to the practice of trying to look at the estimates in a fairly literal way. In addition, the committee was hampered by the absence of expert staff to assist it in the designation of topics for inquiry and in the provision of information. As a result the committee was unable to achieve an acceptable definition of its role. To search for economies in the estimates was to enter a cul-de-sac, productive of conflict with the Treasury and exposed to the inconveniences of the annual cycle of financial business. By 1931, when the Procedure Committee was looking at the complaints of inadequacy in the methods of handling parliamentary business, the Estimates Committee enjoyed a poor reputation and was not taken seriously as a model for procedural development. Slowly in the 1930s it recovered somewhat and began to move towards the type of administrative scrutiny which had been initiated by the National Expenditure Committee after 1917 and which was to be further developed by a committee under the same name set up in late 1939. But once again it was the pressures of a crisis which forced the pace of development rather than the successful resolution in normal conditions of the ambiguities inherent in the idea of looking for economies in the estimates.

The inter-war years saw one major and somewhat unsuccessful review of procedure, that of 1931. Originally set up in late 1930 the committee sat throughout 1931 and was unable to report before the dissolution of that year. Its evidence was referred to a new committee in 1932 which produced a short report on which little action was taken.[1] It is indeed the evidence given to the committee which is of far greater interest than the practical outcome of its deliberations.[2] Basically, there was a cleavage between those who saw the principal problem as one of enabling the will of the majority to be put into effect more quickly and more efficiently, and those who were worried by the declining influence of minorities and private Members generally, and by the impact on House of Commons control of the widening of the sphere of public action and regulation for which the Government had taken over responsibility. Cautious politicians like Baldwin and MacDonald were sceptical of the case for major procedural changes; Churchill enthused over his scheme for an industrial chamber of Parliament; Mosley wanted to see Parliament obediently serving the needs of a strong Government; Lloyd George was full of schemes for strong specialized committees to deal with bills and finance, though it was pretty clear that he had not thought deeply about how these might work in practice; F. W. Jowett and Ramsay Muir (along with others) propounded a view of parliamentary organization which implied not only specialization in committee, but abandonment of the veneration accorded to debate on the floor of the House and of the formalized

[1] H.C. 129, 1931–2.
[2] *Special Report from the Select Committee on Procedure on Public Business*, H.C. 161, 1931–2.

adversary relationship between Government and Opposition.[1]

As far as committee organization went the recommendations of 1932 were modest. There was no support for any major modification of standing committee practices nor for the application of something like select committee procedures to a large number of bills. On select committees there was a recommendation that the Estimates Committee should be strengthened by closer association with the Public Accounts Committee, by the provision of qualified staff drawn either from the Exchequer and Audit Department or in the shape of a new body of advisers, and by the widening of its terms of reference to embrace policy questions and the relationship between public expenditure and national income. These proposals were not put into effect, but have some interest as defining what was to remain an important ingredient in the argument about the place of select committees in the pattern of relationships between Parliament and the Government right down to the present.

On the one hand it was admitted that the Commons as an institution distinguishable from the majority party in it could no longer exercise that control over the activity of government which the theory of its role appeared to demand. Thus, there was a problem: how could the Commons be strengthened so that the gap between theory and practice would not be such as to undermine popular trust in the Westminster form of parliamentary government? On the other hand, the dominant procedures of the House had come to mirror the process of competition between two parties, each of which hoped to exercise unhampered the full powers of government in virtue of possessing a majority of votes in the House. If this postulate was to be maintained—and it was—it became difficult to see what changes could be made which would increase the power of minorities, groups, and individuals in the House and thus require a different mode of political organization. But when

---

[1] It is perhaps worthy of comment that the 1931 committee on Public Business heard as witnesses virtually all the major figures in the House as well as many lesser known procedural experts. The 1976–7 Special Committee on Procedure, appointed to carry out 'a fundamental review', had to be content with a less dazzling roll-call of witnesses. Perhaps this points to a certain change in the status of such bodies.

people find themselves on the horns of a dilemma there are always some who believe that an intermediate resting-place can be found with none of the discomforts of the one horn or the other. The select committees of 1930–2 did not themselves produce a clear case for such a comfortable resolution of the dilemma. Yet much of the evidence points towards what was very soon to become the conventional reformist argument for treatment of the failings of the House of Commons: let us maintain the conventions of debate, the clash of Government and Opposition, and the concentration of authority in the Ministry of the day which the Westminster form of parliamentary government is held to require. But let this be moderated by providing means whereby Members of Parliament can examine closely what Governments are doing and subject all this to the healthy public criticism of representative laymen. In this way, so the argument runs, Members might hope to recover an influence which escapes them on the floor of the House and within the bonds of party disciplines. Even by 1934 this approach finds expression in the writing of Ivor Jennings.[1]

Yet the decade turned out to be an inauspicious one for the further pursuit of parliamentary reform. The mood of criticism of Parliament was quickly modified under the impact of the threat stemming from the success of political extremism on the Continent of Europe. The rapid emergence of the prospect of war with Germany removed the relevance of schemes of institutional reform in the legislature and pointed instead to the need for a more vigorous Executive. Even the concern with economy in public spending which had played a big part in such proposals as the Procedure Committee did make for the development of select committee scrutiny soon gave way to acceptance of a rising curve of expenditure, particularly for defence purposes. So the decade moved to its close with select committees at their most modest level of activity for very many years. The Public Accounts Committee continued to do its job methodically, perhaps enjoying a reputation somewhat out of proportion to the beneficial results it actually achieved. The Estimates Committee had survived and was showing signs of a more constructive approach to efficiency in government

[1] See, for example, *Parliamentary Reform*, by Sir Ivor Jennings (Gollancz, 1934).

operations. But for other purposes, all of which were familiar before 1913, select committees had become less and less used. Investigation of questions of broad public interest was entrusted more and more as a matter of course to officially appointed committees; the sanctity of the 'policy' area had assumed the shape of a doctrine which was held to debar Members of Parliament from active involvement either in the elaboration of policy options or in the scrutiny of bills outside of the debating rules; there was resigned acceptance of the improbability of achieving any *a priori* control of expenditure through the action of the House, or of doing much to check the increasing flow of delegated powers; and there were even signs that where allegations of misconduct or of abuses in public life affected Members themselves, it was thought better to entrust investigation to impartial nominated bodies or persons than to Members of the House.

The Epoch of Contentment 1945–1964

The impact of the Second World War on parliamentary institutions in Britain was favourable. Their survival and that of the country wiped out the critical mood of the previous decade. It appeared that the Government had been enabled to exercise unprecedented powers to mobilize the society and its economy for war purposes, and that this had in no way undermined the principles of parliamentary government nor diminished the ultimate authority of the elected Chamber. Moreover, the election of 1945 brought the two-party system to a level of simple bipolar competition not attained since the days of Gladstone and Disraeli. And they had had to lead parties far less firmly disciplined than the Labour and Conservative parties after 1945. Thus the conditions were ideal for the operation of a model of parliamentary government according to which the Government gets its way by virtue of its majority, subject only to the rights of a vigilant Opposition to oppose and of individual back-benchers of any party to seek the redress of grievances and publicity for whatever they might regard as matters of public concern.

A shrewd and gifted exponent of this doctrine was Herbert Morrison, experienced parliamentarian and business manager of the Labour Government of 1945–50. It was undoubtedly his views which carried most weight in the presentation of the Government's procedural proposals to the select committee on Procedure of 1945–6 and he ensured in the end that they were put into operation, notwithstanding the committee's reservations about some of them. Morrison's aim, broadly speaking, was to clear the decks for a large programme of government legislation. This meant preventing restoration of anything like the pre-1939 allocation of time to private Members and providing for wider and more intensive use of standing committees.[1] More closely related to the subject in hand is, however, the fact that Morrison was a persuasive witness against some of the proposals for the extension of select committee activity put forward by Sir Gilbert Campion, Clerk of the House of Commons. With unerring practical instinct Morrison saw that a Government anxious to put through a large legislative programme and responsible for an immensely wide range of executive activity and public spending programmes could hardly be helped (at any rate within the time horizons of most party politicians) by innovations which would tend to increase the opportunities of the House of Commons to intervene, to amend, to criticize, and to consume time and administrative effort.

How then did Campion see the problems facing the House in 1946? He appears to have been something of a rationalist in the mould of Lord Haldane. He analysed the functions of the House, identified failings in the procedures for their discharge, and devised a coherent pattern of procedural changes which would, he believed, have enabled the House to perform its functions more effectively. Though he had a judicious respect for the traditions of the House he clearly believed in the possi-

[1] It is worth noting, however, that the proposals relating to acceleration of the legislative programme put to the 1945–6 Procedure Committee were based on a scheme originally drafted by a committee of Ministers of the Coalition Government. (See Appendix to the *First Report from the Select Committee on Procedure*, H.C. 9–I, 1945–6.) Thus Morrison was representing what were very widely held views of the needs of the Government *vis-à-vis* Parliament amongst front-bench politicians. For his arguments see his evidence to the Procedure Committee 1945–6 and his well-known book, *Government and Parliament: A Survey from the Inside* (Oxford University Press, 1954).

bility of functionally adequate solutions to correctly identified problems. Not surprisingly, his memorandum on procedural reform has a degree of lucidity, internal coherence, and practical sense which is perhaps unique in the modern history of Parliament. It is equally not a matter for great surprise that his most important proposals were rejected, some by the Procedure Committee itself, some later by the Government.

Campion saw the functions of the House as:

(1) The representation of popular opinion
(2) The control of finance
(3) The formulation and control of policy
(4) Legislation[1]

The first of these could be left aside as involving far more than procedure. The second could no longer be performed by the whole House in so far as it referred to the 'review of expenditure in its *financial aspects*'.[2] To this end Campion made proposals for an amalgamation of the revived Estimates Committee and the Public Accounts Committee. The third concerned primarily the floor of the House, though the Procedure Committee quite rightly switched the emphasis somewhat by combining elements of the second and third functions under 'control of policy and administration'. It was under this umbrella that Campion's proposals for strengthening the newly established (1944) select committee on Statutory Instruments fell. For the fourth Campion concluded that the evident weaknesses of the current legislative methods required a standing committee system which would encourage 'diluted' specialization and permanence as well as withdrawal of certain opportunities for debate from the floor. Needless to say this far-seeing but cautious scheme for a more coherent legislative committee structure could not survive Mr. Speaker Clifton Brown's stern warning that it would represent 'a drastic interference with the rights of private Members'.[3] There is nothing like a reiteration of a venerable doctrine for killing proposals for change in the House of Commons.

[1] Campion's memorandum is published as an Appendix to the *Third Report from the Select Committee on Procedure*, H.C. 189-I, 1945-6, pp. xxi–lv.

[2] Ibid., p. xxiv, para. 9.

[3] 'Reform in Procedure', Memorandum by Mr. Speaker on the Suggestions of the Clerk of the House, ibid., p. 82.

In relation to select committees Campion's proposals were in fact modest in scope and followed closely ideas which had been put forward several times before. But he was also influenced by the experience of the wartime National Expenditure Committee which had issued one hundred reports in just over five years and had been judged on the whole to have been a success. It was from its methods of work that Campion drew the conclusion that his proposed Expenditure Committee should operate through a number of permanent and specialized sub-committees. The committee was to combine the functions of both the Public Accounts and Estimates Committees and would draw on the services of the Comptroller and Auditor-General whose statutory responsibilities would remain unchanged. This scheme was endorsed by the Procedure Committee, but never put into effect. However, it is likely that the discussions of select committees before the Procedure Committee did have some influence both on the future evolution of the Estimates Committee and on the crystallization of the idea of 'scrutiny of administration' as an area which might safely and properly be left to Members of Parliament.

A great deal of time was expended on Campion's proposals for a select committee on expenditure. This is at first sight odd in view of his affirmation that 'It would be only advisory' and his repeated statements to the effect that it would not pre-empt policy discussions in the House. Indeed there appeared to be little prospect of Campion's Public Expenditure Committee doing the dreadful things which Herbert Morrison feared.[1] Nevertheless, it may well be that Campion himself did not reveal all. Frequently he referred the committee to Captain Diver, the clerk to the 1939–45 National Expenditure Committee, and professed not to know himself how exactly the committee he was proposing would work! It is, however, fairly clear that it could not have operated effectively without embracing policy questions, and the evidence from Captain Diver showed that the distinction between policy and administration was nebulous anyway. What is more, as is now known

[1] In much of his oral evidence to the Procedure Committee Morrison was concerned to express the fears of Whitehall about the dangers of creating a counter-bureaucracy ('sleuths over at the Palace of Westminster', as he once remarked).

from the experience of the post-1970 Expenditure Committee, the facility to examine policy makes far less practical difference to the kind of questions which such a committee can tackle than has often been assumed. Thus we see that the crucial element in Campion's proposal, the radical part, was the amalgamation of the auditing function of the Public Accounts Committee with the scrutiny of 'efficiency of expenditure' function, the two to be exercised with the backing of the Comptroller and Auditor-General. In time this would have had a profound effect both on the permanent audit services and on the shape and direction of expenditure scrutiny by the House. In particular, it would have given to a wide-ranging expenditure committee the support of a substantial and experienced staff and this alone would have influenced significantly the kind of broader scrutiny of how policies were implemented which the committee could undertake. As it was, this proposal was rejected and the Estimates Committee had to attempt to follow the precedents established by the National Expenditure Committee which preceded it, but without having any specially qualified staff to support it or a systematic flow of relevant information to guide the choice of topics for inquiry. This was to set the pattern for the whole post-1946 evolution of discursive administrative scrutiny.

Despite relatively modest results, the 1945–6 procedure review remains important. To some extent Campion still thought in rather rigid categories of policy and administration, believing that a separation could be made and that control of the former was really for the floor of the House, whilst control of the latter should be entrusted to select committees. Consistently with this his view of administrative scrutiny also emphasized the financial and legal aspects of the process rather than the interconnections of policy determination, the setting of budgets, implementation of policy, and the adaptation of policy in the light of experience of how it works out in practice. Nevertheless, his principal memorandum and the committee's Third Report contributed much to the development of a wider and more realistic concept of scrutiny of administration. It was seen as a continuing activity which was desirable in the interests of efficient government. Even though the boundaries between policy and administration might be blurred, such scrutiny of efficient government could be entrusted to Members without risk of serious interference with the business of the Government, if only because on the floor of the House the lines of division between Government and Opposition were so clearly drawn. This fact of itself provided a guarantee that committees would be cautious in their inquiries and this outcome was all the more likely if they continued to operate without the aid of 'expert' staffs and avoided anything in the nature of serious subject specialization. It was broadly within this framework that select committees were to develop from 1946 onwards, first the Estimates Committee, then later in the 1950s the Nationalised Industries Committee. Though the years after 1964 were to bring an enhanced diversity in the range of committees charged with the oversight of executive activity, these limiting conditions were to retain their force. They symbolize that accommodation with the realities of competitive two-party politics and single party majority control of the Commons which the advocates of scrutiny of administration by select committees have then and later had to accept as the price for the gradual extension of their schemes.

The procedural revisions of 1946 were intended chiefly to facilitate the handling of government business, and in particular legislation. But they also set the framework within which a steady development of select committees as instruments of general administrative scrutiny could take place. Though the pace of development was gentle, it was in the twenty years after 1946 that the theory and practice of scrutiny by committee were really established. This experience was in turn to be the basis on which a substantial extension of committee scrutiny was to take place after 1966.

There were four major committees in the years after 1946, all of which can be said to have worked well within their limits. The Public Accounts Committee continued to enjoy most prestige and was able steadily to extend its concern for scrutinizing not just financial procedures but administrative methods and organization. The 'candle-ends' approach to expenditure gave way to a more realistic appreciation of the fact that probity alone was not enough. There was need for an active and continuing appraisal of how efficiently resources were being used. The Estimates Committee, re-established again at the end of the Second World War, was concerned with many of the same issues and this meant inevitably that there was some overlap with the work of the Public Accounts Committee. Nevertheless, the Estimates Committee ranged more widely, being unconstrained by the programme of inquiries carried out by an official such as the Comptroller and Auditor-General acting on its behalf, and was able to establish itself as a useful surveyor of how the central administration was organized for the performance of its functions and of how effectively the implementation of policy and the execution of the Government's expenditure programmes were carried out.[1] It was the largest of select committees, with its 49 members normally working through six sub-committees of inquiry, each of which was for practical purposes a separate and independent group. Whilst it remains hard to assess what the committee achieved directly, there is little doubt that it accustomed the departments to the dissemination of a great deal of information about their activities and organization, and that it succeeded in making them willing to listen sympathetically to parliamentary criticism. Thus there was established an educative dialogue which, for a while at least, brought benefit to both Westminster and Whitehall. That a price was paid in terms of an ambiguity about the role of the Estimates Committee cannot be denied, and indeed this was brought out sharply by Mr. Enoch Powell in evidence to the Procedure Committee of 1964–6. The committee had to blur the lines between policy and administration and had to make proposals which effectively implied policy changes.[2] But it is hard to discern who was the worse for that.

Closely following the Estimates Committee in style was the select committee on Nationalised Industries, established first as a temporary body in 1951 and after much argument, prevarication, and hesitation on the part of the Government

---

[1] The absence of support similar to that provided by the Controller and Auditor-General for the Public Accounts Committee also weakened the Estimates Committee by compelling it always to start from scratch: it had next to no analytic basis on which to work. For this reason continuity of membership and dedicated service became very important. See the author's *Parliament and Administration: The Estimates Committee 1945–65* (1966) for a detailed study of this committee and its contribution to the development of the scrutiny of administration.

[2] *Fourth Report from the Select Committee on Procedure*, H.C. 303, 1964–5, *Minutes of Evidence*, Q.349, p. 81.

confirmed in 1956 as a sessional committee.[1] In part the committee owed its existence to determined Conservative backbench pressure to devise ways of getting round what was held to be the excessive insulation of the nationalized industries from parliamentary pressures. But it also reflected a wider uneasiness about the extent to which state enterprises, for which there was in practice a great deal of ministerial responsibility, could safely be left to manage their affairs as they thought fit. In the event the committee satisfied neither the expectations of those who hoped for it to become a scourge of the nationalized industries nor of those like Herbert Morrison who saw it as a serious threat to the 1945–50 concept of the public corporation. Instead it developed a relatively friendly and even protective relationship with the industries whose reports and accounts it was entitled to scrutinize and investigate. Though often critical of the performance of particular industries (e.g. railways in 1959–60) the chief target of criticism became more and more government departments and Ministers whose actions so often tended to subvert the independence which the public corporation had been intended to enjoy.

Once it got going the committee aimed at examining each major industry at roughly a seven-year interval. For approximately two cycles this proved more or less practicable, but became less so as the number of nationalized enterprises began to increase in the later 1960s. But in addition to industry investigations the committee has also tackled horizontal problems, notably in the major report of 1968–9 on ministerial control of the nationalized sector. Though it is hard to demonstrate the direct effects of this report or of others concerned with particular industries, there is no doubt that they made a major contribution to public knowledge of the nationalized industries. Moreover, they generally reveal a sober grasp of the complexities of public enterprise organization and its relations with the Government which is at least equal to that shown by various official bodies which have from time to time reported on the problems of the public sector of industry. It is possible that the

---

[1] The establishment and early history of the Nationalised Industries Committee are dealt with in D. Coombes, *The Member of Parliament and the Administration: the case of the Select Committee of Nationalised Industries* (Allen & Unwin, 1966).

committee was influenced in its style and thoroughness by the fact that it has always been fairly small, never exceeding eighteen members. There have been notable examples of long service and evidence of a considerable ability to set aside party political prejudices in dealing with the economic problems of public enterprise. Like the Estimates Committee the National-ised Industries Committee received no expert assistance during the years when it was getting established, nor has it subsequently ever acquired more than the help of temporary specialist advisers.

The fourth committee of scrutiny was that on Statutory Instruments which operated from 1944 down to its replacement by a joint Lords–Commons committee in early 1973. This has never received the degree of attention given to the other com-mittees of administrative scrutiny, despite the fact that in 1946 Campion and others attached great importance to that aspect of administrative control provided by the vetting of statutory orders. No doubt the reason for this neglect lies in the relatively technical character of the committee's scrutiny, that in turn stemming chiefly from its restricted terms of reference. It has been debarred from considering the merits of delegated legisla-tion nor could it even recommend on broad political grounds that a particular statutory instrument should be considered by the House. Certainly the committee helped to maintain a certain order in an area of forbidding complexity and variety. Whether the task it performed need have been discharged by the House of Commons at all is, however, open to question. Effectively the scrutiny was performed by Speaker's Counsel advising the committee and it would appear that little would have been lost by relegation of a function of this kind to a permanent organ of legal scrutiny.[1]

We have provided no more than the barest outline of the pattern of administrative investigation by select committee established in the twenty years after the Second World War. Inevitably this cannot do justice to the range and interest of the reports and evidence produced, nor can it give any clear indica-

---

[1] This is not intended to suggest complete exclusion of the House of Commons from the examination of delegated legislation. The question is whether the technical scrutiny as such could not have been entrusted to a permanent body entitled to report both to Ministers and to the House.

tion of how effective in terms of an influence on ministerial and departmental action this effort was. Two factors of some importance have to be borne in mind in assessing both the style of operation of select committees of scrutiny and the educative impact which the reports had. One is that many of the leading parliamentary figures on both sides of the House had their roots in the Parliaments of the 1920s and 1930s. They were people who respected parliamentary procedures and for the most part took seriously the idea that Parliament existed just as much to allow minority opinions to be voiced as to facilitate action supported by majorities. Thus they were generally conservatives in procedural matters. But their suspicion of change was not merely reactionary. It expressed rather a certain scepticism about whether the House could devise any better ways of holding a balance between executive needs and respect for the representative principle as manifested in the whole House than had been established in the course of the past century. According to this view Parliament faced a genuine dilemma and the wisest and most courageous course was to sit on that horn which carried the risk of executive dominance, but to do one's best to see that it did not become too uncomfortable. This means that the task of select committees was seen as consisting chiefly in the patient pursuit of an explanatory dialogue with the Executive. This would inform small groups of Members and contribute to the shaping of parliamentary opinion in a way which would command the respect of Governments and party majorities. In other words executive dominance was hopefully mitigated by the persuasive arguments of those minorities prepared to devote time to the scrutiny of executive activities.

The other factor is that despite differences of policy between the two main parties, there was in this period a considerable tolerance of the measures put into effect by the other side. The Conservative party revised but little of the 1945–51 legislative enactments, and at least during the 1950s it is doubtful whether a Labour Government, had it come to power, would as a matter of commitment have immediately repealed what its opponents had done. These attitudes helped to maintain a context favourable to a relatively objective style of administrative scrutiny by select committee and to keep its scale modest.

Both these factors provided a stabilizing background to activity in Parliament. In this context there was a willingness in the House of Commons to leave the task of scrutinizing the formidably complex organization and operations of the state to a relatively small group of Members. Within that group many changed around quickly, so that the burden of maintaining continuity fell on a very small number, those who had a natural gift for the select committee style of inquiry and usually a strong sense of service to the House. In these qualities they were not all that different from their predecessors at the opening of the century. A problem for the future was, however, to lie in the continuing decline of this kind of Member, forced out by economic and social change, by the idiosyncratic predilections of constituencies, by the increasing unattractiveness of the parliamentary profession, and by the pressures of rigid party discipline. There is some irony in the fact that the post-1966 expansion of administrative scrutiny has coincided with the passage of that type of Member most likely to endow it with substance and to earn for it respect.

As far as the other uses of select committees are concerned the trend already established was confirmed after 1945. It continued to be rare to refer bills to select committees, though occasional examples can be found on such subjects as army discipline and obscene publications. Equally rare was reference of a matter on which legislation might be needed, though here too examples occur such as the 1957–8 select committee on Obscene Publications. Nevertheless, parliamentary reformers were to return in the late 1960s to the possibility of using select committees again more regularly in the preparation of bills, at what came to be called the pre-legislative stage. It should, however, be remembered that the conditions in which legislation is drawn up have changed substantially since the beginning of the century. Much legislation confers substantial powers on Ministers or some other public agency and the element of general regulation addressed to the citizen is correspondingly diminished. Apart from the fact that extensive administrative experience is required for the drafting of measures intended to facilitate executive action, it is also usual for them to be contained in some party commitment. Government by party manifesto accords ill with a readiness to refer problems to select committees. Furthermore, there is the factor of speed and urgency. Governments have come to believe far more dogmatically than they used to that they have a right to get their legislation through quickly and that national well-being depends on their enforcement of this right. No matter how spurious these claims may be, they too weigh against a substantial reversion to earlier habits of engaging groups of Members of Parliament in preparing the ground through inquiry for measures of public regulation.[1]

In their working methods select committees changed very little in the years after 1945. They continued to operate through the collection of oral and written evidence, though the quantity of the latter showed some tendency to increase relative to the former. The proceedings were as a rule time-consuming and ponderous, though this had the advantage of ensuring that a large amount of evidence appeared on record when published alongside the report at the end of an inquiry. Attendance at hearings, particularly at smaller sub-committees of the Estimates Committee, was always somewhat irregular. A select committee suggests a body of men and women meeting regularly and working together as a united team. The reality has always been different, and especially in recent Parliaments. A select committee is in fact often a shifting tenuous body, with some members missing numerous meetings, some unable to find time to read the papers, and many given to putting in an appearance before slipping out to attend to some other matter. Inevitably the burden has fallen on a minority of dedicated members and on the chairmen. If they have been hardworking and have had some idea of what they were aiming for, then the committees have had a good prospect of producing useful reports. Inevitably too the committees have depended greatly on the competence of their staffs. The Public Accounts Committee continued to rely on the support of the Comptroller

---

[1] These remarks need to be qualified by reference to the appointment of select committees on Corporation Tax (1970–1), on Tax Credit (1972–3), and on a Wealth Tax (1974–5). Though no trend appears to have been established, these committees did demonstrate that it was not entirely impracticable to revive an earlier function of the select committee. It should be noted too that the tradition persists that morality and taxation are 'safe areas' for select committee inquiry.

and Auditor-General, whilst the Statutory Instruments Committee always enjoyed a measure of support from Speaker's Counsel. The Estimates and Nationalised Industries Committees had throughout the years before 1965 to manage with no specialized help, relying entirely on the clerks drawn from the department of the Clerk of the House. Whether this was a severe handicap must, however, be doubted. Given the task of discursive inquiry and recommendation to which the committees were confined, it remained (and still remains) hard to determine just what kind of qualified staff they might effectively have used. Since the rationale of select committees continued to be expressed in terms of providing a check by laymen on the activities of the Executive, a strong suspicion of 'experts' as potential manipulators survived.

To conclude this section, the scrutiny of administration had by the late 1950s acquired a certain coherence. The appropriation and proper disbursement of funds were still examined by a committee supported by an audit service; delegated legislation received a thorough scrutiny in respect of certain technical standards; there was an ongoing scrutiny of 'value for money' and of the organization and methods of administration conducted on a 'spot-check' basis by the Estimates Committee; and there was a rather similar treatment of the publicly-owned sector of industry entrusted to public corporations. The results of all this work did not have a major impact on how Governments behaved nor on the decisions they took. But the process of inquiry did help to maintain certain standards of conduct both in the public service and in political life, to reinforce the idea of the subordination of administration to political requirements and control, and to sustain a modest degree of confidence in the House of Commons in its own ability to exert at any rate some element of that control over the affairs of government which its claim to final authority required.

The Years of Reform: 1965 to the Present

Fifteen years or so after 1945 it looked as if a point of equilibrium might have been reached in the adjustment of the claims of the Government to safeguard its responsibilities to those of the House to assert its rights of supervision over the execution of policy. But this was not so. A Procedure Committee was appointed in late 1956 and from then on was frequently re-appointed, though it was not until the mid-1960s that the pressures from such bodies began to have noticeable effects. Much of the activity of Procedure Committees after 1957 concerned other aspects of the House's procedure than the use of select committees. Nevertheless, there were already in 1958 calls for the extension of select committee scrutiny[1] and the then Clerk of the House, Sir Edward Fellowes, suggested to the 1958 Procedure Committee that as an experiment a Joint Committee on Colonial Affairs might be set up and a Defence Committee of the House to look at defence estimates.[2] In its 1959 report the committee rejected these suggestions, partly by reference to the work on defence estimates already carried out by the Estimates Committee and partly by invoking a peculiarly rigid interpretation of the theory of the separation of powers. 'The House', the committee said, 'has always been careful not to arrogate to itself any of the executive power. The establishment of a colonial committee would not only invade this principle, but would also lead to the establishment of other similar committees.'[3] Nevertheless there were six Labour members of the committee who opposed this conclusion.

For a while the procedural caution both of successive Procedure Committees and of the Government (notably in the shape of Mr. R. A. Butler) ensured that the call for more scrutiny by select committee or by some curious hybrid committee entitled both to debate and take evidence went unheeded. But after the return of a Labour Government in October 1964 the winds of change began to blow more strongly.

[1] The demand for more specialist committees was voiced in the debate on procedure on 31 January 1958, though in a hesitant way.

[2] Sir Edward Fellowes was influenced in his first proposal by the precedent of the Joint Committee on Indian Affairs 1921–9, though his memorandum makes no reference to its more impressive successor of 1932–4; he also seems to have taken no account of the fact that the Estimates Committee always set one of its sub-committees to examine some aspect of defence spending and was thus substantially performing the task for which the proposed Defence Committee was intended. See *Report from the Select Committee on Procedure*, H.C. 92–I, 1959, General Memorandum on Procedural Reform, *Minutes of Evidence*, p. 18.

[3] Ibid., *Report*, p. xxv.

This is not to imply that the Government formed by Mr. Harold Wilson had any carefully prepared plans for procedural reform in the House of Commons. This was certainly true at the beginning and indeed the available evidence suggests that right down to 1970 procedural reform proposals depended substantially on improvization. The Government was generally guided by its view at any particular point in time of what kind of changes might best facilitate the passage of its own business on the floor, in committee of the whole House, and in standing committees. But it recognized too that in the climate of opinion of the 1960s it was expedient to give some satisfaction to those who were demanding changes which they saw either as compensation for the still greater control of business exacted by the Government, or as the key to developments which would (so it was hoped) eventually transform the relationships between the House and the Executive to the advantage of the former. So the Government tacked its course accordingly, sometimes showing cautious sympathy for the demands of the 'reform by select committee' lobby, sometimes (as in 1966) rushing ahead of them and presenting the House with committee experiments which its own Procedure Committee had not yet recommended, and sometimes simply doing nothing. Not surprisingly, by 1970–1 the outcome was something of a patchwork: the select committee map certainly looked different from what it was in 1960, but it is hard to discern what, if any, principles had shaped the manner in which it had been re-drawn or to identify with precision how the role of investigatory committees had changed in a qualitative sense.

Before making some remarks about the manner in which select committee scrutiny has been extended in recent years, it is important to mention briefly the parliamentary reform movement and the context of opinion in which it grew up. There is little doubt that by about 1960 there was increasing anxiety about the economic performance of Britain. This was felt by people belonging to several professional groups important either for what they do or the influence they have on public opinion. In the search for remedies which then got under way there quickly appeared a strong conviction that the reform of the governmental and administrative machinery was what was needed: here was the key to a reversal of fortune. It is significant that the term 'machinery' has been so frequently used in discussion of the British system of government. It suggests in an obscure manner that it is all a question of organization, of setting up this or that committee, agency, ministry, council, etc., and in so doing completely overlooks the fact that institutions which serve political purposes have to be founded on certain principles or guiding assumptions. Now the peculiarity of British political development is that the principles underlying the major institutions are both hard to define and extremely resistant to change. The convenient effect of the 'machinery' language was, however, that it helped people to push on one side the problem of the principles by which institutions are structured. It enabled them to believe that by changing and adding to the machinery real changes were being made in the terms on which political and administrative institutions were shaped. Thus most of the innovations in government of this period were bound to some extent to be living contradictions: they purported to introduce new ways of conducting business, yet were necessarily limited by a failure to re-define the principles on which they were constructed or on which the underpinning institutions rested.[1]

This pervasive and somewhat shallow belief in the benefits of institutional reform—conceived, however, as the improvement of machinery—affected the House of Commons just as deeply as it influenced other sectors of public activity and organization. Generational changes as well as the return of a Labour majority committed to restoring the country's ailing economy and on that basis to expand its social services meant that the House of Commons contained a higher proportion of Members sympathetic to procedural change than previously.[2] Moreover,

---

[1] The author has developed a critique of the modern cult of organizational reform in Britain in several places, e.g. 'Recent Administrative Reform in Britain', in A. L. Leemans (ed.), *The Management of Change in Government* (Nijhoff, 1976), and at length in *In Search of the Constitution* (Pergamon, 1977). His views of the weaknesses of the case for parliamentary reform through the development of select committees are set out in his contributions to *The Commons in Transition* (Fontana, 1970) and to the successor volume, *The Commons in the Seventies* (Fontana, 1977).

[2] It should be remembered too that an increasing number of the 1966 entry of younger Conservative M.P.s also had great faith in the benefits to be gained from organizational reform in government and were well-

many of them, and especially in the Labour party, were teachers and journalists by profession, people skilled rather in the production of ideas than of goods or services of a more tangible kind. This type of Member was receptive to the pleas for institutional change advanced by such bodies as the Study of Parliament Group founded in early 1964.[1] This latter was a striking example of the manner in which academics began to associate formally and regularly for the study of British political institutions and in so doing necessarily became a discreet pressure group, channelling into the appropriate parts of the system of government their proposals for improvement. This was in some respects a new phenomenon, men and women with an avowedly theoretical knowledge claiming to advise the practitioners who had traditionally claimed something like a monopoly of wisdom in respect of the institutions of government.

Finally, the triumph of the reforming spirit in relation to Parliament was assisted by a belief widely shared by nearly all politicians who had not attained high office as well as by those who had studied Parliament. This was the belief that Parliament had declined seriously in relation to the Executive and that something should be done to strengthen it as a representative institution capable of controlling the Executive. On the other hand there were few who in the early 1960s questioned the postulate of competitive two-party politics, or that of ministerial responsibility understood as the claim to full discretion so long as the Ministry was upheld by a majority in Parliament. Thus, if the House of Commons was to be strengthened and the influence of individual Members restored, this had to be done in a manner which would not disturb these underlying constitutional assumptions and the political practices associated with them. The most promising way of squaring this circle, so many believed, was to develop the function of disposed towards parliamentary reform involving an extension of select committee scrutiny.

[1] One of the founders of the Study of Parliament Group, Professor Bernard Crick, made an influential and persuasive contribution to the diffusion of ideas for parliamentary reform through his book, *The Reform of Parliament* (Weidenfeld & Nicolson, 1964). His main reform proposal was an extension of select committee scrutiny by which the influence of Members of Parliament was to be dramatically strengthened.

scrutiny and advice. True, Parliament could not expect to have a real share in the powers of decision, but at least it could inform public opinion more effectively, advise Governments more insistently, and warn. And the instruments for so doing were to be select committees. Such in outline was the climate of opinion in which the issue of parliamentary reform was approached in the years 1965 to 1970.

The development of select committees did, of course, go forward in the context of other procedural changes made between 1966 and 1968, some of them substantial, in the ways in which business is handled in the Commons. The passage of the Finance Bill was expedited by the relegation of large sections of it to a standing committee; the venerable procedures of Supply and Ways and Means were part simplified, part abolished; the range of standing committees for legislation was extended; experiments were made with morning sittings and committees to take the second reading of bills. But all these changes served on balance to strengthen the Government's capacity to safeguard its business. Intended to point in the other direction were the extensions of select committee activity which were put into effect. The first proposals came from the Procedure Committee of 1964–5 which advocated a strengthening of the Estimates Committee and widening of its terms of reference. Essentially it wanted an Expenditure Committee which would be expected to examine 'how the departments of state carry out their responsibilities and to consider their Estimates of Expenditure and Reports'.[1] It envisaged this committee as functioning through specialized sub-committees and pressed for it to be allowed to employ specialist assistance and to travel abroad when necessary. In making these proposals the committee was reflecting several of the suggestions put to it by the Study of Parliament Group,[2] though it did not go the whole way with the Group and declined to recommend that specialized committees for the scrutiny of policy and administration should be set up with the ultimate objective of bringing them into the committee consideration of bills.

[1] *Fourth Report from the Select Committee on Procedure*, H.C. 303, 1964–5, para. 16, p. ix.
[2] Ibid., *Minutes of Evidence*, pp. 131–43 for the Memorandum submitted by the Study of Parliament Group.

Nothing was done immediately to implement these proposals. However, the then Prime Minister decided to commit himself publicly to an extension of parliamentary committees shortly before the March 1966 election. Later that year the Government approved the setting up of several new committees, though still doing nothing about the proposal for a new Expenditure Committee. It must, however, be remembered that the Government, which now had a substantial majority and was anxious to carry through a legislative programme, was preoccupied with the other procedural changes already mentioned. It was anxious to expand the number of standing committees, whilst the modernization of Supply procedure and completion of the Finance Bill reforms were also more important for it than the expansion of select committees. It is nevertheless striking that the select committee innovations of 1966 had such a purely *ad hoc* character. Despite the arguments already advanced by the Procedure Committee in favour of a coherent pattern of committees to scrutinize expenditure and administration, what was actually done expressed no particular plan for the improvement of parliamentary scrutiny nor did the choice of areas of investigation reveal any priorities or criteria of importance. Though Mr. Richard Crossman, who was responsible for procedural questions from August 1966, refers several times in his Memoirs to having 'a plan' for reform and for specialist committees in particular, he vouchsafed to posterity no precise details of this.[1] The most he did was to indicate some support for 'specialist' committees, and later to suggest a distinction between 'subject' and 'departmental' committees. The first of the 'subject' committees to be appointed was Science and Technology, a subject which was tolerably neutral in political terms and in which a number of Members were known to be seriously interested.[2] This committee appeared in late 1966 and has survived to the present day, having been notable for a relatively high stability in membership and

[1] It is a curious fact that despite R. H. S. Crossman's desire to be a latter-day Bagehot, Vol. II of *The Diaries of a Cabinet Minister* (Hamish Hamilton/ Jonathan Cape, 1976) contain no sustained and coherent reflections on parliamentary reform in general or on select committees in particular.

[2] There had been an unofficial all-party Parliamentary and Scientific Committee for some time which brought together a nucleus of Members interested in scientific and technical matters.

the production of some remarkably thorough and extensive reports, especially in the field of nuclear energy. Another subject committee was Race Relations and Immigration, established at the end of 1968 and also still operating. Four 'departmental' committees appeared between 1967 and 1969, those on Agriculture, Education and Science, Scottish Affairs, and Overseas Aid. The first three of these were short-lived, surviving but a couple of years in each case. Overseas Aid (later Overseas Development) has managed to survive, though occasionally under threat of closure.

Alongside committees with subjects and departments there also emerged a select committee on the Parliamentary Commissioner for Administration following the 1966 Act which provided for the appointment of such an official. This was a natural development, given the terms on which the office was established. The committee provides the sole example of a close analogy with the Public Accounts Committee in that it has a clearly defined task to perform and does this on the basis of reports furnished by a permanent official and his staff.[1]

Undoubtedly there was a quality of improvization and experiment about the 1966–9 innovations. They required the services of far more members than had worked on select committees in the preceding years and this inevitably attracted some members away from the established scrutiny committees —Accounts, Estimates, Nationalised Industries. Nor did these experiments take place without friction between the new committees on the one side and Ministers and departments on the other. The Agriculture Committee ran into such conflict and both the Scottish Affairs and Education and Science Committees expressed irritation at the restraints to which they were subjected both by the Government Whips and the departments. Thus it was not surprising that the Procedure Committee report of 1968–9 on the Scrutiny of Expenditure and Administration[2] should repeat the case for a more coherent approach to the scrutiny of policy and administration by the

[1] Much information and comment on the relationship between the select committee on the Parliamentary Commissioner for Administration and the Office of the Commissioner is provided by R. Gregory and P. Hutchesson, *The Parliamentary Ombudsman* (Allen & Unwin, 1975).

[2] H.C. 410, 1968–9.

creation of an Expenditure Committee, fashioned out of the existing Estimates Committee, but strengthened by wider terms of reference and a structure of functional sub-committees. By implication at least it was acknowledged that the recent specialist committee innovations had been unsatisfactory and that it might not be necessary to continue all of them. A factor to which the Procedure Committee gave great emphasis was the need to adapt the investigatory work of the House to the developments in the Treasury's management of public expenditure and in particular to the annual publication of expenditure white papers covering a period of five years ahead. It was thought that one of the tasks of such an Expenditure Committee would be to prepare the ground for a grand annual debate of the Government's medium term spending plans emerging from the public expenditure survey process. As experience was to prove, the Procedure Committee seriously misjudged the willingness of the House to give sustained attention to matters of such a general and even speculative nature and in respect of which no decisions had to be taken by the House itself.

It fell to the Conservative Government which assumed office in 1970 to approve the proposals just outlined and the Expenditure Committee duly replaced the Estimates Committee at the beginning of 1971. It has subsequently worked chiefly through six sub-committees, one labelled 'General' and five others, viz. defence and external affairs, environment, trade and industry, education, the arts and the Home Office, and social services and employment.[1] Its terms of reference are laid down in broad terms, thus permitting the committee to examine issues of policy as well as efficiency and economy in administration. In addition the committee, like others, has been able to travel freely and to appoint temporary specialist advisers. Though the committee has been productive, it is, however, hard to demonstrate that its reports have differed substantially from those of the Estimates Committee. It is true that it is not inhibited from commenting on matters of policy, but in practice this has had to be done with some caution. It is relatively easy to secure agreement on matters of 'administrative

[1] The distribution of functional responsibilities and the titles of sub-committees have varied from time to time. What is quoted above refers to the position in late 1974 at the beginning of the present Parliament.

policy', for example on criticisms of the way in which policies have been pursued or developed in detail, but if it is a matter of current or prospective Government and party commitment it is hard for the committee itself to avoid dividing on party lines. This has usually meant that the majority party has carried the day and voted down recommendations or criticisms which the Government would have rejected anyway. Awareness of such difficulties dictates restraint in the treatment of policy issues. In addition, the ability to discuss policy has done little to modify the caution of Civil Service witnesses on whom the Expenditure Committee, like other select committees, must extensively rely for information.[1]

Let us try to summarize the main features of the committee pattern which has now emerged. There are two committees with very specific tasks of *post facto* scrutiny—the Public Accounts and the Parliamentary Commissioner for Administration Committees. Alongside these are the Statutory Instruments Committee, operating since 1973 jointly with the Lords, and the select committee on European Secondary Legislation, first appointed in 1974 to scrutinize regulations and proposals emanating from the institutions of the European Community. The first of these continues to have a relatively technical function, whilst the second might in principle acquire something much more like a scrutiny of legislation role. But such a development must depend extensively on the future evolution of Community law-making as well as on domestic political attitudes towards the British role in the Community. Then there are two major committees of financial and administrative scrutiny which are concerned chiefly with efficient administration and the effectiveness of the policies being pursued in the areas remitted to them: here the reference is to the Expenditure Committee and the Nationalised Industries Committee. Additionally there are the two subject committees referred to

---

[1] There has been a tendency since 1968 for Ministers to appear before some select committees. But they are no substitute for officials and indeed their presence tends to sharpen the lines of party division and thus to reduce the effectiveness of the investigatory procedure itself. There has also since the late 1960s been a marked tendency for select committees to widen the range of witnesses called before them, particularly by consulting outside the ranks of the Civil Service.

already—Science and Technology and Race Relations and Immigration—and one rather tenuous departmental committee, Overseas Development. Strictly speaking it has not for some time had a separate department to oversee and might, therefore, be treated too as a subject committee.

The select committees now in operation are all concerned essentially with examining what is done by public agencies. Despite the fact that no attempt has been made to relate their structure closely to the distribution of functions in government, they nevertheless do in a rough and ready way range over a very large part of central administrative activity as well as covering the public enterprise sector. The majority of them are most accurately described as instruments of administrative scrutiny—they investigate what has been done and how. In some cases the genuinely inquisitorial factor is more prominent, notably for the Public Accounts Committee and the Parliamentary Commissioner for Administration Committee, both of which are in the position of examining errors and mistakes brought to their notice by their investigating agents. But nearly all other committees must proceed by discursive and exploratory inquiry. The ground is not prepared for them and they have to pick their way forward by the time-hallowed procedure of sending for papers and examining witnesses. Nor do they have much support in this task. They depend chiefly on the generalist clerks of the House, supplemented from time to time by temporary advisers thought to be qualified to assist committees with particular inquiries.[1] It is not surprising, therefore, that most of the select committees work in a somewhat laborious fashion: they rarely build on a fund of relevant and continuous experience, often they do not know precisely what problems are the most important and the most suitable for analysis, and their procedures (combined with the working habits of so many members) tend to work in favour of diffusion rather than concentration of effort and attention.

As far as specialization goes, it will be clear that there has

[1] Most select committees have made some use of temporary advisers, but all have done so on a modest scale. Some committees have encouraged such advisers to play a major role in assessing evidence and in drafting reports, while others have held them at arm's length and shown no sign of knowing how to assimilate specialist advice.

been but modest progress in this direction. The contemporary pattern of select committees offers to members more opportunities to apply their specialized knowledge and to develop particular interests than was possible earlier in the century. And undoubtedly many committees do tend to attract into membership those who have for a variety of reasons a specialized concern with their field of scrutiny and inquiry. Nevertheless, the committee structure itself is not functionally specialized to the extent familiar in many other parliaments, nor do select committees as a rule have tasks to perform which are as clearly defined as those of the normal legislative committee elsewhere. Consequently the idea of the Member of Parliament as the lay critic still survives, sustained too by the preference which many Members have for maintaining a wide and varied pattern of activities in and around the House. The most that can be said, therefore, is that the ground has been prepared for a much higher level of subject specialization amongst Members and that this possibility is enhanced by the sessional status which most committees now have. The strengthening of such subject specialisation was indeed firmly endorsed by the Procedure Committee in 1978[1] and linked closely with proposals for a systematic pattern of committees of scrutiny based on the functions of Government departments. But it remains to be seen whether such a substantial shift from earlier habits will secure acceptance.

Finally, it is worth stressing that the task of contemporary select committees of scrutiny remains to inquire and to make recommendations to the House. But since their recommendations proceed *proprio motu* from their own investigations they do not represent anything to which either the House or the Government need feel committed. In other words, the committees are not charged with handling parts of the business of the House which someone is anxious to get through. Instead they stand on one side, eliciting information and forming opinions. It is for this reason more than any other that their reports receive comparatively little attention in the House. Though steps were taken in the late 1950s to ensure that at least three days per session were devoted to debating reports

---

[1] Select Committee on Procedure, 1st Report 1977–78, H.C. 588 I–III. This committee was set up specially to carry out 'a fundamental review' of procedure.

of what were then the major committees of administrative scrutiny, it has never been possible to establish a system providing for the regular discussion in the House of all select committee reports. As the number of committees has increased, so inevitably has the number of reports of which the House takes no formal notice at all. In fact, the real addressees of reports have become the departments of government rather than the House itself. Special reports containing the observations of these departments on reports dealing with aspects of their responsibilities and functions are regularly published, though sometimes only after delays of up to a year. Though the departments usually comment in a manner suggestive of careful attention to the views expressed by select committees, they are under little pressure to accept such recommendations as are put to them. A dialogue has taken place, but it is a dialogue at arm's length across the gap established by the conventions of party politics on the floor of the House.

Such conditions go far to explaining why it was unrealistic to believe, as some parliamentary reformers of the 1960s appear to have done, that select committees held the key to a change in the relationships between Government and Parliament. Such effects cannot be expected of bodies which have no powers of decision and are under no obligation to vote, to say nothing of the party political neutralization which remains an important condition of their ability to produce results and to secure attention.

Scrutiny Committees and their Place in Parliament

If account is taken of a number of other select committees—some domestic and procedural and a very small number still set up occasionally either for investigation of a special problem or to consider a bill—it is clear that the House now makes far more extensive use of select committees for scrutiny than it has done since the period before 1914. It is not unusual for something like 35 to 40 committees and sub-committees to be sitting in the course of a session, nor for up to 300 Members to be engaged on such work. However, in case this is considered to be unprecedented, it is worth recalling that in the years between 1878 and 1903 there were rarely less than 30 select committees per session and on average 350 Members of Parliament were involved in them. Thus, it would be unwise to conclude without careful inquiry that the burden of select committee service on Members is much heavier than it has ever been before or that committees themselves are the cause of lower attendance in the Chamber. But it is in the thrust and purpose of select committee work that the major changes have occurred.

Half a century or more ago select committees other than those of a domestic nature or devoted to private bills were still used chiefly to investigate a problem of current importance and concern prior to action, or to examine a public bill. In other words, the select committee was either ancillary to the legislative process or had something nearer a royal commission function, embracing both the analysis of existing administrative methods and the study of policy in a specific context. Sometimes, of course, the remit was narrower and directed a committee affecting the public service or office-holders to make an inquiry into specific allegations. The use of select committees in these ways proceeded from the belief that it was both practicable and desirable for the House to be associated actively with the handling of problems of public concern. Though the area over which Governments claimed responsibility was widening, this had not yet seriously called into question the right and ability of the House to have such opportunities. This pattern then gave way to something much simpler and more restricted, and for the best part of forty years the House limited its select committees to scrutiny on a restricted scale of what government departments and agencies dependent on Parliament for funds had done and how they were organized for their functions. This was a phase which coincided with the rapid expansion of government powers and the strengthening of party discipline. The House's gradual involvement in an ongoing scrutiny of administration can be treated as a response to those trends, the only response which political and constitutional circumstances left open to it. Hesitant before 1939 but gathering strength after 1945 this became the orthodox view of the purposes to be served by select committees.

However, the pursuit of administrative scrutiny could not indefinitely conceal a major difficulty facing the modern House of Commons. It has become chiefly a place for full-time politicians. But at any one time barely a seventh of the Members can expect to enjoy some share in the powers of government. The problem, therefore, is to define the role of the remainder, and more especially to render this role such as will attract capable people into political life. Given the dominance of the Government and of the official Opposition in the House, it is hard to devise a role which offers to professional politicians a firm prospect of constructive activity and of opportunities actually to influence particular outcomes. It was a belief that the range of scrutiny evolved by about 1960 was inadequate to meet these needs that stimulated the recent search for more effective means of widening the scope of such scrutiny and of increasing the quantity of it. Thus quantitative changes were put in hand, but they implied no radical qualitative change either in the relationships between Government and Parliament or in the basic structure of parliamentary business. The extension and to a limited degree the systematization of scrutiny has not resolved the underlying problem to which it was thought to offer hope of a solution.

Nevertheless, within the postulates which determine the character and constitutional role of the British Parliament it remains possible to find a rationale for the extensive use made of select committees. Three postulates or principles have been of decisive significance in the modern evolution of the House of Commons and they remain of great importance. The first is the equality of Members. It is this principle which stands in the way of withdrawing matters of decision from the floor of the House, for only there does each Member have a voice and a vote. This is why, as Redlich discerned long ago, the House has remained hostile to a delegation of powers to a genuine committee system. The second is the majority principle which requires constant appeal to a vote, to the collection of voices. But this has always been interpreted as 'simple majority' and has worked against the power of veto of parts of the House and the growth of conventions of consensus transcending the natural divisions between the majority and the minority. True, the majority principle has to be applied with care if minorities are not to be overridden and rendered sullen and obstructive. The appeal to 'the sense of the House' was for long enough a way of moderating the impact of the majority rule and of appealing to values in the House expressive of respect for the presence of dissent within it. The third has been the responsibility of the Executive, the bearers of the authority of the Crown and of the powers vested in them by statute, to the House of Commons as a whole. But this was and is a relationship which has been held to leave untouched the discretion of both sides—the right of the House to give or withdraw its confidence and the right of a Government to govern according to its judgement of what it is expedient to do so long as it retains that confidence. That the majority principle has in this century fortified Governments in the claims they make is clear. But equally significant is the fact that the three principles together militate against the notion of a sharing of power between Government and Parliament, of the striking of bargains between those in office and those on whose support they depend. And if bargains have to be struck, then at least they should not appear too obviously to have this character.[1]

These postulates reach back into a now distant past. Within the bounds set by them the British Parliament flourished as a great debating assembly, claiming a full and unlimited sovereignty, but delegating the use of that authority extensively to those who acted in its name, that is to say the Government of the day. In these conditions there could not take place that development of committees charged with matters to decide which has been a characteristic of all legislatures which have been in fact or law distinct from the executive power. If Parliament was to control Governments, then it had to do so on the floor of the House. The absence of a committee system reflected the dislike of specialization by Members and hostility to the idea that a man might exert more influence by working

[1] It recognized that these closing remarks refer to a party system which, some would argue, is already changing significantly. Moreover, since early 1977 a Labour Government has agreed to a voting arrangement with the Liberal party for which a price has to be paid in policy concessions. Nevertheless, it is uncertain whether this shift to something nearer to coalition politics will survive an election. There is so far no conclusive evidence that the parties think in different categories about their relations with each other nor has the absence of a simple two-party majority-minority situation had any noticeable impact on parliamentary procedure in general and the functions of committees in particular.

in some segment of Parliament than on the floor of the House.

The counterpart of this dislike of specialization was, however, the faith in laymen, in the straightforward practical citizen who can subject the actions of those in authority to the tests of common sense. That the test of common sense often means no more than the counting of prejudiced likes and dislikes should not obscure the fact that such an appeal has been intimately associated with the British understanding of democratic government. But it was precisely the appeal to the lay opinion which came to be the major justification for select committees. There were matters on which the House wished to be informed. Let it, therefore, send a few of its typical Members to collect the information and to report back. But to make sure that they did the job properly, let them follow the procedures of the Courts, hear witnesses, and write down for the parent body to read what they have heard and concluded.

Such in essentials was the justification for select committees and such it remains even now. They are groups of Members sent off to inquire and to report as laymen on what they discover and what they think about it. Today it is primarily the complex pattern of state activity to which the House directs the attention of those appointed to advise it in this way. This has certain consequences for what select committees of scrutiny can actually do and for the manner in which they operate. The activities of the state are manifold and continuing and impose their own imperatives on Members of Parliament who scrutinize them. As laymen devoting but a part of their time to such tasks they sail between the Scylla of superficial and sometimes emotive criticism and the Charybdis of judicious appraisal which rarely excites political attention. Moreover it has to be remembered that there is an inevitable disjunction between the time-scale of select committees and that of the floor of the House. The floor is dominated by two factors: the Government's desire to get its business through and the desire of both Opposition and individual Members to raise whatever matters appear to them to be of immediate political concern and advantage. Into a flow of activity determined by these two considerations it is rare indeed that the work of critical appraisal to which most select committees are dedicated can be inserted. The price they pay for their relatively wide freedom to inquire as they see fit is that the House attends only fitfully to the results of their labours. This situation is in turn a protection for Governments to whom most select committees *de facto* address their recommendations. Ministers and their officials are rarely under pressure to do what select committees advise or even demand. Benevolent circumspection is what has generally characterized the reactions of the Executive.

The crucial point is that the responsibility of the Government is still asserted on the floor of the House and here it is the firm and public ties of party which count. Such influence as select committees can acquire as well as their ability to work effectively depends, in contrast, on a certain abstinence in respect of party commitment. Political restraint is a condition of their successful operation. Yet political restraint cannot guarantee the support and interest of the House, for in it the Government and party predominate. This has become the Achilles heel of the rationale of scrutiny by select committee. The justification for the activity lies in an appeal to the common-sense judgement of the individual Member of the House. This no doubt represents a noble ideal, but it assumes a representative assembly with more control of its time than the House of Commons and a pattern of political loyalties substantially different from the realities of the later twentieth century. It has its roots in the era which preceded the emergence of highly disciplined and nationally organized parties. And it assumes too that knowledge of a specialized kind is far less important than it has become in the society we now have.

There is a rationale for scrutiny by select committee, but only within postulates which the House of Commons has sought sedulously and with some success to preserve. Yet in the world outside the House much has changed: the structures through which power and influence are exerted, the patterns of communication in society, the scale and character of problems of public concern, and the range of knowledge and skills relevant to handling them. If the ends of representative government by consent are to continue to be served, it may be that the postulates inside the House which have sustained scrutiny by select committee and much else besides will have gradually to change too.

IX

QUESTIONS AND DEBATES

Robert Borthwick

Questions

In the last quarter of the twentieth century Parliamentary Questions are regarded as one of the few surviving opportunities for the back-bench Member of Parliament to have anything like an effective voice on the floor of the House of Commons. Opinions vary about the value of Questions as a means of exercising control over administration but there is less disagreement that the existence of Question Time and other means of questioning provide a necessary outlet for private Members' energies.

Although their origins lie in the eighteenth century it was during the nineteenth that Questions became a significant feature on the parliamentary scene.[1] For much of the nineteenth century, it is true, they represented merely one among a number of ways in which back-bench Members could express themselves on the floor of the House. Towards the end of the century some of these other opportunities were restricted or eliminated and accordingly Questions, which to a large extent survived unscathed, were put under greater pressure and raised somewhat nearer their modern pedestal. For much of the nineteenth century, Questions, like other forms of business, were subject to few restrictions but gradually in the last three decades of the century greater formalization of procedure occurred. The rather easy-going system of the early and middle part of the century was put under strain—for example while gradually Questions were grouped together as one of the items to be taken before Public Business started, until the 1880s it

---

[1] On the early history of Questions see P. Howarth, *Questions in the House* (Bodley Head, 1956). Their subsequent development up to 1960 is well treated in D. N. Chester and N. Bowring, *Questions in Parliament* (Oxford, Clarendon Press, 1962). This whole section owes much to the latter work.

was usual for Questions to be read in full in the House and likewise until that time it was apparently possible (though increasingly frowned upon) to ask Questions without giving written notice.[1] Changes in 1886[2] (subsequently embodied in Standing Orders in 1888) altered both of these situations, though one of the consequences of requiring written notice was the development of the supplementary Question 'put for the purpose of elucidating any answer given in the House.'[3] The growth in the number of Questions in the latter part of the nineteenth century, largely but not entirely due to the efforts of Irish Members, precipitated these changes. Even with these restrictions Question Time in the House posed problems for Governments because it preceded Public Business and its fixed place in the timetable meant that its expansion was at the expense of government business. According to Chester and Bowring by 1900 more Questions were asked in one day than in the whole of the session of 1830.[4]

Thus as the twentieth century opened Questions had grown in volume and some of the main rules governing their place in the parliamentary system had been formalized. The situation at that time was that Questions could be asked on any day on which the House sat but in practice Ministers did not attend to answer Questions on Wednesdays. On the other four days in the week Questions were taken, as we have seen, as one of the items of business preceding Public Business and thus (along with Petitions and Private Bills) had the security of being completed before Public Business was started. The disadvantage from the point of view of Government in terms of the uncertainty which it faced is obvious and, though private Members' rights had been considerably reduced in the nineteenth century, by modern standards they were still very considerable in terms of their ability to delay government business. The tension of the early sessions of the century[5] probably made it inevitable that this situation would be altered.

The changes came in 1902 and took the form of placing a time limit for the first time on the period allowed for Questions.

---

[1] See Chester and Bowring, pp. 18–22.   [2] Ibid., pp. 20–1.
[3] Ibid., pp. 43–8.   [4] Ibid., p. 16.
[5] In 1901 'Question Time took up the equivalent of almost fifteen eight-hour days. Public Business seldom started before 6 p.m.' Ibid., p. 50.

Questions were to be taken from 2.15 to 2.55 p.m. (with Questions of an urgent nature of which private notice had been given taken from 2.55 to 3 p.m.) on each of four days;[1] thus allowing only 40 minutes for Questions. From the Government's point of view this gave it a guaranteed share of the House's time for its business and a much greater certainty as to the time at which that business would start. These changes, from the back-benchers point of view, were less drastic than those their sponsor (Mr. Balfour) had originally proposed. Those would have involved moving Questions away from the early part of business to a period between 7.15 and 8 p.m. with any remaining unanswered being dealt with at midnight. Had such proposals been accepted the history of Questions in the twentieth century would have been very different.

These changes in 1902 laid the basis for the twentieth-century framework of Question Time and, with a modification in 1906, substantially provided the modern position as regards the place of Questions in the parliamentary timetable. In 1906 the fixed starting time was removed so that Questions could be taken as soon as the earlier business (Prayers, unopposed Private Business, etc.) was completed thereby enlarging Question Time by at least five minutes and possibly as much as fifteen.[2] Henceforth Question Time was of uncertain length but of a maximum of 55 minutes.

An important element in the changes made in 1902 was the introduction of the distinction between starred and unstarred Questions. The latter were to receive a written answer as were any starred Questions which were not reached or which Members were not present to ask. Other changes at this time included lengthening the period of notice required for Questions for oral answer.[3] Now Questions would only be answered which had appeared on the Notice Paper for the previous day. The Government had suggested that Questions considered of greatest importance be assured of oral answers by careful

[1] These four days were now to be Monday, Tuesday, Wednesday, and Thursday.

[2] Chester and Bowring, pp. 85–6.

[3] Up to this point it had been possible for a Question to be put down up until the Notice Paper for the relevant day went to the printers (usually late in the preceding day). Ibid., p. 77.

arrangement of the Order Paper but this idea failed to gain much support.[1] In the remainder of the first session in which the new rules applied the time available for Questions proved sufficient on all but five occasions.[2]

As noted above the place of Question Time in the Parliamentary Day was to all intents and purposes settled by 1906 and though the times of sitting have subsequently altered, the overall period of 45–55 minutes has remained unaffected.

It is convenient, having set out the basic position of Questions near the beginning of the century, to consider their subsequent development in a number of sections. So that attention will be given first (and at greatest length) to starred Questions, then to Questions for written answers and finally to Private Notice Questions.

Starred Questions

There has, not surprisingly, been a growth in the number of Questions on the Order Paper since the beginning of the century, but this has by no means been a steady progression. The earlier totals are in general lower than those for recent years but whether expressed as sessional totals or as daily averages[3] the heaviest pressure came in two immediate post-war sessions, 1919 (total 16,378, daily average 126) and 1945–6 (total 21,135, daily average 128). In general the daily averages in the post-Second World War period are higher than those for the 1930s but lower than those for the early 1920s. Of course what these figures do not show is the number of starred Questions actually answered at Question Time. Here the picture is a corrective to the figures above pointing to a fairly steady decline in the capacity of Question Time.

After the changes of 1902 60–70 Questions were answered orally each day and in 1919 'there were many days when 75 or more starred Questions were answered orally'.[4] The daily average in 1938–9 and in 1945–6 was around 60—in the 1960s it dropped to around 40 and by the mid-1970s to around 25. The reasons for this decline are several and include (but only partly) the rise of the supplementary, the lengthening of

---

[1] Ibid., pp. 80–2. [2] Ibid., pp. 84–5.
[3] Ibid., pp. 87–8. [4] Ibid., p. 114.

ministerial replies (both to original Questions and to supplementaries), the lengthening of supplementaries themselves,
and the styles of the Speakers who differ in their attitude to
progress at Question Time.

Surprisingly in view of the increased pressure placed on
Question Time, until recent years unstarred Questions had not
grown much in volume. The daily average in the early years of
the century was around 20 and this was true at the end of the
1950s. There had of course been high spots in between: a daily
average of 30 in 1945–6 for example and of 27 in 1919 and
1939–40.[1] Since 1962–3 however the daily average has risen
very noticeably: from 31 in that year to 37 in 1963–4, to 46 in
1964–5, to 56 in 1965–6, 77 in 1967–8,[2] 79 in 1968–9, 97 in
1971–2, and 110 in 1972–3. There has thus been an explosion
in Questions for written answer over the last decade or so. These
recent increases reflect a change in the use of written Questions
from the search for information to the barrage technique where
an impression is sought merely by the volume of Questions[3]
and are in part also a result of the tighter restrictions on the
tabling of starred Questions.

Given the tremendous expansion in government activity and
in the people's expectations of government activity in this
century[4] it is perhaps surprising that the growth in Parliamentary Questions and the pressure on Question Time has not been
greater. That it has not has been due in part to a number of
limitations that have been placed on Question Time and the
asking of starred Questions. These limitations have taken a
number of forms:

(a) limitations in number
(b) limitations on period of notice
(c) limitations on what is in order
(d) development of the rota system

It will be convenient here to consider briefly each of these
developments.

[1] See Table ibid., pp. 87–8.

[2] D. N. Chester, 'Questions in Parliament' in A. H. Hanson and Bernard
Crick (eds.), *The Commons in Transition* (Fontana, 1970), p. 102.

[3] Unstarred Questions are discussed more fully below at pp. 489–71.

[4] This point is made more fully in a Memorandum to the Select Committee on Parliamentary Questions, 1971–2, by D. N. Chester, H.C. 393
(1971–2), p. 87, para. 3.

(a) *Limitation in number of questions to be asked*

In the nineteenth century there had been no limit on the number of Questions each M.P. might ask on any day. With the introduction of a limit on Question Time a self-denying ordinance had limited to 8 the Questions any Member might ask on one day. This agreement was formalized in 1909. This became four in 1919, three in the following year, and two in 1960.[1] This remained the overall limit until 1972, though a change was made in 1971 so that M.P.s' second Questions addressed to the Minister at the top of the list that day or to the Prime Minister were answered only after all the first Questions to that Minister had been dealt with.[2] In 1972 a further change was made (and introduced in 1973) so that not more than eight Questions for oral answer might be tabled in a period of 10 sitting days ahead with not more than two Questions tabled for any one day and only one Question to any Minister. This had the virtue of being a much simpler prescription than the scheme it replaced. Under that scheme any number of Questions might be tabled for oral answer with a decision being made to remove those in excess of two only two days before they were answered. This opened up the possibility of Members deliberately tabling large numbers of Questions, either to create an impression on government departments or to maximize their chances of securing a high place on the list when the printer put the Questions in order.[3]

(b) *Period of notice*

As noted already it was not until the 1880s that written notice of Questions was required. In 1902 the period of notice was altered so that Questions had to appear on the Notice Paper of the day before. Now it must be two days before the Question is to be asked.[4] The opposite problem of Questions being put

[1] See Chester and Bowring, p. 108.

[2] See *Second Report from the Select Committee on Procedure*, 1969–70, H.C. 198, para. 14. For examples see *H.C. Debs.*, Vol. 815, cols. 640–1. (All references to Commons Debates are from the 5th series.)

[3] See H.C. 393, *Report*, paras. 15–19 and Appendix 7. For the implementation see *H.C. Debs.*, Vol. 848, cols. 994–5.

[4] Except for Expedited Questions see S.O. No. 8(5) (1975 edn. of Standing Orders, H.C. 154 of 1974–5) and Chester and Bowring, p. 232.

down too far in advance was tackled in 1965 by a limit of three weeks (to limit the pre-empting of the Order Paper). This was reduced to ten sitting days in 1971.[1]

(c) *Limitations as to what is in order*
Limits on time available, period of notice required, the rota system, and so on are not the only hazards with which the would-be questioner has to contend. As substantial, though less apparent, are the formal requirements surrounding the content of his Questions. These requirements derive from the basic principle that 'the purpose of a question is to obtain information or press for action'. The rules which flow from this are based on Speakers' rulings, given either in the House or in private, over the years and in practice enforced by the Clerks in the Table Office, subject to appeal in cases of dispute to the Speaker.[2]

The restrictions vary greatly in their importance.[3] Some are merely extensions to Questions of the general rules of the House, for example that offensive expressions should not be included in Questions. Some have appeared trivial or to have had trivial consequences: quotations are not permitted in Questions thereby ruling out anything appearing in inverted commas, except apparently the names of ships.[4] Sometimes the results are puzzling: thus while the Prime Minister may be asked 'whether statements made outside Parliament by Ministers of Cabinet Rank on public occasions' represent government policy, Questions about such statements by other Ministers are not in order. Other rules are more substantial: Questions may not refer to matters *sub judice*, nor reflect on the decision of a court of law. Likewise they must not reflect on the sovereign or on members of the Royal family. Questions must not refer to the confidential advice of Ministers in fields such as the granting of honours, ecclesiastical patronage, the appointment

[1] See *Second Report from the Select Committee on Procedure*, 1969–70, H.C. 198, para. 13. For implementation see *H.C. Debs.*, Vol. 815, cols. 641–3.

[2] *Report from the Select Committee on Parliamentary Questions*, 1971–2, H.C. 393. Memorandum by the Principal Clerk of the Table Office, paras. 15–17.

[3] For a full list see Erskine May, *Parliamentary Practice*, 18th edn. (Butterworth, 1971), pp. 232–9.

[4] H.C. 393 (1971–2). Memorandum by the Principal Clerk of the Table Office, para. 18.

and dismissal of Privy Councillors, or the dissolution of Parliament. Questions which are 'multiplied with slight variations on the same point' are not permitted,[1] likewise Questions 'requesting information set forth in accessible documents or in ordinary works of reference' may not be asked.

Two other categories of restriction deserve rather fuller consideration. The first of these derives from the rule that Questions must relate to matters for which Ministers are responsible or which could be made so by legislative or administrative action. In the immediate post-Second World War period this caused some problems in connection with the extension of industries in public ownership. Questions on the industries were 'restricted to those matters for which a Minister is made responsible by the statute concerned or by other legislation'.[2] In practice this meant that Ministers refused to answer Questions on the day-to-day administration of the industries. Such refusals were not only unpopular but also were sufficient to block further Questions on these subjects for the remainder of a session. In May 1948 the Speaker Clifton Brown announced a new policy on his part for dealing with Questions in this controversial area. While accepting the rules about ministerial responsibility the Speaker indicated that he would in future authorize acceptance of a Question asking for a statement where it had previously been refused on a matter deemed of 'public importance'. At the same time he acknowledged that this left open the possibility that a Minister might still refuse to answer a Question. As Chester and Bowring point out, much of the difficulty was due to the political tension surrounding the issue of nationalization at that time rather than to the inherent problem raised by their constitutional position.[3]

The other area meriting discussion relates to the bar against repeating a Question (or substantially the same Question) in a parliamentary session. Until 1972 this barrier was absolute so that if a Question had been answered or an answer refused the

[1] Apparently no action has been taken under this heading since the 1953–1954 session. See *Select Committee on Parliamentary Questions, Minutes of Evidence* Qs 387–91.
[2] Erskine May, p. 326.
[3] Chester and Bowring, p. 305. Their Appendix II covers this matter in some detail.

Clerks would block any further Questions in that session. The 1971–2 Select Committee on Parliamentary Questions recommended that only where a Question was answered should the rule against repeating it in that session be continued. Where 'a Minister has refused to take the action or give the information asked for in a Question he should be able to be asked the same Question in three months time'.[1] In several areas, for example the arrangements for national security, ministerial refusals had hardened into rules preventing such Questions being asked at all.[2] In these 'closed' areas the Committee recommended that 'Ministers should be able to be asked once every Session whether they will now answer such Questions'.[3] These recommendations were accepted[4] and as a result there has been some softening of previous attitudes.

Evidence presented to the Committee drew attention to the narrowing effect of precedents[5] and in their Report the Committee took an expansive line in encouraging the Speaker to break free from the accumulated weight of previous rulings. Thus they recommended that 'a Question which is otherwise within the rules of order should not be disallowed solely on the ground that it conflicts with rulings previously given'.[6] The result of this has been some liberalization of the rules surrounding Questions. The Clerks now feel freer in allowing Questions. In part this change was inevitable: with the increase in the number of Questions submitted detailed attention lavished on each was bound to be less. The world of 10,000 Questions a session is rather different from that of 25–30,000 Questions a session.

(d) Development of the rota system
In the nineteenth century questions were addressed to Ministers in the order in which they were received by the Clerks; the only

---

[1] *Report from the Select Committee on Parliamentary Questions*, 1971–2, H.C. 393, para. 7.

[2] Ibid., para. 6. An extensive list of such areas is given in Appendix 9 of the Report.

[3] Ibid., para. 7.

[4] See the statement by the Speaker, 20 Dec. 1972. *H.C. Debs.*, Vol. 848, cols. 1335–7.

[5] H.C. 393 (1971–2), *Minutes of Evidence* Qs 428–39.

[6] Ibid., *Report*, para. 10. See also *H.C. Debs.*, Vol. 848, cols. 1335–7.

exception to this being Questions to the Prime Minister which, originally as a kindness to the elderly Mr. Gladstone, were arranged last on the Order Paper from 1881 onwards. Clearly this rather easy-going system was threatened by the introduction of a time limit for Questions and as part of the 1902 reform package it was agreed that Questions in the first 50 each day should be grouped for each Minister. According to Chester and Bowring this practice was extended to all starred Questions on the daily list without any announcement to this effect being made.[1]

In 1904 Questions to the Prime Minister were put not later than number 51 and then 45 to ensure that they were reached. The arrangements regarding other Ministers were still in a sense haphazard, the grouping depending entirely on the Questions that were put down for answer. This system was viable only so long as, even with the time limit, there was a reasonable chance of all Questions being reached. Inevitably the system did not always function to maximum satisfaction: where Questions remained unanswered these could involve matters of substance and major Departments. The first step towards a rota system was to give certain Departments a fixed place; thus in 1906 it was announced that Questions to the Foreign Secretary would come first on Tuesdays and Thursdays and that Questions to the Irish and Colonial Secretaries would also have some priority.[2] This system which seems to have operated until the end of the First World War brought a very large increase in the number of Questions.

Exactly when the pre-war system changed is not easy to say. The first typed rota appeared in 1924 but Chester and Bowring believe that the new system which it reflects had already been in existence for some years before 1924.[3] The new system involved giving most Departments a fixed order at each of the four Question Times. There were in effect four groups of Departments at each Question Time: the beginning group whose questions started before the Prime Minister, then the Prime Minister himself (and the Treasury Minister on Tuesdays) whose Questions started not later than No. 45, then the

[1] Chester and Bowring, pp. 128–9.   [2] Ibid., pp. 129–31.
[3] Ibid., p. 134. Developments down to 1961 are clearly set out in pp. 134–44.

Departments who were most unlikely to be reached, and finally Departments unlisted for that day whose Questions would come before the Prime Minister if less than 45 Questions were down for the beginning group or otherwise after the beginning group's Questions had been completed.

This stage, it will be seen, was not a rota in the full sense in that the position of Departments on any day remained the same from week to week. That next stage was reached in 1929 when it was laid out that on Tuesdays four Departments (Lord Privy Seal, Board of Trade, War Office, and Scottish Office) would take turns at being first, second, third, and fourth—though on Tuesdays, as before, the Prime Minister, the Chancellor of the Exchequer, and the Financial Secretary to the Treasury were to come at no later than Question No. 45. Thus the principle of a rota was introduced; at first for only one day a week and involving only four Departments—one of the four was changed in 1930 and a fifth added in the same year. A further refinement came in 1938 when an element of rotation was introduced on Wednesdays and Thursdays: in the case of Wednesdays the Foreign Office and Air Ministry were to occupy the first two places with three Departments rotating behind them. On Thursdays the Ministry of Labour was to be first and then four Departments were to have rotating places. It will be seen that these additional elements of rotation were not in quite the same form as the Tuesday system. This rather piece-meal system was overhauled in 1945. Then the rota system was extended to all four days of Questions and covering six Departments each day over a six-week cycle though some seven Departments continued to have a fixed place (and did not appear in the rota) beginning after the Prime Minister's Questions, which continued at no later than No. 45.

The final stage in the evolution of the rota came in 1952, as a response to the demands upon Question Time, when the fixed place of all except Prime Minister's Questions was eliminated. All Departments were now placed on the rota—on Mondays a seven-Department seven-week cycle; on the other three days an eight-Department eight-week cycle applied. The changes since then have involved altering Departments within this framework to take account of changes in their existence and in parliamentary interest in their affairs. A further refinement in recent years, with the growth of large (conglomerate) Departments, has been the appearance of the parent Department at several points in the rota taking over the spots occupied by hitherto separate Departments. This has raised problems of reaching the areas of previously separate Departments.[1] The Prime Minister has retained his special place on the rota though his position was advanced from not later than No. 45 to not later than No. 40 in February 1960 but this did not solve the problem of reaching him and in 1961 his position was changed to 3.15 p.m. on Tuesdays and Thursdays, thus giving a guaranteed 15 minutes on each of these days. In 1961 too the reference to Prime Minister's Questions on Mondays and Wednesdays was allowed to drop from the rota.

More recently Britain's entry into the European Communities has placed a further demand on Question Time. The problem of gathering information on Common Market affairs was discussed by a select committee in 1972–3 who recommended that 'a place for questions relating wholly to EEC matters should be inserted in the rota at a fixed time'.[2] This recommendation was accepted by the Government[3] and they now have a separate slot within Foreign Office Questions.

Growth of Supplementaries

Part of the explanation for the decrease during this century in the number of Questions reached at Question Time is the growth in the number and length of supplementary Questions. From its original purpose of clarifying ministerial reply supplementary has grown to become almost the main point of the oral Questions. While already by the start of the century the supplementary had acquired something of its modern purpose as a means of harassing Ministers,[4] the use made of it was modest by present-day standards. As Chester and Bowring point out, in the early part of this century 'there were fewer

---

[1] H.C. 393 (1971–2), *Report*, para. 30.

[2] *Second Report from the Select Committee on European Secondary Legislation*, 1972–3, H.C. 463–I, para. 92.

[3] *H.C. Debs.*, Vol. 872, cols. 523–55 (written answers). See also M. Ryan and P. Isaacson, 'Parliament and the European Communities', *Parliamentary Affairs*, Vol. XXVIII, pp. 209–10.

[4] Chester and Bowring, p. 44.

supplementaries than starred Questions; on average one supplementary for every two to three main answers'.[1] In the early 1960s when they were writing there were roughly three supplementaries for every two main Questions.[2] By 1974 for the same week of the session the ratio had dropped to two supplementary Questions for each main Question. Question Time has become supplementary time. Moreover, it would be rare nowadays for a Question not to attract a supplementary; yet in a selected week in 1937 or 1946 no supplementaries were asked on a daily average of 19 and 18 Questions respectively.[3]

However, it is not merely that supplementaries have grown in number, they have grown also in length. In 1919 the average was just over four lines of *Hansard* since when there has been a growth as shown in Table V.1.[4]

TABLE V.1

Average length of supplementary (lines in Hansard)
(week before Christmas in each case)

1937	5·0
1946	5·1
1949	6·5
1954	8·5
1959	10·0
1964	8·7
1969	7·9
1974	9·7

So too has the length of ministerial replies to supplementaries grown. From just over 3·5 lines in 1919 it was only 3·0 in 1937, had reached 4·0 by 1949, 4·7 in 1954, 7·8 in 1959, and had dropped to 6·6 by 1964. More recently these have lengthened again: 1969 to 8·6 lines and by 1974 to 10·3 lines. Against this however there has been some shortening of ministerial replies to original Questions. Thus they occupied an average of 9·2

---

[1] Ibid., p. 115.
[2] *Second Report from the Select Committee on Procedure*, 1964–5, H.C. 188. Memorandum by the Second Clerk Assistant, Table 1, p. 9.
[3] Loc. cit., Table 1, Note 2.
[4] Loc. cit., Table 1, updated.

lines in 1919, 10·0 in 1937, 8·6 in 1949, 6·2 in 1954, 7·1 in 1959, and 6·7 in 1964 (and only 5·5 in 1962). By 1969 they were down to 5·9 lines and in 1974 to 4·8 lines.

Inevitably there is a conflict between supplementaries and original Questions. That more original Questions be answered almost certainly means fewer supplementaries. But this may go against the object of Question Time in the sense of pursuing a point at some length and exposing a Minister to detailed scrutiny. The dilemma is insoluble—though various palliatives have been suggested over the years: printing initial ministerial answers, shorter supplementaries, settling for mini-debates on a small number of issues, and so on. None has achieved much support.

Questions for written answer

Questions that were unstarred, that is for written answer, were part of the reforms on 1902 when for the first time a definite time limit was placed on Question Time. One of the initial attractions of unstarred Questions was that answers to them were to be printed and circulated with the Votes, thus providing a permanent record of the answer—something which did not become reliably available for answers to oral Questions (or on a daily and weekly basis) until *Hansard* became an official verbatim record in 1909.[1]

It remained true that one of the advantages that starred Questions had, apart from the opportunity of putting a supplementary, was that an answer was required on a particular day whereas there was no due date for unstarred Questions. The early assumption was that answers to unstarred Questions circulated with the Votes would be as quick as for starred Questions. In practice answers have not always been forthcoming as quickly as Members would like and throughout this century there have been promises from Governments that this would be improved. In 1937 Departments were instructed to inform questioners if no reply could be provided within four days. In 1946 the Government accepted a recommendation of the Select Committee on Procedure that replies to unstarred Questions should be provided within seven days of the Question

[1] Chester and Bowring, p. 66.

appearing in the Notice Paper. This period was reduced in 1960 to three working days.[1]

The aspirations for a speedy answer to at least some unstarred Questions were endorsed by the Select Committee on Parliamentary Questions in 1972. They recommended in effect that in future there should be two types of unstarred Questions. The existing sort would continue but a new category would be created, 'where a Member particularly wants a written answer on a named day'.[2] These were to be distinguished by the letter 'W' and to be subject to the same minimum notice as oral Questions. The proposal was adopted at the end of 1972 and the change embodied in Standing Orders.[3] The result has been of considerable significance: the category has become popular with Members, partly, no doubt, because its introduction coincided with the much tighter rules about the tabling of starred Questions, and partly because its advantages became known to Members. There is perhaps some danger that the addition of a 'W' to a Question will become almost automatic for many Members with consequent problems for Departments. This may result in a greater use by them of 'holding' answers as they are faced by greater pressure of time.

Despite these efforts to make the unstarred Question more attractive and despite the congestion surrounding starred Questions at Question Time it is only in recent years that unstarred Questions have shown a marked rise in popularity.

As noted earlier, the average number of unstarred Questions per day in the 1950s was much the same as in the pre-First World War period (20 per day on average for 10 sessions after 1902, 18 per day in 10 sessions in 1950s).[4] Between these times there are periods of greater activity such as 1919–25 but also periods of lesser activity, e.g. 1930 and especially 1931–6. In the past the periods of higher volume for unstarred Questions tended to parallel those for starred Questions. In part this is, as Chester and Bowring point out, because in such periods any surplus over individuals' daily maxima, unless deferred, are automatically 'destarred'.[5] This factor is of course likely to be compounded when the individual's daily ration of starred

---

[1] Ibid., pp. 111–12.   [2] H.C. 393 (1971–2), *Report*, para. 28.
[3] *H.C. Debs.*, Vol. 848, cols. 1070, 1336.   [4] See above p. 480.
[5] Chester and Bowring p. 110.

Questions is reduced as it was in 1919 and 1920. The interesting point remains, however, that it was not until the mid-1960s that there was any marked increase in the number of unstarred Questions.

Thus in 1967–8 for the first time the number of unstarred Questions exceeded the number of starred ones: 13,601 against 11,588. This has been true in every session since then. In 1970–1 for example there were 20,300 unstarred compared to 13,646 starred Questions.[1] By 1972–3 there were 17,836 unstarred and 7,952 starred Questions and in 1974 11,777 written and 3,824 starred Questions. The figures are slightly misleading in that not all unstarred Questions are handed in in that form and with the increase in the volume of Questions the process of unstarring has taken a heavier toll. However in 1970–1 48 per cent of all Questions were handed in as unstarred and from 1972–3 onwards unstarred Questions have been a great majority of those Questions handed in.[2] Why has this happened? In part undoubtedly for the reasons suggested above but also because their potential for mounting mini-campaigns by way of a large number of Questions on a particular topic has been belatedly recognised. This of course raised the question whether such use will lead eventually to some limit on the number of unstarred Questions allowed.[3] One partial solution to this problem that has been suggested is to allow longer written Questions. In evidence to the Select Committee on Parliamentary Questions 1972 the Principal Clerk of the Table Office suggested that the ruling that Questions should not exceed 70 words in length might be relaxed.[4] The Committee did not take up this suggestion in their Report. According to one authority on this subject the problems created by the increased case of unstarred Questions are likely to require the attentions of a select committee in the near future.[5]

[1] H.C. 393 (1971–2). Memorandum by the Principal Clerk of the Table Office, para. 35.

[2] The change in the rules regarding starred Questions undoubtedly encouraged this trend.

[3] A possibility raised in H.C. 393 (1971–2). Memorandum by the Principal Clerk of the Table Office, para. 40.

[4] Ibid., para. 42.

[5] H.C. 393 (1971–2). Memorandum by D. N. Chester, para. 12.

Private Notice Questions

As part of the reforms of 1902 there was made available a period
of five minutes after other Questions for the answering of
Questions asked by Private Notice. The intention was to
restrict the period to Questions 'of an urgent character' (and
also to Questions relating to the business of the House).[1] In the
changes of 1906 this meant that Private Notice Questions could
be taken at 3.45 p.m. at the end of Questions. The procedure
has survived largely unchanged since that time. The rules
governing such Questions are strict: it must be 'of an urgent
character, and relate either to a matter of public importance or
to the arrangement of business'.[2] The acceptance of such a
Question is at the discretion of the Speaker. The advantage of
the procedure is that it permits a Question to be answered on
the day on which notice is given (providing notice is given to
the Speaker by 12 noon). According to Chester and Bowring
about forty such Questions a year are allowed[3] and this figure
seems not to have altered much over the years. The rules
surrounding admissability are rather strictly adhered to—
though even so such Questions are a regular feature of the
House's business. In deciding whether to allow a Private Notice
Question Speakers have considered themselves bound by
precedents. One result has been that Questions on certain
categories of events (for example fatal railway accidents) have
acquired an almost automatic right to be asked. Attempts have
been made in recent years to loosen some of these restrictions.
As a result of a Report from the Select Committee on Procedure
in 1967 the Speaker was given greater flexibility in accepting
Private Notice Questions. Previously he had been obliged to
refuse such Questions where there was a Question down for oral
or written answer on the same subject or where such a Question
was subsequently handed in before he made his decision. The
change in 1967 enabled him to disregard such Questions for
written answers and to take account only of Questions that were
'liable to be answered orally within a reasonable period of time,

---

[1] Chester and Bowring, p. 72.
[2] S.O. 8(3) (1975 edn., H.C. 154 of 1974–5).
[3] Chester and Bowring, pp. 105–6.

having regard to the urgency of the subject matter'.[1] The Select Committee on Parliamentary Questions in 1972 recommended that the Speaker 'should no longer feel bound to follow individual previous rulings in deciding whether to allow a Question to be asked after Private Notice'.[2] This has meant that the Speaker and his advisers are freer to decide whether to allow a Private Notice Question,[3] though it is unlikely to mean any great increase in the number of such Questions accepted.

Questions to the Prime Minister

The way in which a special place for Prime Minister's Questions has been carved out has already been traced.[4] What these changes reflect is a greater desire to question the Prime Minister and certainly an unwillingness to risk, due to the increase in the pressure on Question Time, being unable to question him twice a week. Under the system of the Prime Minister answering at a Question of fixed number (whether number 51, 45, or 40), there could be no guarantee that his Questions would be reached and even less that all Questions to him would be reached. So it was that in July 1961 the change was made to take the Prime Minister's Questions at 3.15 p.m. on Tuesdays and Thursdays while by later the same year the explicit references to Prime Minister's Questions on Mondays and Wednesdays had been allowed to wither away.

The move to a fixed time on two days a week both reflected and encouraged the growth in the importance of the event. According to G. W. Jones, Mr. Macmillan was responsible for a take-off in Prime Minister's Questions which none of his successors has either been able or wanted to reverse. He points

---

[1] *Fifth Report from the Select Committee on Procedure*, 1966–7, H.C. 410, para. 6.

[2] H.C. 393 (1971–2), *Report*, para. 29. This was in part a response to the suggestion that perhaps it was no longer necessary to automatically allow a Private Notice Question whenever there was a fatal railway accident. See Memorandum by the Principal Clerk of the Table Office, para. 34.

[3] For the implementation of this suggestion see *H.C. Debs.*, Vol. 848, cols., 1335–7.

[4] On Questions to the Prime Minister see G. W. Jones, 'The Prime Minister and Parliamentary Questions', *Parliamentary Affairs*, Vol. XXVI, pp. 260–73.

out that such Questions grew from about three per week in
1953–4 to about fifteen per week in 1958–9. 'Between 1964 and
1969 more starred questions were handed in to the Table
Office for the prime minister than for any other minister.'[1] In
the 1970s the creation of conglomerate Departments altered
this but the Prime Minister still leads in Questions answered
orally. In another sense the pressure on the Prime Minister's
Question period has increased: while the average number of
Questions answered remained fairly constant through the 1960s
(about six or seven Questions or groups of Questions in each
quarter-hour period), because of the increase in the number of
Questions tabled, this represents a declining percentage from
nearly 80 per cent in 1962–3 to about 40 per cent in 1969–70
and 1971–2.[2]

The result has been a complete change in the nature of
Prime Minister's Question period. No longer is it simply a
search for information in those areas where the Prime Minister
has some special responsibility or where he has taken a special
interest. Instead it has become in Jones's words 'a twice-weekly
confrontation about the competence of the government'.[3]

Inevitably there has been interest in extending the Prime
Minister's Question period. The Select Committee on Parliamentary Questions in 1972 devoted a good deal of attention
to the subject and recommended that 'for an experimental
period the time of Prime Minister's Questions on Tuesdays shall
be extended by fifteen minutes until 3.45 p.m.'.[4] This suggestion
was not accepted. Concern has been expressed also about the
need to make the Prime Minister's period more topical and to
avoid repetition of Questions. These desires arise because of the
regularity of the Prime Minister's slot in the timetable. A
further problem is the vagueness felt necessary in framing
Questions to the Prime Minister so as to avoid their being transferred to an appropriate departmental Minister. Necessarily
Questions are of the sort asking whether the Prime Minister
has plans to visit a particular area, which enable the real point
to be made in the supplementary where it could technically,
but is unlikely practically, to be ruled out of order. In the words
of the Select Committee on Parliamentary Questions: 'The

---

[1] Ibid., pp. 261–2.   [2] Ibid., p. 264.   [3] Ibid., p. 263.
[4] H.C. 393 (1971–2), *Report*, para. 27.

principal cause of discontent amongst Members appears to be the contrast between the difficulty in tabling a straightforward Question to the Prime Minister which will not be transferred, and the ease with which almost any proposition can be put to him in the form of a supplementary Question.'[1] There is no easy solution to this problem: a stricter policy of transfers to departmental Ministers would be unpopular and would in any case be difficult precisely because of the element of disguise in the Questions; likewise stricter interpretations of what was permissable in supplementaries might well produce greater discontent, and thereby cause greater loss of time, than a continuation of the present interpretations. From the point of view of the Civil Service one of the major weaknesses in the present system is that it has, because of the necessarily vague nature of many Questions to the Prime Minister, to prepare for a wide range of possible supplementaries. To meet this and other objections to the present operation of Prime Minister's Questions it was suggested to the 1972 Select Committee on Parliamentary Questions that consideration might be given to allowing one of the weekly Prime Ministerial slots to be used for oral Questions without notice. It was argued that this would make Questions more topical, obviate the need to use 'disingenuous devices' at present in vogue to keep Questions in order and to avoid their being transferred.[2] This proposal did not meet with the approval of the Select Committee who argued that it would be 'to surrender to the tendency to trivialise Prime Minister's Question time', as well as placing an unfair burden on the Speaker.[3]

Questions and Questioners

So far we have looked at Questions mainly in procedural terms; it is necessary now to turn to their more political features: in particular their value as an instrument of parliamentary control or criticism of the executive, and as an outlet for private Members.

[1] Ibid., para. 22.
[2] Ibid. Memorandum by the Principal Clerk of the Table Office, paras. 22–32 and especially paras. 29–32.
[3] Ibid., *Report*, para. 23. See also paras. 20–2 and 24–7.

There is no doubt that Question Time is regarded as a prime parliamentary occasion. Its traditional status is based on the view that it provides a profound test of ministerial quality, an occasion when the affairs of Government can be scrutinized and a time for Governments to defend their policies against searching inquiry. For the individual M.P. there is the opportunity to present and air grievances (providing ministerial responsibility is, or can be plausibly argued to be, involved), to act as the representative of his constituency and as a partisan party member attacking poor quality policies, decisions, or individuals represented in the Government of the day.

The literature on British politics is full of references to the value of Questions and Question Time. In the first decade of the century Redlich wrote of the Questions put to Ministers as playing 'a very important part in the proceedings of the House of Commons'.[1] Another foreign observer, Lowell, seems to have been even more impressed when he wrote that Questions turn 'a searchlight upon every corner of the public service'.[2]

More recently a glowing testimonial to the institution has come in these terms: 'There is no test of a Minister's worth so searching as question-time. Nothing brings out his qualities of moral strength and perspicacity so clearly . . . [Questions] are one of the most effective methods of control of the executive ever invented.'[3] These are bold claims and are not to be accepted entirely without hesitation for others have taken less optimistic views. Before the First World War Sidney Low was writing of the questioning of 'the advisers of the Crown' as an ancient and valuable privilege but one which had limitations: 'this method of extracting information on the actions of the Executive is in practice considerably circumscribed'.[4] More recent writers have often expressed themselves more bluntly. Mackintosh for example sees a decline in the efficacy of the institution in recent times: 'Question Time began to lose its

---

[1] J. Redlich, *The Procedure of the House of Commons* (Constable, 1908), Vol. II, p. 241.

[2] A. L. Lowell, *The Government of England* (New York, Macmillan, 1920) (first published 1908), Vol. I, p. 332.

[3] E. Taylor, *The House of Commons at Work* (Harmondsworth, Penguin, 1963, 5th edn.), pp. 113–14. By the 7th edition in 1967 this last phrase had become 'a most effective method of control of the executive'.

[4] S. Low, *The Government of England* (Fisher Unwin, 1904), pp. 91–2.

force after the Second World War as so many members wanted to ask questions in the same limited period of time that the Speaker decided to limit each member to one supplementary question and the whole process was so speeded up that any reasonably competent minister has no difficulty in parrying criticism.'[1] While Mackintosh may be exaggerating both the consciousness of the Speaker's decision and the impact which it may have had, the general point he is making serves as a corrective to some of the grander claims for Questions.

What then are we to conclude? It is probably the case that some of the claims made for Question Time as a device for mercilessly throwing light on the far corners of Governments are overstated. It would be generally accepted now that for this purpose Question Time has considerable limitations: it is partly, as Mackintosh points out, a matter of the pressure of time, partly a matter of information. M.P.s are unwilling or unable to develop their critical capacity to the point where the telling question can be formulated. But even if it could it is doubtful whether it would have a devastating effect as Governments of all persuasions have developed a defensive, some would say secretive, habit of mind when dealing with the House of Commons.[2]

Yet all this is not to say that the institution is without value, merely that as a means of finding out things it is severely limited. One has to balance the rather gloomy observations above by noting both the tremendous popularity of Questions among M.P.s and the fact that Question Time has become more than ever part of the inter-party battle. In that sense it is a legitimate and necessary part of the conflict model of politics that is at the heart of British parliamentary Government. Many of those who look for a different (even a more elevated) style at Question Time are in effect seeking to replace the existing model of politics with a consensual one. Those more critical of this attitude would of course say that it is an attempt to take

[1] J. P. Mackintosh, *The Government and Politics of Britain* (Hutchinson, 1970), p. 27.
[2] In part it depends on what is regarded as an accurate description of the constitution: this has some parallels with what Professor Birch calls the 'liberal' and 'Whitehall' views. See A. H. Birch, *Representative and Responsible Government* (Allen and Unwin, 1964).

the politics out of Question Time but it probably cannot be dismissed simply as anti-political in that sense.

Even those inclined to take a somewhat unsympathetic attitude to the effectiveness of Question Time usually admit that it is important to retain the device. There is, they feel, something salutary for Governments to be required, on four days a week during the session, to publicly justify themselves (whatever the limitations imposed by lack of time or lack of depth, freshness, and unpredictability in the Questions). In this sense Question Time serves both as a general pressure on Ministers to be always liable to account for their responsibilities and a safeguard which by its existence can be mobilized if unsatisfactory situations are rumoured.

It is important also to see Question Time from the point of view of the individual M.P. This is to view it not primarily as a check on administration or as a means of scoring points in the continuous election campaign of which the House of Commons is alleged to be the forum but as one of the devices open to the M.P. to raise a constituency point or an individual or group grievance. In this sense it is one of a range or mechanisms available to the M.P. to press his case. As such it comes somewhere between the private letter to a Minister and the raising of an issue in an adjournment debate or, more rarely, in a debate under Standing Order No. 9. As such the Question for oral answer serves a valuable purpose for the individual M.P. either as a threat of something to be resorted to or as a device for indicating publicly concern over some issue.

It would be impossible to measure in any meaningful way how influential Questions have been as a means of altering decisions, achieving actions, or influencing policy. As Johnson argues,[1] one can point to celebrated examples where positive results were achieved by Questions, for example the 1928 Questions about police treatment of Miss Savidge or in 1959 in the case of the Thurso boy. But, he points out, Question Time worked in these cases because they were matters which were 'fairly precisely defined' and which did not 'involve the political standing of the government too seriously'.[2] In such

[1] See N. Johnson, 'Parliamentary Questions and the Conduct of Administration', *Public Administration*, Vol. 39, pp. 131–48.
[2] Ibid., p. 144.

areas a Question may be successful in that information may be obtained, a mistake corrected, or a decision altered. But, suggests Johnson, 'immediately the Question strays on to wider issues involving more general policy matters and issues of political concern, then little, if anything, of practical significance can be achieved'.[1] The most that is likely to be gained in that situation is some loss of prestige by the Government of the day as it has to face perhaps a series of Questions on a topic.

Writing in 1962 Chester and Bowring attempted to correct any impression of the spectacular success of Question Time: 'As there have been some half a million starred Questions answered on the floor of the House since 1902 it would indeed be remarkable if a few examples of spectacular results could not be found.'[2] They add, however, that probably as much success was achieved by Members privately. Rather they preferred to stress the value of Questions and Question Time in terms of its being a device for 'emphasizing the individual responsibility of Ministers' and as a means of enabling 'a large number of miscellaneous issues to be dealt with quickly within the framework of parliamentary procedure'.[3]

Whatever the importance of Question time in the eyes of M.P.s (of this as reflected in demand see below) and of the public there is little dispute as to the importance of Question Time in terms of the attention given to it by the Civil Service. Given the points made above it seems unlikely that this attention arises from a fear of damaging inquiries arising in supplementaries (though the unexpected can never be ruled out) so much as from a concern to protect the reputation of the Minister and of the Department. Here we have to pay attention to the concept of the village society where a small but informed audience pass judgement. This may overlap, but need not, with the reactions of Parliament and the outside public.[4] One should add of course that Ministers themselves are likely to be concerned with their reputations, ambitious men anxious to advance their careers. 'A Minister cannot make a great Parliamentary reputation by the manner in which he answers

---

[1] Ibid., p. 143.   [2] Chester and Bowring, p. 286.   [3] Ibid., p. 287.
[4] For a discussion of this idea see H. Heclo and A. Wildavsky, *The Private Government of Public Money* (Macmillan, 1974). See especially in this context, pp. 11–12.

Questions, but if he cannot handle them effectively in the House he is unlikely to go far or even last long as a Minister.'[1] Answering Questions thus provides Ministers with an opportunity to reveal their capacity and the House with an opportunity to evaluate their performance.

Procedurally, as Johnson points out, the Civil Service treat Questions (especially starred ones) with a good deal of respect. 'It is customary for the permanent head of a department to see and approve replies to all Questions and this seems to be standard practice throughout Whitehall.'[2] Moreover, because of their urgency Questions take precedence in Departments over other business and this too gives them an importance in the eyes of civil servants.

Of course not all Questions pose fierce and difficult problems for Ministers and civil servants. As long ago as 1908 Redlich was pointing out that Questions 'are often arranged by the Government itself, so as to give them an opportunity of making announcements in a somewhat informal way'.[3] This facility is useful for Governments (especially favoured here is the unstarred Question since it rules out the felt need in modern times to raise a supplementary) as it enables them to make announcements of fact or policy or to get something on the record. It also helps to preserve the fading convention that all important announcements should first be made in the House of Commons.

In the 1970s this modestly useful, and essentially harmless, device acquired a new fame with allegations that far from resorting to the inspired Question merely to enable information to be provided a government Department was actually encouraging Questions from government back-benchers so as to head off hostile attacks from the Opposition. This so called 'planting' of Questions gave rise to a select committee to look into the affair.[4]

The evidence presented to this Committee suggested that there had indeed been some excess of zeal in the Department of the Environment in providing government back-benchers with Questions that would be helpful to the Department in terms

---

[1] Chester and Bowring, p. 237.　　　[2] Johnson, p. 132.
[3] Redlich, Vol. II, p. 242.
[4] Select Committee on Parliamentary Questions. In fact as will already be apparent the Committee dealt with more than just this limited issue.

both of their substance and of occupying a slice of the Order Paper. This practice was defended by the Minister concerned as a legitimate response to Opposition pressure at Question Time: '. . . the Opposition launched a campaign designed to pre-empt the Order Paper at Question Time on 10th and 31st March (1971). As a result of this they succeeded in having 30 questions answered orally as compared with six from Government supporters.'[1] At the same time, however, the Minister acknowledged that there was nothing improper in the Opposition tactics. The preparation of a 'bank' of Questions was further defended on the grounds that it had been done before, though where and when remained a little obscure.

In their Report the Committee drew a distinction between 'the use by the Government of "inspired" oral and written Questions to enable them to give information to the House, and the preparation of a "bank" of Questions the answers to which are of secondary importance to their use as a means of increasing the proportion of Questions on the Order Paper favourable to the Government.'[2] On the latter activity the Select Committee noted tartly that it was not for the Government 'to seek to redress the party balance of Questions on the Order Paper and Civil Servants should not in future be asked to prepare Questions for this purpose'.[3] When in December 1972 this Report was considered by the House of Commons it was announced that instructions were being issued to Departments to ensure that civil servants were not again involved in the preparation of this kind of Parliamentary Question.[4]

The Questions

In a survey of this sort it would be useful to offer some assessment of how the type of Questions asked has changed. Unfortunately this is not a matter that is easy to assess. The volume of Questions has already been dealt with both in terms of the number presented and the number answered orally. One can also say something about changing fashions in the subject matter of Questions as different topics have risen and fallen as matters

---

[1] H.C. 393 (1971–2), *Minutes of Evidence* Q.226.
[2] Ibid., *Report*, para. 36.   [3] Loc. cit.
[4] *H.C. Debs.*, Vol. 847, col. 462 and Vol. 848, col. 998.

of public concern. For example the casual reader of *Hansard* for the pre-First World War period cannot fail to be struck by the large number of Questions devoted to Ireland, often on points on minute local detail. Chester and Bowring refer to this: 'In the Session of 1905 the Ministers primarily responsible for Irish affairs answered a quarter of the written and nearly a third of the oral Questions.'[1] They go on to suggest that in the period 1906–14 perhaps one-third of all Questions related to Ireland.

In more recent times too one can see in Question Time some reflection of contemporary concerns. Thus in 1945–6 the War Office was extremely popular with a large number of Questions about demobilization; by 1947–8 attention had moved to the Ministry of Food while in the late 1950s the Colonial Office was the most questioned Department. Between 1964 and 1969, as Jones noted, 'more starred questions were handed in . . . for the prime minister than for any other minister'.[2] Behind came such Departments as Transport (second most popular in 1964–5 for example). By the end of the 1960s the large Departments such as Technology and Environment had taken over the leading places.

In terms of the changes in style and quality of Questions, however, it is difficult to be more than impressionistic. If one reads a selection of Question Times before 1914 and in the 1970s it seems that Questions for oral answer have become somewhat more general by the 1970s and perhaps also more argumentative in tone. This latter comment applies particularly to supplementaries where Questions are increasingly prefaced by remarks such as 'Is the Minister aware that I am disappointed with that answer?' This is perhaps the most general peg with which to preface the supplementary. By contrast Questions in the earlier period tended to be more concerned with gaining information and even supplementaries seem to share that aim. No doubt there is some connection here with the diminishing proportion of Questions that fail to attract a supplementary.[3] Probably also the change in tone reflects the fact that the answers to the original Questions are frequently known by the questioners and the purpose of the Questions is

[1] Chester and Bowring, p. 91.   [2] Jones, p. 262.
[3] See above pp. 487–8.

not to obtain information but to make some point via the supplementary. Johnson calls this '. . . perhaps the most significant change which there has been in the character of Question time'.[1]

Several changes have taken place in this area. Up until perhaps the Second World War a Question to a Minister was regarded 'as a matter between the Minister and the Member', whereas now it is seen as 'the possession of the House'.[2] Moreover until the post-war period there was apparently no presumption of a more or less automatic right to a supplementary on the part of the Member asking the original Question.

As regards the style of ministerial answers Johnson has argued that they were different early in the century. Then Ministers seem to have had less background information, to have been more willing to confess ignorance, and the House more willing to accept such confessions. The pressures on the Minister were arguably less also as the Questions were not concentrated as they are now thanks to the rota system.[3]

One of the ways, it seems agreed, in which Question Time has changed is that it has become less of a back-benchers occasion and rather more of an official Opposition occasion. This is not to say that the tabling of Questions does not remain primarily a back-bench affair but rather that Opposition frontbench spokesmen feel it appropriate (or perhaps required of them) to join in the supplementaries. It is, of course, possible to exaggerate the change that has taken place here. Chester and Bowring refer to a study[4] which indicated that in the 1929–30 session 10·9 per cent of the starred Questions and 17 per cent of the supplementaries were asked by 30 former Conservative Ministers; though they go on to suggest that much of the questioning was done by former Junior Ministers and many more prominent ex-Ministers had little part in it.[5] Moreover

---

[1] Johnson, p. 142.
[2] *Second Report from the Select Committee on Procedure*, 1969–70, H.C. 198, para. 3. See also J. Rose, 'Questions in the House', in D. Leonard and V. Herman (eds.), *The Backbencher and Parliament* (Macmillan, 1972) pp. 99–100.
[3] These points are discussed by Johnson, pp. 133–4.
[4] R. W. McCulloch, 'Question Time in the British House of Commons', *American Political Science Review*, Vol. 27, pp. 971–5.
[5] Chester and Bowring, pp. 217–18.

they believe increased questioning is normal where the Government is in a weak position. Thirty years later 29 Members of the Opposition had shadow departmental responsibilities[1] and between them were responsible for 1,300 Questions, some 10 per cent of the total starred and unstarred Questions for the session. Their conclusion is that, at that time, Questions remained a predominantly back-bench device.[2] These figures do not take into account supplementaries and they acknowledge that Opposition spokesmen are more active in supplementaries than in tabling Questions of their own. The motive here may be partly a matter of Opposition prestige and morale, partly to gain some political advantage from a topic, and partly to support or rescue the original questioner.[3]

More recent evidence supports the Chester and Bowring thesis: comparing the first 28 Question Times of the 1969–70 session (under a Labour Government) with the first 28 Question Times after Christmas in the 1971–2[4] session we find that in 1969–70 Conservative front-bench spokesmen were responsible for 67 (or 6·30 per cent) of the Questions asked at Question Time and 274 supplementaries (or 15·7 per cent of the total). In the 1971–2 sample Labour front-bench spokesmen asked only 33 of the Questions that received oral answer (3·8 per cent of the total) and 279 supplementaries (16·4 per cent of the total). It would seem that Question time does indeed remain a back-benchers occasion. However, to this a number of qualifications must be added. The first is that these figures ignore the Liberal Party's contribution (and more recently those of the Scottish National Party and Plaid Cymru spokesmen). Secondly a slightly different picture is presented for supplementaries if one assumes that each original questioner had, almost as of right, one supplementary. If one deducts these supplementaries from the total then in the two periods considered Opposition front-bench spokesmen were responsible for 36·2 and 35·1 per

[1] The identification of Opposition spokesmen is very much easier after 1955. See R. M. Punnett, *Front Bench Opposition* (Heinemann, 1973), esp. pp. 59–65.

[2] Chester and Bowring, p. 219.

[3] Ibid., pp. 219–20.

[4] The slightly different parts of the sessions were chosen for convenience, to avoid the complication caused by a re-shuffle of Opposition front-bench responsibilities in December 1971.

cent respectively of the remaining supplementaries. It is perhaps this level of participation which gives rise to the widespread impression that Question Time is becoming less of a back-benchers occasion. A third factor to be considered is the extent of Opposition organization at Question Time. Punnett referred, in the case of the Conservative Party, to the involvement of the back-bench subject committees. Each committee in 1969–70 held a meeting the day before its subject was to come up at Question Time and 'tactics for supplementary questions were worked out in advance with the spokesmen concerned'.[1] This seems to imply that Opposition activity at Question Time extends beyond the ranks of those formally designated as 'spokesmen'.

One of the problems at least partly responsible for the congestion at Question Time is the unevenness of demand among M.P.s. Reference has already been made to the declining volume of Questions dealt with at Question Time, the increasing restraints on the number of Questions allowed to M.P.s, and the more complex rules about such things as period of notice that are now required to make the machinery function at all. It is perhaps fortunate that M.P.s' demands do differ: were all those eligible to do so to make maximum demands then clearly the situation would be impossible. Even so it is not satisfactory that only a proportion of starred Questions are asked orally. This has been likened to a company issuing a bogus prospectus.[2] It is not merely a matter of a large volume of starred Questions not being reached, or of inevitable conflict between depth and breadth, at Question Time, as Chester points out: 'The more elaborate the rules, the greater the advantage given to the professional questioner.'[3] The changes made in 1972 have helped somewhat here. By limiting the number of Questions that may be tabled the imbalance between Questions for the Order Paper and Questions answered orally has been checked.

Almost certainly there has throughout the century been considerable variations in the number of Questions asked by

[1] Punnett, p. 304.
[2] The simile is Chester's, see his Memorandum in H.C. 393 (1971–2), para. 20.
[3] Ibid., para. 7.

Members; there have always been the 'professional questioners'. Unfortunately the available statistics do not make for easy comparisons between different periods but broadly their message points in the same direction. For example, in the 1905 session '(t)wo thirds of the 4120 starred Questions were asked by 35 of the 679 members' with eight Members each asking over 100 Questions and, at the other extreme, 200 Members not asking any.[1] According to a calculation for the period 1924–31 50 Members were responsible for 45,000 of the 80,000 starred, unstarred, and supplementary Questions.[2] More recent figures[3] tend to be based on numbers of notices given of oral Questions, which of course is rather different from the number of Questions receiving oral answers. For the 1968–9 session 452 out of a potential Question-asking population[4] of 538 gave notice of at least one Question. Twenty-three of these Members gave 100 or more notices of Questions (accounting for one-third of all such notices) while 74 Members gave notice of 50 or more Questions which accounted for 55 per cent of the total of such notices.[5] In 1972–3, and looking at Questions actually asked, 12 Members had 40 or more oral Questions (with the highest individual figure of 81). In the same session 17 Members asked 200 or more Questions receiving written answers and of these only three were in the top 12 for Questions receiving oral answers. Two hundred and fifty-seven Members asked no oral Questions but of these 79 were members of the Government or occupied one of the excluding House positions.[6]

These figures suggest that in addition to those whose office precludes their tabling Questions of their own, there is a group of Members who have little recourse to Questions and, at the other extreme, a small group who exploit the opportunities much more fully. As noted already, the effect of increasing

[1] Chester and Bowring, p. 194.
[2] McCulloch, p. 974.
[3] In *Fifth Report from the Select Committee on Procedure*, 1966–7, H.C. 410, Appendix 9, and *Second Report*, 1969–70 (H.C. 198), Appendix 1 (II).
[4] Defined as the total membership minus all holders of government office, the Speaker, the Chairman of Ways and Means, the Deputy Chairman (since 1971 there have been two Deputy Chairmen), the Leader of the Opposition, and the Opposition Chief Whip.
[5] H.C. 198 (1969–70), Appendix 1 (II).
[6] Based on figures in *The Political Companion*, No. 17, pp. 118–43.

restrictions on the number of Questions permitted has been to limit the number of Questions which the 'professional questioners' are able to ask. It seems likely that throughout the century the House has contained a number of Members who delight in their role of professional questioners. Their motives no doubt are varied but self advertisement must be assumed to be high on the list.

It is partly because of this tendency among a small minority of Members to exploit the available opportunities that any suggestion for extending Question Time meets with opposition. Why should, the argument runs, the opportunities be increased for those who already enjoy more than their share of the cake. The dilemma goes to the heart of the problems facing Question Time. Should its evident popularity be acknowledged by trying to squeeze more into the available time or into additional time? Or, as Chester has persuasively argued, should the limitations of time be recognized and ways sought to gain maximum value from what is available?[1] In particular, should it not be recognized that concentration on a limited number of interesting topics would probably be more valuable than trying to cover a large number of less interesting matters? Practice has already in the 1970s moved in this direction with the virtual abandonment of 'progress' as an index of success at Question Time. If there are a limited number of topics that merit this extended attention then an intensification of the present trend to ventilate few topics at Question Time seems likely. All this is to recognize the overtly political, rather than the purely informational, role of Question Time. But for the final quarter of the twentieth century it is likely to be in this direction that change will point.

Debates

With debates, perhaps even more than with Questions, the most prominent feature of their twentieth-century development is the stability of outward form, especially if one regards the century in this context as starting in 1902. The latter part of the nineteenth century saw a decline in the very wide opportunities

---

[1] H.C. 393 (1971–2), Memorandum by D. N. Chester, para. 15–20.

hitherto available to the back-bencher so that by the time the century opens his rights have already been restricted into very much their modern pattern. What this century has shown is merely a tinkering with the basic pattern established in 1902 and 1906.

Times of sitting

In 1900 the normal arrangement was for the House to sit from 3 p.m. until midnight when the 'interruption' occurred, after which certain categories of business were permitted up to 1 a.m. During the sitting there was an 'interval' from 7 p.m. to 10 p.m. during which important Members did not speak, leaving things to the lesser mortals.[1] On Wednesdays the sitting began at midday and ended at 6 p.m.

Under Mr. Balfour's reforms of 1902 a system of double sittings on the first few days of the week was introduced.[2] The House was to sit from 2 p.m. to 7.30 p.m. and from 9 p.m. to midnight (or 1 a.m. at the latest). As before, midnight was the time for the interruption of business (though this was now the second interruption) after which only unopposed or exempted business could be taken. Thus in the afternoon session interruption and closing of the sitting were virtually synonymous but not in the evening sitting. The short sitting was removed to Fridays when there was to be a single (or 'morning') sitting from 12 noon until 6 p.m. with the interruption at 5.30 p.m. In addition private Members' business had precedence at the evening (i.e. second) sitting on Tuesdays and Wednesdays.

This system did not prove entirely popular and in 1906 further changes were made in order, according to Sir Courtenay Ilbert writing shortly afterwards,[3] to do two things. The first was to delay the start of the sitting which under the 1902 scheme 'trenched severely on necessary morning work at Government offices, in committee, in the city or at home'. (Jennings adds a further argument that the early start provided

[1] J. Redlich, op. cit., Vol. 1, p. 194 fn. 3.
See also A. L. Lowell, op. cit., Vol. 1, pp. 302–3 fn. 1.
[2] Redlich, op. cit., pp. 194–201.
[3] See his Supplementary Chapter in Redlich, Vol. III, esp. pp. 202–3.

inadequate time for lunch.)[1] The second aim was to enable the House to rise under normal circumstances at a time 'when the man of small or moderate means could make sure of getting home with the help of a public conveyance'.[2]

To achieve these objects double sittings were abandoned and replaced by a single sitting beginning at 2.45 p.m. and ending formally at 11 p.m. with unopposed or exempted business possibly lasting until 11.30 p.m. An attempt to return private Members' business to Wednesdays was unsuccessful and Friday was kept for this purpose as the day of the short sitting[3] with business starting at noon and being interrupted at 5 p.m. with adjournment at 5.30 p.m. From 1921 onwards it was the practice for Friday sittings to be from 11 a.m. to 4 p.m. (or 4.30) but the change was not embodied in Standing Orders until 1927.[4]

This basic pattern of business survived until the Second World war when 'the blackout, evening air-raids and transport difficulties rendered earlier sittings necessary'.[5] During the war the hours of sitting were more variable but the House tended to meet at 11 a.m. and to go on until some time in the afternoon, usually about '4 or 4.30 p.m. in the winter, or an hour or two later in the summer'.[6] Both the times of the daily sittings and the days on which the House met were secret. From March 1945 the time of meeting was 2.15 p.m. with the interruption at 9.15 p.m. and the half-hour adjournment to 9.45 p.m., though with a not infrequent suspension of this rule to add an hour to these times. This schedule survived for less than a year after the war for it was in April 1946 the change was made to what are the present hours of sitting.[7] Then the Labour Government after discussions through the usual channels (though rather less with their own back-benchers) announced that the House would move to 2.30 p.m. as the starting time

[1] Sir Ivor Jennings, *Parliament* (Cambridge University Press, 1957, 2nd edn.), p. 97.
[2] Ilbert, loc. cit.
[3] Lowell notes that the habit of passing 'what is known as the weekend in the country' accounts for this change. Vol. 1, p. 303.
[4] *H.C. Debs.*, Vol. 212, cols. 516–17.
[5] Jennings, p. 96.
[6] Lord Hemingford, *Back-bencher and Chairman* (Murray, 1946), p. 220.
[7] *H.C. Debs.*, Vol. 421, cols. 2217–58.

with 10.30 p.m. (after the now customary half-hour adjournment debate) as the normal time for adjournment. On Fridays the sittings were to continue to begin at 11 a.m. and end at 4.30 p.m. Complaints at the time of this change from some back-benchers suggested that the convenience of members of the Government and those back-benchers who had other employment had ranked above the wishes of some of the full-time M.P.s. This charge in various forms has continued to be heard in the thirty years since. One small concession to the feeling was the experiment initiated in 1967 with morning sittings.[1] These took place on Mondays and Wednesdays and were intended as continuations of the previous Thursday and Tuesday sittings respectively (though the choice of Monday from this point of view was not ideal—it was governed by the need to keep clear Tuesdays and Thursdays when standing committees meet), rather than the start of that day's proceedings. As such they were intended to reduce late (i.e. past midnight) sittings. In fact they did not succeed in doing this: 'Despite the extra hours of morning sittings the amount of late night work was the same, or slightly more than it had been in the last comparable session 1962–3. The gainer was the Government not the back-bencher.'[2] This, plus their unpopularity with the Conservative Opposition, meant that the experiment was not repeated, though occasional morning sittings were held after that to avoid a late sitting.[3]

The types of Debate

Debates in the House of Commons fall into a number of categories depending on one's basis of classification. It is possible to group them according to their purpose or their source. If the former basis is used, then one distinguishes between debates on legislation, and on delegated legislation, the various financial or quasi-financial debates, the general debates either on substantive motions or on occasions such as the Address in Reply to the Speech from the Throne, and debates in private Members' time. Finally, there are the various adjournment debates, first, those that properly belong in that group where the motion is used as an alternative to a substan-

---

[1] Ibid., Vol. 738, cols. 471–608.　　[2] Ibid., Vol. 754, col. 253.
[3] E.g. 21 May 1968.

tive motion, second, the adjournment motion at the end of each day, third, those held before each holiday break and, last, the Emergency or Urgency Adjournment debates. Alternatively, it is possible to classify debates according to whether they are promoted by the Government, the Opposition, or back-benchers and likewise whether they take place in time conventionally allocated to each of these groups. In general, however, the first of these bases for classification seems the most satisfactory. Fortunately to make this section more manageable several types of debate fall to be considered elsewhere: debates on legislation and those with a financial basis are considered in the chapters dealing with those subjects;[1] so that it is convenient here to consider debates in three broad groups. First, the 'general' debates, second, the adjournment debates, and, finally, debates on private Members' motions.

Debates on substantive motions

It is convenient to subsume under this heading debates on the Address in Reply to the Queen's (or King's) Speech at the opening of each parliamentary session. As a class of business this has a fixed place in the timetable and procedurally has altered hardly at all during the course of the century. The Address in Reply itself had already, by the beginning of the century, become formal rather than, as it had been, a detailed response to the monarch's speech. Less time is now devoted to the Debate on the Address than was the case at the beginning of the century. In 1902 the debate took up ten sittings, in 1903 this had dropped to eight sittings, and by 1906 to six. Campion's figures show that for the period 1919–26 the average was five sittings, for the period 1928–9 to 1935–6, six sittings, and for 1945–6 to 1954–5 again six.[2] This remains a representative figure.

While the pattern of the debate has remained broadly the same with a first section of general discussion on the Government's programme followed by a series of debates on amendments regretting omissions from that programme again there

---

[1] See Chaps. v and vii.

[2] Lord Campion, *An Introduction to the Procedure of the House of Commons* (Macmillan, 1958), Appendix III, pp. 335–7.

has been a decline in activity. In 1902, for example, twelve amendments were proposed (many of them by Irish Members) and in 1903 the figure was thirteen. By 1906 it had dropped to nine. However, for many years the number has been much smaller. In 1926, for example, three days of general debate were followed by two days on a Labour Opposition amendment and one on a Liberal amendment. In 1936–7 three days of general debate were followed by two days on each of two amendments. In 1956–7 there were four days of general debate and one day on each of two amendments both from the Opposition. In 1966–7 five days of general debate were followed by one day on the only Opposition amendment. In 1974–5 the pattern was four days plus one day on each of two Opposition amendments.[1] It seems clear therefore that the pattern is now fairly rigid with the official Opposition taking over almost completely the moving of amendments not only from back-benchers but also from other parties not in Government.

Of substantive motions themselves Campion has said 'Stated generally, [they] are the least technical and most intelligible form in the procedure of the House.'[2] They come in a variety of forms and have the advantage (over adjournment motions) that they permit a clearer definition of the views of the House in that they are subject to modification to record disagreement or to head off opposition. Such motions may derive from the Government as an invitation of support for a policy or as a means of testing opinion. Alternatively they may be moved by the Opposition; for example as a motion of censure or as some form of criticism falling short of censure. In fact such motions (as opposed to using Supply Days for this purpose) occupy a comparatively small proportion of the House's time. Motions of censure between 1919 and 1926 averaged but one half sitting per session; from 1928–9 to 1935–6 they averaged two sittings and from 1945 to 1954–5 again two sittings. Other Opposition motions in government time in these three periods accounted for an average of one, two, and one sittings respec-

[1] In 1974–5 session the main Question was pressed to a division which is unusual.

[2] *Third Report from the Select Committee on Procedure*, 1945–6, H.C. 189–I, Appendix: Memorandum by the Clerk of the House, p. 26.

tively; while government motions occupied on average four, six, and thirteen sittings.[1] These figures would suggest that in the post-war period the House has spent more time on general debates than it did in the inter-war period. This impression is strengthened by two more recent sessions, chosen for no better reason than that they were of roughly normal duration. In 1967–8 the House spent about 15 sittings on debates on substantive motions (usually on motions to take note or to approve). In 1972–3 the figure was about 20 sittings.[2]

Adjournment Motions

As already noted these fall into four main categories: when moved by the Government as an alternative to a substantive motion, when moved each evening at the conclusion of the day's business, when moved before each of the recesses, and finally Urgency or Emergency Motions.

(a) *Government Adjournment Motions*
The first of these overlap, as we saw, with the previous category of debates. Their disadvantage, as compared with that category, that they do not easily provide a clear verdict or decision, may in certain circumstances be an advantage. In the most famous such debate in this century, on the conduct of the Norway campaign in May 1940 and as a result of which the Chamberlain Government fell, the impact was heightened precisely because the motion lacked specific critical language. Between 1919 and 1926 such motions occupied an average of one-and-a-half sittings per session; from 1928–9 to 1935–6 an average of two sittings and from 1945 to 1954–5 an average of seven sittings.[3] This figure has been maintained in the more recent sessions examined: in 1967–8 it was seven-and-a-half sittings and in 1972–3, eight sittings.

(b) *Daily Adjournment Motions*
As we have already seen the normal time for the interruption of

---

[1] Campion, op. cit., Appendix III.
[2] 'About' because in several cases the debates occupied part of a sitting and one cannot be absolutely precise in adding the fractions.
[3] Campion, op. cit., Appendix III.

business at the end of each sitting has varied during the course of the century. Beginning at midnight (with exempted and unopposed business permissible to 1 a.m.) it became 11 p.m. in 1906 (with exempted business to 11.30). There it stayed until the Second World War. After the war the normal time for interruption became 10 p.m. with a further half-hour to 10.30 p.m. Under the modern rules, however, if exempted business is being taken or, if for some other reason, the ten o'clock rule is not in force, there is still half an hour for an adjournment debate at the end of the sitting. From the back-benchers point of view this is a great improvement on the pre-war situation where the half-hour was available only if there was no exempted or other business for discussion after the time of interruption and if the normal rule about interruption had not been suspended. Even a division at the end of the previous debate could render the time available quite worthless. During the Second World War the period became a more regular feature as a compensation to private Members for the loss at that time of their other opportunities.[1] In 1946 its length was guaranteed in a Sessional Order as half an hour and this was enshrined in Standing Orders in the following year. The result of this has been that in the post-war period the Adjournment Debate has become an important and guaranteed outlet for back-benchers: even after an all-night sitting half an hour will be solemnly devoted to such a debate. Nowadays there are few sittings not ended with such a debate. Compare this, for example, with session 1936–7 when out of 155 sittings of the House there were only 21 days on which such debates were held: a proportion of one in five.

Jennings has pointed out that during the Second World War the popularity of adjournment debates grew to the point that a system of control was required.[2] The result was the introduction in 1945 of a ballot to determine the right to raise an issue on the evening adjournment. Up to 1960 there was a weekly ballot for three places each week with the subject for debate on the other two days being chosen by the Speaker. Since that date the Speaker has chosen the subject on only one day a week and there has been a fortnightly ballot for the remaining eight slots. One further change at the same time was that whereas those

---

[1] Chester and Bowring, p. 206.   [2] Jennings, p. 118.

unsuccessful in the weekly ballot had stayed in for subsequent ballots unless they were successful or withdrew their name, since then the reverse system has applied with unsuccessful Members being excluded from subsequent ballots unless they positively indicate a wish to stay in.[1]

The conventional reaction to an answer at Question Time which does not satisfy a questioner is for him to announce that he will seek to raise the matter on the adjournment. Such announcements of course have no validity but this reaction in part explains the tendency for adjournment debates to be seen as an extension of Question Time. But they are not just this and despite the fact that they take place late at night (or early in the morning), usually in an almost empty house, they have a value in making 'the workings of the Government and the administration more open'.[2]

(c) *Holiday Adjournment Motions*

By custom the day on which the House adjourns for each recess is devoted to a series of short debates in which private Members have an opportunity to raise any matters except legislation. The actual motion fixing the period of the recess is now moved several days before the actual date of adjournment and nowadays provides an opportunity for a debate of two or three hours in which various reasons are adduced as to why the recess should be shorter. This debate is a relatively recent innovation. Until the early 1950s (and even into the 1960s on occasion) this motion was agreed to without debate (though Campion records that in earlier times this motion was debated[3]). The debates on the actual day of adjournment now number usually four days a year as compared with an average of two-and-a-half days between 1919 and 1926 and three-and-a-half days in the period 1928–9 to 1935–6. The explanation for this change lies in the longer sessions that are now customary and the fact that the parliamentary year no longer coincides with the calendar year.

[1] *Report from the Select Committee on Procedure*, 1958–9, H.C. 92–I, para. 32.
[2] V. Herman, 'Adjournment Debates in the House of Commons' in D. Leonard and V. Herman (eds.), *The Backbencher and Parliament* (Macmillan, 1972), p. 125.
[3] Campion, op. cit., pp. 105–6.

(d) *Emergency Adjournment Motions*

Until the 1880s it was relatively easy for a private Member to move the adjournment of the House and then raise any matter he wanted to. The over-use of this possibility led to restrictions in 1882 designed to limit the number of occasions when the adjournment of the House might be moved before Public Business was begun. These took the form of moving the adjournment being possible only to discuss 'a definite matter of urgent public importance'. To be accepted, this motion required 40 Members to rise in their places to support it or, if less than 40 but not less than 10 did so, then a majority supporting the proposition in a division. If the motion was accepted in either of these ways it was debated immediately. After 1902 emergency motions were still brought forward at the beginning of the sitting but if accepted they stood over to the beginning of the evening sitting (i.e. at 9 p.m.). In 1906 when the House reverted to single sittings, emergency motions were debated at 8.15 p.m. on the day they were accepted.[1] In 1927 this was changed to 7.30 p.m. which was a more accurate mid-point of the sitting.[2] When the House revised its hours of work after the Second World War the time for debating urgency motions became 7 p.m. and it was provided that the sitting should be extended by a period equal in length to the time taken on the adjournment debate, which itself was to be limited to three hours. This change had been proposed as long ago as 1907 as a means of limiting the moving of emergency adjournments for the purpose of disrupting the Government's programme.[3] Following a Report from the Select Committee on Procedure of 1966–7 the normal time for holding the debates was changed to 3.30 p.m. on the day after the acceptance of the motion (except that when moved successfully on a Thursday, the debate would be held on the following Monday). Provision was however retained for holding a debate at 7 p.m. the same day where matters were sufficiently urgent.[4]

[1] See Lowell, Vol. 1, Chap. XVIII, esp. pp. 334–6.
[2] *H.C. Debs.*, Vol. 212, col. 525.
[3] See *Second Report from the Select Committee on Procedure*, 1966–7, H.C. 282, para. 5.
[4] Ilbert, op. cit., pp. 222–3.

In the early life of this Standing Order a great deal of the decision whether to accept a motion lay with the House itself: the Speaker decided only whether a matter was definite, leaving it to the House to decide, by its support, whether it was 'urgent' and 'of public importance'.[1] Gradually Speakers extended their power over all aspects of the Standing Order and in the course of time they took a more restrictive view of what the Standing Order permitted. Thus each of the three main terms was progressively narrowed;[2] for example, 'definite' meant that a motion must not deal with more than one subject, it must deal with a particular case and one that was not based on an uncorroborated report but where official information was available. To be deemed 'urgent', the matter upon which a motion was based had to have happened recently and be raised at the first opportunity; it had to require the action of the House and the Government and could not be postponed until a later moment where it might be discussed (for example, on a Supply Day). To be of public importance a matter had to be more than an individual grievance. Moreover, other principles were developed and refined, for example that the responsibility of the Government be clearly involved and that the matter must involve official action beyond the ordinary administration of the law.

Concern about the weight of these and other restrictions was expressed to the Procedure Committees of 1945–6 and 1958–9, but in neither case were any changes made despite modest recommendations from the Committee.

Some indication of the extent of this problem can be gained from figures in Table V.2.

These figures indicate a dramatic change in the period after 1920 compared with the period before that date. The point of change seems to have been around 1921: in that session of 11 applications 8 were allowed and 3 refused, whereas in the following session of 14 applications 4 were allowed and 10 refused.[3] In no session since then has the number of applications allowed exceeded the number refused. In the 1960s the situation

---

[1] Jennings, p. 111.

[2] See H.C. 282 (1966–7), *Minutes of Evidence*, Appendix 1 for examples of this narrowing.

[3] See Jennings, pp. 112–13, Table III.

became particularly acute: the number of applications in 1960–1 at 22 was the highest since 1920 (and of these only two were accepted) while in the three sessions from 1963–6 not a single application was successful.

TABLE V.2

Emergency Adjournment Debates

Average per Session in period	Offered	Refused	Allowed
1882–1901	8·1	1·2	6·9
1902–20	8·6	2·5	6·1
1921–39	6·0	4·5	1·5
1939–40 to 1948–9	1·9	1·5	0·4
1950 to 1958–9	7·3	6·8	0·5
1959–60 to 1965–6	10·8	10·1	0·7

The matter was considered again by a procedure committee in 1966–7. They were generally sympathetic to the idea of liberating the Standing Order from the restricting hand of precedent and suggested the replacement of the words 'a definite matter of urgent public importance' with the words 'a specific and important matter that should have urgent consideration'.[1] In addition they suggested that the Speaker should be encouraged to be more willing to allow debates and that some of the other restrictions (for example the narrow interpretation of ministerial responsibility or the fact that an arranged adjournment might already have been moved) should not be regarded as overwhelming reasons for refusing a request. These recommendations were accepted in November 1967.[2] The immediate impact was not all that dramatic: in the 1967–8 session there were 20 applications for debates of which four were allowed. In 1972–3 there were 32 applications of which only one was allowed.

As part of the effort to free Speakers from the bounds of precedent (and to prevent the growth of a new series of precedents) it was agreed in 1967 that they should no longer be

[1] H.C. 282 (1966–7), *Report*, para. 10.
[2] *H.C. Debs.*, Vol. 754, cols. 258–9 and 371–2.

obliged to give reasons for their refusal to grant an application for a debate. This has not worked entirely satisfactorily: inevitably it leaves applicants somewhat in the dark and Speaker Lloyd has expressed some regret about this aspect of the change: 'I was a member of the Select Committee on Procedure and this discretion [not to give reasons] was to some extent my own idea. I have subsequently regretted it because it puts a great burden on the Chair.'[1]

Private Members' Motions

Writing early in the present century Redlich noted that one of the main features of the preceding 25 years had been the complete suppression of the private (or unofficial, as he was referred to then) Member.[2] A particular manifestation of this was the gradual reduction in the amount of the House's time allocated to the private Member. By the end of the nineteenth century this change had largely been accomplished and the final stage in the process was the Balfour reforms of 1902 which gave the Government virtually complete control over the time-table, making their lives predictable and their business more or less assured.[3]

After 1902 private Members had (for both bills and motions) Fridays, until Whitsun and after Michaelmas, plus the third and fourth Fridays after Whit Sunday. In addition their business had priority at the evening sittings on Tuesdays (up to Easter) and on Wednesdays (up to Whitsun and after Michaelmas). Under this arrangement the Friday sittings were kept for bills with only the Tuesday and Wednesday evening sittings for motions. In the 1906 changes private Members' business was not substantially affected. They kept such Fridays and Tuesday and Wednesday evenings as they had had before with the minor modification necessary for the new single sitting that their business was to begin at 8.15 p.m. This pattern

---

[1] Ibid., Vol. 852, col. 1500.

[2] Redlich, Vol. 1, p. 206.

[3] Lowell however notes that the change in 1902 was less dramatic than it appeared: in practice before 1902 Governments had considerable control. As he put it the changes 'merely sanctioned by permanent standing order a practice that had long been followed in an irregular way by special resolutions adopted during the course of the Session', Vol. 1, p. 312.

survived until 1927 (though with the risk that has been present throughout the century, that the Government would comandeer all or part of private Members' time). In that year private Members were given one whole day up to Easter instead of two evenings up to Easter and one between Easter and Whitsun. Under the new arrangement two motions would be debated during the day with 7.30 p.m. as the point of division between them.[1] In the years after that private Members fared rather badly: the Government took the whole of their time in 1928–9, 1931–2, 1934–5 and from 1939 to 1948. In 1948–9 they regained some time for bills but it was not until the 1950 session that they had an opportunity once again to introduce motions. Since that time their motions have shared with bills the 20 Fridays customarily allocated to private Members.[2] At first the split on Fridays was 10–10 but in the 1966–70 Parliament to facilitate the passage of private Members' legislation, sixteen of the Fridays were allocated to that and only four to motions. Since 1970 the split has been 12 for bills and eight for motions. In addition to this since 1959 four half days have been allocated to private Members' motions; initially these were on Wednesdays but more recently Mondays has been the preferred day for this when the debates are held until 7 p.m.

In the early part of the century one of the most contentious aspects of private Members' motions was the practice of blocking. By setting down a motion for a long way ahead or without specifying a definite day an individual M.P. or the Government could effectively prevent discussion of a subject, thereby severely restricting the scope of private Members' motions. Redlich records, for example, that in the 1902 session this technique was used to block discussion of Protection and of the employment of Chinese labourers in the Transvaal.[3] This power of blocking was held to apply to other occasions also such as the debates before each holiday adjournment. The subject was tackled by a select committee in 1907 after the Government had been hoist with their own petard.[4] The Committee recommended that 'In determining whether a discussion is out of order on the ground of anticipation, regard

---

[1] *H.C. Debs.*, Vol. 212, cols. 516–18.
[2] P. G. Richards, *The Backbenchers* (Faber and Faber, 1972), pp. 114, 142.
[3] Redlich, Vol. 1, p. 205.   [4] Ilbert, op. cit., p. 220.

shall be had by Mr. Speaker to the probability of the matter anticipated being brought before the House within a reasonable time.'[1] This was taken, verbatim, into Standing Orders in 1914 since when the problem has been much less serious.[2]

Throughout the century the problem of allocating scarce resources in relation to private Members' motions has been dealt with by recourse to lot. The rules for balloting have varied considerably during this time. After 1902 the limit on the period of notice was four motion days ahead (i.e. two weeks in normal circumstances); and apart from the start of the session (when the ballot covers two weeks) the ballot was held weekly until Easter.[3] This system, although perhaps the only one available in the circumstances, gave rise to the practice of 'syndicating' whereby groups of Members interested in a topic would enter the ballot in the hope that one of them would be lucky. As with other procedural innovations the idea was started by the Irish Members. Up to 1927 there were separate weekly ballots for the Tuesday and Wednesday debates. When these were combined a change was made to a single ballot with two first places for the main slots of the two-part debate. In 1933 the maximum period of notice was reduced from the fourth to the second motion day in the hope that this would produce debate whose subject matter was somewhat fresher. In the post-war period there have been as many ballots as days for the discussions of motions. For each motion day it is the practice to select three motions though in practice only the first one each day is likely to be discussed.[4]

The attitude of commentators to private Members' motions debates has not been over-kind. The best that Lowell could find to say about them in the first part of the century was that they helped 'to keep alive the salutary fiction that members of Parliament still possess a substantial power of independent action'.[5] He pointed to the fact that the topics chosen were sometimes too parochial in their scope to interest enough M.P.s to keep a house: in 1903 the House being counted out on seven out of 17 private Members' nights.[6] This problem was present in the inter-war period too.

---

[1] Ibid., pp. 222–3.　　[2] *H.C. Debs.*, Vol. 62, cols. 149–59.
[3] Lowell, Vol. 1, p. 314.　　[4] Richards, op. cit., p. 114.
[5] Lowell, Vol. 1, p. 316.　　[6] Ibid., p. 315.

A modern commentator generally well disposed to private Members' debates nevertheless records that 'on Fridays the House is even less compelling as a debating society than as a legislature'.[1] Richards goes on, however, to point out that these debates allow discussion of topics that might not otherwise be aired, permit M.P.s to raise pet subjects, enable them to raise matters relating to their constituencies and so on. They are thereby not to be despised in the total of back-benchers' activities.

The position of the private Members

Reference has already been made to the extent to which the Government gained control over the timetable of the House leaving private Members with a small share of the business they could call their own. This of course takes no account of the fact that much of the time designated as Government or Opposition time, is in fact occupied by back-benchers. Nevertheless there is a real sense in which the House is run by and through 'the usual channels' whose interests may from time to time be different from those of back-benchers. Yet what Lowell expressed more than half a century ago remains valid: 'while many private members loudly bewail their wrongs, they make no organized effort for mutual protection'.[2] There are of course good reasons why they do not.

A good example to fit Lowell's thesis concerns the class distinction between those who are and are not Privy Councillors. The 1958–9 Select Committee on Procedure gave some attention to the convention that Privy Councillors had a prior claim to be called in debates (and also to put supplementaries at Question Time) ahead of other back-benchers. The origins of this tradition are obscure and although not a Standing Order it had acquired the force of one. In the debate prior to the setting up the Committee considerable unhappiness had been expressed on the subject and although most of those who gave evidence to the Committee about the matter were noticeably complacent about it, the Committee in their Report suggested a modification of the practice.[3] This was a very modest change

[1] Richards, loc. cit.   [2] Lowell, Vol. 1, p. 314.
[3] *Report from the Select Committee on Procedure*, 1958–9, H.C. 92–I, para. 29.

of emphasis to the effect that 'the Chair should give due weight to the experience and standing of Privy Councillors, but should not be bound to call them in preference to other Members'.[1] In fact even this proved too strong a recommendation and nothing happened as a result except that it was agreed to leave things to the Speaker. Rumbles of this discontent continue to be heard from time to time.

This problem can be seen as part of the wider issue of the structuring of debates. Formally, of course, participation in debate depends on 'catching the Speaker's eye'. In practice matters are a good deal less spontaneous than this would imply. For a long time (though exactly how long is not clear) it has been the practice for the Speaker to prepare a batting order from those who have notified him (either directly or via the Whips) of their desire to participate in the debate. The Speaker is not bound by his list and does not necessarily confine himself to it. It is of course from time to time a source of complaint. But such complaints, like the lists themselves, are manifestations of the problem caused by more Members wanting to speak than there is time for.

An alternative way of facing up to this problem would be to encourage or to enforce shorter speeches, thereby enabling more Members to participate. In fact the House has always been reluctant to go beyond encouragement when the issue has been raised as it has throughout the century. As far back as 1901 a motion was proposed in favour of a time-limit for speeches; again in 1904 the topic was raised.[2] Shortly afterwards Redlich commented: 'It may reasonably be doubted whether strict rules of this kind, which are a negation of free parliamentary action, will ever find favour in the House of Commons.'[3] The seventy years since that was written have done nothing to suggest that he was mistaken in his judgement. In his evidence to the 1945–6 Procedure Committee Campion suggested a time-limit for speeches but the Committee did not agree, arguing that 'the influence of the Chair with the general support of the House is the only effective and practical check'.[4] The 1958–9 Procedure Committee was slightly more adventurous: in addition to repeating their predecessor's appeal for brevity

---

[1] Ibid.   [2] Redlich, Vol. I, p. 204.   [3] Ibid.
[4] H.C. 189–I (1945–6), *Report*, para. 56.

in speeches, they endorsed a suggestion that an hour in major debates be devoted to five-minute speeches.[1] Even this was too radical and the House confined itself to the familiar exhortations. Sixteen years later yet another Select Committee on Procedure looked at the matter with results that would not have surprised Redlich. They recommended that 'the matter should be left to the self-discipline of Members and their sensitivity to the general atmosphere of the House and the wishes of their fellow Members, reinforced by the ultimate power of the Chair to refrain from calling Members who have flagrantly abused this freedom of debate'.[2]

In fact it seems agreed that speeches have become shorter. The oration of several hours is now rare: 'Front bench speakers rarely talk for more than hour, and twenty minutes is the usual time for a private member.'[3] In part this reflects changing styles of oratory and in part the greater pressure of Members wanting to speak. Observers are agreed that the modern House contains more Members who want and expect to speak compared to the situation at the beginning of the century.

Not only have speeches become shorter, it is probable their style has also changed.[4] By its nature this is not a matter amenable to measurement but it is likely that changes in the composition of the House, in the prevailing style of society outside, together with competing attractions have combined to produce a less flowery, more prosaic style. It may well be that Parliament retains much that is traditional and even artificial in its favoured speaking styles which makes the contrasts with previous eras less obvious than they would otherwise have been. Inevitably there are those who lament the change, feeling that oratory has disappeared from the parliamentary scene.[5]

---

[1] H.C. 92–I (1958–9), *Report*, paras. 26–7.

[2] *Fourth Report from the Select Committee on Procedure*, 1974–5, H.C. 671, para. 23.

[3] Jennings, p. 148.

[4] See J. V. Jensen, 'Clement R. Attlee and Twentieth Century Parliamentary Speaking', in *Parliamentary Affairs*, Vol. XXIII, pp. 277–85.

[5] E.g. J. Critchley, 'As we mumble our way through the House, where oh where have the good speakers gone', *The Times*, 26 July 1975.

The point of debate

Fundamental to the question of debate in the House of Commons is to decide what it all means. If it has a point is this the same point that it has always had? Behind this lies the prior question of what the proper function of the House is. Running through the operation of the House in the twentieth century has been a tension between the House as seen from the point of view of the Government (or perhaps one should say front-benchers) and as viewed by back-benchers. From the Government's point of view the House is a place which plays a part, albeit a subordinate part, in legitimizing action. This represents a change from the nineteenth-century conception of the House: the rise of disciplined mass parties and the extension of the functions of Government has meant that the private Member has been demoted and that the business of the House is necessarily what the Government wants it to be. In this sense the House has become a euphemism for the Government. The result of this change has been an almost perennial self-doubt on the part of the House of Commons. It expresses itself in this context by taking the form of questioning whether debate has a point, wondering whether anyone is listening, and asking how debate can be improved. In part this dilemma is insoluble: the notion of debate as the stage prior to decision lost some of its glamour when divisions became largely predetermined. It would not, however, be fair to conclude that it has no point: as with Questions some are listening and of course one can see debate as a valuable safeguard because it can on occasion provide a necessary forum (May 1940 must be the outstanding example in this century).

Parliament faces the future with a lack of confidence. It seeks more time for debates (e.g. under S.O. No. 9 or on European Affairs) without quite knowing why. Two factors are crucial here. The first is that discontent with Parliament is only partly Parliament's own fault since it inevitably becomes an object of the wider discontent with the system as a whole.[1]

[1] On this see R. Butt, *The Power of Parliament* (Constable, 2nd edn., 1969), esp. Chaps. 4 and 5.

Secondly, Parliament functions only as well as the party system: if that is thought irrelevant or out of date so Parliament must suffer. It may be that changes in this will lead to some revival in the attention given to debates in the House of Commons.

X

PARLIAMENT AND MASS COMMUNICATIONS IN THE TWENTIETH CENTURY

Colin Seymour-Ure

'Do not run after a Minister or Private Member.' So begins one of the rules for journalists with access to the Members' Lobby at Westminster. 'It is nearly always possible', the rule continues, 'to place oneself in a position to avoid this.'[1] Although drafted in the late 1940s, the rule typifies the ambivalence and mutual suspicion always characteristic of relations between Parliament and the press. On the one hand Parliament curbs the Lobby man: on the other, his usefulness is tacitly admitted.

Parliament and the press are so continuously involved that a detailed account of their relationship through the century would be quite impossible in this essay. The emphasis, rather, will be on factors determining the attitudes of each institution towards the other and on the resulting machinery of parliamentary coverage.

Tension, ambivalence, and suspicion are undoubtedly the most important characteristics of press–parliamentary relations. Their degree has varied over the years as Parliament and press have changed. Occasionally the tension manifests itself forcibly. In extreme cases, in 1956 as in 1901, offending editors were summoned to the Bar of the Commons to apologize for contemptuous remarks.[2] Mostly the tension remains latent; but so

---

[1] The Lobby rules. Version dated July 1956, published in Jeremy Tunstall, *The Westminster Lobby Correspondents* (Routledge and Kegan Paul, 1970), pp. 124–8.

[2] 99 *H.C. Deb.* 4s. c. 1189, 16 Aug. 1901, editor and publisher of the *Globe*: 563 *H.C. Deb.* 5s. c. 403, 7 Feb. 1902, editor of the *Sunday Express*. References to House of Commons debates are to the 5th series unless otherwise indicated.

long as certain basic features of Parliament and press survive to shape their attitudes it can never disappear.

First and foremost Parliament obviously needs the press (in which word radio and television will generally be included here) to report its proceedings—a need given physical recognition in 1850 in the construction of a separate press gallery in Sir Charles Barry's House of Commons. Yet, from the provision of tickets for the reporters of Harmsworth's *Daily Mail* at the turn of the century to the arrangements for broadcasting debates in 1976, Parliament has insistently sought to control the terms of its publicity. Press Gallery records are sticky with the honeyed words of parliamentarians about the Fourth Estate. Yet the best remembered quotation of all about the press by a politician is 'power without responsibility, the prerogative of the harlot throughout the ages'—Stanley Baldwin's indictment of the ambitions of Lord Beaverbrook and Lord Rothermere in 1930. The press parliamentarians variously want is, naturally, that which most reflects their individual interests and partisanship. In particular, Parliament likes publicity at the time of its own choice. It has been continuously resentful of premature disclosure of information which Parliament ought to be the first to hear. Where such disclosure concerned parliamentary papers it has been treated as a contempt. On other occasions it has brought strong disapproval from the Chair—and the chance, evidently, of private protest too. When *The Times* in 1920 published the final draft of the Speaker's Conference on Irish Devolution, Speaker Lowther sent for the paper's Lobby man 'but was, of course, unable to obtain from him any indication as to how the document had been obtained. The most that I could do was warn him that in the event of a repetition of such an event as publishing a document headed "Private and Confidential" I should strike him off the list of those admitted under the Speaker's authority to the Press Gallery.'[1] The downfall of Hugh Dalton as Chancellor of the Exchequer was occasioned in 1947 by the premature disclosure of Budget details by the London *Evening Star*. This was a technical offence if ever one was: Dalton gave a few details to a Lobby journalist while actually on the way to the Chamber to

[1] Vt. Ullswater, *A Speaker's Commentaries* (Arnold, 2 vols., 1925), Vol. II, pp. 278–9.

deliver his speech. They were published in a small number of copies of one edition of the paper, and (according to one account) it was only because the *Evening Standard* tipped off an Opposition M.P. that the matter became an issue.[1] The disclosure of Budget details, of course, has traditionally been a special sin; and in this case the journalist too fell under suspicion until it was clearly established that he had stuck faultlessly to the conventions of Lobby journalism.[2] 'Routine' premature disclosure still earned sufficient opprobrium in 1975 to lead the Privileges Committee to recommend that the editor and responsible correspondent of *The Economist* be banned from the precincts of the House for six months (except for the purpose of consulting their respective Members) and that the paper be fined, as a penalty for disclosing a draft report of the Select Committee on a wealth tax.[3] No evidence was produced by the Privileges Committee to show that the offence was not merely technical. Nor were the suggested punishments adopted. The episode was another reminder of the touchiness of the House.

Just as much as for publicity, Parliament needs the press for a source of information. This is more difficult to measure across the century since it lacks the kind of landmarks associated with arrangements for publicity. But the results can be seen in any Question Time or Adjournment Debate. If one thinks more broadly, of a 'parliamentary agenda' consisting in a number of topics to which at a given moment M.P.s attach priority, then the press can be said to have a major influence over it—now as in 1900, no doubt. Harold Wilson remarked in a letter to *The Times* in 1973 (about a legal dispute involving the *Sunday Times*): 'Parliament is hamstrung in its discussions of, and decisions on, matters of public importance if it cannot draw both on the facts and opinions freely published in the press. . . . For the raw material of parliamentary debate is in fact what members read in the press.'[4] Similarly definitions of what constitutes a 'political crisis'—whether it be the shell shortage in the First World War, a *Times* leader about Sudetenland Germans in 1938, or vaguer crises like the 'energy crisis' of the

---

[1] Patrick Gordon Walker, 667 *H.C. Deb.* c. 509, Nov. 14, 1962.
[2] *Select Committee on the Budget Leak, Report*, H.C. 20, 1947.
[3] H.C. 22, 1975–6.
[4] Letter to *The Times*, 24 July 1973.

1970s—have often been influenced for M.P.s by the constructions put upon them in the press. Again, however, M.P.s have persistently berated the press in this century for its superficiality and sensationalism. With the growth of political broadcasting after 1959 came a comparable refrain about broadcast 'triviality'.[1]

There is a deeper sense in which Parliament accepts but resents the importance of mass communications. The shape of Parliament is necessarily conditioned to some extent by the communications technology of the day. The parliamentary idea of consultation preceded Parliament as an institution.[2] The growth of newspapers and of parliamentary responsibility to the electorate encouraged the institution continually to adapt its behaviour to the needs of the press, just as in the earliest days its timetable was geared to the cycle of seedtime and harvest. At the extreme one may argue that communications media are 'bigger' than institutions; so that if Parliament fails to adapt to a new medium like television—whose parliamentary coverage it has continually limited—Parliament not the new medium will in the long run be the loser.

While much tension derives from the ambivalence of parliamentarians who both recognize and dislike their dependence on the press, some derives also from the dependence of the press on Parliament. Newspaper competitiveness and the obvious attractions of Parliament as a news source (though less, compared with Whitehall, than in 1900), mean that papers have always been willing to suffer the indignities of parliamentary control over reporting facilities—epitomized in the fact that it remained technically a breach of privilege to report the proceedings of the Commons at all until archaic resolutions were rescinded in 1971. Up to a point press and Parliament share common values. Despite the growth of committee activity after 1945 (and particularly after 1960), the focus of parliamentary

[1] See particularly R. H. S. Crossman, *The Politics of Television* (Granada Guildhall Lecture, 1969).

[2] 'The parliamentary idea of consultation is older than Parliament as an institution and the seniority of the parliamentary idea is a useful reminder that institutions of government depend for their character and evolution not primarily on procedural rules and mechanisms but on the political climate in which they arise.' Ronald Butt, *The Power of Parliament* (Constable, 2nd edn., 1969), p. 31.

procedure remains the floor of the Commons Chamber. The constant presentation of questions for debate in terms of Aye and No, reinforced by a Government–versus–Opposition, party-confrontation model of doing business—even down to the winner-takes-all method of choosing M.P.s from the electorate and the executive from M.P.s—all fit in well with newspaper preferences for clashes, conflict, and excitement. They are symbolized by the faithful reporting of the exact votes in Commons division lists whose arithmetic totals have usually been politically unimportant.

Neither press nor Parliament, on the other hand, defines its goals exclusively by reference to the other. Parliament wants publicity for what its Members consider important, and at the time of its choice. Newspapers, by contrast, have to take account of factors like the presumed and expressed interests of a target audience; their partisanship and attitude to the Government; conventional news values; and overriding economic factors that determine things like space. Both institutions, moreover, can claim a rival popular legitimacy; Parliament, because it is the elected representative body of the people; the press, because its readers 'vote' with their money and have a relationship to their papers untrammelled by the intermediary of parties. It is precisely when parliamentarians are unsure of their own standing with the people and fear that the mandate of the press is the more solidly based that the tensions can be highest—as is illustrated, for instance, in parliamentary hostility to the 'anti-waste campaign' after the First World War (when the Harmsworth press pinpointed M.P.s who supported 'wasteful' expenditure)[1] and to critical comment during the Suez crisis of 1956.

Tension derives also, finally, from the fact that the House of Commons is not a monolith. Some group or other in it has nearly always seen the press as an ally—back-benchers of any party against the Leadership, Opposition parties against the Government, individual Ministers, perhaps, against each other. The partisan element in the press, which was past its peak early in the twentieth century but remained a factor in press relations with Parliament, ensured that every Government

---

[1] See, e.g., complaints in the Commons on 8 Dec. 1920, 135 *H.C. Deb.* c. 2116–19, 2406–7.

apart from the first Labour administration enjoyed some press support—at least on entering office. In short, different parliamentarians see different parts of the press as allies or enemies at different times.

One result of the ambivalence of parliamentary attitudes has been the endurance of a golden age myth—the belief that at some earlier period the press was more thoroughly in tune with Parliament's needs. (Newspapers in turn share a myth about the quality and influence of Parliament, especially in their comment on elections.) In a Commons debate in 1875 Lord Hartington noted the tendency for papers to substitute 'somewhat sensational descriptions of the proceedings' in place of their formal reports.[1] An anonymous writer in the *Contemporary Review* remarked in 1877 that 'newspapers do not lay so much stress upon the fulness of their reports' as they used to.[2] In his memoirs in the 1920s Lord Asquith commented on the decline.[3] Aneurin Bevan thought a good reason for broadcasting debates was their inadequate coverage in the press.[4] Within weeks of becoming Leader of the Commons in 1976 Michael Foot complained that 'Most newspaper reporting is an absolute travesty of what it used to be, even when I came to the House.'[5]

Was there a golden age? It may be that particular parties or individuals (leaders in the metropolitan press and local Members in the provincials) felt themselves ideally served at one time or another in the nineteenth century; but surely never in the twentieth. More probably the myth stems from the belief that there is an activity called 'politics', of an unchanging character, independent of the peculiar qualities of the communications media of the time and liable, therefore, to be distorted by them. If one's own experience as a parliamentarian seems to be distorted, one may be tempted to think that previous ages were more truly recorded. If, on the other hand, one takes the view that politics has no existence outside the media through which those involved communicate with each other, the idea of distortion has little place; for one will more readily accept that

[1] 224 *H.C. Deb.* 3s., p. 54, 4 May 1875.   [2] June 1877, p. 165.
[3] Earl of Oxford and Asquith K. G., *Fifty Years of Parliament* (Cassell, 2 vols., 1926), ii. 179.
[4] 612 *H.C. Deb.* c. 865–7, 3 Nov. 1959.
[5] 909 *H.C. Deb.* c. 1227, 13 Apr. 1976.

the nature of parliamentary activity—the form, style, and subjects of discourse alike—inevitably change with changes in communications technology.

The golden age attitude means that when Parliament has adapted to the needs of the press it has done so slowly, if not grudgingly. Its desire for publicity ensures that sooner or later the adaptation takes place. No one could hear a word in the Press Gallery at a trial sitting in the new House of Commons in 1850. 'What's to be done?' asked the Prime Minister, Lord John Russell, having been up to hear for himself. 'The House has been built.'[1] The implied shrug was belied by the consequences. The windows were blocked up and a false roof was put in. The opening was delayed until 1852. This was typical. Whether it has been facilities, formal procedure, or informal behaviour, Parliament has adapted when obliged to. Newspaper deadline times in the late nineteenth century, when the London papers were expanding into the provinces, meant that if speeches were to be reported they must be shorter and made much earlier in the day than before. The *Westminster Gazette* editor J. A. Spender, comparing the mid-nineteenth-century Commons with the 1920s, remarked that the great moments then 'were nearly always after dinner and generally after midnight, but in these days the newspapers which impose their timetable upon Parliament are more and more aggrieved if anything important is said after the dinner-hour.'[2] The decision in 1902 to change Question Time to the early afternoon took account of newspaper convenience: 'We must arrange our proceedings, I presume', said A. J. Balfour, Leader of the House, in words that carry an almost audible sigh, 'so that they may be reported in the newspapers that have currency all over the country.'[3] The same year Lord Londonderry refused to start the sitting of the Lords on 2 December at 4 p.m. because the press reporters thought it was starting at 4.15 p.m. and did not turn up until then.[4] Unlike Question Time, an attempt to change the timing

[1] Memorandum by T. T. Clarkson (*Daily News*), 1889, in Press Gallery archives.

[2] J. A. Spender, *The Public Life* (Cassell, 2 vols., 1925), i. 131.

[3] 102 *H.C. Deb.* 4s. c. 784.

[4] Michael MacDonagh, *The Reporters' Gallery* (Hodder and Stoughton, n.d.), p. 423.

of the Budget was unsuccessful in 1973. The provincial evening papers wanted it brought forward from 3.30 p.m. to 2.30 p.m. so that more of it would catch their editions. The Procedure Committee canvassed other interested parties and turned the suggestion down.[1]

One result of the growth of provincial papers in the late nineteenth century was an increase in speech-making. 'Time was', recalled the veteran parliamentary journalist Henry Lucy in 1909, 'when 660 members were content to form an audience enraptured by the eloquence of eight or ten. Now with special wires feeding local papers, every Member feels called upon to deliver a certain number of remarks on important bills or resolutions brought before the House.'[2] 'His speech might empty the House,' remarked another journalist of such back-benchers, 'but it would be certain to fill the columns of his local journal.'[3] Lucy was writing near the end of an era, however. The expansion of the popular press, the decline of provincial dailies, and the increasing monopolization of parliamentary time by the Government all reduced the speech-making tendency. In the 1970s the private Members who received coverage were mainly the exhibitionists, the specialists in news-worthy subjects and parliamentary questions, and (in local papers) the publicity-minded constituency M.P.s.

Informal adaptation of this kind is difficult to trace precisely. Two other examples may be quoted in which it is difficult to be sure whether adjustment to the needs of the press reflects a new, publicity-conscious attitude in the M.P.s concerned, or whether they are simply post-Second World War expressions of long-standing attitudes. One example refers to the Opposition; the other to Select Committees.

The Opposition—more strictly, here, the organized collective leadership in the Shadow Cabinet—has become more institutionalized since Mr. Attlee adopted a system of designated Shadow Ministers in 1945. R. M. Punnett, in a full-length study, observes one of the consequences: 'The more formal the organisation of the Opposition front bench, the more publicity the arrangements are likely to be given, and thus the more

---

[1] *Select Committee on Procedure, Report*, H.C. 152, 1972–3.
[2] Henry W. Lucy, *Sixty Years in the Wilderness* (Smith, Elder, 1909), p. 420.
[3] R. D. Blumenfeld, *The Press in my Time* (Rich and Cowan, 1933), p. 110.

easily the Opposition leaders can be identified by the electorate as a *team* of possible Ministers.'[1] Oppositions may not always want to avoid the appearance of a one-man band. (If they do, they must fight a tendency clearly discerned by Punnett for the Leader to get disproportionate coverage.) Even if they do not, publicity remains essential. In comparison with Government, Opposition is all talk and no action, and Shadow Cabinets must make the most of the forum provided by the floor of the House. There, talk *is* action, and there the press focuses. Thus, in Punnett's words, 'there is a great temptation for the Opposition to try to attract news coverage to itself by all means possible, including dramatic and vigorous outbursts against the Government's "villainy"'.[2] The limited scope for amendment of bills may paradoxically have exaggerated such techniques since 1945. Certainly one Shadow Chancellor in the 1970s was said to feel privately that he had to go 'beyond the mark' and be more sensational than his predecessors between the wars, in order to get reported. Away from the floor of the House Oppositions have become more skilful, as they have become institutionalized, in keeping the press informed of Shadow Cabinet meetings and of their important 'decisions'. The Opposition Leader has had regular weekly meetings with the Lobby correspondents at least since 1955. The Opposition can also be said to 'need' the press too for the newspapers' frequently superior expertise and capacity for research. That need may well have grown during the century with the complexity of government legislation, though it is doubtful whether it has required any change of attitude by Opposition leaders.

Select Committees as they developed after 1945 did not take an active interest in publicity until the institution of the so-called Crossman (or 'Specialist') Committees in the 1966 Parliament. These and their successors typically invited the press to report their proceedings as they went along instead of waiting for the final report; and their subjects (e.g. immigration and race relations) often made them interested in seeking a wider range of witnesses than before. A crucial factor, though it rarely seems to have been made explicit, was the increasingly apparent fact that if the Committees' inquiries were to in-

---

[1] *Front-Bench Opposition* (Heinemann, 1973), p. 71.   [2] Ibid., p. 196.

fluence policy they must do so on the basis that 'knowledge is power'; that is, they must bring into the arena of discussion information which would otherwise be ignored.[1] To get publicity the Committees had to overcome several difficulties: the tendency of the press to concentrate on the floor of the House, the absence of relevant subject specialists among the gallery men, and the sheer problem of journalists not knowing in advance such details as the programme of witnesses giving evidence. Some parliamentary officials considered it a minor triumph to get the weekly list of public committee sessions published in *The Times* and the *Daily Telegraph*. Committees announced themselves in press releases at the start of new inquiries, usually including an open invitation to submit evidence. Lists of specialist journalists were assembled by Committees that had a well defined ambit (e.g. Science and Technology, Public Expenditure Committee General Sub-Committee). Advance copies of reports were made more widely available, up to 48 hours before publication. Reports having predictable news value, like those of the Select Committees on Abortion (1976) and Violence in the Family (1975–6), were launched with press conferences. Sometimes subjects seem even to have been chosen for their newsworthiness—the personality of the chairman being an important factor. The result of these developments was an undoubted impact on specialist and semi-specialist literature in policy areas like social services, science and technology and the economy and a discernible shift in the emphasis of parliamentary reporting, including the reassignment of staff in one or two papers.

   Much the best example of Parliament's toe-dipping approach to the waters of changing mass media was its treatment of broadcasting. The best illustration of this, in turn, was the extraordinary Fourteen Day Rule—a vain effort by the institution to withstand a new medium in a situation that forced it at last, Canute-like, to yield. In essence the rule stated

---

[1] For example, Sir Henry d'Avigdor-Goldsmid, Chairman of the Public Expenditure Committee, observed that the Report of the Committee's General sub-committee on Public Expenditure to 1976–7, published in 1972 (Cmnd. 5178), 'set the keynote for the debate on the White Paper and for subsequent discussion in the press'. *The Parliamentarian*, Vol. LIV, No. 4, 1973, p. 208.

that the BBC must not broadcast discussions on any subject to be debated in Parliament within the next fortnight, or on any legislation currently before either House. The result was that programmes were continually being replanned or withdrawn. On the BBC's estimate, at any one time 'some hundreds' of items in various stages of preparation were potentially vulnerable. Cancelled items often had to be replaced by something 'of much less concern and value'; and programme producers developed the habit of ignoring 'risky' subjects in favour of 'safer but less significant enterprises'.[1] When the rule became formalized into a legal obligation the wastage increased (hitherto, for instance, the Budget had not been included); but much of the time, as before, the public did not know what they were missing. The external services alone of the BBC were exempt from the rule. 'Parliament', the Director-General of the BBC, Sir William Haley, wrote in 1949, 'is the only grand forum of the nation.' Once a matter was under discussion there, 'it should not also be being discussed in the ether'.[2]

Incredibly the BBC Governors invented the rule themselves in 1944, in a defensive spirit typical of their pre-war attitude to powerful outside bodies. Their aim was to prevent pressure by Ministers who wanted to broadcast on the eve of debates about current legislation which, as the war-time coalition began to strain, might be controversial. The Governors passed a broad resolution that included other broadcasts in addition to ministerial ones. After the war the rule was to put into a general *aide-mémoire* about political broadcasting agreed between the BBC, the Government, and the Opposition. This was really the turning-point for the BBC, since the agreement introduced safeguards against controversial ministerial broadcasts and thus removed the danger that the Fourteen Day Rule was invented to combat. From now on the rule was maintained at the insistence of the party leaders. Trying to wriggle out of it, the BBC promised to stick to factual or explanatory statements about relevant subjects if the rule was abandoned: the parties were not impressed. The BBC gave earnest assurances that it had

[1] *Report from the Select Committee on Broadcasting (Anticipation of Debates),* H.C. 288, 1955–6, memorandum from the B.B.C., pp. 30–1.
[2] Sir William Haley K.C.M.G., 'Parliamentary Institutions and Broadcasting', *Parliamentary Affairs,* Vol. II, No. 2, Spring 1949, p. 112.

'no intention of becoming an alternative, simultaneous debating forum to Parliament': the parties noted the fact.[1] The Beveridge Committee recommended the rule's abolition in 1951, but successive Governments did nothing.[2] In 1953 the BBC said flatly that it wanted the rule dropped and asked for the parties' agreement: the period of a fortnight was arbitrary, the public thought it was absurd and wrongly blamed the BBC for its continuance, and it was difficult to administer because broadcasts were planned before the parliamentary timetable.[3] Despite the BBC's promise not to include M.P.s in discussion programmes during the appropriate periods, Government and Opposition were still immovable.

Now the BBC acted unilaterally. It announced its intention to withdraw the rule. The party leaders advised it not to. The BBC proposed a looser version, which the parties again rejected. The BBC view was that if there was to be a rule they would prefer it to be a legal directive by the Postmaster-General under the Corporation's licence. The Government accepted this suggestion and a directive was issued (covering the ITA as well) on 27 July 1955. The BBC published a statement that they accepted it unwillingly.[4]

The effect of the rule was to shut off the broadcast media completely from discussion of issues before Parliament precisely at the time when they were most topical—and to keep its own Members away from the media too. The institution simply closed its eyes and ears and pretended the media did not exist. The party leaders' stated reason for their insistence was that the rule protected M.P.s from undue outside pressure before a parliamentary debate. It probably appealed also to party

---

[1] *Select Committee on Broadcasting (Anticipation of Debates)*, op. cit., pp. 23, 25.

[2] *Report of the Broadcasting Committee 1949*, Cmd. 8116 (1951), pp. 68, 197.

[3] *Select Committee on Broadcasting (Anticipation of Debates)*, op. cit., p. 26.

[4] The directive prescribed '(a) that the Corporation shall not, on any issue, arrange discussions or ex-parte statements which are to be broadcast during a period of a fortnight before the issue is debated in either House or while it is being so debated: (b) that when legislation is introduced in Parliament on any subject, the Corporation shall not, on such subject, arrange broadcasts by any Member of Parliament which are to be made during the period between the introduction of the legislation and the time when it either receives the Royal Assent or is previously withdrawn or dropped'. Ibid., p. 28.

managers by removing an outlet for the views of back-bench dissidents—specially as these, the BBC felt, often gave better broadcasts.[1] It was certainly not forced on the back-benchers, however. In a Commons debate in November 1955 the rule's basic principle was upheld in a free vote by 271 to 126.[2] But the motion also called for a Select Committee to review the method of implementing it. This recommended that any limitation should be for seven days only and not at all after a bill's second reading. Then in December 1956 the Prime Minister announced the trial suspension of the rule subject to the broadcasting authorities' undertaking to continue to observe its spirit. Six months later it was suspended indefinitely.[3]

Why did the Commons change their minds? The year 1955 saw a new Parliament, a second, commercial, television service, an autumn Budget subject—for the first time under the formal directive—to limitations on the broadcasters' ability to cover it, and two new party leaders. All those factors may have made a difference. Sir Winston Churchill and Mr. Attlee both reflected strongly the simple 'threat' view of broadcasting: either Parliament must be the grand inquest of the nation or broadcasting must. Churchill's defence of the rule has an archaic, patrician ring, asserting with purple extravagance the supremacy of Parliament:

It would be shocking to have debates in this House forestalled time after time by expressions of opinion by persons who had not the status or responsibility of Members of Parliament. . . . I am quite sure that the bringing on of exciting debates in these vast, new robot organisations of television and B.B.C. broadcasting, to take place before a debate in this House, might have very deleterious effects upon our general interests, and that hon. Members should be considering the interests of the House of Commons, to whom we all owe a lot.[4]

This same 'necessity of upholding the primacy of Parliament in debating the affairs of the nation' was the only justification the

[1] Ibid., p. 27. See also the comments of Mr. Crookshank, Leader of the Commons, on 30 Nov. 1955, 546 *H.C. Deb.* c. 2440. Cf. Burton Paulu, *British Broadcasting in Transition* (Macmillan, 1961), p. 96.

[2] 546 *H.C. Deb.* c. 2315–446, 30 Nov. 1955.

[3] 562 *H.C. Deb.* c. 1095–7, 25 July 1957, 574 *H.C. Deb.* c. 91–2W, 18 Dec. 1956.

[4] 537 *H.C. Deb.* c. 1277, 23 Feb. 1955.

Select Committee could find for the rule.[1] Yet it was not one enforced on the press nor, obviously, on the individual.

That habit of mind had only to be changed which saw outside discussion as a challenge to Parliament, for the rule to fall away.

A more long drawn-out history of suspicion—still unfinished in the mid-1970s—was Parliament's attitude towards the broadcasting of its proceedings. As early as 1925 two or three individualists like Commander Kenworthy broached the topic in the Commons but were stalled by the Prime Minister, Stanley Baldwin. Similar requests, including one for cine-filming, met with blank refusal in 1936, 1938, 1939, and several times during the Second World War. Even a proposal by Winston Churchill to record some of his wartime speeches for broadcast was withdrawn when certain Members indicated their hesitation about a precedent with propagandist peacetime implications.[2] Late in 1945 a few further requests were rebuffed by Mr. Attlee.[3] The Beveridge Committee dismissed the idea in 1949 as having probable effects 'which most people in Britain would think harmful'.[4] These views may seem less surprising when it is remembered that until 1940 the BBC did not even have representatives in the Gallery. They relied on agency copy. In May that year the authorities promised to keep one seat free each day in the Members' Gallery—but without the right to take notes. Not until September 1941 did the BBC get regular reporting facilities.[5]

Interest in televised debates built up around 1959, partly perhaps as a result of commercial television's pioneering coverage of the Rochdale by-election in 1958; partly because the opening of Parliament was televised the same year; and possibly too because the medium now reached the majority of the population (75 per cent of households had TV in 1959 compared with 40 per cent in 1955).[6] Several Labour leaders went on

[1] H.C. 288, 1955–6, p. iii.

[2] 377 *H.C. Deb.* c. 199–202, 382–3, 20–1 Jan. 1942.

[3] W-Cmdr. Cooper, 413 *H.C. Deb.* c. 444, 21 Aug. 1945; P. Gordon Walker, 417 *H.C. Deb.* c. 213–14, 11 Dec. 1945.

[4] *Report of the Broadcasting Committee 1949*, p. 68.

[5] Haley, op. cit., p. 115.

[6] D. E. Butler and D. Stokes, *Political Change in Britain* (Harmondsworth, Penguin, 1971), p. 269.

record in favour, largely, in the case of men like Aneurin Bevan, because they believed it would counter the conservative bias of the press (to which, having lost three successive elections, the party was sensitive). Other influential voices began to be raised. By 1963 Iain Macleod, then Leader of the Commons, agreed there was much to be said for the idea. Jo Grimond, the Liberal leader, was firmly in favour. (Both of them were good parliamentary and TV performers.) By then, too, the parties had been able to taste the quite pleasing experience of their annual conferences being televised, and articles and pamphlets arguing the case had begun to appear. A Select Committee was set up to investigate the question of televised proceedings soon after the Labour Government took office in 1964. It came out against continuous live broadcasts but suggested a closed circuit experiment, on the basis of which M.P.s could decide whether to make permanent arrangements to supply the BBC and ITV with recordings for use in edited form. This proposal was rejected on 24 November 1966 by one vote (131–130) in a division cutting clean across party lines.[1] Some M.P.s who supported it may have stayed away in the mistaken belief that it was bound to be accepted and that their votes would not be needed.

The House of Lords was less timid. The motion for an experiment was easily carried and early in 1968 four different kinds of broadcast were tried out: a continuous closed circuit performance for two days, an edited version of one day's debates reduced to 30 minutes, a 10-minute summary, and an even shorter 5-minute summary suitable for insertion into news bulletins. The peers' reactions, *The Times* reported, ranged from 'terrible' to 'excellent'. But even the most unfavourable impression could always be swept away by enthusiasts with the argument that the House of Commons would be much more successful. For example, the Government Leader in the Lords, Lord Shackleton, said he was 'a little bit disappointed'; but he thought 'the Commons would come over a great deal better because they move much more quickly, particularly at Question Time'.[2] *The Times* reporter felt that only the 5-minute version would really be worth having: 'Here we had a far stricter assertion of

[1] 736 *H.C. Deb.* c. 1730.   [2] 14 Feb. 1968.

news values and audience interest, with the right pace of picture and voice.'[1]

Although the Commons had rejected television they did proceed, a few months after the Lords' experiment, with one of their own in radio.[2] For four weeks proceedings in certain Committees as well as debates in the House were recorded and then edited into half-hour and 15-minute summaries. Reaction to these was not unfavourable.[3] A sub-committee of the Committee responsible for the trial warmly recommended making such programmes regularly available for broadcast. The Committee as a whole, however, rejected the idea on the grounds that public money should not be spent on 'a project which is known to be controversial'.[4] In 1971 the Services Committee also turned down a BBC request to broadcast the debates on British entry to the EEC.[5] A further radio experiment was more warmly received, however, in 1975. This time recordings were made public. They were included, for one month beginning on 9 June, in the regular radio report 'Today in Parliament'. The programme's audience (normally about 1¼ million) rose by some thirty per cent.[6] In the next session the House decided to adopt the arrangement as a routine practice. Whether this would help or hinder the cause of televised proceedings remained to be seen. Enthusiasts had continued to press their case even after the closed circuit experiment had failed.[7]

The objections to televised debates changed little over the years. Nearly all came under one or another of four headings. Television would change the nature of debate, by reducing spontaneity, by Ministers hogging the floor, and by encouraging

[1] 19 Feb. 1968.
[2] The resolution was passed on 11 Dec. 1967, 756 H.C. Deb. c. 94–137.
[3] The Times, 30 Apr. 1968.
[4] Select Committee on House of Commons Services, 9th Report, H.C. 448, 1967–8; 1st Report, H.C. 48, 1968–9.
[5] Report, H.C. 510, 1970–1.
[6] The House decided on the radio experiment by 354 votes to 182, in a free vote; and against a TV experiment by 263 votes to 275. 887 H.C. Deb. c. 48–178, 24 Feb. 1975. The increased audience for Today in Parliament was quoted by William Hamilton, 897 H.C. Deb. c. 822, 7 Aug. 1975.
[7] e.g. the debate initiated by Robert Sheldon, a Labour back-bencher, on 21 Nov. 1969, 791 H.C. Deb. c. 1617–718. The debate faded out without a quorum, it being a Friday morning.

the temptations of demagoguery and speeches aimed at the audience beyond the cameras. It would mislead the public about the work of Parliament, emphasizing the theatrical at the expense of the workshop elements and the floor of the chamber at the expense of committee and constituency work. It would change the qualities required of M.P.s, so that they would have to be 'telegenic'. Lastly, it might exaggerate the significance of Parliament in the public mind at a time when the focus of publicity should increasingly be Downing Street, Whitehall, and the powerful pressure groups. Common to each argument was the feeling that change would come about not as the result of a conscious decision based on relevant criteria but, on the contrary, as an undesirable by-product of the new medium. As one back-bencher asked defiantly in one of the debates, 'Why should we have our changes in procedure dictated by television?'[1] Wherever television gets in, complained another, 'it wants to start moving furniture about'.[2]

Apart from reporting debates, the broadcasters' treatment of Parliament was conditioned from the start by the BBC's fear of controversy, typified in its attitude to general elections. Until the 1959 election the BBC maintained absolute silence about the campaign in its news bulletins and current affairs programmes for fear of contravening the Representation of the People Act (1949) by appearing to 'promote the election of a candidate'. The parties' own, strictly rationed, broadcasts had the air to themselves. Due to the initiative of the independent companies this policy was abandoned in 1959 and elections thereafter saw a variety of broadcasts. The governing principle of party 'balance' remained but was interpreted ever more flexibly: for example, balanced party representation was not required on each programme in which parliamentarians appeared, but it was maintained over a range of programmes. The 1969 Representation of the People Act reflected this new flexibility, which applied both to elections and to discussion programmes between elections.

Until the radio broadcasts of its proceedings, then, Parliament bent broadcasting to a rather simple and narrow conception of its needs. The principles of balance and—between

[1] Dame Joan Vickers, 736 *H.C. Deb.* c. 1650, 24 Nov. 1966.
[2] William Deedes, 713 *H.C. Deb.* c. 1050, 28 May 1965.

1944 and 1956—the Fourteen Day Rule curbed or silenced independent debate of parliamentary affairs; while 'Today in Parliament' ensured a regular precis of Parliament's own debates. This programme too was a BBC initiative, first broadcast on 9 October 1945. It was written into the BBC's licence as a legal obligation about a year later. Another parliamentary radio discussion programme, 'The Week in Westminster', started in November 1929 but was never made obligatory.

A study of the Gallery's facilities provides a further illustration of the tension and ambivalence in press–parliamentary relations. The Gallery has consistently been treated as a poor relation. Facilities that cost little or nothing—the right of access to the Members' Lobby, advance copies of answers to parliamentary Questions—have been granted readily (unless some point of high principle is involved). Facilities using space and money have always been at risk. The Gallery in Barry's building had nineteen boxes at the front, with the same number of seats behind. There were two writing rooms at the rear. (The Lords' gallery had twelve boxes and fourteen seats.) Long before 1900 these proved insufficient. In 1878, when a select committee inquired into the advisability of having an official report of debates (*Hansard* was still a private enterprise), there were 123 reporters.[1] This inquiry led to five boxes being added on each side of the Gallery, with more seats behind. They were given to provincial and Scottish papers. The original boxes had always been reserved for the London papers, the press agencies, and *Hansard*. At the turn of the century there were thus seats for 65 reporters and standing-room inside the doors at each corner for another couple of dozen. The number of tickets of admission issued by the Serjeant-at-Arms was over 250 (it was 230 in 1889, representing 73 newspapers and agencies). Only a rare parliamentary occasion actually drew that sort of number.[2]

At this time three categories of journalist were inconvenienced

---

[1] The reporters are worth categorizing, in the absence of a comparable list for 1900: *The Times*, 16; *Morning Post*, 11; *Standard*, 17; *Morning Advertiser*, 15; *Daily Telegraph*, 12; *Daily News*, 10; *Daily Chronicle*, 7; *Globe*, 6; *Pall Mall Gazette*, 2; *Echo*, 2; Press Association, 10; Central News, 7; *Sun* and Central Press, 3; *Hansard*, 4; Reuter's, 1. Some of these tickets were used by editors and leader writers.

[2] Michael MacDonagh, *The Book of Parliament* (Isbister, n.d.), p. 314.

by the imbalance between space and membership. One was the rapidly growing class of popular halfpenny newspapers—notably the *Daily Mail* and the *Daily Express*. Parliamentary inertia and the obstinacy of the entrenched members forced these to adopt extraordinary expedients. Alfred Harmsworth had to buy a provincial newspaper with rights to a box in order to get access for the *Daily Mail*. The *Daily Express* resorted to hiring the box of a moribund Irish newspaper (which saw the strength of its bargaining position and extorted a large fee).[1] By such techniques the halfpenny press probably came to occupy nearly half the gallery accommodation by 1909. The position of the entrenched papers was understandable on competitive grounds; and this was still an era of verbatim reports, requiring papers to keep staffs of up to a dozen circulating on duty. There may well have been an element of traditionalism too. R. D. Blumenfeld, who was involved with the *Daily Express* at the time, reckoned that once the privilege of reporting Parliament was granted to the press 'a traditional procedure grew up in regard to it which soon became sacrosanct; and to suggest a modification of the established usage seemed almost like tampering with the British Constitution itself'.[2]

Another example of the rigidity of the membership rules also involved the *Daily Express*. H. W. Lucy had spent more than thirty years in the Gallery with the *Daily News* and other papers. He was famous as 'Toby, MP' for his notes in *Punch*. In 1904, having dropped his old-established connections and contracted to write a column for the *Daily Express*, he found himself without a gallery ticket. Tickets were issued to papers, not to individuals, and the *Daily Express* was not entitled to one. Within a week between 70 and 80 Members offered to ballot daily for a place for him in the Strangers' Gallery. But his dignity was preserved when the Speaker, 'whilst pointing out that the jurisdiction of the Press Gallery rested not with him but with the Serjeant-at-Arms, gave instructions that whenever there was room below the Strangers' Gallery on the floor of the House I should be passed in by the doorkeeper without the necessity of making formal application for admission'.[3]

Foreign journalists were a second excluded group. This was

[1] Blumenfeld, op. cit., p. 111. [2] Loc. cit.
[3] Lucy, op. cit., p. 236.

already a longstanding grievance in 1900. For example, the United States' ambassador had directly approached Speaker Peel on behalf of an American newspaper in 1884. In 1908 overseas journalists pressed their case to the Select Committee on the Reporting of Debates,[1] but again without success. The official view was allegedly that since Reuter's had men in the Gallery the foreign press would have to make do with agency copy.[2] An equally plausible excuse may well have to do with gallery exclusiveness. It was common for reporters to earn extra money as stringers for papers not represented; and profitable arrangements were possibly maintained by some of them with foreign papers.

The third excluded category, numerically less significant at the time, was women. One of the new directions of journalism in the 1880s and 1890s was an increased appeal to women readers. In 1890 Miss Julia Blain of the *Women's Penny Paper* applied to the Serjeant-at-Arms for a gallery ticket. She received a courteous but firm reply: 'Not only have I no authority to admit ladies into the Reporters' Gallery, but the Gallery is already quite filled, and there is a long list of journals which are applicants for admission in the event of a vacancy taking place.'[3] The account of a gallery member of the day, Michael MacDonagh of *The Times*, makes clear that sex prejudice was an equally strong reason. When Charles Bradlaugh raised the matter in the Commons, Speaker Peel replied that admission of women 'would lead to consequences which at present it is difficult to conceive'. The Serjeant-at-Arms, Sir Henry Erskine, was also supposed to have told Miss Blain that 'the male journalists would . . . much resent the intrusion of women into the Gallery, and he was afraid that the consequent outcry would be terrific'.[4] MacDonagh felt that opposition in the Gallery was mainly composed of two elements—the trade union feeling and the club man's feeling. 'Some were apprehensive of being ruined by female cheap labour, and others supposed that their free and unfettered social intercourse would be fettered and made artificial by the presence of women.'[5] In the manner of club prejudice, the Gallery's chief attendant was evidently the most hostile of all. Miss Blain's attempt failed and women

[1] H.C. 358, 1908.   [2] MacDonagh, *The Reporters' Gallery*, p. 11.
[3] Loc. cit.   [4] Ibid., p. 12.   [5] Loc. cit.

continued to be excluded at least until after the First World War. In 1912 there was even a fuss by the Serjeant-at-Arms (still Sir Henry Erskine) when the gallery committee engaged Miss Victoria Fer to sing at the Annual Dinner. He could find no precedent for a woman appearing at such an entertainment within the precincts and he had to be 'induced to modify his views'.[1] The admission of women resulted eventually in the provision of a separate rest room for them in 1932. Even by 1964, however, there was only one woman regularly attending the Gallery, plus a few occasionals.

Space for the big new 'popular' halfpenny papers was found partly by the expedients described; partly by the deaths of so many newspapers in the first quarter of the century; and partly by the decline of interest generally in verbatim reporting. In 1935 the Services Committee found that the Gallery's accommodation appeared to meet its needs. By then the number of daily attenders was down to about seventy-five. But in the next ten years it rose again. It continued to do so after the war, both because of the expansion of the Lobby correspondents, who use the Gallery's facilities (even although they are primarily interested in what happens off the floor of the House), and also because provincial evening newspapers—one of the growth areas of the post-war newspaper industry—were admitted for the first time in 1947. By 1948 daily attenders had increased to 135, to 163 in 1953, and to between 180 and 190 by 1964—with the total number of ticket holders up to 297. The list of regular members was broken down by a gallery working party that reported in detail on status and conditions as follows:[2]

News Agency staffs	49
BBC and ITN	5
National dailies	56
London evening papers	7
National Sunday papers	8
Provincial morning and evening papers	38
Hansard reporters	23
Political parties liaison officers	3
Transmission staffs and messengers	17
	206

[1] *The Times*, 7 May 1912.

[2] *Partners in Parliament: a Report to the Press Gallery* (Mercury Press for the Parliamentary Press Gallery at Westminster, n.d.), pp. 35–6.

Increased numbers were taken care of in theory when the House was rebuilt after 1945. Justice was at long last attempted, for example, for the overseas reporters. By 1939 a row of the public gallery had been reserved for them; but at first they had been allotted only a few seats, they were not allowed to take notes (like the public), and they had to seek Foreign Office approval whenever they came. William Barkley, a sketch-writer on the *Daily Express* from the 1930s to the early 1960s, recorded 'a crowning illustration of the harm done by the exclusion of the foreign press'. On 12 April 1943, Sir Kingsley Wood, Chancellor of the Exchequer, delivered his Budget speech:

The meeting-dates of Parliament in the war were a guarded secret passed around by word of mouth and never published in advance. Parliament rarely met on Mondays in the war. Moreover, by long usage Tuesday is Budget Day. The date in question was a Monday. On that day American newspapermen in their London offices were astounded when the tape suddenly began to announce that the House was in Session and to report Sir Kingsley Wood's speech. This was a speech in which the British Chancellor gave some account of reverse Lease Lend—of the financial efforts made by Britain for the common advantage. Who would be surprised—and who could complain—if these matters were reported in the American newspapers from the jaundiced angle of scandalously ill-used reporters?[1]

When the post-war House was planned the Gallery was rebuilt to twice its former size, providing a total of 161 seats and a capacity on major occasions of more than 250. Typically, the size at first proposed by the planning Select Committee was only half that. It was increased as a result of evidence submitted by gallery members. The gallery Annual Meeting on 10 May 1948 agreed that foreign reporters could become members on equal footing with the British. In fact the foreign journalists could never satisfactorily agree between themselves on the allocation of their tickets after the House opened in 1950, and practically none became members. About seventy seats were available and more than double that number of applicants had been expected. Part of the problem was that few of them needed to attend the Gallery several days a week: indeed they were usually more interested in the Lobby correspondents'

[1] *The Press Gallery at Westminster* (Kemsley Newspapers for the Press Gallery, n.d.), p. 6.

privileged access to Ministers, away from the Gallery itself.[1] When the working party reported in 1964 the situation was that foreign reporters—even daily attenders—were having to get a ticket from the Serjeant-at-Arms office every time they wanted to use the Gallery. Their accommodation on the floor above left much to be desired too. One Commonwealth reporter complained to the working party: 'We are expected to write serious dispatches in what is little better than a public thoroughfare.' The trouble was that their room was used as a route from the Press Gallery staircase to the Committee corridor.

Accommodation in the Gallery itself has become less of a problem as the century has passed. Even finer points like audibility were settled with the introduction of microphones into the new Chamber in 1950. Hitherto, the front boxes in the Gallery were reserved for verbatim reporters so that they missed as little as possible. In the House of Lords microphones were installed much earlier—in 1925. Accommodation off stage has always given rise to complaint—the Commonwealth reporter being heir to a long tradition. It is as though the Commons, satisfied that the visible arrangements for reporters are adequate, assume that everything out of sight must be adequate too. The Gallery has been its own worst enemy in this respect. Keen to defend its foothold at Westminster it early took its exclusiveness to the point of asserting—successfully—that Members of Parliament should not be admitted to the premises except as guests. As guests, they attended only roast-beef not scrag-end occasions: breeding in ordinary Members a lack of familiarity with the reporters' working conditions. The working party in 1963 had to take Sir Alec Douglas-Home and Mr. Selwyn Lloyd on special briefing trips during their deliberations.

The needs of reporters and the facilities available have coincided variously. The turn of the century seems to have been one of the better periods, partly because of the reporters' success in keeping newcomers out. Writing just before the First World War, MacDonagh was able to refer to the facilities as 'to all intents and purposes a spacious and well-equipped club'.[2] 'The time came', recalled Sir Alexander Mackintosh (who also

[1] See, e.g., Boyce Richardson, *New Statesman*, 22 Mar. 1965.
[2] MacDonagh, *The Reporters' Gallery*, p. 416.

talked of a 'well-equipped club'), 'when we were able to have a bath.'[1] There were four comfortably furnished writing rooms, including a library, and a dining room, bar, and buffet. For reporters in between turns, club facilities were exactly what was necessary, and the atmosphere was evidently redolent of tobacco smoke, the rustle of magazines, and the quiet slide of pawns across the chess board.

MacDonagh was a sentimentalist about the Gallery and a parliamentarian in his bones (one story holds that before 1914 he was promised the Clerkship of the projected Irish Parliament). The Edwardian years may well have been an untypical period of elegance in the Gallery's accommodation: certainly at no other time has a reporter described his colleagues as 'not only tolerated but petted'.[2] Some of the rooms were given to the Gallery only in 1899, probably appropriated from the residence of a retiring Clerk of the House. Others had been added earlier from the flat of a deceased assistant Serjeant-at-Arms. Even MacDonagh referred to 'the curious twists and turns, and the rambling irregularity of the whole place'.[3] Until a lift was installed in 1905 access was by climbing several steep flights of stairs.

Such convenience was comparative. Most writing rooms would seem convenient if the alternative was walking back to the office to write up your turn—as it was until No. 18 Committee Room on the Committee corridor was opened to reporters late in the nineteenth century. In the limited space of the Palace of Westminster and in the absence of an independent gauge of space required, the history of the Gallery's accommodation has been a periodic tug of war with the authorities. The Gallery has gained inches of ground from concerted heaves. In 1908 two extra writing rooms were requested on the Committee corridor, and two completely new rooms were constructed. In 1912 the library was enlarged. In 1914 the First Commissioner of Works was surprised at the limited facilities after a visit to the Gallery. The House authorities agreed that radical alterations were needed. In 1920 gallery improvements were included in a Vote of £14,000 but cut-backs forced their

---

[1] Sir Alexander Mackintosh, *Echoes of Big Ben* (Jarrolds, n.d.), p. 160.
[2] MacDonagh, *The Book of Parliament*, p. 314.
[3] *The Reporters' Gallery*, p. 14.

cancellation next year. Stanley Baldwin, Financial Secretary to the Treasury, declared himself privately to be wholeheartedly in favour of reconstruction.[1] Pressure was eased by the annexation of the top floor of the Clerk of the House's residence. When in 1930 the Office of Works asked for three of the rooms back the Gallery refused and were supported by the Serjeant-at-Arms. In 1934 the installation of a lift in the house of the Serjeant himself absorbed half one of the Gallery's writing rooms. In 1953 gallery witnesses to the Select Committee on House of Commons Accommodation acknowledged that 'we are content at present', although numbers had increased substantially since the rebuilding: but that if numbers went on growing 'we shall certainly have to ask for more accommodation'.[2] One extra writing room was subsequently added. By 1964 the Gallery's working party was probably able to derive a perverse satisfaction from the calculation that, with the exception of the BBC's room, all the thirteen reporters' rooms in the Gallery failed to meet the minimum of forty square feet per occupant specified in the Offices, Shops and Railway Premises Act of 1963. The average was below thirty feet and one of the news agencies, Exchange Telegraph, had only fifteen feet. These calculations excluded *Hansard* and *The Times*, which both had rooms outside the gallery premises. The working party's 30,000 words of evidence included a plague of grumbles—too few rooms, too few desks, too much noise and heat, not enough air and telephones. The complaint of one Lobby correspondent is worth contrasting with MacDonagh's 'spacious and well-equipped club'. Reporting Parliament

is only possible at the cost of the tension and nervous strain of those who are trying to overcome intolerable physical conditions. . . . [T]he cost of this is the risk of ill-health of those who have to work against the appalling obstacles that now stand in the way of the efficient reporter . . . First any Lobby Correspondent is dealing not with one story but with probably half a dozen. He must listen to Question Time, listen to statements after Questions, attend Lobby meetings, visit MPs who wish to see him, or whom he wishes to see in the Members' Lobby, and then set to work in conditions which would daunt anyone. He must work in a room with perhaps a dozen or more other people, all of whom are typing busily at the peak hours. The noise alone would be enough to prevent anyone in any other profession

[1] *Partners in Parliament*, p. 50.   [2] Quoted, ibid., p. 35.

from concentrating. . . . No journalist that I know working inside a news-paper office is quite so unaided as we are and I have met none who has seen the writing conditions in the House of Commons who has not been appalled by them. . . . On a big day the work is concentrated between the hours of say four to eight o'clock. At that period I think about fifteen people are liable to be in the room I occupy. The noise is fearful: there are no facilities for records: there are no outgoing telephones. At the same time there are two incoming telephones. These ring constantly. They are answered by the people nearest them or by people who happen to be in the room. The calls are seldom for the man who answers the telephone. Thought is thus interrupted. . . .[1]

Changes since 1964 have alleviated some of these problems but it is difficult to see how the Gallery will ever be treated as anything other than a poor relation.

One occasional focus of attention has been catering. The Gallery's dining room is an important symbol as well as a useful facility. In 1958 Speaker Morrison, an ally, called it essential to the tradition and dignity of the Gallery. Like the convention that M.P.s may not enter the premises, it reflects the Gallery's desire to have as autonomous a status as possible, rather than to be just a featureless extension of Parliament. 'What is wrong with the Press Gallery conditions', commented a journalist to the 1964 working party, 'stems from one basic fact—the relationship between members of Parliament as a body and journalists as a body. It is on the MP's side a relationship akin to that between first class and second class citizens. A good many journalists, including some of those most senior, share this attitude.'[2] The twentieth century has lacked brave causes like the very right to report debates, and catering seems sometimes to have been a substitute.

The dining room dates from the innovations after 1880. Previously reporters often went out to eat since only a mono-chrome diet of bread, cheese, coffee, and boiled beef was available, provided by the gallery door-keeper. The problem with the dining room has been its perennial loss of money, due to late hours and long recesses. (The bar, in contrast, seems always to have made a profit.) After a ten-year experiment contracting it out, catering returned in 1900 to the Commons Refreshment Department, where it subsequently stayed. The ambiguous tone of later press–parliament relations is reflected in a report

---

[1] Press Gallery archives.   [2] Ibid.

of the Select Committee on House of Commons Accommodation in 1901: 'A very considerable addition was made last year to the accommodation in the Reporters' rooms, but there still seems to be need for more space for dining. This is a matter involving, it is understood, some structural difficulty and expense, and the Committee recommend that the matter should be considered.'[1] Relations never reached the level of a major crisis until February 1958, although they had had more downs than ups since 1945. Without warning the Secretary received from the Clerk of the Select Committee on Kitchen and Refreshment Rooms a formal letter announcing that after the Easter recess the dining-room facilities would be withdrawn. The reaction was strong. Speaker Morrison wrote to the Chancellor of the Exchequer in support. Emergency protest meetings and deputations ensured that the threat was lifted. The 1964 working party reported: 'Our objective there is plain: to keep [the dining room] by whatever means is necessary.'[2]

The incident illustrates well the tenuousness of the Gallery's position. The outrage seems to have been as much to members' dignity as to their stomachs. 'It is true that when I entered the Gallery we received little consideration from the Authorities', remarked Sir Alexander Mackintosh (talking of the 1880s from the vantage point of the 1940s): 'But gradually we received more and more the rights of self-government until we enjoyed a sort of Home-rule under the Speaker and the Serjeant-at-Arms.'[3] The reporters remain at Westminster on sufferance, however, even now that their reports are no longer technically an offence. The authorities control admission tickets, and the executive power of the Gallery Committee, set up in 1881 and numbering about ten members and three officers, relates only to strictly internal affairs. Speakers may pledge, as did Speaker Fitzroy in 1940, that 'the Speaker will always be ready to uphold the rights and privileges of the gallery in the House of Commons'.[4] Serjeants-at-Arms may make comparable pledges: Sir Henry Erskine, having received from the Gallery

---

[1] *Select Committee on House of Commons Accommodation, Report*, H.C. 234, 1901, p. v, section 5.

[2] *Partners in Parliament*, p. 29.   [3] *Echoes of Big Ben*, pp. 161–2.

[4] *Partners in Parliament*, p. 16.

on the occasion of his silver wedding in 1911 a silver inkstand and a verbal bouquet (and having seen his wife receive a floral one), claimed that no one could appreciate more fully the difficulties of the Gallery, and that 'his endeavour had always been to do everything in his power to grease the wheels of their coach'.[1] But Parliament is the ultimate judge of the rights and privileges; Parliament supplies the accommodation free of charge; and while reporters are no longer the social inferiors of parliamentarians, as they commonly were in 1900, their bargaining position cannot be strong. The ambiguousness of their position was nicely illustrated by an incident in the 1972 session. The Serjeant-at-Arms, presumably protecting the Lobby's traditional secretiveness, refused to give a copy of the Lobby list to an M.P. who wished to circularize its members. He raised the matter as a question of privilege. While the Speaker refused to give the complaint precedence over Orders of the Day—thus leaving it unsettled—the Services Committee were prompted to issue a special report affirming the right of Members to have the list made available and recommending that henceforth it be published quarterly.[2] The 1964 working party called its report *Partners in Parliament*. From Parliament's viewpoint, the partnership has never been one among equals.

A different kind of facility, causing fewer problems, is the provision to gallery members of advance copies of documents. This started earlier than one might think. Not only were bills, amendments, and parliamentary papers in general supplied by 1900, but M.P.s had begun to appreciate in the 1870s and 1880s the advantages of making sure that their speeches were recorded as accurately as possible. They started to adopt the habit of sending up their notes to the Gallery. Copies of Ministers' answers to Questions were routinely placed in one of the writing rooms. Without them, in the days before amplification, detailed answers could be lost altogether. Lloyd George was creating a precedent, however, when he sent up at intervals of fifteen minutes the succeeding sections of his crisis-provoking Budget speech in 1909, so that the reporters could be sure to have the facts and figures right.

These practices were significantly changed only with the

[1] *The Times*, 27 June 1911.

[2] 885 *H.C. Deb.* c. 1475–8, c. 1637–8, 3rd of May 1978; H.C. 331, 1972–3.

proliferation of departmental Press Officers in Whitehall during the Second World War. The tendency was increasingly for them to make themselves available in the Gallery at Question Time or before ministerial statements with copies of what was being said and any background information that might be necessary. The Gallery also established a 'statements secretary' through whom such information could be distributed if a Press Officer was not present. Departments have obviously varied in their efficiency, in the opinion of reporters; but there is periodic liaison with gallery officials, and there have even been conferences of Press Officers and gallery man.

In this account of facilities no distinction has yet been drawn between the Lobby correspondents and other Westminster journalists. The work of the Lobby men is described in more detail below. Here one need simply note that, broadly, the gallery man is concerned with reporting or describing proceedings on the floor of the House, and the Lobby man explains and interprets them in the context of what happens outside the Chamber. Lobby men use the Gallery's facilities, as the earlier grumbles by one of them indicate. In addition they have their own organization and committee. Numbers have, again, always been controlled by the Serjeant-at-Arms. Editors of eligible papers nominate journalists whose names are put on the Serjeant's list. 'The journalist then (compulsorily) joins a 'voluntary' lobby association and pays a nominal subscription.'[1]

The Lobby is a more competitive place than the Gallery. Relations with Ministers are closer and confidential. The opportunities for a member to offend are greater. While the Lobby has been accused since 1945 of the comfortable vices of pack journalism, its Committee's writ does not extend to control over whom editors nominate. Nor can the Committee therefore explicitly enforce the detailed rules set down for newcomers in the booklet 'Lobby Practice', first drafted in the late 1940s. The Lobby's facilities are not the kind which take much administering either. The original 'facility', which gave the job its name, was the privilege of frequenting the Members' Lobby immediately outside the House of Commons. It is a good place

---

[1] Tunstall, op. cit., p. 5. The punctuation, brackets around compulsorily and the quotation marks around voluntary are intended to convey some of the nuances of the relationship.

for making contact with Members. All other journalists and the public are excluded from it. Secondly, Lobby men get from the Vote Office free copies of parliamentary papers as soon as they are published (in a technical sense which does not mean they are widely available, even to Members). This includes *Hansard*, Votes and Proceedings, the Order Paper, Bills, Motions and Amendments, White Papers, Blue Books, Departmental Reports, and a large variety of Stationery Office publications. Thirdly, there are Lobby meetings, which originated in the early 1930s. These take place in a distant committee room allocated to the Lobby, with details of former office holders on the wall. They are chaired by the Lobby Chairman—a symbol of the fact that they are held at the invitation of the Lobby and not at the behest of the Ministers and party leaders who are the chief guests. This is not the pretence it might seem. Ministers have quite often sought an invitation through their press relations staff and have been rebuffed because the Lobby are too busy or feel the exercise would be fruitless. A last 'facility' worth mentioning are the Lobby lunches. As late as 1914 these were probably held two or three times a session. Between the wars they were always twice a year and after 1945 once a year. Not only were the speeches of the guests off the record: they were so numbingly secret that according to the one-time Lobby Chairman, Guy Eden, writing in 1950, 'it is bad form even to discuss in private what may be said'.[1] The reason for this was a characteristic paradox: some of the 'most interesting, important and revealing speeches' ever made by public figures (and therefore eminently worth discussing) were made at these lunches. The practice came to a sad end in 1964. At a special meeting the Lobby decided to abandon it because of the friction and jealousy aroused. More and more editors and news executives wanted invitations to the lunches, and more and more M.P.s grumbled because they were left out.[2]

What most of those facilities boil down to is the definition of a number of places at Westminster where Lobby journalists and politicians can meet and talk, individually and in groups. The facilities gain their significance from the kind, purposes, and

[1] *The Press Gallery at Westminster*, p. 21.
[2] Tunstall, op. cit., p. 77.

uses of the talk which goes on. These are all examined further below.

The work of the Gallery has been affected not just by its facilities and Parliament's attitudes but also by developments in the newspaper industry. At the turn of the century basic changes were taking place which influenced the shape of the industry right into the 1970s. They were typified in the foundation of the *Daily Mail* by Alfred Harmsworth (Lord Northcliffe) in 1896. The first number sold 397,215 copies, more than any English daily paper had sold before. Within four years the *Mail* was printing in Manchester as well as in London, and had a circulation of nearly one million. Most of the ideas that made this achievement possible as well as the technical developments facilitating large print runs (i.e. large circulations) came from America. Harmsworth was the first to exploit them. Above all, he matched the vast potential lower middle class readership who were prepared to pay one halfpenny for a daily paper, but not one penny, with the growing supply of advertising (especially for branded goods—sewing machines, food products, etc.). The *Daily Mail*'s masthead proclaimed it 'The Penny Newspaper for One Halfpenny'. The Victorian newspapers were heavily political—appealing primarily, as R. D. Blumenfeld (a Harmsworth contemporary) put it, 'to the business and professional classes whose private interests were always directly affected by the issues of party politics'.[1] In contrast the *Mail* and its competitors—both new, like Arthur Pearson's *Daily Express*, and rejuvenated like the Cadbury's *Daily News*—were lively, entertaining, full of snippets of inconsequential news, with particular appeal to women and those in the lower middle classes with a modicum of purchasing power and leisure.

You could search the Victorian newspapers in vain [Harmsworth reminisced years later] for any reference to changing fashions, for instance. You could not find in them anything that would help you to understand the personalities of public men. We cannot get from them a clear and complete picture of the times in which they were published, as one could from the *Daily Mail*. Before that was published, journalism dealt only with a few aspects of life. What we did was extend its purview to life as a whole.[2]

[1] Blumenfeld, op. cit., p. 109.
[2] Quoted in Harold Herd, *The March of Journalism* (Allen and Unwin, 1952), p. 241.

In addition to its low-price, large-sale strategy, its dependence on advertising revenue, and its new stress on profit (the *Daily Mail* was the first daily paper in which the public could buy shares), the burgeoning popular press had severe consequences for the rest of the industry. First, it contributed to a drastic decline in the number of provincial morning papers—from 52 in 1900 to 25 in 1940 (Table VI.1). London morning papers were less affected. A few, certainly, went out of business (e.g. the *Standard* in 1917), but newcomers kept the overall number around ten—and continued to do so throughout the century. The *Daily Mirror* started, in the mid-1930s, to expand into the working class, the last great market, using exactly the same method as the *Daily Mail* forty years earlier, but in a tabloid format borrowed from the United States. The post-1945 deaths of the *News Chronicle* (1960), *Daily Herald* (1964), and *Daily Sketch* (1971) were matched by the foundation of the *Sun* (1964) and the emergence of the *Guardian* and the *Financial Times* as fully-fledged national dailies. But as early as 1928 *The Economist* could comment: 'Unless assisted by the earnings of an associated evening paper, secure in its appeal to "racing and football" readers, a provincial daily is, broadly speaking, no longer a very profitable asset.'[1] Evening papers, as the remark indicates, were less vulnerable to London-based competition. Their number actually rose slightly up to the 1920s and did not fall steeply afterwards. The decline of provincial mornings led finally, of course, to the virtual elimination of towns with competing newspapers.

A second effect of the popular press, following the size and national penetration of their circulations, was the growth of chain ownership, linking provincials with each other and with the London papers. In 1921 five out of 41 provincial mornings belonged to chains. By 1939 ten out of the diminished number of 25 did so—mainly to the Berry brothers or the Westminster Press. Forty per cent of the provincial evenings were in chains by 1934, and half the Sundays and London mornings. The Berry's division of family holdings in the later 1930s reduced the totals somewhat.

The provincial press suffered in circulation too. Figures

---

[1] *The Economist*, 1 Nov. 1928.

before 1920 are unreliable. Between the wars the London mornings doubled their circulation in the process of becoming national papers. By contrast the London evenings remained static and the provincials dropped. Separate figures for provincial mornings are particularly scarce, but it seems probable that their total circulation was at least half that of the London mornings in 1920. Twenty years later—and after—it was down to one seventh. A 'quality' provincial morning paper like the *Manchester Guardian* and the *Yorkshire Post* might sell anything between 25,000 and 50,000 copies in 1921. This did not look completely ridiculous beside *The Times* or the *Morning Post*; and 'populars' like the *Daily Dispatch* (203,000) could compare with the *Daily News* (300,000) or the *Daily Express* (579,000). By 1939 that was finished. The London papers, led by the *Daily Express* (2,546,000), were nearly all over one and a half million; and *The Times* (204,000) and the *Daily Telegraph* (737,000) were out of reach.

TABLE VI.1

Provincial Daily Papers (England, Scotland, and Wales)
1900–1970

	Morning	Evening	Towns with two or more Morning Papers
1900	52	81 (?)	17
1910	45	?	15
1920	45	89(?)	15
1930	32	82	8
1940	25	76	7 (1938)
1950	25	76	4 (1948)
1960	19	74	1
1970	18	75	1

Sources: Royal Commissions on the Press, 1947, 1962; Press Council Annual Reports; D. E. Butler and Jennie Freeman, *British Political Facts 1900–1967* (Macmillan, 1968).

A last change to mention—though less clearly a product of the growth of the popular press—was the rapid decline of the London evening papers. In 1900 there had been almost as many of these (nine) as of morning papers (ten). At the end of the First World War there were still six, selling well over one-third as many as the morning papers. Two of them, however, the *Pall Mall Gazette* and the *Westminster Gazette*, were 'club-land' papers with matchstick circulations in the twenty-thousands. In their heyday before the war, they had enjoyed a quite disproportionate political influence and a close connection to parliamentary life. By the mid-twenties only the *Star*, the *Evening Standard*, and the *Evening News* remained.

These changes can be summed up inelegantly by saying that the press changed in the twentieth century from a large number of London-based (or 'metropolitan') morning and evening papers and a very large number of provincial morning and evening papers, to a small number of national morning papers (sharply distinguished into 'quality' and 'popular' types) and a small number of provincial morning and evening papers.

The implications for parliamentary coverage were considerable. The new breed of proprietor, firstly, did not see his paper so exclusively as a party political instrument. Before the First World War at least four London papers—the *Observer*, the *Standard*, the *Globe*, and the *Pall Mall Gazette*—were in regular receipt of Unionist subsidies. When Max Aitken (Lord Beaverbrook) bought the *Globe* in 1911 for £40,000, £15,000 came from his own pocket and the rest from party funds.[1] On the Liberal side, families like the Cadburys and Colmans ran papers in the party interest without regard to profitability. Weetman Pearson spent three-quarters of a million pounds keeping the *Westminster Gazette* going as a morning paper from 1921–8. By 1929 the TUC had sunk half-a-million into the *Daily Herald* and seen a profit only once, in the first six months of 1924. In the 1930s all that stopped. The *Daily Herald* was made profitable by J. S. Elias of Odhams, using aggressive salesmanship that had nothing to do with politics (let alone socialism). Despite a plea to Neville Chamberlain the *Morning Post*, rescued by a Conservative syndicate in 1924, found no backers when it tottered again in 1937. (Its circulation was said

[1] A. J. P. Taylor, *Beaverbrook* (Hamish Hamilton, 1972); see e.g., pp. 61–2. For a general discussion of the press and the party system between the wars, see Colin Seymour-Ure, 'The Press and the Party System between the Wars', in Gillian Peele and Chris Cook (eds.), *The Politics of Reappraisal 1918–1939* (Macmillan, 1975), pp. 232–57.

to decrease each day by the number of deaths reported in its columns.) No Liberals saved the *Daily Chronicle* in 1930; it merged with the *Daily News*.

Proprietors like Beaverbrook, Northcliffe, and his brother Rothermere, were certainly engrossed in politics. But their mass circulation papers needed profits (notwithstanding Beaverbrook's later boasts to the contrary) and advertising revenue. Their papers therefore tended to become 'depoliticized'. Readers were won partly by a low price and partly by the extraordinary insurance and free-gift circulation wars of the late 1920s and early 1930s. (A whole Welsh family, it was rumoured, could be clothed for the price of eight weeks reading of the *Daily Express*.) The premium on brightness and entertainment meant that the popular press developed a broad social function rather than a narrowly political—still less partisan—one. Editors became technicians like Arthur Christiansen of Beaverbrook's *Daily Express*, not trenchant political essayists. Had he and his like been put in charge of a really popular paper, admitted the *Westminster Gazette* editor, J. A. Spender, in 1927, they 'could have been relied upon to kill it in about a fortnight'. Such papers had a power which was a serious rival to Parliament, he grumbled sourly, 'and upon which Parliament in the last resort depends'.[1] Lloyd George wrote of Northcliffe: 'He owed no allegiance to any party, so that every genuine party man deplored his paper. Most of them bought it and read what was in it and then damned it.'[2]

'In broadening the basis of journalism,' R. D. Blumenfeld reflected, 'the modern newspaper has also broadened the basis of politics.'[3] He was sceptical—probably quite rightly—how far the old verbatim reports of speeches were read. Lord Rosebery, for instance, confessed at a Press Club lunch in 1913 that except among those whose painful duty it was to read speeches for professional reasons he could never find anybody who read them.[4] The new mode of journalism took this view for granted. The historian of the *Birmingham Post* noted that in the 1920s 'Parliament and Whitehall had become only one of several

[1] *Life, Journalism and Politics* (Cassell, 2 vols., 1927), Vol. II, p. 136.
[2] David Lloyd George, *The Truth about the Peace Treaties* (Gollancz, 2 vols., 1938), Vol. I, p. 266.
[3] Op. cit., p. 125.   [4] Quoted, ibid., p. 120.

public topics, and their treatment in the papers tended to move away from the spacious solemnity of earlier times.' The *Post's* new London correspondent in 1923 'had to reflect this change of emphasis'.[1] Similarly Blumenfeld noted in 1933 that 'the cutting down of newspaper reports of Parliamentary debates and political speeches generally is one of the most significant changes that have taken place in British journalism during my time'.[2] Long reports gave way progressively to digests and summaries supplemented by a sketch. Colin Coote, who wrote *The Times'* sketch for some years in the 1920s, described the work as 'really precis-writing with a few frills'.[3] For the popular press, however, the sketch was a more exciting feature. In Blumenfeld's words, 'It is the dramatic asides, the lively incidents, the witty backchat, the idiosyncrasies of speakers, the tense moments of conflict between the dominant personalities, the whole human setting of the Parliamentary scene, that the public likes to read about, and it is this that the popular newspaper sets out to give.'[4] J. B. Atkins, the *Manchester Guardian's* sketch-writer in 1899, caught his employers' eye partly by his sports writing.[5] The decline in verbatim reporting, whose practitioners prided themselves on their non-partisanship, provided new opportunities for biased parliamentary coverage too. This is obviously extremely difficult to measure over a period of time, but Blumenfeld for one felt that in the 1930s unbalanced treatment was far too common.

The popular press signalled also, finally, an increased role for the Lobby correspondent. A broader, less politically-minded readership needed politics interpreted to it more than hitherto.

Some of the changes in newspaper attitudes to parliamentary coverage can be charted by simple content analysis. Table V.2 shows the percentage of their editorial copy (that is, of their total space less advertisements) given to parliamentary coverage in London-based morning daily papers. The *Yorkshire Post* and

[1] H. R. G. Whates, *The Birmingham Post 1857–1957* (Birmingham Post and Mail Ltd., 1957), p. 152.

[2] Op. cit., p. 112.

[3] *Editorial* (Eyre and Spottiswoode, 1965), p. 142. Coote was an M.P. after the war until 1922. His varied journalistic career ended as editor of the *Daily Telegraph*, 1950–64.

[4] Op. cit., p. 122.

[5] David Ayerst, *Guardian: Biography of a Newspaper* (Collins, 1971), p. 262.

the *Scotsman* are included as examples of major papers outside London. The *Manchester Guardian* comes in this category too for all the sampling dates except 1960 and 1972. Coverage was measured for every twelfth year, starting in 1900. This had the advantages of regularity combined with a fairly late end date and of avoiding a war year. A war year would have been interesting in itself but difficult for comparison. The effects of the war economy remain clearly visible in the figures for 1948, when newspapers were still obliged to keep their pages down. File copies of a few papers were not available for particular years; and some papers that were short-lived or did not survive long into the twentieth century are excluded. Figures are not presented in column inches or square inches since fluctuations in type size and design make a considerable difference to the number of words per inch. For a broad comparison across the century percentages are better. In addition, all percentages have been linked to an index number of 100 based on the coverage of *The Times* (the fullest coverage) in 1936, the mid-year of the sample. Coverage was measured of ten parliamentary days per calendar year—two of each weekday. (Full details of the sampling method are given in the bibliographical note.) All kinds of coverage were measured, including reports, sketches, Lobby pieces, leading articles, gossip, letters, pictures, and cartoons.

Figure VI.1 shows the trend of coverage for all the papers averaged together. Between 1900 and 1972 coverage dropped almost exactly in half, from 7·3 per cent of editorial space to 3·6 per cent. The peak, however, proves not to have been the turn of the century but the austerity year of 1948 (7·9 per cent). Papers had only half a dozen pages or so and there was a heavy, controversial legislative programme. But that period represented a kind of hiccup. Without it the path is a steady decline, the steepest drop taking place between 1924 and 1936. In those years the popular papers competed most aggressively for a mass readership. For instance the *Daily Express* rose from a circulation of 850,000 in 1925 to 2,546,000 in 1939; the *Daily Mirror* from 964,000 to 1,571,000 (entirely after 1935); and the *Daily Herald* from 350,000 to 1,850,000. In those years the general pattern of modern newspaper values was set.

None of the papers in Table VI.2 fits at all closely to the

Figure VI.I. Parliamentary coverage as a percentage of total editorial space: average for all selected daily newspapers, 1900–1972

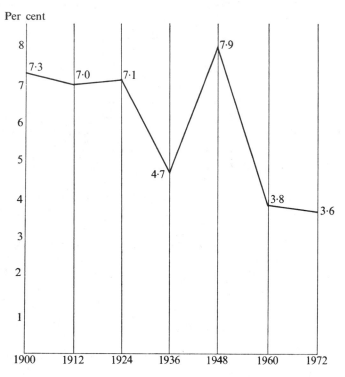

Note: for selected papers, see Table VI.2.

golden age view of the newspaper as a heavily political product. Obviously much imperial and foreign news was political, as well as some domestic non-parliamentary news. But by 1900 even in the two oldest and traditionally most 'serious' papers, the *Morning Post* (1772) and *The Times* (1785), the proportion of parliamentary news was only about 10 per cent. Other papers like the Liberal *Daily News* (1846), the *Daily Chronicle* (1869), the *Morning Leader* (1892–1912), and the Unionist *Daily Telegraph* (1855) were already affected by competition from the newly founded *Daily Mail* (1896) and the *Daily Express* (1900). (The *Daily Express* was the first paper to put news on the front page.) Even so, most of them were publishing at least twice as much parliamentary copy, proportionately, as the newcomers. By 1912 Northcliffe's *Daily Mirror* (1903) was established too. This was essentially a genteel illustrated paper with a completely different audience from the massive working-class readership it gained in the late 1930s. The *Daily Sketch*, also, was founded in 1908. The older 'popular' papers still had a significantly larger parliamentary coverage. After the First World War the distinction disappeared. Indeed the *Daily Chronicle*, bought by Lloyd George as a mouthpiece at the end of the war, fell below all the newcomers—although there was not very much difference between any of them. This was due partly to an actual increase in the coverage given by the *Daily Mail* and the *Daily Express*. The drop between 1924 and 1936 was uniform (except, oddly, for *The Times*, for which the low 1924 figure was exceptional). It is deceptively steep for the *Daily Herald*. The *Herald*'s 1924 coverage (14 per cent) was the highest for any paper in any of the sample years and reflected that paper's connection with the Labour movement. In 1924 it was directly owned by the TUC and the Labour Party. After commercial control (but not political policy) passed to Odhams in 1929 the paper became less distinctive.

Among the surviving populars in 1960 and 1972 coverage was down to the same level (or less) as in 1900. A large part of the overall decrease, however, was made up of decreases in the coverage by the 'quality' papers. *The Times* in 1972 was giving proportionately only three-quarters of the coverage it gave in 1900. The *Daily Telegraph* was down on its 1912 figures (and on the 1900 figures of the *Morning Post*, which it absorbed in 1937). The provincial papers especially gave up the attempt to compete with the London papers. In 1924 the *Scotsman* and the *Yorkshire Post* were still sufficiently entrenched in their areas to carry on much as before, but the *Manchester Guardian* had dropped its coverage by a third. After the Second World War the other two papers fell similarly, although the *Scotsman*'s status as a national paper for Scotland gave it an incentive to keep the level up. In 1972 the *Scotsman* carried more parliamentary news proportionately than did the *Guardian* in its national guise.

With a twelve-year interval between the sample dates these figures must be treated with caution. They are consistent with

TABLE VI.2

Parliamentary Coverage in Daily Newspapers, 1900–1972: Percentage of Editorial Space, and Index
(The Times, 1936=100)

Name and Lifespan date of Newspaper	1900 %	1900 index	1912 %	1912 index	1924 %	1924 index	1936 %	1936 index	1948 %	1948 index	1960 %	1960 index	1972 %	1972 index
Morning Post (1772–1937)	10·0	111	10·2	113	13·8	153	6·0	66	—	—	—	—	—	—
The Times (1785–)	12·5	138	12·2	135	3·9	43	9·0	100	10·3	114	6·9	76	9·4	104
Daily News (1846)/News Chronicle (1931–60)	5·3	59	8·8	97	5·8	64	3·6	40	5·5	61	2·3	26	—	—
Daily Telegraph (1855–)	3·6	40	9·1	101	8·0	88	5·7	63	13·8	153	6·9	76	7·0	77
Daily Chronicle (1869–1931)	7·3	81	n.a.	n.a.	4·6	51	—	—	—	—	—	—	—	—
Daily Graphic (1890–1926)	5·3	59	5·3	59	5·2	58	—	—	—	—	—	—	—	—
Morning Leader (1892–1912)	5·8	64	—	—	—	—	—	—	—	—	—	—	—	—
Daily Mail (1896–)	n.a.	n.a.	3·2	36	5·5	61	4·2	46	8·0	88	3·3	36	3·0	33

Daily Express (1900–)	2·7	30	2·8	31	5·3	59	2·6	29	10·9	121	1·6	18	2·0	22
Daily Mirror (1903–)	—	—	1·5	17	4·7	52	2·0	21	4·6	51	1·3	14	1·8	20
Daily Sketch (1908–71)	—	—	2·9	32	4·0	44	1·0	11	4·9	55	n.a.	n.a.	—	—
Daily Herald (1912–64)	—	—	—	—	14·1	155	4·6	51	9·8	108	1·9	21	—	—
Westminster Gazette (1921–28)	—	—	—	—	7·5	83	—	—	—	—	—	—	—	—
Sun (1964–)	—	—	—	—	—	—	—	—	—	—	—	—	1·1	12
Manchester Guardian (1821–)	11·4	126	12·0	133	8·0	88	5·2	58	12·0	133	5·3	59	4·3	47
Scotsman (1817–)	9·6	107	10·2	113	9·8	108	8·0	88	10·6	117	5·8	64	4·8	53
Yorkshire Post (1866–)	n.a.	n.a.	6·9	76	7·6	84	4·7	52	2·1	23	3·4	38	2·9	32

Note: 'editorial space' is total space less advertisements.

Daily Sketch was named *Daily Graphic*, 1946–52. *Westminster Gazette* was an evening paper 1893–1921.

the impressions of journalists, however. At the very least, one can say that in 1900 it was not uncommon for morning papers to give 10 per cent of their space to Parliament and rare for them to give less than 5 per cent. By 1972 5 per cent was rare and 10 per cent unheard of (though *The Times* came close).

As those changes indicate, the emphasis in party coverage has shifted considerably during the twentieth century. There were five types of parliamentary journalist in 1900; reporters (the largest group), sketch-writers, Lobby men, writers of London letters for provincial papers, and artists. The latter included such specialists in parliamentary caricature as Francis Carruthers Gould of the *Westminster Gazette* (and earlier the *Pall Mall Gazette*), the first staff cartoonist on a British daily paper. As photographs rapidly replaced drawings in the illustrated press the number of artists dwindled. London letters continued well into the inter-war years but with decreasing parliamentary content, so that their authors ceased to be a significant distinguishable group in the Gallery.

The reporters in 1900 were probably just past the height of their importance. If any one occasion was their apogee, perhaps it was 8 April 1886, when Gladstone introduced his Home Rule Bill in a speech of nearly 25,000 words, lasting three and a half hours. London and provincial papers alike took it down verbatim, some of them using up to twenty reporters in a kind of fire-bucket relay. Gladstone sat down at 8 o'clock and before midnight Manchester, Leeds, and Edinburgh had the speech in type.[1] Lloyd George's Budget in 1909 was a comparable exercise; the demand for gallery seats was so great that sketch-writers were allotted a section of the Strangers' Gallery (an unprecedented step) and the Press Gallery was reserved as far as possible for reporters.[2] But this was a kind of *reprise* and not to be repeated. Ever since the provincial papers had been admitted to the Gallery in 1881 the habit of sketch-writing had grown more important and the straight reporting of extensive speeches less so. David Ayerst, historian of the *Manchester Guardian*, describes James Drysdale's sketch as 'one of the highlights of each day's *Guardian*'.[3] In 1900 the two kinds of

[1] J. D. Symon, *The Press and its Story* (Seeley Service, 1914), p. 84.
[2] MacDonagh, *The Reporters' Gallery*, p. 9.
[3] Ayerst, op. cit., p. 348.

reporting coexisted quite happily, since there was space for both.

Reporting and sketch-writing both basked, moreover, in the reflected glory of Parliament. J. D. Symon, writing in 1914, could refer to the Gallery as 'the height of reportorial ambition'.[1] MacDonagh called it every young reporter's goal. He played fancifully with the idea that no reporter on his first day would dream of taking the lift up to the Gallery but would trudge the narrow stairway—'to make the stairs stepping stones to higher things'.[2] Paradoxically, therefore, one reason for the gallery man's status was that he might not stay there long but move on to the higher grades of journalism, to law, politics, and, in those days, religion. A young reporter off to join the *Scotsman*'s parliamentary staff in 1924 was told by Sir Robert Bruce, editor of the paper he was leaving, the *Glasgow Herald*, that the Gallery was as good as a university education. In the days before the expansion of state education there was much truth in that—not least in the literal sense that the gallery man's routine provided plenty of opportunity to study for Bar exams and the like. Beyond that, parliamentary work was considered good experience generally. Despite the decline of interest in political news, for example, the editor of the *Birmingham Post* chose as the new head of his London office in 1923 a man with parliamentary experience in the Gallery.[3] Geoffrey Dawson took Alan Robbins out of the Lobby in 1938 to become news editor of *The Times*. When Barrington-Ward wanted to groom someone in the late 1940s to succeed Robbins he insisted that it should be a man with parliamentary experience.

Those considerations applied to gallery men indifferently. The reporter still had his own distinct professional status in 1900, rooted essentially in the claim to possess a kind of judgement. MacDonagh contrasts the reporter, a touch scornfully, with the mere shorthand writer.

A reporter is a person with a quite different capacity. He must have a knowledge of the subject under discussion, and such judgement and discretion, and gift for condensation as will enable him to divest the ideas and arguments of the speaker of diffuseness and verbiage, and present them clearly and concisely in print. . . . There is no limit to the subjects, no

[1] Op. cit., p. 75.   [2] *The Reporters' Gallery*, p. 4.
[3] Whates, op. cit., p. 152.

boundaries to the places, that the House of Commons may not get in touch with on any night of a Session. That being so, the reporter, besides being a rapid note-taker, must be acquainted with the history and geography of the world, and especially of the British Empire, and also have so complete an understanding of current politics and economics as to appreciate the subtle illusions which play about every great debate, for, without this equipment, he will not be able, on the one hand, fully to report the important speeches of Ministers and ex-Ministers, and, on the other, to condense judicially the remarks of speakers who, while they do not bear to be reported verbatim, have yet something of value and interest to say.[1]

In other words the reporter must be a renaissance man. Such a conception turns completely on the assumption that the floor of the House is where the important parliamentary business is done; that readers need and want to follow it in some detail; and that its full significance will be manifest in a scrupulously accurate and proportioned report. (Sir Alexander Mackintosh once asked a reporter why he did not insert the name of a Member to whom Gladstone had referred in a scathing passage, since the report left the man's identity in doubt. 'It is not my duty', the reporter replied, 'to add to Gladstone's words.')[2]

The machinery of parliamentary reporting was finely tuned in 1900 to meet that kind of need. Most papers had from three to a dozen reporters. One or two, like *The Times*, had rather more. During the years when *The Times* was contracted to produce *Hansard* its staff was as high as eighteen. *The Times'* chief of staff occupied the central place in the Gallery, immediately above the Speaker's chair, with two more *Times'* men on his left and the *Daily Telegraph* on his right. Reporters did their work in 'turns', usually of a quarter of an hour, but as short as five minutes when press time was near. A carefully worked-out timetable was prepared, including instructions about length and first/third person. After each turn the reporter would write up his notes ready for the office. Then he would be free until his next turn, perhaps a couple of hours later. Well into the present century copy was sent by messenger. *The Times*, uniquely, started a system in 1951 of marking up the parliamentary copy and setting type actually at Westminster.

That routine remained the same throughout the century. The number of newspapers using it declined drastically. Already by

---

[1] *The Reporters' Gallery*, p. 19.   [2] Mackintosh, op. cit., p. 161.

the First World War many of the smaller provincial papers had begun to rely on agency copy and to use their staff men simply for sketches and London letters. Three agencies supplied a service—the Press Association (PA), Central News, and the Exchange Telegraph (Extel). All were nineteenth-century foundations. A subscription to Extel cost £50 per annum before the First World War. A fourth agency, Reuters, supplied the foreign press. Eventually the agencies themselves reduced in number. First went Central News, whose parliamentary service was taken over by the Press Association in 1947. Then Exchange Telegraph, whose staff fell sharply in the 1950s, stopped its service on 31 December 1965. The result—a *de facto* monopoly for the PA—led to comment in both Houses of Parliament. But only a handful of provincial papers and not even all the nationals had still been subscribing to Extel and the service had lost money for years.[1] By the 1970s only four organizations were collecting a full, or fairly full, verbatim report: *Hansard*, The Press Association, *The Times*, and the *Daily Telegraph*. Accompanying the progressive disappearance of verbatim work went a decline in the number of gallery men who could write shorthand. What in 1900 had been an indispensable qualification, the source of much professional pride,[2] was by the 1920s merely a convenience for most reporters. *Hansard* found the Gallery ceasing to be a reliable recruiting ground for its own staff.[3]

The high status of the parliamentary reporter endured to the First World War, but it was increasingly displaced by that of the sketch-writer. We have seen the reasons why sketch-writing appealed to publishers and editors. They coincided clearly too with developments in Parliament—notably the declining importance of the set-piece debate in the Chamber as a source of significant political news. It would be a mistake to see the roots of sketch-writing wholly in the last fifteen or twenty years of the nineteenth century, however. Already in the 1840s and 1850s enterprising journalists knew that there was room for

---

[1] J. M. Scott, *Extel 100* (Ernest Benn, 1972), pp. 90, 208–9.

[2] Out of session, parliamentary reporters were commonly put onto comparable work—annual conferences of many kinds and, in those days, formal dinners.

[3] L. W. Bear, 'Parliamentary Reporting at Westminster (Part I)', *The Parliamentarian*, Vol. LIII, 1972.

descriptive as well as narrative parliamentary reporting. 'The curious thing', Disraeli wrote to his sister about one of his performances in 1840, 'is that *The Times*, which gives an admirable report of what I said, gives a most inefficient impression of the effect produced.'[1]

The sketch-writers' increasing success bred resentment in old gallery hands. 'We are simply crowded out by sketchwriters,' grumbled J. F. McCallum, head óf the Press Association staff, in 1908, 'and these gentlemen, who are rather lofty, have very little regard to the convenience of the reporter, thinking that they are a cut above him. They will chatter when he is busy taking notes, making his task sometimes excessively difficult.'[2] It was not surprising if the likes of Henry Lucy and T. P. O'Connor felt their skills were less mechanical than the reporters'. They were stylists and sometimes more highly educated. At root theirs was a journalism of comment. They enjoyed a higher status in their offices and they caught the eye of M.P.s. O'Connor, for example, got away with copy which would surely not have been acceptable from an ordinary reporter. He invented a sort of typewritten shorthand and used an inadequate machine: 'Spkr lookd surprisd at hon mbrs interptn and gd. natrdly remarkd tt twas impossible make hhway if hon mbrs wr alld to intervene on soh slight notice, which evokd ld cheerng.'[3] Again, the proprietor of the *Birmingham Post* 'enjoyed the occasional flurries' stirred up by his sketch-writer and had a relationship 'on a plane of confidence and friendship' with him. ('You're a cantankerous old devil, Whates,' Charles Hyde said at the close of a private conversation, 'but you tell me the truth.') His sketches were a daily column on the leader page—'an almost sacrosanct feature of the paper'.[4]

The measure of Lucy's esteem with M.P.s (apart from his knighthood in 1909) was the reaction in 1905 to a libel case in which he was the defendant, as 'Toby, M.P.' An all-party committee was formed to raise the £300 fine. Lucy's personal friends among M.P.s were circularized, but others, including peers, made contributions unsolicited. The contributors inclu-

---

[1] Quoted, MacDonagh, *The Reporters' Gallery*, p. 43.
[2] Quoted, ibid., p. 44.   [3] Quoted, Blumenfeld, op. cit., p. 115.
[4] Whates, op. cit., pp. 149–50.

ded many Cabinet Ministers. Subscriptions actually had to be limited to one guinea. Even if some of them may have been in recognition of *Punch* as much as of Lucy himself, it was still an impressive episode.

Extra weight was given to the sketch-writers' position because parliamentarians saw that they had a certain power. 'I suppose for one person who reads the report there are thousands who read the summary and the sketch', remarked Mr. Asquith in 1908.[1] The sketch-writer is universally read, observed Lloyd George a few years later, 'and therefore he is very dangerous. . . . [P]eople depend for their impressions of Parliament on his writings'.[2] Lloyd George's feeling was that an impression was conveyed that rather underestimated Parliament's capacity. Politicians were also concerned, of course, at the possible partisanship of sketch-writers. A Liberal Minister before the First World War told Sir Alexander Mackintosh 'with ill-concealed petulance' that it was 'the duty of the Press to report the speeches, not to comment on the manners and idiosyn-cracies [*sic*] of the members'.[3]

In due course the sketch-writers in their turn were to diminish in importance. Before 1914, however, they and the reporters leave the impression that the Gallery was a successful, self-confident place—and without too many worries, at that time, about facilities. The club atmosphere went beyond the exclusive attitude to women, foreigners, and M.P.s. There was a flourishing golf club, the high point of whose calendar was a match against parliamentarians (with Mr. Balfour a coveted opponent). Members helped each other out in difficulties: the occupational hazard of the sketch-writer, for instance, was to be out of the Gallery at the one moment when something he should not miss cropped up. (The risk of missing a speaker altogether was removed when annunciators were installed in the writing rooms.) There were gallery outings to the seaside; and an annual dinner at which the guest of honour was always a party leader (Balfour in 1908, Asquith in 1909, Grey in 1912, Bonar Law in 1913). Their speeches were reported in *The Times*.

An unavoidable problem in days of long reports and bad acoustics was the misheard or mistranscribed remark. William

---

[1] MacDonagh, *The Reporters' Gallery*, p. 45.   [2] Loc. cit.
[3] Op. cit., p. 161.

Law published a list in his history of *Hansard*, from which these examples are drawn.[1] The correct words are in brackets:

Not one jot or tickle (tittle)
That was good enough in the citizen (cities and) towns
This was a patriotic and audible (laudable) move
A self-denying audience (ordinance)
The proposal is that the Capital should be evaporated (evacuated) immediately on the declaration of war
The colonel (kernel) of the whole matter
The gum (Government) became unstuck
Security for ten years (of tenure)
Half a chair (Hertfordshire)
Some call him a strong man, but I say he is potty (putty)
Taxes on Norwich (knowledge)
Higher (hire) purchase

Changes after the First World War were mainly in degree, along lines and for reasons already described. Reporters and sketch-writers alike were supplanted progressively by the Lobby correspondents. The commonest form of reporting debates by the 1970s was the combination of sketch and report in one story, a technique probably pioneered by William Barkley of the *Daily Express* in the mid-1930s. Among national dailies only *The Times*, the *Guardian*, the *Daily Telegraph*, and the *Financial Times*, maintained the older practices into the 1970s. Among provincial dailies only the *Yorkshire Post*, the *Birmingham Post*, and Darlington's *Northern Echo* still had a regular report of debates, plus the *Scotsman* and the *Glasgow Herald*. Parliamentary news continued to find a place in such London letters as survived—for example in the *Eastern Daily Press* and the *Western Morning News*. If Westminster remained 'the height of reportorial ambition' at all, the Lobby was its undoubted focus.

'The Gallery are as it were outside people,' remarked a Conservative Whip in the early 1960s; 'the Lobby are inside people. I am not meaning to be rude.'[2] The remark echoes the decline in the status of reporters. By the 1960s about one-third of the gallery members were Lobby men. In 1900 the proportion was one-seventh of that; and the changing ratio reflects the Lobby man's increased importance. The Whip did not intend to be rude but if he had not said so he might reasonably have

[1] William Law, *Our Hansard* (Pitman, 1950), ch. 9.
[2] Private Communication.

been misunderstood. In a general sense Lobby men have not in fact enjoyed much higher status with M.P.s than have reporters. As late as the 1960s a senior Conservative party manager could confide that Lobby men were not really the sort of people one had down for the week-end. In the gatherings of politicians beyond Westminster—and not just at week-ends —Lobby men never featured prominently throughout the century. On the Conservative side, money and social background doubtless had something to do with it—although even before the Second World War a number of Lobby men (William Deedes on the *Morning Post*, Anthony Winn on *The Times*) had advantages of birth and education that put them at least on an even footing on that ground. The main reason, rather, was that Lobby men were reporters just as much as their colleagues in the Gallery; whereas journalists who carried weight outside Westminster were editors and feature writers—'heavies' like Geoffrey Dawson, C. P. Scott, J. L. Garvin, Evelyn Montague, and a catalogue of others. Dawson chose his Lobby men with enormous care and learnt a great deal from them every day, much of which was no doubt useful in his own relations with politicians. But if Stanley Baldwin, say, wanted to enjoy a personal intimacy with *The Times* it was obviously going to be with the editor; with the Lobby man he would have at most a measure of professional intimacy.

In the late 1960s a few Lobby men found the opportunity to write weekly 'think-pieces'—but this was in addition to their reporting routine. The basis of the routine has always been that the Lobby man's job is a hard-news job, not an 'ideas' job; and this was the principle according to which papers' applications for Lobby privileges were traditionally considered. The Lobby man, it was noted above, interprets what happens on the floor of the Chamber in the context of what happens outside. His general function is to keep in close touch with government and party activities behind the scenes so that he can explain and amplify matters both of policy and personalities. He must keep abreast—or ahead—of the formulation of policy, alert to shifts in opinion and support for the leadership; anticipating the contents of White Papers and parliamentary reports; sniffing out the business of the Cabinet. A very large part of his time must be spent simply analysing and recording the details of bills and all the wide variety of parliamentary, government, and party documents when they are released. In 1900 the scale of the job was incomparably smaller but its core—anything in politics that touched the Westminster scene—was the same as in the 1970s.

Unchanged too in 1976 were the conventions of confidentiality governing the acquisition and use of much information off the record. Keeping ahead of events means publishing news before some at least of those concerned would like it published —and publishing much that they would not like published at all. The peculiar character of parliamentary government—a collective executive responsible to a continuing majority of the Commons—produces contradictory pressures of party discipline and factionalism, and of cabinet solidarity and ministerial ambition. These lead to news being available—but often on condition that it is muffled and unattributed.

The facilities for the Lobby men have already been described. The system originated partly as a by-product of sketch-writing in the 1880s. Once parliamentary journalists began to describe debates as well as to report them it was a short step to producing paragraphs that sought to interpret them as well as to fill in the background. Thus the father of the Lobby system was that innovative journalist H. W. Lucy. He happened to mix more than most gallery men with M.P.s, and the *Daily News* started printing his casual political notes. These were such a success that he gradually spent more and more time in the Lobby and less in the Gallery.

The other cause of the Lobby system was the growth of the provincial papers. Political news-gathering on the London papers had typically been an editorial function. The provincial editors needed someone to do it for them, and parliamentary journalists were the obvious people. *The Times*, by contrast, did not appoint its first Lobby man (W. E. Pitt) until 1892, as its editor's wealth of contacts made one at first unnecessary. (Pitt stayed on until 1908.)

The looseness of the system in its early days is illustrated by the fact that until 1884 access to the Members' Lobby was virtually unrestricted. Up to 1870 it was open to the world at large, and the crush became so great that Speaker Denison instituted a rule prohibiting entry by the public. This had largely lapsed when, in 1884, Irish-American demonstrators set off dynamite in Westminster Hall. In the subsequent tightening of security the 'Lobby List' was started for journalists, bringing with it the implied notion of membership and privileges.

The period before the First World War was a golden age for the Lobby system. The party battle at Westminster was the nerve centre of politics. Success as a Lobby man meant mainly the intelligent anticipation of party developments and the decisions of parliamentary committees and Royal Commissions. There was little of the complex routine of explaining White Papers and government policy which later came to occupy so much of the Lobby man's time. F. J. Higginbottom, who was in the Lobby throughout the 1890s, described those as the palmy days.[1]

The work was particularly suited to individual sleuthing, since so much of it consisted in competition for early information. The numbers involved were small too; there were only about thirty Lobby men in 1914. Even then, however, a notable feature of Lobby journalism had already been developed—the combination of collaboration and competition. London morning papers might compete against each other, for example, but not be concerned about evening and certain provincial competition. Thus Higginbottom, contributing to the evening *Pall Mall Gazette* and various provincial dailies like the *Manchester Guardian*, used to swap information with Pitt of *The Times*. Jeremy Tunstall, in a comprehensive survey of Lobby practice in the late 1960s, found a 'general exchange of information between all, or nearly all members' and 'more specific partnership arrangements between two, three, or four correspondents'.[2] Two-fifths (15) of Tunstall's thirty-seven correspondents said they co-operated with a specific partner; talking to each other almost every day, dividing news-gathering activities, and sometimes swapping carbons of their stories. Moreover collaborators tended to work not for non-competing but actually for competing news organizations. The relationships did not necessarily exclude competition (competition includes interpretation as well as speed and completeness). They were a kind of professional self-protection against the demands of the journalists'

[1] F. J. Higginbottom, *The Vivid Life* (Simpkin, Marshall, 1934).
[2] Tunstall, op. cit., p. 83.

employers. They also reflected the principle that 'not being last with the news' is almost as important as 'being first with the news'. In the intricate Lobby system of the 1960s, Tunstall noted several types of exchange:

1. Loose formations of up to six Lobby men, perhaps including provincial men who may have good contacts with 'their' local MPs . . . 2. Cohesive partnerships of the men who work closely together on a wide variety of stories. 3. Partnerships which only operate on some types of story or task—such as sharing the reading of long documents. 4. Arrangements between men who are in very active competition over perhaps 90 per cent of the field, not to compete in the other 10 per cent.[1]

In the much smaller Lobby before 1914, and with a more limited field of operation too, collaboration was probably less diverse. But its advantages must have been obvious on the simple ground that two (or more) heads are better than one. Certainly Higginbottom and Pitt brought off between them a number of scoops. More complicated arrangements were already common in the 1930s. One Beaverbrook Lobby man, for instance, worked then in a syndicate of four, including Alan Robbins of *The Times* and a man from the *Scotsman* and a stringer for some overseas papers. Arrangements were so sophisticated that occasionally they used to let each other have scoops. Another syndicate included the *Daily Telegraph*, Reuters, and the representative of a provincial chain. There were at least two other syndicates.

The confidentiality of relations with M.P.s meant that methods of getting information were as devious before 1914 as later. MacDonagh quotes a characteristic example. A provincial Lobby man was called to meet his local Member in the Committee Rooms corridor of the House. After a brief general chat the Member hurried off and the journalist noticed he had omitted to take with him a document he put on the window-ledge. The document was the draft report of a select committee then sitting upon a subject of great public interest. The Member had left it, of course, on purpose. The journalist returned it simply with a note saying he had found it on the ledge when the Member left—and his paper had an exclusive scoop.

The success of Lobby men in discovering information which Members wished to conceal (if only for the time being) brought

[1] Ibid., p. 85   [2] MacDonagh, *The Reporters' Gallery*, pp. 63–4.

out the familiar ambivalence in Parliament towards the press. By 1900 the Lobby system was securely established, if uncomfortable. 'The way of the Lobbyist was hard in contrast with what it is today', wrote Higginbottom in 1934. 'Then one had to walk warily and calculate the chances of rebuff in approaching a Minister or member for the first time; now, information is asked for and expected almost as a right, and even Ministers are canvassed for news with a freedom that forty years ago would have been resented.'[1] Acceptance came for two reasons. One was the Lobby men's circumspect behaviour. They knew they were in the House on sufferance and that the nature of the work depended on confidentiality. There quickly grew up a corporate Lobby interest in correct behaviour by individuals: lack of integrity in one could damage the confidence of politicians in the whole system—a fact well illustrated by the disillusion of many Labour parliamentarians in the late 1960s. By 1900 the Lobby had shown its integrity was extremely high. The second reason was that M.P.s, in a time of widened suffrage and party organization, quickly saw the value of being well in with their local papers. Lobby men had a bit of leverage in building up their contacts.[2] By 1900, therefore, the Lobby found itself accepted as part of the Westminster scene. While complaints in the House about leakages of committee reports were regular, for example, the remedy was accepted as in the hands of Members themselves. The attitude of the Prime Minister, Campbell-Bannerman, to a complaint of 1906 was typical. He suggested Members should 'button up the recesses of their minds' against the Lobby's encroachments; and the Speaker said: 'The best way to stop a leakage is to fill up the hole.'[3] Neither suggested that the behaviour of the newspaper was blameworthy.

With the First World War the work of the Lobby began to grow. Partly this was just because the work of the Government

---

[1] Op. cit., p. 149.

[2] Cf. Alfred Kinnear, *Our House of Commons* (W. Blackwood and Sons, 1900), p. 101: 'A very large number of members of the House of Commons keep up relations with the 'gentlemen of the press' for purely personal reasons. These are political "log-rollers". They are men with motions to make or questions to ask.'

[3] 167 *H.C. Deb.* c. 692, 13 Dec. 1906.

expanded as the parties assumed wider and positive responsibilities in matters like employment, pensions, and housing. Lobby men increasingly had to explain and interpret official policies as well as (or rather than) simply record the details. This kind of work was much less adaptable to individual initiative and bred less scoops. During and after the Second World War it grew enormously. It was work which led Higginbottom to reminisce: 'the Lobby in the 1930s seems a tame and colourless place'.[1]

Despite the increase in work the size of the Lobby remained much the same right through the Second World War. There were still about thirty members, only two-thirds of whom were very active. Provincial newspapers applied for membership at intervals but were rebuffed. Throughout the inter-war years the Lobby was a thoroughly accepted and respectable group in the parliamentary world, with a solid reputation for discretion and integrity. Baldwin had found it an efficient news machine in the events surrounding the General Strike in 1926. Ramsay MacDonald badly needed it if he was to be 'understood' after the formation of the National Government in 1931. Baldwin, again, was glad to have the Lobby handle the Abdication crisis story in 1936, from beginning to end. Neville Chamberlain was his intermediary: once he briefed the Lobby three times in a single day. (The strategy of the Abdication was another matter entirely. Baldwin's liaison for that was with an editor—Geoffrey Dawson of *The Times*. The episode illustrates well the officers/other-ranks distinction between editors or proprietors and reporters, in the eyes of politicians.)

One extremely important development in the system occurred between the wars—possibly upon the formation of the National Government, and certainly at about that time. This was the institution of Lobby Meetings—collective gatherings at which Lobby men question a Minister (or his Press Relations Officer) or a member of the Opposition and hear expositions of government or party policies. This led, perhaps after the outbreak of war, to a distinction between membership of the 'inner' Lobby, with the right to attend collective briefings, and ordinary membership without that right. The *Daily Worker*, for example,

---

[1] Op. cit., p. 154.

was not allowed into the 'inner' Lobby until after Soviet Russia entered the war on the Allies' side. During the war the Lobby as a group established an especially close *rapport* with Parliament. Partly this was for social reasons: gallery members of all kinds shared fire-watching and Home Guard duties with M.P.s and officials. More importantly it was because of its convenience as a group representing the national press, meeting regularly and having a proven reliability at keeping secrets. Guy Eden, Secretary and father of the modern Lobby, was thus the only man outside a limited circle of Cabinet and Service people to be told in advance of Mr. Churchill's journey to the Atlantic Conference in 1941. At the appropriate time Eden was to pass the information on to the other Lobby men. The Lobby was also used as the channel for information about Dunkirk, the preparations for D-Day, and other wartime secrets.

After the war the Lobby changed more rapidly than before, not only in type of work but also in composition. First the provincial evening papers clamoured at length successfully to get in. Previously these papers had to use the sort of expedient the new populars had used in the 1900s for ordinary gallery access. Some employed stringers. A few had a morning paper 'partner' with a Lobby ticket. Others made devious arrangements like that of the three papers in the Portsmouth and Sunderland Newspapers Group (*Portsmouth Evening News*, *Sunderland Echo*, and *Northern Daily Mail*). The Lobby man serving these papers was technically employed by the Central News Agency, and they had first call on his services.

Several evening papers took the opportunity provided by the setting-up of a Royal Commission on the Press in 1947 to air their grievances. The *Bristol Evening Post* was particularly bitter. Its representatives were frankly sceptical of the Serjeant-at-Arms' explanation that lack of space prevented admission of the provincial evenings. They put their exclusion down to professional jealousy and restrictive practice. (As with gallery reporters in the old days, Lobby men on the less demanding papers were certainly running profitable sidelines as stringers between the wars.) Guy Eden not surprisingly rejected this view. 'We take no sides whatsoever in either the admission or the exclusion of people', he told the Press Commission. 'The authorities of the House have always, in the last twenty-three or twenty-four years that I have been there, accepted that view.'[1] He repeated the official view: 'It is entirely a matter of physical accommodation. It is a question of whether you are to have, say, fifty or sixty people floating around the Lobby when Members are there; and the bigger the body the more difficult it is to supervise, so to speak.' This argument was by no means specious: the working relationships permitted by a small Lobby group no doubt did involve a useful intimacy. But it was not the whole story. The provincial evenings won the day and were allowed membership in the newly opened House in 1950.

Sunday papers also began to grumble. Part of the idea of Lobby journalism as a hard-news job was that Lobby men had to be writing for a daily paper. Otherwise they were not allowed to join. By 1939 Sunday papers had won the concession of a one-day-a-week ticket. This did not, however, include access to the crucial Lobby meetings. Charles Eade, editor of the *Sunday Dispatch*, told the Press Commission:

I hold, as the editor, a Lobby ticket for the one day, the Wednesday, when I can walk around the Lobbies of the House of Commons; and as they were holding a meeting on a Wednesday I went to the meeting, and as soon as they saw me (they all knew who I was) they had a little conference among themselves and decided I was not to be admitted, and I had to leave. I pointed out at the time to Brendan Bracken, who was Minister of Information, that if the Government wanted to get information to the Press it was not sufficient to give it to the Lobby correspondents, because if they did they were excluding the Sunday newspapers. . . . Nothing has ever been done about it.[2]

Nothing was done about it after the Royal Commission either. Most Sunday papers did not mind their exclusion: they were not greatly concerned with the routine explanatory work Lobby meetings existed to facilitate. By 1960, however, Sunday papers were changing. The growth of background journalism and 'investigative' techniques (plus a much greater acreage of space) made papers like the *Sunday Times* and the *Observer* fretful. The newly launched *Sunday Telegraph* forced the issue in 1961. Determined to have a hard-news political correspondent as well as the kind of reflective essayist typical of such

[1] *Royal Commission on the Press 1947–1949*, Cmd. 7700, *Minutes of Evidence*, Q.8482.
[2] Ibid., Q.10,660.

papers, it won agreement from the Lobby establishment. Sunday Lobby men became full members, with rights to attend the collective meetings. Other weekly publications (*Spectator*, *New Statesman*, etc.) followed some ten years later.

A different type of change in membership was the growth in the 1950s of what were at first known as 'alternate' Lobby men. Papers were permitted a deputy, who could attend the Lobby (and Lobby meetings) instead of, but not at the same time as, the senior Lobby man. Until then only *The Times* had been allowed two Lobby men of right. Other papers wanting two had to acquire them by roundabout means. One of the *Daily Telegraph* men, for instance, owed his place to the *Morning Post* —amalgamated with the *Telegraph* in 1937. The *Daily Express* made a complicated manoeuvre in the early 1930s. The Westminster Press, by dint of buying up provincial dailies, 'owned' about four Lobby tickets. An *Express* man was technically 'hired' by a Westminster Press subsidiary, and his work with their ticket was then sold exclusively to the *Express*.

By the mid-1970s, then, membership of the Lobby was open to a milling crowd compared with the snug group of thirty at the end of the Second World War. In the 1972–3 session the Serjeant-at-Arms' list contained no less than 202 names of whom 69 were 'alternates'.[1] It was small wonder that the previous year the House of Commons Services Committee approved in principle an extension to the Lobby room.[2] The degree of intimacy with M.P.s—even of recognition—was bound to decline. This need not affect the individual Lobby man who stayed in the job a long time. It made an enormous difference to the amount Ministers unbent in Lobby meetings. This in turn reduced the value of exclusiveness, and the inner/outer distinction came largely to disappear. Effective Lobby journalism was seen once again as a more individualistic activity.

An early sign of declining homogeneity was the Lobby Committee's decision to put in writing the Lobby rules—probably just before the provincial evening papers were admitted. Previously newcomers used to be 'coached in the etiquette of the place' (Guy Eden's phrase). Two parliamentary incidents

[1] *Select Committee on Services, 5th Report*, H.C. 331, 1972–3.
[2] H.C. 72ii, 1971–2.

may have influenced the decision. One was Mr. Dalton's Budget leak in 1947, referred to earlier. The Select Committee inquiring into the affair cleared John Carvel, the *Star* Lobby man; but some initial hostility probably shook the Lobby. The other incident, in the same year, was the Allighan breach of privilege case. Allighan, himself a journalist as well as an M.P., suggested that journalists got news from M.P.s by standing them drinks until they became 'lubricated into loquacity'.[1] The Lobby rose at the suggestion that it relied on such ruses. It was on its initiative that the matter was raised in the House and became the subject of lengthy inquiry.

Those two incidents were enough to show the Lobby that there was some confusion, if nothing more, in the new Parliament about the methods and conventions of the Lobby. The result was the drafting of the booklet *Lobby Practice*, which is given to new entrants. Latterly, this does not seem to have been taken too seriously (one or two Lobby men claimed in the 1970s not to have bothered to read it); and the Committee never had more than a moral authority to enforce the rules, since the sanction of exclusion rests in theory with the Serjeant-at-Arms. None of that matters much, however, since the rules are no more than common sense, aimed to make it possible for journalists to gather confidential information without threatening the formal principles of parliamentary government or embarrassing those who work them. In other words the rules enable the Lobby to find out what goes on in private party meetings, for example, but without making it impossible for parties to claim that those meetings are, and should be, confidential. The first and fundamental rule, therefore, on which the whole system depends, is that a Lobby journalist must never reveal his sources of information ('. . . experience has shown that Ministers and M.P.s talk more freely under the rule of anonymity').[2] Several other rules are variations of this theme—'Sometimes it may be right to protect your informant to the extent of not using a story at all', and so on. (That applies to information 'off the record'. Information published but without attribution is 'on Lobby terms'.) There are warnings about observing embargoes, watching out for breach of

---

[1] *Committee of Privileges*, H.C. 138, 1947–8.
[2] Quoted, Tunstall, op. cit., p. 125.

privilege, and doing 'nothing to prejudice the communal life of the Lobby, or the relations with the two Houses and the authorities'. A long section lays down the conventions governing Lobby meetings. These mainly have to do with competition ('Stay to the end of meetings'), confidentiality ('Do not talk about meetings BEFORE or AFTER they are held . . .'), and discretion ('Do not make political or debating points at Lobby meetings'). A section of 'general hints' has to do with behaviour in the Lobby itself and protects the clublike privacy of the House. Out of context these are little short of hilarious. One is quoted at the start of this chapter. Another runs: 'Do not "see" anything in the Members' Lobby, or in any of the private rooms or corridors of the Palace of Westminster.'[1] Perhaps the key rule of this kind is 'Do not crowd together in the Lobby so as to be conspicuous.' Lobby men, after all, are not part of the formal, explicit, parliamentary machine. Political realities make them necessary, but ideally they should be invisible.

The relationships which these rules govern have probably changed in kind very little since 1900. But the Lobby have become progressively more interested in Ministers than in back-benchers: a more apt name for Lobby men in the 1970s, indeed, might be 'Downing Street Correspondents'. The exception are the Lobby men for provincial papers (over half the total), for whom good contacts with local Members are essential. Typically, a provincial Lobby man will so arrange things that his local Members tell him when they are going to speak or put down questions; and he will bounce ideas or stories off them for comment. When the press was more partisan, contact doubtless varied also with the politics of a Lobby man's paper. He would be little use if he had no 'balance' of sources, however, so he was almost bound to be *persona grata* to all parties.

---

[1] '. . . if I went down into the lobby now and I saw . . . one member striking another, I could not go and send a report to my newspaper and say: "I saw Mr. X striking Mr. Y". What I should do is to go up to another Member who had seen this incident and he could tell me about it and I could report that I understood that Mr. X had struck Mr. Y, but the reader would have no inkling of the fact that I had been there.' Chairman of the Lobby Journalists, in evidence to the Select Committee on Parliamentary Privilege, H.C. 34 (1967), Q.223.

The average back-bencher since 1945 has not really had very much to contribute to a Lobby man. Some always give the party line assiduously: others are less discreet. In any case a Lobby man always checks and re-checks with other M.P.s. The most useful thing probably that a Member can do is leak about a private meeting; and of course his views on current party controversies—about policies or personalities—help to build up the pile upon which the Lobby man forms his own overall view. A friendly M.P., too, may sometimes put down parliamentary questions on subjects in which a Lobby man is interested and out of which he hopes to make a story. But the journalist may well know more of interest to back-benchers. Because it is his job to be in touch he may be a better judge of opinion in the back-bencher's own party and specially in certain sections of it; and of course he will know much more than the back-bencher about opinion in the party opposite. In addition, back-benchers are interested in a Lobby man's views because he is somewhat detached compared with M.P.s. On the whole, then, the Lobby have a better hand of cards to play with back-benchers than they need. This relationship reflects once again the ambivalence in parliamentary attitudes to the press. Lobby men are useful because they are a channel to the public and they know what is going on; but also they are a menace—precisely because they are a channel to the public and they know what is going on. The best general illustration of this attitude is the treatment of leaks from back-bench party meetings—mainly the Conservative 1922 Committee and the Parliamentary Labour Party Committee. Nearly always someone has wanted these meetings to leak and the Lobby have been able to piece together the gist of what was said. The ultimate paradox has been when the party itself wants a meeting to leak—usually to emphasize party solidarity or the strength of the leadership. Meetings of the P.L.P. were a particular provocation to the Lobby in the 1930s and 1940s because the editor of the *Daily Herald* attended them for 'background' purposes. The party considered no favouritism was involved, since press notices were issued to the Lobby after each meeting, with details of the subjects discussed and such decisions as were not confidential. This in turn was an excuse for dissident Members to leak their own versions of events. 'Putting the record straight' has always been the general justification for leaking; and this may mean either making sure that a minority view is put on the record or that the majority view is given its full weight. In the 1950s the Labour Party's habit of issuing a press release lapsed, but it was revived in June 1967, in more detail, after a number of rows about unofficial leaks. It would be a heavy labour to trace all such rows across the years—and an unnecessary one, as they have all involved the same arguments.[1]

Back-benchers, then, are of interest to Lobby men mainly as sources of information about their reactions to policy developments and to parliamentary or political events, and about their attitudes to the party leadership. Reports of party meetings and generalized comment about back-bench opinion are the product of their interest. The Lobby's interest in party leaders follows naturally from wanting to look at these developments from the other end. The majority party leaders, obviously, are of interest as members of the Government; and the interest emerges in reports of Cabinet affairs and stories about the interplay of personalities and the trend of policies. Much of the work—on White Papers, for example—is not strictly of parliamentary concern and cannot be explored in detail here.

The Lobby meetings are an important aspect of routine relationships with Ministers (flanked by their civil servants), especially on the administrative (or departmental) side of their work. The Prime Minister's Press Relations Adviser has normally held two meetings a day, at least since the Second World War. One, late in the morning at Downing Street, is mainly for the benefit of the provincial evening papers. The other, for those with night-time deadlines, takes place in the Lobby room at Westminster. Since the early 1960s there has also usually been a Saturday briefing for Sunday journalists. Ramsay MacDonald was the first Prime Minister to have a Press Officer to maintain links with the Lobby during the 1929 Labour Government. Arrangements were haphazard throughout the 1930s, however, with civil servants in the Cabinet Office and the Treasury briefing the Lobby at various times. The Chief Press Relations Officer regularly attached to the Prime Minister's staff from the early 1930s apparently took a

---

[1] For a detailed examination of some disputes since 1945, see Colin Seymour-Ure, *The Press, Politics and the Public* (Methuen, 1968), pp. 216–26.

fairly negative view of the job and concentrated on keeping the press away from busy Ministers as much as possible.

The first of the modern Press Relations Advisers was Francis Williams, an ex-editor of the *Daily Herald*, who was brought into Downing Street by Mr. Attlee in 1945 to help interpret to the press a Labour philosophy which it was not the business of civil servants to expound.[1] Williams's background included work in the wartime Ministry of Information. He stayed two years, working partly as Press Secretary, partly as chairman of various departmental committees dealing with particular information issues, and partly as overseer of government public relations as a whole. (These latter jobs have often subsequently been done by a Cabinet Minister.) His successor, Philip Jordan, had been a *News Chronicle* journalist and was a less explicitly Labour Party man. On his death in 1951 the Lobby intimated that a regular civil servant might be better, so that political ambiguities were minimized. This was an assertion of the Lobby's traditional hard-news outlook, and it was accepted. A journalist–turned–civil servant from the Treasury Information Division, Reg Bacon, was appointed.

The importance of prime ministerial personality was reflected in Mr. Churchill's dislike of the whole idea of public relations advice. Mr. Bacon was discouraged from having much contact with the Lobby. Indeed he seems not to have had much to do at all. But after some six months of the Churchill administration Lobby protests led to a resumption of what had become a convenient practice—this time with a different Treasury man, Fife Clark, serving Mr. Churchill and Lord Swinton, Minister in charge of co-ordinating Home Information Services.

With that short hiatus, regular Lobby meetings with the Prime Minister's Press Relations Advisers continued uninterruptedly after 1945. The Adviser's office grew a little, so that he came to have two or three assistants as well as secretarial staff. The number of Lobby men entitled to attend grew much more, as we have seen. The result was that by the time of the 1974 Wilson administration both Lobby and Advisers were finding the meetings increasingly fruitless as off-the-record occasions. They began to leak badly, and were seen by the

[1] Francis Williams, *Press, Parliament and People* (Heinemann, 1946); Marjorie Ogilvy-Webb, *The Government Explains* (Allen and Unwin, 1965).

journalists as no longer a good news source. Mr. Wilson's Adviser, Joe Haines, decided to discontinue them in their traditional form, but his office continued to release information on the record about prime ministerial plans and activities.[1]

Lobby meetings with individual Ministers were subject to less change in their character, though the consequences of the Lobby's increased size made them less intimate and Ministers more cautious. The Leader of the House of Commons has had a weekly meeting about forthcoming business ever since that job became conventionally separated from the Prime Minister's after 1945. The same day the Leader of the Opposition has a briefing about his or her plans. The value of these and other ministerial meetings has fluctuated enormously, depending on subjects and personalities. Some leaders, like R. A. Butler, established a very close *rapport* with the Lobby. The heyday of the collective briefing, however, was undoubtedly the 1940s and early 1950s. The Labour Government's post-war legislative programme was of a scale and technicality imposing on the Lobby men a need for much straightforward guidance and help in expounding it to their readers. Subject specialists in defence, social services, economics, and so on were far less common on newspapers then than in the 1960s. The Lobby man needed to be a remarkable polymath if he was to keep on top of the parliamentary side of government work. For political stories—'Who's in, who's out'—individual sleuthing remained the key news-gathering mode. But a great acreage of print was sown with seed from the Lobby briefings.

Prime Ministers themselves have never had much direct contact with Lobby men. Gladstone was almost never seen in the Lobby, though his son Herbert (who leaked his father's conversion to Home Rule for Ireland in 1885) was helpful. Asquith went into the Lobby on rare occasions only to post a letter. Lloyd George preferred 'the use of intimates with personal connections in the higher reaches of journalism'.[2] Baldwin was probably the first Prime Minister to see the Lobby— initially on an individual basis—and he grew cautious after being let down by a Sunday paper. Ramsay MacDonald is said

[1] B.B.C.-TV, *The Editors*, 4 July 1976.
[2] Francis Williams, 'The Office of Public Relations Adviser to the Prime Minister', *Parliamentary Affairs*, Vol. IX, No. 3, 1956, p. 260.

to have been eager and helpful: *The Times* Lobby man, for one, was at 10 Downing Street all through the Sunday evening in 1931 during which MacDonald went to the Palace to resign as Labour Prime Minister and came back again as the head of a National Government. Neville Chamberlain got on very well with the Lobby. Churchill, allegedly, had almost nothing to do with it until his black swans flew away from Chartwell and he wanted the press to publicize the fact widely. In his post-war premiership, though, he was persuaded to see the Lobby now and again. Eden saw little of the Lobby—he had been more at home with Diplomatic correspondents. Macmillan saw individual Lobby men occasionally and went to Lobby meetings a few times a year. Wilson was closer to the Lobby at first than any of his predecessors. 'He wanted the journalists to feel he accepted their wish that he should be accessible and he made himself so', wrote Wilson's secretary, Marcia Williams.[1] When frequent contact did not provide the kind of coverage Wilson was after, he tried the so-called 'White Commonwealth' experiment, involving 'fortnightly evening meetings at No. 10 with Senior Lobby Correspondents from a number of daily and Sunday papers'.[2] These did not work well either. The press disliked the selectivity; Wilson wanted them to be reflective occasions; the Lobby wanted hard news. Eventually Wilson's contact with Lobby men was probably no greater than many of his predecessors'.

Governments never get the publicity they want, of course, and the Lobby has often been the object of ephemeral hostility. In the 1960s a more persistent stream of criticism developed. Source anonymity, critics claimed, means that the reader does not know what to believe; that guesswork may be deliberately presented as fact; that trivial sources can be magnified; that news is distorted because some politicians more willingly talk off the record than others; that an air of cosiness surrounds Lobby journalism, and an air of 'knowingness' stemming from access to a small private world; that conspiracy theories of politics are encouraged; and that some Lobby men may even use their position to carry on public relations work. The defence of source anonymity in the Westminster system is in a simple

[1] *Inside Number 10* (New English Library paperback edn., 1975), p. 182.
[2] Ibid., p. 184.

paradox; upon secrecy rests openness. 'Unless news is to be reduced to a bleak and uninterpreted account of public statements,' one ex-Lobby man has written, 'there must be a good deal of non-attributable exchanges between the press and politicians.'[1]

Another criticism has been of Lobby men's lack of specialized knowledge of important areas of Government, like management of the economy. Lobby men can reply that theirs is a political, not a subject, expertise; and that subject specialists outside the Lobby have grown considerably since the early 1960s. The Lobby, again, have been accused of being 'managed' by Governments through the collective daily briefings and the control of information.[2] Governments, in contrast, have tended to see themselves as victimized by the Lobby (a view strongly held by Harold Wilson's advisers, for example).[3] Lastly, the increased size of the Lobby has been seen as reducing its standards of discretion and integrity, so that confidential news is no longer safely entrusted to Lobby men.[4]

Some of these criticisms mistake the news-orientation of the Lobby or the context in which Lobby men work. Others are difficult to substantiate and perhaps unprovable. But the fact that for a period in the Wilson administrations the effectiveness of the Lobby system almost became an issue *in* politics itself reflects the importance of the institution.

This importance is shown in the Lobby's status in the news industry. Inside their offices Lobby men (except on some provincial papers) enjoy very high status among journalists. They get paid better than most reporters (and about the same as M.P.s). Even before the First World War the *Manchester Guardian* Lobby man, G. H. Mair, was paid more than his London editor.[5] They have exceptional and often daily access to their editor (usually by phone: Lobby men spend little time actually in their papers' offices). They have considerable autonomy in their choice of stories and their stories lead the

---

[1] Butt, op. cit., p. 416.

[2] e.g. Charles Wintour, *Pressures on the Press* (Andre Deutsch, 1972).

[3] e.g. Marcia Williams and Joe Haines, op. cit.

[4] e.g. Marcia Williams, Joe Haines, and George Brown, *In My Way* (Harmondsworth, Penguin, 1971).

[5] Ayerst, op. cit., p. 566.

paper frequently. The quality of their work is seen by editors (perhaps too much) as growing with experience. Many acquire a *gravitas* through spending long years at Westminster. Some get bitten by the job—just as in the golden days of the gallery reporters men like MacDonagh became priests of the place. Others stay because there is nowhere else to go: suitable public relations jobs—the most common outlet for specialist journalists—are few. Tunstall's survey in 1968 found that eight out of 36 Lobby men in national news organizations had been in the Lobby twenty years or more. The median time for all 36 was eight years.[1] Earlier in the century such longevity was certainly no less and probably more. Exceptional examples were Sir Alexander Mackintosh—in the Gallery and Lobby for fifty-seven years from 1881 to 1938; R. G. Emery, who spent fifty years there for the *Morning Post* over the same period; and John Martin of the *Daily Telegraph*, whose gallery career started in the 1870s and who still attended the gallery masonic lodge in his nineties. Guy Eden joined the Lobby in 1923 and stayed some thirty-five years. E. P. Stacpoole was Extel Lobby man from 1936 to 1966. Harry Boardman was the *Manchester Guardian* Lobby man from 1931–45 and sketch-writer until his death (while correcting a proof) in 1958. The Lobby's importance in news organizations at large may eventually be seen to have peaked in the 1950s. Other kinds of political analyst less tied to Westminster or possessing a subject expertise (e.g. economics) gained importance relatively. In the Westminster news arena, however, the Lobby man's importance remained unchallenged in the 1970s.

Across the twentieth century the tensions in the relationship between Parliament and the news organizations have endured, while the forms of parliamentary coverage have shifted from reporting to description and to interpretation. Compared with their interest in other political institutions the interest of news organizations in Parliament has declined, giving the tension extra tautness. The decline has been caused less by changes in news media than in politics. News media are interested in the points of decision in politics—about people, policy, and events. They are concerned with Parliament to the extent that Parlia-

---

[1] Tunstall, op. cit., p. 33.

ment shares in those decisions; and their shifting coverage reflects their perception (rightly or wrongly) that Parliament's share has dropped, even if the institutions challenging it remain, like Whitehall and Downing Street, linked to it.

That is an institutional perspective. One may consider as well the parliamentary idea of consultation. Here the devout parliamentarian may have less to regret. Modern communications, both in travel and in broadcasting, have made the physical constraints on consultation less and less binding. The Palace of Westminster—indeed the floor of the Chamber—was still in 1900 the primary focus of parliamentary activity. By the 1970s parliamentary work had diversified and disintegrated, both at Westminster (into party and parliamentary committees) and elsewhere. At first sight the parliamentarian's fear that broadcasting might usurp Parliament seemed justified on the evidence of the growth of political programmes after 1959. Ironically that growth was stimulated in part precisely because the cameras were kept out of Westminster not because they were let in. Yet the growth 'usurped' Parliament only in a limited institutional sense. For political broadcasts remained heavily influenced—in style, content, and choice of participants—by parliamentary values. Many aspects of the parliamentary idea were thus being expressed as effectively in the forum of a broadcasting institution as in the Palace of Westminster. Moreover Westminster institutions themselves started to lose their physical limitations when select committees began to take evidence outside the precincts. Parliament and the Palace of Westminster, in other words, had been more nearly identical in 1900 than they now were in the 1970s. Some of the changes in news media coverage, therefore, could be seen as the result of diversification in the forms of expression of the parliamentary idea and not as an erosion of interest by media. If the institutional perspective is preferred to this interpretation, however, and if declining coverage of debates is seen as a cause as well as a reflection of declining parliamentary status, the remedy must lie with Parliament. News media report Parliament if Parliament matters. As J. A. Spender once remarked: 'The Press might get on without politics; but politics cannot get on without the Press.'[1]

---

[1] Spender, op. cit., ii. 106.

NOTES ON SOURCES

Some of the research for this essay was undertaken in the early 1960s. The author is grateful to the Press Gallery committee of those years for access to the Gallery's library and archives. In a few passages he has drawn substantially on material published in chapters VI and VII of his book *The Press, Politics and the Public* (Methuen, 1968) and in chapter V of his book *The Political Impact of Mass Media* (Constable, 1974).

The content analysis of parliamentary coverage was financed by a grant from the Nuffield Foundation and carried out by Miss Ruth Shaw. The sample of newspapers was drawn for each year as follows. The number of parliamentary days in the year was divided into ten equal units. From the first five of these a set of weekdays, Monday to Friday, was chosen; and likewise from the second five. From the first five units one unit was drawn at random (e.g. 'the third unit'). Next a weekday was drawn at random (e.g. 'Tuesday'), to be chosen from the several examples of that day in that unit. (There were up to four in some units.) The particular example (e.g. 'the third Tuesday') was chosen also at random. Another unit was then drawn from the remaining four; another day from the remaining days of the week; and the particular day from the total number of that day in the unit. The fifth unit and the day of the week in it were decided, necessarily, by elimination—but the choice of a particular date for that day could still be determined by chance. The process was repeated for the second set of weekdays in the second five units. The units were then arranged in proper sequence. The choice was modified by including arbitrarily the day of the Budget, which always fell in the first half of the year but not always in the same unit. Since the parliamentary timetable varies a different sample had to be drawn for each year. As an example the procedure produced this result in 1912 (a busy year).

Number of parliamentary days in calendar year: 170 = 17 days per unit.

Unit	Day of week	Partic. day and no. possible	Date
1	Thursday	Third of four	29 Feb.
2	Friday	Second of four	15 Mar.
3 (Budget)	Tuesday	First of four	2 Apr.
4	Monday	Third of three	20 May
5	Wednesday	Second of four	12 June
6	Wednesday	Second of three	10 July
7	Thursday	Second of three	1 Aug.
8	Tuesday	Second of four	22 Oct.
9	Monday	First of three	1 Nov.
10	Friday	First of three	6 Dec.

APPENDIX I: THE DEPARTMENT OF THE CLERK OF THE HOUSE

Anthony Barrett

A distinguished member of the department of the Clerk of the House was once asked for his comments on an essay on the history of the department. 'The first Clerk to emerge from obscurity . . .' it began. The distinguished clerk read no further. 'The fellow obviously knows nothing about the subject', he remarked scornfully. 'No Clerk ever emerged from obscurity.' The department has had its share of strong personalities, formidable intellects, and eccentric characters. But with rare exceptions they have recognized that the House is normally best served by comparative anonymity and absence of fuss. For that reason this chapter will be confined to the description of institutional changes and will allow those clerks who are still living to continue to enjoy their obscurity, and the House to profit by it.

For over six hundred years, since the time of the first recorded appointment of a Clerk of the House of Commons (or 'Under-Clerk of the Parliaments') in 1363, the Clerk and his various assistants have provided the essential clerical services for the House. As the needs of the House have changed, so the Clerk's department has adapted itself to meet them, although its attitude to change has never been purely passive and successive clerks have frequently, by their advice, been instrumental in bringing about reforms.

At the beginning of the present century the main services required of the Clerk and his department by the House were to keep records of its proceedings, to advise the Speaker and Members on the law of Parliament and its procedure, to handle all the procedural business connected with the process of legislation, both public and private, to provide secretaries for select committees, and to perform the duties of Accounting Officer and Paymaster for the whole House of Commons Vote.

To do all this the Clerk had two Clerks Assistant and a staff of thirty-three other clerks. The Clerk himself and the two Clerks Assistant were primarily responsible for recording the minutes of the proceedings of the House and for advising the Speaker and Members on procedure. The rest of the department was organized in four offices, each under a principal clerk.

The *Journal Office*, under the Clerk of the Journals, converted the notes in the minute books of the Clerks at the Table first into the Votes and Proceedings—published daily and written rather in the style in which telegrams might have been composed in the seventeenth century, if that had been possible— and subsequently into the narrative form of the Journal. This is the final and authoritative record of the proceedings of the House and to ensure accuracy the proofs are checked meticulously several times. It is not, of course, a record of Members' speeches, which are contained in the Official Report of Debates (*Hansard*), whose Editor is on the staff of Mr. Speaker's Department. The Journal Office also prepared the massive annual and decennial indexes to the Journals, which enable them to be used to provide the necessary precedents on which to base procedural advice—another function of this office.

The *Public Bill Office*, as its name implies, was responsible, under the Clerk of Public Bills and in co-operation with the parliamentary draftsmen, for work connected with public bills. Such work is, of course, particularly heavy during the committee and report stages. The duties of clerks to the standing committees appointed to consider public bills were mostly performed by the clerks in the larger Committee Office. The Clerk of Public Bills himself also acted as accounting officer and paymaster for the whole House of Commons Vote, a task which involved a great deal of detailed accounting work.

The *Private Bill Office*, whose head was the Clerk of Private Bills, performed similar functions with regard to private legislation, the principal differences being that the drafting of such bills was the concern not of the parliamentary draftsmen, but of private firms of solicitors appointed by Mr. Speaker as parliamentary agents, and that the committee stage was taken, not in standing committee, but in quasi-judicial committees of four members.

The largest office was the *Committee Office*, whose clerks, under the Clerk of Committees, attended to all the secretarial work of select committees: arranging meetings, conducting correspondence, keeping formal minutes, advising on procedure, and drafting reports. At this time, however, it was not unusual for the chairmen of committees to draft their own reports.

Such were the main duties and the organization of the department at the beginning of the century. To carry out those duties the Clerk of the House was assisted by three dozen other clerks of various grades and a few messengers. The clerks normally did their own routine work, relied on memory rather than filing systems, and wrote their letters, minutes, and reports themselves in longhand, though probably not always with quill pens.

The career of a clerk, though not usually unduly arduous, was unsatisfactory in two respects. Promotion was slow, and although this did not invariably give rise to the financial hardship which it would today, since it was not unusual at that time for clerks to have private incomes, it must have contributed to the high turnover of the younger clerks.[1] One began as a junior clerk[2] at a salary of £120, and proceeded very slowly through the grades of assistant clerk and senior clerk until, towards the end of his career, a clerk might be the principal clerk of one of the four offices or, if very fortunate, he might, at an earlier age, 'go to the Table' as Second Clerk Assistant. From there promotion first to Clerk Assistant and then to Clerk of the House was fairly automatic, but the principle was by no means unshakeably established. In 1902, according to Mr. Speaker Lowther, who was at that time Chairman of Ways and Means, Sir Courtenay Ilbert, the eminent parliamentary draftsman then engaged on the Education Bill, 'had not been able to work with Mr. Balfour on the terms of complete confidence and mutual trust which are indispensable in such a position and was offered the position of Clerk of the House'.[3]

---

[1] The Maclean Report in 1918 (see below) drew attention to the number of clerks transferring to government departments.

[2] This grade was abolished in 1912 and thereafter the lowest grade was assistant clerk.

[3] Viscount Ullswater (Mr Speaker Lowther), *A Speaker's Commentaries*, Vol. I, p. 324. The subsequent passage, giving details of the other promotions

The second unsatisfactory feature of a career in the Clerk's department was that it tended to be spent entirely in the office into which the clerk was recruited. There were two consequences of this: his work lacked variety and his prospects of promotion depended not so much on his abilities or his seniority in the department as on the office which he had joined. A clerk starting in a small office like the Journal Office would, if his colleagues in that office were a good deal older than he, obtain quite rapid promotion. For a clerk in the Committee Office promotion was likely to be heartbreakingly slow by comparison and a sense of injustice inevitably arose. It is not surprising that many clerks left for employment in government departments and elsewhere.

The organization of the department changed very little between the turn of the century and the Second World War. The number of clerks had fallen to 27 by the end of the First World War and remained at about that number until 1939. The Committee and Private Bill offices were amalgamated in 1912. More important, the transfer of clerks from one office to another was gradually introduced.

This last reform followed a recommendation of a committee under the chairmanship of the Rt. Hon. Donald Maclean appointed by Mr. Speaker in 1918 to

consider the method of appointment, conditions of service, and scale of remuneration and allowances of the Clerks and other Officers of the

---

at the Table, shows how it was possible to function with a stranger to the department at its head and also indicates that Ilbert's appointment was exceptional. It is worth quoting in full as it conveys the flavour of the period so well: 'Mr Jenkinson, the Clerk Assistant, whose health had given way, was replaced by Mr A. Nicholson. The latter was a tall, stalwart specimen of humanity, well acquainted with all the intricacies of House of Commons procedure and the minutiae of the various departments, and often rendered me great assistance in the discharge of my duties at the Table. In his time he had rowed in the Oxford eight, and his love of flowers and of stalking (he was a Scottish laird) formed a bond of union between us. He met with a terrible misfortune for one day, whilst shaving, his hand slipped and the razor cut into his left eye, with the result that he lost the sight of it. Mr Nicholson had been Second Clerk Assistant, and he was succeeded by Mr T. L. Webster, a cousin of Lord Alverstone, the Lord Chief Justice. He has now deservedly mounted the ladder of promotion and, as a reward of his abilities, finds himself the Clerk of the House.'

Department of the Clerk of the House; and to report whether it is expedient that any changes should be made in the same; and, if so, to assist the Speaker by the preparation of a scheme to that effect, for the consideration of the Commissioners for regulating the Offices of the House of Commons.

On the subject of appointments, this committee, having noted that they were made by the Clerk of the House, 'who can lay down what conditions he thinks fit', went on to recommend against recruitment by open competition, as a similar committee had done in 1899. The reason given was that 'by the nature of their work, the Clerks of the House are necessarily brought into close personal relations with Members of the House, and the smooth and harmonious working of the House depends to a considerable extent upon the possession by these Officers of qualifications which cannot be tested merely by a competitive examination'. It is possible that another consideration was that the change might make it more difficult for candidates recommended by Members and others to obtain appointments. It was fairly common for successful candidates before the First World War to have some connection with Members or officers of the House. In spite of the Maclean Committee's recommendation, however, recruitment through the Civil Service first division competition was introduced, although the Clerk of the House retained the right of nomination, which meant that any candidate whom he thought unsuitable would not be considered for appointment. It is impossible to say whether the introduction of competitive entrance raised the intellectual level of the department. The clerks still came almost exclusively from the major public schools and from Oxford and Cambridge, but this is hardly surprising and was true to almost the same extent of the Diplomatic and Home Civil Services between the wars.

Towards the end of the Second World War a clerk was appointed to help the Clerks at the Table to deal with Parliamentary Questions. It was often difficult to deal with these adequately at the Table itself, and it was not unknown for a Question to be refused a place on the notice paper with no other reason given than that it was 'not a proper Question'. The creation of the Table Office, of which this new appointment was the modest beginning, meant that in future clerks could discuss adequately with Members the reasons for rejecting their Questions and, in consequence, could frequently help to redraft them in such a way as to bring them into order. Of course, Members could still deal with the Clerks at the Table, if they wished, and any disagreements with the Table Office were referred to the Clerk at the Table and, if necessary, to the Speaker. After the war, when the House, which had been sitting in the Lords' chamber, moved back into its own re-built chamber, a small room near the Speaker's chair end was found for the new office, which was increased to four clerks to deal with the growing number of questions and motions and which took on general responsibility for the preparation of the 'Orders of the Day and Notices of Motions'.

It is worth noticing too that the rebuilding of the Commons' chamber also gave an opportunity to provide new accommodation for the Journal and Public Bill Offices—previously dispersed in the Cloisters and off Westminster Hall—immediately above the rebuilt chamber.

The third quarter of the century has been a period of almost continual change in the department. The causes have been various: modifications in the practice and procedure of the House; demands for more assistance or new kinds of assistance from Members; the consequent need to devolve more duties on junior staff; and the need to offer a reasonable career in order to maintain recruitment. A chronological account of the developments of this period would be disjointed and confusing. It is more convenient to look at the present structure of the department and identify the changes which have taken place and then to draw some general conclusions.

The Clerk of the House is still the principal permanent officer of the House and since 1935 its accounting officer. The Clerk Assistant and Second Clerk Assistant still assist him at the Table, but other clerks at the senior and middle levels also perform short spells of duty at the Table, leaving the regular Clerks at the Table free to deal with the increasing burden of administrative work. This change is a logical extension of the principle of circulation first laid down in the Maclean Report and has been accompanied in recent years by a much greater flexibility in the disposition of the department's listed manpower. Thus, for example, a clerk in the Journal Office might take a standing committee on two mornings a week, or assist in the work of a select committee.

The only major difference in the work of the Journal Office is that since October 1969 the Votes and Proceedings and the Journal have been written in an almost identical form. Both now resemble an expanded version of the old Votes and Proceedings.

The Public Bill Office took over responsibility for the staffing of Standing Committees after the war. It therefore felt the effects of changes in Standing Orders which have reduced the size of Standing Committees in order to make possible an increase in their number. In session 1974–5 there were ten standing committees,[1] compared with four twenty years earlier. The former practice of providing two clerks for each committee —the junior keeping the minutes and calling the names in divisions to keep himself occupied while he learned the procedure—has had to be virtually abandoned. Most standing committees have only one clerk and clerks from the other offices have to share in the work of standing committees.

The Private Bill Office has, perhaps, changed least, although the number of 'clerk-hours' spent on the work of this office has been drastically reduced as the number of bills per session has fallen from 273 in 1900–1 to 32 in 1974–5.

It is in the Committee Office that the upheaval has been greatest. First, the number of select committees, like that of standing committees, has increased. In 1900 there were nineteen (of which four were dealing with the committee stages of bills) and no sub-committees. In 1974–5 the numbers were 23 select committees and 19 sub-committees respectively.[2] Second, they now tend to cover much broader and less clearly defined fields, whereas in 1900 the matters referred to select committees tended to be narrow and specific: Hospitals (Exemption from Rates), Burial Grounds (Remuneration), Census (Expenses), Great Indian Peninsula Railway Bill (Annuities), Lunacy

---

[1] In addition to the Second Reading Committees and Committees on European Commission Documents and on Statutory Instruments.

[2] These numbers do not include committees performing procedural functions in connection with public or private legislation, such as the Court of Referees, Committees of Selection, Standing Orders Committee, and Business Committees on Bills.

Board (Scotland) (Salaries &c.), and so on. Of course, the Committee of Privileges still endures, and *ad hoc* committees are still set up to deal with particular cases, like that of the Rt. Hon. Member for Walsall North, but in addition there are, for example, select committees on Science and Technology, on Overseas Development, on Nationalised Industries, and on Race Relations and Immigration. There is the Committee on European Secondary Legislation and its sub-committees which try to sift and examine the mass of regulations and directives which originate with the Commission of the European Communities and to draw the attention of the House to those which give grounds for concern. There is also the Expenditure Committee, descendant of the Select Committee on Estimates and the National Expenditure Committee. This has no fewer than six sub-committees, each charged with examining and drafting reports on a particular field of government expenditure.

The development of these committees has been dealt with in chapter VIII. Changes in the numbers and scope of select committees have naturally resulted in demands from Members for more clerks. They have also meant demands for a wider range of assistance. Whilst a committee like Privileges works in much the same way as it did seventy years ago, the newer committees, wrestling with the enormous complexities of modern government activity and trying to explain them to the House and criticize them constructively, have often found they need more help than one clerk (who usually has other duties as well) can give.

The demand for more clerks could be met to only a limited extent by recruitment straight from the universities, partly because there was a sudden and immediate need for experienced committee secretaries and partly because it was not known whether the 1960s experiments with specialist committees and with increasing the scope of other committees would become a permanent part of the committee system, or whether they would be abandoned after a few sessions. The obvious source of recruitment for temporary committee secretaries was the Civil Service, but there was a traditional reluctance to employ as officers of the House of Commons civil servants whose first loyalty was to the Executive, to whose service they would be returning. The problem was solved by recruiting officials who were nearing retirement and who would thus be able to sever their connection with the Civil Service and finish their careers in the service of the House of Commons.

The increasing technicality of the inquiries undertaken by select committees led also to a demand for technical or 'specialist' assistance. This demand was first voiced by the Select Committee on Nationalised Industries[1] which recalled that in 1921 a select committee on the Telephone Service had appointed an assessor to advise it on technical matters. There were two major objections to the regular employment of specialist advisers: one practical, the other one of principle. The practical difficulty was that the House of Commons could not offer a career suitable for experts of the calibre required, nor, in most cases, even the possibility of permanent employment. A highly qualified engineer, or even an accountant could not be fitted readily into the Clerk's Department or the Library and in any case his services might be required for only one session. The alternative was to offer short-term contracts, but it was feared that the sort of fee which would be permitted by the Treasury would not prove acceptable to the experts. In fact this fear proved groundless and over the past decade a succession of distinguished experts in many fields—economics, industry, military affairs, agriculture, education, and so on—have assisted committees in return for the reimbursement of modest expenses.

The other uncertainty about the employment of experts was more fundamental. Committees of the House of Commons had always been composed mainly of laymen and they reported in layman's language to the House. True, some of the evidence submitted to them was technical, but it was always possible for the clerk to ensure that it was expressed as plainly as possible and for Members to clear up technical misunderstandings during the examination of witnesses. An expert, on the other hand, might take over the committee. At worst the inquiry might be a dialogue between expert and witnesses conducted through the chair. An expert might exercise too great an influence on a committee which would adopt his point of view too uncritically. The House might be presented with a report

[1] *Special Report from the Select Committee on Nationalised Industries (Reports and Accounts)*, H.C. 276, 1959.

which even the Members who had served on the committee did not fully comprehend. And so on.

In practice these fears, too, have proved largely unfounded, partly because of the care taken by chairmen, clerks, and specialist advisers to keep in step with their committees. As a result, select committees have derived great benefits from their advisers without accepting their advice uncritically. The dangers still exist, but in most cases have been outweighed by the deeper understanding of the subject of the inquiry which has resulted from the use of specialist advisers.

In addition to the great changes which have taken place in existing offices, the post-war period has seen the creation of new offices. The Table Office has already been referred to. Another development arose from the rapid spread of independence among Britain's former colonies. Each newly independent state set up its own Parliament based on the Westminster model and it was not enough to present them each with a mace and a copy of Erskine May and tell them to get on with it. Standing Orders had to be drafted, advice given on procedural problems, and clerks even went out to act temporarily as Clerks or Speakers of the new Parliaments. More and more overseas clerks came to Westminster for training. To cope with these problems a new post, that of Fourth Clerk at the Table, was created in April 1953. As his title implied, this officer was to sit at the Table whenever possible, so as to have first-hand experience of procedure in the House, but most of his time was to be spent in dealing with relations between the Clerk's Department and Commonwealth Parliaments.

The development of relations between the House of Commons and European parliamentary assemblies also brought fresh responsibilities to the Clerk's Department. It had begun by providing procedural assistance to the Consultative Assembly of the Council of Europe and to the British delegation to the Assembly from its creation in 1949.[1] Subsequently similar assistance was provided at the assemblies of Western European Union and the NATO Parliamentarians (later the North Atlantic Assembly). This help had been organized by the Clerk of the House who delegated the various tasks to those clerks

[1] The first Clerk of the Assembly was Lord Campion, a former Clerk of the House of Commons.

who could be spared from the existing offices. It gradually became clear that greater continuity would be required. An Overseas Office was set up in 1967 to handle all work for Commonwealth Parliaments and international assemblies, and within it a small European section to deal on a part-time basis with the Council of Europe and WEU. At the same time the post of Fourth Clerk at the Table was allowed to lapse. When the United Kingdom joined the European Community in 1973 the Clerk's Department was required to provide regular assistance to the delegation to the European Parliament. The European section was expanded and a clerk was given the full-time job of serving the delegation.

A very different problem was presented by the gradual accumulation of the unreported and unpublished records of select committees in the Record Office in the Victoria Tower, and the constant demands for access to and consultation of these records by scholars and others. In 1976 a Clerk of House of Commons Committee Records was appointed to survey the great bulk of these documents and to advise if and how they could be released to the public under a sort of thirty-year rule.

The increasing complexity of the work of the House and of the services required by its Members led to growing support among them for the view which had long been held by a few, that the House should exercise more control over its own accommodation and services. On 26 April 1965 control of that part of the Palace of Westminster which was occupied by the House of Commons passed from the Queen to the House. In the same year a select committee recommended that this control should be exercised by a Services Committee, which was accordingly set up. Then, on 1 January 1968, an Administration Department was created. It combined the existing Fees Office and Establishments Office and handles the routine financial and personnel work of the House. The Clerk to this Committee was given the title of Clerk Administrator and, in addition to his duties as a committee clerk, was placed at the head of the new department. These changes brought a greater measure of supervision by Members, but all the existing departments of the House retained a large measure of autonomy and the successful working of the system has been due to willing co-operation between them. Nevertheless, although the system works it is obviously untidy, a fact which must have offended the eyes of Sir Edmund Compton[1] and his team of civil servants, who were appointed by Mr. Speaker in 1973 to review the administrative services of the House.

His main recommendation was that the existing departments of the House (Clerk, Speaker, Serjeant-at-Arms, Library, and Administration) should be unified under a Chief Officer who would have two deputies, one responsible for procedural matters and the other for administration. Sir Edmund argued that 'the time has come for a significant shift from procedural services to administrative and management services'. His arguments and conclusions tended to equate the House of Commons as far as (or rather farther than) possible with a government department, and this tendency seems to have been recognized by a committee of Members whom Mr. Speaker appointed to consider his report. Whilst they rejected his proposals they came out in favour of 'more closely co-ordinated services' and made several recommendations aimed at bringing this about. On his proposals concerning the Chief Officer, they commented:

We fear that a new official at Permanent Secretary level would cut off the Speaker from Heads of Departments and other senior Officers and would not be consistent with the maintenance of the necessary degree of Departmental autonomy in day-to-day matters; the 'co-ordination', on a Civil Service Departmental pattern, of advice to the Speaker at this level seems unnecessary, and more likely to confuse than to clarify. Nor are we satisfied that there is a continuing body of work, in addition to that done at present by Heads of Departments, which would justify a further post at this level.[2]

Here this history must break off, for the final outcome of all these deliberations rests in the future.[3] For the moment the

[1] A former Comptroller and Auditor General and Parliamentary Commissioner for Administration.

[2] *House of Commons Administration. Report to Mr Speaker by Committee under Chairmanship of Mr Arthur Bottomley MP*, H.C. 624, 1975, p. 12.

[3] One decision, of both historic and administrative importance has been taken already. The post of Second Clerk Assistant has been abolished. His duties have been transferred mainly to the Principal Clerk of the Table Office. Before this change the Second Clerk Assistant might be appointed whilst in his late forties and expect to be promoted to Clerk Assistant and then Clerk of the House. In effect, the choice of the future head of the department was made when he was appointed Second Clerk Assistant. The choice could now remain open for several years longer.

Clerk of the House, as its principal procedural adviser and Accounting Officer remains its senior permanent officer. However, he is at the head of a department very different from that of his predecessor in 1900. It now numbers 108, of whom only a minority are 'clerks' as the term would have been understood at the beginning of the century. This is because of an enormous increase in the numbers of staff in what, until recently, the Civil Service termed the executive and clerical grades. Again, this change has occurred almost entirely in the last two decades. In 1900 the clerks were assisted by only a few messengers. In 1918 the Maclean Committee recommended against the employment of 'second division clerks' but in favour of 'shorthand typewriters'. By 1953 there were eleven clerical officers or 'office clerks' as they were known in the House, but only three personal assistants and three shorthand typists. In the 1960s the first executive officers were appointed, to take over some of the duties previously performed by clerks.

In spite of all these changes, the function of the department remains what it has always been: to provide the House of Commons with the professional knowledge of the law and practice of Parliament and with the clerical services necessary to enable it to carry on its business. However much the scope of those services has broadened, the department has always recognized that its work cannot be an end in itself, as it may in the case of a government department, but must always be directly related to the demands of the House and its committees. The two most important innovations of the present century in the Clerk's Department have been, in fact, not the practical changes already described—the elaboration of parliamentary services—but the gradual establishment of two principles.

The first was restated as recently as August 1975 in the Bottomley Report: 'The staff of the House of Commons must continue to be recognised as a wholly distinct body, with a quite separate function, from the Civil Service whose duty is to serve the Executive.'[1] This principle had not always been recognized, as the appointment of Sir Courtenay Ilbert to the Clerkship of the House showed, but as the century progressed, such appointments became increasingly unlikely. The controversy

[1] Op. cit., p. 11.

which surrounded the appointment of former civil servants to the staff of select committees in the late 1960s showed how firmly this principle had taken root. Nevertheless, the final solution was a breach of the principle in the same way that Ilbert's appointment had been, and it was followed by a more serious, though unavoidable, breach a few years later when civil servants in mid-career were brought in to help with the overwhelming work-load of the Select Committee on European Secondary Legislation. It is sometimes argued that a greater interchange between the Civil Service and the Clerk's Department would be to their mutual benefit, and this is probably true. But if such interchange were to result in any weakening of the loyalty of clerks towards the House of Commons, then the price would be too high, because clerks frequently have to give advice which goes against the wishes of the Executive. If divided loyalties were to inhibit them in giving such advice, the House of Commons would suffer.

The other principle which has, fortunately, become even more firmly established over the last hundred years is the clerks' total independence of political parties. The days when relationship to or friendship with a Member of Parliament helped a candidate to obtain a clerkship are past (although, of course, such connections do not and should not hinder his appointment). Moreover, clerks, whatever their personal political views, are expected not only to behave with impartiality, but to keep their political opinions to themselves, lest they should even be suspected of bias. It may be thought that all this should be taken for granted, but it would be regarded with astonishment in several other Western European parliaments and international parliamentary assemblies, where it is quite normal to appoint senior officials who have openly declared their allegiance to a particular political party. Under this system it is quite accepted that politicians will press for the appointment or promotion of their own candidates and the latter will not hesitate to seek the support of politicians in the advancement of their careers.

As in the question of interchange with the Civil Service, there is a case to be made for this system. Again, however, it is difficult to reconcile it with the idea of a secretariat owing allegiance to the House as a whole, rather than to any section of it.

It is most unlikely that the House would gain by abandoning the present system, which has contributed much to the relatively smooth working of the machinery of Parliament in a period of great political and administrative upheaval.

APPENDIX II: THE HOUSE OF COMMONS LIBRARY

David Menhennet

The Library round about 1900

'So, from very modest beginnings, the Library as an institution has developed at Westminster. In its present magnificence and importance it offers a picturesque contrast to the surroundings and equipment of the small Committee-room in which it found a home in 1818. How insignificant beside it to-day would look its old neighbours the Smoking-room and Bellamy's Coffee-room! What progress, Lord Farnborough [Thomas Erskine May, later Clerk of the House] must have continually noted, was being made in the Department from the time when he entered it as an Assistant! In short, the Library of the House of Commons has grown and expanded with the growth and expansion of the Empire, until to-day it is an essential factor in the great organisation of the Imperial Parliament.'[1] Daniel Crilly, M.P., who wrote the above resounding words in concluding four articles on the Commons' Library which he wrote in February and March 1899,[2] was expressing an apparently widespread satisfaction and current sense of achievement at Westminster in the matter of library amenities and services. Sir Richard Temple, M.P., recorded a few years earlier that 'for study, for letter-writing, for culture generally, the highest standard of convenience prevails in this Library'.[3] 'This suite of apartments would have satisfied the highest aspirations of the most ardent of bibliophilic members of the pre-Reform times', noted Arnold Wright and Philip Smith in their encyclopaedic account of the Palace of Westminster published at the turn of the century. 'Ample in proportions, lofty and airy, and possessing, with the

[1] *Lords and Commons: An Illustrated Parliamentary Paper*, edited by F. Moir Bussy. No. 4, 4 Mar. 1899, p. 104.

[2] Ibid., Nos. 1–4, 11, 18, 25 Feb., and 4 Mar. 1899.

[3] *Life in Parliament . . . from 1886 to 1892 inclusive* (John Murray, 1893), Chap. 2, p. 16.

attractions of a delightful outlook, the advantages of quiet and seclusion, the Library constitutes perhaps the most desirable establishment of the kind there is in London.'[1]

Seventy-eight years ago the Commons' Library occupied, as it does today, a prime position in the 'new' Houses of Parliament which were built by Sir Charles Barry and A. W. Pugin after the Great Fire of 16 October 1834 had destroyed almost the whole of the old Royal Palace of Westminster. Daniel Crilly, Richard Temple, and their contemporaries could reach their Library in less than one minute's walk from the chamber, and found themselves in a fine suite of four large and two small adjoining rooms running along the river front, with views over the Terrace towards St. Thomas's hospital, Westminster Bridge, and Lambeth Palace.[2] Situated on the principal floor of the building, the Library was thus well placed for ease of access not only from the chamber but from the lobbies, restaurants, and smoking rooms on the same floor and from the committee rooms on the floor immediately above. This strategic position was, and remains, a factor of crucial importance. Barry and Pugin intended that the Library should be a central amenity for Members during the long hours which they spent at Westminster and they must have seen that however handsome or spacious the apartments themselves might be, the latter would be under-used unless they were close to the chamber itself. Photographs taken at or towards the turn of the century show that the overall appearance of the Library, despite differences of detail in the arrangement of furniture, was very similar to the first impression which a visitor to the Library, at a time when the House is not sitting, has today. Dark-painted ceilings with their patterns reflected in the carpets, fine carved woodwork, silver-plated stationery racks and penholders on the long writing tables, green leather chairs and armchairs, large Gothic-style windows looking east across the Thames: these features have given the Library an air of dignity and comfort

[1] *Parliament Past and Present* (Hutchinson & Co., 1902), p. 262.
[2] One of the four large rooms was intended for the private use of the Speaker. This fourth room was handed over to Members by Mr. Speaker King in 1966, and now forms an integral part of the Library suite.

from the start. One other physical feature should be mentioned —namely the high bookshelves lining the walls in all six rooms. Whilst these undoubtedly enhance the appearance of the Library, the absence in all four large rooms of any sort of gallery[1] means that Members and staff alike must use ladders to retrieve books from the upper shelves. This is a fairly common feature in many private libraries, and it does not appear to have worried men like Gladstone and Disraeli: but it does not add to the ease and comfort with which the users may browse among the books!

The present suite of rooms came into use shortly before 1852 with the exception of the Map Room—or Reference Room, as it is now called—which was appropriated for the Library in 1856. With the appointment of Benjamin Spiller as the first Librarian in 1818, a home was found for the Library in a small committee room 17ft. 6ins. long by 16ft. 9ins. wide situated above the outer Lobby between the Smoking Room and Bellamy's famous Coffee Room.[2] Select Committees of 1825 and 1826 recommended that a new Library near the chamber should be built; and a new, larger room designed by Sir John Soane was duly completed in 1827. It measured 55ft. by 23ft.—almost ten times the area of its predecessor[3]—and it looked out over what was then Cotton Garden to the river. However, this accommodation was soon found to be inadequate and, although extra space was found in 1833, it is likely that the piecemeal expansion of existing accommodation would have continued had not the Great Fire of 1834 presented itself as an unsolicited, ruthlessly efficient ally.

The Report from the Standing Committee on the Library of the House of 10 June 1852 stated that, in October 1834, 'two-thirds of the books which had been accumulated were burned; and the volumes saved were much injured by water and exposure'.[4] At first, the Library had contained little but

---

[1] A gallery ran round three sides of the small Map Room (now the Reference Room) from the start. A gallery was added to the second of the smaller rooms, the Oriel Room, in 1955.

[2] See *Evidence* (Q. 19) by the Librarian, Thomas Vardon, to the *Standing Committee on the Library of the House of Commons*, H.C. 104, 30 Mar. 1835. This important Report, published shortly after the Great Fire of 1834, is full of fascinating information concerning the early history of the Library.

[3] Ibid., *Evidence* (Q. 20).   [4] H.C. 453, *Report*, p. 3.

the official printed records of the House and volumes of parliamentary papers: collections which, thanks largely to the inspiration of Speaker Charles Abbot from 1802 onwards,[1] were themselves of great importance. By 1828, the growing usefulness of the Commons' Library was clear enough for the Government to authorize the expenditure of £2,000 on books —'in addition to the great store of Parliamentary and Record Volumes already accumulated'[2]—and by 1832 the holdings totalled 5,650 volumes.[3] It was this collection, together with priceless accumulations of manuscripts scattered within the precincts of the Palace, which suffered so grievously in the 1834 conflagration.[4]

In the new Library the holdings leapt to upwards of 30,000 bound volumes in 1857; as a former Librarian noted in 1953 in evidence submitted to the Select Committee on House of Commons Accommodation, 'the extent of the new shelving must have seemed enormous at first'.[5] What sort of books were being purchased or—frequently—accepted as gifts? The Standing Committee on the Library of 1835 re-affirmed the view of an earlier committee that the House of Commons required a 'Library of Historical and Constitutional Information'; and this principle was followed faithfully enough, as successive printed catalogues of the Library up to 1900 reveal. However, a great deal of general literature was also acquired, and the emphasis on strictly relevant literature undoubtedly became less pronounced. A critical view of this trend was contained in a report by Sir Charles Oman, M.P., written in 1923 at a time when H. A. L. Fisher was Chairman of the Library Committee:

. . . in the Catalogue of 1851 we find that there are numerous books of general literature already on the shelves—good early Victorian editions of

---

[1] On this and other aspects of the Library's early history, see Appendix D.II, pp. 111–13, to the *Report from the Select Committee on House of Commons Accommodation, &c.*, 1953–4, H.C. 184.

[2] Preface (p. 3) to the printed *Catalogue of Books in The Library at The House of Commons*, H.C. 80, 27 Feb. 1830. The Preface (by John Rickman, Clerk Assistant) and the Classified Catalogue are of considerable historical and bibliographical interest.

[3] 1953–4, H.C. 184, Appendix D.II, p. 112, para. 4.

[4] Lists of the books lost and saved in 1834 are available.

[5] 1953–4, H.C. 184, Appendix D.II, p. 112.

the Latin and Greek Classics, and much standard English poetry are now recorded—Shakespeare, Milton, Pope and Swift are forthcoming—Bacon is represented by the *Novum Organum* and the *Essays*, no longer by the *History of Henry VII* alone. Sir Thomas More's *Utopia*, Locke's and Hume's complete works and much more in the way of philosophical thought has come to hand. But the absolute denial of the original precepts of the founders of the Library best appears in the work of a Committee of 1856. This most distinguished body—it included Lord John Russell, Mr. Disraeli, Sidney Herbert and fourteen others—was charged with the expenditure of a legacy of £400 for the benefit of the Library, left by the will of Mr. Phillips, once Secretary to Speaker Manners-Sutton. They selected as appropriate purchases the whole of the scientific works of Cuvier, the great French anatomist, costing no less than £236, also the *Corpus Scriptorum Byzantinorum* at £25 5s. 0d., and *Biblia Sacra Polyglotta* at £42, with several other similar but less expensive items.

After this one can only say that *anything* might have been put into the Library, and that one is not quite certain whether the Committee of 1856 were aiming at setting up the most glorified 'County Home Library' conceivable, or whether they were not filled with a desire to emulate the all-embracing ambitions of the British Museum. By the action of our predecessors in 1840–60 the House of Commons Library was definitely committed to the policy of becoming a 'general' library, not merely a 'Library of Historical and Constitutional Information'. The only branch of literature which was never admitted was fiction, and I am not sure that even some fiction does not lurk in the collected editions of the works of such authors as Swift and Moore, while we certainly possess the erotic romances of Longus, Achilles Tatius and Heliodorus, as well as Lucian and Apuleius—all of which ought to have come under the original ban.

Since the Catalogue of 1856 was printed the Library has developed in a somewhat irregular fashion, according as the interest of those in charge of it swayed in one direction or another; to one Political Economy, to another Law, to another Foreign History, to a fourth political thought, to a fifth original documents of early date may seem a neglected section requiring instant reinforcement. The result is that in some provinces the Library is for the time up-to-date, while in others it is not.[1]

Sir Charles Oman may have had some grounds for criticizing the wide-ranging bibliophilic tastes of successive Librarians and Library Committees during the nineteenth century and the first quarter of the twentieth century; but his criticisms obscure a number of important points. First, there could be no crime in making classical fiction available to Members: on the contrary, debates of the period leading up to 1900 and following it owed much to Members' acquaintance with the writings of Swift and Dickens, to mention only two authors. The same may

[1] Cited ibid., p. 113.

be said of the Latin and Greek classics acquired for the use of legislators, and of much of the French literature which adorned the shelves.[1] Latin and French, moreover, had once been official languages of the Government, and many Members of the Victorian era were trilingual. What was true of Virgil and Voltaire was of course even truer of Shakespeare and Milton, Locke and Hume, and so on.

Equally important in assessing the value and relevance of the principal book collections round about 1900, however, is the *function* of the Library in the context of parliamentary life at that time. It is not possible to judge the book selection (or any other) policy of a particular period realistically without asking oneself: what was the essential purpose of the Library itself?

Thomas Vardon, the Librarian, was asked by the Committee of 1835 to distinguish between the duties of a 'parliamentary' and a 'public' librarian, as he understood them. He replied:

The distinction is very strong in practice when properly worked out. My duties, as attending the parliamentary department of the Library, I consider to embrace the attendance on Members generally, or select committees specially, and upon the House during the progress of public business. The attendance on Members generally is rather indefinite, but it amounts in fact to this, that to the extent of time which I can give, which is day and night during the sitting of the House, the practice is, that there is no subject connected with parliamentary business, on finance, or the forms of the House, or the progress of Bills, or the contents of Acts, on which I am not called upon to afford instant information. In respect to select committees, the notes continually sent me from the Chairmen or members of Committees do not specify—'I want such and such a volume of such a work' but their notes contain generally queries whether there be law upon such and such a subject; if there be, where it can be found; in what Acts: or regarding parliamentary papers, whether such information can be given, and whether, without troubling the Members with long papers, I can state briefly the information desired in their queries, which of course involves a great deal of indefinite labour during the whole of the day. Then, to the House at night, every Member must be aware of the sort of applications which are made to the Librarians, by the minute, I may almost say, for the debates, or the divisions which have taken place on particular occasions; for information concerning Finance Papers, Trade or Acts of Parliament relating to the subject under discussion, &c.: this necessarily involves (and it cannot pos-

---

[1] An expert appraisal of the Library's French holdings in 1952 revealed that out of a total of 722 titles examined only three were considered 'valueless'.

sibly be stopped) a great deal of conversation, which must take place between the Members and the Librarians.[1]

Vardon was giving evidence shortly after the first Reform Act had brought into the House some 200 new Members—an influx of 'new blood' which has been likened to the big Labour intakes of 1945, 1964, and 1966.[2] This situation, plus the impetus for a fresh start provided by the Great Fire of 1834, probably explains the prescient nature of Vardon's declaration, over 140 years ago, regarding the active information-giving role of the parliamentary librarian. Had this policy been systematically followed, then the book-selection policy of Librarians and Library Committees over the ensuing 70 years or so would no doubt have been very different. In fact, this information-giving function was not developed during the nineteenth century. From Library Committee reports, from scattered observations by Members and other writers, and from the evidence contained in successive printed catalogues of books, it is clear that in 1900 the Commons' Library was a good general library: offering on the one hand the essential parliamentary and official literature and, on the other, the cultural amenities associated with a good club or country gentleman's private library. There is evidence that the average Member of the late nineteenth century, far from resenting the leisurely atmosphere and somewhat passive role of his Library, actually approved of it.[3] The short chapter devoted to the Commons' Library in Arnold Wright and Philip Smith's *Parliament Past and Present* is a revealing commentary on the sort of parliamentary library considered desirable by most Members round about 1900.[4] No criticism is intended by this remark. The Commons' Library matched the spirit of the age and rightly reflected the more leisurely, self-contained approach to literature, and to the business of keeping informed, of the typical cultivated, reasonably well-off Member at the time. As Barker

[1] H.C. 104, 30 Mar. 1835, Q. 3.
[2] A. Barker and M. Rush, *The Member of Parliament and his Information* (Allen & Unwin, 1970), p. 290.
[3] See for example Sir Richard Temple, op. cit., p. 16; A. Wright and P. Smith, op. cit., p. 262; D. Menhennet, *The Library of the House of Commons*, in *Political Quarterly*, Vol. 36, No. 3, July–Sept. 1965, pp. 324–5.
[4] Op. cit., Chap. XX, pp. 260–4.

and Rush, among others, have pointed out in their study of *The Member of Parliament and his Information*, 'public affairs' could be followed at that time, without great difficulty, by means of conversations and parliamentary proceedings themselves, backed up with the perusal of parliamentary blue books, *The Times*, the *Morning Post* and a selection of other informative periodical publications.[1]

The Select Committee on the Library of 1945–6

From the comparatively scanty evidence available it appears that the Library's book-buying policy and its cautious approach to any sort of current affairs or information service altered very little during the first 45 years of the present century. What suited the Victorian Member of Parliament, however, became increasingly less acceptable as the complexity, pace, and volume of parliamentary business steadily increased. Two distinguished observers who were not Members commented unfavourably during the 1930s on what they regarded as a failure on the part of the Library to provide the modern services required by the House of Commons. H. G. Wells, an unsuccessful parliamentary candidate himself, took time off from examining *The Work, Wealth and Happiness of Mankind* to criticize the legislature's Library as follows:

The enquiring stranger will naturally wish to be shown the library and the organization for prompt information. He will find three or four rooms lined chiefly with files of State papers and with collections of books on British birds and field sports—dating from the times when the majority of elected members were country gentlemen. True, a selection of the customary reference books to be found in clubs and hotels, and a few recently published political biographies, along with a small shelf of current books from a circulating library, indicate a faint recognition of modern requirements. But no effort is made, even from such pathetically inadequate material as this library comprises, to assemble for the use of members from time to time such books or papers as bear on subjects under discussion in the legislative chamber. There are no research workers, preparing synopses or abstracts of information: no effort, indeed, at all to relate the library, as such, to the specific needs of those who might use it.[2]

Ivor Jennings, at the time Reader in English Law at London University, published a book on *Parliamentary Reform* in 1934

[1] Op. cit., p. 291.   [2] Op. cit. (Heinemann, 1932), p. 570.

in which a short chapter is devoted wholly to the Commons' Library. Jennings argued that no attempt was being made to provide relevant literature and current information to Members at a time when the legislature was having to cope with an ever-widening range of matters, many of them complex and highly technical:

Steps should therefore be taken for making the library adequate to its task. This means not only the provision of a really first-class library, especially on commercial, economic, and constitutional questions; it means also the appointment of a sufficient staff to catalogue and index the material which it ought to contain. Especially necessary is an adequate index of the Parliamentary debates and of official papers of all kinds, foreign and dominion and colonial, as well as British. Also, the average member has no time for research, and comparatively few can afford a competent private secretary. It should be one of the functions of Parliament to inform its own members. The library staff should therefore be able to produce information on any topic with which the House, or a committee thereof, is dealing. If, for instance, the problem under discussion is local taxation, the library should be able to produce a memorandum referring to official statistics, the reports of the numerous commissions and committees which have investigated the problem in the past, reports on foreign experience, and the investigations of private research workers.[1]

Jennings's perceptive criticisms were obviously shared by a growing number of Members during the 1930s and, but for the advent of the Second World War, this feeling of dissatisfaction would undoubtedly have led to earlier remedial action. Sir George Benson, M.P., wrote:

As a back bench Member in 1930, I was appalled to find the House of Commons served by a Library which had hardly progressed since 1850. It seemed inadequate, unbalanced and in many ways inefficient. . . . Latin and French classics still occupied front-row space in the exact positions where they had been originally placed in 1852. . . . There was no research. . . . The atmosphere was that of a country gentleman's private library.[2]

The staff of the Commons' Library—a Librarian and Assistant Librarian with supporting clerical staff—had always been small and, until 1945, it never exceeded seven. For many years during this period, moreover, the annual estimate to cover book buying, binding, and the purchase of newspapers,

[1] Op. cit. (Gollancz), Chap. X, p. 162.
[2] In *Second Report from the Estimates Committee, on the House of Commons Library*, 1960–1, H.C. 168, *Evidence*, pp. 1–2.

periodicals, stationery, and stores was only £1,200. With such limited means, it is small wonder that the Library was not able to provide that modern type of legislative library service which H. G. Wells, Jennings, and others considered essential. Some official impetus and support from the House of Commons itself was clearly required; and this was duly provided by the Select Committee which was appointed in October 1945 to 'inquire into the Present State of the Library of the House of Commons', and which published two important reports.[1]

The services which libraries provide vary greatly according to the different functions which they seek to fulfil. At one end of the scale are those national and other very large libraries whose principal purpose is the acquisition and preservation of literature for posterity; at the other extreme are those whose main task is the active provision and evaluation of information. In retrospect, the most important of the tasks which the 1945–6 Select Committee of Members set themselves was to ask: 'What sort of library do we require?'

In their First Report, the Committee decided that the essential purpose of the Commons' Library was to supply Members with information rapidly on any of the 'multifarious matters' which came before the House, or which Members had to deal with in the general course of their parliamentary duties.[2] The Second Report returned to this definition of functions: 'Your Committee feel that the Library of the House of Commons can, and should, be made into a unique organisation. It should be far more than a repository of books and parliamentary papers. It should aim at *providing Members rapidly with precise and detailed information on subjects connected with their duties*'.[3]

In other words, the House of Commons' Library was to be expanded and developed into a first-class reference library, with all the basic materials and means of quick reference which such a commitment entailed. Only in this way could it begin to meet the requirements of a busy legislature. But the 1945–6 Select Committee went further. In their First Report they stated:

[1] *First and Second Reports from the Select Committee on Library (House of Commons)*, 1945–6, H.C. 35, 99–I.
[2] 1945–6, H.C. 35, 99–I, p. iii, para. 5.
[3] Ibid., p. vi, para. 8. [Author's italics.]

Your Committee are of the opinion that, if skilled advice upon choice of books and possible sources of information were available, the utility of the Library would be very greatly increased. As the present staff are fully occupied with their existing duties Your Committee recommend the appointment of two Assistant Librarians. For these posts very special qualifications will be required, including a wide knowledge of the social and political sciences. They should not be responsible for any of the routine work of the Library; their duties should be to give *specialist active assistance* to Members in every possible way. In order to attract candidates of the very high standard and mature age which Your Committee feel will be needed to fill these posts adequately, they recommend that salaries should commence at £800 rising by annual increments of £25 to £1,000.[1]

In this recommendation lies the genesis—admittedly not explicitly stated—of the Library's research services which to-day form a major and highly distinctive feature of its work. In their Second Report, the Committee referred to these two new appointments, which were quite highly paid, as posts for 'two Research Assistants with special qualifications in the Social Sciences', and went on to doubt whether two would be an adequate number to deal with the range of subjects and publications involved.[2]

'Reference' and 'research', then, were the two arms of the new-style post-war Commons' Library which the Select Committee of Members under the chairmanship of Sir (then Mr.) George Benson envisaged. There was one other basic requirement, which the Committee did not overlook, and that was the building-up of an adequate modern bookstock. Although some of its holdings had been damaged during the war years—over two-thirds (about 60 tons) of them were sent for safe keeping to the Bodleian, to the National Library of Wales, and elsewhere—the Library still possessed in 1945 an extensive and valuable collection of books acquired over the past 100 years. But the Committee found the stock to be 'woefully short' of modern literature in a number of subjects. Among the subjects in which the Library was deemed to be deficient were: finance and political economy; social science; history; constitutional law; the Dominions and Colonies; the U.S.S.R. and the Asiatic countries.[3] The Committee therefore recommended that

[1] Ibid., p. iv, para. 5. [Author's italics.]
[2] Ibid., p. vi, para. 9.
[3] Ibid., p. iii, para. 2.

the Library should take steps, as urgently as the difficult post-war conditions allowed, to enlarge and update its bookstock and, equally important, its range of newspaper and periodical literature. It also proposed that a new author catalogue and a new alphabetical subject catalogue should be compiled, both on cards, and that a suite of cellars two floors below the Main Library should be prepared for reserve stock. Finally, the Committee heard evidence from Sir Giles Gilbert Scott, the architect of the new Commons' chamber, and from Mr. Albert Bossom, M.P., that the building of galleries in three of the large Library rooms (Rooms A, B, and C) would not harm the aesthetic and architectural character of those areas. It accordingly recommended that, with a view to accommodating more books and making them more accessible to users, galleries should be so constructed.[1]

This last recommendation has not been implemented. However, despite the fact that the Select Committee's two reports were never debated in the House, an encouraging start was made with all the other major recommendations. The Government of the day, no doubt aware that among the large post-war intake of new Members were many who could not afford personal libraries, or research, or even secretarial assistance, provided what was for the times a generous amount of money in order to modernize and enlarge the Library's holdings of books, periodicals, and newspapers and to prepare for the Library's emergent role as a reference and information service. The book holdings were overhauled by experts and serious gaps in certain basic sections such as economics, politics, constitutional history, law, and biography were filled. Card catalogues, both author and subject, were begun; and cellar space was provided for the overflow of materials from the main suite of rooms. A separate Reference Room was established in 1946, and quickly became the nucleus of the new Library's quick-reference services. Almost unbelievably, in 1946 only a single newspaper and some 50 periodicals were regularly taken; by about 1950, this provision had increased to over 100 British and foreign newspapers and over 1,000 journals. Members had been able to borrow most of the Library's books since shortly before the war, but an important new facility was now instituted

[1] Ibid., p. v, para. 4.

when the Library systematically began to borrow copies of wanted books from other libraries on a subscription basis. In this way, a partial solution was found to a very real problem. It was (and remains) a frequent occurrence that twenty or more Members wished to borrow a personal copy of a topical or politically important book; the system of borrowing multiple copies of such a book has meant both that Members' waiting lists can be kept within reasonable proportions, and that the Library has not had to buy for permanent retention more copies of a particular book than it actually needs.

The first Handbook, or guide, to the services of the Library was issued in March 1950,[1] and in itself constituted a step forward in the Library's public relations with its important clientele. This Handbook shows that, five years after the Select Committee had been set up, the Library consisted of two principal Divisions—Parliamentary and Reference. The former handled the considerable intake of official publications, and housed the catalogues and main collection of books. The Reference Division is described as 'an information department'.[2] In addition to its reference material, it was initially the home of the Library's International Affairs Desk and of its Statistical Section, although the latter was already designated a 'special service'.[3] Finally, in 1950, there existed a very small but quite separate Research Department, staffed by two research assistants.

The definition of the latter's duties was given in the Handbook as follows:

To carry out the 'long term' researches the Research Department was set up in May, 1946. Its staff are free to pursue their enquiries on behalf of Honourable Members wherever they think the answers to those enquiries are likely to be. They work in an office near the Library and are available to make enquiries into all matters relating to the Parliamentary duties of Honourable Members. The research they undertake is usually and normally bibliographical; they seek the latest references in books, periodicals, newspapers and official publications (including *Hansard*), to material published on the matter before them and they arrange for the works cited to be obtained, photo-copied or translated as necessary, and placed before the Honourable

---

[1] *The Library of the House of Commons*, March 1950.
[2] Ibid., p. 5.   [3] Ibid., p. 6.

Member requiring the information. At the same time they prepare memoranda and bibliographies which are issued in a mimeographed form, on important matters due or likely to be raised on the floor of the House. Before the second reading of all important and controversial Government and Private Members' Bills they issue bibliographies on the subjects dealt with in those Bills. These bibliographies contain references, annotated to shew their scope, to the Parliamentary Papers and non-Parliamentary publications dealing with the subject before the House, to previous debates on that subject and to relevant books, pamphlets and periodical articles.[1]

In his evidence to the 1945–6 Select Committee the then Librarian Designate, Mr. H. A. St. G. Saunders, had emphasized the need to cater for those more complex and protracted inquiries from M.P.s which could not be handled within the context of the Library's normal reference and information services.[2] He also stressed that the minimum of two research assistants recruited for the purpose should be exempted from the normal, time-consuming Library routines. Finally, he suggested that financial provision should be made available for journeys to be undertaken by them with the object of consulting other libraries and sources of information 'in any part of the globe'. It seems that this last particular suggestion was not fully endorsed by the Select Committee or by the Government—although the research staff in 1950 were described as being free to pursue their inquiries 'wherever they think the answers to those enquiries are likely to be'. Certainly the idea of longer-term research, set somewhat apart from the other Library services, was fully accepted in 1950. The 1950 Handbook also stated that the research undertaken was 'usually and normally bibliographical': great stress was laid, in those early days, on the compilation of careful and lengthy bibliographies.[3] A feature of the subsequent development of the Library's research services has been a move away from primarily bibliographical research in favour of shorter explanatory 'briefs' in the form of letters to Members, in the compilation of which both published and unpublished, written and oral, sources are used. This trend was certainly helped and accelerated by the transfer at an early stage of the Statistical Section to the research,

---

[1] Ibid., p. 7.

[2] 1945–6, H.C. 35, 99–I, *Evidence*, p. 28.

[3] The *Handbook* for 1950 lists 64 such bibliographies prepared between August 1947 and December 1949: op. cit., Appendix 1.

as opposed to the reference, side of the Library's activities. Already in 1950 the two qualified statisticians were supplying precise figures in written form in response to Members' individual inquiries and, by 1953, the Librarian was able to link the 'Research and Statistical Sections' in his account of the Library's special services to Members.[1]

From 1945–6, therefore, dates the real beginning of the House of Commons Library as a modern legislative reference service: a reference and research library for the House, its Committees, and, above all, for individual Members. By happy coincidence, the Legislative Reference Service of the United States Congress (since re-named the Congressional Research Service) was substantially expanded and reorganized by the Legislative Reorganization Act of 1946. Since then, both organizations have developed along basically similar lines, although the Washington Service has far outstripped its Westminster counterpart in terms of numbers of staff. This type of post-war development has not, of course, been confined to Britain and the United States. Now is not the time to discuss the comparative aspect of the question, but it is worth registering that, whenever the role of modern parliamentary libraries is discussed in a realistic and international context, the notion of an active 'legislative reference service' is bound to figure prominently. In seeking to offer such a service, parliamentary libraries are responding, essentially, to the requirements of their special users. As was pointed out over ten years ago:

The use which students and teachers make of a university library differs fundamentally from the type of service which Members expect from the House of Commons Library. Here, the emphasis is on the provision of information—of facts and figures as opposed to the mere production of source material. Often, the straightforward presentation of published data just will not suffice in itself. These must be evaluated by the staff of the Library, supplemented from oral sources of information, condensed and written up in the form of a balanced assessment which a Member can assimilate in a matter of minutes. Mistakes are costly and potentially embarrassing—not least to the Member himself. Naturally, the scope and calibre of such a library service can vary enormously according to the available resources of staff and material, and according to the wishes of the particular representative assembly concerned. But the basic functional concept of a legislative reference service, big or small, is a *sine qua non* of a modern

---

[1] 1953–4, H.C. 184, Appendix D.II, p. 107, para. 15.

parliamentary library. It follows that the present-day services of the House of Commons Library are not simply the arbitrary outcome of specific recommendations made twenty years ago: they also derive, automatically, from the way in which Members use their Library.[1]

More precisely, it may fairly be said that today's House of Commons Library derives from the wish of Members, over 30 years ago, to have a library service that was relevant to their requirements.

Developments since 1950: Expansion, Reorganization, Control

By 1950, the 'new-look' Commons' Library was in being; a sound start had been made, but progress had necessarily been slow and uneven. Sir George Benson told the Estimates Committee which examined the Library in 1960 that in 1950 'The rooms looked depressing . . . The catalogue was in arrears . . . Every step towards improvement was blocked by economy warnings and lack of staff.'[2] It was therefore decided that a comprehensive overhaul of 'every corner of the Library and its administration and services' was required—and by 1960 the Librarian was able to report substantial progress.[3]

Apart from what may be fairly described as a general physical tidying-up of the Library, and obvious improvements in the standards of comfort and routine services provided for Members, the marked progress in Library services (other than research, which is dealt with separately) over the ten-year period up to 1960 may be outlined as follows:

(a) The design of the Reference Room and that of the other main reception point for Members' inquiries, the Oriel Room, were modernized. A gallery was constructed around three sides of the Oriel Room, and purpose-built newspaper chests and periodical fitments were provided in the small, busy Reference Room.

(b) The author and subject card catalogues were completed and

---

[1] D. Menhennet, in *Political Quarterly*, Vol. 36, No. 3, July–Sept. 1965, p. 325.

[2] *Second Report from the Estimates Committee, on the House of Commons Library*, 1960–1, H.C. 168, *Evidence*, p. 3, para. 8.

[3] Ibid., pp. 3–8, paras. 9–40.

a duplicate catalogue was begun. In any working library, the catalogue is a key tool: and its completion (to 1960) and the subsequent care with which it was kept up to date was a major achievement.

(c) A series of visible strip indexes, listing up-to-date references to a wide range of parliamentary and other official material, both British and foreign, was begun in 1955. The Commons' Library may justly claim to have pioneered this method of jotting down current references to debates, parliamentary questions, parliamentary papers, legislation in both Houses, reports from committees, and much else besides; and these indexes, which have been systematically extended since their introduction, have been a crucial factor in the Library's efforts to provide Members with a fast, accurate, and comprehensive information service.

The staffing establishment of the Commons' Library was also expanded over this period, though not without difficulties and setbacks. From two university graduates and five men of junior grades in 1945, it rose to 20 in 1950, to 30 in 1955, and to 32 in 1960. The senior grade of Library Clerks—university graduates with good honours degrees and often professional or other postgraduate qualifications as well, linked to the various Museum Keeper grades—had risen to 11 by 1960, while the organization of the Library into a Parliamentary (or Reference) Division and a Research Division had also been formalized and completed. The total cost of the Library had risen considerably: from about £11,000 in 1946 to about £40,000 in 1960. Given the negligible size of the House of Commons Library in 1946, however, this near-quadrupling of expenditure was not really surprising.

These upward trends continued into the 1960s. As the numbers of staff available to serve Members of Parliament rose, so too did the demands placed upon the staff. Research inquiries showed a marked increase following the general election of 1959, when a large number of younger men and women entered Parliament for the first time: by the end of 1963 it was possible to observe that the annual average of inquiries from Members during the four-year period 1959–63 (813) was nearly 50 per cent greater than that for the preceding four years. The research figures for 1964 revealed a further increase of 42 per cent—to 1,154 inquiries—over the annual average for 1959–63.[1] In addition, 35 Reference Sheets—select, annotated reading lists on current legislation and on other topics of parliamentary interest—were compiled by research staff during 1964; their popularity testified to the growing awareness among Members of the assistance which their Library, if properly stocked and staffed, was capable of offering them. This awareness was strengthened, no doubt, by a rising tide of public interest during the early 1960s in the developing role of Parliament and in the research and information services which Members required to do their jobs effectively. The Study of Parliament Group (S.P.G.), consisting of university teachers of politics and government and of certain senior staff from the House of Commons and House of Lords Departments, was formed in 1964. One of the Group's earliest pre-occupations was with the adequacy, or otherwise, of the Library's services to Members: its academic members published their views individually[2] or, when opportunity occurred, submitted evidence to select committees of the House. The detailed study by Anthony Barker and Michael Rush on *The Member of Parliament and his Information*, published jointly for Political and Economic Planning and the Study of Parliament Group in 1970, resulted directly from the setting-up in 1966 of a working party within the S.P.G. to study the problem. The book is still a standard source of reference in its field.[3]

During this initial period of gradual expansion, from 1950 to about 1965, the Librarian had been helped and advised by an informally constituted committee of Members of Parliament. It was this advisory committee of Members, known as the Library Committee, which replied to the Estimates Committee's Report on the Library in 1961.[4] However, this method of control, by Members, of their own Library and of its services had never been entirely satisfactory since the Speaker first appointed such an informal, advisory group in 1922. In 1965,

---

[1] A. Barker and M. Rush, op. cit., p. 296.

[2] See, for example, B. Crick, *The Reform of Parliament*, first published in 1964, 2nd edn., 1968, and revised 2nd edn., 1970.

[3] Chapter VI of this book deals with the Library and with Members' views on its services.

[4] 1960–1, H.C. 246.

therefore, the members of the then Library Committee submitted evidence to the Select Committee on the Palace of
Westminster, which was currently considering the whole question
of Members' control of their own accommodation and facilities:

From 1818 to about 1834 the Library was under the Speaker's direction.
From 1834 until 1861 a powerful 'Standing Committee' on the Library was
appointed sessionally to help him. There next ensued a long period, again
under the Speaker's sole direction, until 1922, since when he has regularly
appointed his own informal Advisory Committee of Members (ourselves).
The method of control, despite certain advantages, has never closely fitted
the changing needs of the Library. In the 1834–61 period names like Peel,
Lord John Russell, Palmerston, Disraeli and Gladstone, not to mention the
Chancellor of the Exchequer of the day, filled the Committees. The business
connected with a comparatively leisurely Library was apparently too
restricted to hold their interest. Since 1945, however, the needs of Members
for documentation and research have greatly increased, both in quantity
and scope, and the difficulties of control have been of a very different kind.
Whilst the Library's obligation to provide Members rapidly 'with precise
and detailed information on subjects connected with their duties' is generally accepted, opinions of both Members and others as to the precise
extent of the Library's functions as a research and reference library vary
considerably. Owing to their informal status, the Library Committee find
themselves largely unable to secure the provision of the library services
which they believe Members require. They have always felt free to advise
the Speaker upon improvements which they consider to be desirable or
which other Members bring to their notice; as well as upon matters remitted
to them by the Speaker; unfortunately they cannot press this advice. They
have no formal channel for discussions with the Treasury and cannot even
make a report to the House.'[1]

The Library Committee went on to propose that what was
needed was a select committee of Members, or a sub-committee
forming part of a larger House of Commons 'Commission',
which would exercise control on Members' behalf of the
Library's policy and services.[2] The Select Committee on the
Palace of Westminster did in fact recommend that, in future,
the Library Sub-Committee should form an integral part of a
new and important Select Committee on House of Commons
Services, which was to advise the Speaker in all matters regarding House of Commons accommodation and services.[3] Since
1965, therefore, there has existed an official channel of

---

[1] Appendix 2, p. 92, to the *Report of the Select Committee on the Palace of
Westminster*, 1964-5, H.C. 285.

[2] Ibid., Appendix 2, p. 93.   [3] Ibid., *Report*, p. vii.

communication between Members and the Librarian—a link which, as the more recent Committee on House of Commons (Administration) recorded—has proved both long-standing and beneficial.[1]

The Advisory Library Committee, in their memorandum to the 1964–5 Select Committee on the Palace of Westminster, also recommended that the Library should cease to form a part of the Speaker's Department and should become instead a separate department of the House of Commons.[2] This proposition reflected in part the wish of the Library Committee to have a more effective say in the policy and general development of library and research facilities, and partly the continuing growth in the size and range of services of the Commons' Library itself. The Palace of Westminster Select Committee did not recommend accordingly. However, by 1966, the Library had expanded its services still further in step with Members' wishes and requirements—the staff now totalled 48—and a Treasury Organisation and Methods review carried out in 1966–7 recommended that the Library should form a separate department under the day-to-day administrative control of the Librarian. This was duly approved by the House and, since August 1967, the Library has formed one of the five largely independent Departments among which the permanent staff who serve the House are distributed.[3] More recently, the Committee under Mr. Arthur Bottomley, M.P., which examined the administrative services of the House of Commons, recommended a number of important organizational changes; these changes, when implemented in 1979, will not affect the Library's position as one of five Departments of the House, but will bring the Vote Office (which issues and circulates parliamentary papers to Members) into the Library Department: a welcome addition.[4] The Bottomley Report also recommended that the

[1] Report by a Committee under the Chairmanship of Mr. Arthur Bottomley, M.P., on *House of Commons (Administration)*, 1974–5, H.C. 624, p. 21, para. 4.43.

[2] 1964–5, H.C. 285, Appendix 2, p. 94, para. 4(c).

[3] Erskine May, *Parliamentary Practice*, 18th edn. (Butterworth, 1971), pp. 234–6. A full account of the 'Departmental' organization of the House staff is contained in M. Rush and M. Shaw (eds.), *The House of Commons Services and Facilities* (Allen & Unwin, 1974).

[4] 1974–5, H.C. 624, pp. 21, 23, paras. 4.43, 4.56.

Librarian should become a member of the new House of Commons Board of Management, which has been set up to advise the Speaker and a reconstituted House of Commons Commission on all matters affecting the work of more than one Department of the House, and on staffing policy generally.[1]

By 1970, the House of Commons Library had a total annual budget of £175,000, and a staff complement of 54, of whom 20 belonged to the senior grades of Library Clerk and above.[2] Following a series of reviews and investigations, and with the full knowledge of the Library Sub-Committee, the Research Division had been reorganized in 1968 into four Sections— Home and Parliamentary Affairs, Economic Affairs, Statistical, and Science and Technology respectively. Inquiries from Members involving research[3] were distributed among the staff of these four Sections and, within each Section, individual members of the graduate staff were beginning to specialize in particular areas of public affairs such as agriculture, education, employment, and science policy. The Statistical Section differed (and still differs) from its three counterparts in two respects: it had employed specialist, statistical staff right from its inception in 1946, and it dealt with all statistical inquiries, whatever their subject area or areas might be. Writing in February 1971 Geoffrey Lock, at that time the Head of the Library's Statistical Section, had this to say of the work involved:

[1] Ibid., p. 14, para. 4.2. See also House of Commons (Administration) Act, chap. 36 of 1978.

[2] See M. Rush and M. Shaw, op. cit., Chap. 5, 'The House of Commons Library', pp. 138 et seq.

[3] The Library's use of the term 'research' has given rise to some discussion over the years. Broadly, the Commons' Library has interpreted 'research' in the sense that other large parliamentary libraries have interpreted it. The most recent definition was offered by senior Library staff in their evidence to the Select Committee on Assistance to Private Members in January 1975: 'The distinction between "secretarial" and "research" assistance, and the proper definition of the latter, are also important. "Research" in the context of this Memorandum differs from both academic research and secretarial or reference work (tracing passages in Hansard, finding addresses, etc.); it is the supply of information, advice and documentation, at varying levels of sophistication and generally with some speed, on all matters with which Parliamentarians become involved.' 1974–5, H.C. 191–i, p. 2, para. 4.

The Statistical Section of the House of Commons Library meets a growing need on the part of Members (and to some extent Peers) for statistics more extensive than can be obtained by a parliamentary question, without the publicity involved and without the need for a wait of some days. Enquiries can only rarely be answered by the straightforward extraction of figures from a single source. We usually have to bring together figures from a wide range of different sources, do calculations on them, annotate them on conceptual points, and generally adapt them to the Member's specific needs. Only very rarely can we give to one Member material prepared for another; the enquiries all differ, so the replies are individually tailored. We work largely from printed material, of which we maintain a large collection, and for recent figures Hansard answers and press notices form an important source. . . . The clientele consists mainly of backbenchers and some front-benchers of the Opposition of the day, though it is not unknown for Ministers to consult us, even on matters connected with their own Departments. The work can vary from the supply of figures to a front-bench spokesman for a winding up speech in a major debate, through such things as assistance with a note of dissent to a Report of a Royal Commission, to (as it turned out) provision of material for a filibuster in Committee. As far as possible we have somebody present to assist Members with figures as long as the House sits, even when it sits very late.[1]

The above passage gives a good thumb-nail sketch of the type, range, and pressures of work performed today by the Library's research staff for individual Members of Parliament. Since 1970–1, the number of inquiries handled by the Research Division has continued to grow. In 1970, 1,659 written answers were sent to Members; the progression since then has been as follows:

Year	Number of Research Inquiries
1971	2,114
1972	2,208
1973	2,394
1974	2,345
1975	3,670
1976	4,493

Today (October 1978) the Library has an overall complement of 88,[2] of whom 30 work in the Research Division. Since 1976, in the light of a growing workload and with the important

[1] *Statistical News* No. 12, February 1971, pp. 5–6. See also G. F. Lock on 'The Role of the Library' in *The Commons in Transition*, ed. A. H. Hanson and B. Crick (Fontana/Collins, 1970), Chap. 7.

[2] The Librarian is assisted by a Deputy Librarian, two Assistant Librarians, six Deputy Assistant Librarians, 16 Clerks, professional and executive staff, and by clerical, secretarial, and other supporting staff.

aim of increasing the degree of subject specialization possible among research staff, a new unit—dealing with inquiries on education and the social services—has been formed within the Home and Parliamentary Affairs Section of the Research Division. Each Section is headed by a senior member of the research staff who, in turn, is responsible to one of the Library's two Assistant Librarians. The International Affairs Section, which handles a vast intake of European and foreign documentation in addition to answering those research inquiries on international affairs which do not fall within the scope of research subject specialists, forms a part of the Library's Parliamentary Division. In addition to answering inquiries from individual M.P.s, research staff also prepare Reference Sheets and Background Papers for the general use of Members, the latter documents being pamphlet-length, factual briefs by subject specialists on such different topics as Devolution, Chemical and Biological Warfare, Metrication, Murder Statistics, Proportional Representation, Animal Feeding Stuffs, and a Bill of Rights. Always, the emphasis is on subjects of interest, or subjects likely to be of interest, to Parliament. In October 1970, an article on the Library recorded that perhaps the most interesting development of the past three years had been an increasing involvement by Research Division staff in the work of specialist select committees such as those on Science and Technology, Agriculture, Education, Overseas Development, and Race Relations:

Library staff who undertake this work are usually specialists in a particular field (for example, agriculture); over a period of time they work alongside the Clerk to the Committee and, in some cases, an outside expert brought in to advise on certain aspects of the matter under investigation. They attend meetings and, on request, provide technical advice as well as specific research assistance and bibliographical guidance.[1]

At the time of writing, this involvement of Library staff in committee work of the above type is tending to diminish somewhat—partly at least owing to the Library's full workload of inquiries from individual Members. This sort of longer-term

[1] 'Inside the Commons Library', in *Library Association Record*, Oct. 1970, Vol. 72, No. 10, pp. 330–1. See also D. Menhennet and J. B. Poole in *New Scientist*, 7 Sept. 1967, p. 501.

research work nevertheless remains a highly desirable feature of the Research Division's terms of reference, and provides a welcome opportunity of co-operation with the staff of another Department, that of the Clerk of the House.

Whilst it is relatively easy to trace the upsurge over the last 20 years in the work performed by research staff the increasing pressures on the Parliamentary Division, though none the less real and substantial, are difficult to quantify in specific terms. It is certain, however, that the specialist work of the Research Division could not be carried out without the support of the 125,000 or so books, the full collections of British and foreign official publications, the newspapers and periodicals, and the catalogues, special collections, and indexes maintained by its 'main library' counterpart. Here, too, the authorized establishment has had to be expanded; and, not surprisingly, many of the Department's professionally qualified library staff work in the Parliamentary Division. When the Select Committee on Assistance to Private Members recently recommended a doubling of the research services in the Library, it also accepted that any such increase would have to be accompanied by some expansion of the reference and supporting staff in the Parliamentary Division,[1] thus recognizing the integration and interdependence of the research and reference arms of the Library's services. Indeed, it has been an important point of Library policy since 1945 that the two Divisions, Parliamentary and Research, should form equal partners within the overall organization.[2]

Very approximately, the Parliamentary Division to-day deals with 1,500 mainly short-term requests from Members for information and documentation each week that the House is sitting. These requests are placed not only direct by Members themselves coming to the Library, but also by letter and by telephone—and the need to provide good telephone access to the Library means that there are fifteen such instruments in the main suite of rooms alone. Small wonder that the requirements of the 'information explosion' sometimes conflict with the other traditional role of the Commons' Library as a place for relaxation and quiet study! To help reduce the pressure on

[1] 1974–5, H.C. 662, para. 6, p. v.
[2] 1974–5, H.C. 191–i, para. 24, pp. 8–9.

the main library telephone services, and also to cater for those
Members who were allocated rooms in the newly renovated
Norman Shaw (North) building[1] in 1975, the Library opened
a branch reference library on the top floor of that same building
in June 1975. In addition to servicing Members, the Norman
Shaw (North) Library admits Members' secretaries and personal research assistants, and handles a substantial amount of
telephone inquiries received from outside bodies and the
public. Since its inception, the branch reference library has
been increasingly used and now forms an essential part of the
House of Commons Library's services. Two recent reports from
the Select Committee on House of Commons (Services)—on
Members' Secretaries and Research Assistants and on Services
for the Public respectively[2]—seem certain to add to its responsibilities. Indeed, since this chapter was first written, the branch
library has been expanded into a Public Information Office,
and a Weekly Information Bulletin is now published.

The Library has a long-standing interest in the use of computers for storing and retrieving information. In 1970 a team
from Aslib (formerly the Association of Special Libraries and
Information Bureaux) carried out an exhaustive survey of the
Library's manual indexing methods and, in their 276-page
report, recommended that 'the computer should be put to work
to enhance the information services available to Members of
Parliament'.[3] For a number of reasons, including the cost factor,
the phased introduction of automatic data processing suggested
by the Aslib Report of 1971 was not authorized by the House at
that time. However, the Library was allowed to recruit a qualified computer specialist to its staff, and continued to take an
active interest in the potential usefulness of a computer-based
information service in Parliament.[4] Various short-term experiments, in conjunction with International Computers Ltd. and

[1] Formerly New Scotland Yard, on the Victoria Embankment.
[2] 1976–7, H.C. 508 and 509. On the Library's growing services to
Members' research assistants, see J. B. Poole and A. M. Gould, 'Information
for Parliament', *Aslib Proceedings*, June 1977, pp. 224–6. See also 1974–5
H.C. 662, pp. vi–viii.
[3] *Computer support for Parliamentary Information Service*, by B. C. Vickery and
H. East (Aslib, January 1971), p. 12.
[4] Cf., e.g., J. B. Poole, 'Computers in the House of Commons: Retrospect
and Prospect', in *The Parliamentarian*, 1973, Vol. LIV, pp. 214–22.

with IBM (United Kingdom) Ltd., were mounted. Most importantly, the Library proceeded to work out with the Central Computer Agency the best way of transferring its manual *indexing* systems to a central, computer-based system which might be consulted from a number of visual display units scattered throughout the Library's premises—and no doubt, in due course, elsewhere. On-line retrieval of information was and remains the primary aim: but such a system would have a number of other important advantages, of which some form of regular Selective Dissemination of Information (SDI) service for Members could certainly be one. The House of Lords had also shown a great deal of interest in computerized information retrieval, and on 29 March 1976 the then Lord President of the Council announced that he hoped shortly to set up a small, informal Joint Committee of both Houses to advise on the prospects for a computer-based parliamentary information retrieval system.[1]

The Report of this Informal Joint Committee on Computers to the Leaders of both Houses, under the chairmanship of Lord Darling, was published in January 1977.[2] It noted that a start had already been made in the House of Lords with the indexing of the titles of EEC legislation, and it recommended that the computer-based indexing system proposed for the Commons' Library should be proceeded with. In May 1977, following detailed evidence given to the Library Sub-Committee by Library staff and by the Central Computer Agency, the Select Committee on House of Commons (Services) published its Report, recommending that the Librarian should be authorized to proceed with the introduction of computer-based indexing in the House of Commons Library, as soon as possible.[3]

The Library's proposals for the step-by-step introduction, over a period of several years, of a computer-based indexing system to parliamentary and other material are set out in full in the Evidence to the above Report.[4] The House of Commons itself agreed to these plans for computer-based indexing on

[1] *H.C. Debates*, 908, c. 332 Written Answers.
[2] 1976–7, H.C. 78.
[3] 1976–7, H.C. 377, on Computer-Based Indexing for the Library.
[4] 1976–7, H.C. 377, pp. 2–9. See also J. B. Poole and A. M. Gould, 'Information for Parliament', pp. 221–36.

26 January 1978; and the Library thus stands on the threshold of an important development in its services to Members.[1]

Parliamentary Libraries

No mention has been made until now, in this brief historical survey of the House of Commons Library in the twentieth century, of its counterpart in the House of Lords. The latter dates from 1826. It is quite separate from the Commons' Library, serving Peers and House of Lords staff on the same official footing that the Commons' Library accords absolute priority to Members and to the staff of the Commons. The staffing establishment of the Lords' Library is, by comparison, small: but it is expanding, and a working group chaired by Viscount Eccles recommended in March 1977 that the House of Lords Library 'should be organised to provide Peers with more reading material relating to current affairs and the business of the House, and with an information service more nearly comparable to that provided by the House of Commons'.[2] There has always been much informal and useful co-operation between the two Libraries. For example, the Commons' Library is glad to take advantage of the excellent law collections available in the House of Lords, where service to the Lords of Appeal remains a primary duty; on the other hand, the larger staffing resources of the Commons' Library enable it to help Peers and House of Lords staff in their current information and specialized research requirements, subject always to the overriding priority of Members' own needs. Recently, a joint working party drawn from the staff of the two Libraries has been meeting at regular intervals to discuss matters of common concern.

Returning to the House of Commons, one may fairly say that today's Member of Parliament finds himself well and truly at the centre of a continuing 'information explosion'. Thanks to the ever-widening scope of governmental activities, there are very few areas of public policy which do not impinge on the work and representative responsibilities of the modern Member

[1] On the wider issue of computer applications in Parliament, see 1977–8, H.C. 617–i.

[2] 1976–7, H.L. 84, p. 23.

of Parliament—agriculture, education, employment and unemployment, environmental questions of every description,
health, housing, regional affairs, social security, and scientific
and technological policy, to mention but some, in addition to
those more traditional long-standing areas of parliamentary
concern such as foreign affairs, national defence, trade, and
financial control. To help them carry out their functions of
parliamentary criticism and scrutiny, Members need a great
deal of precise and accurate, sometimes complex, information,
over a tremendously wide range of subjects;[1] moreover, they
frequently require this information at very short notice and in
a pre-digested analytical form of presentation.

In their full and valuable study of *The Member of Parliament
and his Information*, Barker and Rush have shown that M.P.s
obtain their information from a great diversity of sources.
Similarly, in their memorandum to the Select Committee on
Assistance to Private Members, in January 1975, senior Library
staff conceded the obvious point that there were some important
tasks—for example, the provision of party-political assistance
and the settlement of certain purely constituency problems—
which the House of Commons Library either should not, or
could not, carry out.[2] Nevertheless, Barker and Rush point out
that, in 1970, the term 'parliamentary information services' was
'95 per cent synonymous with the work of the Library' at
Westminster.[3] And the above Select Committee, reporting its
investigations to the House, stated that: 'In general we believe
that the Library provides the best means of meeting the purely
research needs of most Members.'[4]

It is generally accepted, then, that the parliamentary library
should be at the centre of those information services which
Members need in order to perform their duties. In countries
where economic resources permit, this important principle is
recognized through that provision of finance and other facilities,
ranging from the adequate to the generous, which is made for
the parliamentary library and its associated services. The

[1] A recent study in this general field is Janet Morgan's *Reinforcing
Parliament* (Research Publications Services, 1976).
[2] 1974–5, H.C. 191–i, Memorandum, pp. 1–2.
[3] Op. cit., p. 290.
[4] 1974–5, *Second Report*, H.C. 662, p. vi, para. 9.

Congressional Research Service in Washington is usually quoted as an illustration of a truly extensive legislative research and reference facility: in 1977, its overall staff numbered just over 800. However, the legendary resources of the Congressional Research Service are, in terms of size, untypical—Rush and Shaw have referred to 'the deviant American example'.[1] When seeking to consider parliamentary libraries in international perspective, it is much more realistic to compare the House of Commons Library at Westminster, and its 1978 staffing complement of 88, with its Australian and Canadian counterparts. In Canberra, the Commonwealth Parliamentary Library had an overall establishment of 126 in 1976 to serve both the Senate and the House of Representatives (total membership 187); in Ottawa, the Library of Parliament serving both the Senate and House of Commons (total membership, 368) had just over 180 staff at its disposal for this purpose in 1977. At the other end of the scale are those legislatures, mostly in newly independent or developing countries, where library and information facilities are extremely modest and, in some cases, rudimentary. In his contribution to an International Symposium on 'The Member of Parliament: His Requirements for Information in the Modern World', held in Geneva in January 1973, Ian Grey of the Commonwealth Parliamentary Association emphasized the plight of many smaller countries where there were simply not enough resources of finance or trained manpower to provide an adequate parliamentary library or information service.[2] The House of Commons Library at Westminster, then, would probably occupy a fairly high position in any international 'league table' based on size of staff and range of resources. However, in view of the fact that the Library today serves 635 Members of Parliament, the overall establishment of 88 appears relatively modest in comparison with, for example, its Australian and Canadian counterparts. The Select Committee on Assistance to Private Members, in 1975, reported as follows: 'On the evidence we have received we believe that there is wide agreement that the Library's research division should be expanded as far as possible.' The

[1] *The House of Commons Services and Facilities*, pp. 252–3.
[2] Op. cit., pp. 184–6.

Committee went on to recommend increases in the research services and in the reference and supporting library staff.[1]

A parliamentary library is, in terms of subject coverage, a general library; however, it serves an important and, in terms of information requirements, special clientele. The job of the House of Commons Library—like that of its counterparts abroad—is to provide Members with books and documents, and with oral and written information, in connection with the whole range of their parliamentary duties. These are simply defined terms of reference, although their implementation is complex, changing, and challenging. As in the past, it is likely that the developing requirements of Members, and the interest (critical or otherwise) which they take in their Library, will do much to determine the pattern of its future growth and development.

[1] 1974–5, *Second Report*, H.C. 662, p. v, paras. 6–7.

INDEX

Abraham, L. A., 177–8, 216, 235, 242, 243, 244
ad hoc committees, 440–1
adjournment debates, 170–5, 514
adjournment motions, 164n, 513–19; ballot for, 514–15; daily, 513–15; emergency, 516–19; government, 513; holiday, 515
administrative scrutiny, 277, 470–3; see also select committees
Alderman, R. K., 26
Allocation of Time Orders, 271–2
amendments: carried against the government, 250–1, 287; in select committees, 280; selection of, 166–70; to substantive motions, 511–12
Anson, Sir William, 208
anticipation, 178–80
Appropriation Act, 353
appropriations in aid, 353
aristocracy, 7
Ashton, J., 228
Asquith, Herbert, 589
Attlee, Clement, 392, 539

backbench Members, 430; adjournment debates and, 514; communication and, 23–5; debates and, 522–4; financial procedures and, 401, 418; legislation and, 252, 284, 290; press coverage of, 534; Question Time and, 476, 498; resistance to innovation by, 3; scrutiny committees and, 471–2
Baldwin, Stanley, 55
Balfour reforms (1902), 361–3, 477–8, 510, 519
Barker, Anthony, 422, 424, 628, 638
behaviour, parliamentary, 71–2
Benson, George, 619
bill of aids and supplies, 358–9
Birmingham Post, 574
blocking motions, 179–80, 520–1
Blumenfeld, R. D., 545, 561
Boundary Commissions, 197
Bowles, Chester, 348–9
Bowring, N., 499, 504
Boyd-Carpenter, John, 148–9n

broadcasting, 536–44, 593; B.B.C.'s fear of controversy, 543
Brockway, Fenner, 191
Brogan, Colin, 233n
Brown, W. J., 223–4
Butler, R. A., 55, 459

Cabinet, the: legislation and, 251, 289
Callaghan, James, 228
Campion, Lord, 162–3, 269–70, 274, 283, 420; changes in supply procedure and, 406–8; his proposals for select committees, 447–50
censure motions, 512–13
Chamberlain, Neville, 590
charges, 331
Chester, D. N., 499, 504
Chief Whip: as Prime Minister's adviser, 12; Conservative, 14, 18; extra-parliamentary party and, 13; Labour, 15; Liberal, 14–15, 18; private secretary to, 16
Churchill, Winston, 253–4, 316–17, 539
Clerk, department of the, 596–610; Administration Department, 606–7; appointments to, 600; careers in, 598–600; Committee Office, 598, 599; committee records and, 606; European section, 605–6; functions of, 596–7, 608; independent of party, 609; Journal Office, 597, 601, 602; overseas clerks trained by, 605; Private Bill Office, 597, 599, 602; Public Bill Office, 597, 601, 602; review of (1973), 6–7; select committees and, 602–3; staff, 597, 601–2, 603, 607–8; Table Office, 600–1, 605
Clifton Brown, Speaker, 138–40, 145, 155, 158, 168, 173, 176, 179, 185, 187, 188, 199, 201, 283, 448, 483
closure: Speaker's power of, 162–4
Committee of Privileges, 177
Committee of Selection, 259, 263
Committee of Supply, 186, 349–50; 1900–1919, 367–8; 1919–1945, 392–4; abolition of, 410; debates in, 351–2, 364

Committee of the Whole House, 251, 253, 264
Committee of Ways and Means, 349–350; abolition of, 410
Committee on Defamation (1975), 214
Committee on National Expenditure report (1918), 389–90
communication and consultation: between front and back benches, 23–5; in the PLP, 44–5; over choice of Speaker, 151; Whips role in, 60
Comptroller and Auditor General, 449, 450, 457–8
Conference of Speakers and Presiding Officers of Commonwealth Parliaments, 201–2
Conservative Parliamentary Party, 27–30; committees in, 32–41, 66; election of leader, 54–9, 64–5; M.P.s, 97–102; Unionist Agriculture Committee, 34; unofficial groups in, 48
Conservative Party, 4
conservatism (of the Commons), 2
Consolidated Fund: charges on, 310–11, 331
Consolidated Fund Bills, 335, 352–4, 391, 410, 417–18
Consolidated Fund Standing Services, 336
contempt: by newspapers, 227, 229–30; concept of, 219–30; defined, 242; punishment for, 205, 206, 207; redefinition of, 235–6
Crick, Bernard, 462n
Critchley, Julian, 39
Crossman, Richard, 290, 306–7
Cunningham-Reid, Captain, 138–9
Curzon, Lord, 55

daily adjournment motions, 175–7
Daily Chronicle, 565
Daily Express, 564, 583
Daily Herald, 560, 565
Daily Mail, 557–8, 564
Daily Mirror, 558, 565
Daily Telegraph, 559, 565, 574, 583
Dalton, Hugh, 528–9
debates, 507–26; broadcasting of, 214–215; irrelevance and repetition in, 165–6, 263; length of speeches, 523–524; misrepresentation of, 226–7, 229; on adjournment motions, 513–519; on Consolidated Fund Bills, 354; on the Queen's speech, 511–12; on private Member topics, 175–6; on substantive motions, 511–13; point of, 525–6; privilege and, 211–16, 226–7; publication of, 215, 246; reporting of, 554, 574, 593; Speaker's role in, 154, 170–6, 187–9; standard of, 71; style of, 524–5; televised, 540–4; times of sitting and, 508–10; types of, 510–11; see also Supply debates
Defence vote on Account, 411
delegated legislation, 439; scrutiny committee for, 3
Deputy Speaker, 167, 186
Devlin, Bernadette, 192–3, 217
devolution, 200–1
dilatory motions, 164–5
discipline: in the PLP, 25–6; of Members by Speaker, 189–94; Whips, role in, 12–13, 18–19, 61–2
dissolution, threat of, 12
Douglas-Home, Sir Alec, 55–6

Economist, The, 529
Eden, Anthony, 590
elections: deposits, 85; family seats, 88; unopposed returns, 85
electoral finance, 84–5, 86, 95
electoral reform: speaker's conference on, 199–200
electoral system, 79; seats and votes relationship, 80
electoral threshold, 79
emergency adjournment procedure, 170–5
enabling Acts, 267
English, Michael, 221
Essex University privilege case, 220–1
estimates, 339; amendments to, 351; consideration of, 349–52; defence, 408; form of, 350; growth in number of 368–9; Navy and Army . . ., 369, 373,374, 381, 392; see also supplementary estimates
Estimates Committee, 3, 262, 445; organization of, 452; origin of, 341, 436–7; re-establishment of, 441–3; report on control of expenditure (1958), 411–12
European Economic Community, 202
executive power: House of Commons and, 444, 455, 462–3, 473

expenditure: optimization of, 345; volume of, 339–40
Expenditure Committee, 421, 466–7; advocated, 465–6
expenditure control, 466; concept of, 342–7; debates and, 338–9; in *1900*, 346–59; indirect, 343; legislation required for, 331–2; Lords' role in, 332; principles of, 329–34; procedure for, 334–42; restriction of borrowing powers and, 338; select committees and, 340–1; stages at which exercised, 345; *see also* Supply
expenditure investigation, 261–2

Fellowes, Sir Edward, 274, 399, 459
Fellowes schedules, 399
Finance Bill, 274
financial committees: *1900–1919*, 387–9; *1919–1945*, 404–5; *1945* to date, 420–421; *see also specific committees*
financial procedure, 329–425; *1900–1919*, 359–89; *1919–1945*, 389–406; *1945* to date, 406–21; Crown and, 332–3, 335; Lords' role in, 355–9, 365–6, 419–20; policy debates and, 339, 344, 385–6, 400–1, 422, 423; telescoping of, 391; *see also* estimates *and* Supply
Fitt, Gerard, 233n
Fitzroy, Speaker, 135, 167, 178, 183, 185, 188, 193
Foot, Michael, 214, 245
Fourteen Day Rule, 536–40
free speech: privilege and, 213–14, 233, 236, 245
free votes, 315

Gallery journalists, 544–55; accommodation for, 549–53; advance copies of documents for, 554; as a club, 573; catering for, 552–3; foreign, 545–6, 548–9; membership of, 545–9; number of, 547–8; status of, 553–4, 569; women, 546–7
Glasgow Herald, 574
government legislation, 247–91; delegation of, 252; drafting of, 251–2; in the nineteenth century, 248–9; planning of, 264–7; priority for, 360; select committees and, 279–82; speaker and, 163; time spent on, 277

grievances, raising, 348, 383; Question Time and, 496
Grey, Ian, 639
Griffith, J. A. G., 286, 287–8
Guardian, 574
guillotine: selection of votes and, 362–3; used in financial procedure, 360–2, 368, 385, 396, 407, 410
Gulley, Speaker William, 133–4, 156–7, 202

Hansard, 551, 571
Harcourt, Sir William, 344, 364
Heath, Edward, 63; leadership elections and, 56–7, 64–5
Herbert, A. P., 304
Hogg, Quintin, 232–3
Herman, Valentine, 288
hours of sitting, 364
House of Commons: as a club, 177–78; communications technology and, 530; composition of, 73–80; control of government by, 444, 455; loss of power by, 62–3; deficiencies of, 6; times of sitting, 508–10
House of Commons (Services) Committee, 198
House of Lords: broadcasting and, 542; Library, 637
Hylton-Foster, Speaker, 137, 138, 143–145, 165, 181, 182, 183–4, 185, 189, 194, 201

Ilbert, Sir Courtney, 250, 598
Independent Labour Party, 25–6, 111, 197
Independent MPs, 74
information, disclosure of, 528
interest groups: consultation with, 250; private members' legislation and, 311–12, 327; relations with MPs, 228
interests, representation of, 96–7, 98, 103
Irish Nationalists, 74, 76, 78–9; procedure changes caused by, 77, 161–2, 170, 477, 521

Jennings, Sir Ivor, 4, 202, 318, 445, 618–19
Joint Select Committee on the Publication of Proceedings in Parliament, 215
Jordan, Colin, 218–19

Jowett, F. W., 443–4
Junor, John, 229

kangaroo closure, 166–7
King, Speaker Horace, 127, 137, 146, 147, 159, 160–1, 164, 165–6, 168–9, 173–4, 175, 189, 191

Labour Party: Conference, 23n; Constitution, 22; effect of nationalist parties on, 77–8; intra-party democracy in, 9; National Executive Committee, 25
Labour Representation Committee, 110, 111
Lansbury, George, 190–1
Laski, Harold, 317
law reform, 312–13
legislation: contentious, 289–90; growth in volume of, 73, 277; introduced in the Lords, 278, 357–8; non-controversial, 286–7; the Speaker and, 125; uneven spread of, 278; see also government legislation and private Members' legislation
Liberal Labour Pact (pre 1914), 85
Liberal Parliamentary Party, 30–1; cross voting and, 18; decline of, 73–4; groups in, 48–9; leadership of, 54, 58, 67; M.P.s, 103–7; organization of, 21
Liberal Unionist M.P.s, 108–9
Library: Bottomley report on, 630–1; branch reference library, 635; budget, 631; committee, 628–9; compared to other legislatures, 638–9; functions of, 614, 616–17, 640; general literature in, 614–15; handbook, 623; holdings, 614–16, 621–2; in 1900, 611–18; information services in, 617, 620–1; location of, 612; Members' information, 637–8; Parliamentary Division, 634–5; Research Department, 623–4, 625–6, 631–3; Select Committee on (1945–6), 618–626; services, 626–7, 630; since 1950, 626–37; staff, 619–20, 627–8, 630, 631, 632–3; use of computers by, 635–637
Lidderdale, Sir David, 409–11
Lloyd, Speaker Selwyn, 137–8, 145, 160–1, 164, 169, 175, 181, 184, 186, 187, 192–3, 200, 519; election of, 147–50

Lloyd George, David, 317, 573, 589
Lobby correspondents, 555–7, 574–92; alternate, 583; back-benchers and, 586–7; careers, 592; confidentiality and, 576, 578–9, 584–5; copies of parliamentary papers for, 556; exchange of information between, 577–578; explanation of policy by, 580; facilities for, 556–7; golden age for, 577; hostility towards, 590–1; increased importance of, 574–5; 'inner' Lobby, 580–1; leaks to, 586–7, 588–9; membership of, 576–7, 582–3; Ministers and, 585, 589; 'off the record' briefings, 576; Prime Minister and, 587–91; provincial, 581–2; role of, 575–6; rules for, 555, 583–7; social status of, 575; status among journalists, 591–2; subject specialists and, 589, 591; Sunday papers and, 582–3
Lobby lunches, 556
Lobby meetings, 556, 580–1
Lock, Geoffrey, 631–2
Low, S., 496
Lowell, A. Lawrence, 8, 248–9, 254, 383, 431–2
Lowther, Speaker James, 134, 156–7, 166, 178–9, 185, 188, 203
Lucy, Henry, 572–3, 576

MacAndrew, Sir Charles, 140–1
MacDonagh, Michael, 549–50, 569–70
MacDonald, Ramsay, 23, 50, 589–90
Mackintosh, Alexander, 70–1
Mackintosh, John, 249, 278, 496–7
Macmillan, Harold, 55, 493, 590
machinery of government, 460–2
Manchester Guardian, 559, 565
marginal constituencies, 90–1
mass communications, see broadcasting and press, the
Maxwell-Hyslop, Robin, 149, 151–2
Maybray-King, Lord, see King, Speaker Horace
Members of Parliament, 69–123; achievement of office by, 92–3; adverse reflections on, 226–34, 241; age at first election, 89–90; attempts to influence, 219–25; career length, 5, 90–2; career patterns, 83–96; committee system and, 430, 440; competition for seats, 87; Conservative, 97–102; educational background of,

99–100, 104–5, 108, 110, 112, 113, 115, 121–2; electoral experience of, before election, 86–7; end of career, 93–6; financial burdens on, 85, 95; freedom from arrest, 209–11; full time, 94–5, 120; interest groups and, 228; Labour, 111–17; Lib-Labs, 109–110; Liberal 103–7; Liberal Unionist, 108–9; local connections of, 87–9, 121; local government experience of, 89; financial inducements to, 222–5; nationalist, 117; newspaper criticism of, 227, 229–30, 241–2; obstruction of, 220; occupational background of, 100–2, 106–7, 108–9, 111–13, 122; press and, 579; remuneration of, 84–85, 120; sartorial style of, 69–70; selection of, 84; socio–economic backgrounds, 96–120; suspension of, 190; turnover of, 80–2, 103–4; welfare officer role, 119–20; women, 69; working class, 106–7, 109–10, 114–15; workload, 118–19; *see also* backbench Members

Ministers: party committees and, 40–1, 42–3; relations with the Lobby, 555; select committees and, 453

minority government, 78

money bills, 354–5, 365–6; starting in the Lords, 419–20

money resolution, 310–11, 354–5; *1900–1919*, 386–7; *1919–1945*, 402–4; *1945* to date, 418–20; deferred till second reading, 404; drafting of, 403, 419; moved by Ministers, 336–7; private Members' bills and, 337; required before legislation, 334; significance of, 337–8

Monk resolutions, 408–9, 411

Morley, Lord, 251–2

Morning Post, 560–1, 564

Morrison, Herbert, 4, 266, 466–7

Morrison, Speaker, 135, 141–2, 145, 156, 158–9, 183, 186, 188–9, 195

Muir, Ramsay, 323–4, 443–4

naming a member, 190

National Expenditure Committee, 405, 441–2, 449, 451–2; administrative scrutiny by, 442; proposed, 392–3

National Loans Fund, 336

nationalist parties, 76–80 *passim*; M.P.s, 117

newspapers, *see* press, the

Nicolson, Nigel, 225

Nineteen Twenty–Two Committee, 15–16, 27–30; origin of, 27

Nineteenth-century politics, 7–8

Northern Ireland political parties, 77

Opposition, the: institutionalization of, 534–5; Speaker and, 197; Supply debates and, 381–2, 406, 409, 317, 424

Pall Mall Gazette, 560

Pannell, Charles, 133, 140, 145, 218–19

Pardoe, John, 149

Parker, John, 325–6

Parliament: discontent with, 525; upholding primacy of, 539–40; workload, 73, 118–19

Parliament Acts (1911, 1949), 196, 365–366

Parliamentary business: control of, 154; precedence of, 177–8

Parliamentary Commissioner for Administration Bill, 287

Parliamentary Labour Party: committees in, 32, 41–8, 66; conservative approach to procedure of, 4; discipline within, 19–21; early growth of, 74; election of leader, 50, 51–3, 59; electoral practice, 51–3; Executive, 24; extra-parliamentary party and, 23, 63–4; liaison committee, 24, 44–5; meetings, 26–7; Ministers and, 24; organization of, 21–7; socio–economic changes in, 111–17; Speakership and, 140–3; suspension from, 20; unofficial groups in, 48

Parliamentary parties, 7–68; defining, 74; development of, 7–58; differences between, 30–1, 66–7; effect of, 59–65; extra-parliamentary parties and, 63–64; meetings, 9, 29; number of, 75–6; organization of, 21–31; *see also specific parties*

Parliamentary Party committees, 32–49; attitude, 33–4; chairmen of, 34–35, 36; effect of, 62–3; influence of, 39–40, 45, 47; meetings of, 36, 38; sectional, 34; subject, 34–9, 41–7

Parliamentary timetable: Government control of, 14

party leader: election of, 9–10, 29, 49–
59, 64–5; power of appointment, 54,
57; press coverage of, 535; Prime
Minister as, 49–50; re-election of, 50
Peel, Speaker, 171
Plaid Cymru, 31, 67, 76–8, 80
Plowden report on Control of Public
Expenditure (1961), 345–6, 412,
423
points of order, 187–8
policy: distinguished from administration, 428–9, 449–50, 452
political parties, 526; effect of changes
in, 6; in the nineteenth century, 7–8;
local organizations, 13; organization
of, 14–15; select committees and, 440,
444–5; see also Parliamentary parties
political structure, 5
post-legislative scrutiny, 282–3
pre-legislative committees, 433–4, 435;
private Members' legislation and, 324
press, the: agencies, 571; as a political
ally, 531–2; as a source of information,
529–30; changes in Parliamentary
coverage, 562–8, 594; circulation,
558–60, 563; dependence of, on
Parliament, 530–1; depoliticization
of, 561; development of, 557–62;
distortion by, 532–3; evening, 559–
560; golden age of, 532; ownership of,
558; Parliamentary attitudes to, 586;
Parliament's need for, 528, 529;
popular, 545, 557, 563; proprietors,
561; provincial, 558–9, 574, 576,
581–2; subsidized by political parties,
560
Press Officers, departmental, 555
Prime Ministers: Labour, 50–1; choice
of speaker and, 152–3; chosen by the
Monarch, 55; Press Relations Adviser, 587–9
private Members' legislation, 292–328;
ballot for, 292–3, 298–9, 311, 325;
closure and, 163–4, 299–300, 326;
contentious and non-contentious, 304,
318–19; drafting of, 306, 322–3;
extra time for, 294, 295, 296, 306–7,
319; ideas for, 308–13; in the Lords,
297; in the nineteenth century, 247–
248; insufficient study for, 320; Members' attitudes to, 316–22; mandate
for, 320–1; money resolutions and,
337; moved to Fridays, 301; objec-

tions to, 318–22; preparation of, 305–
306; priority for, 302–3; procedure
for, 323–6; public opinion and, 327;
referred to Select Committees, 324–5;
report stage and, 294; Standing Committees and, 259, 294, 301, 306;
standing Order, 37 and, 296; subject
of, 313–16; success of, 307–8; time for,
73, 293, 297–9, 303, 305, 324, 326–7,
508, 509, 519–20; two-party system
and, 319; value of, 327–8; voting on,
321–2; withdrawn in favour of
government bills, 315
private Members' motions, 520–1
privilege, 204–46; adverse reflections on
Members, 226–34; broadcasting and,
214–15; Commons' jurisdiction on,
207–8; complaints procedure, 235–6,
240; complaints raised by Members,
177–8; defence of justification, 234–5;
defined, 206, 242; forced resignations
and 225; freedom from arrest, 209–
211; freedom of debate, 211–16;
incidence of complaints, 230–1; intimidation and molestation and, 216–
225; judicial aspects of, 204–5, 207,
236–7, 242–5; money bills and, 356;
nature of, 204–9; overseas legislation
and, 205, 207–8; press criticism and,
190–2; Speaker's role in, 131, 177–8,
192–4; The Economist case (1975),
215; United States practice, 243–5;
use of the term, 240–1
privilege amendments, 358
Privy Council Judicial Committee, 210
privy councillors: given precedence in
debate, 126, 522
procedural innovations: executives' control over, 2–3
procedure, 1–2; for private Members'
bills, 323–6; political nature of, 3, 5;
Speaker and, 130–1, 153–85;
Profumo, John, 213
Public Accounts Committee, 420, 421,
436, 446, 451, 467; origin of, 341;
subjects considered by, 434
public expenditure, see expenditure
Punnett, R. M., 534–5

Questions and Question Time, 476–507,
515; answers to, 503; backbenchers',
476, 504; changed to suit press, 533;
Civil Service and, 499–500; conflict

and, 497–8; effect of, 498–9; grouping of, 156; growth in number of, 73, 159–60, 477, 480, 490–1, 494; limitations in numbers, 481; Members' use of, 505–7; notice required for, 178, 481 a; on nationalized industries, 483; Opposition and, 503; planting of questions, 500–1; private notice, 492–3; rota system, 484–7; rules for, 482–3, 491; Speaker's role in, 154–61, 492–3; starred, 478, 479–487, 502; status of, 496; supplementary, 156–61, 487–9, 502, 503, 504–5; time for, 154–5, 477–8, 479; to the Prime Minister, 485, 487, 493–5; type of questions, 501–7; unstarred, 478, 489–91

Redlich, Josef, 1, 51, 247–8, 252, 346–7, 356, 426, 431–2, 496
reform of Parliament, 460–2; comprehensive schemes of, 4; conservatives and, 455
Renton Committee (1975), 289
Report committees, 275
report stage, 274; amendments selection at, 168–9; lengthening, 267; private Members' Bills and, 294, 326–327
reporters, 568–71
Royal Commission on Standards of Conduct in Public Life, 222–3
Royal Commission on the Press (1947), 581
Rush, Michael, 628, 638

safe constituencies, 83–4, 90
Sandys, Duncan, 212
Saunders, H. A. St. G., 624
Scotsman, 565, 574
Scottish Grand Committee, 261
Scottish National Party, 31, 67, 76–7, 78, 80
Scottish standing committee, 259–60, 274, 275, 408
Second Readings, 286; for private members bills, 293, 325
Select Committee on Agriculture, 465
Select Committee on European Secondary Legislation, 467
Select Committee on House of Commons Services, 629–30

Select Committee on National Expenditure (1903), 387–8
Select Committee on Nationalised Industries, 421, 452–4, 467
Select Committee on Parliamentary Privilege (1966–7), 177–8
Select Committee on Parliamentary Questions, 494
Select Committee on Procedure, reports from: (1886), 255; (1906), 257–258, 263; (1930), 316–17, 443; (1932), 390, 443–4; (1945), 266–7; (1945–6), 447; (1946), 168, 171; (1956), 274; (1959), 173; (1964–5), 463; (1965–6), 409; (1966–7), 173–4, 276; (1968–9), 276–8, 465–6; (1972), 147; (1970–1), 278
Select Committee on Procedure relating to Money Resolutions, 403–4
Select Committee on Race Relations and Immigration, 465
Select Committee on Science and Technology, 464–5
Select Committee on Statutory Instruments, 448, 454, 457, 467
Select Committee on the Parliamentary Commissioner for Administration, 465, 467
Select Committee on Privilege (1967), 234–45; recommendations, 237–9
Select Committee on Procedure on Public Business (1931), 157, 254, 262
Select Committee on the Official Secrets Acts (1939), 212
select committees, 426–75; 1914–1939, 439–46; 1945–1964, 446–58; 1965 to date, 458–70; administrative scrutiny by, 449–51; assistance for, 601–5, 633; before 1914, 429–39; considered unnecessary, 427–8; delegation of power to, 472–3; discussion of reports, 469–70; expenditure control and, 340–1; for scrutiny of bills, 279–282, 290, 437, 441, 456; function of, 431–2, 468; innovations (1966), 464–465; investigative, 435, 436, 439–46; membership of, 438, 456, 457; operation of, 437–9, 457; prelegislative, 433–4, 435, 456; press and, 535–6; relationship of, to Commons, 474–5; scrutiny by, 470–3; specialization of, 469, 473–4; witnesses at, 438–9, 467

services, legislation for specified, 336
sessions: lengthening of, 73; number of
days in, 277
Silverman, Sydney, 231
Sinn Fein, 74, 76
Sketch writers, 562, 568, 571–3
social reform Bills, 294, 310, 313, 317;
select committees and, 435
Speaker, the, 124–203; adjournment
motions and, 514, 518–19; amendments selected by, 166–70; censure
motions on, 163, 172–3, 181; certification of money bills by, 196; choice
of members in debate, 126; constraints
upon, 126–7; contact with Members,
186–7; continuity of, 131–2; debates,
126, 523; death of, 146–7; department of, 198; dissolution and, 197;
election of, 132–5, 147–51; electoral
reform and, 199–200; emergency
debates and, 170–5; his constituency,
136–7, 138; impartiality of, 125;
judicial aspects of, 129; Labour Party
and, 140–3; lawyers as, 128–9;
minorities and, 125–6; money bills
and, 365–6; new election procedure
(1974), 150–1; parliamentary elections and, 132, 135–8, 153; prestige
of, 127–8; previous offices held by,
143–4, 148; Prime Ministers and,
152–3; procedural powers of, 130–1,
153–85; qualities required of, 203;
retirement of, 128, 139–40, 194–6;
role of, 124; statutory duties, 196–8;
strains of the post, 185–7; *sub judice*
matters and, 180–5; supply debates
and, 407–8, 410
speech-making: increase in, 534
Spender, J. A., 533
Stacey, Frank, 287
standing committees, 3; allocation of
business to, 257; beginning of, 255–6;
business sub-committee of, 269;
chairmen, 168, 257, 260, 263; composition of, 262–3, 289; controversial
bills and, 270–1; government defeats
in, 288; guillotine and, 269, 271–2; in
the nineteenth century, 255–6; legislation and, 253–60 *passim*; 301, 447;
number of, 261, 268; private members' business and, 259, 325; Procedure Committee (1906) and, 257–
258; sittings, 268–9, 286; size of, 260,

274, 275; specialization and, 259,
283–4; whips appointed to, 17, 272–4
Standing Orders: Speaker and, 153
Study of Parliament Group, 235–6, 277,
278, 282, 325, 327, 463; foundation
of, 462; view of the Library, 628
sub judice matters, 180–5
Sunday Express, privilege case, 229
Sunday Theatres Act (1972), 297n
Supplementary estimates, 335–6, 351,
407, 416; debates on, 384–5, 393,
396–7; growth in number of, 399
supply, 329–425; consideration of votes,
361–3; process of, 335–6; withholding
of, 343
Supply days, 307, 363–4, 424; number
of, 407, 410
Supply debates, 399, 351–2, 364; *1900–
1919*, 365–88; *1919–1945*, 394–402;
1945 to date, 412–18; adjourned,
395–6; amendments in, 384, 400, 407,
417; Chairmen of, 383–4; changes in
style of, 402; choice of subjects for,
380–82, 385, 401, 406; government
defeat, 415–16; inadequacy of, for
scrutiny, 340; on administration, 373;
on reports of committees, 391–2;
used for opposition business, 349,
381–2, 406, 409, 417, 424
Supply procedure: *1900–1919*, 359–64;
1919–1945, 389–94; *1945* to date, 406–
412; Balfour reforms, 347–9; limiting
time for, 348; timing of, 391
suspension of the House, 72

Taverne, Dick, 225
Ten-Minute Rule Bills, 180, 292, 294–6,
300–1, 308
Thatcher, Margaret, 57
Times, The, 551, 559, 563, 564, 565, 568,
570, 571, 574, 583
trade union sponsored M.P.s, 85, 111,
116; privilege and, 223–5
Transmire, Lord, 138
Treasury borrowing, 353
tribunals of inquiry, 182–4
Tunstall, J., 577–8
two-party system, 78–9; select committees and, 446, 451, 455

Ulster Unionist Parliamentary Party,
31
United Ulster Unionist Coalition, 31, 67

Vardon, Thomas, 616–17
Votes, *see* estimates
Votes of Credit, 378, 397
Votes on Account, 335, 350–1, 418

Warbey, William, 230–1
Warren, Chief Justice, 244
Ways and Means Committee: Chairmen of, 134–5, 146
Ways and Means 'spending' resolution, 252–3
Wells, H. G., 618
Westminster Gazette, 560
Whips, 10–12, 31; communication and, 11–12; effect of, 59–62; functions of, 10–13, 60; junior whips selected by, 53; Labour, 20–1; number of, 17;

private Members' business and, 310; voting cohesion and, 8; withdrawal of the whips, 19, *see also* Chief Whip; work-load, 15–17
Whitaker, Sir Thomas, 302–3
White Papers, 276
Whitelaw, William, 246
Whitley, Speaker John, 134, 180, 188
Wigg, George, 232
Williams, Francis, 588
Wilson, Harold, 589, 590–1
Winterton, Lord, 70
Wood, Sir Charles, 247
written whips, 12

Yorkshire Post, 559, 565, 574

FAC